READER'S DIGEST

Natural Wonders of the World

READER'S DIGEST

Natural Wonders of the World

The Reader's Digest Association, Inc.

Pleasantville, New York   Montreal

Natural Wonders of the World

Editors: Richard L. Scheffel, Susan J. Wernert
Art Editor: Donald D. Spitzer
Associate Editors: James Cassidy, Valentin Chu,
Suzanne E. Weiss
Art Associate: Janet G. Tenenzaph

With special assistance from Senior Staff
Editor Alma E. Guinness and Associate Editors
Robert V. Huber and W. Clotilde Lanig

Consultant

Rhodes W. Fairbridge, *Professor of Geological Sciences,
Columbia University*

Contributors

Writers: Oliver E. Allen, Patricia Ellsworth,
Peter R. Limburg, Alan Linn
Copy Editor: Harriet Bachman
Research Associate: Kathryn D. Kudla

The credits and acknowledgments that appear on pages 462–463
are hereby made a part of this copyright page.

Based on the book first published in France as *Dictionnaire
Illustré des Merveilles Naturelles du Monde*
Copyright © 1978, 1977 Sélection du Reader's Digest, S.A.

Library of Congress Catalog Card Number 80-50353
ISBN 0-89577-087-3

Printed in the United States of America
Fifth Printing, July 1984

Summary of Contents

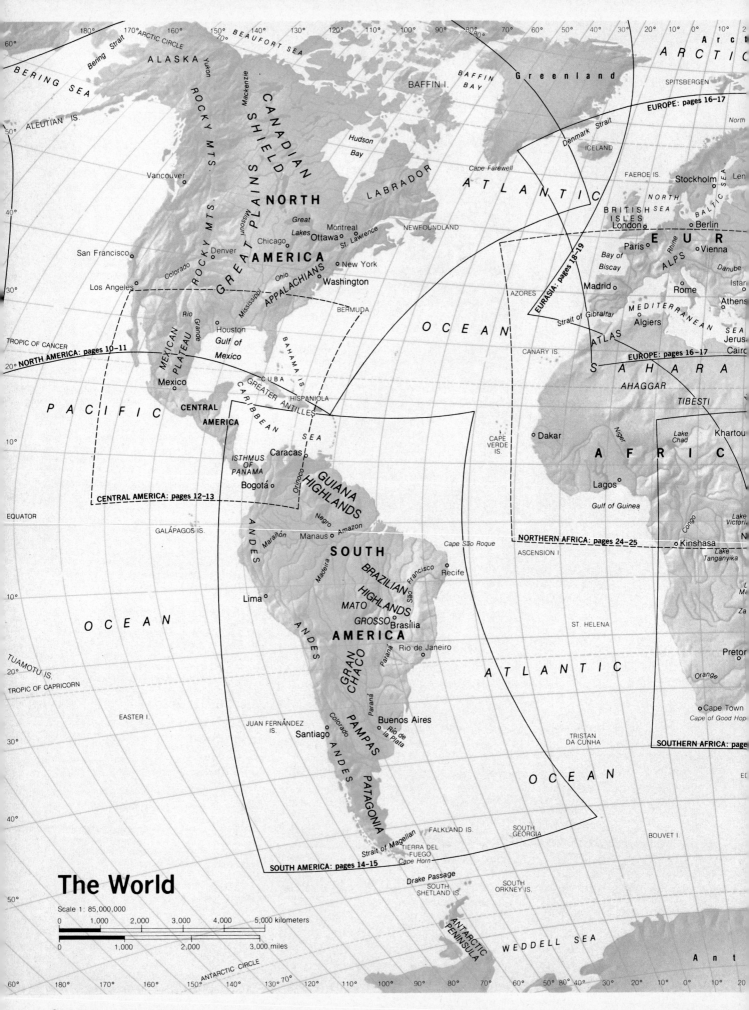

The World

Scale 1: 85,000,000

0   1,000   2,000   3,000   4,000   5,000 kilometers

0   1,000   2,000   3,000 miles

North America

Scale 1 : 19,600,000

0 100 200 300 400 500 600 700 800 900 1,000 kilometers

0 100 200 300 400 500 miles

10

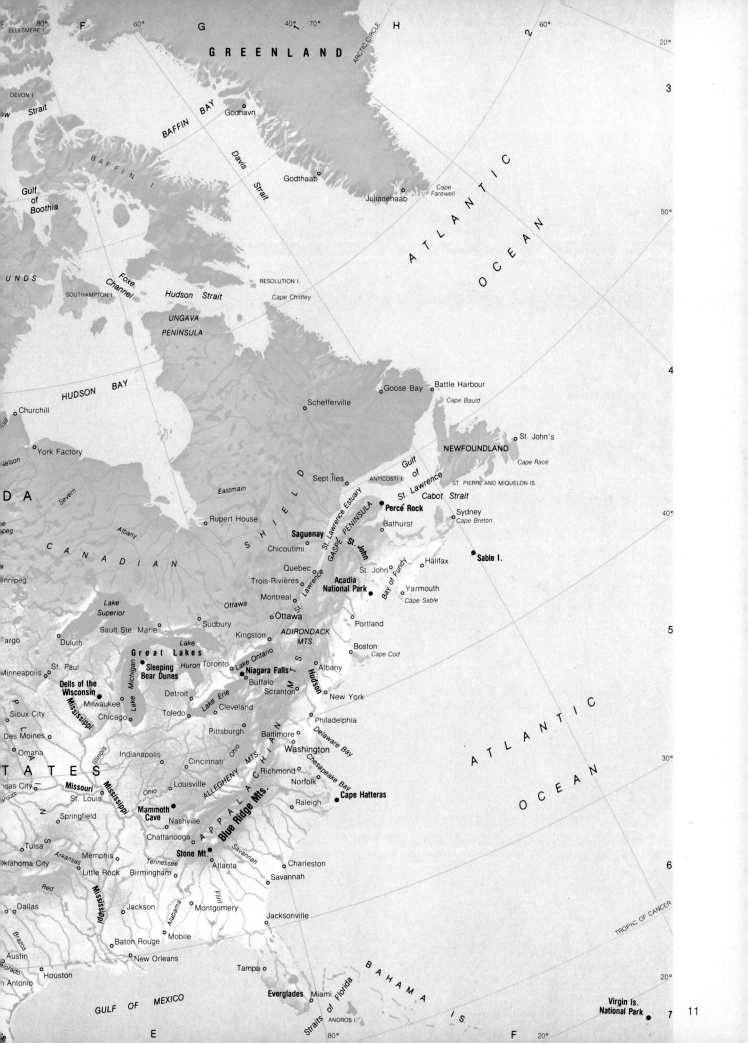

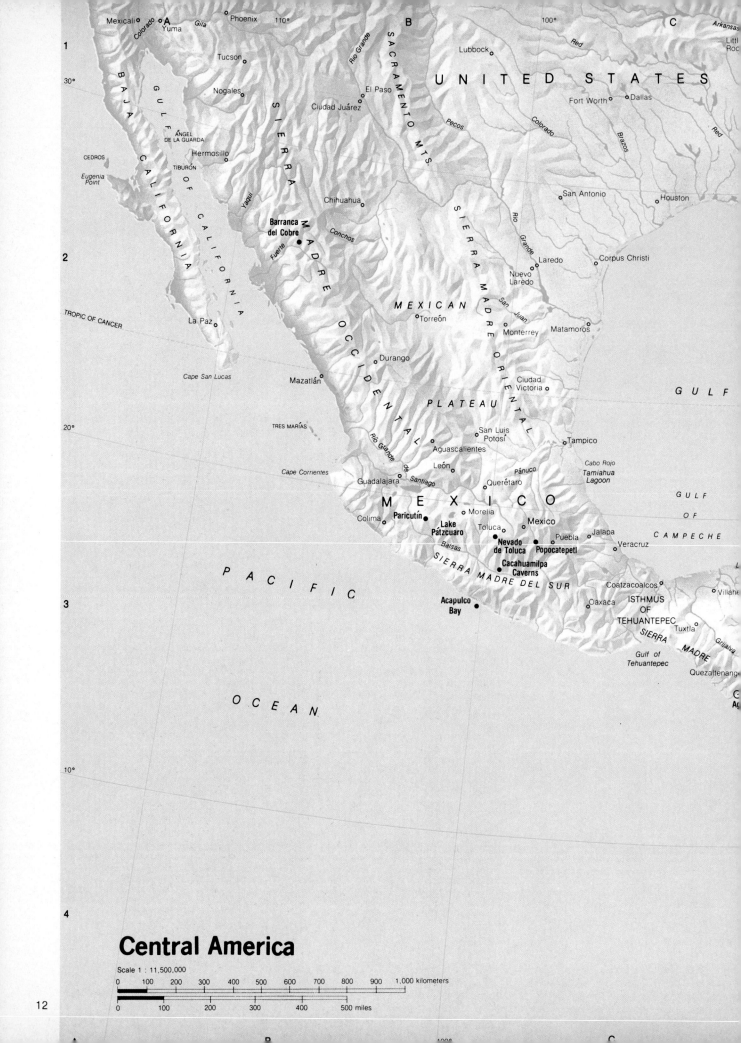

Central America

Scale 1 : 11,500,000

| 0 | 100 | 200 | 300 | 400 | 500 | 600 | 700 | 800 | 900 | 1,000 kilometers |

| 0 | 100 | 200 | 300 | 400 | 500 miles |

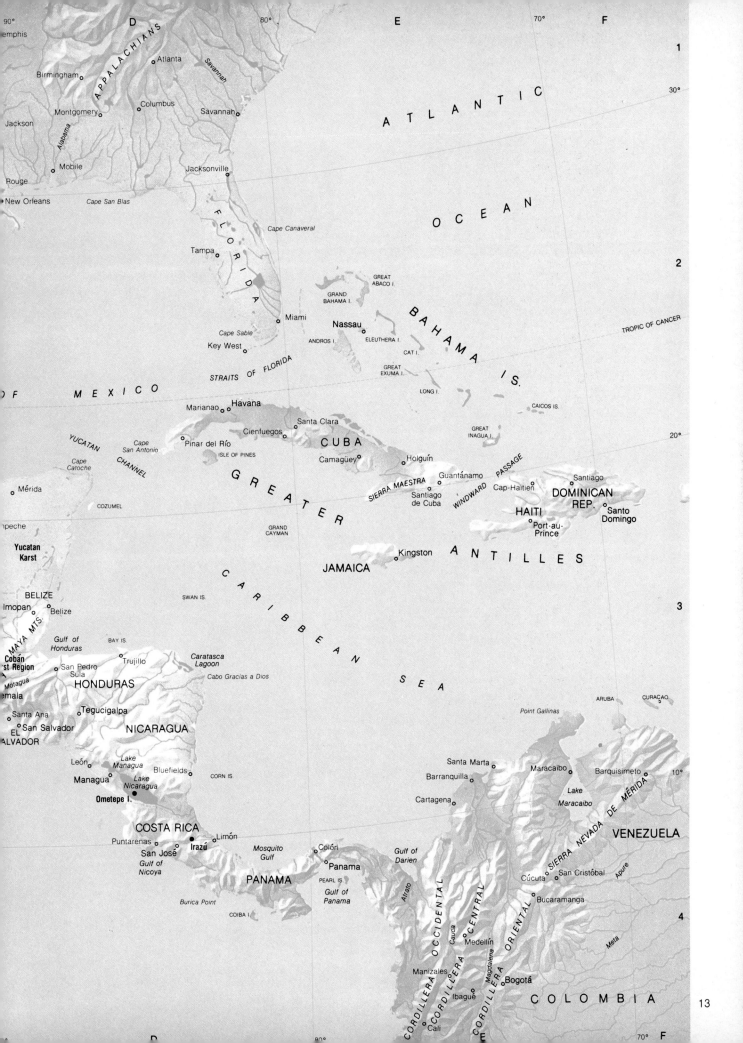

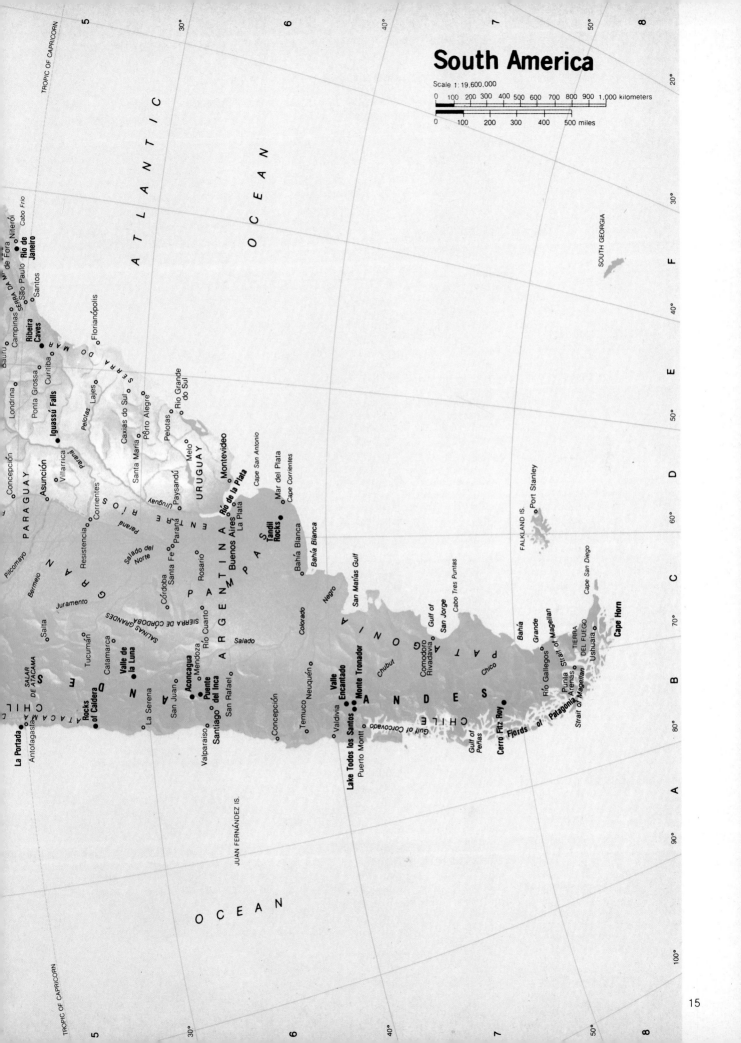

South America

Scale 1:19,600,000

0 100 200 300 400 500 600 700 800 900 1,000 kilometers

0 100 200 300 400 500 miles

TROPIC OF CAPRICORN

ATLANTIC   OCEAN

SOUTH GEORGIA

Cabo Frio
Niterói
Rio de
Janeiro
São Paulo
Santos
Campinas
SERRA DA MANTIQUEIRA
Ribeira
Caves
Florianópolis
Bauru
Londrina
Ponta Grossa
Curitiba
Iguassú Falls
SERRA DO MAR
Lajes
Caxias do Sul
Rio Grande
do Sul
Pôrto Alegre
Pelotas
Pelotas
Santa Maria
Villarrica
Paraná
Concepción
Asunción
PARAGUAY
Melo
URUGUAY
Paysandú
Uruguay
Montevideo
Río de la Plata
La Plata
Cape San Antonio
Mar del Plata
Cape Corrientes

Port Stanley
FALKLAND IS.

Pilcomayo
Bermejo
Juramento
Salta
Tucumán
Catamarca
ENTRE RÍOS
Corrientes
Resistencia
Paraná
Santa Fe
Córdoba
Rosario
Buenos Aires
Tandil
Rocks
GRAN   CHACO
SIERRA DE CÓRDOBA
SALINAS GRANDES
Río Cuarto
ARGENTINA
PAMPAS
Bahía Blanca
Bahía Blanca
Salado del
Norte
Salado
Negro
San Matías Gulf
Gulf of
San Jorge
Cabo Tres Puntas
Cape San Diego

SALAR
DE ATACAMA
Rocks
of Caldera
La Portada
Antofagasta
ATACAMA
CHILE
DESERT
ANDES
Valle de
la Luna
Aconcagua
Mendoza
Puente
del Inca
San Juan
La Serena
San Rafael
Colorado
Concepción
Temuco Neuquén
Valle
Encantado
Monte Tronador
Valdivia
PATAGONIA
Chubut
Comodoro
Rivadavia
Bahía
Grande
Chico
Río Gallegos
Punta
Arenas
TIERRA
DEL FUEGO
Ushuaia
Cape Horn
Strait of Magellan
Strait of Magellan
Patagonia
Fjords of
Cerro Fitz Roy
Gulf of
Peñas
Gulf of Corcovado
Puerto Montt
Lake Todos los Santos
Santiago
Valparaíso
ANDES
CHILE

JUAN FERNÁNDEZ IS.

OCEAN

TROPIC OF CAPRICORN

Europe

Scale 1: 11,400,000

| 0 | 100 | 200 | 300 | 400 | 500 | 600 | 700 | 800 | 900 | 1,000 kilometers |

| 0 | 100 | 200 | 300 | 400 | 500 miles |

17

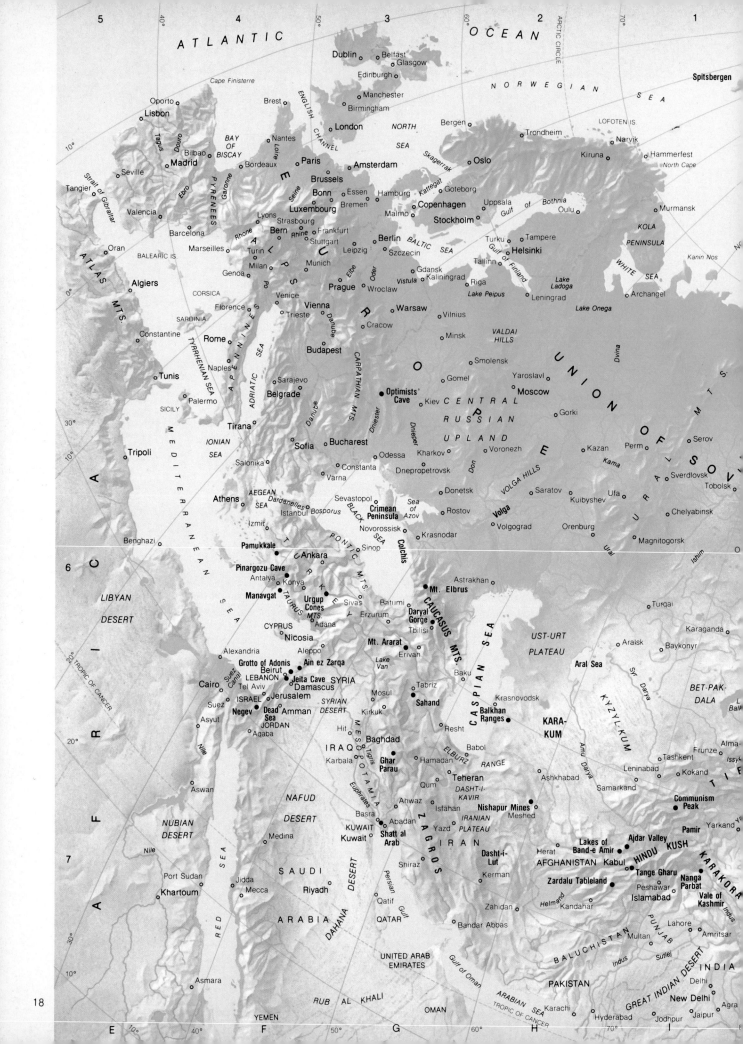

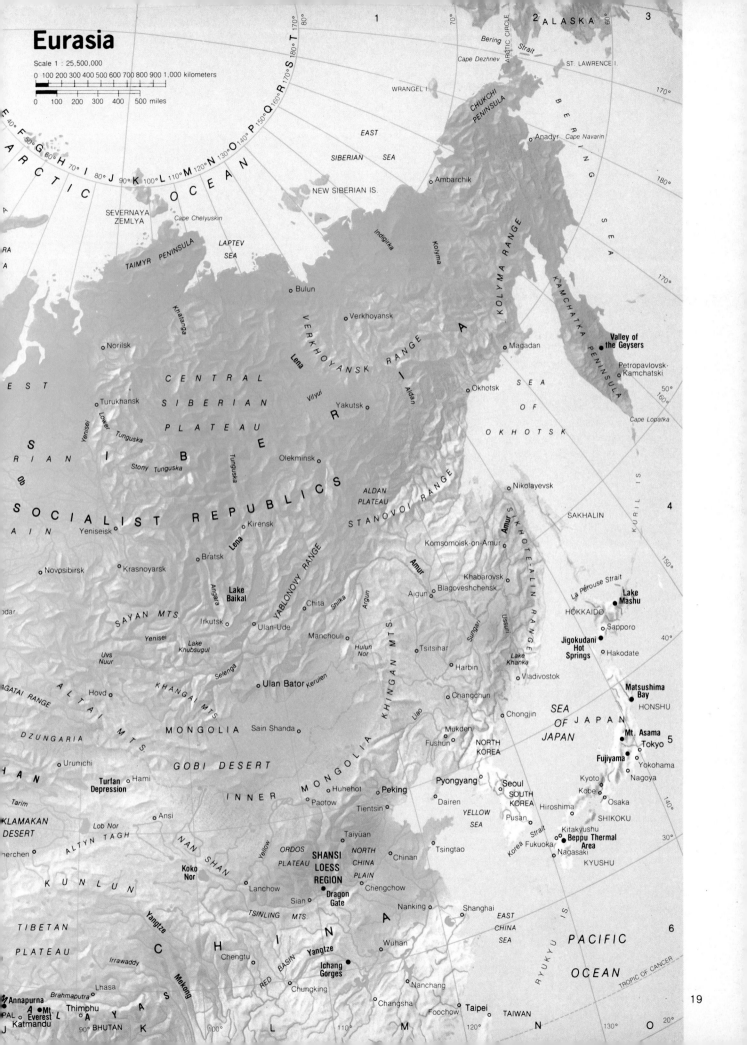

Eurasia

Scale 1 : 25,500,000

0 100 200 300 400 500 600 700 800 900 1,000 kilometers

0 100 200 300 400 500 miles

ARCTIC OCEAN

ALASKA

Bering Strait

Cape Dezhnev

ST. LAWRENCE I.

WRANGEL I.

CHUKCHI PENINSULA

Anadyr Cape Navarin

EAST SIBERIAN SEA

Ambarchik

NEW SIBERIAN IS.

B E R I N G S E A

SEVERNAYA ZEMLYA

Cape Chelyuskin

TAIMYR PENINSULA

LAPTEV SEA

Indigirka

Kolyma

KOLYMA RANGE

KAMCHATKA PENINSULA

Bulun

Verkhoyansk

Valley of the Geysers

Norilsk

Lena

V E R K H O Y A N S K R A N G E

Magadan

Petropavlovsk-Kamchatski

CENTRAL

Turukhansk

Vilyui

Yakutsk

Okhotsk

SEA OF OKHOTSK

Cape Lopatka

SIBERIAN

Yenisei

Lower Tunguska

PLATEAU

Aldan

S I B E R I A

Stony Tunguska

Tunguska

Olekminsk

ALDAN PLATEAU

Nikolayevsk

SAKHALIN

KURIL IS.

SOCIALIST REPUBLICS

STANOVOI RANGE

Yeniseisk

Lena

Kirensk

Komsomolsk-on-Amur

Amur

SIKHOTE-ALIN RANGE

HOKKAIDO

Lake Mashu

Novosibirsk

Krasnoyarsk

Bratsk

YABLONOVY RANGE

Khabarovsk

Ussuri

Sapporo

Jigokudani Hot Springs

Hakodate

Angara

Lake Baikal

Chita

Shilka

Argun

Amur

Aigun

Blagoveshchensk

Sungari

SAYAN MTS.

Irkutsk

Ulan-Ude

Manchouli

Tsitsihar

Lake Khanka

Vladivostok

Matsushima Bay

Yenisei

Lake Khubsugul

Selenga

Hulun Nor

KHINGAN MTS.

Harbin

HONSHU

Uvs Nuur

Kerulen

Ulan Bator

Changchun

SEA OF JAPAN

Mt. Asama

Tokyo

AGATAI RANGE

Hovd

KHANGAI MTS.

Chongjin

JAPAN

Fujiyama

Yokohama

ALTAI MTS.

MONGOLIA

Sain Shanda

Mukden

NORTH KOREA

Kyoto

Kobe

Nagoya

DZUNGARIA

GOBI DESERT

Fushun

Pyongyang

Seoul

Osaka

SHIKOKU

Urumchi

INNER MONGOLIA

Huhehot

Peking

Dairen

SOUTH KOREA

Hiroshima

Turfan Depression

Hami

Paotow

Tientsin

YELLOW SEA

Pusan

Kitakyushu

Beppu Thermal Area

Tarim

Ansi

Taiyuan

Fukuoka

Nagasaki

KYUSHU

KLAMAKAN DESERT

Lob Nor

ALTYN TAGH

NAN SHAN

Yellow

ORDOS PLATEAU

SHANSI LOESS REGION

NORTH CHINA PLAIN

Chinan

Tsingtao

Korea Strait

cherchen

KOKO Nor

Lanchow

Sian

Dragon Gate

Chengchow

Nanking

Shanghai

EAST CHINA SEA

RYUKYU IS.

PACIFIC OCEAN

KUNLUN

TSINLING MTS.

C H I N A

Wuhan

TIBETAN PLATEAU

Yangtze

Chengtu

RED BASIN

Yangtze

Ichang Gorges

Nanchang

Irrawaddy

Chungking

Changsha

Foochow

Taipei

TAIWAN

Lhasa

Mekong

Annapurna

Brahmaputra

Thimphu

Mt. Everest

NEPAL

Katmandu

BHUTAN

H I M A L A Y A S

TROPIC OF CANCER

19

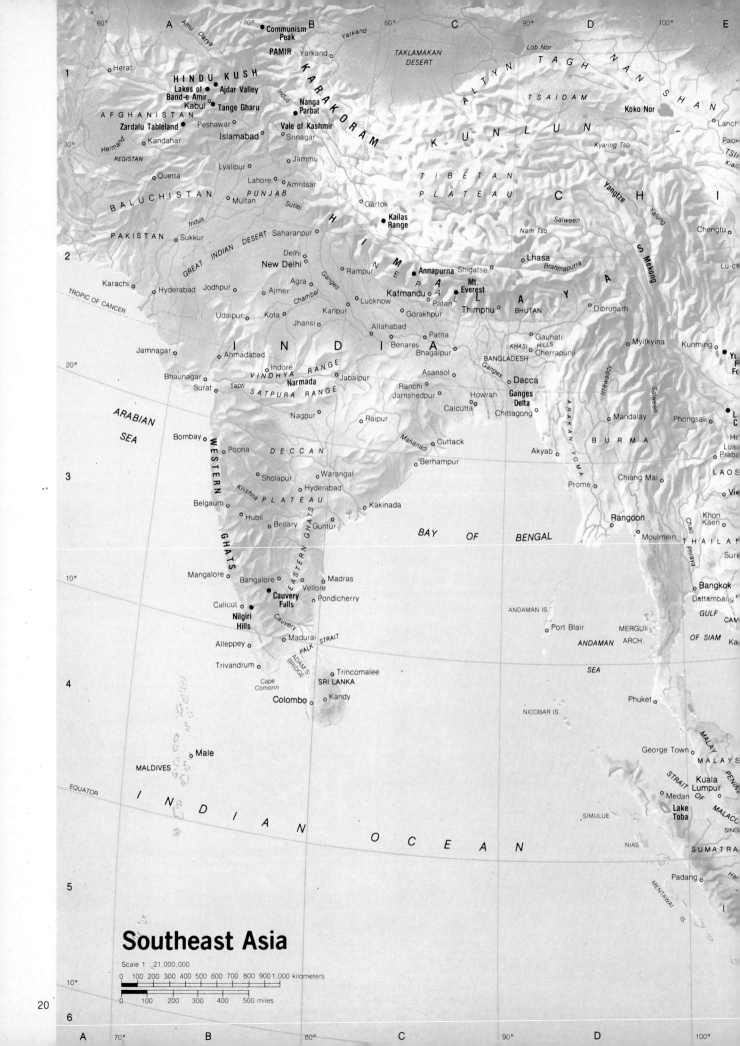

Southeast Asia

Scale 1 : 21,000,000

0 100 200 300 400 500 600 700 800 900 1,000 kilometers

0 100 200 300 400 500 miles

20

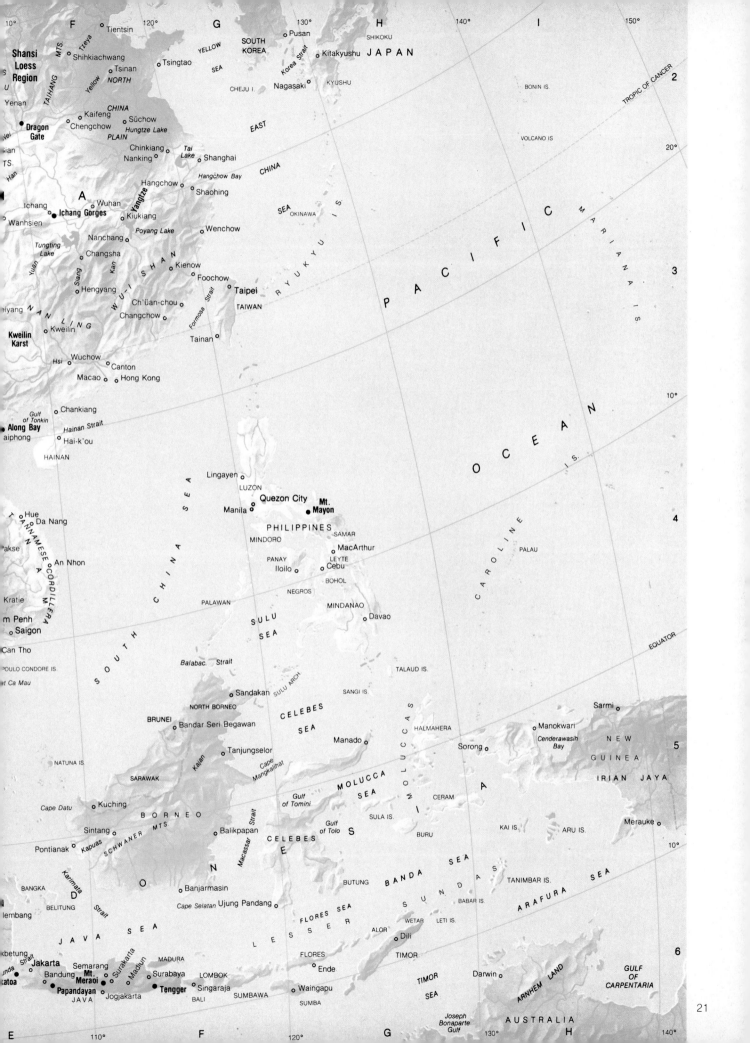

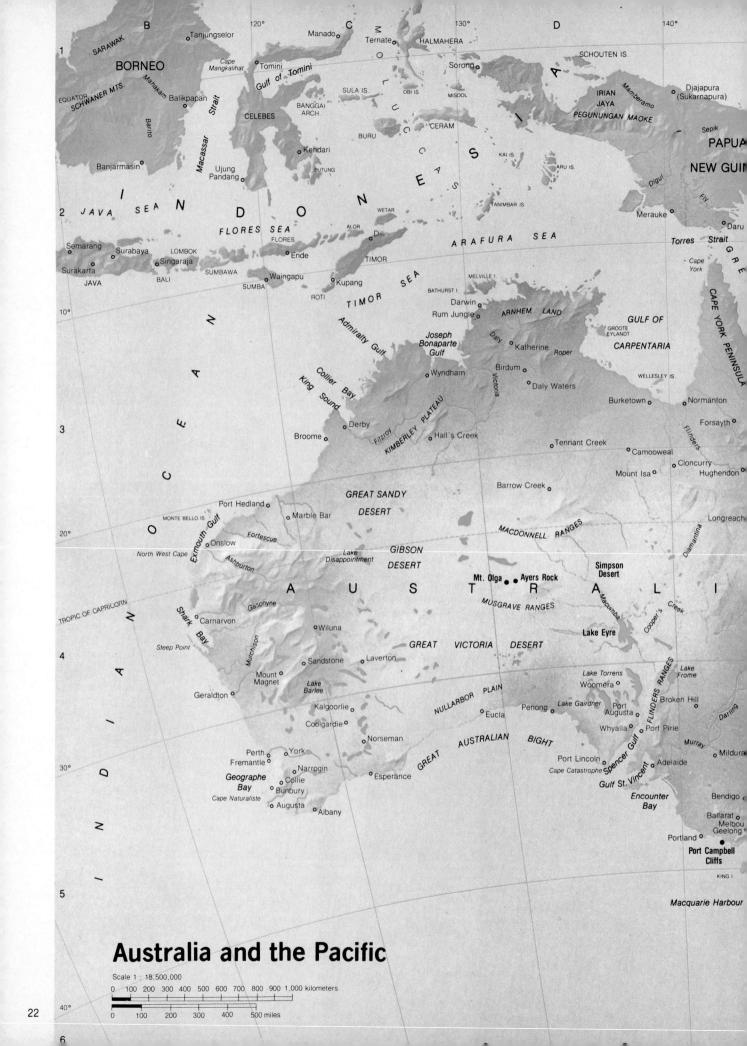

Australia and the Pacific

Scale 1 : 18,500,000

0   100   200   300   400   500   600   700   800   900   1,000 kilometers

0   100   200   300   400   500 miles

22

150° F 160° G 170° H 180°

MELANESIA   MICRONESIA

ADMIRALTY IS.

NEW
IRELAND

BISMARCK ARCH.

MAIANA

EQUATOR

NONOUTI

NEW BRITAIN   BOUGAINVILLE   SOLOMON   TABITEUEA

ARORAE

2

FERGUSSON I.   NEW GEORGIA   MALAITA   NANUMEA

D'ENTRECASTEAUX IS.   NIUTAO

LOUISIADE   Honiara   SAN CRISTOBAL
ARCH.   GUADALCANAL

RENNEL I.   SANTA CRUZ IS.   FUNAFUTI

10°

VANIKORO   ANUTA I.   NIULAKITA

PACIFIC

ESPIRITU SANTO

CORAL   VANUATU   VANUA
LEVU

SEA   MALEKULA

3

Townsville   FIJI

Bowen   EFATE   Vila   VITI LEVU   Suva   LAU
GROUP

Mackay   REEF   ISLE OF PINES

Capricorn   CHESTERFIELD IS.   NEW   Hienghene Bay
Channel   CALEDONIA

Rockhampton   ONO I.

Mount Morgan   St. Vincent   Nouméa   20°
Bay   ISLE OF PINES

Bundaberg

Roma   DIVIDING   Gympie   OCEAN   TROPIC OF CAPRICORN

Toowoomba   Brisbane
Ipswich
Cape Byron   NORFOLK

4

Dubbo   LORD HOWE I.

Newcastle

Bathurst   Mts.   Sydney   KERMADEC IS.   30°

Jenolan Caves   Blue

anberra   Wollongong

North Cape

Bairnsdale   TASMAN   Whangarei   Hauraki Gulf

son's Promontory   Auckland   Bay of Plenty

Strait   Hamilton   White Island

FURNEAUX IS.   SEA   NORTH I.   Whakarewarewa   East Cape
ks Strait   Thermal Area   Waimangu Hot
Launceston   NEW   Springs   5
St. Mary's   ZEALAND   Gisborne

TASMANIA   Napier

Hobart   Nelson

utheast Cape   SOUTH I.   Cook   Wellington
Greymouth   Strait
Franz
Josef Glacier   ALPS
Milford   SOUTHERN   Mt. Cook
Sound   Christchurch
Puysegur   Sutherland
Point   Falls
Fovea   Dunedin   CHATHAM I.   40°

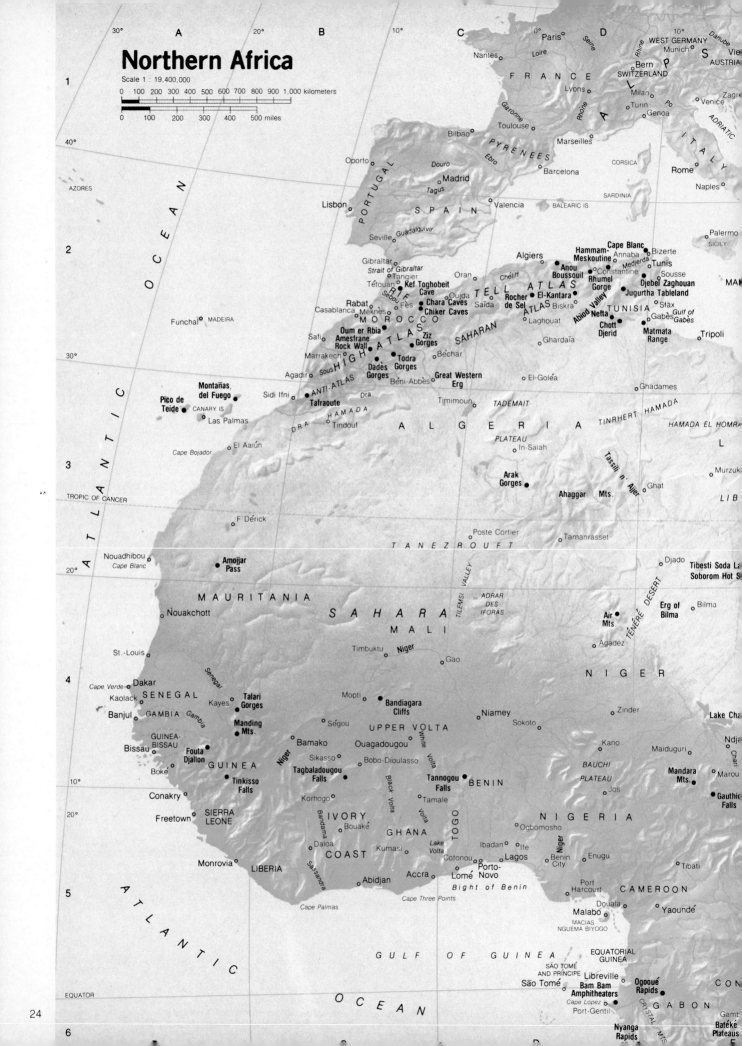

Northern Africa

Scale 1 : 19,400,000

0 100 200 300 400 500 600 700 800 900 1,000 kilometers

0 100 200 300 400 500 miles

A 30° 20° **B** 10° **C** 0° **D** 10°

AZORES

OCEAN

ATLANTIC

Nantes
Paris
Loire
Seine
FRANCE
Lyons
Garonne
Toulouse
Rhône
Marseilles
RHINE
WEST GERMANY
Munich
Danube
Bern
SWITZERLAND
Milan
Po
Turin
Genoa
Venice
AUSTRIA
Zagr
ADRIATIC
ALPS
PYRENEES
Bilbao
CORSICA
ITALY
Oporto
Douro
Ebro
Rome
Madrid
PORTUGAL
Tagus
SPAIN
Naples
SARDINIA
Lisbon
Seville
Guadalquivir
Valencia
BALEARIC IS.
Palermo
SICILY
Gibraltar
Strait of Gibraltar
Tangier
Algiers
Cape Blanc
Bizerte
Hammam-Meskoutine
Annaba
Tunis
Tétouan
RIF
Chéliff
Anou Boussouil
Medjerda
Sousse
Kef Toghobeit Cave
Oran
TELL ATLAS
Constantine
Rhumel Gorge
Djebel Zaghouan
Oujda
Rocher de Sel
El-Kantara
Jugurtha Tableland
Rabat
Sebou
Fès
Chara Caves
ATLAS
Biskra
Abiod Nefta
TUNISIA
Casablanca
Meknes
Chiker Caves
SAHARAN
Sfax
Gulf of Gabes
MOROCCO
Saïda
Laghouat
Chott Djerid
Funchal
MADEIRA
Safi
Oum er Rbia
Amestrane Rock Wall
Ziz Gorges
Ghardaïa
Matmata Range
Gabès
Marrakech
HIGH ATLAS
Todra Gorges
Béchar
Tripoli
Agadir
Sous
Dadès Gorges
Great Western Erg
Ghadames
Sidi Ifni
ANTI-ATLAS
Béni-Abbès
El-Goléa
Montañas del Fuego
Dra
Timimoun
TADEMAIT
TINRHERT HAMADA
HAMADA EL HOMRA
Pico de Teide
CANARY IS.
Tafraoute
HAMADA
DRA
Tindouf
A L G E R I A
PLATEAU
Cape Bojador
El Aaiún
In-Salah
Tassili n' Ajjer
Murzuk
Arak Gorges
Ghat
LIB
TROPIC OF CANCER
Ahaggar Mts.
F' Dérick
Poste Cortier
Tamanrasset
Djado
Tibesti Soda La
Soborom Hot S
TANEZROUFT
Nouadhibou
Cape Blanc
Amojjar Pass
TILEMSI VALLEY
Erg of Bilma
Bilma
MAURITANIA
SAHARA
ADRAR DES IFORAS
Aïr Mts.
TÉNÉRÉ DESERT
Agadez
Nouakchott
MALI
St.-Louis
Timbuktu
Niger
Gao
N I G E R
Cape Verde
Dakar
Senegal
Kaolack
SENEGAL
Kayes
Talari Gorges
Mopti
Bandiagara Cliffs
Niamey
Zinder
Lake Cha
Banjul
GAMBIA
Gambia
Manding Mts.
Ségou
UPPER VOLTA
Sokoto
Kano
Maiduguri
Ndja
Chari
Bissau
GUINEA-BISSAU
Niger
Bamako
Ouagadougou
White Volta
BAUCHI PLATEAU
Mandara Mts.
Marou
Boké
Fouta Djallon
GUINEA
Tagbaladougou Falls
Sikasso
Bobo-Dioulasso
Black Volta
Tannogou Falls
BENIN
Jos
Gauthio Falls
Conakry
Tinkisso Falls
Korhogo
Volta
NIGERIA
SIERRA LEONE
Freetown
Bandama
IVORY
Bouaké
GHANA
Tamale
TOGO
Ogbomosho
Ibadan
Ife
Benin City
Enugu
Tibati
Monrovia
LIBERIA
COAST
Daloa
Kumasi
Lake Volta
Niger
Lagos
Cotonou
Porto-Novo
Lomé
Port Harcourt
CAMEROON
Abidjan
Accra
Bight of Benin
Douala
Yaoundé
Cape Palmas
Cape Three Points
Malabo
MACIAS NGUEMA BIYOGO
ATLANTIC
OCEAN
GULF OF GUINEA
EQUATORIAL GUINEA
SÃO TOMÉ AND PRÍNCIPE
Libreville
Ogooué Rapids
CON
São Tomé
Bam Bam Amphitheaters
GABON
EQUATOR
Cape Lopez
Port-Gentil
Gamb
CRYSTAL MTS.
Batéké Plateaus
Nyanga Rapids

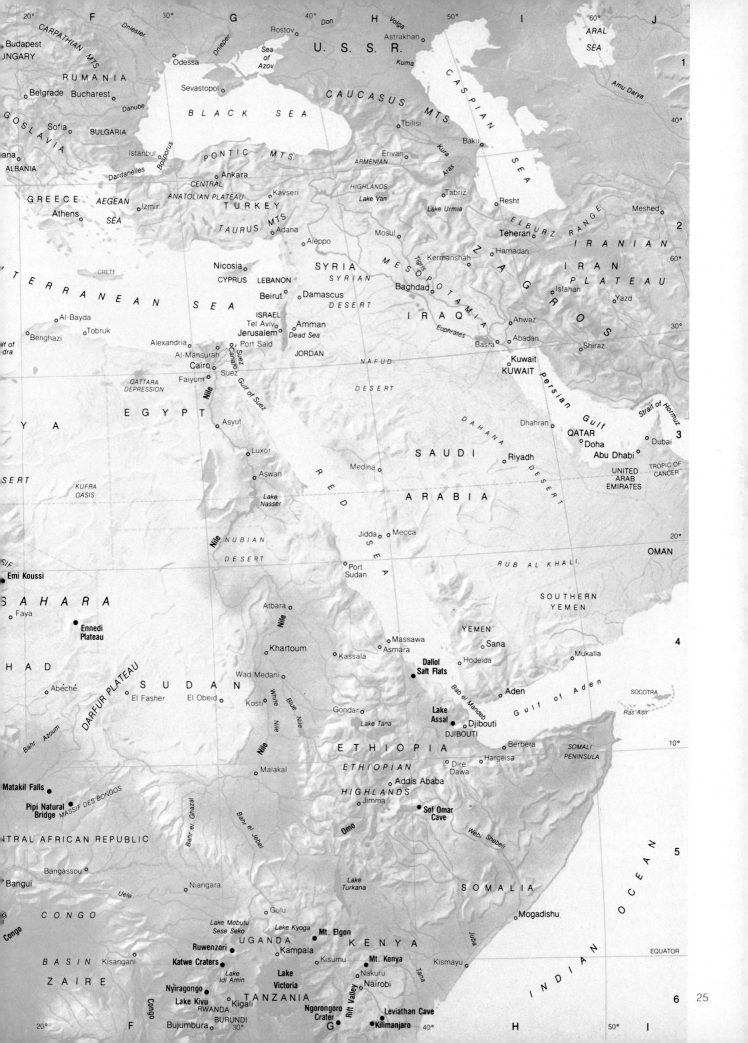

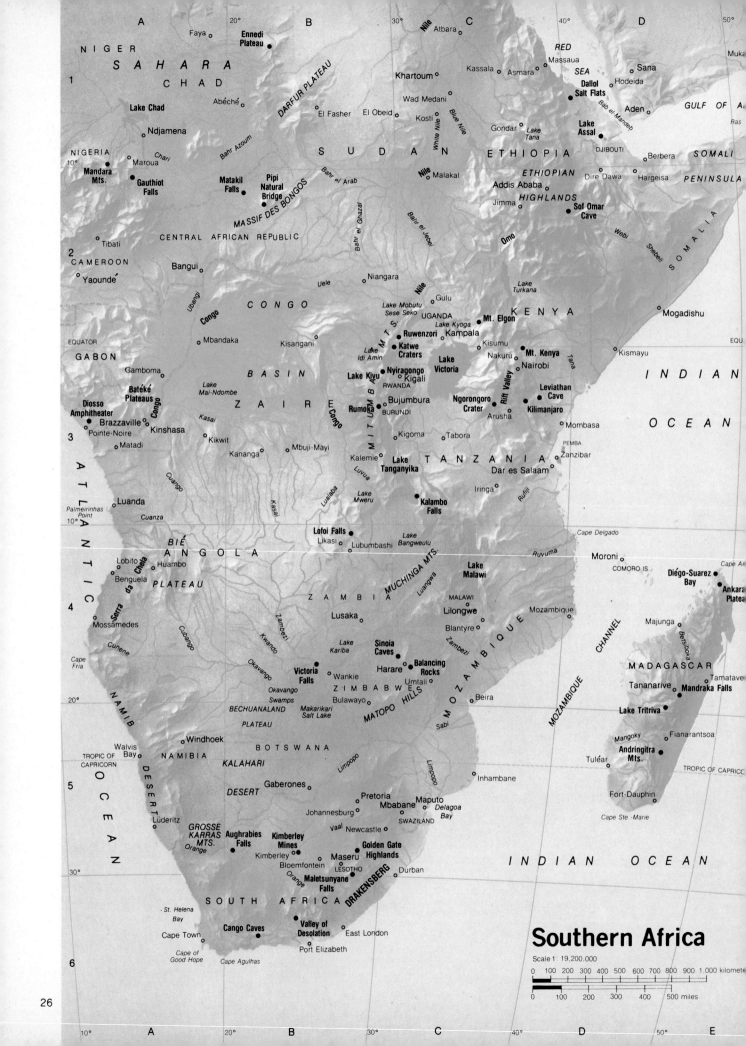

Southern Africa

Scale 1 : 19,200,000

0   100   200   300   400   500   600   700   800   900   1,000 kilometers

0   100   200   300   400   500 miles

26

A

Aar Gorge

- Switzerland
- Map: page 17, D–4

A glacier-fed river has sculpted this deep, breathtaking gash across a limestone barrier in the Swiss Alps.

From its source in the Bernese Alps to its confluence with the Rhine, the Aar River winds northward through some of Switzerland's loveliest scenery. But few sectors can rival its passage through the Aar Gorge, a slot carved through a limestone ridge near the little town of Meiringen.

Just as the river rises today from a glacier on the flanks of the Finsteraarhorn, the highest peak in the Bernese Alps, the gorge is an indirect product of glaciation. As the Ice Age came to an end some 10,000 years ago, torrential runoff water from melting glaciers eroded a deep, narrow chasm through the limestone barrier.

The result is truly spectacular. Although the gorge is scarcely 1 mile (1.6 kilometers) long, it is bounded by sheer cliffs up to 165 feet (50 meters) high. And at the bottom the cleft in places is no more than three feet (one meter) wide.   □

AAR GORGE. *The Aar River churns between the sheer walls of the gorge, carved when melting glaciers released torrents of water at the close of the last ice age.*

ABIOD VALLEY. *In the lower part of the valley, barren plateaus contrast with the lush greenery in oases irrigated by the Algerian river as it descends toward the Sahara.*

Abiod Valley

- Algeria
- Map: page 24, D–2

Near the northern fringes of the Sahara, a ribbon of greenery traces the course of a life-giving river.

The Aurès massif, a range of the Saharan Atlas in northeastern Algeria, has long been a formidable barrier to travel. Lines of rugged cliffs border the mountains on the north; to the south they slope down toward a Saharan basin that lies below sea level.

One of the few passes across the massif is the Abiod Valley, a route that has been known since Roman times. The Abiod River rises near the foot of Djebel Chélia ("Shield Mountain"), which, with an elevation of 7,638 feet (2,328 meters), is the highest peak in northern Algeria. Flowing southward toward the Sahara, the river winds through a valley lush with greenery nurtured by its waters.

Plentiful precipitation on the high peaks of the Aurès sustains the flow of the Abiod River. Djebel Chélia and other summits are covered by snow for three months of the year, and rainfall is substantial in other seasons.

The highlands bordering the upper valley have a distinctly Mediterranean look. Dense forests of oaks, pines, and ancient cedars mantle the slopes. But beyond the narrow Tighanimine Gorges, where the walls bear an inscription left by Roman legions, the scene begins to change. The forests give way to low shrubs, and eventually they too disappear.

But the valley itself is dotted with oases watered by the Abiod. The most beautiful is at the village of Rhoufi, where stark cliffs and barren plateaus contrast with the greenery on the floor of the valley. In addition to groves of date palms, there are orchards of figs, pomegranates, and apricots, as well as plots of vegetables and flowers. A road on the rim of the cliff overlooking the valley provides travelers with spectacular views of the oasis.

Other villages dot the valley farther downstream, but by now travelers are aware of hot desert winds blowing in from the south. Finally, beyond the last few scattered oases, the Sahara, whose influence has long been felt, stretches to the horizon. And there the life-sustaining waters of the Abiod, reduced to a trickle, at last are completely absorbed by the parched desert sands.   □

ACADIA NATIONAL PARK. *Rugged granite hills and headlands beside the restless sea epitomize Acadia and the rocky coast of Maine.*

Acadia National Park

- United States (Maine)
- Map: page 11, F–4

The passage of glaciers long ago and the continuing onslaught of the waves have combined to mold the landscapes of this splendid park.

Acadia National Park on the coast of Maine, though comparatively small, includes landscapes and seascapes of incredible beauty and variety. Granite mountains drop precipitously to the sea, where battering waves crash thunderously against rocky cliffs and headlands. Elsewhere along the scalloped shoreline there are bays and coves, sea caves and tranquil tide pools, picturesque fishing villages and sedate resorts, while inland, freshwater lakes and ponds are surrounded by magnificent forests, rolling meadows, and steep valleys.

Most of the park is situated on Mount Desert Island, but it also includes part of Schoodic Peninsula (the only portion of the park on the mainland), the wilderness of Isle au Haut, and several smaller islands. The highest point in the park—and on the entire eastern seaboard of the United States—is Cadillac Mountain, at 1,530 feet (466 meters). Its summit, accessible by road, overlooks an incomparable panorama of the island-studded sea and long headlands of Maine's famous rocky coast.

The rocks exposed on the mountains and along the shore are mostly coarse-grained pink and gray granite. They were formed some 275 million years ago when a pocket of molten magma welled up into even older overlying layers of sedimentary rock, then slowly cooled and hardened into granite. Most of the sedimentary rocks have since been worn away, and today little more than the granite remains.

The most distinctive features of Acadia National Park were sculpted during the Ice Age, which began about 2 million years ago. An ice cap centered on eastern Canada slowly spread southward, eventually covering the Maine coast with ice more than 5,000 feet (1,500 meters) thick.

Advancing and retreating several times across the land, the debris-laden ice scoured the entire region. Mountaintops were rounded off, and the polished bedrock was grooved with long striations. Basins were deepened in the lowlands, later to be filled by lakes and ponds such as lovely Jordan Pond. Steep, river-carved valleys were widened and deepened into characteristic glacial valleys with distinctive U-shaped cross sections.

One of the valleys was subsequently invaded by the sea, forming Somes Sound, which nearly splits Mount Desert Island in two. The only true fjord in the eastern United States, it is about 6 miles (10 kilometers) long and is flanked by steep slopes that descend to depths of 150 feet (45 meters) below the water.

As a result of the Ice Age, moreover, Maine's coast is a classic example of a drowned coastline. The tremendous weight of the ice cap caused the earth's crust to warp downward. The eventual melting of the ice, in turn, caused the sea level to rise. Former valleys were flooded, becoming long, narrow bays and inlets; the intervening mountain ridges remained as headlands pointing out to sea. Offshore, only the highest mountain crests remained visible as islands both large and small.

Even today Acadia's landscapes are still being altered by one of the most visible forces of erosion: the relentless, pounding waves. Attacking fractures in the rock, they undermine the cliffs and in time reduce even the largest boulders to rubble and sand.

Today a network of roads and trails provides tourists with a number of ways to sample the full range of Acadia's landscapes, richly varied forests, and plentiful wildlife. Perhaps the most memorable is an early morning pilgrimage to the summit of Cadillac Mountain, where visitors can be bathed by the first rays of sunlight that daily touch the United States. □

Acapulco Bay

- Mexico
- Map: page 12, B–3

From the time of its discovery by the conquistadores, the mountain-girt bay has been a magnet for travelers.

Sometimes known as "the pearl of the Pacific," Acapulco Bay is one of the finest natural harbors in the world. A broad, deep, oval indentation on the southwest coast of Mexico, it is partially enclosed on one end by a sheltering peninsula. An island, Isla la Roqueta, in the mouth of the deep-water bay further protects it from ocean swells. Inland, beyond a narrow strip of lowlands, the bay is almost completely encircled by the mountain barrier of Sierra Madre del Sur, which rises steeply to heights of 3,000 feet (900 meters) above the water.

The soldiers of the conquistador Hernán Cortés first arrived on the shores of Acapulco Bay in the 1530's, and the Spaniards quickly recognized its potential. Acapulco soon became the main port for Spain's China trade. Galleons laden with gold and silver regularly set sail across the Pacific and returned from the Far East with rich cargoes of silk, porcelain, and spices.

Today, however, the bay is best known as the focal point of a flourishing resort. The ramparts of luxury hotels rise all along its shores. The slopes are dotted with homes and villas surrounded by gardens brimming with blossoming bougainvillea and poinciana. And fringing the deep blue bay are long stretches of golden, palm-lined beaches, some favored for their morning exposure, others for their afternoon hours in the sun. □

ACAPULCO BAY. *Deep, broad, and sheltered from the sea, the bay was once a thriving seaport. Today a fine climate and golden beaches have made it a flourishing vacation resort.*

Aconcagua

- Argentina
- Map: page 15, C–6

Rising toward the heavens in the southern Andes is the "rooftop" of the Americas, the highest peak in the entire Western Hemisphere.

To the east of the capital city of Santiago in central Chile, the magnificent mountain wall of the Andes rises toward the sky along the border with Argentina. Rugged and windswept, several of the jagged peaks reach to heights of 20,000 feet (6,100 meters) and more.

The undisputed giant of them all, some 70 miles (110 kilometers) northeast of Santiago in Argentina, is the lofty summit of Aconcagua. With an elevation of 22,835 feet (6,960 meters) above sea level, it is the highest mountain in the Western Hemisphere. Its summit stands some 2,500 feet (750 meters) higher than that of Alaska's Mount McKinley, the highest peak in North America.

Steep, glacier-carved slopes descend in all directions from the barren crest. At the southern foot of the mountain, the slopes end at Uspallata Pass, one of the most important in the Andes. Located some 12,500 feet (3,800 meters) above sea level, the pass is traversed by a road, and the Transandine Railroad tunnels beneath it. In 1817 the great South American liberator José de San Martín led his army across the pass into Chile, a feat considered comparable to Hannibal's crossing of the Alps. Today the pass is crowned by the famous statue of the Christ of the Andes, commemorating boundary settlements between Argentina and Chile.

As might be expected, this king among American mountains has been an irresistible challenge to climbers. Many have made it to the top since the first successful ascent in 1897. But many have also died in the effort, for the mountain is subject to sudden fierce storms accompanied by winds of up to 160 miles (260 kilometers) per hour. Strangely enough, however, despite the obvious hazards a number of dogs have successfully accompanied climbers to the top.

The mountain, a mass of volcanic rock atop older, intensely folded sedimentary rock, was severely glaciated during the Ice Age. And glaciers persist on its slopes to this day. Among the several rivers nourished by their meltwater is the Aconcagua, which flows westward to the Pacific Ocean. Rising on the frigid heights, it descends to irrigate a fertile subtropical valley on its journey to the sea. □

Adonis, Grotto of

- Lebanon
- Map: page 18, E–5

The nearby ruins of a Roman temple attest to the antiquity of human association with this cave, said to be the place where Adonis was slain.

At the village of Afqa, some 25 miles (40 kilometers) northeast of Beirut, the dark mouth of a cave interrupts the face of a high limestone cliff. Water cascades from the opening, especially in spring, and flows into the Mediterranean via the Nahr Ibrahim. The river was once known as the Adonis, and the cave itself is still known locally as the Grotto of Adonis.

According to one version of the legend of Adonis, the handsome youth beloved by Venus, it was at this cave that he was gored to death by a wild boar. The river's water, reddened by silt after the winter rains, is said to be the blood of the slain youth.

The cave is also of interest for its size. Beyond the pool inside the entrance, more than two miles (three kilometers) of passageways have been explored, some of them dry, others the beds of underground streams. □

Agua

- Guatemala
- Map: page 12, C–3

A graceful volcano never known to be active suddenly caused a city's ruin—not with fiery ash but with a devastating flood of mud and water.

In the autumn of 1541 the town of Ciudad Vieja, the first capital of Guatemala, was destroyed by an upheaval that no one could have foreseen. The majestic cone of the volcano Agua, towering some 7,000 feet (2,100 meters) above the city nestled at its foot, showed no signs of activity, nor has it ever actually erupted in the centuries since. Yet in the early morning hours of September 11, 1541, the volcano unleashed a devastating torrent of destruction that engulfed the entire city.

According to an early account of the catastrophe, it had been raining steadily for three days before disaster struck. Suddenly, at 2 a.m., the earth began to shake with violent tremors. It was then that a wall of mud and water surged down the mountainside, uprooting trees and sending boulders hurtling down the slopes. Ciudad Vieja was buried by the torrent, and by the time the violence ended, more than 1,000 people had been killed.

Agua, or the "water volcano," was named for this strange and lethal flow of water and mud. Scientists attribute its occurrence to a fatal combination

ACONCAGUA. *In the brilliant light beneath frigid, cloudless skies, the mountain stands as a king among giants, towering high above all of its lofty Andean neighbors.*

GROTTO OF ADONIS. *Water flowing from the mouth of this cave is the overflow from an extensive network of underground streams that penetrate the limestone massif.*

AGUA. *While its neighbor Fuego emits a plume of smoke and steam, Agua, once the cause of great destruction, now stands silent and serene.*

of unprecedented rainfall and violent earthquakes. Three days of heavy rain had filled the volcano's summit crater to overflowing and at the same time transformed the loosely packed ash and debris on the slopes into a sea of mud. The earth tremors caused a breach in the crater rim, and the escaping water triggered the mudflow that engulfed the town.

Located in southern Guatemala, Agua is but one in a long chain of volcanoes that run parallel to the Pacific coast from Mexico through Central America. (Agua's neighbor Fuego, meaning "fire," is the most active volcano in Guatemala.) Rising to an elevation of 12,310 feet (3,752 meters) above sea level, Agua is distinguished by its strikingly symmetrical slopes that curve gracefully down to the surrounding valleys. Agua is also notable for the relatively small size of its crater: the interior walls are only about 325 feet (100 meters) high, and in one section they are only 40 feet (12 meters) high. It was through this notch in the crater's rim that the torrent of water escaped in 1541, carving a channel that is still clearly visible down the mountainside.

As with other volcanoes, those same slopes are covered by exceptionally fertile volcanic soil. Sugarcane, coffee, and corn are cultivated on the mountainsides, while near the top Agua is still mantled with tropical forest. Visitors frequently trek to the now-tranquil summit for superb views of the surrounding countryside. □

The Pacific Ocean's Restless "Ring of Fire"

Any map detailing the world's principal volcanoes makes it clear that the great majority are located around the margins of the Pacific Ocean. From the mountain chains of South America, a line of volcanoes extends north to Alaska and then continues in a great arc down through the islands of the western Pacific as far as New Zealand.

What is the reason for this long chain of volcanoes and earthquake zones, this "ring of fire" that encircles the Pacific? The so-called theory of continental drift suggests that it is the result of disruptions caused by rapid growth of the ocean floor. In the eastern Pacific a belt of new material is constantly being added to the crustal plate on the ocean floor. This causes older parts of the plate to move east and west like giant conveyor belts. The leading edges move toward—and are finally forced below—the adjacent continental plates.

These collisions result in both earthquakes and intense volcanic activity. When the oceanic plate meets a continental plate, as in the Americas, mountains are formed by the folding of the rock and the accumulation of the lava. When the plates converge beneath the sea, as they do in Japan and Indonesia, curved chains of volcanic islands rise from the floor of the ocean.

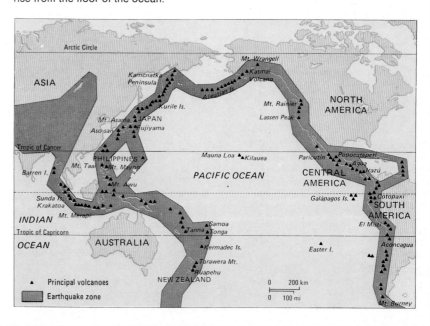

AHAGGAR MOUNTAINS. *Once a nearly flat plain, this uplifted landscape in North Africa is gradually being eroded to more rugged relief.*

Ahaggar Mountains

- Algeria
- Map: page 24, D–3

Baking beneath the Saharan sun, a craggy massif exposes some of the oldest rocks in Africa.

Remote, mysterious, yet dramatically beautiful, the crags and crests of the Ahaggar Mountains rise like islands above desolate plateaus in the heart of the Sahara in Algeria. Covering an area of about 212,000 square miles (550,000 square kilometers), they are sharply bounded on the north, east, and south by abrupt sandstone cliffs at the edge of the encircling Tassili plateaus. The boundary is less distinct toward the west, where the ancient rocks of the Ahaggar region sink beneath the sandstone formations of the Tanezrouft country, the notorious Land of Thirst.

The mountains of the Ahaggar, also known as the Hoggar, are not especially high. Around the edges of the massif they vary between 1,600 and 2,600 feet (500 and 800 meters). Even in the center, in the Atakor Range, they do not rise much above 6,600 feet (2,000 meters); the highest point, Tahat, only reaches 9,574 feet (2,918 meters). Yet they are fascinating, not only for the way they project above their flat surroundings but also for their complex geological history.

In contrast to the relatively young sedimentary formations that surround them, these mountains are composed of metamorphic rocks about 2 billion years old, overlain in places by much more recent volcanic formations. They are in fact one of the few exposed portions of the West African Shield, part of the ancient basement rocks of the continent that are buried beneath sedimentary deposits across most of the Sahara.

Following their formation, the rocks of the shield underwent a long period of folding, faulting, and changing in other ways. By at least 700 million years ago, their surface had been worn down to a vast peneplain, or nearly flat eroded surface. This surface was further planed down by two periods of intense glaciation, one about 650 million years ago and the other about 450 million years ago.

The ancient bedrock is exposed in the Ahaggar because the earth's crust in the area has gradually bulged upward in a broad dome. Any sedimentary deposits that may once have covered it have long since been eroded away, and the old peneplain surface itself is now being sculpted once again to a more rugged relief. In fact it is probable that the dome has been buried and reexcavated several times. No one knows for certain when this happened last, but the evidence suggests that the shield rocks had already been stripped clean of any sedimentary deposits by about 100 million years ago.

From Peneplain to Mountain Peaks

In many areas ancient massifs of crystalline basement rocks have been worn down to nearly flat surfaces known as peneplains. Most of Canada east of the Rocky Mountains, for example, is a peneplain, where metamorphic rocks known as the Canadian Shield have remained relatively stable for a billion years or more.

Elsewhere, certain peneplains have been rejuvenated, or raised again, and subjected to renewed erosion. In some places the rejuvenation has been brought about by a simple doming of the earth's crust. The Adirondacks were formed in this way. The Appalachians, in contrast, were formed by upward arching of the ancient basement rocks on an elongated axis. In other places the old eroded surface has been broken up by faults, followed by up and down movements of great blocks of the crust. The Grand Tetons are dramatic examples of fault-block mountains.

More often, however, the rejuvenation of peneplained surfaces has resulted from a combination of forces. In the Ahaggar Mountains (below left), the crystalline basement rocks domed upward, and volcanoes then spilled lava on the uplifted surface. The Vosges Mountains in France (below right), in contrast, were formed by doming of the surface combined with massive movements along fault lines that produced horsts (uplifted blocks) and grabens (down-dropped blocks). The Rhine now flows through the graben that separates the Vosges from the Black Forest.

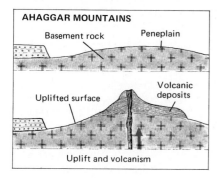

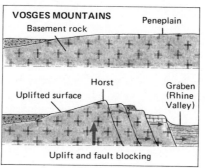

Further upwarping of the Ahaggar dome has taken place since that time, probably as a result of the formation of a pocket of molten material lying deep beneath the crust. Although the pocket has been only partially emptied by volcanic eruptions, this activity has created some of the most impressive scenery in the area. Millions of years ago, domes of volcanic material developed atop broad plateaus of basalt. Now, after the forces of weathering have worked on the rock, only the more erosion-resistant material that plugged the volcanic cores remains. These plugs, which were split into vertical columns when the molten material cooled, stand as extraordinary towers starkly silhouetted against the horizon. The most magnificent of all these peaks, Ilamen, rises to 8,760 feet (2,670 meters).

The recent "rejuvenation" of the Ahaggar uplift has led to the carving of the once flat peneplain into more rugged mountainous relief amplified by repeated cycles of change in rainfall and temperature. Radiating outward from the Atakor Range at the center of the uplift, for example, is a series of river valleys. Although these are mostly dry today, all are very deeply incised into the surface of the land—the products of vigorous erosion during successive wet periods that alternated with drier times.

Among the evidence of past cold intervals occurring in the Sahara are hollows on the lower slopes of Ilamen, which were carved out by long periods of snow accumulation and sliding. Here too are found solifluction lobes, curious puffy bulges on hillsides that were caused by the gradual downward flow of soil as a result of repeated freezing and thawing of the surface.

But the most dramatic signs of more favorable climates in the not-so-distant past are the implements of Stone Age men that have been discovered here. And on the nearby Tassili plateaus are many rock paintings depicting hunters and herdsmen, elephants, cattle, and sheep—creatures that could have thrived only when the desert truly bloomed.

Even today, however, the Ahaggar Mountains are not completely barren. Rainfall, though meager, is sufficient to support a sparse cover of grasses and other plants in lowland valleys and in the Atakor highlands. Here and there are a few stunted olive and pistachio trees. And surrounding each of the many *gueltas,* or permanent water holes, that dot the mountain slopes is a small oasis of greenery, including an abundance of colorful oleanders.

A population of Tuareg tribesmen, who continue to tend their flocks of goats and sheep, still survives in this strangely haunting region. Although their traditional nomadic way of life is gradually being modified by intrusions of the modern world, their tall, blue-shrouded figures striding across the horizon provide a living link with the long history of this remote, majestic Saharan landscape. □

AHAGGAR MOUNTAINS. *Towering volcanic plugs, the resistant cores of volcanoes that have been worn away by erosion, are some of the region's most dramatic landforms.*

Ain ez Zarqa

- Lebanon
- Map: page 18, E–5

After a mysterious underground journey the waters of the Orontes rise in an artesian spring.

Not far from Lebanon's Mediterranean shore is a desertlike plateau that is constantly attacked by wind and dust storms. Suddenly, in the midst of this desolation, a surprisingly green area, rich in trees and other plants, interrupts the landscape. The reason for this unexpected relief is Ain ez Zarqa, a natural artesian spring (*ain,* or *ayn,* is an Arabic word meaning "spring").

Fed by meltwater from mountain snows, the waters of Ain ez Zarqa emerge on the surface at this location because of a fault (a fracture in the rock) that intersects a thick limestone formation, allowing the groundwater to escape. Flowing from the spring at the average rate of 3,435 gallons (13 cubic meters) per second, the water not only irrigates this area; it also supplies the Orontes, Lebanon's most important river and one that crosses

An artesian spring occurs where water in a water-bearing rock layer (an aquifer) is trapped between two impermeable rock layers. The water escapes to the surface through a natural outlet, such as a fault, in the upper rock layer.

Water flows beneath surface

Impermeable rock

Artesian spring

Water flows through permeable rock

Impermeable rock

Fault

Syria and Turkey before emptying into the Mediterranean Sea.

Stone Age sites near Ain ez Zarqa attest to a human presence in the area for thousands of years. A monument decorated with hunting scenes and estimated to be about 2,000 years old squats on a nearby hill. In addition, a honeycomb of cells has been excavated in the sheer rock walls of a steep canyon near Ain ez Zarqa—the ruins of dwellings used in the seventh century by Maronites, a religious group that sought refuge there. □

Aïr Mountains

- Niger
- Map: page 24, D–4

Known to man for thousands of years, the Aïr region is an unexpected haven in the midst of the Sahara.

The Aïr can well be considered the Switzerland of the desert," proclaimed Heinrich Barth, a widely renowned German explorer who reached this region in 1850. This mountainous area extends 250 miles (400 kilometers) north to south and 125 miles (200 kilometers) east to west in the West African country of Niger. An extension of the Ahaggar massif in Algeria, it is a land of contrasts: here there are both arid rocks and lush vegetation, running water and oppressive heat, flat deserts and steep mountain slopes.

The Aïr (also known as Asben and Azbine) began to develop 2 billion to 3 billion years ago, when extreme heat and pressure caused the formation of metamorphic rocks (gneiss, schist, and granite). Then about 150 million years ago, as a result of activity deep within the earth, its crust bulged in this area. This bulge created a circular and radial network of faults that have guided the forces of erosion. Eventually the faulted blocks became separate peaks. Sometime later, volcanic activity produced the cone-shaped summits—for instance, Mounts Gréboun (at 6,562 feet, or 2,000 meters, the Aïr's highest) and Bagzan.

Mount Bagzan is unique among the Aïr Mountains because it has good water resources and supports a permanent farming population. Its irrigation system dates back to ancient times. Harnessed cattle walk around a well to pump the water, which is placed in large goatskin buckets and then emptied into the hollowed-out trunks of palm trees. When the water is needed, it is sent down a network of tiered canals to the rows of crops (among them, dates and olives).

In the east the Aïr Mountains terminate abruptly at the formidable Ténéré Desert. Caravans cross this partly sandy, partly stony expanse as quickly as possible, stopping only at the oases at Fachi and Bilma or at the well at Achegour. Except for a few brief, violent rains in summer, the Ténéré is almost totally dry. Shepherds must find water for their animals where they can: in rock basins and springs.

AIN EZ ZARQA. *The endless stream of water welling up from the spring supports a welcome oasis of greenery in a parched desert landscape. Water that is not used for irrigation eventually flows by way of the Orontes River to the Mediterranean Sea.*

AÏR MOUNTAINS. *Even in this dry region a few spiny acacia trees manage to survive beside giant dunes heaped up at the foot of the mountains.*

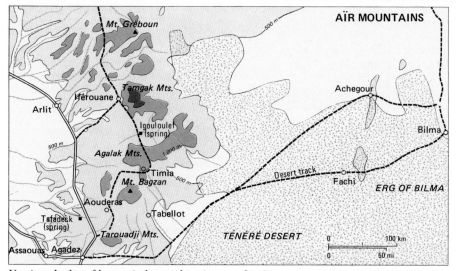

Varying shades of brown indicate elevations in the Aïr, a mountainous region in the West African country of Niger. Part of the Sahara, the Aïr is scored by streambeds that are usually dry (blue dotted lines). Vast areas of sand dunes (stippling) lie to the east.

A desert people called the Tuaregs inhabit the Aïr. Generally nomadic, some of them are now farmers living in the valleys, while others are tradesmen living in the towns. The largest of these settlements is Agadez, an oasis and market town with a population of about 7,000.

Cave murals found in the Aïr indicate that Neolithic man occupied the region some 8,000 years ago. Curiously, the cave pictures portray an area with a much wetter climate, indicating that the desert has advanced greatly in the last few millennia. The region's excessive dryness and extraordinary heat (up to 122° F, or 50° C, in the shade) probably account for the current diminishing of the population in the region. The repeated droughts prevent extensive farming, and this type of climate does not attract industry. The mountains do have, however, a number of natural resources, including substantial deposits of salt, tin, and tungsten. And the recent discovery of an especially valuable mineral, uranium, near Agadez may prove a great boon to the population and the economy of the Aïr. □

Ajdar Valley

- Afghanistan
- Map: page 18, H–5

A natural dam blocks the barren Ajdar Valley. Reputed to be a petrified dragon, the barrier is actually made of travertine.

An impressive rock dam about 260 feet (80 meters) high and 40 feet (12 meters) wide blocks this arid valley deep in the heart of Afghanistan. *Ajdar* is the Persian word for "dragon," and legend has it that the dam is really a petrified dragon that was slain by the son-in-law of the prophet Mohammed after it demanded a daily tribute of one maiden, two camels, and a ration of fodder.

Actually, the dam is a natural barrier anchored to an outcrop of limestone and consisting of accumulations of travertine, which is made of the same substance (calcium carbonate) as limestone. Even in this dry area the underground water is rising to the surface in springs. As it does so, it dissolves calcium carbonate from the limestone. Upon reaching the surface, the pressure decreases, and the calcium carbonate is redeposited as travertine. (Specially adapted plants living here also help in its precipitation.) As long as the groundwater continues to flow upward in this dry region, the natural dam will continue to grow. □

ALAND ISLANDS. *A labyrinth of rocky islands clutters the entry to the Gulf of Bothnia, an arm of the Baltic Sea. Low-lying and well wooded, they are a popular vacation area.*

Aland Islands

● Finland
● Map: page 16, F–2

Relieved of the weight of Ice Age glaciers, the earth's crust continues to rise upward in this area, causing islands to emerge from the sea.

An enchanting world of islands and islets—about 6,500 in all—lies in the entrance to the Gulf of Bothnia, the arm of the Baltic Sea that juts north-ward between Finland and Sweden. Capped with fragrant groves of ever-greens and bare near the waterline, the gently rounded, rocky Aland Islands seem to drift in a labyrinth of picturesque channels.

From a low-flying plane the islands look like pieces of a giant jigsaw puzzle thrown at random across the placid sea. From water level they look like a vacationer's dream come true, and in fact visitors by the thousands arrive each year to camp and boat.

The Aland Islands have a long geological history, and they continue to change perceptibly to this day. The exposed bedrock is a type of granite estimated to be more than 1 billion years old. Composed of large scattered feldspar crystals embedded in masses of fine-grained white or gray quartz,

the rock is tinted with various shades of red and pink.

During the last ice age the entire region was covered by thick sheets of ice. As the masses of ice ground slowly southward, they stripped away most of the soil and the deeply weathered sur-face rock, polishing the granite and planing it to gently undulating con-tours. Over thousands of years the great weight of the ice also caused the earth's crust to bend downward.

When the glaciers melted, immense amounts of water raised the level of the ocean. Waves of the ancestral Bal-tic Sea, which was much larger than it is today, came flooding over the area, drowning the landscape and washing away much of the debris of rocks and clay that the melting glaciers had de-posited on the surface.

But during the past 10,000 years the earth's crust, relieved of the immense weight of the ice sheets, has been slowly rising. More and more land is emerging from the sea, forming more and more islands that grow larger and larger. (The main island now covers 285 square miles, or 740 square kilo-meters.) Because of this movement, it is possible that someday all the islands may be united in a solid neck of land linking Finland to Sweden and trans-forming the Gulf of Bothnia into a broad landlocked sea. □

Aletsch Glacier

● Switzerland
● Map: page 17, D–4

Though every year this glacier is slightly smaller than the year before, it is still the largest in the Alps.

The Aletsch Glacier flows down the valley from its beginning high in a pass between two massive mountains, the Jungfrau and the Mönch. Located in south-central Switzerland, it mea-sures some 15 miles (25 kilometers) in length and encompasses about 50 square miles (130 square kilometers), making it both the longest and the largest glacier in the Alps.

Glaciers are often thought of as rivers of ice—rivers that are made of snow that has compacted under pres-sure. Like ordinary rivers, they have their sources, tributaries, and outlets. In the case of the Aletsch, three ice streams—the Great Aletsch Firn (*firn* is the name used for compacted snow), the Jungfrau Firn, and the Ewig-schneefeld ("Eternal Snow Field") —come together in the region called the Concordia Platz. From this point the great glacier moves south toward the Rhone Valley, flowing at an av-erage rate of 500 to 650 feet (150 to 200 meters) per year.

Along the way small tributary gla-ciers feed into the main glacier. How-ever, most of the tributary glaciers are melting back and have become dis-connected from the main glacier, so that ice from them no longer reaches the Aletsch.

On its left bank the Aletsch Glacier forms a wall, damming up the waters of a small tributary valley and creat-ing a lake called the Märjelensee. In the past the lake sometimes drained unexpectedly into channels beneath the ice, but now the drainage has been controlled to avoid flooding.

The last big ice advance occurred in the 17th century, but today there is not enough snow to compensate for loss by melting. Since 1892 the terminal snout of the Aletsch has receded more than 3,300 feet (1,000 meters), and the glacier now occupies only about half of its former basin. Traces of irrigation canals, which were dug into the old valley floor and then buried by the ice during the late Middle Ages, have now become visible again. Along the sides of the glacier a line of boulders and rocky debris (lateral moraines) shows the former extent of the ice.

ALETSCH GLACIER. *Grinding relentlessly down the mountainside, the great river of ice is streaked with dark ribbons of rock debris.*

But even at its present size, the Aletsch Glacier stores a tremendous amount of water. In fact the Massa River, which is a tributary of the Rhone, consists entirely of meltwater from the Aletsch. Though in winter the stream almost runs dry, its torrential summer flow supplies a seasonally operated hydroelectric station.

At one time difficult to reach, the Aletsch region now attracts many visitors, who can take a train up the side of the Jungfrau to the highest point in Europe that is reachable by rail. Also, several cable cars run up from the Rhone Valley to vantage points above the glacier itself.

The glacier provides exceptional terrain for skiers, even in spring, and the Aletschhorn (the highest peak in its basin) offers a challenge to the most experienced mountain climbers. In addition, there is a nature reserve (the Aletschwald), as well as two resorts at Belalp and Riederalp, which provide accommodations for visitors interested in glacier excursions. The beautiful scenery and the pure air are clearly reasons enough for visiting Switzerland's Aletsch Glacier.   □

ALONG BAY. *Riddled by tunnels and caves, the towering islands and islets scattered across the bay are the disjointed remnants of a once-continuous limestone formation.*

Along Bay

- Vietnam
- Map: page 21, E–2

Tall, rocky towers rise from the placid waters off the coast of Asia. Mythology attributes them to a dragon, modern geology to erosion.

Along Bay has one of the most extraordinary landscapes in the world. In this arm of the Gulf of Tonkin, a chain of jagged peaks—some carved into arches, others excavated into tunnels, and still others into caves hung with menacing stalactites—protrudes from the sea as if suddenly engulfed by an immense cataclysm.

The rock formations in Along Bay are so fantastic in shape and extent that Vietnamese mythology credits them to a dragon; the name Along, or Halong, means "the place where the dragon came down." Individual formations bear the fanciful names bestowed on them by the French geographers who mapped the area in the 19th century: Les Marionnettes ("The Puppets"), Ile du Grand Singe ("Island of the Great Ape"), Grotte des Merveilles ("Grotto of Marvels"), Ile de la Surprise ("Island of Surprise").

Made of 250-million-year-old limestone, these rocks have been shaped by karst erosion. In effect, this means that their structure is a result of the dissolving of limestone by the acidic action of carbon dioxide contained in groundwater. Karst landscape often includes caves—for example, Carlsbad Caverns in New Mexico and Mammoth Cave in Kentucky.

Some karst regions are more impressive than others, for the degree of erosion varies according to the type and thickness of the limestone, the amount of rainfall, the content of carbon dioxide in the water, and other factors. The karst in Along Bay, which is part of a rock formation that extends into China, is exceptional because the erosion is extremely advanced. In this tropical region of Asia, both the annual precipitation rate and the carbon dioxide content are very high, the limestone is thick at the base, and the rock is especially vulnerable because of folding and fracturing of the earth's crust here. Thus erosion has contoured even the residual peaks, carving them into tortuous channels, deep caves, and high arches—a type of relief that is known as tower karst because of the steep-sided hills.

Sculpted when the rocks were above sea level, the karst in Along Bay is all the more spectacular because it is now partially submerged. As sea level rose because of the melting of the Ice Age glaciers, the water drowned the bases of the rocks, transforming the landscape into an islet-strewn sea. In some places deep bays and supersaline lakes developed in the depressions between the towers. Though these lakes seem cut off from the sea, their water level rises and falls with the tide, because they are connected with the sea by the network of karst tunnels and caves that honeycomb the highly eroded sculptures of rock. □

Alps

- Europe
- Map: page 17, D–4

Rising like a jagged spine across Europe, the Alps swing through seven countries and divide the continent into two distinct climatic zones.

About 180 million years ago, according to many geologists, a spectacular upheaval took place on the earth's surface. The Atlantic Ocean began to spread, increasing in size and causing Africa to move northward and initiate a series of collisions with southern Europe. The climax was reached approximately 40 million years ago, when the earth's crust in the Alpine area crumpled and buckled, and the distorted landscape developed into the highest mountains in Europe. Even today the Alps continue to grow, thrust farther upward by movements of the earth's crust.

The central axis, or core, of the Alps is made up of hard crystalline rocks such as granite, gneiss, and mica schist. Spreading out from this core region is a wide zone of somewhat softer sedimentary rocks, mainly hard limestones with weaker sandstones and shales.

The Alps are neither straight nor symmetrical. They extend in an arc from southern France through Italy, Switzerland, Austria, and Germany (where they reach their northernmost point) and then cut into Yugoslavia and Albania. The mountains are at their highest in the west and south, falling away to the east and north. At all points, however, the Alps form a climatic barrier between the warm air of the Mediterranean and the colder temperatures of northern Europe.

In their long span (750 miles, or 1,200 kilometers), the Alps hold virtually every kind of natural wonder. There are the famous peaks—the Matterhorn, the Jungfrau, Mont Blanc—that tower snowcapped above the clouds. There are the massive glaciers—the Aletsch and the Gorner, for example—that flow slowly down the mountain valleys. The great rivers of Europe—the Rhine, Rhone, and Danube—rise in the Alps, and sparkling lakes—Lucerne, Maggiore—nestle in the heights. Spectacular waterfalls, such as the Giessbach, cascade down the slopes, and deep caverns, such as the recently discovered Jean-Bernard Cave, penetrate the mountains.

ALPS. *Above gentle slopes of softer rock the bold limestone summit of France's Mont Aiguille—"Needle Peak"—looms like castle battlements.*

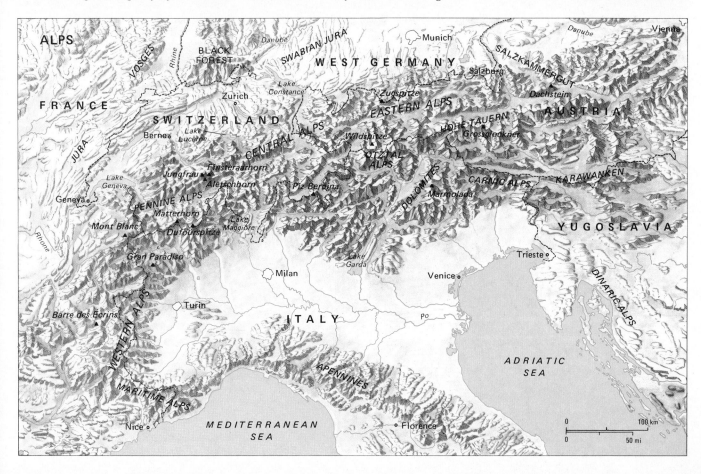

39

ALPS. *In Italy's Gran Paradiso National Park snowcapped peaks contrast with verdant forests beside a rock-strewn stream. Both valleys and mountains were carved by glaciers.*

Amazon River

- Brazil
- Map: page 14, D–3

Largest but not the longest of rivers, the Amazon glides through luxuriant jungles across equatorial South America.

The fertile valleys of the Alps have attracted settlers ever since prehistoric times, providing a refuge for many different peoples. Some found the mountains a challenge. For nearly 2,000 years the greatest feat of Alpine daring (as well as one of the most phenomenal achievements in history) was the epic journey of the Carthaginian general Hannibal, who led a great cavalcade of troops, supplies, and elephants through the western Alps to defeat the forces of Rome in the second century B.C. Then in 1786 two Frenchmen, Jacques Balmat and Michel Paccard, succeeded in reaching the top of Mont Blanc—at 15,772 feet (4,807 meters) the tallest peak in the Alps. This exploit opened the era of Alpinism for mountain climbers and has led to the development of tourism as the main industry of the Alps. Today vacationers from all over the world travel there to enjoy the excellent skiing and mountain climbing, pure air, and splendid scenery. □

The first European to discover the Amazon was the Spanish explorer Vicente Yáñez Pinzón, onetime captain aboard Christopher Columbus's ship the *Niña*. Cruising the coast of Brazil in 1500, he sailed into at least one of the mouths of the Amazon and realized that he had found a very large river indeed.

But real exploration did not begin until 1541, when Francisco de Orellana, another Spaniard, set out on a journey down one of the Amazon's tributaries in eastern Ecuador. Drifting with the current into ever-larger streams, Orellana and his band of soldiers reached the Atlantic nearly a year and a half later. Along the way they battled with tall, fierce female warriors whom Orellana likened to the Amazons, the legendary female warriors of Greek mythology. And so the river got its name.

The name is appropriate, for the Amazon is a giant among rivers. Only the Nile is longer—and only slightly

AMAZON RIVER. *Heavy rainfall throughout the vast drainage basin supports lush jungle and accounts for the enormous volume of water.*

longer. But the Amazon's total length (almost 4,000 miles, or 6,500 kilometers) is still impressive: it is equal to about 1½ times the distance from San Francisco to New York.

Its drainage basin is the largest of any river in the world. Fed by more than 1,000 tributaries, including 7 that are themselves more than 1,000 miles (1,600 kilometers) long, it drains more than half of Brazil as well as parts of Bolivia, Peru, Ecuador, Colombia, and Venezuela. Its total drainage basin of some 2,722,000 square miles (7,050,000 square kilometers) encompasses about one-third of South America—an area more than 10 times the size of Texas and nearly as large as the entire contiguous United States.

Over most of this vast region the climate is very warm and humid. Rain falls about 200 days each year, and total rainfall exceeds 80 inches (2,030 millimeters) per year. One result of so much rain is that Amazonia, as the central region is known, is covered by the largest tropical rain forest in the world. Another result is that the river carries by far the largest volume of water of any river in the world. On the average, some 28 billion gallons (105 trillion liters) per minute flow into the sea—about 10 times the flow of the Mississippi. The discharge is so great, in fact, that it noticeably dilutes the salinity of the Atlantic's waters for

more than 100 miles (160 kilometers) offshore.

The great river begins as hundreds of tiny streams high in the Peruvian Andes, some of them within 100 miles (160 kilometers) of the Pacific Ocean. Rushing down the slopes, stream after stream continues to merge to form larger and larger rivers. Near Iquitos in eastern Peru, the northeastward-flowing Ucayali and the Río Marañón, the two main headwaters of the Amazon, unite to form a truly major river. Iquitos is the point farthest upstream that shallow-draft freighters

and passenger vessels can penetrate (deepwater ships can reach as far as Manaus in central Brazil).

Beyond Iquitos the river changes both its character and course. Turning abruptly eastward, it more or less parallels the equator as it meanders over lowland plains. At Iquitos the river also changes its name. Locally it is known as the Solimões from Iquitos to its junction with the Rio Negro at Manaus and is called the Amazon only from Manaus to the sea.

Crossing the low interior basin of Brazil, the Amazon flows along a very

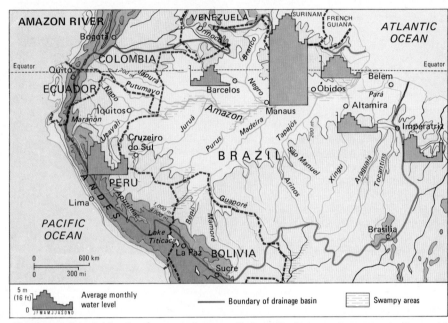

Nearly continentwide, the Amazon's drainage basin is the largest of any river in the world. Crossing a nearly flat interior basin, the river is flanked by broad swampy zones that are periodically flooded. Because of seasonal differences in the climate, the high- and low-water levels of various tributaries occur at different times of the year.

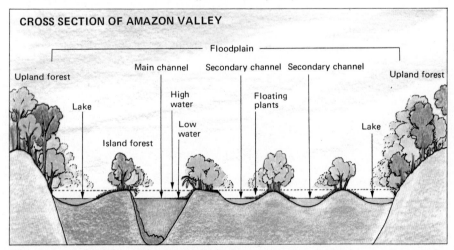

The Amazon's floodplain, 25 miles (40 kilometers) or more in width, is a vast swampy zone laced with an intricate network of secondary channels, lakes, and islands. Inundated at each high-water stage, the islands are heavily forested with trees adapted to withstand periodic flooding. Beyond the floodplain on permanently dry land, the taller species take over, including many trees that are valuable as timber.

gentle gradient—only about 1¼ inches per mile (20 millimeters per kilometer). Sluggish now, it branches into numerous secondary channels, which are separated by very densely forested islands. Beyond the riverbanks are broad, swampy floodplains dotted with lakes (*varzéas*) and covered with lush, periodically flooded forests.

All along the course of the river there are seasonal floods. Tributaries flowing from the south tend to reach their highest stages from February to April, while those coming from the north tend to crest in June or July.

On its long journey to the sea the Amazon also varies in color. Some of its tributaries are called *ríos blancos* (white rivers), though their color is oftener a murky yellow or tan. Others are known as *ríos negros* (black rivers), their waters dark but crystal clear. The white rivers rise in the Andes, and their turbidity results from the heavy loads of mud and silt they carry. The black rivers, in contrast, rise in areas of ancient basement rock where little sediment remains to be washed away; only dissolved organic matter stains their clarity.

Clearly the most dramatic union of a black-water stream and a white one occurs at Manaus, where the Rio Negro flows into the muddy Amazon. For many miles the black and white waters flow side by side in separate, clearly defined streams before they finally intermingle.

About 600 miles (965 kilometers) from the coast, at Óbidos, the ocean begins to affect the river. Tides are able to penetrate this far upstream because of the extremely gentle slope of the land.

Beyond the point where the Xingu flows in from the south, the Amazon splits up into a maze of channels clogged by larger and larger islands. (Marajó, the biggest island in the delta, is about the size of Vermont and New Hampshire combined.) Finally, beyond its several mouths, the river merges with the sea.

Although there are a few sizable cities along the river's banks and scattered settlements inland, Amazonia is largely uninhabited. Here and there plantations have been cleared in the jungles, and natives ply the streams in search of latex and Brazil nuts. But mostly the great green luxuriant rain forest is still pristine wilderness, one of the few large areas left on earth where nature's creation remains more or less unspoiled and intact. ☐

AMESFRANE ROCK WALL. *Unequal erosion of hard and soft rock layers created horizontal grooves in the "columns" that make up this massive wall of stone.*

Amesfrane Rock Wall

- Morocco
- Map: page 24, C–2

Towering above a dry riverbed, the wall of gray and ocher rock looks like a row of pillars carved by giants.

Complete with rows of tall, pillarlike shapes and a crest that resembles a steeple, this spectacular formation in the High Atlas Mountains was long ago dubbed the Cathedral. The main part of the wall rises straight up for some 1,650 feet (500 meters) above a dry riverbed. At the top there is a setback, and then the rock continues up again to a maximum height of 2,300 feet (700 meters).

The wall is composed of alternating layers of hard and soft rock. Because the soft, clayey layers have eroded more easily than the harder layers of sandstone and conglomerate, the surface of the wall is patterned with nearly horizontal grooves and ridges. In addition, when the mountains were uplifted, the rock mass was cleaved by many vertical fractures. Erosion in these zones of weakness resulted in the formation of the gigantic, partially rounded columns.

A rather hazardous trail leads to the setback at the top of the main rock wall. But a magnificent panoramic view rewards anyone who attempts the climb to the top. ☐

Amojjar Pass

- Mauritania
- Map: page 24, B–3

Incised in terrain as flat as a tabletop, the stark desert canyons were carved by rushing water in a part of Africa where today it practically never rains.

Rainfall is rare in the Amojjar Pass, as it is in most of this part of northwestern Africa. At the nearby town of Atar, rainfall averages only about 4 inches (100 millimeters) annually, in some years dropping to as little as 1.2 inches (30 millimeters). Yet over millions of years, water provided by recurring wet cycles has been sufficient to carve this wadi, or dry riverbed, in the nearly flat-topped plateau.

Composed of ancient pinkish to brownish sandstones, the meandering canyon walls are topped by craggy vertical cliffs. Their bases are hidden in surprisingly uniform talus slopes—slopes covered with rocks and sand loosened by erosion from the cliffs and pulled by gravity toward the floor of the valley.

A visitor to this awesomely silent, seemingly unchanging landscape can hardly visualize the rare torrents that caused its formation. A few drought-resistant plants, chiefly acacias, dot the valley floor. Nourished by traces of moisture that seep into the sandy soil after the infrequent storms, they are reminders that rain and the resultant erosion affect the landscape all over the globe. ☐

AMOJJAR PASS. *The canyon follows lines of fractures in the original rock formation. Over time, erosion widened the cracks to form the broad openings that exist today.*

Amur River

- U.S.S.R.
- Map: page 19, O–3

Sweeping down from Siberia, the mighty Amur snakes across the plains, making giant loops and meanders as it heads eastward toward the Pacific.

To the Mongols it is known as the Black River, and to the Chinese, Black Dragon River. But it seems that to the early inhabitants of the region the name *A-mur* meant simply "Big River." Flowing for nearly 2,800 miles (4,500 kilometers), the Amur is the longest river in Siberia and the eighth longest in the world. Its drainage basin, which includes areas of China and Mongolia as well as the U.S.S.R., covers approximately 712,000 square miles (1,844,000 square kilometers). And the river is 10 miles (16 kilometers) wide at its mouth.

The Amur proper is formed by the union of the Shilka and the Argun, which flow down from high, rolling plateaus in Mongolia and Siberia. In its upper reaches the Amur is a mountain river. Rushing down the slopes, its bed encumbered by enormous boulders, it cuts through deep gorges and flows between steep banks blanketed by coniferous forests.

As the Amur River flows downstream, the surroundings gradually change. The mountains fade away, and more and more cedars and deciduous trees appear along the shores. At Blagoveshchensk the river divides into numerous branches and begins to wind through a lowland that is subject to frequent flooding. One meander is particularly striking: the river flows in

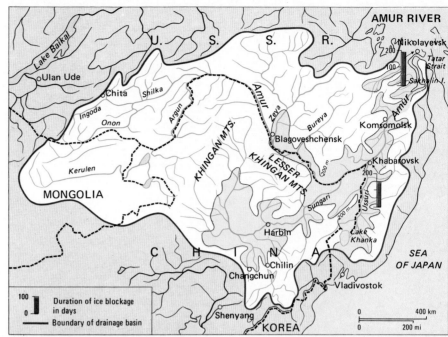

Formed by the merging of the Shilka and the Argun, the Amur is the only major river in Siberia that flows eastward and empties into the Pacific Ocean. Most of its immense drainage basin (outlined in red) is uplands and high plateaus, but it also includes vast lowland plains (green area). An important transportation route, the Amur River is navigable for its entire length except when its channel is blocked by ice. The pink bar graphs compare the yearly duration of ice blockage at two points along the river's course.

an enormous loop that extends for 28 miles (45 kilometers) but covers a distance of only three-tenths of a mile (half a kilometer).

Gathering more and more tributaries, the middle Amur continues on its gentle, majestic course across the very broad floodplain. At the Lesser Khingan Mountains it disappears into a narrow gorge 95 miles (150 kilometers) long, then reappears once more on a vast open plain.

At Khabarovsk, though still about 600 miles (1,000 kilometers) from its mouth, the Amur lies only 230 feet (70 meters) above sea level. Because of the very gentle gradient that prevails during the rest of its journey to the sea, the lower Amur River wanders very sluggishly across the swampy plain, its bed choked with countless islets and shifting sandbars. Finally, after one last turn toward the north, it flows into an immense estuary. The other great rivers of Siberia flow into the Arctic Ocean; the Amur River is unique in that it flows instead into the Pacific Ocean—into a narrow passage called the Tatar Strait.

The Amur is also unusual because it is fed primarily by monsoon rains, not by glaciers or by springs. From November to March, when there is little precipitation, the river reaches its low-

water stage. In spring the water level rises slightly as the light winter snowfall over the plains and mountains begins to melt. But in summer low-pressure systems that develop over Siberia tend to draw in warm, humid air from the Pacific. Violent rainstorms result, each one leading to an abrupt rise in the water level—and often to catastrophic flooding.

Since the beginning of this century, flood-control measures have gradually been containing the river and have been converting its valley into rich agricultural land. Fisheries, especially salmon fisheries, are another important river resource. But above all, the Amur is valuable as a transportation route. Though ice jams block its channel in winter (for up to six months in some places), the river is navigable along its entire course. Thus oil from Sakhalin Island, just offshore from the mouth, can be ferried upstream to the interior, while timber from the Siberian taiga is transported downstream, along with grains, machinery, and other manufactured goods from western Siberia and European Russia. The river, in short, is the basic transportation corridor in this sparsely populated part of the world, and in some cases it is the sole means of access to isolated taiga outposts. □

ANDES. *High in the Peruvian Andes a lake fed by glacial meltwater fills a valley that was dammed by a barrier of glacial debris.*

Andes

- South America
- Map: pages 14–15

Volcanoes and glaciers continue to leave their mark on the longest mountain system in the world. Sinuously winding down the western coast of South America, the Andes eventually disappear into the sea.

The longest and the second highest mountain system in the world, the Andes curve in a gentle S shape along the western edge of South America, all the way from the warm Caribbean to the frigid waters off Cape Horn. The Spanish conquistadores coming upon the mountains in the 16th century called them a cordillera, or rope. More precisely, the Andes are a series of parallel ropes—tall mountain chains

with high plateaus in between. More than 40 Andean mountains are higher than Mount McKinley, the highest peak in North America.

This immense system is still being built and changed by the forces of nature. Some 600 million years ago, the Andes region was a seabed where sediments and other deposits gradually hardened into shale and limestone. About 225 million years ago, thick layers of sandstone developed on top of the shale and limestone.

Then movements within the crust of the earth shaped the rock, folding and lifting the thick formations above the surface of the sea. About 70 million years ago, these high folds were sculpted by running water into gently rolling plains. New upheavals lifted parts of these highlands again, and

again they were deeply grooved by the forces of erosion. In parts of the range the process was repeated yet a third time. Today active volcanoes and slow uplift continue to build the Andes, which are rising about 4 inches (10 centimeters) per century.

A relatively new force has also shaped the mountains. During the last ice age great sheets of ice, some probably as thick as 4,000 feet (1,200 meters), spread over the mountains, carving many of them into characteristic sharp profiles. Between the peaks the slowly moving ice scooped out broad U-shaped valleys. In some places the glaciers dropped piles of boulders and clay, damming the valleys and creating such long, narrow lakes as Lake Buenos Aires.

As the ice melted, the oceans rose and the water filled many of the valleys, forming picturesque fjords along the southern coast. Glaciers and their meltwater are still wearing away parts of the Andes. In the southern part of the continent one small remnant of these ice sheets continues to cover approximately 9,000 square miles (23,000 square kilometers) and nearly fills a valley about 300 miles (500 kilometers) wide.

The Andes Mountains themselves measure some 5,500 miles (8,850 kilometers) long and 200 miles (320 kilometers) wide, except in Bolivia, where the width is almost double that. The northernmost section is split into three major ranges, or cordilleras: the Oc-

cidental, Central, and Oriental. In the Central Andes (the widest region) the two main ranges enclose a large Altiplano, or high plain, at an elevation of 12,000 to 14,000 feet (3,700 to 4,300 meters). In the south the Andean massif narrows to one single ridge topped by Aconcagua, at 22,835 feet (6,960 meters), the highest peak in the Western Hemisphere. The mountains diminish gradually toward the southern tip of the continent, disappearing into the sea as mountainous islands near Cape Horn.

In the highest regions the Andes are a frigid desert whipped by ice-cold winds. The mild climates of the lower Altiplano support some agriculture, including such crops as grains, potatoes, and fodder for livestock. In the Andean foothills some regions receive more than 180 inches (4,500 millimeters) of rainfall annually and are covered with lush tropical vegetation.

A Spanish explorer who sought gold in the 1530's, Diego de Almagro, was probably the first European to reach the interior of the mountains. Though he failed to find what he was looking for, he discovered the ruins of an Inca empire. Almagro followed valleys that run between the fortresslike ranges—valleys that feed some of the mightiest rivers in the world, including the Amazon and Orinoco. Despite the valleys, the mountains remain impassable in some areas, and caravans of sure-footed llamas are still a major means of transportation. □

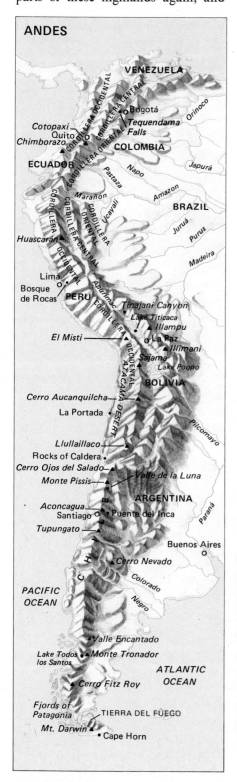

ANDES. *Rimmed by chains of high peaks in the Central Andes is the Altiplano (the "High Plateau"). Frigid, windswept, and generally dry, it is dotted with sparkling lakes.*

Andringitra Mountains

- Madagascar
- Map: page 26, D–5

Tropical vegetation and elaborately sculptured rocks compete for attention in a rugged mountain landscape.

North to south, east to west, and top to bottom, this mountain range in southeastern Madagascar abounds in contrasts. A mass of granite and similar rocks generally running from north to south for approximately 40 miles (65 kilometers), it is part of a much longer escarpment separating the island's eastern coastal lowlands from a broad central highland.

The Andringitras begin in the north as a chain of giant isolated domes that stand 1,640 feet (500 meters) high. In its main central area the chain broadens to a maximum width of 6 miles (10 kilometers), then tapers again to the south. In this region it encompasses a series of massive, dramatically eroded mountains, including Boby Peak—at 8,721 feet (2,658 meters) the highest point in the range. Finally, in the extreme south, separated from the rest of the chain by a low pass, is isolated Ivohibe Peak, which rises to 6,788 feet (2,069 meters).

The mountains also change dramatically from west to east. From their crests they slope down rather gradually to the west and are partly overgrown with forests. The east side is a series of barren domes and abrupt, fluted escarpments. Buffeted by tropical storms that drop an annual rainfall of more than 70 inches (1,780 millimeters), the mountains have been severely eroded by torrential streams that have scoured out deep channels and ravines and carved the domes into titanic sculptures. The overall effect amply justifies the mountains' name, which means "desert of rocks."

Another interesting feature of the Andringitras is the striking change in vegetation as elevation increases. A tropical rain forest filled with orchids gradually gives way to a zone draped with thick, beardlike festoons of lichens. At 6,600 feet (2,000 meters) begins a belt of giant shrubs that form a virtually impenetrable barrier. Finally the "desert of rocks" opens to a grassland habitat.

In the past these rugged mountains served as a refuge for the lowland Betsileo people. Today much of the area has been made into another type of refuge—a nature reserve that is visited by scientists and sightseers. □

ANDRINGITRA MOUNTAINS. *Scoured by torrential rains, the rocky domes and escarpments are deeply channeled with crevices and ravines.*

Angel Falls

- Venezuela
- Map: page 14, C–2

Sluggishly wandering across the top of a plateau, the Río Churún leaps to life as its waters plunge down the tallest waterfall in the world.

Until 1935 this splendid plume of water was known only to local Indians. That was the year that an American pilot-adventurer, Jimmy Angel, saw the falls for the first time from his plane while exploring the wilderness of Venezuela's Guiana Highlands in search of gold. He found immortality instead.

The waterfall that bears his name is a spectacle of extraordinary beauty. Spilling over the edge of a reddish-white sandstone escarpment, the jet of glistening white water knifes downward and dissolves in a frenzy of spray in a dark green jungle setting. The water first plummets in a single unbroken cascade of 2,648 feet (807 meters), hits an obstruction, then hurtles down for another 564 feet (172 meters). With a total drop of 3,212 feet (979 meters), Angel Falls is the tallest waterfall in the world.

The falls originate on a giant plateau that reaches an elevation of 9,700 feet (2,950 meters) above sea level and towers above the surrounding jungle. Often shrouded in mist and pelted by rain, the plateau is known by its Indian name of Auyán Tepuí ("Devil's Mountain").

The horizontal layers of sandstone forming the massif are intersected by innumerable vertical joints and fractures that permit water to trickle in and open up fissures. As a result, underground streams spurt out of the rock wall below the main lip, in addition to the water that spills over the edge of the cliff.

Although the area was once virtually inaccessible, tourists can now reach it by plane or by motorized dugout canoe. The view of the falls from ground level is impressive. Surrounded by a thundering roar, visitors see first the tremendous plunge pool, then the falls themselves, and finally the enormous escarpment that fills the horizon. Just as unforgettable is the experience of seeing Angel Falls from the air: the plane seems about to graze the high rocky vertical walls as it skims through the iridescent spray of falling water. □

ANGEL FALLS. *From the top of the escarpment to the foot of the gorge, the waters plummet for a distance equal to nearly 20 times the height of Niagara Falls.*

ANKARANA PLATEAU. *At the western edge of the deeply eroded limestone plateau, the rugged cliffs of Madagascar's Wall of Ankarana rise abruptly above the grassy plains.*

Ankarana Plateau

● Madagascar
● Map: page 26, D–4

Trickling waters have transformed this limestone massif into an impenetrable domain bristling with sharp spikes and jagged ridges.

Near the northern tip of Madagascar a broad limestone plateau slopes gently to the east. On the west it ends abruptly in a steep cliff ranging from 650 to 920 feet (200 to 280 meters) in height. Known as the Wall of Ankarana, the cliff extends north to south for 15 miles (25 kilometers).

The Ankarana Plateau itself is composed of 150-million-year-old limestone, soft and chalky in the upper part, hard and crystalline at the base. Located in a region of high rainfall (70 inches, or 1,800 millimeters, per year) and riddled by fractures when the plateau was uplifted, the rocks are ideally suited for the formation of karst. This is the type of terrain caused by the dissolving of limestone in water, noteworthy for the development of such features as caves and underground streams.

On the wall of the escarpment running water has sculpted deep channels along joints, or fractures, in the rock. But something else has happened as well. Saturated with dissolved limestone, the water has redeposited the minerals on the eroded surfaces in the form of long draperies of rock. At the foot of the cliff, underground water emerges from the limestone, where it has also created immense caverns.

To the south, the edge of the escarpment has been eroded into a series of tall, freestanding blocks. Remnants of the once-continuous plateau, they are known as turmkarst, or tower karst.

In contrast, the limestone at the center of the plateau is broken up into much larger masses separated by narrow gorges. Some of the gorges follow faults in the rock; others were caused by the collapse of the roofs of caves and tunnels that formed along the network of fractures. The masses themselves are pocked with sinkholes near their steep edges.

In those places where the crystalline limestone has been stripped of its chalky cover, the bare surface has been dissolved into a pattern of channels and ridges called lapies by geologists and known locally as *tsingy*. Normally of low relief and rounded contours, they have grown to giant proportions such as are rarely seen elsewhere. Bristling with jagged ridges, sharp pinnacles, and knifelike blades, these areas are impassable to anyone traveling on foot.

The tortured relief and the covering of dense, scrubby thickets assure the Ankarana Plateau of protection from human intrusion. Only from a plane or from a helicopter is it possible to appreciate the grandeur of this spectacular karst landscape, considered to be among the most impressive in the entire world. □

Annapurna

● Nepal
● Map: page 20, C–2

Revered as the realm of gods, this towering Himalayan massif seems to defy attempts at human intrusion. Yet a few climbers have made it to the top.

Towering above lush green foothills and lowlands cloaked with dense jungle vegetation, the jagged crests of Annapurna rise toward the heavens like a solid wall. Steep slopes gashed by deep gorges and covered with glittering fields of ice and snow make the summits all but inaccessible. Regarded by local people as the dwelling place of gods, the peaks are both forbidding and inspiring.

For sheer contrast in elevations, the Annapurna range is most impressive when seen from the Pokhara basin. The basin is only 2,625 feet (800 meters) above sea level. Yet just 20 miles (32 kilometers) to the north the steep southern slopes of Annapurna rise to a maximum elevation of 26,503 feet (8,078 meters).

The Annapurna range is a massif, or group of connected peaks, cut off from the nearby ranges of the central Himalayas by a deep valley at each end. Some 30 miles (50 kilometers) long, the giant ridge includes four crests that have elevations of about 25,000 feet (7,600 meters). The tallest of the peaks is Annapurna I at 26,503 feet (8,078 meters). The other three high points are Annapurna II at 26,041 feet (7,937 meters), Annapurna III at 24,860 feet (7,577 meters), and Annapurna IV, which reaches 24,630 feet (7,507 meters).

Geologically, the structure of Annapurna is quite similar to that of the

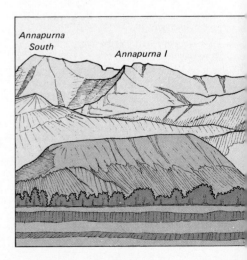

Annapurna South

Annapurna I

Himalayas as a whole. Very steep on its south face and sloping gradually down to the north, it is believed to represent a gigantic monocline, or steplike fold, in the earth's crust. In addition to being folded, however, the entire mass was subsequently thrust southward over a foothill zone. In some places it was overturned completely, forming some of the highest mountain peaks in the world.

Annapurna's dramatic crests and ridges were sharply chiseled during the last ice age, when they were covered by extensive glaciers. At their maximum extent the glaciers reached all the way down to an elevation of 6,600 feet (2,000 meters) in one valley. When the glaciers retreated, meltwater rushing down the steep southern slopes of Annapurna dropped enormous quantities of sediments in the Pokhara basin. It was these sediments, deposited in a layer about 500 feet (150 meters) thick, that gave the basin its flat surface, an unusual feature in the Himalayan region. Glacial debris also dammed some rivers in the basin, creating a series of lakes, the largest of which is Lake Phewa.

Annapurna still has glaciers, though those present today are midgets compared to the great Ice Age glaciers. During the summer monsoons humid air is forced upward by the high ridge of mountains, and heavy loads of snow are dropped down on the crests. Because of the extraordinarily steep slopes, no long valley glaciers have been able to develop on Annapurna's southern flanks; the largest, the Sanctuary Glacier, is only about 5 miles (8 kilometers) long. But on the north slopes glaciers are extensive—and a real hazard to mountain climbers.

Because it is so difficult to approach, the Annapurna massif was explored by mountaineers later than some other Himalayan ranges. Yet Annapurna I was the first peak more than 8,000 meters, or 26,250 feet, high to be scaled by man (a French expedition led by Maurice Herzog reached the top in 1950). Annapurna was back in the news in 1970, when a British expedition led by C.J.S. Bonington successfully completed an ascent of the terrifying southern wall. And with its incredibly difficult terrain, the Annapurna range undoubtedly will continue to challenge even the most skillful mountain climbers from around the world in the years to come. □

ANNAPURNA. *Reflected in the placid waters of Lake Phewa are the craggy connected peaks of the Annapurna massif; the various peaks are named in the panorama below. The glacier-carved spire of Macchapuchare, near the center of the photo, dominates this view from the south. Though Macchapuchare is actually lower than Annapurna III, its flat-topped neighbor, it appears taller because it is closer to the photographer. The highest peak in the entire massif, Annapurna I, is nearly hidden by intervening crests and foothills.*

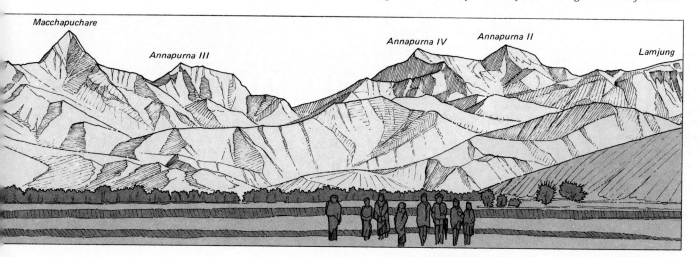

ANOU BOUSSOUIL. *Beyond the dark entry to the cave lies a series of winding passageways and vaulted chambers that were dissolved from the rock by running water.*

Anou Boussouil

- Algeria
- Map: page 24, D-2

Perched high on a mountainside, the entrance to the second deepest cave in Africa gapes like an open wound, gathering a torrent of water from the melting snows.

Unlike most of the caverns carved into the limestone peaks of the Djurdjura Mountains in northwestern Algeria, Anou Boussouil is an active cave, for running water continues to erode and enlarge it to this day.

A riverbed that is dry much of the time disappears into the mouth of the cavern, located 3,524 feet (1,074 meters) up on a rugged mountainside.

When it rains, the channel funnels the runoff into this great yawning chasm. But the major work of erosion takes place in spring. As late as April, snow continues to blanket the mountaintops. When it finally melts, a torrent pours down the slopes and is swallowed up by Anou Boussouil. Even in summer, when the stream dries up, water continues to seep into the cavern as the snow trapped in deep crevices gradually melts.

Scientific exploration of the cave did not begin until 1933. Since that time it has been discovered that the cave system actually includes two separate parts. The first segment, following a twisted course, ends in a spacious gallery. A sinkhole 209 feet (65 meters) deep then opens the way to the second section, where a series of pits leads to a vaulted chamber. Beyond this point, the passageway is completely filled with water. No one knows exactly where the flooded portion of the cavern goes. Ultimately, however, the underground river emerges in the Acif el-Hammam gorge.

For many years the Anou Boussouil was thought to be the deepest cavern in Africa. Only recently did it yield that title to the cave of Kef Toghobeit, which is located in Morocco. □

ANTARCTICA. *Ringed by an ocean filled with floating pack ice, the continent is almost entirely covered by permanent ice and snow.*

Antarctica

● Map: pages 8–9

Nine-tenths of the earth's entire supply of fresh water is locked up in the great ice cap, glaciers, and ice shelves of this frozen continent.

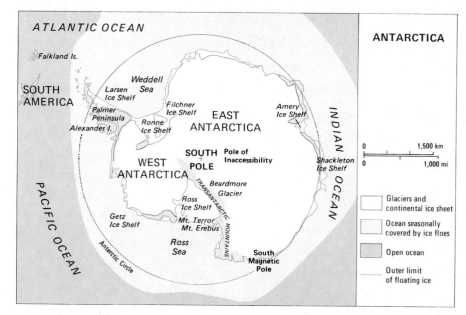

Among the most dazzling examples of human courage and endurance are those provided by early explorers of Antarctica, the desolate, icy continent at the southern end of the earth's axis. Since its discovery in 1820, explorers from many nations have struggled against turbulent seas, floating ice, raging storms, and sub-zero temperatures to chart its frozen wastes. Yet nearly 100 years passed before man was able to penetrate inland as far as the South Pole, which lies near the center of the continent.

The conquest of the South Pole brought triumph to one man and tragedy to another. The British explorer Robert F. Scott and the Norwegian Roald Amundsen had been in competition in a race won by Amundsen; it was the latter's expedition that planted a flag at the Pole on December 14, 1911. Scott's five-man team arrived about a month later and found that their rivals had preceded them. The Scott party perished of cold and exhaustion on the return trip.

With an area of about 5,500,000 square miles (14,245,000 square kilometers), the frozen continent is larger than any country in the world except the U.S.S.R. And virtually all of Antarctica is covered with ice; less than 2 percent of its surface is bare rock or uncovered soil.

The climate is extremely severe. At the Pole of Inaccessibility (the point farthest from any coast), the average annual temperature is a chilling −70° F (−57° C). During blizzards, winds blow with a force of as much as 185 miles (300 kilometers) an hour.

Geologically, the continent is divided into two distinct parts. East Antarctica is an almost perfect semicircle covered by a dome-shaped ice cap with an average thickness of 9,800 feet (3,000 meters). Weighted down by this heavy load of ice, the earth's crust is depressed as much as 1,970 feet (600 meters) below sea level. In West Antarctica, in contrast, the surface relief reflects many more of the irregularities of the terrain lying beneath the ice: in some places subglacial mountains emerge as prominent peaks.

In addition to the ice cap, the surface is streaked with glaciers, which slowly creep down mountainsides and ooze through gaps between mountain barriers. One of them, the Beardmore, is the largest glacier in the world.

Much of the coastline is fringed by ice shelves—giant platforms of ice that partially float and are also partially grounded in shallow water. About 650 feet (200 meters) thick at their outer edges, they are the source of enormous flat-topped icebergs that break off and float away. Beyond the ice shelves the entire continent is ringed by jumbled blocks of frozen seawater—the slowly drifting pack ice that grows wider in winter and shrinks again when summer returns.

Because of the inhospitable conditions, life is relatively sparse in Antarctica. The most conspicuous inhabitants are birds, especially penguins, which nest in enormous rookeries. The surrounding seas, in contrast, abound with life, including seals, whales, and many smaller creatures.

Earlier in this century Antarctica's strategic location and potential mineral resources made it the site of intense territorial competition among the nations of the world. In 1959, however, a 12-nation compact was signed, reserving the continent for peaceful scientific investigation. Thus it has become a huge natural laboratory where nations collaborate on research to enrich our understanding of the earth's climate, wildlife, and geological history. □

The Birth of an Iceberg

Icebergs are formed when large masses of ice calve, or break off, from the front of a glacier or the edge of an ice shelf. Winds and currents then carry them out to the sea. In Antarctica the biggest and most beautiful icebergs are the great flat-topped ones that separate from the ice shelves.

The biggest one on record, spotted from a U.S. icebreaker in 1956, was 60 miles (96 kilometers) wide and 208 miles (334 kilometers) long. Because of their huge dimensions, these icebergs survive a long time, despite the inevitable melting as they drift into warmer water. They last so long, in fact, that schemes have been proposed for towing them to arid regions to provide new sources of fresh water.

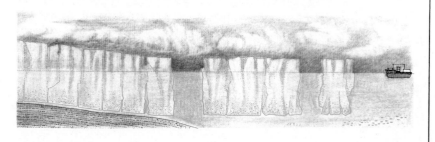

Apuane Alps

- Italy
- Map: page 17, E–4

Source of the famed Carrara marble, the Apuane Alps house some of the busiest stone quarries in the world.

Though from a distance parts of the Apuane Alps seem covered with snow, their white patches are actually marble, the stone for which the mountains are famous. Located in west-central Italy in the Tuscany region near Pisa, the mountains seem all the more impressive because of their proximity to the sea. Less than 10 miles (16 kilometers) from the Ligurian Sea (an arm of the Mediterranean), the Apuane Alps climb very suddenly, their steep slopes and sharp peaks rising to 6,384 feet (1,946 meters) at Monte Pisanino, their highest summit. The total length of the chain, however, is only about 35 miles (55 kilometers).

This region of Italy was once an inland sea. Two depressions in the sea gradually filled in with sediments, which hardened into limestone, dolomite (magnesium limestone), sandstone, and shale. Then about 25 million years ago there were several overthrusts: that is, rock was overturned and pushed into a depression to the east, creating intense pressure that transformed the limestone and dolomite into marble.

More uplifting occurred approximately 20 million years ago, producing the mountains known as the Apennines. The Apuane Alps are a direct continuation of the Northern Apennines, separated from the main section by the Magra Valley. Although the neighboring mountains are rather rounded, the Apuane Alps have steep, jagged peaks and deep, narrow valleys—a result of the heavy precipitation in this coastal region, which has carved the mountains into their present shapes.

Although the Apuane Alps may appear impenetrable, they are easily accessible by roads that go up to the marble quarries and also lead to hiking trails. One of the highlights of a trip through these mountains is a visit to the Grotta del Vento ("Grotto of the Wind") at Fornovolasco. Here cavities have developed in the thick mass of marble. Because there is a temperature difference between openings on opposite slopes, a movement of air is produced inside—hence the descriptive name of the cave.

But by far the most interesting sight in the Apuane Alps is the quarrying of Carrara marble. Named for a town at the foot of the mountains, this marble is a fine white stone that has been quarried for 2,000 years and has been used by sculptors (including Michelangelo) since the time of the Roman Empire. To extract the marble, mountainsides are sometimes blasted with dynamite, a procedure that tends to shatter the rock. A less destructive mode of removal is to saw enormous pieces of marble from the face of the mountain and then send them down to the valley to be cut up for sale. The cutting process involves wearing down the marble with sand: long steel wires moving over pulleys scrub sand and water into grooves that become deeper and deeper until finally the blocks can be separated. □

APUANE ALPS

West   East

Mt. Pelato
1,431 m
(4,695 ft)

2,000 m
(6,560 ft)

0   3 km   6 km (3.7 mi)

▨ Shale   ▦ Dolomite   ▥ Marble   ▧ Quartzite

A slice through the Apuane Alps shows that the layers of rock are tilted toward the east. Because the shales are relatively soft, they have been eroded into valleys; the more resistant rock types, such as marble and dolomite, make up the peaks.

Apurímac River

- Peru
- Map: page 14, B–4

From a source high in the Peruvian Andes, the Apurímac plunges through sheer-walled gorges and canyons as it rushes north toward the Amazon.

Fed by meltwater trickling from glaciers, the Apurímac River is born about 16,500 feet (5,000 meters) high in the Andes of southern Peru. Its channel, interrupted by frequent rapids and waterfalls, hurtles down mountain slopes and then across high-elevation plateaus. Finally, after flowing some 545 miles (880 kilometers) along a generally northward course, it merges with the Urubamba River to form the Ucayali, one of the main headwater streams of the Amazon.

For most of its length the Apurímac flows through deep, narrow canyons. The most spectacular are at Incahuasi, about halfway down the river's course, where the wildly turbulent stream is hemmed in by towering, almost vertical walls.

Since the river flows across a variety of geological formations, rocks exposed in the canyon walls differ from one place to another. In some areas the walls are lava and other volcanic rocks. Elsewhere they are formed of limestone, sandstone, shale, and various igneous rocks, resulting in an amazing variety of colors and textures in the canyon walls. □

APUANE ALPS. *The "eternal snows" gleaming on the steep mountainsides are actually exposed rock in marble quarries, along with centuries-old accumulations of quarry debris.*

APURÍMAC RIVER. *Curving through the mountains of Peru, the glacier-fed river is hemmed in by craggy cliffs and steep gorges along much of its circuitous course.*

Fair, held around July 20, which opens with a loud blaring of shepherd's horns and draws thousands of peasants who live on the mountains.

The Apuseni region also attracts visitors appreciative of varied scenery, for it boasts many caves, sinkholes, underground rivers, and other examples of a particular kind of landscape (called karst) that develops in limestone. A trip to the Apusenis might include the labyrinthine Meziad Cave, as well as the Citadels of Ponor, where there are three giant sinkholes along the course of an underground river. Petrifying springs in the area contain water with so much lime that any object falling into it becomes fossilized almost immediately.

Not all the impressive features of the landscape are karst features. The Detunate is a basalt wall that resembles a breaking wave, and the Citadel of Gold is a maze of mountain tunnels constructed by Roman miners searching for gold in the second century A.D. For just as the Apuseni Mountains are rich in outstanding landforms, so are they rich in gold, copper, iron, and other valuable metals. □

Apuseni Mountains

- Rumania
- Map: page 17, F–4

Surrounded by striking limestone rocks, this small branch of the great Carpathian mountain system contains a wealth of valuable metals.

The Apuseni Mountains rise in Transylvania, the Rumanian region that is steeped in the legend of Dracula. Extending for 55 miles (90 kilometers), they are part of the great Carpathian mountain system, which runs in a large semicircle from Czechoslovakia to Rumania and connects the Alps with the Balkans. Although the Apusenis are not extraordinarily high, reaching a maximum of about 6,070 feet (1,850 meters), they stand over a region of impressive limestone formations that attract many visitors.

People also travel to the Apuseni area to visit the villages scattered halfway up the mountains. The houses there are especially picturesque because of their unusual architecture: the roof is twice as tall as the rest of the house. Mountain visitors can attend fairs where the peasants show their traditional folk art, songs, and dances. One of the most popular is the Gaina

APUSENI MOUNTAINS. *In an idyllic setting in the heart of Transylvania, a fast-flowing stream has chiseled a deep gorge into the flat-topped limestone massif.*

ARAK GORGES. *Like the turrets and battlements of an abandoned desert fortress, the towering sandstone walls of the canyon stand out against the cloudless Saharan sky.*

Arak Gorges

● Algeria
● Map: page 24, D–3

Unearthly silence and an awesome sense of solitude pervade these winding desert gorges. Yet even here there are—and long have been—signs of life.

Following an old caravan route toward the central Sahara, the traveler comes upon tall cliffs and suddenly enters the majestic Arak Gorges. The canyons were incised into the surface of a plateau by an ancient river that was much more active than any remaining there today. Flowing from south to north, this river cut its way down through thick sandstone formations to the bedrock of crystalline schist. Subsequent wind erosion modified the contours of the canyon walls, which range in height from 800 to 1,600 feet (250 to 500 meters). Now all that remains is the dry bed (wadi) of the Arak, meandering between castle-like cliffs flanked by the steep slopes of fallen rocks.

Though the area is extremely dry—rainfall is only 2.3 to 2.9 inches (60 to 75 millimeters) per year—it is not without life. Just where the canyon walls close in to their narrowest point, a little military outpost stands guard over a water hole fed by a permanent spring and inhabited by several kinds of fish. All around the water hole is a lush oasis of greenery, including reeds, rushes, and a type of cattail with leaves as much as 13 feet (4 meters) long that are used in the building of thatched huts.

Like the rest of the canyon, the area around the water hole is enveloped in uncanny silence. Yet many kinds of small animals, such as gerbils, rats, and snakes, live there. Lizards with blue bodies and red heads scuttle across the sunbaked rocks. Robinlike wheatears linger near human visitors as if awaiting handouts. Small vultures wheel and turn in the brilliant blue, cloudless sky.

Man is rarely seen in the gorges today. A few dozen families of nomads who pass through from time to time formerly tended gardens in the area, using a system of irrigated terraces to cultivate corn, barley, beans, and especially tomatoes, which were sold to travelers.

But man has known the canyon a long time. Burial mounds built more than a thousand years ago have been discovered in the area, and even earlier primitive stone tools, dating from perhaps 100,000 years ago, have also been found among these ancient rocks honed by vanished rivers. □

Aral Sea

● U.S.S.R.
● Map: page 18, G–4

Glimmering at the heart of an immense desert basin, the vast, landlocked Aral Sea is the fourth largest lake in the world.

Like Utah's Great Salt Lake, the Aral Sea is landlocked at the center of a broad basin. Rivers flow in but not out; water escapes only by evaporation from its surface. Although the water level has risen and fallen substantially in the past, yearly inflow at present is about equal to evaporation, and the water level is stable.

Vast but rather shallow, the Aral Sea is approximately 270 miles (435 kilometers) long and 180 miles (290 kilometers) wide. More than a third of its area is less than 33 feet (10 meters) deep, with just one small area reaching the maximum depth of 225 feet (69 meters).

Astonishingly clear and intensely blue, the sea is bounded by a variety of contrasting shorelines. To the north, where it borders on the undulating wastelands of the Turgai Desert, the shore winds in and out around several enormous embayments. The western coast, in turn, is abrupt, bounded by tall cliffs that form an almost straight shoreline. The east coast, in contrast, has invaded the dunes of a sandy desert, resulting in a series of long, narrow bays and a profusion of islets.

To the south is the enormous delta of the Amu Darya, and in the northeast is the great delta of the Syr Darya. Two of the most important rivers in Central Asia, they rise high in the mountains and carry large quantities of sediment—as well as water—downstream, so that their deltas continue to grow each year. □

Ararat, Mount

- Turkey
- Map: page 18, F–5

And in the seventh month, on the seventeenth day of the month, the ark came to rest upon the mountains of Ararat.—Genesis 8:4

Traditionally revered by many Jews and Christians as the landing place of Noah's ark, Mount Ararat was long considered sacred and unclimbable. But it was probably the high elevation and dangerously loose boulders that delayed its conquest until 1829, when Johann Jacob von Parrot, a German naturalist, finally succeeded in reaching the summit after two unsuccessful attempts.

Overlooking the borders of Turkey, Iran, and the U.S.S.R., Ararat is the highest peak in Turkey. Technically speaking, Ararat is a massif, consisting of several connecting peaks. Great Ararat reaches a height of 16,945 feet (5,165 meters), and Little Ararat, 7 miles (11 kilometers) to the southeast, is 12,877 feet (3,925 meters) high. Both of these mountains are symmetrical and cone-shaped.

The location of Ararat coincides with one of the key geological sutures of the earth's surface, a boundary where great crustal plates have collided. In this region a plate coming from the south converges on the Eurasian plate, coming from the north. The boundaries between the plates here are not yet sealed and continue to jostle one another, as evidenced by the devastating earthquakes that repeatedly ravage the area around eastern Turkey.

According to many geologists, plate boundaries may also be marked by volcanoes. Both Great Ararat and Little Ararat are composite volcanoes, composed of alternating layers of lava and ash. (The latter material is widespread across the landscape, forming a grayish-white rock known as andesitic tuff.) Most of Great Ararat was formed about 2 million years ago atop a block of uplifted rock. Little Ararat is a younger volcano.

Great Ararat stands out not just because of its height and cone-shaped symmetry; it also has a permanent snowcap retained by three natural, high-elevation terraces. Nine glacial "tongues" escape downslope from this ice field. Where they meet the snow line they melt and give rise to streams. The snow line is at a relatively high elevation (15,420 feet, or 4,700 meters, on the south face) because the region is so dry. In summer there is no precipitation on the plateau around the mountain, although some rain falls on the massif.

The entire massif has only two springs: one on the main mountain and one on the ridge connecting the two peaks. Owing to the lack of water, Ararat is relatively uninhabited and barren. Though Kurdish shepherds venture into the limited grassy areas in the high elevations, the entire massif seems desolate except for some junipers and a clump of birches on Little Ararat. The present emptiness contrasts sharply with medieval accounts of Mount Ararat. In the 10th century Thomas of Arazroun described it as a beautiful forest-clad mountain dotted with hamlets and populated by deer, wild pigs, and mountain lions. Since that time overgrazing and woodcutting have taken their toll. And a particularly ravaging earthquake in 1840 precipitated a landslide that destroyed everything in its path, leading to the abandonment of permanent habitation on Mount Ararat. □

MOUNT ARARAT. *No longer active, this permanently snowcapped volcano was built up by alternating eruptions of ash and lava.*

ARCHES NATIONAL PARK. *Landscape Arch, with a span of 291 feet (89 meters), is the longest natural arch known anywhere on earth.*

Arches National Park

- United States (Utah)
- Map: page 10, D–5

Created by erosion, these famous sandstone arches will eventually be destroyed by the same forces.

This dry region bordering on the Colorado River in southeastern Utah has the greatest concentration of natural stone arches on the continent. Dozens of arches have developed here, along with needles, towers, domes, and other rocks beautifully sculpted by the forces of nature.

The Landscape Arch is the world's longest natural arch, measuring 291 feet (89 meters). The famous Delicate Arch rises in isolation atop a large mass of sandstone, looking so fragile that one wonders why it has not fallen down. The tall Courthouse Towers stand above huge expanses of red rock. The Fiery Furnace, with its bright red walls and extremely narrow, rocky passages, seems to blaze at sunset. The rocks in the Windows section balance very precariously atop one another amid numerous arches large and small. Many more arches in the park remain unnamed, allowing visitors here to let their imaginations wander as they will.

Formation of the rocks found in Arches National Park (known until 1971 as Arches National Monument) began about 150 million years ago when layers of Entrada sandstone formed from the sand and sediment of an inland sea. Although there are other kinds of sandstone in the area, this salmon-tinted type, which takes its color from minute quantities of iron in the almost pure quartz, is especially susceptible to the formation of arches.

Natural arches are a product of erosion—products that visitors to the park can see in the making. The inevitable weathering, especially by water, follows cracks in the sandstone. Slowly the cracks become wider and wider, and eventually only narrow walls of rock, known as fins, remain. Ice, snow, rain, and wind attack the fins, undercutting them and perforating their softer layers. In some cases, depending on the hardness and balance of the rock, a hole may enlarge to such an extent that only an arch-shaped piece of rock remains. So although such arches look as if carved by a river, they are in fact formed by the disintegration of the weakest part of the sandstone. (Rivers do shape rocks into natural *bridges*—for instance, the famous limestone Natural Bridge that spans Cedar Creek in the western part of Virginia.)

Of course, erosion does not stop when the arches form, and the arches that visitors see in the park today will eventually collapse. At the very least, these arches will differ tomorrow from what they are today, because those forces that created them are progressively destroying them, even as new ones are being formed. □

50° F (10° C). This line more or less parallels the Arctic Circle except in Canada and the Bering Sea, where it dips quite a bit to the south. Still others maintain that the tree line, the northern limit of forest growth, marks the southern boundary of the Arctic. As it happens, this line is about the same as the 50° F (10° C) isotherm.

However it is defined, the Arctic is like no other place on earth. At its center is the Arctic Ocean. Five times the size of the Mediterranean Sea, it covers about 4,732,000 square miles (12,256,000 square kilometers). But there is little water to be seen. In winter the sea is sealed beneath ice from shore to shore, and at other times much of its surface is well hidden beneath a permanent ice pack.

Three distinctive types of ice float on arctic waters. Most abundant are the floes—large, flat sheets of frozen seawater. More massive and much more irregular in form are the icebergs calved from glaciers, especially from the western coast of Greenland. Finally, here and there are ice islands—huge, raftlike slabs of ice that have broken off the ice shelf fringing northern Ellesmere Island. Drifting very slowly across the ocean, several of these large, stable platforms have become excellent sites for floating scientific research stations.

The shallow margins of the Arctic Ocean are underlain by the continental shelf, which is relatively narrow off North America and Greenland but as much as 1,100 miles (1,770 kilometers) wide off Eurasia. Beyond this broad expanse of shallow sea the ocean floor

The Arctic Ice Pack: A Mass of Ice in Constant Motion

Much of the Arctic Ocean is covered by a permanent ice pack—a mass of slowly drifting floes joined together into a more or less continuous cover of ice. In fall, the surrounding zone of open water also begins to freeze. At first the water takes on an oily and then a greasy texture as more and more floating ice crystals form. When the crystals fuse together, they sometimes form pancake ice—sheets resembling gigantic lily pads with their edges turned up as a result of collisions with other ice masses. Gradually the sheets of ice merge and thicken to an average depth of approximately 6.6 feet (2 meters). The surface, however, is far from smooth. Wind and water movements cause the ice to crack and then to drift apart and form large ponds of open water, which are known as polynyas, and long, wide channels, which are known as leads. When the leads close up again, hummocks are formed where slabs of ice pile up atop one another, and high, jagged pressure ridges result when floes collide. In spring, floes on the margins of the permanent ice pack gradually melt and drift apart, and large areas of open water reappear on the surface of the sea.

Arctic Region

● Map: pages 8–9

Glaciers, tundra, wilderness islands—diverse scenic wonders beckon in this remote region.

The top of the world is a unique place—a frozen sea ringed by frozen land. The sun never sets in summer yet stays below the horizon throughout the long winter night. Majestic and mysterious, the region is brightened by the play of the northern lights against the winter sky and by the blooms of myriad wildflowers in the long summer day.

The Arctic is sometimes considered to include the entire region north of the Arctic Circle, the line beyond which, because of the tilt of the earth's axis, the sun never sets for part of the year. Others define the Arctic as the region north of the 50° F (10° C) isotherm, the line along which the average temperature in July is only

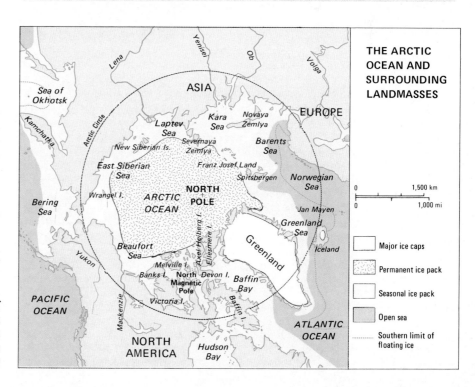

THE ARCTIC OCEAN AND SURROUNDING LANDMASSES

ARCTIC REGION. *Glacial tongues, sweeping down from an ice cap on Canada's Ellesmere Island, all but engulf the mountaintops.*

drops abruptly into a huge central depression crossed by three towering submarine mountain ranges. Here the depth in places exceeds 14,000 feet (4,270 meters).

The Arctic Ocean is almost completely encircled by land, including northern Europe and Siberia, northernmost Alaska and Canada, Greenland and several major islands. And like the ocean, much of the land is permanently covered with ice in the form of glaciers and ice caps. The biggest arctic ice cap is the one that almost completely covers Greenland. A great dome of ice as much as 11,000 feet (3,350 meters) thick, it is second only to the antarctic ice cap in size. If it were to melt, estimates are that the runoff water would raise all sea levels by 20 feet (6 meters).

Other major ice caps and glaciers are found on Ellesmere Island and several other Canadian islands, Norway's Spitsbergen archipelago, and Novaya Zemlya and some of the other Russian islands. Iceland has rather extensive ice fields that are especially interesting because of the volcanic activity on the island. When an eruption takes place under the ice, large-scale melting occurs and causes a sudden flood of mud, ash, and water.

Much of the glacier-free land in the Arctic is treeless tundra, either flatlands or gently rolling plains underlain by a deep foundation of permafrost (permanently frozen ground). In summer the soil thaws to a depth of about 3 feet (0.9 meter), but because the meltwater cannot percolate down into the permafrost, the surface is cov-

ered by marshy areas and studded with lakes and ponds.

One result of the repeated freezing and thawing of the soil is the landscape known as patterned ground: stones of different sizes have been sorted out over time to form more or less symmetrical patterns, usually circles or polygons. Another result is solifluction, the slumping of soil on hillsides into broad, tonguelike lobes.

Although the arctic summer is brief, much of the tundra supports a dense growth of mosses, lichens, wildflowers, and dwarf shrubs. Wildlife also is abundant, with large populations of insects, lemmings, caribou, reindeer, and waterfowl. And roving over the ice pack, sometimes even in winter, is one of the most majestic predators, the elusive polar bear. □

ARMAND CAVE. *Multicolored lighting enhances the unearthly beauty of the cave, where a meandering path guides visitors through the maze of baroque, pillarlike stalagmites.*

Armand Cave

- France
- Map: page 17, D–4

A fantastic forest of fragile columns sprouts from the floor of this jewel among caves.

When in 1897 cave explorer Louis Armand first penetrated the cave now bearing his name, he gasped in astonishment at what he saw. For at the base of a chimneylike sinkhole some 250 feet (75 meters) below ground, the high vaulted chamber known as the Grande Salle ("Great Hall") opens out like the interior of a cathedral.

About 325 feet (100 meters) long and 180 feet (55 meters) wide, its sloping floor is covered by an extraordinary forest of stalagmites. Bristling with projections that resemble the branching of trees, the fragile columns have been deposited by water that seeps through the limestone ceiling. Rank upon rank, 400 in all, they rise to heights of nearly 100 feet (30 meters).

Tourists nowadays approach the remarkable Grande Salle through a man-made tunnel. From a platform that provides a panoramic view of the cave, a walkway circles through the magical forest of stalagmites, where artificial lighting enhances the unearthly beauty of the scene. □

Arrábida, Serra da

- Portugal
- Map: page 17, C–5

On one side the Serra da Arrábida slopes gently, providing splendid terrain for farming. The other side drops abruptly to the ocean.

Covered with dark green pines and cypresses, the pink and white cliffs of the Serra da Arrábida rise serenely above the blue water. Although the vegetation here more closely resembles that of the Mediterranean seacoast, this *serra* ("mountain range") borders the Atlantic.

The mountains, composed primarily of marine limestone, stand in a region that was the eastern edge of a rift that began to open between Europe and North America about 180 million years ago. Matching limestone can be found today off eastern Newfoundland, which was connected to Europe at that time.

This rather low range (its maximum elevation is about 1,600 feet, or 500 meters) is asymmetrical. The slope facing the ocean is very steep, while the other side inclines gently, allowing easy cultivation. Visitors often stop at the ruins of the convent of Arrábida for an overview of the area and then stay in the little fishing village at the foot of the cliffs, where there are excellent beaches. □

SERRA DA ARRÁBIDA. *The long ridge of limestone mountains, flanked by a wall of cliffs, overlooks an ocean of matchless blue.*

Asama, Mount

- Japan
- Map: page 19, O–5

Built on the ruins of older peaks, Asama is an exceptionally active volcano in a volcano-rich land.

Located about 85 miles (140 kilometers) northwest of densely populated Tokyo, Mount Asama is the highest point in a chain of volcanoes stretching along the middle of the island of Honshu. Its summit lies 8,200 feet (2,500 meters) above sea level.

Until about 2 million years ago Mount Asama did not exist; up to that time the place where it now stands was a rocky plateau. Then during a long series of eruptions a volcanic mountain known as Kurohu-yama developed on the plateau. Geologists call Kurohu-yama a composite volcano because it consisted of a number of layers—loose deposits of cinders and ash alternating with layers of consolidated lava.

After the massive eruptions of Kurohu-yama ceased, the eastern section of its cone collapsed. Next, a shield volcano—a large, dome-shaped accumulation of lava—formed over part of the collapsed cone. Two voluminous eruptions of pumice spread over the shield volcano. Finally, a composite cone with two craters developed over the shield volcano. Thus Mount Asama is actually a double-cratered composite cone atop a shield volcano atop another composite cone.

Mount Asama's major eruptions have been explosive in type, throwing out ash, rounded masses of lava (known as bombs), fragments of lava (lapilli), and sometimes pumice. The famous eruption in 1783, which took the lives of more than 1,300 people, began with a rain of ash and pumice and was followed by several rapid flows of hot lava.

Since the beginning of this century scientists have kept close watch over Mount Asama. Minor eruptions occur there with some regularity—almost 2,000, for example, between 1933 and 1960. Slight, persistent earth tremors, a swelling of the crater, and other signs suggest that eruptions will continue to occur there. □

MOUNT ASAMA. *Among the world's most violent volcanoes, Asama is constantly monitored by scientists for warnings of potential eruptions.*

LAKE ASSAL. *Supersaturated with salts, the briny waves build up glistening encrustations of calcite, gypsum, and other minerals.*

Assal, Lake

- Djibouti
- Map: page 25, H–4

Ten times saltier than the ocean, this African lake is the most saline body of water in the world.

Lying 510 feet (155 meters) below sea level, Lake Assal is the lowest point in all Africa and, excluding the ocean basins, the third lowest surface in the world. Like the Dead Sea and the Sea of Galilee (also known as Lake Tiberias), it occupies a rift valley—a depression where the earth's crust has split and adjacent areas have moved with respect to one another.

Located in the Danakil Desert near the southern end of the Red Sea, Lake Assal has no outlet; streams flow into the lake but not away from it. Though springs supply some water, the main source is the seasonal flow in the wadis. In summer these usually dry riverbeds become raging torrents that can raise the lake level 15 inches (380 millimeters) in just a few hours.

This dry region formerly had a wet climate, and the water level of the lake about 10,000 years ago measured 260 feet (80 meters) above the present-day sea level. In fact the former shoreline of this ancient lake can still be seen on the slopes of the surrounding hills. But as the climate became drier, the level of the lake progressively dropped.

Lake Assal has a high evaporation rate. The air temperature is very high. Strong winds cause further evaporation. In the dry season the hot, dry winds often blow from the interior of Africa; in the wet season the monsoon winds bring rain to the hills, but heated and dried as they pass over hot lava rocks, the winds pick up moisture from the lake.

All this evaporation leads to an increasing concentration of salt in the water, making the lake a mineralized brine that is the saltiest body of water in the world. During the last few thousand years the mineral salts (calcite, halite, and gypsum) have been crystallizing on the shores and the bottom of the lake. The surrounding plain, once the lake floor, is a glistening expanse of salt. During each wet season the lake level rises, and as the water slowly evaporates, another band of salt is laid down on the plain.

Any animal unfortunate enough to fall into the briny water is killed almost instantly. In the southeastern part of the lake, small fish inhabit the springs; but if they are accidentally carried out into the main part of the lake, they die at once. Transported by the waves, their bodies are thrown onto the plain, rapidly covered with salt, and thus preserved. Similarly, twigs, branches, and debris carried into the lake are immediately coated with a preserving layer of salt. □

Assynt Region

- United Kingdom (Scotland)
- Map: page 16, C–3

Like islands in the sea, a series of steep-sloped mountains towers over a stark landscape in a wild and lonely corner of Scotland.

Immortalized by many generations of painters and celebrated by a host of poets, the region surrounding Loch Assynt in Scotland's Northwest Highlands has fascinated geologists as well. It is an austere and treeless landscape formed of glacier-carved, light gray metamorphic rock known as Lewisian gneiss. Nearly 3 billion years old, this ancient basement rock is rounded into hills and ridges and dotted with numerous lakes.

Rising above this rugged base, in striking contrast, is a series of imposing, steep-sloped mountain peaks. Unlike the ancient gneiss on which they rest, they are composed of massive layers of reddish-brown sandstones. These so-called Torridonian sandstones are more than 600 million years old and are capped in places by a somewhat younger layer of white Cambrian quartzite.

Ranging from about 2,000 to 2,800 feet (600 to 850 meters) in height, the enormous, distinctive profiles of these mountain masses looming on the horizon form one of the most unusual landscapes in Great Britain. Farthest to the north is the many-peaked hulk of Quinag, overlooking Loch Assynt. South of the loch is Canisp. An elongated, isolated massif shaped like an inverted ship, its rose-colored, rocky debris contrasts with the bare gray gneiss at its foot. Veins of reddish porphyry, a once hot material, were long ago injected in sheets between the layers of sandstone, giving the slopes a stepped profile.

To the west of Canisp is Suilven, by no means the biggest but certainly the most famous of all the peaks. With a simple form and steep profile, it has been compared to a pillar, a sugarloaf, and a fortified castle. Almost bare of vegetation, this so-called Matterhorn of the Highlands clearly reveals the sequence of beds of Torridonian sandstones that form it.

Farther south is Cul Mor, at 2,786 feet (850 meters) the tallest peak in the group. And finally, rising from the shore of Loch Lurgainn, is Stac Pollaidh, an eroded stump of sandstone with a jagged profile.

How do we account for the presence of these dramatic sandstone mountains, standing like intruders on a platform of an entirely different type of rock? The sequence began with the formation of the basement rock, the Lewisian gneiss, nearly 3 billion years ago. Over a long period of time its surface was eroded down to broad, rolling hills and valleys.

Then the land became covered by the sea, and the thick beds of Torridonian sandstones were deposited on the eroded surface of the gneiss. The deposition of younger rocks on an older eroded surface produces what geologists call an unconformity.

A second unconformity between the Torridonian sandstones and the Cambrian quartzite that caps them in some places reveals that a second cycle of erosion and deposition took place. After the sandstones were formed, they were uplifted from the sea and partially eroded. Then they were submerged again and the quartzite was eventually produced.

Following another period of uplift, much of the quartzite was eroded away, along with most of the sandstone. Glaciation provided the finishing touches, honing the landscape to the contours that remain today. The mountains of the Assynt region are thus the isolated remnants of a once continuous sandstone formation that originally covered the entire area. And in time it is likely that these survivors will also disappear. ☐

ASSYNT REGION. *Carved to their present forms by Ice Age glaciers, the steep slopes and deep lochs are the end results of nearly 3 billion years of geological history.*

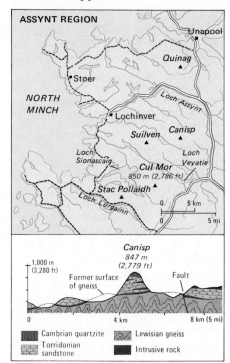

A cross section of rocks in the Canisp area reveals the repeated cycles of deposition and erosion that have taken place in the Assynt region in northwestern Scotland.

AUGHRABIES FALLS. *A torrent of water divides into a multitude of cascades at the brink of the falls, then plunges to a deep, dim gorge.*

Aughrabies Falls

- South Africa
- Map: page 26, B–5

The waters of the Orange River roar and tumble over a spectacular cataract and rush into the confines of a deep, narrow granite gorge.

The longest river in southern Africa, the Orange crosses almost the entire width of the continent. Extending from the Drakensberg range in the east to the Atlantic in the west, it alternately widens and narrows during its journey of 1,300 miles (2,100 kilometers). Near the border of South Africa and South-West Africa (Namibia), it splits into several channels, spanning a total width of 9,800 feet (3,000 meters). Shortly thereafter, the river narrows very dramatically and plunges 480 feet (146 meters) from the edge of a plateau in a drop even greater than that of Africa's more famous Victoria Falls.

From the plunge pool at the base of the Aughrabies Falls—a deep basin reputed to contain valuable diamonds as well as a giant serpent—the water speeds down a spectacular gorge. Scientists consider this gorge, which precisely follows a geological fault, to be the world's best example of the erosion of granite by water.

Of all the great rivers in the world, the river that feeds the Aughrabies has the largest variation in flow. During each dry season the Orange River diminishes to such an extent that mere trickles of water flow down the gorge. But during the rainy season (October to March) the flow increases so much that water may tumble down to the gorge in as many as 19 separate waterfalls. A thundering sound fills the air as the water roars downstream; in fact the name Aughrabies (or Augrabies) is derived from the Hottentot word for "the place of great noise." The falls are often called by their older name, King George's Falls (after George IV of England).

Although the Aughrabies Falls were first seen by a European (Hendrick Wiker, an official of the East India trading company) in 1778, they were basically inaccessible until 1963, when a highway was built nearby. The establishment of Aughrabies National Park in 1966 finally opened the area to tourism, and present-day visitors to the park even have the opportunity of viewing the falls from the air as they fly over them in a small plane. ☐

AYERS ROCK. *The giant of the Australian Outback is the eroded remnant of a mountain that was once even larger in size.*

Ayers Rock

- Australia
- Map: page 22, D–4

The massive hulk of Ayers Rock, one of the world's largest monoliths, looms like a sleeping giant on a desert plain.

A mass of golden-red sandstone some 1,100 feet (340 meters) high and nearly 6 miles (9 kilometers) in circumference, Ayers Rock is visible from a distance of more than 60 miles (100 kilometers). Stark, barren, and overwhelming in size, it completely dominates its surroundings.

The rock is composed of arkose, a type of sandstone that is rich in the mineral feldspar. Weathering of the feldspar gives the rock its overall reddish cast, but its exact color changes rather dramatically under differing light throughout the day.

The rock was formed more than 450 million years ago from horizontal layers of soft sands deposited on an ocean floor. Subsequent movements of the earth's crust upended the formation, turning the layers to their now nearly vertical position.

The projecting remnant of a mountain that was once much larger, Ayers Rock was whittled to its present size and contours by long periods of wind and water erosion. The differences in the hardness of the upturned layers of sandstone have caused them to erode at different rates, resulting in the pattern of ridges and furrows across the surface of the rock. Some of the debris worn away from the rock mass long ago can still be seen nearby in the form of sand dunes.

The more recently eroded debris, washed down by the infrequent rainstorms, forms an apron of soft sediment all around the rock. Although sparse patches of tough, drought-resistant vegetation are able to grow and survive in this sandy soil, the mountain itself is completely bare, supporting no life whatever.

In desert environments a special form of weathering sometimes results in the accumulation of larger chunks of debris at the base of a rock. Under the alternating influences of intense heating by day and rapid cooling at night, the surface of the sandstone tends to expand and contract.

Eventually the rock cracks, and thin plates split away from the surface and slide down to form chaotic heaps of broken debris. One enormous flake of this sort slid down the north face of Ayers Rock but did not break; it remains as a long curving arc that is known popularly and picturesquely as the Kangaroo's Tail.

Another peculiar feature of Ayers Rock is the development of tafoni, or honeycomblike hollows, and even caves in its surface. These are caused by the disintegration of the natural cement that holds individual grains of sand together in the rock. Rainwater seeps in and loosens the sand grains until they are eventually carried away by wind or water. In one place on the north face of the rock, this type of weathering has resulted in an extraordinarily intricate network of convolutions that resemble a human brain—a feature that has come to be known, of course, as the Brain.

Large caves are most numerous near the base of the rock. They have been used since time immemorial by the Aborigines, who decorated their walls with paintings and pictographs. Mute testimony to primitive man's reverence for Ayers Rock, these archeological relics add to the majestic beauty of the colossus of the Australian Outback.   □

B

Badlands

- United States (South Dakota)
- Map: page 10, D–4

"Bad" and barren yet fascinating as well, this landscape is perpetually being altered by the brief but violent rains that sweep across the plains.

As barren as a moonscape, this region in western South Dakota was known to the Indians as *mako sica.* The first Europeans to see it, fur trappers coming down from Canada, called it *les mauvaises terres.* Both terms mean the same thing—bad lands.

The formation of this incredibly eroded plateau began about 80 million years ago with the accumulation of sediments in a shallow sea. Eventually an upward movement of the earth's crust caused these deposits to emerge as dry land. Plants covered the former ocean floor and over eons rains molded the surface into rounded hills and broad valleys.

About 35 million years ago, rivers rushing down from mountains to the west began spreading layers of clay and other sediments over the undulating plain. Now and then violent eruptions in the mountains also spread layers of volcanic ash over the landscape. Gradually the area became a vast marshy plain that was transformed into an immense grassland as the climate changed.

Then severe erosion began. Wind and freezing both played a part in shaping the landscape, but most of all the Badlands were sculpted by flowing water. Runoff from the short, extraordinarily violent cloudbursts, which are typical of semiarid climates, easily eroded the extremely weak rocks and clayey deposits.

Gradually the region was transformed into the gullied topography that remains today. Stretching on for miles are astonishing vistas of spires, fins, jagged peaks, pinnacles, and sawtoothed ridges—all laced with mazes of tortuous, steep-sided ravines and banded by layers of different colors.

And the process goes on. With each summer storm, ridges are eaten away, gullies grow deeper. Slowly but surely, the rugged contours of this harsh landscape are gnawed away.

Life in the Badlands is sparse today. Here and there a few plants have gained a foothold. Rock wrens nest in sheltered crannies, and mammals such as coyotes wander by. Yet in the past the area teemed with life—a different sort of life. Among the many fossils discovered in the Badlands are the remains of three-toed horses, saber-toothed cats, and a type of camel no larger than a dog. □

BADLANDS. *Crisscrossed by ravines and cut up into jagged pinnacles, the ever-changing landscape is all but devoid of vegetation.*

LAKE BAIKAL. *Fed by rain and snow fall on surrounding mountains, overflow from the great lake escapes northward to the Arctic Ocean.*

Baikal, Lake

- U.S.S.R.
- Map: page 19, L–3

The world's deepest lake is a huge natural reservoir that holds as much water as all five Great Lakes.

Cradled between forested mountain slopes in central Siberia, the vast expanse of Lake Baikal is always a surprise to visitors. Reflecting clear blue skies or veiled in mist, frozen from January until the last few ice floes melt in May, alternately placid and stirred up by violent storms, Lake Baikal presents the ever-changing spectacle of a freshwater sea.

Not especially wide, the lake averages only 30 miles (48 kilometers) across. But its sickle-shaped basin is a full 395 miles (636 kilometers) long. And its surface area of 12,160 square miles (31,500 square kilometers) is greater than the entire state of Massachusetts.

Even more impressive is Baikal's depth. Going down to a maximum of 5,315 feet (1,620 meters), it is the deepest lake in the world. It is also the world's largest body of fresh water, with a total volume of some 5,500 cubic miles (23,000 cubic kilometers); it contains about as much water as all five of North America's Great Lakes combined. It has been calculated that

it would take almost a year for the total outflow of all the rivers in the world to fill Lake Baikal.

The lake's great depth, the abrupt drop-offs to deep water, and the relatively straight shorelines are all explained by Lake Baikal's unusual geological history. Located along a series of great faults, or cracks in the earth's crust, the basin was formed when a belt of rocks sank downward in huge segments along the fault lines. At the same time that the fault blocks were subsiding, the lake's mountain borders were rising. The result was the formation of a gigantic trench, or trough, in the earth's crust—Lake Baikal's enormous elongated basin.

The earth movements that formed this great trench began more than 20 million years ago, making Lake Baikal one of the oldest lakes in the world. And the process continues even today. Since the beginning of the last century, about 30 large-scale earth tremors have been recorded in this particularly earthquake-prone region. From time to time whole segments of Baikal's shoreline have subsided, leaving bays where there had been dry land. Indeed, some scientists have predicted that in time Asia will split apart in this area, forming a vast new sea.

Just as remarkable as Baikal's history is the array of plants and animals that inhabit it. More than half of the 600 kinds of plants and 1,200 animal species living in its waters are found nowhere else in the world. Among the most unusual inhabitants are large numbers of freshwater seals; among the most important economically are the salmonlike fish known as omul, which make Lake Baikal the most productive fishing ground in Siberia.

A vital transportation route, the lake is a valuable natural resource. Its dependable year-round outflow down the Angara River (its only outlet) powers the many hydroelectric plants located along the river's course. Pulp mills have been built on the lakeshore. The mineral hot springs in the area are considered curative, and there is a variety of recreational opportunities in and around the lake. □

Balancing Rocks

- Zimbabwe
- Map: page 26, C–4

Although a gentle push will set them swaying, the Balancing Rocks always return to their original positions.

With a history that stretches back 3½ billion years, the enormous formations that make up the Balancing Rocks of Epworth are among the oldest on the planet. Poised on granite hills about 7½ miles (12 kilometers) south of Harare, the capital of Zimbabwe, the rocks appear to be so precariously balanced, one on top of another, that even a light push could send them rolling down into the surrounding scrub. But as the thousands of tourists who have tried can testify, no shove can dislodge the Balancing Rocks. They sway, but they never fall.

How did these rocks assume their peculiar seemingly gravity-defying balance? Time, Africa's tropical climate, erosion, and the structure of the rock provide the answers. The rocks were once part of the earth's crust, which in this section of Africa exceeds 20 miles (32 kilometers) in thickness. The crust is mainly granite, which originally lay molten deep within the earth. Over millennia it gradually rose toward the surface, cooled, shrank, and cracked in such a way as to produce a series of massive granite blocks that were more or less rectangular. As time passed, groundwater seeping in through the cracks weathered these blocks and eventually rounded off the once angular corners.

After the rocks became exposed on the surface of the land, the sun, wind, and rain completed the rounding-off process. Daily heating and cooling helped flake off the surface layers already loosened by water, and wind and rain carried away the debris. The end result: a once-solid mass of granite has eroded into a heap of giant boulders, some poised at such delicate angles that a hand can rock but never dislodge them.

Formations similar to the Balancing Rocks of Epworth also can be found in Zimbabwe in Rhodes-Matopos National Park. In addition, there are balancing rocks in England (Dartmoor), in Australia (Yellowdine), and in Argentina (Tandil). □

BALANCING ROCKS. *Seemingly piled up by playful giants, the boulder heaps were formed as forces of erosion gradually enlarged the fractures in an ancient mass of granite.*

Balaton, Lake

- Hungary
- Map: page 17, E–4

The largest lake in Central Europe is a health spa, a popular vacation resort, and an oasis of natural beauty.

Noted for its warm, inviting, opalescent waters, Hungary's Lake Balaton is an internationally famous vacation resort. The low, flat southern shore, fringed by long, sandy beaches, is studded with resort villages. On the very picturesque northern shore, the eroded volcanic peaks of the Bakony Mountains rise to heights of more than 2,300 feet (700 meters). Densely forested in places, their slopes elsewhere are covered with carefully tended vineyards and orchards. Here too are resorts, including some with mineral hot springs and baths that are said to have special curative powers.

With a total surface area of about 230 square miles (600 square kilometers), the so-called "Hungarian Sea" is the largest lake in Central Europe. Long and narrow, it extends for about 50 miles (80 kilometers) from the southwest to the northeast but is nowhere more than 8.7 miles (14 kilometers) wide. Although one spot reaches a depth of 36 feet (11 meters), most of the lake is less than 13 feet (4 meters) deep. The water along the south shore is so shallow, in fact, that in some places it is possible for bathers to wade out as far as 1,300 feet (400 meters) from the shore.

This idyllic expanse of water did not always look as it does today. Formed by a downwarping of the earth's crust, it was originally a chain of five separate lakes. Over time the barriers between them eroded away to form a single basin. The lobe-shaped Tihany Peninsula, jutting abruptly from the north shore and reaching more than halfway across the lake, is a remnant of the barrier between two of the former lake basins.

Nor was the water level of Lake Balaton always the same as it is today. Traces of former shorelines are easily recognizable on the slopes some 20 to 26 feet (6 to 8 meters) above the present level of the lake. They testify to times when the climate was much wetter and the lake much deeper than it is today. At other times in the past, in contrast, Lake Balaton is believed to have dried out completely.

Another change that took place in fairly recent times was the silting up of a large bay at the southwestern end of the lake. Known as Kisbalaton, or "Little Balaton," it is now a vast marsh that shelters spectacular concentrations of spoonbills, herons, egrets, and other water birds. □

Balkhan Ranges

- U.S.S.R.
- Map: page 18, G–5

Two mountain ranges, separated by a valley that descends below sea level, were created by folding of the earth's crust many millions of years ago.

More often than not, the twin Balkhan Ranges are obscured from view by swirling clouds of yellow dust blown in by sandstorms over the vast Kara-Kum desert. But when the winds die down, passengers on a railroad to the east of the Caspian Sea get a chance to witness an impressive sight: like mighty fortresses, a pair of barren, flat-topped mountain ranges rises unexpectedly from the glistening, salt-encrusted plain.

To the north of the railroad route, stretching east and west for about 40 miles (65 kilometers), lies the Greater Balkhan Range, with a maximum height of 6,168 feet (1,880 meters). To the south are the Lesser Balkhans, reaching 2,549 feet (777 meters).

Though neither range has any permanent rivers, many deep gorges and ravines corrugate their very steep, sparsely vegetated slopes. The gulleying is caused by brief but heavy seasonal rains in an otherwise dry climate. During violent storms veritable torrents of mud pour down the slopes, gouging out the ravines. At the base of the mountains these seasonal streams fan out and drop their loads of liquid mud in apronlike cones of sediment. Similar cones of debris, known as alluvial fans, can be seen at the foot of mountains in very arid parts of the American West such as Death Valley.

The Lesser Balkhan Range is also notable for its impressive badlands. The term, originally coined for the Badlands of South Dakota, refers to landscapes where extensive erosion has carved the surface into barren labyrinths of narrow gorges separated by steep, sharp crests. □

LAKE BALATON. *Bordered by the volcanic peaks of the Bakony Mountains in Hungary, the lake fills a long, narrow basin that was formed by a downwarping of the earth's crust.*

Bam Bam
Amphitheaters

- Gabon
- Map: page 24, D–6

Remote and rarely visited, these African cliffs are capped by grassland contrasting with dense rain forests that crowd in at their foot.

Accessible only by air, these strangely eroded basins gouged out of the flanks of low sandstone hills and plateaus lie almost directly on the equator in West Africa. Heading south from Gabon's capital city of Libreville, the small plane crosses mile after mile of dense tropical rain forest that masks the monotony of the coastal plain. Suddenly the jungle is interrupted by a series of low sandstone uplands, which are covered with savanna grasses that ripple in the breeze.

Here and there, scooped from the sides of the hills, are semicircular bowl-shaped depressions—deeply gullied, devoid of vegetation, glistening with an array of ocherous hues. The most impressive of these erosional amphitheaters are known today as the Grand and Petit Bam Bam, or the Great and Little Bam Bam.

The plane lands at the tiny settlement at Wonga-Wongue, the only inhabited place in the area. Except for a gamekeeper's house and a visitors' lodge, the only signs of civilization are rough tracks opened in the past by lumbermen. Four-wheel-drive vehicles carry visitors to the cliffs.

The basins are eroded into the sides of hills that rise, islandlike, about 325 feet (100 meters) above the surrounding jungle. Torrential equatorial rains have carved them from the relatively soft sandstone and shaly rock formations that make up the hills. Deeply gullied into a maze of narrow ravines and sharp crests, they are examples of the badlands type of erosion similar to that found in the American West.

The unique combination of steaming jungle on the surrounding plain, the "islands" of grassland atop the sandstone hills, and the abrupt slopes furrowed by erosion accounts for the special beauty of this region of Gabon. Because of the difficulties of access, relatively few visitors have seen the Bam Bam Amphitheaters; fortunately for future generations, the area has been preserved as the Wonga-Wongue National Park. □

BAND-E AMIR. *Guarded by a stone sentry, two lakes lie at different elevations. Water from the higher one spills over the natural dam in the distance, then flows into the lower lake.*

Band-e Amir,
Lakes of

- Afghanistan
- Map: page 18, H–5

High in a dry land, these sparkling mountain lakes have been backed up behind natural stone dams.

Like jewels in an elaborate necklace, the mountain lakes of Band-e Amir glitter in a network of slow-moving streams. Milky white in some places, azure, turquoise, or dark green elsewhere, the lakes sparkle in breathtaking contrast to the arid land nearby. High, steep cliffs border the lakes, complementing their dramatic beauty.

Varying in length from a minuscule 300 feet (90 meters) to more than 4 miles (6½ kilometers), the lakes nestle along a river valley located in the central highlands of Afghanistan. In this mountainous country of south-central Asia, the average elevation is more than 4,000 feet (1,200 meters) above sea level; the highest peak reaches nearly 25,000 feet (7,600 meters). The lakes themselves lie at an elevation of about 9,800 feet (3,000 meters) above sea level.

Throughout the country precipitation is sparse, occurring mainly in the form of snow that blankets the mountains from November to March. Fed by meltwater, the rivers of Afghanistan fluctuate drastically from season to season; small streams dry up completely by July. Lakes are few and far between, their rarity adding to the appeal of Band-e Amir.

The lakes of Band-e Amir seem all the more spectacular because of the effort it takes to reach them. Travelers starting out from the ancient city of Bamian, famous for its two immense rock-hewn sculptures of Buddha, must negotiate approximately 50 miles (80 kilometers) of very treacherous road before suddenly coming upon the shimmering panorama of lakes, ponds, and streams that make up what

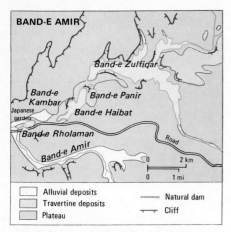

BAND-E AMIR

Band-e Zulfiqar

Band-e Kambar

Band-e Panir

Band-e Haibat

Japanese garden

Band-e Rholaman

Band-e Amir

Road

0   2 km

0   1 mi

Alluvial deposits
Travertine deposits
Plateau

Natural dam
Cliff

Nestled among high cliffs and plateaus, the lakes of Band-e Amir are bordered by deposits of travertine, which has formed several natural dams. Soil (alluvial) deposits support the growth of "Japanese gardens."

is sometimes called the eighth wonder of the world.

The lakes are widened portions of the Band-e Amir River, which has backed up behind several natural stone dams. Each lake is at a slightly different elevation, and together they form a series of steps along the course of the river.

Sluggish streams connect the lakes, creating places that are neither water nor land. Fancifully referred to as "Japanese gardens" because of their mixture of plants and rocks, these "amphibious" areas are characterized by deposits of soil and by dark green mounds, or hummocks, that alternate with pale-colored willows and patches of aquatic growth. The plants add a touch of living color to a landscape noteworthy for its harshness and severity, and they play an essential role in the continuing development of the natural stone dams.

Band-e Amir's dams are made of calcium carbonate, a substance coming from the limestone and marl (a clayey rock) that make up the nearby plateau. Surface water on the plateau, originating as rain or snow, dissolves the calcium carbonate and carries it down to the low-lying areas along the Band-e Amir River. There a chemical reaction between the aquatic plants and the water causes the calcium carbonate to come out of solution.

Laid down in layers, especially in warm weather, the deposits of calcium carbonate harden into travertine—a light-colored, semitranslucent, porous stone that is often used in walls and in interior decoration. Travertine deposits are not unique to this region; they

BAND-E AMIR. *Cliffs rimming these Asian lakes succumb to the onslaught of rain and snow. The light-colored patches of stone below are debris eroded from the cliffs.*

also occur in caves, along rivers, and around springs, including hot springs in Yellowstone National Park in the United States and cold ones in Afghanistan's Ajdar Valley.

Travertine deposits along the shores of Band-e Amir's largest lakes have accumulated to form dams measuring up to 33 feet (10 meters) high and 10 feet (3 meters) thick. These dams—and the lakes behind them—are so striking that a Moslem legend has developed to explain their origin. It credits the molding of the landscape not to a chemical reaction but to the actions of Ali, son-in-law of the prophet Mohammed. The name Band-e Amir, in fact, means "Dam of the Prophet" (or "Dam of the Saint").

According to the legend, Ali was furious because a tyrant had tried to hold him prisoner. So he climbed a mountain, and with a vigorous push of his foot he initiated a landslide that blocked the river and created the dam

that is now called Band-e Haibat ("Dam of Wrath").

But Ali didn't stop there. He used his sword to slice off another rock, which became Band-e Zulfiqar ("Dam of the Sword"). His servant Kambar created the third dam, Band-e Kambar. The tyrant's slaves, liberated by Ali, built Band-e Rholaman ("Dam of the Slaves"). And when a woman who witnessed these exploits offered Ali some unripened cheese (*panir*), he promptly tossed it into the river to form Band-e Panir.

It was in this way, according to legend, that the dams of Band-e Amir were created. But one problem remained: the dams blocked the water flow so completely that the downstream stretch of the river became a dry streambed. To placate the alarmed villagers, Ali used his fingers to trace out a series of channels that restored the flow of water, and the landscape was changed to its present form. □

Bandiagara Cliffs

- Mali
- Map: page 24, C–4

Towering above an endless African plain, a dramatic wall of multicolored sandstone forms a natural fortress.

South of the great bend of the Niger River not far from the legendary city of Timbuktu, a massive sandstone plateau rises abruptly above the plain. Its main wall of cliffs, some 125 miles (200 kilometers) long, varies from about 300 to 600 feet (90 to 180 meters) in height, while in one nearby area the cliffs rise almost vertically for as much as 1,650 feet (500 meters) above the plain.

The eroded remnant of a once much more extensive plateau, this great slab of sandstone was deposited in an inland basin more than 600 million years ago. Subsequently the earth's crust domed gently upward in this area, exposing the sandstone and the much softer underlying limestone and shale. Over the eons, fast-flowing streams eroded away the underlying formations, undermining the harder sandstone and leading to great landslides and collapses along the cliffs. Little by little the edges of the ancient plateau were gnawed away, leaving only the cliff-bounded upland that remains today. □

BANDIAGARA CLIFFS. *Though parched and dry today, the cliffs were carved by rushing water in past epochs when the climate was wetter.*

Baradla Caves

- Czechoslovakia—Hungary
- Map: page 17, F–4

Concerts are sometimes held in this large network of caves running between Hungary and Czechoslovakia.

Beneath the Baradla Valley lies a complex maze of caves. This labyrinth includes two large systems: the Aggtelek Caves in Hungary and the Domica Caves in Czechoslovakia. Together called the Baradla Caves, they extend over a distance of nearly 20 miles (32 kilometers) beneath the border of the two countries.

This subterranean network, housing one of the few underground biological research stations in the world, has ten entrances (seven natural, three artificial). The main Aggtelek entrance is the starting point for the tour to the Astronomical Tower, a stalagmite that measures 65 feet (20 meters) high and is one of the tallest known stalagmites in Europe. (A stalagmite is a conical structure on the floor of a cave, produced by the dripping of lime-saturated water from the roof; a corresponding cone called a stalactite often grows down from the roof.) Although the tour leading to this giant stalagmite is a long one (it takes about 5½ hours), it includes several other halls rich in the dripstones (stalagmites and stalactites) for which these caves are justifiably famous.

A variety of shorter excursions enables visitors who have less time to see those sections of the cave network that are the most heavily decorated with stalactites and stalagmites. A short excursion, for example, also starts at the main Aggtelek entrance. This tour includes a descent down a flight of stairs to see archeological excavations and a walk along the Acheron (a small underground stream) to view such outstanding cave formations as the Turtle, the Eagle, and the two Pheasants. Leaving the course of the Acheron, visitors climb up to the next level to visit the ominous-looking Black Hall. Close at hand is the Concert Hall, a big chamber with excellent acoustics where more than 1,000 people can attend performances (symphonies and other types of concerts are held during spring and fall). In the Tiger Hall a dripstone formation suggests this feline's silhouette; the Hall of Columns contains a veritable forest of stalagmites. Finally, visitors to the Baradla Caves proceed through the Labyrinth and emerge by way of a nearby exit into the valley. □

BARADLA CAVES. *Massive floor-to-ceiling columns resembling frozen waterfalls are among the varied dripstone formations found in this popular tourist attraction.*

Batéké Plateaus

- Congo
- Map: page 26, A–3

These rolling hills and plateaus near the Congo River resemble enormous grass-covered dunes.

Brazzaville, capital of the People's Republic of the Congo, stretches for 6 miles (10 kilometers) along the Congo River near the boundary of two very different geological regions. To the southwest lies the Inkisi belt, made up of sedimentary rocks more than 500 million years old; to the east and north are the Batéké Plateaus (named for the people who inhabit the area), which are composed of younger sediments deposited 100 to 200 million years ago.

Two distinct formations underlie the Batéké region, which covers an area of 5,000 square miles (13,000 square kilometers). At the base are white or yellow sands, sometimes interfingered with layers of sandstone hundreds of feet thick. Above this are white or ocher-colored clayey sands. Because of the absence of fossils, the precise history of these deposits is still a mystery. What is certain, however, is that the formations were laid down not in the ocean but after the continent assumed its present form (until about 200 million years ago Africa was part of a large continental mass called Gondwanaland).

Resembling giant steps, the Batéké Plateaus rise to various heights. The

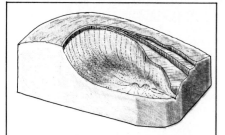

Natural amphitheaters scar a number of the sandy hillsides in the Congo's Batéké Plateaus. The large bowllike openings result from soil erosion and from the slumping of entire hillsides in massive landslides.

lowest level, the Mbe Plateau, stands 1,600 to 2,300 feet (500 to 700 meters) above sea level and is separated from the other plateaus by the Lefini, a tributary of the Congo River. North of the Lefini River is a higher tier of more than 2,600 feet (800 meters), which is fragmented into tilted plateaus. Several still higher plateaus rise above these and overlook a sea of hills covered with tall savanna grasses.

This very unusual rolling topography may be a result of the absence or scarcity of surface runoff water; instead of streaming over the land and smoothing it down, water seeps into the porous sands and disappears underground.

Particularly extraordinary are the enormous bowllike amphitheaters, or cirques, with sharp rims that contrast quite dramatically with the gentle rounded slopes of the hills. These basins are caused by the slumping of entire hillsides—again as a result of the seepage of surface water.

Surprisingly, in this hot, humid climate where the dry season lasts only three months, vegetation is relatively sparse. In an area so close to the equator, it would seem that the land should be covered by mature rain forests. But the only dense forest in the region grows in impenetrable belts or patches along rivers and streams. The hills and plateaus, in contrast, are covered by tall grasses and small, scattered trees and shrubs. Since savanna vegetation normally grows in much drier areas, its presence here is difficult to explain. Some scientists have suggested that the combined effects of the sandy substratum, occasional dry periods, and human intervention (setting fires and clearing the land for habitation) may have led to the disappearance of the original, quite possibly different vegetative cover. □

BATÉKÉ PLATEAUS. *Here and there on the plateaus, water-saturated soil has created landslides, scarring the rolling hillsides with bowllike natural amphitheaters.*

Belogradchik Crags

- Bulgaria
- Map: page 17, F–4

The inspiration for many a legend, a swath of intriguingly shaped rocks angles across the landscape.

Bristling with sandstone towers, a natural fortress used by Roman and Turkish invaders dominates the small city of Belogradchik in northwestern Bulgaria. Located near the Danube River and surrounded by lush greenery, it is an extraordinary belt of rocky spires about 20 miles (32 kilometers) long and 2 miles (3.2 kilometers) wide.

A traveler on the winding road to Belogradchik crosses a scenic pass, then continues through groves of leafy trees, and suddenly approaches these spectacular, colorful towers and obelisks, some more than 325 feet (100 meters) high. Needless to say, these intriguingly shaped natural structures have fired many an imagination and stimulated a host of local legends. There is, for example, the legend of the nun who fell in love with a handsome knight and was turned into one of the rocks by her mother superior. The "Dialogue of Adam and Eve" is a gigantic formation about 65 feet (20 meters) high, located at the foot of the fortress. Nearby are so-called monks, a knight on horseback, and a schoolgirl. An easily recognized dog, a surprisingly lifelike bear, and a cuckoo that emits strange noises when the wind blows are all part of the menagerie at Belogradchik.

The story of Belogradchik is one of erosion. The sandstone and conglomerate rocks were formed about 200 million years ago, when this area was covered by the sea. Limestone later developed on top of them. Then, some 20 million years ago, this part of the Balkans rose above sea level, and the rock formations here became folded— so much so that the sandstone and conglomerate were exposed to the elements. As erosion set in, it carved away the rock, except where erosion-resistant boulders in the formation protected the sandstone beneath. As a result, pyramidal shapes were formed, each capped by a mass of more resistant rock.   □

Benbulbin

- Ireland
- Map: page 16, C–3

A legendary dwelling place of bygone warriors, Benbulbin completely dominates the heart of "Yeats country."

Rising abruptly above the low coastal plain near Sligo Bay in northwestern Ireland are the Dartry Mountains, a series of impressive, flat-topped massifs bounded by spectacularly steep slopes. The westernmost of the group is Benbulbin, which reaches 1,722 feet (525 meters) above sea level. (*Ben* is the Gaelic word for mountain.)

Bleak, austere, frequently battered by storms that sweep in from the Atlantic, the great plateaulike mass of rock has always had the power to stir the imagination. According to legend, it was a dwelling place of the Fianna— bands of warriors who flourished in the third century A.D. Since that time they have been heroes of Irish folklore, and their names and exploits are evoked in the verse of the famed lyric poet William Butler Yeats. Yeats, who loved this countryside, is buried in a

BELOGRADCHIK CRAGS. *Creased by ravines and capped by balanced rocks, a cluster of eroded sandstone crags rises like a natural fortress.*

BENBULBIN. *Sculpted long ago by passing glaciers, the austere massif still bears the full brunt of storms that sweep in from the sea.*

cemetery in the village of Drumcliff at the foot of the mountain.

Benbulbin is a huge block composed of horizontal layers of sedimentary formations that were deposited here about 320 million years ago. The nearly straight-walled, furrowed cornice at the top of the mountain includes thick beds of two limestone formations: the massive, light-colored Dartry limestone on top of the thinner, darker Glencar limestone. The gentler lower slopes, largely mantled by debris, are composed of much softer Benbulbin black shale.

The mountain's particularly distinctive cliffs were sculpted by glaciers during past ice ages, which alternated over hundreds of thousands of years with temperate interglacial periods. At their greatest extent, massive ice sheets covered nearly all of Ireland and Great Britain. Their modeling action resulted not only from grinding by debris as the ice sheets slowly advanced, but also from the powerful runoff of meltwater when the glaciers retreated.

The remains of spectacular landslides can be seen in nearby valleys, while a smaller but nonetheless impressive landslide has scarred Benbulbin's northwestern face. That dramatic wall of stone, directly exposed to the full violence of ocean storms, is also corrugated by deep, evenly spaced vertical channels, apparently caused by both abrasion and dissolution of the limestone.

More sheltered and less rugged, the southwestern and northeastern sides of the mountain permit easy access to the flat summit. At the top of the mountain the surface is a patchwork of peaty areas covered by dwarf, windblown heaths alternating with coarse rubble.

Several arctic-alpine plant species, which are relics of ancient glacial periods, thrive in hollows in the limestone on the mountaintop. Normally found in colder climates much farther to the north, these species extended their ranges southward during the ice ages. Then, as the glaciers retreated and the climate warmed again, they managed to survive only in the cooler habitats found at high elevations.

But the greatest reward for climbing to the top of Benbulbin is not its plant life. From that vantage point the view includes the whole dramatic sweep of "Yeats country"—a panorama of Sligo Bay and its surroundings, with lakes, woods, and mountains that would inspire any poet. □

Ben Nevis

- United Kingdom (Scotland)
- Map: page 16, C–3

With its foot near sea level and its head often hidden in clouds, the tallest mountain in the British Isles towers above its surroundings.

Ben Nevis: some say its name means "hill of heaven," while others claim it means "cloud-capped mountain." Either interpretation is appropriate, for the brooding summit of Ben Nevis, frequently shrouded in mist, certainly seems to reach up to the sky. This great massif in northwestern Scotland, with a total height of 4,406 feet (1,343 meters), is in fact the tallest mountain in all of the British Isles.

For anyone who makes the fairly easy climb to the top, the reward is a breathtaking panorama. (On a clear day the view extends for some 75 miles, or 120 kilometers, in all directions.) Far off in the distance along the western horizon are the dark hills of Mull, Skye, and the other islands of the Inner Hebrides, rising above the shimmering Atlantic. To the north the majestic crests of the Western Highlands billow off into the haze, with lakes glittering in the intervening straths (wide valleys) and narrower glens. To the south and east are still more rumpled ranges of hills and glens—the wild and lonely Grampian Mountains. And stretching off to the northeast is the Great Glen, or Glen More, an extremely straight valley that extends all the way across Scotland along a giant fracture in the earth's crust. The most famous of the several lakes strung out along its length is Loch Ness, a sheet of water some 25 miles (40 kilometers) long and up to 754 feet (230 meters) deep.

The dramatically rounded hulk of Ben Nevis, overlooking this grand sweep of scenery, began to take form some 350 million years ago during a very intense mountain-building episode known as the Caledonian Revolution. In contrast to most of the other mountains in the area, which were formed by the folding of ancient basement rocks, Ben Nevis is the product of volcanic activity. A gigantic plug of very hard, erosion-resistant lava, it is encircled by two rings of granitic rocks that also welled up from deep down in the earth's crust. The subsequent slow but general upheaval of the Scottish Highlands raised the summit of Ben Nevis to its present height.

Further refinement of the mountain's contours took place during the recurring ice ages over the last 2 million years. Grinding repeatedly across the landscape, the great ice sheets tended to scrape away the soil and plane less resistant rock formations. Valleys such as Glen Nevis along the southern foot of the mountain were deepened and greatly enlarged. A lovely wooded glen today, enlivened by several waterfalls on the rushing Water of Nevis, the valley is strewn with glacial erratics—large boulders that were picked up elsewhere and dropped there by the melting glaciers. (The nearby Great Glen is a large-scale example of valley glaciation.)

On Ben Nevis itself, the most conspicuous Ice Age remnants are spectacular cirques on the northeastern side. These deep steep-sided, basinlike depressions were hollowed out when glaciers formed in the heads of formerly shallow mountain valleys. Snow blown over the mountaintop by prevailing southwesterly winds tended to accumulate in sheltered hollows on the northeastern side. As glaciers grew and began their slow creep down the mountainside, the great masses of ice scooped out the bedrock to form these characteristic bowllike hollows.

Glaciers persisted on Ben Nevis until less than 10,000 years ago, and even today it would not take much of a climate change to trigger their return. The area is wet and cool, without much real summer. In nearby Fort William, which stands slightly above sea level at the foot of Ben Nevis, the average annual rainfall is about 80 inches (2,000 millimeters), and the average temperature in July reaches only 58° F (14° C). The sun, moreover, shines on the average for only 2.7 hours per day the year round.

On Ben Nevis, with its much higher elevation and more continual cloud cover, conditions are even cooler and wetter. Snow accumulates very rapidly on the mountain slopes, especially in spring, and often remains throughout summer and into autumn. At elevations above 3,900 feet (1,200 meters), semipermanent snow fields are found in sheltered cirques and ravines where the sunlight rarely penetrates. It has been estimated that if it were only about 1,000 feet (300 meters) higher, authentic glaciers could form on the mountain. Even as it is, just a very slight drop in average temperatures could bring about renewed glaciation on Ben Nevis. ☐

BEN NEVIS. *The windswept, sparsely vegetated peak, the highest in the British Isles, is composed of a very hard, erosion-resistant mass of ancient volcanic rock.*

Beppu Thermal Area

- Japan
- Map: page 19, O–5

Geysers, hot springs, and boiling caldrons of mud reveal restless forces beneath the surface of the earth.

Throughout the world few places can match Beppu's abundance of geothermal phenomena. Near this city in northeastern Kyushu are more than 3,500 hot springs, geysers, and fumaroles (vents emitting gases, especially steam). These emissions, which together eject more than 2 million cubic feet (55,000 cubic meters) of water per day, are signs of relatively recent volcanic activity. The city of Beppu, in fact, lies at the base of a slope of volcanic debris, and several volcanoes (presently inactive) are located nearby.

Beppu's most spectacular emissions come from the *jigokus*. Also called fire pits and hells, these boiling ponds give off varying combinations of gases, hot water, and minerals, often accompanied by loud, explosive sounds. The largest one is Umi jigoku, which has sediments that reflect the color of the sky. Chinoike jigoku has blood-red water, colored by the products of underwater oxidation. Juman jigoku has the biggest fumarole, Bozu jigoku emits grotesque bubbles of mud, and Tatsu-maki jigoku is an active geyser that erupts jets of pressurized steam every 17 minutes.

Because Beppu is the site of such extraordinary geothermal activity, it has become one of Japan's major resorts. Visitors can soak in hot sand

BEPPU THERMAL AREA. *Turbulent gases create miniature craters and streams in a boiling mud pot. Slightly cooled mud is used for "baths," as are pockets of hot sand.*

BEPPU THERMAL AREA. *A puff of steam and hot water tops an erupting geyser, one of an abundance of geysers, hot springs, and related phenomena near a city in Japan.*

"baths," cook eggs in hot puddles, and watch hippopotamuses, pelicans, and other animals enjoying the warm water in a small zoo.

But Beppu is not just a tourist attraction: the thermal areas provide treatment for people with a variety of illnesses as well as supply heat and hot water to the communal baths, public buildings, greenhouses, and even henhouses. A university laboratory in the city specializes in the study of hot springs, and researchers are investigating ways of further utilizing both geothermal and volcanic energy in Japan and in other countries. □

Berlenga Island

● Portugal
● Map: page 17, C–5

This tiny island has more than its share of precipitous cliffs, sheltered coves, and other dramatic seascapes.

Ilha Berlenga, or Berlenga Island, is basically a continuation of Cape Carvoeiro, a piece of Portugal that juts into the sea north of Lisbon. This oddly shaped bit of land, only nine-tenths of a mile (1½ kilometers) long and less than half a mile (800 meters) wide, is the principal island in the small Berlengas archipelago.

With its granite cliffs, narrow valleys, deep caves, and sheltered coves, Berlenga Island has a striking array of scenery for such a small place. The island's red rock, composed primarily of quartz and feldspar, vividly contrasts with the surrounding blue-green water. Erosion has carved the rock into steep-walled valleys and precipitous cliffs. Deep caves such as Gruta Azul ("Blue Grotto") scallop the coastline, and marine tunnels such as Furado Grande ("Big Hole") penetrate the shoreline.

Furado Grande is about 230 feet (70 meters) long and opens into a dramatic bay. Walled in by sheer granite cliffs some 200 feet (60 meters) high, the bay is noted for its wild beauty. Although it resembles a fjord, it is actually a ria—a valley carved by a river and then flooded by the sea. (Fjords, in contrast, are flooded glacial valleys.)

Though Berlenga's scenery is spectacular, the landscape itself appears quite barren. Its skimpy soil can support only limited vegetation, and strong winds batter any trees that manage to survive. Lacking agriculture, the islanders' livelihood depends on the abundant fish—mackerel, mullet, swordfish—and other marine life in the surrounding waters. Though fishermen generally head for the deeper waters, many fish can be caught in the island's sheltered coves.

The waters around Berlenga also attract divers, while hikers come to the island to climb among the cliffs and wend their way to the 16th-century monastery, the 17th-century fortress (complete with drawbridge), and the 19th-century lighthouse. Visitors can also take boat trips to the caves and coves or venture to other islands—the Estrelas, Forcadas, and Farilhões—in the lovely little archipelago. □

BIG SUR. *Sweeping slopes, rugged headlands, and sheltered beaches attract an endless stream of visitors to this California coast.*

Big Sur

- United States (California)
- Map: page 10, C–5

A wild and windswept California coastline is famed as one of the world's most dramatic meeting places of solid land and surging sea.

Paralleling California's Pacific shoreline is a line of mountain chains, the Coast Ranges. One of them, the Santa Lucia Range, extends about 140 miles (225 kilometers) southeast of Carmel Bay, rising as a barrier between the sea and the rich agricultural lands of the Salinas Valley.

The special beauty of the place results from the way the slopes in the northern part of the range swoop down dramatically from the heights to end abruptly in the sea. Here along the Big Sur coast, stretching some 50 miles (80 kilometers) south of the village of Carmel, the mountain flanks form rocky headlands alternating with deep coves.

Battered constantly by the crashing surf, the headlands end in rugged cliffs, while offshore the ocean is dotted with freestanding rocks and pinnacles. The rocks, once part of the mainland, are eroded remnants of headlands that once extended much farther out to sea. Pounded by the waves, they too in time will topple and be reduced to sand that will eventually be washed ashore.

A popular tourist destination, the Big Sur is best seen from the highway that snakes along the coast. Leaping across canyons on towering bridges and winding in and out across misty headlands, it ranks among the finest scenic drives in the world. □

Bilma, Erg of

- Chad–Niger
- Map: page 24, E–4

A vast Saharan sea of sand has been modeled by the wind into an intricate mosaic of imposing dune forms.

Contrary to a common misconception, the Sahara is not an endless shifting sea of sand. In fact, only one-fifth of its area is covered by ergs, the Arabic word for such sandy expanses. Much of the remainder of the Sahara is made up of gravelly plains (regs), stony upland plateaus (hamadas), and isolated, islandlike mountain massifs.

ERG OF BILMA. *Ceaseless winds have modeled the surface of the Saharan sand into a delicate pattern of ripple marks, interrupted here and there by drought-resistant plants.*

Typical of the many ergs that dot the desert is the Erg of Bilma, which covers extensive areas of Chad and Niger in the south-central Sahara. Fanning out to the southwest from the Tibesti Massif, the highest mountain mass in the desert, it is about 750 miles (1,200 kilometers) in length and 175,000 square miles (455,000 square kilometers) in area. From horizon to horizon it extends, a billowing expanse of sand dunes interrupted only by a few waterholes, oases, and areas where bare rock is exposed.

The source of all this sand is the rugged Tibesti, which has been attacked over many millennia by wind and water erosion. Transported by the prevailing wind—the harmattan, which blows in constantly from the northeast for eight months of the year—the sand grains are scattered across the Erg of Bilma and modeled into dunes of various forms.

Dominating the center of the erg is a sand sea—a thick covering of very high, billowing dunes. Along the eastern border are numerous barchans—extremely mobile, crescent-shaped dunes with the tips, or horns, pointing downwind. Other areas are dominated by ghourds—extraordinarily complex, pyramidal, star-shaped dunes having arms radiating in all directions. (Open corridors between ghourds, known as gassis, are often the only available routes for the passage of caravans.)

In the southern half of the erg most of the dunes take the form of long, parallel sand ridges. Known as seif dunes, they are generally separated by troughlike gassis, just as the ghourds are. Some of the ridges are enormous, reaching 110 miles (175 kilometers) in length, with an average width of 3,300 feet (1,000 meters). Although the main sand ridges generally are aligned in the direction of the prevailing harmattan wind, sometimes the pattern becomes more complex. In addition to the parallel rows of seif dunes, diagonal ridges have also developed, creating checkerboard patterns of ridges and depressions.

Although the overall shapes of the various dune forms are more or less stable, their surfaces are constantly being altered. Shifting about before the wind, individual sand grains are piled up into innumerable ripples that texture the surfaces of the dunes with an infinite variety of patterns.

At the extreme southern margin of the erg the dunes have been stabilized by vegetation, and on gently sloping sand mounds the local tribes cultivate crops of millet and sorghum. Yet the balance is a delicate one. If the plant cover should be destroyed by overgrazing or lack of adequate rainfall, the wind would mobilize the sand once again, remodeling it into new, ever-shifting dune forms. □

Blanc, Cape

● Tunisia
● Map: page 24, D-2

*In northernmost Tunisia, a pair
of gleaming white headlands
juts dramatically into the sea.*

Like arms embracing a sheltered cove,
the twin headlands at Cape Blanc
project boldly into the Mediterranean
at the northernmost tip of Tunisia.
Shimmering in brilliant sunlight, the
sheer white limestone cliffs contrast
dramatically with the clear blue waters of the sea.

The cliffs facing each other on opposite sides of the cove are the highest
parts of the two promontories, with
nearly vertical drops of about 325 feet
(100 meters). From these high points
the tops of the headlands slope gradually downward to lower—but still impressive—cliffs on the outer edges of
the promontories.

At one time the two headlands were
a single promontory, formed as a result of an upward arching of the
earth's crust along a north-south axis.
The outer layers of this arch were
composed of massive deposits of limestone about 260 feet (80 meters) thick,
lying over a central core of marl,
which is a chalky clay.

Because it is much more easily
eroded than limestone, the underlying
core of marl was gradually hollowed
out, causing the overlying limestone to
collapse. The result was the formation
of a deep, steep-sided trench down the
center of the original headland. Thus
what was once a single promontory
became two, and the trench that separated them is the cove we see today.

No one can say for certain when the
upward arching of the rock took place,
though deformations of the earth's
crust are known to have occurred in
this region about 3 to 5 million years
ago. In any case, it is believed that by
about 1 million years ago Cape Blanc
looked much as it does today.

Erosion is responsible for the white
color of the cliffs that gives the area its
name. Outcrops of the same limestone
formation lying farther inland have
weathered to a grayish hue. But here
waves are constantly gnawing away at
the cliffs and undermining the rocks.
In addition, rainwater is seeping into
fractures in the limestone, causing
whole sections of the walls to tumble
down and exposing gleaming white,
unweathered rock surfaces.   □

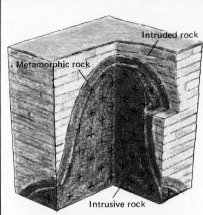

A batholith is a large mass of once-
molten rock, usually granitic in nature,
that welled upward into older overlying rocks. The intense heat of the
molten material causes a thin layer of
metamorphic rock to form in the older
material that surrounds it.

Blanca, Cordillera

● Peru
● Map: page 14, B-3

*High in the Andes, glacier-carved
peaks glisten with ice and snow.
Beneath the whiteness are rocks that
once were a deeply buried batholith.*

The Cordillera Blanca, or the "White
Range," is without doubt one of the
mightiest masses of the Andes. Crisscrossed by dizzying ravines, the range
includes some 30 jagged summits with
heights of 20,000 feet (6,100 meters) or
more. Tallest of all is Huascarán, at
22,205 feet (6,768 meters), the highest
mountain in Peru.

The range, which extends about 125
miles (200 kilometers) from northwest
to southeast, is only 100 miles (160
kilometers) from the Pacific Ocean.
Yet it forms part of South America's
continental divide—the boundary that
separates waters flowing into the Pacific from those that eventually reach
the Atlantic. The western slopes of the
Cordillera Blanca drop down abruptly
to the valley of the Río Santa, which
flows north and then west into the
Pacific; on the east is the valley of the
Río Marañón, one of the principal
headwaters of the eastward-flowing
Amazon River.

Although the mountains are only
about 600 miles (960 kilometers) south
of the equator, they are so high that
their summits have a permanent cap
of snow. Above an elevation of 15,750
feet (4,800 meters), a broad cover of

perpetual ice and snow cloaks the
steep slopes, extending upward for
some 6,000 feet (1,800 meters) to the
top of the highest peaks. The Cordillera Blanca takes its name from these
massive glaciers, standing out in glittering contrast to the blue Andean sky.
To the west lies a lower range of
mountains—the Cordillera Negra, or
"Black Range."

The granitic rocks that rise so high
in the Cordillera Blanca were once
buried deep beneath the earth's surface. They formed after the development of a batholith (from the Greek
for "deep rock")—a geological feature
that also forms the core of the Sierra
Nevada in California and Pikes Peak
in Colorado.

In the distant past a huge mass of
molten material welled upward inside
the earth. When it cooled, it created an
enormous elongated bulge of granitic
rock—a batholith—which was about
125 miles (200 kilometers) long, up to
9 miles (15 kilometers) wide, and more
than 18 miles (30 kilometers) deep.
Then the Andes were uplifted, and the
overlying layers of sedimentary and
metamorphic rocks were gradually
stripped away by erosion. Eventually
all that remained was the harder, considerably more resistant core of granitic rocks.

Yet even these hardest rocks have
been sculpted by erosion. Just as glaciers cap the Cordillera Blanca today,
much larger ice masses gouged its
flanks during past ice ages. Glacial
features abound throughout the entire
range, especially along the western
slopes. Rock surfaces are scarred with
parallel grooves carved by angular
debris trapped in the passing glaciers.
There are streamlined, whale-shaped
knobs of rock, known as *roches moutonées,* that were planed and polished
by the glaciers. Along the mountain
slopes there are many cirques—hollow
bowls carved into the bedrock at the
heads of glacial valleys.

The valleys themselves are among
the most impressive relics of past ice
ages. Deep, narrow, and characteristically U-shaped in cross section, these
troughlike valleys were scooped out
by glaciers as they crept down the
sides of the mountains. Most are located along the weakened zones of
fault lines, where the bedrock fractured as the mountains were uplifted. The most spectacular glacial valleys are the deep *quebradas,* or gorges,
which run down between the high
mountain peaks.

But the glaciers did more than just erode the mountainsides. They also built up entirely new landscape features, called moraines, as they deposited the loads of boulders, rocks, sand, silt, and other eroded debris that had been carried along by the ice. Lateral moraines developed where the debris was dropped along the sides of the glaciers. Terminal moraines—semicircular heaps of rocks and rubble—were deposited along the line of a glacier's snout as the ice melted. Today many of these terminal moraines act as natural dams, blocking the streams of meltwater that continue to flow down from the remaining glaciers and transforming the upstream waters into beautiful jewellike lakes.

Occasionally, one of the moraine dams bursts. In this earthquake-prone region, tremors sometimes trigger avalanches that result in disastrous torrents of ice, mud, and water. Flooding down the *quebradas* and out onto settlements in the Santa valley, they bring instant devastation to the people who live in the shadow of these mighty summits. Thus the gigantic mass of glaciers that account for so much of the beauty of this remote mountain landscape also represents a constant threat to people residing below. □

CORDILLERA BLANCA. *Storms blowing in from the Pacific constantly replenish the glaciers that cap the mightiest peaks in Peru.*

BLUE MOUNTAINS. *Dramatic rock formations such as these sandstone towers, known as the Three Sisters, were carved by rivers cutting downward into the edge of a plateau.*

Blue Mountains

- Australia
- Map: page 23, F–5

Misty blue mountains, dense green forests, and steep cliffs await visitors to this popular vacation area not far from Sydney. Beneath the dissected slopes lie seams of coal.

Seen up close, the Blue Mountains of Australia are green, colored by dense forests. But viewed from the city of Sydney about 40 miles (65 kilometers) away, the mountains appear as a faint bluish line on the horizon, a color change caused by the filtering of light through the airborne oils emitted by eucalyptus trees.

Part of the Great Dividing Range in

New South Wales, the Blue Mountains are about 300 miles (480 kilometers) long and 50 miles (80 kilometers) wide. Nowhere more than 3,900 feet (1,200 meters) high, they are really a deeply dissected plateau.

The geological history of the plateau goes back about half a billion years; traces of limestone, shale, and granite from this time appear on some of the valley floors. Layers of shale 250 million years old, which contain coal seams (constituting a large part of the New South Wales coalfield), lie beneath massive beds of sandstones that are 200 million years old.

The sandstones of the Blue Mountains are the same age as those surrounding Sydney harbor. However, over the course of the last 65 million years the Blue Mountain sandstones were uplifted several times, accompanied by considerable fracturing. The resulting joints and fissures are extraordinarily susceptible to erosion, and even today there are occasional rockfalls on the slopes.

Perhaps the most spectacular phase in the development of the mountains began after the uplifts, when a network of streams began to dissect the plateau. The water cut giant gorges in the sandstone—some with very high, steep sides, some deep enough to expose the underlying shale. In many places the streams create beautiful waterfalls: at Govett's Leap, for example, the water suddenly drops 520 feet (158 meters) in a particularly dramatic cascade.

Although the Blue Mountains were sighted by Europeans as early as 1788, it was not until 25 years later that an explorer, Gregory Blaxland, first crossed their precipitous slopes. Since then their proximity to Sydney and the excellent access roads have turned the mountains into one of Australia's most popular attractions. The resort area of Katoomba provides accommodations for visitors to Echo Point Lookout, where the vista includes the Three Sisters (a trio of gigantic sandstone formations) and the Giants' Stairway (high vertical cliffs resembling steps). The Jenolan Caves, located in a large wildlife preserve about 50 miles (80 kilometers) from Katoomba, contain some of the most remarkable limestone formations in Australia. And the Blue Mountains National Park features the Grose River Gorge, where visitors can hike into an extraordinarily deep valley of multicolored rocks. □

Blue Ridge Mountains

- United States
- Map: page 11, E–5

Shrouded by a constant haze, the Blue Ridge Mountains are rounded in form and subdued in height.

Famed for their high-elevation forests, the Appalachians sweep southwestward from Quebec to Alabama. Highest in New England and North Carolina, this broad system extends for more than 1,200 miles (1,900 kilometers) to form the rocky backbone of the eastern United States.

The Blue Ridge Mountains form a substantial part—615 miles (990 kilometers)—of the far-reaching Appalachians. They begin as a narrow, low ridge in Pennsylvania, then slowly spread and rise until they reach a height of 5,938 feet (1,810 meters) at majestic Grandfather Mountain in North Carolina. The Blue Ridge technically includes among its major spurs the Great Smoky Mountains and the Black Mountains; Mount Mitchell, in the latter range, is at 6,684 feet (2,037 meters) the highest peak east of the Mississippi River.

Two of the world's most scenic highways follow the crest of the Blue

Appalachian Relief

The classic ridge-and-valley relief of the Blue Ridge and other parts of the Appalachian Mountains is the result of events that took place during hundreds of millions of years. First, movements in the earth's crust created large folds in the thick formations of sedimentary rocks (1). Erosion wore down the elevated portions to a nearly flat surface, called a peneplain (2). Crustal upheavals again occurred, and further erosion took place. The softer formations were eroded into valleys; the more resistant rocks became mountains or high ridges (3). This rather uncommon ridge-and-valley system, which can be further complicated by additional crustal movements, is known as Appalachian relief and is also found in Switzerland, Morocco, and Bolivia.

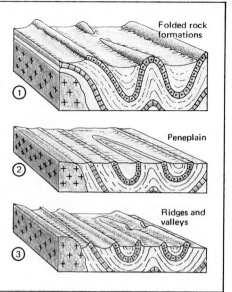

Folded rock formations

Peneplain

Ridges and valleys

Ridge: the Skyline Drive, which runs through Shenandoah National Park in Virginia, and the Blue Ridge Parkway, which links Shenandoah with Great Smoky Mountains National Park in North Carolina and Tennessee. The parkway's northern section straddles a steep, rugged mountain area. But south of Roanoke, Virginia, the Blue Ridge becomes a gentle highland. Beyond Crabtree Meadows, North Carolina, the mountains grow loftier; thick evergreen forests and cloud-swept summits loom above the park-

way. In many places the panorama is much as it was in the early 1700's, when a visitor described the Blue Ridge as "An Ocean of Woods swelled and depressed with a Waving Surface like that of the great Ocean itself." Elsewhere are relics of human history—a gristmill, rough-hewn cabins, and other reminders of a bygone way of life remembered in a wealth of ballads and folklore.

Like the rest of the Appalachians, these mountains were once substantially higher and bolder. Their uplift was nearly completed some 280 million years ago, and they have been drastically eroded since that time.

More recently, immense continental glaciers covered the land as far south as Pennsylvania. Although they did not spread over the Blue Ridge, flora and fauna far beyond their reach became adapted to the cold. When the climate warmed and the ice melted, the cold-adapted species retreated northward, surviving in the South only at higher, cooler elevations. Red spruces and Fraser firs are remnants of the Ice Age, thriving in the higher elevations of the Blue Ridge, and local beeches, birches, and red oaks are typical of forests farther to the north.

Sharing the high peaks is another distinctive plant community. This is the bald—a treeless area covered with grass or, more commonly, with broadleaved shrubs. Often large and vigorous, the latter include huckleberries, mountain laurel, and most especially, rhododendron—an evergreen shrub that blossoms in June and creates some of the most spectacular wild gardens on earth. □

BLUE RIDGE MOUNTAINS. *Blanketed by forests and dissected by snow-covered ravines, the Blue Ridge forms a picturesque part of the ancient Appalachian system.*

Bora-Bora

● French Polynesia
● Map: page 9

This South Pacific island is an enchanting blend of verdant peaks, coral reefs, and a blue lagoon.

Bora-Bora is not a very large island. From north to south it extends only about five miles (eight kilometers) and from east to west only three miles (five kilometers). Nor is it especially high: its tallest peak, Mount Taimanu, is a mere 2,385 feet (727 meters) high, while nearby Mount Pahia rises to a maximum elevation of only 2,169 feet (661 meters).

Yet this island gem, located about 125 miles (200 kilometers) northwest of Tahiti and, like Tahiti, part of the Society Islands, seems to cast a spell over every visitor. Jagged crests and ridges, lush with vegetation, rise dramatically from the coastal strip of soil washed down from the mountains. Along the shoreline, deeply indented by picturesque bays, coconut palms rustle in the trade winds. An enor-

mous almost circular coral reef fringes the island; its top emerges as long, narrow islands (*motus*) enclosing one of the most beautiful lagoons in the Pacific Ocean.

Like most of the neighboring islands, Bora-Bora is the much-eroded exposed tip of a long-extinct volcano built up by a succession of basaltic lava flows. The deep depression now filled by Turaapuo Bay was the main

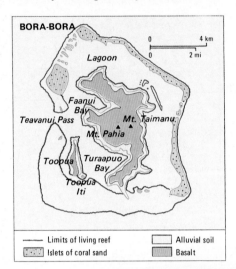

crater of the volcano, while Faanui Bay probably occupies a large side vent. Mount Taimanu and Mount Pahia are believed to be particularly erosion-resistant remnants of the north wall of the main crater. Toopua and Toopua Iti, two islets in the lagoon, are assumed to be remnants of the western wall of the crater.

The coral reef that almost completely encircles the island developed over thousands of years on the submerged slopes of the mountain. Like other coral reefs, it is made up of deposits of calcium carbonate built up by enormous colonies of microscopic coral animals. To the north and east the reef is capped by an almost continuous chain of islets made of sand and coarse coral fragments. To the west a narrow gap in the reef, Teavanui Pass, enables ships to enter the sheltered waters of the lagoon.

First described by Captain James Cook, the British explorer, who anchored there in 1769, Bora-Bora has since attracted many travelers and writers. As further testimony to its beauty, it has served as the setting for several motion pictures. □

BORA-BORA. *Rising from a lagoon almost completely encircled by a coral reef, the island is the eroded summit of a long-extinct volcano.*

Coral Reefs: Where and How They Grow

A coral reef can grow to enormous size: the Great Barrier Reef extends for nearly 1,300 miles (2,100 kilometers) along the northeastern coast of Australia. Yet its basic components are tiny animals—fleshy, tentacled creatures with skeletons of calcium carbonate (the substance that makes up limestone). Reef-building corals generally reproduce by budding off new individuals that remain attached to the "parent." Once a colony forms, it grows upward and outward, building on the skeletons of dead coral.

Microscopic plants live in the soft tissues of coral animals. Because these plants require light for photosynthesis, living coral occurs only in water less than 200 feet (60 meters) deep. Living reefs also require clear, warm, turbulent saltwater; reefs do not develop along the western coasts of continents, where cold currents prevail.

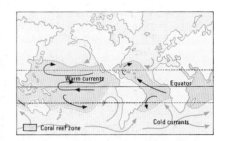

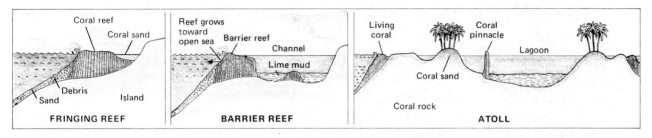

FRINGING REEF   BARRIER REEF   ATOLL

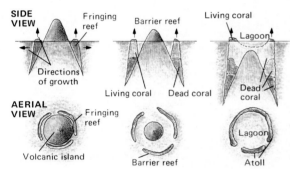

The three types of coral reefs—fringing reefs, barrier reefs, and atolls—develop in sequence. According to the widely accepted theory of Charles Darwin, fringing reefs are the first to develop, forming near the shore of a volcanic island or along the edge of a continent. Because of shifts within the earth's crust or a rise in sea level, the land sinks slowly into the sea. The reef continues to grow upward as the land subsides; and a barrier reef, separated from the land by a broad, deep channel, takes shape. Eventually all of the land may disappear, transforming the barrier reef into an atoll—a ring of coral circling a lagoon. Some scientists attribute the drowning of land entirely to the postglacial rise in sea level. Regardless of how the land became submerged, this theory resolves an apparent paradox: though coral is able to live and grow only in shallow water, some fossil reefs extend more than 15,000 feet (4,600 meters) beneath the surface of the sea.

BOSQUE DE ROCAS. *The product of fire and ice, the eroded pinnacles are composed of volcanic rocks sculpted into their present form by alternate freezing and thawing.*

Bosque de Rocas

- Peru
- Map: page 14, B–4

During the last ice age, nature sculpted a unique landscape of furrowed towers and pillars in central Peru.

Not far from Lima, Peru, rises a remarkable landscape of intricately fluted pillars, honeycombed columns, and creviced towers topped by balanced rocks. The surrounding flat fields further emphasize the extraordinary relief of this rock forest, or Bosque de Rocas, which is a product of both intense heat and extreme cold.

The Bosque de Rocas is in the foothills of the Andes, where there are numerous volcanoes. Millions of years ago the volcanoes exploded and covered vast areas with what eventually became a coating of ignimbrite, or hardened ash, as well as other kinds of volcanic debris.

Near the small village of Huarón, the volcanic rocks formed a plateau on top of layers of different kinds of sandstone, limestone, and conglomerate. This fantastic forest of stone developed on the edge of the rocky plateau and on the slopes of the neighboring valleys.

Because ignimbrite is a porous rock, it is particularly susceptible to frost erosion. About 20,000 years ago, during the last ice age, there was snow on the plateau year-round (today temporary glaciers develop there only during the cool season). As freezing and thawing took place, meltwater filtered into cracks in the porous rock and froze. There its erosive power was intensified, since freezing water always expands, causing rock to crumble along its joints.

Eventually, when the climate here became warmer, the ice melted away, and what remained was the incredibly eroded rock formations, sculpted into deeply grooved towers and pinnacles. The extraordinary topography of the Bosque de Rocas was most likely formed in a relatively short time, geologically speaking, that is—perhaps in one or two millennia. □

Bryce Canyon

- United States (Utah)
- Map: page 10, D–5

A kaleidoscope of ever-changing hues, the colors of the eroded rocks vary with the time of day, weather conditions, and the season of the year.

In the late 1800's Ebenezer Bryce, a pioneering rancher, grazed his cattle in the shadows of the spectacular and colorful rock formations in southern Utah that now bear his name. The area, which is preserved in a national park, was in his words "One heck of a place to lose a cow."

A multicolored maze of pinnacles, columns, spires, and craggy colonnades, the "canyon" actually is not a single canyon but a mass of ravines eroded into the edge of a high plateau. And the erosion continues to this day: the rim of the plateau is receding approximately 1 foot (30 centimeters) every 50 years.

The escarpment, known as the Pink Cliffs, winds more or less north to south for about 20 miles (32 kilometers) along the eastern edge of the Paunsaugunt Plateau. It is composed of limestone, siltstone, sandstone, and shale. The rocks are tinged with me-

BRYCE CANYON. *The fantastic maze of craggy columns marks the eroded edge of a plateau.*

tallic elements, especially iron, that produce a rainbow of hues ranging from pink to red to orange and even lavender.

The horizontal layers of rocks were formed from sediments that began washing into inland lakes from the surrounding highlands some 60 million years ago. About 13 million years ago, after the sediments had been compacted into stone, the entire region underwent a period of general upwarping. Fractured along major fault lines, huge blocks of the earth's crust were heaved slowly upward from what was then sea level to their present elevation. One of the blocks became the present-day Paunsaugunt Plateau, bounded on the east by the towering Pink Cliffs.

Then erosion began its work, gnawing away at the edge of the escarpment and creating a myriad of rock forms. Several physical forces contributed to

the process. For one thing, limestone is very durable and resistant to erosion in an arid climate. Where it forms a wall or acts as a protective cap atop a spire, erosion is slowed down and freestanding conical pillars remain. Shale, conglomerate, and poorly cemented sandstone, on the other hand, are much more easily eroded and so are more likely to be washed away by running water.

In addition, stresses that were created within the rock as the plateau was being uplifted caused the entire mass to become crisscrossed with a pattern of vertical cracks, or joints. Over time the joints gradually widened and then deepened as a result of rainwater seeping in and alternately freezing and thawing. Penetration by plant roots, together with chemical changes in the rock caused by exposure to air and water, also played a role in enlarging the openings. Over long pe-

Bucegi Mountains

- Rumania
- Map: page 17, F–4

Dense forests and rocks of unique shapes adorn these slopes; deep, mysterious caverns hide within.

A segment of the vast Carpathian system, the Bucegi Mountains begin 80 miles (130 kilometers) northwest of Bucharest and cover 115 square miles (300 square kilometers) of the renowned Transylvania region of Rumania. They are not especially tall: their highest point, Omu Peak, reaches only 8,238 feet (2,511 meters).

The mountains' history dates back about 100 million years to the time when sandstone, shale, conglomerate, and limestone began forming in this region, which marks the boundary of two major crustal plates. About 6 million years ago the plates collided, uplifting the mountains and causing the bedrock formations to fold and actually overturn. The plates are still converging, causing occasional earthquakes; a serious one devastated this region in 1977.

Within the Bucegis lie sinkholes and caverns, while strange rock formations rest upon the slopes. This variety in landform results from the rocks' differing degrees of resistance to water and wind erosion. Where limestone predominates, water may dissolve it, forming sinkholes and caverns. Where conglomerate and sandstone prevail, the harsh wind and weather may cut peculiar shapes—for example, Babele ("Old Women"), which is said to resemble human forms bent under the weight of heavy burdens.

Glaciers and rivers also modeled the Bucegi terrain. At the head of some of the highest valleys, glacial ice chiseled semicircular hollows known worldwide as cirques. Rivers have carved the mountains, creating deep ravines and gorges; five steep-walled gorges have been cut by the Ialomita, the region's major stream.

Within the Bucegis is a national park, a preserve for the extraordinarily diverse plant and animal life found there. Wild boars, bears, and wolves prowl the area, and some 1,100 species of plants thrive on the mountain slopes, including a rare iris (*Iris dacica*), an unusual willow (*Salix myrtiloides*), and 33 more that grow nowhere else. □

riods of time the cracks were eventually widened into channels to create the rugged landscape and strangely eroded, freestanding forms that remain today.

The process, however, is never-ending and continues to this day. In late summer, brief, torrential rainstorms cause flash floods at Bryce Canyon. Streams sweep through established channels, scouring them down farther and washing away accumulations of fallen debris. Openings in the rocks are enlarged, parts of walls are split off, and isolated columns are undermined and collapse.

Just as the colors of the rocks at Bryce Canyon change under different lighting conditions, their very contours are also changing over the course of time. As the canyon rim retreats slowly toward the west, the craggy rockscape beneath it is gradually being sculpted anew. □

BUCEGI MOUNTAINS. *Wind, water, and ice, attacking outcrops of rock on the mountainsides over long periods of time, have modeled them into unearthly sculptural forms.*

Cacahuamilpa Caverns

- Mexico
- Map: page 12, C–3

Crisscrossing a limestone massif, a network of subterranean passages forms an eerie but fascinating underground museum.

Hidden in a valley near Taxco, about 95 miles (150 kilometers) southwest of Mexico City, are the most famous caves in Mexico: Las Grutas de Cacahuamilpa. Carved by running water, they are part of an intricate network of underground river channels that riddle a massive limestone formation. Some of the rivers are still active: two surface streams, the San Gerónimo and Chantolcoatlan, disappear underground, flow into each other, and reemerge as the Río Amacuzac. Many former river channels, in contrast, are now high and dry.

The caves (their Aztec name means "place where the coca grows") include a remarkable gallery 4,528 feet (1,380 meters) long, as much as 325 feet (100 meters) wide, and up to 230 feet (70 meters) high. Everywhere the surfaces are lavishly decorated with stone formations deposited layer upon layer by slowly dripping water. Stalactites hang like icicles from the ceiling, and even more impressive stalagmites jut up from the floor. Given such fanciful names as the Puente de los Cuerubines ("Cherubs Gate") and Las Fuentas ("The Fountains"), some of these remarkable domelike structures are up to 130 feet (40 meters) high and 65 feet (20 meters) in diameter.

Once used as hideouts by bandits, the caves have been partially developed for sightseeing and continue to be explored today. Among the maze of passageways, chambers of extraordinary size have been discovered. In some of them the roofs have caved in to form giant, well-like sinkholes and collapsed depressions known as dolinas. Openings in the walls of the dolinas provide access to still other underground river channels.

Many more caverns are found in this limestone terrain, including the Cave of Carlos Pacheco, the Cave of Acnitlapan, and others. It seems likely that further exploration will lead to the discovery of connections between them forming a single vast subterranean river system. □

Caldera, Rocks of

- Chile
- Map: page 15, B–5

Like monsters carved from stone, an array of bizarre contorted rocks forms a fantastic natural sculpture garden in the coastal desert of Chile.

North of Caldera, in the coastal desert of northern Chile, the Pan American Highway passes through a rocky landscape like none other on the Pacific coast of South America. Reared up like giant monsters are great masses of stone, with their insides hollowed out like enormous gaping mouths and their outsides pocked with strange spherical holes and honeycomb cavities. Some of the rocks are huge, with their tall entrances beneath overhanging roofs leading into cavelike shelters as much as 10 feet (3 meters) deep.

The curious cavities in the rocks, known to geologists as tafoni, are the result of a process called honeycomb weathering. The depressions, which may take the form of shallow pits, spherical holes, and even caves, characteristically occur in dry climates and are typically found in crystalline rocks such as these granitelike quartz diorites.

In the cool night air, moisture condenses on the surfaces of the rock, chemically altering and decomposing the rock just beneath the surface so that tiny individual flakes fall off or are transported away by the wind. The hollowing out of cavities in this manner takes place primarily on the shaded side of the rocks, where the dampness prevalent at night persists into the day. On the hot, sunny side of the rocks, in contrast, the materials that dissolve at night are redeposited on the surface during the day to form a hard crust that rings like an anvil when struck with a hammer.

The term tafoni is taken from a Corsican word meaning hole or hollow. The tafoni found in Corsica, however, are generally not as impressive as those produced in Chile, where the coastal fogs generated by the cold Humboldt Current and the intense subtropical sunshine combine to create nearly ideal conditions for the evolution of these fantastic forms. The only comparable development of tafoni, in fact, is found in the Namib desert in South-West Africa (Namibia) and in certain parts of southern Australia. □

CACAHUAMILPA CAVERNS. *Giant chambers in Mexico's most famous caves were hollowed out by water, then ornamented with huge stalagmites and other dripstone formations.*

ROCKS OF CALDERA. *Moistened by fog at night and heated by sun during the day, the strangely pockmarked rocks have been modeled by "honeycomb weathering."*

Cango Caves

- South Africa
- Map: page 26, B–6

A sightseer's delight today, these caves were once dwelling places of ancient man. Nature has decorated them to an extraordinary degree.

A herdsman hunting for lost cattle is said to have discovered this remarkable series of caverns in 1780. In fact, he had only rediscovered them: wall paintings and other artifacts reveal that primitive people—possibly of the Late Stone Age—long ago found shelter in their dim recesses.

Today tourists can follow in their footsteps; for the caverns, though by no means the largest in the world, are notable for the exceptional variety and beauty of their cave formations. Visitors can wander from chamber to illuminated chamber—among them, the Crystal Palace, the Devil's Workshop, and the Crypt—each one filled with new surprises.

There are stalactites and stalagmites, many of them covered with rippled draperies of rock, that were built up by the slow dripping of mineral-enriched water. Cleopatra's Needle, a stalagmite 33 feet (10 meters) tall, is estimated to have been 150,000 years in the making. Curtainlike formations hang down where water has seeped in along fractures in the limestone overhead. Bubblelike formations, fluted columns, clusters of needlelike crystals, and even a curtain that reverberates like a drum all vie for attention.

The caves have never been completely explored, and their full extent is still unknown. As recently as 1972, a whole new sequence of chambers was discovered, and another even larger series was found in 1975. And no one knows what new marvels future exploration may reveal. □

CANGO CAVES. *The easily accessible, artfully illuminated caverns are notable for their great variety of elaborate formations.*

CARLISTA CAVERN. *Though not as large as the immense main chamber, even this secondary gallery dwarfs the human visitor.*

Carlista Cavern

- Spain
- Map: page 17, C–4

A colossus among caves, the Carlista Cavern boasts the largest underground chamber found anywhere in the world.

Near the northern coast of Spain, in the Cantabrian Mountains about 22 miles (35 kilometers) west of Bilbao, there is a slotlike opening in the ground. A mere 3 feet (1 meter) wide and 10 feet (3 meters) long, it is not a particularly impressive sight. Only the whistling of stones thrown into the abyss hints at its depth and the wonder that lies underfoot.

According to a local legend, the Carlista Cavern—Torca del Carlista—owes its name to political rivalry and bloody warfare: a Carlista, a supporter of Don Carlos (the 19th-century pretender to the Spanish throne), decided to throw himself into the yawning chasm rather than surrender to a pursuing band of Royalists. In reality the cavern was probably named for nearby Carlista Peak, which is thought to take its name from the same political movement.

Exploration of the cavern did not begin until 1958, when a group of local speleologists first descended into the void. Like everyone who has followed, they were astonished by what they found. For the first 148 feet (45 meters) below the surface, the entrance to the cave is a narrow, vertical, chimneylike opening in the limestone massif. Then the shaft widens to 66 feet (20 meters) in diameter before opening out into a chamber whose dimensions are difficult to perceive. Even the beams of the strongest headlamps fade away in the enveloping darkness without revealing any trace of a distant wall.

Down through space the explorer continues, until finally gaining a foothold on an enormous accumulation of fallen limestone blocks. At the bottom of the abyss, galleries and chambers, some decorated with impressive stalactites, wind off in various directions. But none of them can compare with the immensity and grandeur of the vast main chamber. More or less oval in form, it is approximately 1,700 feet (520 meters) long and 800 feet (245 meters) wide. Its total surface area of more than 20 acres (8 hectares) is equivalent to about 18 football fields. And at its greatest height the vaulted

ceiling arches some 400 feet (120 meters) above the floor. In surface and volume the main chamber of Carlista Cavern is in fact the largest natural underground opening in the entire world. It surpasses even the Big Room of Carlsbad Caverns in New Mexico and the biggest chamber of the Pierre-Saint-Martin Cavern in southwestern France.

Geologically, it seems likely that this colossal void, littered with a chaos of fallen rocks, is the product of collapse. Following a long period of intensive dissolution of the enveloping limestone formation, the ceiling simply caved in, producing the magnificent chamber that remains today.

A number of similar caves that apparently developed in the same way are found in this part of the Cantabrian Mountains. Like Carlista Cavern, all have vertical, chimneylike entrances, but none has an underground chamber of such overwhelming size. Yet considering the fact that Carlista's enormous cavern remained unknown until as recently as 1958, it seems entirely possible that future exploration in the area may reveal even more astounding secrets still hidden beneath the surface of the earth. □

Carlsbad Caverns

- United States (New Mexico)
- Map: page 10, D–5

The King's Palace, the Queen's Chamber, and other caves enchant human visitors to Carlsbad. For the local bats, however, it is merely a good place to sleep.

A vast network of subterranean passageways and chambers cuts deep into the Guadalupe Mountains in southern New Mexico. More than 60 caves are included in Carlsbad Caverns National Park; the largest has a room the size of 14 football fields, and the deepest explored to date penetrates 1,013 feet (309 meters) beneath the surface of the earth.

The caverns occur in a limestone formation deposited about 250 million years ago in an inland arm of the sea. Its core is a massive fossil reef built by lime-secreting algae and other marine life. After the reef stopped growing, it became buried under a number of layers of sediment. A pattern of cracks then developed in the rock, setting the stage for the development of caves.

Rainwater seeped into the cracks, worked its way downward, and circulated through the limestone. Slowly it dissolved the rock, carving out immense underground galleries. Then, as mountain-building forces uplifted the limestone, air replaced water in the hollowed-out chambers. Mineral-laden water dripped down into the caves and evaporated, depositing the minerals as stalactites, stalagmites, and other dripstone formations. Today only a few formations are still growing at Carlsbad, and these are increasing so slowly that no visible changes occur during a human lifetime.

Three miles (4.8 kilometers) of trails take visitors past a splendid assortment of natural sculptures in this subterranean world. The Queen's Chamber is decorated with shiny "curtains" made of stalactites that grew together along cracks in the ceiling; draperies in the Papoose Room and teeth in the Whale's Mouth have a similar origin. The Green Lake Room contains the Veiled Statue (a dripstone column) and the Frozen Waterfall (a spectacular stalactitic cascade). Many other impressive formations, including the Chinese Temple, Rock of Ages, and Totem Pole, are visible along the trail, which ends with an elevator ride back to the surface.

The landscape above the caverns is as remarkable as the caverns themselves. Deep canyons, bearing intriguing names like Slaughter, Lefthook, and Midnight, slice through the harsh and rugged backcountry. Steep, rock-strewn Guadalupe Ridge reaches an elevation of 6,350 feet (1,935 meters). Wildlife abounds, although the nocturnal habits and subdued coloration of many species keep them hidden from most visitors.

Carlsbad's famous bat population is the exception. For thousands of years bats that winter in Mexico have used one of the caverns (Bat Cave) as a sleeping area in summer. From late spring until autumn's first major frost, these small mammals spiral out of the cavern at sunset to feed on insects along the Black and Pecos rivers. Under peak conditions some 5,000 bats fly out each minute, awing expectant visitors with their numbers and the whirring sounds of flight. □

CARLSBAD CAVERNS. *This giant column formed when an upward-growing stalagmite merged with a downward-growing stalactite.*

Casiquiare Channel

- Venezuela
- Map: page 14, C–2

A maverick link between two river systems, the Casiquiare diverts water from the Orinoco River into the basin of the Amazon.

From its source on the border between Venezuela and Brazil, the Orinoco River flows in a great arc as it heads northward toward the Atlantic Ocean. Crossing jungles and grasslands, it is fed by tributaries all along the way, just as most rivers are. Yet not far from its headwaters there is one side stream where water flows out of—not into—the Orinoco.

By the time it reaches the tiny settlement of Esmeralda, the Orinoco is already a substantial river; its flow is 88,300 cubic feet (2,500 cubic meters) a second. Passing between highlands to the north and a wide plain to the south, it flows steadily toward the sea. Then about 12 miles (20 kilometers) west of Esmeralda, a broad gap appears in the Orinoco's south bank—the beginning of the Brazo Casiquiare, or Casiquiare Channel.

In flood stage, some 20 percent of the Orinoco's flow escapes through the opening, which is about 720 feet (220 meters) wide, and even at low water 12 percent is diverted down the Casiquiare Channel. Swollen by about 100 tributaries along its length of 250 miles (400 kilometers), the channel finally merges with the Río Negro, which flows in turn into the Amazon. Thus the Casiquiare forms a link carrying water from one river system to another—a great rarity among the rivers of the world.

Although the link formed relatively recently, it is the result of a long period of erosion. In the area where the two rivers are joined, they flow across the vast Guiana Shield—metamorphic rock that formed about 3 billion years ago. This was subsequently covered by sedimentary deposits of the Roraima Formation. Then, approximately 1 billion years ago, the whole mass was uplifted above sea level, where it has remained ever since.

Erosion over the next billion years stripped away all of the Roraima Formation and honed the surface down to a nearly flat plain. Eventually, only a very low divide separated the watersheds of the Orinoco and the Casiquiare, which at that time was simply a tributary of the Río Negro.

The final breakthrough came about 17,000 years ago, during the last ice age. With fluctuations in sea level and climatic change, a tributary of the Casiquiare extended its headwaters farther and farther to the north. Finally, during a period of intense flooding, the Orinoco spilled over the low divide between the two river systems. Part of its water has been flowing through the breach ever since. □

Caspian Sea

- Iran—U.S.S.R.
- Map: page 18, G–4

The Caspian, the largest inland sea in the world, is a vast landlocked basin where rivers flow in but not out. Water escapes only by evaporation.

Ancient and immense, the Caspian Sea is not part of any ocean. Completely landlocked, with its surface 92 feet (28 meters) below sea level, it is actually the largest inland sea in the world. Stretching north to south for about 750 miles (1,200 kilometers), it averages 200 miles (320 kilometers) across. Its surface area of 143,000 square miles (370,000 square kilometers) is 1½ times the size of all five Great Lakes combined.

The sea, cupped in a huge depression that probably dates back at least 250 million years, is encircled by a band of lowlands that are also below sea level. To the west it is hemmed in by the picturesque peaks of the Caucasus, while the southern shores are fringed by the towering, deeply forested slopes of Iran's Elburz Mountains. Stretching off toward the east,

Cupped in a depression, the Caspian has two deep basins (dark blue). Arrows indicate currents; hatch marks show winter ice cover in the sea's shallow northern part.

beyond the Balkhan Ranges, is the desolate expanse of the Kara-Kum desert and, farther north, the arid Ust-Urt plateau. Beyond the broad band of lowlands to the north of the Caspian are the rolling Volga uplands, the source of most of the water that flows into this great inland sea.

Far from being a single uniform expanse of water, the Caspian Sea is a place of tremendous variety from north to south and from top to bottom. The northern part of the basin is a flat sedimentary plain with an average water depth of less than 20 feet (6 meters). Near the broad Volga delta, which has an intricate pattern of channels very similar to the Mississippi delta, the water measures only about seven feet (two meters) in depth far beyond sight of land.

Farther south the bottom of the Caspian drops off abruptly into two deep basins, which are separated by an underwater ridge that links the Apsheron Peninsula and the Balkhan Ranges. The maximum depth of the southern basin is greater than 3,200 feet (975 meters), while the northern basin reaches depths of about 2,600 feet (790 meters).

One of the Caspian's most extraordinary features is found along the eastern shore. Almost completely cut off from the main body of water by long, low sandspits is a gulf called the Kara-Bogaz-Gol. With a surface area of about 7,000 square miles (18,000 square kilometers), this one small arm of the Caspian is almost as big as Lake

CASPIAN SEA. *Wild horses watch as waves, stirred up by the wind, lap endlessly at the sea's rock-strewn shoreline in Iran.*

Ontario. Since the water level in the gulf is lower than that of the rest of the sea, a steady flow of water rushes in through a narrow channel that separates the two. But in this particularly arid region the water evaporates rapidly from the shallow gulf, which generally is no more than about 33 feet (10 meters) deep.

Just as the Caspian's basin varies in depth from north to south, so does the nature of the water that fills it. Though the water temperature in the shallow northern part of the sea is more or less uniform from top to bottom, it varies from about 75° F (24° C) in summer to 30° F (–1° C) in winter. From mid-December to the end of April the sea freezes over from shore to shore.

In the south, in comparison, the surface temperature ranges from 81° F (27° C) in summer to a low of 48° F (9° C) in winter, and freeze-ups are rare. Below depths of 1,300 feet (400 meters) the temperature remains constant at 41° F (5° C). At these depths the waters support little life. The virtual absence of dissolved oxygen and high concentrations of hydrogen sulfide create a poisonous environment

in which bottom-dwelling plants and animals are unable to survive.

Even more striking are the variations in salinity throughout the sea. Off the mouth of the Volga, the source of 80 percent of the water flowing into the Caspian, the water is virtually salt-free. Elsewhere in the basin the water contains 1.3 percent salt, about one-third as much as seawater. But in the shallow Kara-Bogaz-Gol, the salt content is 35 percent—10 times as much as seawater. The bottom of the gulf is covered by a layer of salts seven feet (two meters) thick, and the waves throw tons of salts up on its banks.

The Caspian has also changed over the course of its history. Until about 12 million years ago, for example, it was linked to the Mediterranean (by way of a connection with the Black Sea). Similarly, about 2 million years ago the Caspian and the Mediterranean were briefly linked once again.

Climatic changes during the ice ages resulted in fluctuations in the Caspian Sea's depth and surface area. When the inflow of glacial meltwater exceeded the rate of evaporation from its surface, the water level rose. When

the inflow was less than the amount lost through evaporation, the water level dropped and the surface area shrank. Traces of former shorelines can be seen in many places: remnants of a line of ancient ports and villages, for example, have been discovered up to 30 miles (50 kilometers) north of the present shore.

Currently, the water level is slowly dropping, not because of any drastic climate changes but because of the works of man. Construction of dams and diversion of water from feeder streams—especially from the Volga—have greatly reduced the inflow. Heroic schemes have been proposed to remedy this situation. One plan involves diverting water from the north-flowing rivers of Siberia into the Volga and thence into the Caspian. An even more ambitious project would close off the shallow northern end of the sea with huge dikes and embankments in order to raise the water level and maintain navigation. Whatever the outcome of these projects, one thing remains certain: the Caspian Sea will retain its preeminence as the largest inland body of water in the world. □

CATHEDRAL GROVE. *High rainfall and a relatively mild climate account for the extraordinarily lush forests that flourish on the western slopes of Canada's Vancouver Island.*

Cathedral Grove

- Canada (British Columbia)
- Map: page 10, C–4

Rising majestically toward the sky, the tall trees resemble gigantic pillars in an immense outdoor cathedral.

Vancouver Island, at the western end of the U.S.-Canadian border, is the largest island off the Pacific Coast of North America. Its terrain is dramatic—a rugged, rocky coast, sparkling blue fjords cutting far inland, snowcapped mountains, and wilderness lakes and rivers. But perhaps the most impressive features are the island's dense forests, for its mild winters and very abundant rainfall promote extraordinary growth.

About 30 miles (50 kilometers) inland from the western coast stands the most impressive forest of all: Cathedral Grove in Macmillan Provincial Park. The trees here, which grow straight and tall until they reach a height of about 200 feet (60 meters), tower like immense columns in the giant cathedral of the forest. The interior of the woodland has an eerie cast. A greenish-blue hue, the result of the filtering of sunlight by the evergreen needles, surrounds the trees. Occasionally the sun pierces an area where a limb has fallen, but much of the time a dense fog shrouds the atmosphere. This humid environment causes ferns, mosses, and lichens to grow profusely, clinging to the tree trunks and carpeting the ground. Otherwise, because of the darkness created by the dense canopy, there are very few low-growing plants.

Although Cathedral Grove has a variety of trees, including western red cedars, western hemlocks, grand firs, and broad-leaved maples, it is best known for its Douglas firs. Some of them are up to 800 years old, survivors of a devastating fire that occurred about 300 years ago.

Except for redwoods, Douglas firs are the tallest trees in North America. The highest tree in Cathedral Grove measures 275 feet (83 meters), which is the approximate height of a 23-story building; the broadest trunk is more than 30 feet (9 meters) in circumference, requiring six adults with arms outstretched to encircle it. Still larger Douglas firs can be found across the border in Washington's Olympic National Park, which has a climate similar to Cathedral Grove's. □

CAUCASUS MOUNTAINS. *Stretching from the Black Sea to the Caspian, these rugged ranges rise as a nearly impenetrable barrier.*

Caucasus Mountains

- U.S.S.R.
- Map: page 18, F–4

The Caucasus figures prominently in Greek myth. Zeus chained Prometheus to a mountain here, and Jason pursued the legendary Golden Fleece nearby.

Geographers consider the Caucasus Mountains, which occupy the region between the Black Sea and the Caspian, as part of the natural boundary between Europe and Asia. Although the mountain system is relatively narrow (its width varies from 60 to 90 miles, or 100 to 150 kilometers), the mountains are surprisingly difficult to cross. For the most part they have no passes lower than 7,550 feet (2,300 meters), and the one road that crosses the mountains—the Georgian Military Highway, which winds through the Daryal Gorge and Krestovy Pass—is sometimes closed by avalanches.

There are sharp distinctions between different sides of the mountain system. Although most of the peaks are on the north (the highest, Mount Elbrus, reaches 18,481 feet, or 5,633 meters), this side rises more gradually than the lower, very steep southern face. In addition, the northern side is composed mainly of limestone, while the southern side is made of shale and sandstone. The eastern end is different again, with irregular valleys and folds that dip away in all directions.

The climate also varies from one region to another. The western slopes, toward the Black Sea, get 10 times as much rain as the slopes by the Caspian. And the slopes facing south, toward Turkey and Iran, receive considerably more precipitation than the northern slopes.

Precipitation contrasts help explain the distribution of snow and ice in the Caucasus. The snow line, or the elevation above which there is permanent snow, goes from about 9,800 feet (3,000 meters) in the west to as high as 13,100 feet (4,000 meters) in the drier eastern section. Although the Caucasus has some 2,000 glaciers, only 7 percent of the glaciated surface lies in the eastern part, where the glaciers are limited to high valleys.

A relatively young mountain system, the Caucasus was uplifted about 25 million years ago as part of the great Alpine upheaval. Although glaciation in the Alps occurred about 1 million years ago, none of the Caucasus peaks appear to have been glaciated until 100,000 years ago. This would seem to indicate that until that time the mountains were still rising and were too low to sustain extensive ice caps. Frequent earthquakes testify to the fact that even today the earth's crust is unstable in this area. □

Cauvery Falls

- India
- Map: page 20, B–3

Spilling over the edge of a plateau, the river has carved its valley upstream to these splendid twin waterfalls.

The Cauvery River is a placid stream as it wanders across a high plateau in southern India. Flowing southeastward in a broad, shallow valley, it meanders lazily among gently rolling hills worn down by eons of erosion.

Then, suddenly, at Sivasamudram island, the river plunges downward in a series of waterfalls that send up dense clouds of spray. Dividing into two arms that circle the island, the river forms twin cascades that drop a total of 320 feet (98 meters) before the branches reunite downstream.

The Cauvery River does not resume its peaceful course immediately. For the next 50 miles (80 kilometers) it is interrupted by several rapids as it flows through a deep valley that occasionally contracts into very narrow gorges. Then it sweeps out across an open plain as it continues on its journey to the Bay of Bengal.

Cauvery Falls (also known as Sivasamudram Falls) and the rapids downstream from the cataracts occur where the river passes from a higher to a lower plateau. An abrupt, fairly recent uplift of the earth's crust increased the difference in elevation between the two plateaus, resulting in vigorous erosion. Thanks to the presence of a structural trough in the surface, the valley floor has been progressively deepened all the way up the stream to the falls. Because of the downcutting of the valley floor, some of the tributaries that formerly flowed smoothly into the mainstream now occupy hanging valleys; perched at a higher level, they are forced to plunge over waterfalls in order to reach the Cauvery River. ☐

Chad, Lake

- Central Africa
- Map: page 24, E–4

In the southern reaches of the Sahara, the desert is winning the battle between land and water.

Lake Chad is an unusual body of water. Located at the junction of the nations of Chad, Cameroon, Nigeria, and Niger, it is one of a mere handful of lakes bordering the Sahara. And although most desert lakes have a high salt content, Chad is a freshwater lake. But the most dramatic feature of Lake Chad is its history—specifically, its drastic shrinkage over time.

Scientists believe that 2 million years ago the Paleochadian ("Ancient Chad") Sea encompassed more than 100,000 square miles (260,000 square kilometers) of central Africa. Lake Chad, the remnant of this enormous stretch of water, today covers only

LAKE CHAD. *Low sand dunes become floating islands when the water level of this enormous lake rises after the seasonal rains.*

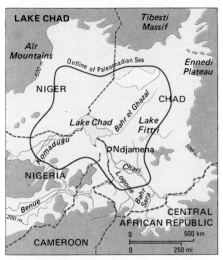

Lake Chad has shrunk dramatically in size over the last 2 million years. The red outline on the map indicates its former boundaries, the patch of blue its present-day size.

6,000 square miles (16,000 square kilometers)—a reduction in size of more than 90 percent.

Why has the lake shrunk so dramatically? Changes in climate, especially rainfall, are certain to have played a role. And some geologists believe that movements of the earth's crust may have reduced the amount of water flowing into Lake Chad. According to this theory, as land in the region was uplifted, the course of certain streams shifted; instead of eventually reaching the lake, their waters were diverted into the drainage basin of the Congo River.

Lake Chad continues to dry up. Several rivers still flow into the southern section, but the water they bring in, plus the minimal rainfall, does not equal the amount lost through evaporation and drainage. At the same time the lake basin itself is slowly filling up with debris.

Though a mere relic of its former size, Lake Chad is still an enormous body of water: it is the fourth largest lake in Africa and the 17th largest in the world. From year to year and from season to season, its depth and boundaries fluctuate. The northern section, which is almost completely cut off from the southern part by a ridge known as the Great Barrier, is especially vulnerable to any short-term changes. This section dried up completely during the droughts of the 1970's. Yet when heavy rains periodically flood the region, the lake expands far to the north, engulfing sand dunes and transforming them into islets in a vast desert sea. □

Chara Caves

● Morocco
● Map: page 24, C–2

Beneath a Moroccan mountain lies the most extensive cave system in the northern part of Africa.

An abundance of limestone and plentiful rainfall combine to produce a great number of spectacular caves in northeastern Morocco, some of them still unexplored. Near the town of Taza, on the fringes of the Atlas Mountains, there are at least three outstanding systems of caverns, including the Chara Caves—the largest series of underground galleries in all of northern Africa and among the most extensive on the entire continent.

Like other limestone caves, those of Chara have been fashioned by the dissolving action of water. An underground river flows through parts of this subterranean maze, while other former river channels are now dry galleries festooned with thick growths of stalactites and stalagmites.

The main underground river in the Chara Caves, which flows along the lines of a fracture in the limestone, has eroded a deep passageway. Here and there the passage is partially blocked by rocks that have caved in along the walls. But in three places the passageway's ceiling has collapsed entirely. Along these sectors the whole riverbed is clogged by fallen debris, while above it the passageway opens up into spacious chambers with ceilings as much as 130 feet (40 meters) high.

In the upper levels of the limestone formation, collapses are even more numerous. In many places openings communicate directly with the surface in the form of sinkholes and dolinas (collapsed valleys). Though these and other entrances provide easy access to the limestone labyrinth, the full extent of the Chara Caves has yet to be completely explored and mapped. □

CHARA CAVES. *A rushing torrent suddenly disappears into an opening in a wooded limestone massif, one of several entrances to the longest series of caves in Morocco.*

SERRA DA CHELA. *Rising abruptly to dizzying heights, steep escarpments overlook hot, semidesert coastal lowlands.*

Chela, Serra da

● Angola
● Map: page 26, A–4

**Rugged cliffs towering above
an African coastal plain mark the
broken edge of two continents.**

The Serra da Chela, running more or less parallel to the coast of Angola in southwestern Africa for about 100 miles (160 kilometers), rises above the Atlantic in a single giant step. Scalloped by promontories and indented by valleys, its rugged slopes tower more than 7,000 feet (2,100 kilometers) above the narrow coastal plain, then slope downward to inland plateaus.

The "mountains" are, in effect, a severely eroded escarpment at the edge of the ancient African continental shield, composed of rocks up to several billion years old. At one time all the continents were united in a single landmass, Pangaea. Beginning about 200 million years ago, Pangaea broke up along major rift zones, and the continents as we know them today began to drift apart. The Serra da Chela is the margin of the crustal plate where Africa was once connected to South America. As the two continents drifted apart and the Atlantic Ocean formed, the ancient crustal rocks of Africa rose slowly upward to their present elevation. Subsequent erosion of the escarpment along the continental margin resulted in the contours of the mountain range that remain up to this day. □

Chiker Caves

● Morocco
● Map: page 24, C–2

**Hollowed out by running water, the
underground river channels that form
the caves are flooded after heavy rains.**

South of the ancient city of Taza in northeastern Morocco is a limestone massif riddled by extensive cave systems. Sinkholes pock the surface, and disappearing streams reemerge elsewhere from holes in the ground.

Among the best known of the many caverns in the area are the Chiker Caves, where an underground lake is found at the bottom of a gaping sinkhole about 33 feet (10 meters) in diameter. There are also galleries, some of them beautifully decorated with cave formations, totaling more than three miles (five kilometers) in length.

Following heavy rains, floods come rushing through many of the underground passageways. Although it is believed that the Chiker Caves may be connected with some of the other nearby cave systems, no direct links between any of them have yet been established.

Just as interesting as the caves' hidden grottoes are the springs where their waters reemerge on the surface in a series of foaming cascades. The water tumbles down stepped waterfalls, over barriers built up by the deposition of calcium carbonate that once was dissolved in the water. □

CHIKER CAVES. *Just as water flows into the caves, it later reemerges from gushing springs and tumbles down the mountainside across a series of travertine barriers.*

CHIMNEY ROCK. *Rising like a lighthouse above the rolling plain, it is an eroded remnant of rocks that once blanketed the entire area.*

Chimney Rock

- United States (Nebraska)
- Map: page 10, D–4

Visible from afar, Chimney Rock was a major landmark for pioneers traveling west on the Oregon Trail.

Pioneers traveling across the Great Plains on the Oregon Trail reckoned their progress in terms of the famous landmarks they passed along the route—Scotts Bluff, Courthouse Rock, Jail Rock, and many others. But few of the natural landforms had as great an impact as Chimney Rock, towering like a beacon above the North Platte River Valley in western Nebraska.

Visible from a distance of 30 miles (50 kilometers) or more, the rock is indeed an impressive sight. A steep-sided conical mound topped by a vertical sandstone column, the formation rises about 325 feet (100 meters) above its surroundings. (The spire alone is about 120 feet, or 35 meters, high.)

The pioneers almost always described it in glowing terms. Nearly all agreed that it did indeed look like a chimney, though a few likened it to Cleopatra's Needle or a church spire. The more prosaic dismissed it as a "haystack with a pole stuck in the top."

To geologists, however, Chimney Rock is an erosional remnant, one of the few remaining outcrops of rock formations that once covered a far more extensive area. The conical base of the rock is composed of hard pink sandy clay that was deposited by the wind over a long period of drought more than 25 million years ago.

Then, following a period of erosion, the climate became more humid. Over the course of several million years, streams flowing across the region deposited a thick layer of sandstone on top of the clay formation.

The sculpting of the rock itself has taken place during the last 2 million years. Streams carved their way down through the sandstone, gradually widening their valleys. As they undercut the sandstone cliffs, great chunks of rock collapsed and were carried away. Eventually almost all the sandstone and clay were eroded from the region. Only here and there did a small, more resistant remnant of the original blanket of rocks remain.

Even today, the sculpting of Chimney Rock is not completed. Between 1897 and 1965 the lofty sandstone spire lost more than 16 feet (5 meters) of height—the result of natural erosion and thoughtless vandalism. Yet even if in time it crumbles to a featureless heap of debris, the rock will be remembered as a symbol of America's movement to the west. □

Ciudad Encantada

- Spain
- Map: page 17, C-4

Bizarre rock formations in the mountains near Madrid resemble the ruins of an enchanted city.

Bridges, theaters, prisons, and convents are not unusual structures. What makes them unique in Ciudad Encantada ("Enchanted City") is that these fancifully named "buildings" were not constructed by man but were carved from rocks by the forces of nature.

The ruined "city of rocks" stands on a plateau of about 500 acres (200 hectares) not far from Madrid. This area is a superb example of karst relief. Water saturated with carbon dioxide gas and organic acids has infiltrated and dissolved portions of the plateau, which is composed of limestone embedded with dolomite.

Though they are similar in composition, limestone erodes faster than magnesium-rich dolomite. As a result, the plateau is wearing away unevenly. Irregular shapes made up of more resistant rock project above their surroundings, seeming to form the skyline of a city. ☐

COBÁN KARST REGION. *Though partially masked by jungle vegetation, the distinctive topography of the eroded limestone landscape stands out plainly beneath the tropical sky.*

CIUDAD ENCANTADA. *Capped by a slab of resistant rock, an eroded limestone remnant forms a giant pillar in Spain's "enchanted city" of strangely sculpted rock forms.*

Cobán Karst Region

- Guatemala
- Map: page 13, C-3

A limestone landscape in Central America is dramatic on the surface and full of surprises underground.

The city of Cobán, in the Guatemalan province of Alta Verapaz, is built on the edge of an extensive expanse of the eroded limestone terrain known as karst. Over a long period of time heavy tropical rains, made acidic by decomposing jungle vegetation, have seeped into crevices and gradually dissolved the limestone to create the landforms typical of karst.

Now the surface is studded with steep-sided knolls (known as *mogotes*) separated by little enclosed valleys where the limestone has been dissolved. The land is pockmarked by sinkholes (known as *ojos*, or "eyes"), which lead to underground river networks. Here and there streams and rivers disappear into sinkholes, only to reemerge elsewhere after flowing long distances through subterranean channels. In addition to active underground streams, there are many "fossil" river networks—cave systems that are dry today but were hollowed out by running water when the water table was at a higher level in the past.

Many of these fossil river channels can be seen from the surface by looking into the *ojos*. Often decorated by formations, these channels can be easily explored. In some places it is possible to enter a cave on one side of a *mogote* and emerge on the opposite slope. Or the explorer can make his way from one *ojo* to the next along a dry underground streambed.

Among the most spectacular features of the Cobán karst, however, is the magnificent underground course of the Río Candelaria. Surmounted by at least two fossil stream networks, the active river channel today extends through a series of limestone hills for more than 6 miles (10 kilometers). The channel, an opening 100 feet (30 meters) across and 165 feet (50 meters) high, broadens occasionally to enormous chambers. In many places the ceiling bristles with hanging forests of stalactites. Elsewhere it is pierced by small windows where rays of light, filtering through the surface vegetation, are reflected in the waters of the underground river. □

Cobre, Barranca del

- Mexico
- Map: page 12, B–2

Almost as deep as the Grand Canyon, Mexico's rugged, steep-walled "Copper Canyon" is a breathtaking sight.

Dizzying views of incredibly deep canyons reward the intrepid traveler who ventures along parts of the western slope of the Sierra Madre Occidental, the great mountain chain that parallels the Pacific coast of Mexico. Near the southwestern corner of the state of Chihuahua, tributaries of the Río del Fuerte ("Strong River") have carved their way down into pine- and cedar-covered plateaus, creating a deeply dissected, genuine "badlands" topography on a giant scale.

Most impressive of all these great gorges is the Barranca del Cobre—the Copper Canyon, named for ancient copper mines in the region. The cre-

BARRANCA DEL COBRE. *As the Sierra Madre was slowly uplifted, the Río Urique continued to gnaw its way downward into the rocks and gouge out the gigantic abyss of the canyon.*

ation of the Río Urique, the canyon is an enormous trench some 30 miles (50 kilometers) long with almost vertical sides that extend 4,600 feet (1,400 meters) from rim to base. (With a depth of about 1 mile, or 1,600 meters, the Grand Canyon of the Colorado is only slightly deeper.) In this arid region plant life is rather sparse on the canyon's upper slopes. The depths of the chasm, in contrast, are masked beneath lush tropical vegetation—the result of moisture from the river and the warmer climate that prevails at the much lower elevations.

The remarkable development of canyons in this area results primarily

from two factors: climate and geological history. The region's long dry season alternates with a short rainy season. And when it rains, torrential downpours transform the rivers into very powerful erosive forces capable of carrying off tremendous loads of soil and debris.

The river courses, moreover, were established long before the Sierra Madre was uplifted to its present elevation. Thus as the mountains slowly rose higher and higher, downcutting by the rivers kept pace with the uplift, resulting in ravines and canyons of exceptional dimensions such as the Barranca del Cobre. □

COLCHIS. *Abrupt escarpments, lush vegetation, and limpid waters all contribute to the charm of this fabled haven beside the Black Sea.*

Colchis

- U.S.S.R.
- Map: page 18, E–4

The mythical home of magical Medea, Colchis today is a popular resort area noted for its climate and scenery.

At the eastern end of the Black Sea, hemmed in by towering peaks of the Caucasus, is Colchis, long the inspiration of myths and legends. According to Greek mythology, the princess Medea, renowned for her magical powers, was born in this land of incredible wealth and enchantment. And Jason, who later would be her husband, came to Colchis in search of the Golden Fleece, which was said to be hidden there in a sacred grove.

Mountain slopes on the southwest flank of the Caucasus, plunging almost directly into the sea, account for part of the special beauty of Colchis. Composed of complexly folded sedimentary rocks overlain by volcanic formations, they are covered with dense forests overgrown with vines.

In vivid contrast are the fertile coastal lowlands, such as the broad, flat sedimentary plain along the Rion River. Like the lower mountain slopes, the plains are garden spots planted with plums, citrus trees, tea, vineyards, and olives.

This lush vegetation is a result of the region's warm, humid climate. The Caucasus to the north acts as a barrier, keeping out cold air masses in winter, while moist air moving in off the Black Sea accounts for the high precipitation (up to 120 inches, or 3,050 millimeters, per year). Thus, just as Jason came long ago to Colchis on his mythical quest, visitors continue to flock to its seaside resorts to enjoy the mild climate and idyllic scenery. □

Columbia Icefield

- Canada (Alberta—British Columbia)
- Map: page 10, D–3

The largest icefield in the Rockies spawns glistening glaciers and feeds great rivers that rush to distant seas.

High in the Canadian Rockies, amid mountain peaks that exceed 11,500 feet (3,500 meters) in elevation, there is a massive permanent accumulation of ice and snow. Straddling the border between two of Canada's oldest and most famous national parks, Jasper and Banff, the Columbia Icefield is not large compared with the ice caps that blanket Greenland and some of the Arctic islands. Even so, its dimensions are impressive: up to 3,300 feet (1,000 meters) thick, it covers an area of about 120 square miles (310 square kilometers).

The Columbia Icefield, in a sense, is a leftover from the last ice age, when gigantic ice sheets covered much of northern North America. As the climate warmed at the end of the ice age, the ice sheets gradually retreated to the north. Now isolated remnants persist only in the extreme far north and atop high mountain ranges where, because of altitude, a cold "ice-age" climate still prevails.

The Columbia Icefield is not a static thing, however. Each winter, moist air masses moving in from the Pacific continue to drop more snow on the mountaintops. Under the pressure of its own weight, the huge accumulation of snow and ice slowly but continuously spreads outward in all directions, with lobes of ice creeping down valleys in the form of glaciers.

The largest of several glaciers radiating from the icefield is the Saskatchewan Glacier. (It covers an area of about 23 square miles, or 60 square kilometers.) But by far the most accessible is the Athabasca Glacier, a tongue of ice about 6 miles (10 kilometers) long. The Athabasca's imposing snout is easily approached from a nearby highway, the Icefields Parkway. Touring the glacier on snowmobiles, visitors can begin to comprehend its awesome erosive power—and perhaps imagine the former much larger glaciers that scoured out the deep valleys between the surrounding peaks of the Rocky Mountains.

Perched astride the Continental Divide, the Columbia Icefield has been aptly nicknamed "the mother of rivers." Cascading at first across alpine meadows and then plunging down forested mountain slopes, its meltwater ultimately reaches far-flung destinations. The Saskatchewan Glacier is the source of the North Saskatchewan River, whose waters eventually flow into Hudson Bay and finally into the Atlantic Ocean. The runoff from the Athabasca Glacier feeds the Athabasca River, which empties, by way of the Mackenzie, into the Arctic Ocean. And still other glaciers nourish the headwaters of the mighty Columbia River, whose ultimate outlet is the Pacific Ocean. □

COLUMBIA ICEFIELD. *Through an outlet between the rugged peaks, the massive lobe of a glacier spills downslope from the icefield.*

Communism Peak

- U.S.S.R.
- Map: page 18, I–5

The highest mountain in the U.S.S.R. tops the elevated region known as Bam-i-Dunya—"the roof of the world."

For many years the highest mountain in the U.S.S.R. was thought to be Lenin Peak, near the border of Afghanistan. Then in 1928 a German-Soviet exploration team discovered a higher peak nearby, which has undergone several name changes since its discovery. Originally known as Mount Garmo, it was called Stalin Peak until that leader fell into disrepute. Today it is known as Communism Peak.

Reaching a height of 24,590 feet (7,495 meters), Communism Peak rises in the Pamirs—a remote mountainous area known to local inhabitants as Bam-i-Dunya, or "roof of the world." Formerly a low plain, the Pamirs were uplifted between 30 and 100 million years ago as part of the great alpine system that extends from the western Mediterranean to southeastern Asia. Since that time the mountains have been carved up by both rivers and glaciers. The Pamirs, in fact, boast the second largest glacier in Asia, the Fedchenko. It is a remnant of the extensive ice cap that covered nearly the entire region during the Ice Age, when only the highest mountains—such as Communism Peak—protruded above the frozen landscape. □

Congo River

- Central Africa
- Map: page 26, A–3

Africa's second longest river is a vital transportation route and potential source of electric power.

Sweeping northward in a broad arc across the equator and then south again to its outlet on the Atlantic, the Congo, also known as the Zaire, is among the great rivers of the world. The major waterway of central Africa, it drains virtually all of Zaire, most of the People's Republic of the Congo, and portions of several neighboring countries. Its total drainage basin of about 1.5 million square miles (3.9 million square kilometers) is in fact the second largest in the world. (Only the Amazon drains a larger area.) And

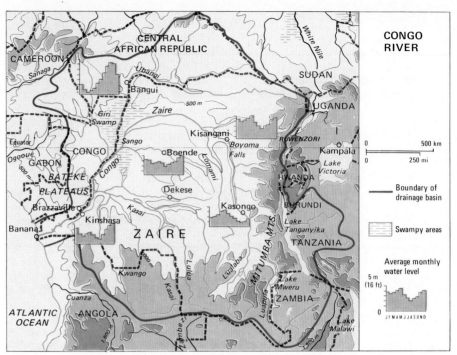

The flow of water in the mainstream of the Congo remains fairly constant throughout the year because the flood stages of its various tributaries occur in different months.

with a length of some 2,900 miles (4,700 kilometers), it is the second longest river in Africa, exceeded only by the Nile.

On its long journey to the sea, the Congo is a river of many moods. From its source in Zambia in the highlands between Lake Tanganyika and Lake Malawi, it drops from an altitude of 5,760 feet (1,755 meters) to sea level. In some places it broadens into lakes and spills over its banks to form great marshes; elsewhere its flow is constricted by narrow gorges. Portions of the river flow lazily between shorelines that are green with dense jungle vegetation; other sectors roar over impressive waterfalls and across long stretches of cataracts.

Despite its many cascades, however, much of the Congo and its major tributaries is navigable. Because the river basin lies astride the equator, rainy seasons to the north and to the south occur at different times of year. With floodwaters from different feeder streams constantly replenishing its volume, the flow in the mainstream remains fairly uniform throughout the year. In all, the Congo and its tributaries make up a navigable river system of more than 8,000 miles (13,000 kilometers).

Geographically, the river is usually considered to include three distinct sectors: the Upper, Middle, and Lower Congo. In its upper reaches, the young

northward-flowing river is called the Lualaba. Formed by the union of highland streams with water flowing westward from Lake Tanganyika, it is an alternating series of placid navigable sectors separated by dangerous zones of rapids and cascades. (At the Portes d'Enfer rapids—"the Gates of Hell"—the river enters a wild gorge and foams down a series of rapids that continue for about 75 miles, or 120 kilometers.)

Just north of the equator the river plunges abruptly down a series of cataracts at Boyoma (formerly Stanley) Falls and enters its middle course. Curving westward and then southwest, the Middle Congo traverses the vast lowlands at the center of its basin. A sluggish river now, it is in places as much as 8 miles (13 kilometers) wide. Enormous tributaries such as the Lomami and Ubangi enter the mainstream, carrying with them heavy loads of silt. Dividing and rejoining in numerous channels, the river is dotted with countless islands. The silt has also built up natural levees all along the banks, but even so the river regularly spills over them and causes flooding.

The Middle Congo lives up to the traditional image of an African river. Dense tropical forests crowd in along the shores; exotic birds abound on the endlessly shifting islands that clog its course; and crocodiles infest its muddy, slow-moving waters.

CONGO RIVER. *The major river of equatorial Africa is constantly replenished by year-round rainfall over its enormous drainage basin.*

Beyond its junction with the Kasai, the Congo narrows abruptly to no more than a mile (1.6 kilometers) wide as it enters a gorge cutting across the Batéké Plateaus. Deep and swift, it flows between steep slopes as much as 1,300 feet (400 meters) high. And then the river slows down again as it enters a long, broad lake, the Malebo Pool (once known as Stanley Pool). On the south shore is Kinshasa, Zaire's capital, while on the opposite shore is the Congo's capital, Brazzaville.

At its outlet from Malebo Pool, the Lower Congo begins its final turbulent passage to the sea. Over the course of some 200 miles (320 kilometers), it plunges downward for about 900 feet (275 meters). Hurtling once again through narrow gorges, the river's immense energy has been harnessed in a tremendous hydroelectric power plant. (Although only a fraction of the Congo's water resources has been developed, some estimate that the river's potential for hydroelectric power generation amounts to one-sixth of the world's known resources.)

Finally the river slows down once again as it enters its long, broad estuary and gradually mingles with the Atlantic. Laden with silt, its shallow outlet to the sea must constantly be dredged to keep the channel open. And then the river disappears beneath the ocean, hiding one of its most impressive features from view: offshore the Congo has carved a submarine canyon nearly a mile (1.6 kilometers) deep and about 100 miles (160 kilometers) long into the edge of the continental shelf. □

MOUNT COOK. *Fed by storms blowing in off the Tasman Sea, a glacier crisscrossed by crevasses and broken up into jagged pinnacles begins its long descent down the mountain.*

Cook, Mount

- New Zealand
- Map: page 23, H–6

Known to native Maoris as Aorangi, the "cloud piercer," Mount Cook is the loftiest peak in New Zealand.

The rugged spine of New Zealand's picturesque South Island is a towering mountain range known as the Southern Alps. Stretching more or less north to south over a distance of about 185 miles (300 kilometers), they include 17 peaks that exceed 10,000 feet (3,000 meters) in height. Capped by glistening snowfields and streaked by long tongues of glaciers, this magnificent maze of jagged crests and saw-toothed ridges is an irresistible lure to mountain climbers, skiers, and anyone who enjoys spectacular alpine scenery.

Looming above all its neighbors near the center of the range is the majestic summit of Mount Cook—at 12,349 feet (3,764 meters), the highest peak in New Zealand. The mountain and its surroundings are protected in a national park that encompasses some of the finest glacial landscapes in the Southern Hemisphere.

The glaciers that adorn this portion

Glaciers Vary From Place to Place

No two glaciers are alike. They vary from place to place depending on climate, elevation, and the contours of the land. Even so, three general types of glaciers are recognized: the Alpine, Himalayan, and Alaskan types.

Glaciers in the Bernese Alps (below center), like those in New Zealand, are Alpine glaciers. Only the highest peaks are capped by ice. Although individual tongues of ice extend down the slopes, they are not long enough to merge and fill major valleys, such as the Rhone valley.

Typical Himalayan glaciers are found in the Karakoram Range

(below right). While the mountains are much farther south than the Bernese Alps, they are also much higher and thus much colder. Here the glaciers in tributary valleys have merged in major valleys, and much of the land is covered with ice.

Alaskan-type glaciers, such as those found in the Chugach Mountains (below left), are somewhat similar to Himalayan glaciers. Although the mountains are not especially high, they are located in the far north. Again, much of the land is covered with ice. But the climate is so cold that glaciers have descended all the way down to the piedmont plains at sea level.

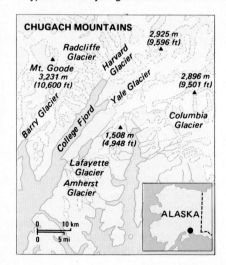

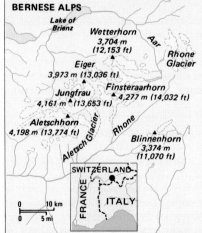

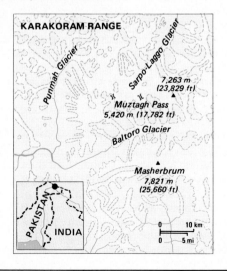

COTOPAXI. *Built up, layer upon layer, of erupted volcanic material, the majestic peak completely dominates its surroundings.*

of the Southern Alps are fed by moist westerly winds that blow in off the Tasman Sea. Diverted upward by the mountain barrier, they drop the heavy snowfall that constantly replenishes the glaciers clinging to the flanks of the mountains.

The glaciers on the western slopes tend to be quite short and steep, ending very abruptly in dense evergreen forests. On the gentler eastern slopes of Mount Cook, in contrast, the glaciers frequently are extremely long and descend to low elevations.

The most impressive of them all, on the eastern slope of Mount Cook, is the Tasman Glacier, a narrow tongue of ice 17 miles (27 kilometers) long and up to 2 miles (3 kilometers) wide. As much as 2,000 feet (600 meters) thick and covering an area of about 20 square miles (50 square kilometers), it is the largest glacier in New Zealand. Its snout, which descends all the way down to the 2,500-foot (760-meter) level, almost reaches the island's central plain.

The glacier is extremely active: it creeps down the mountain at a rate of about 20 to 25 inches (50 to 60 centimeters) per day. But because it reaches such low elevations, there is a great deal of melting and evaporation. The snout of the glacier, in fact, has receded considerably upslope since the turn of the century. Even so, the Tasman Glacier remains the crowning glory of Mount Cook. □

Cotopaxi

- Ecuador
- Map: page 14, B–3

Beautiful but deadly, this Andean volcano devastates not with lava but with torrents of mud and meltwater.

Cotopaxi is a sight to behold. Towering above the neighboring Andean peaks in north-central Ecuador, it is an almost perfectly symmetrical volcanic cone. Its flanks, furrowed with deep ravines, slope gracefully up to a commanding height of 19,348 feet (5,897 meters) above sea level—high enough so that though the mountain is located just a bit south of the equator, it is largely covered by permanent fields of ice and snow. And it is the snow that presents the greatest peril when the volcano intermittently erupts.

Cotopaxi's shapely profile was a long time in the making, for it is actually composed of two volcanic structures, with the newer one superimposed on its ancient ancestor. The older volcano, called Picacho, was formed long before any of the neighboring extinct volcanoes in this area of the Andes. Traces of its caldera still are visible on Cotopaxi's flanks. (A caldera is a giant craterlike cavity formed when a volcano's top collapses or is blown off in an explosion.)

Following the extinction of Picacho, eruptions began again about 70,000

years ago. Little by little, with each new eruption the older mountain was gradually buried by the newer volcanic cone, called Incaloma. The process probably has not yet ended, however, for Cotopaxi has erupted from time to time throughout recorded history—sometimes with disastrous results.

Technically, Cotopaxi is known as a stratovolcano: it is built up of lava flows alternating with layers of ash and other volcanic materials that were exploded from its vent. But the deadliest effects of its eruptions result from the so-called *lozadales*—gigantic avalanches of mud and meltwater—that periodically come flooding down its flanks. Ill-fated offspring of the marriage of fire and ice, they are triggered by the instant melting of ice and snow on Cotopaxi's upper slopes by the intense heat that always accompanies eruptions.

The first recorded eruption of Cotopaxi, in 1533, was chronicled in accounts by the Spanish conquistadores. Of the many that have occurred since then, the worst took place in 1877. The explosions were heard over a radius of more than 200 miles (320 kilometers), clouds of ash and pumice completely darkened the midday sky, and the accompanying *lozadales* killed thousands of people. The steam that still issues from Cotopaxi's vent is a grim reminder that such devastation could occur again. □

Crater Lake

- United States (Oregon)
- Map: page 10, C–4

The history of the deepest lake in the United States began when a great volcano in Oregon blew its top.

Volcano after volcano, the majestic Cascade Range extends for a distance of 700 miles (1,100 kilometers) from northern Washington to northern California. Mount Rainier is here, covered with numerous glaciers; so is Mount St. Helens, one of the few volcanoes in the United States that have erupted in this century. The story of Crater Lake, however, is the story of a peak that no longer exists.

Like the other large volcanoes in the Cascades, a mountain now referred to as Mount Mazama began to develop a million years ago, growing higher and higher as periodic eruptions sent avalanches of molten rock, cinders, and ash down its slopes. By about 7,000 years ago the mountain had reached a height of 12,000 feet (3,600 meters).

Then, in a seeming paradox, the violent forces that had built Mount Mazama brought about its destruction. Huge amounts of frothy lava were ejected from the top of the volcano; molten rock flowed out through cracks along the sides and base. With so much of its inner substance removed and the foundation of the mountain weakened, the top of Mount Mazama eventually collapsed. This, scientists believe, probably happened about 4600 B.C., according to results obtained by analyzing samples of charred wood.

The collapse produced a depression 6 miles (10 kilometers) wide and 4,000 feet (1,200 meters) deep. Such vast depressions are technically known as calderas (the Spanish word for "caldrons"); craters are their smaller, more familiar cousins.

Although the actual collapse of Mount Mazama may have taken only a matter of days, the region was slow to quiet down. Milder eruptions followed, raising several smaller peaks within the caldera. Then finally, about 1,000 to 2,000 years ago, the volcanic activity came to a halt.

As rainwater and melting snows collected in the caldera, the immense basin was transformed into a lake—a lake with neither inlet nor outlet. Today the amount of water draining into the lake roughly equals what is

lost through evaporation and seepage, so that the volume of the water stays about the same. Crater Lake, with a depth of 1,932 feet (589 meters), is the second deepest lake in the Western Hemisphere. Canada's Great Slave Lake, which was dug by glaciers, is deeper by a mere 83 feet (25 meters).

A view of Crater Lake is an image that never leaves the mind. Called Deep Blue Lake by early mining prospectors, it is outstanding because of its color, a sapphire hue that indicates both extreme depth and extreme purity. The water is so pure, in fact, that there was no food for the fish that anglers wanted to stock in the lake decades ago. The problem was solved by adding food (freshwater shrimp), and today trout and other species con-

CRATER LAKE. *Three volcanoes rise from the floor of the enormous lake, but only one, Wizard Island, protrudes above the water.*

tinue to attract many fishermen to Crater Lake.

The lake's surface, protected from the wind by cliffs that rise as high as 2,000 feet (600 meters) above the water, is an enormous mirror. Near the western shore the mirror is broken by the conical contours of Wizard Island. Supposedly named for its remarkable resemblance to a wizard's hat, the is-

land is itself a volcano, one of the small cones that formed after the collapse of Mount Mazama. (Lake soundings have shown that there are two completely submerged volcanic cones.) Visitors to Crater Lake National Park can reach Wizard Island by boat, hike to the summit, and then actually climb down into the crater.

Phantom Ship, a smaller island near

the lake's southern edge, has a different history. Its mastlike projections of dark volcanic rock were formed when molten material was squeezed out through cracks in the enveloping rock. Made of a harder material than its surroundings, this volcanic remnant, or dike, was all that remained when the softer rocks were worn away by the passage of time. ☐

CRATERS OF THE MOON. *As barren as a moonscape, the great lava plateau was built up by a long series of volcanic eruptions.*

Craters
of the Moon

- United States (Idaho)
- Map: page 10, D–4

The Apollo astronauts visited this stark lunar landscape for a preview of what they might find when they landed on the moon.

To Washington Irving, this black and barren moonscape in southern Idaho was "a desolate and awful waste, where . . . nothing is to be seen but lava." To tourists by the tens of thousands who visit the area, which is preserved as a national monument, it is an awesome showcase of volcanic forces. Extending from horizon to horizon is an unearthly panorama of lava flows, cinder cones, and craters.

This eerie setting resulted from volcanic activity, but not in the form of a single explosive eruption. Instead, a great crack, or fissure, about 50 miles (80 kilometers) long developed in the earth's crust. Through this zone of weakness, known as the Great Rift, lava welled up to the surface time and again over the course of thousands of years. With each successive series of eruptions, older volcanic formations were buried and new ones were superimposed on their surfaces. The barren black lavas, which are so prevalent throughout the general area, were all emitted during the most recent eruptions, which probably occurred approximately 2,000 years ago.

The most prominent volcanic features are the numerous cinder cones aligned along the Great Rift. Steepsided and conical, they were built up of ash and eruptive debris that accumulated where fiery fountains of lava shot high into the air. The finest and tallest cinder cone in the area, Big Cinder Butte, rises about 600 feet (185 meters) above its surroundings.

There are also many spatter cones, which are much smaller—up to about 50 feet (15 meters) high—and have steeper sides. The creation of less powerful fire fountains, they were built up of lava that shot up into the air and then piled up in the form of viscous clots or blobs.

Everywhere there are other signs of

volcanism, including lava bombs, craters, molds of tree trunks engulfed by lava, and especially massive lava flows. Some of the lava flows are so-called *pahoehoe* (a Hawaiian term). Their wrinkled, ropy texture resulted from hardening of the surface crust while fluid lava within the flow continued to push the mass forward and heap it up in billowy cascades and festoons. In contrast, the many *aa* lava flows (also known by their Hawaiian name) have jagged, clinkery surfaces and were formed by the movement of less fluid streams of lava.

Penetrating many of the flows are lava tubes. These tunnellike caves were formed when the surface of the molten material cooled and hardened, while a river of lava underneath gradually drained out, leaving an opening. Some of them are even decorated with lava stalactites where hot lava dripped down from the ceiling. □

Crimean Peninsula

- U.S.S.R.
- Map: page 18, E–4

Flat plains and soaring mountains result in striking contrasts on this picturesque Russian peninsula.

Barely anchored to the mainland by an isthmus a mere 2½ miles (4 kilometers) wide, the Crimean Peninsula is almost completely encircled by the Black Sea and the Sea of Azov. To the north the peninsula is a seemingly endless expanse of flat plains. To the south, in contrast, the coast along the Black Sea is bordered by a magnificent range of mountains about 100 miles (160 kilometers) long.

Composed primarily of extensively folded limestone formations, the Crimean Mountains are geologically related to the Carpathians and the Cau-

casus, and are believed to have been uplifted at the same time as the Alps. From north to south the mountains rise gradually but steadily above the plains, with the ascent interrupted by two series of terraced ridges. The Crimean Mountains reach their highest point (5,062 feet, or 1,543 meters) in a peak called Roman-Kosh.

But the special beauty of the Crimea results from the way the mountain slopes drop off abruptly to the south. In many places high cliffs provide a dramatic backdrop along the narrow coastal plain at the edge of the Black Sea. The mountains, moreover, act as a climatic barrier, moderating the effects of cold winds from the north. The result is a balmy climate similar to that of many Mediterranean regions. Because of the lush vegetation and spectacular scenery, seaside resorts flourish at Yalta and many other towns along this "Russian Riviera." □

CRIMEAN PENINSULA. *In the lee of craggy mountain slopes, the southern coast of the Crimea is a sheltered oasis of flourishing greenery.*

Dachstein Massif

- Austria
- Map: page 17, E–4

Honed down long ago by glaciers and dissolved by seeping meltwater, the imposing limestone massif still towers above its surroundings.

Southeast of the city of Salzburg is a region known as the Salzkammergut. Famed for its multitude of lakes and magnificent mountain scenery, it is among the most popular tourist destinations in the Austrian Alps.

One of the ranges that form the southern border of the Salzkammergut is the high, rugged Dachstein Massif. Bounded by cliffs and steep slopes, it is actually a high plateau. Its surface is far from flat, however. Still topped by glaciers, it was once covered by a much more extensive ice cap that gouged out its undulating contours. In addition, a number of high peaks and massive crests rise well above their surroundings. The tallest of all the peaks is the Hohe Dachstein ("High Dachstein"), which reaches an elevation of 9,826 feet (2,995 meters).

The massif is composed mainly of thick beds of limestones and dolomites that were deposited about 200 million years ago. In addition to the effects of past glaciation, the rocks have been eroded in two different ways.

The climate of the region is quite wet, with about 120 inches (3,050 millimeters) of precipitation per year, much of it in the form of snow. As a result, there has been a great deal of frost wedging: water that seeps into cracks and crevices expands when it freezes, and so acts like a wedge that splits off chunks of rock.

In addition, the limestone in the Dachstein is easily dissolved. Water cascading down the steep slopes has carved out many ravines and gullies. Elsewhere summer meltwater has seeped into cracks, gradually dissolving the rock and enlarging the openings. In places, sizable sinkholes and whole collapsed caverns dot the surface. But the most impressive results of this type of erosion are the extensive cave systems that penetrate the massif. Among the biggest ones, the Dachsteineishöhle ("Dachstein Ice Cave") is especially notable for the elegant natural ice formations that decorate its chambers and passageways. □

DACHSTEIN MASSIF. *Hemmed in by sheer cliffs, the calm waters of the Gosau See reflect the craggy snow- and glacier-covered ramparts of the looming mountainous plateau.*

Dadès Gorges

- Morocco
- Map: page 24, C–2

A North African river has carved a miniature version of the Grand Canyon through rocks that once lay deep beneath an ancient sea.

Although it is small and frequently dries up completely, the Dadès River has carved some of the most rugged gorges found anywhere in northern Africa. The river rises in the High Atlas range of the Atlas Mountains in central Morocco. From its source the river runs southwest for about 220 miles (350 kilometers) before joining the Dra River at Ouarzazate, an oasis community at the edge of the Sahara. The lower part of the Dadès Valley is noted for its palm and almond groves, as well as the many roses that are grown there for the production of fragrant rose water. But the river's most distinguishing feature by far is the series of four deep gorges that hem in its upper course.

Winters are severe along the headstreams of the Dadès, and snow persists on the mountain peaks well into summer. During the rest of the year precipitation is quite sparse and intermittent. When storms arrive, however, the rain often falls in tremendous downpours. Streams that were dry before a storm become raging torrents within a matter of hours, and then the flow quickly subsides once again. Geologists call such streams ephemeral, since they are dry much of the time and filled with water only immediately following a rainfall. In the arid American Southwest, streambeds of this sort are known by their Spanish name, arroyos, while in the Arab world they are called wadis or oueds.

The sporadic but intense runoff in the Dadès River results in awesome erosive power. When the river is flowing at flood stage, it carries immense loads of debris down from the mountains. Each particle, large or small, acts like a bit of sandpaper, rasping away at the soft rock of the riverbed and gradually deepening it. In some places the winding gorges are so narrow, deep, and nearly straight-walled that a person standing on the rim can barely make out the river at the bottom of the abyss.

Ranging from about 650 to 1,600 feet (200 to 500 meters) in depth, the gorges vary from narrow defiles to broader, more open canyons. In some places the horizontal layers of rock resemble piles of shelves stacked haphazardly one upon another. Elsewhere the canyon walls are interrupted by terraces or masked by heaps of debris. Where tributaries join the Dadès, they have in places cut off isolated bastions shaped like tabletops, stepped pyramids, and jagged peaks.

Because of the gorges' great depths, their ocher-colored walls become an ever-changing palette of tones as the angle of the sun changes with the time of day and season of the year. In spring and summer, their somber hues are accented by the delicate pastels of blossoming oleanders and a variety of wildflowers, as well as bright clumps of grass that cling tenaciously to the cliffs. In fall, the rust and golden leaves of figs and pomegranates enliven the scene.

The gorges' distinctive profiles are due to their geological origin. Millions of years ago the area now traversed by the Dadès River lay at the bottom of an ocean. Giant coral reefs developed on the sea floor, and huge quantities of sediment were washed in and deposited there. Over the millennia all this material was compacted into layers of limestone, sandstone, and other kinds of rock.

Shifting movements of the earth's crust eventually elevated the region above sea level and, in the process, created the immense folds of rock that now form the Atlas Mountains. The Dadès River, however, established its course relatively early in the upheaval. As land surfaces rose higher and higher, the river incised its serpentine valley ever deeper into the uplifted rocks. Local variations in the cutting power of the river and the hardness of the rocks resulted in the present-day variations in the contours of the walls throughout the gorges.

Portions of the gorges are accessible by an unpaved road that winds up and down and in and out, offering superb views of the valley. Elsewhere footpaths within the narrowest sectors of the chasms provide new surprises at every turn.

Anyone who has seen the Dadès Gorges will understand why they have been likened to the Grand Canyon of the Colorado. The comparison is apt, both scenically and geologically. Although the Dadès's valley is much smaller than the Colorado's, the two rivers have carved their unique gorges in much the same way. □

DADES GORGES. *Barely more than a trickle—or even dry—much of the time, the mountain stream becomes a raging torrent after storms and carves its fantastic gorges ever deeper.*

DALLOL SALT FLATS. *Enriched by salts from sources deep beneath the surface, bubbling springs have built up conical mounds of mineral deposits on the surface of the flats.*

Dallol Salt Flats

- Ethiopia
- Map: page 26, D–1

Over tens of thousands of years, thick salt deposits have accumulated in a deep, dry African depression.

In eastern Ethiopia, near the southern end of the Red Sea, an immense, more or less triangular depression in the earth's crust descends far below sea level. Known as the Danakil Depression or Danakil Desert, this extremely hot, dry area is actually a part of Africa's Great Rift Valley. To the east a low mountain range, the Danakil Highlands, rises between the lowland and the Red Sea. To the west the land ascends to the Ethiopian Plateau.

At one time the basin was connected to the Red Sea and was periodically inundated by its waters. As the seawater evaporated, the dissolved salts remained, so that the surface is now patched with salt flats and briny lakes. One spot, near the southern end of the depression, is now occupied by Lake Assal, which is both the saltiest lake in the world and the lowest point in Africa.

Another relic of these former invasions of seawater is the Dallol Salt Flats near the northern end of the depression. Covered by glistening salt deposits similar to the Bonneville Salt Flats in Utah, as well as a shallow, brackish lake, the surface of the basin

now stands about 400 feet (120 meters) below sea level. But at one time the floor of the depression must have been much lower: in some places the salt deposits are about 3 miles (5 kilometers) thick.

The onetime lagoon now occupied by the Dallol Salt Flats was probably last flooded by the sea about 8,000 years ago. But even today its surface is periodically altered during the annual rainy season when streams pour down from the mountains. The shallow lake expands, dissolving some of the salts; then the water evaporates and the salts settle out once again. □

Danube River

- Central Europe
- Map: page 17, F–4

Following a remarkable course from the Black Forest to the Black Sea, the Danube touches eight countries—and much of the history of Europe.

The Danube, the second longest river in Europe (after the Volga), meanders across the continent for 1,750 miles (2,800 kilometers). From its source in the cool depths of the Black Forest to its outlet on the sun-drenched shores of the Black Sea, the river varies dramatically in mood. Born as a mountain stream, along parts of its course it flows lazily across broad plains, while elsewhere it roars across rapids in deep, narrow gorges.

"Mother Danube" has long been an avenue for exploration, conquest, and commerce. Some of the first civilized tribes to reach Europe followed the Danube west from Asia, establishing agricultural settlements along the way. About seven centuries before the Christian Era, Greek sailors conducted a thriving trade with communities along the river's lower course. Later, fleets of the Roman Empire patrolled its waters, and Roman legions built strongholds along its banks, including settlements on the sites of Vienna, Budapest, and Belgrade. Crusaders followed it east to the Holy Land, and Turks, traveling west, later captured the lower valley.

The Danube begins its long journey to the sea as an alpine stream formed

The Danube carries more water than any other river in Europe, although the flow varies greatly with locality and time of year along various segments of its lengthy course.

DANUBE RIVER. *Flowing toward its outlet on the Black Sea, the river is hemmed in by steep walls of the gorge known as the Iron Gate.*

by the merging of its two main headwaters, the Breg and Brigach, in West Germany. Heading east into Austria, the river picks up speed as it flows through canyonlike valleys hemmed in by wooded hills crowned with the ruins of medieval castles. Eventually the river reaches Vienna, where it flows through the city's outskirts near the Vienna Woods. (This sector of the river inspired Johann Strauss's famous *Blue Danube* waltz.)

The upper course of the Danube ends dramatically in a deep gorge upstream from Bratislava, Czechoslovakia. Crossing the Little Hungarian Plain and then, beyond Budapest, the limitless expanse of the Great Hungarian Plain, the Danube slows down and becomes a flatland river somewhat similar to the Ohio or the Mississippi. With its current reduced to a placid flow, much of the silt carried down from the mountains settles to the bottom, clogging the channel with

numerous islands. Although the middle course of the river is marshy and shallow in many places, this section of the Danube also receives the largest of its 300 tributaries, including the Drava, Tisza, and Sava.

Beyond Belgrade, the capital of Yugoslavia, the river enters the Danube cataracts. At its narrowest point here, known as the Iron Gate, the river boils between sheer rock walls 800 to 1,000 feet (250 to 300 meters) high and only 500 feet (150 meters) apart. In some places the river reaches a depth of 175 feet (50 meters). Dams and canals make the gorge navigable, but boats moving against the swift current must be assisted by locomotives.

Below the cataracts the Danube changes character once again. Sluggish for much of its lower course, the river forms the boundary between Rumania and Bulgaria. To the north, in Rumania, it is bounded by a zone of lakes and marshes that give way to a

broad lowland plain. To the south the banks rise steeply to the wide expanse of Bulgaria's Danubian Plain.

About 50 miles (80 kilometers) from the Black Sea, the river begins to spread out into its delta, dividing into three major channels and multitudes of minor ones. The second largest delta in Europe, it covers an area of about 1,650 square miles (4,300 square kilometers).

This superb mosaic of land and water—including marshes, lagoons, islands, lakes, sandbars, and floating reedbeds—is the home of an almost unbelievable array of plants and wildlife. Best known for its birds (some 300 species have been sighted there), it also harbors 60 kinds of fish, herds of wild boar, and an astonishing assortment of other creatures. Famed as one of the most prolific wildlife sanctuaries in Europe, the Danube Delta attracts tourists and nature lovers from all around the world. □

TORS OF DARTMOOR. *Towering above the grassy moor beneath a stormy sky, some of the massive boulders of Dartmoor rise as much as 50 feet (15 meters) above their surroundings.*

Dartmoor, Tors of

- United Kingdom (England)
- Map: page 16, C-3

Like ruins of castles on the hilltops, craggy outcrops of massive boulders accentuate the beauty of the moor.

Looming above pastoral surroundings in the heart of Devonshire in southwestern England is a wild, lonely, strangely picturesque upland known as Dartmoor. Site of the infamous Dartmoor Prison, it also served as the setting for Sir Arthur Conan Doyle's haunting mystery, *The Hound of the Baskervilles.*

An eroded granite plateau some 23 miles (37 kilometers) by about 10 to 12 miles (16 to 19 kilometers) in extent, it rises to an average elevation of about 1,600 feet (500 meters). The gently undulating surface of the moorland, covered by peat bogs and grasslands where the native ponies roam at will, is broken up by low hollows and winding valleys.

But the most arresting features of the landscape are the huge, barren rock formations that crown the ridges and low hilltops. Resembling the ruins of ancient fortifications or cairns piled up by some bygone race of giants, these stacks of enormous boulders are called tors by the local people.

How did they get there—these odd formations with names such as Vixen Tor, Yes Tor, Hound Tor, Hare Tor, and highest of all, High Willhays (at 2,038 feet, or 621 meters)? Their story began about 250 million years ago when a molten granite massif welled upward into much older overlying rock layers and cooled. Gradually the older rocks

were worn away, exposing the granite in the form of a low dome.

The formation of the tors resulted from the fracturing of the granite along joints that cross each other at more or less right angles. Chemical weathering, water erosion, and alternate freezing and thawing (especially during the ice ages) gradually enlarged the cracks to form rectangular boulders with rounded corners.

As runoff water washed away the sand and gravel from the gradually widening cracks, some of the boulders slowly migrated downslope under the force of gravity and came to rest in the intervening valleys. Those that remain in stacks and clusters on the hilltops form the dramatic tors of Dartmoor that punctuate the landscape today. □

Daryal Gorge

- U.S.S.R.
- Map: page 18, F–4

Steeped in legend and filled with wild beauty, the mountain gorge is a vital route through the Caucasus.

Stretching from the Black Sea to the Caspian, the Caucasus rises as a formidable mountain barrier. The range is not very wide, but the peaks are tall, reaching up more than 18,000 feet (5,500 meters). And passes across the massif are virtually nonexistent.

The only major north-south route, in fact, is through the Daryal Gorge, which the Roman Pliny aptly called the Gates of Caucasus. Carved mainly by the Terek River, the narrow, wild gorge is hemmed in by steep granite cliffs as much as 5,900 feet (1,800 meters) high. Because of its strategic importance, the gorge has long been guarded by fortifications. Today it is the route of the only highway across the mountains, the heavily traveled Georgian Military Road.

In addition to its military importance, the gorge has inspired its share of legends. According to Greek mythology, Mount Kazbek, overlooking the pass, was the mountain to which Prometheus was chained. On another rocky summit are the ruins of the castle of an evil queen who, it is said, lured travelers with her charms, then hurled them to their deaths in the murky Terek far below. □

Tors, Balancing Rocks, and Boulder Fields

Granite and certain similar rocks, which are prone to disintegrating into sandy gravel, are responsible for some very picturesque erosional landforms. Usually found perched on hilltops, they consist of geometrical piles of more or less rounded boulders, known as tors, and even balancing rocks (one boulder perched atop another). In cold climates the process of boulder formation is accelerated by alternate freezing and thawing, which loosens the blocks. In arid regions the wind plays a role too, by blowing away the fine debris. On the slopes the boulders form rock streams, slowly but surely sliding downhill on the beds of sand and gravel washed out from crevices between the rocks. Finally the blocks of stone accumulate in the valley bottoms as boulder fields.

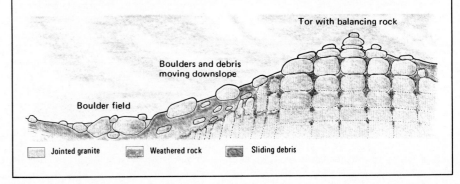

Tor with balancing rock

Boulders and debris moving downslope

Boulder field

Jointed granite   Weathered rock   Sliding debris

Dasht-i-Lut

- Iran
- Map: page 18, G–5

Ridges of salt and billowing dunes of sand contrast with the rocky borders of this vast desert in Iran.

The ancient nation of Iran, once known as Persia, is almost entirely hemmed in by mountain ranges of various heights. Much of the interior of the country is a high, dry, sparsely populated plateau. Far from being a single uniform expanse, however, the interior plateau is cut up by highlands and lesser mountain ranges into several large enclosed drainage basins. Possessing no outlet to the sea, the basins are watered only by intermittent seasonal streams that rush down from the mountains and die out in salt flats and in dried-out lakebeds.

One of the largest, driest, and hottest of all these desert basins is the Dasht-i-Lut in east-central Iran. Some 300 miles (480 kilometers) long and about 200 miles (320 kilometers) wide, it is one of the most forbidding—yet fascinating—deserts in the world. Remarkably varied in terrain, Dasht-i-Lut is an intricate mosaic of rock, sand, and salt deposits.

The rocky deserts are found at the foot of bordering mountain slopes, especially the Kerman range to the west. During the spring wet season, torrents rage briefly down the mountainsides and drop their heavy loads of stones and debris in deltalike deposits known locally as *dasht*. Toward the basin's center, the streams die out in dry lakebeds encrusted with salts and sediments of clay.

Much of the eastern part of the desert is a low plateau covered by flat salt deposits. In the center of the basin, in contrast, the plains of salt and clay have been scoured by northwesterly winds into a spectacular expanse of parallel ridges and troughs. Sometimes rounded in form, sometimes topped by jagged crests, the rumpled ridges extend over a distance of about 90 miles (150 kilometers) and are as much as 250 feet (75 meters) high. In places the salty ridges, which rise like the waves on a storm-tossed sea, are dissected by ravines and punctuated by sinkholes that have been hollowed out by the infrequent rains.

Finally, to the southeast, the Dasht-i-Lut is a vast sea of sand similar to a Saharan erg. Billowing from horizon to horizon are gigantic dunes as much as 1,000 feet (300 meters) in height—among the tallest sand dunes found anywhere in the world. □

DASHT-I-LUT. *Relentless winds have sculpted ancient deposits of salts and clays into a turbulent pattern of jagged crests and troughs.*

Dead Sea

- Israel—Jordan
- Map: page 18, E-5

The lowest body of water in the world —as well as one of the saltiest—has been the site of great events in history.

Descending the dry hills and valleys of Judaea east of Jerusalem, travelers come upon a sign indicating that they are passing below the level of the Mediterranean. Yet they still have a long way to go before reaching the shores of the Dead Sea. Cupped at the bottom of a long, narrow desert valley, the glittering expanse of brilliantly blue water lies 1,296 feet (395 meters) below sea level—making it the lowest body of water in the world.

Despite its name, the Dead Sea is not quite dead nor is it a sea in the usual sense of the word. Although its waters are seven to eight times saltier than the ocean and even brinier than Utah's Great Salt Lake, certain bacteria are able to survive in it. And although it is called a sea, it is actually a landlocked lake: water flows in but escapes only by means of evaporation.

Some 50 miles (80 kilometers) long and about 10 miles (16 kilometers) wide, the Dead Sea occupies only the lowest part of a much longer depression. Its basin, in fact, is part of the Great Rift Valley, a giant fracture in the earth's crust that reaches all the way from Syria to Mozambique. The rifting began about 25 million years ago when two immense plates in the earth's crust started to drift apart, leaving a great indentation between them. And the shifting of the crust continues today, as evidenced by the occasional earthquakes that occur throughout the region.

The peninsula of El Lisan ("The Tongue") divides the Dead Sea into two unequal basins. The southern basin is smaller and shallower, with an average depth of only 20 feet (6 meters). The northern basin reaches a maximum depth of 1,300 feet (400 meters). In parts of the northern basin, mountain slopes plunge directly into the water, their flanks gullied by deep ravines. Known as wadis in Arabic and as nahals in Hebrew, these seasonal streambeds are filled by raging torrents after the infrequent rains.

But the main influx of water into the Dead Sea is from the Jordan River. In this hot desert region, however, evaporation keeps pace with the inflow of water. Each year the equivalent of 55 inches (1,400 millimeters) of water evaporates from the surface of the sea, often obscuring it in veils of mist.

Though the moisture leaves on the winds, the dissolved minerals that its affluents carry into the sea are left behind. As a result, each ton (0.9 metric ton) of water contains 560 pounds (255 kilograms) of mineral salts, including common table salt and other commercially valuable chemicals such as potash, magnesium, and bromine.

The hills and the narrow plain surrounding the sea—austere, nearly devoid of vegetation, yet strangely beautiful—have been the site of many momentous events in history. Near the northern shore is the city of Jericho, site of the oldest known settlement in the world. Not far away, in the River Jordan, Jesus was baptized by John. According to some experts, the ruins of the evil cities of Sodom and Gomorrah lie beneath the waters of the sea. Above the western shore rises the mountain fortress of Masada, where in A.D. 73 some 960 Jews of the Zealot sect committed mass suicide rather than surrender to Roman soldiers. And just to the north of Masada, in a hillside cave at Qumran, a shepherd boy in 1947 discovered the first of the famed long-lost Dead Sea Scrolls. □

Saltwater Samples

Mean concentration of mineral salts in major bodies of water

	parts per thousand
Dead Sea	280
Great Salt Lake	205
Red Sea	40
Mediterranean Sea	39
Ocean (average)	35
Black Sea	18
Caspian Sea	13
Aral Sea	11

DEAD SEA. *Miniature castles made up of salt deposits are reflected in briny moats along the shoreline of the historic sea.*

DEATH VALLEY. *Though rainfall is rare in the valley today, running water has left its indelible imprint on the exquisitely eroded landscape.*

Death Valley

- United States (California)
- Map: page 10, D–5

Lowest, hottest, and driest all in one, the forbidding desert valley is also a place of startling beauty.

To the local Indians, Death Valley, near California's Nevada border, was known as Tomesha–"Ground Afire." And with good reason: soil temperatures in this hottest, driest spot in North America have been known to reach a scorching 190° F (88° C). Air temperatures are equally ovenlike. One summer day in 1913 the temperature in the shade reached a record 134° F (57° C), the highest ever reported in the United States. Rainfall on the valley floor, in turn, averages less than 2 inches (50 millimeters) per year, and in some years no rain falls at all.

Yet the valley is far from lifeless. Mesquites, creosote bushes, cactuses, and a wealth of wildflowers all thrive there. Animal life ranges from tiny desert pupfish that inhabit isolated springs to lizards, coyotes, bighorn sheep, and even herds of wild burros.

The valley–the central feature of Death Valley National Monument–extends north to south for some 140 miles (225 kilometers). Hemmed in to the east by the Amargosa Range and to the west by the Panamints, its width varies from 5 to 15 miles (8 to 24 kilometers). Geologically, the valley is known as a graben. It formed as an enormous block of the earth's crust shifted downward along fault lines while neighboring blocks moved upward to form the fringing mountains.

The down dropping of the valley floor over the course of time was tremendous. One spot near a small salt pond known as Badwater stands at 282 feet (86 meters) below sea level–

the lowest bit of land in the Western Hemisphere. Just a short distance away, in spectacular contrast, Telescope Peak, the highest point in the monument, rises to an elevation of 11,049 feet (3,368 meters).

To the north of Badwater is an area known as the Devil's Golf Course. Modeled by the wind and infrequent rainfall, thick salt deposits form a fantastically corrugated expanse of jagged spires, ridges, and troughs. Still farther to the north is the Racetrack, a flat, clay-filled former lakebed. Scattered across its surface are boulders, each with a track in its wake tracing the movement of the boulder across the clay. Apparently the rocks are pushed by strong winds after rains, when a film of water makes the surface slippery. Elsewhere in the monument, spectacular sand dunes, rugged badlands, deep canyons, and snowcapped peaks vie for attention in one of North America's strangest landscapes. □

Desolation, Valley of

- South Africa
- Map: page 26, B–6

Very dry and austere, the Valley of Desolation lives up to its name. Its fascination lies in the huge rocks that reach boldly toward the sky.

Though often portrayed as a tremendous expanse of level plain, the southern part of Africa is a series of steps leading from a vast inland plateau down to the coast. The main drop is a long line of cliffs known as the Great Escarpment; below it lies an arid plain called the Great Karroo. Then comes another escarpment, another plain, and so on south to the Cape Ranges and then the sea.

The Valley of Desolation is a low-lying portion of the Great Karroo formed by intensive erosion along a fault in the earth's crust. As its name implies, there are no lush forests in this barren valley, no sparkling lakes to delight the eye and soul. Its austere beauty stems from its array of huge natural sculptures, some reaching up more than 400 feet (120 meters). Cast into battlements and humanlike forms strewn across the land, the rocky prominences create a vista so impressive that the valley has been declared a national monument.

At one time these rocks were buried deep within the earth. Millions of years ago this part of Africa was covered by layers of sandstone and shale. Then molten material (magma) rose up from deep in the interior. Before arriving at the surface, the magma spread out between the layers of older rocks, where it cooled and hardened into a dark crystalline rock called dolerite. Thus patches of dolerite came to be distributed within the layers of sandstone and shale.

Over the millennia the forces of erosion ate away at the top layers, gradually wearing down the surface until the dolerite became exposed. Dolerite is far more resistant to erosion than are sandstone and shale. Thus as the softer rocks disappeared, the dolerite slowly came into view. Today huge chunks of dolerite are scattered across the land, along with formations of softer rock that are protected by caps of dolerite. But even the dolerite is vulnerable and will eventually succumb to erosion. □

DELLS OF THE WISCONSIN. *The intricately eroded cliffs, capped by fragrant groves of conifers, are products of an age when ice sheets covered much of the surrounding landscape.*

Dells of the Wisconsin

- United States (Wisconsin)
- Map: page 11, E–4

Golden-hued cliffs, calm blue waters, and narrow chasms contribute to the beauty of the sandstone gorge.

In few places in North America have the forces of erosion created a more picturesque ravine, or dell, than this one along the Wisconsin River. For a distance of more than 7 miles (11 kilometers), the river twists and turns between colorful, deeply eroded sandstone cliffs as much as 80 to 100 feet (24 to 30 meters) high. Squeezing through narrow chasms (at the "Jaws" the canyon is barely 50 feet, or 15 meters, wide), then gliding majestically past stone pillars that seem balanced in defiance of gravity, the river attracts admirers all year long.

The sandstone that makes up the cliffs was formed hundreds of millions of years ago when this part of North America lay at the bottom of a shallow sea. Bit by bit, individual grains of sand accumulated in thick layers near the shoreline, and over the eons were transformed into solid rock.

The formation of the gorge itself, however, was a relatively recent development. Over the course of the past 2 million years or so—the Ice Age—great sheets of ice alternately advanced and retreated across much of northern North America in four successive waves, scarring the landscape as far south as southern Illinois. Diverted by uplands, however, the advancing lobes of ice left portions of Wisconsin and adjacent states relatively unscathed. (The unglaciated region is known as the driftless area, since the landscape was not masked by drift, or glacial deposits.)

The Dells, located near the very edge of the driftless area, were untouched by the grinding sheets of ice. But the glaciers carved the gorge indirectly. As the ice sheets melted, gushing streams of water rushed across the land, scouring out the Wisconsin River's serpentine channel. Because the meltwater wore away softer layers of sandstone more easily than the harder layers, the walls of the gorge are deeply corrugated and in many places are capped by shelflike overhangs. Where the river undercut the edges of small islands, it left behind tall, mushroom-shaped pedestals.

The river also ground down into fractures that crossed the sandstone layers, enlarging them and making angular chasms that turn at nearly right angles. Even today, alternate freezing and thawing, rainfall and melting snow continue to alter the contours of the canyon walls. □

VALLEY OF DESOLATION. *Rocky sentinels watch over a South African landscape, survivors of the battle between rocks and erosion.*

DETTIFOSS. *Veiled by swirling mist, a glacier-fed river plunges over a precipice of dark volcanic rock on its way to the Greenland Sea, a southern arm of the Arctic Ocean.*

Dettifoss

- Iceland
- Map: page 16, B–2

The largest waterfall in Iceland is nourished by a huge glacier but was formed by fiery volcanic activity.

The roar of falling water and a haze of mist alert the tourist as he approaches Dettifoss, Iceland's most impressive waterfall. (*Foss* means "waterfall" in Icelandic.) Plunging abruptly over the edge of a precipice, the water drops 144 feet (44 meters) into a swirling caldron of foam and then continues along on its journey northward to the Greenland Sea.

The falls, in a stark, treeless setting, are best visited in summer when the bright hues of wildflowers contrast with the somber tones of the rock along the canyon walls. Composed of basalt, a type of volcanic rock, the cliffs are broken up into tall hexagonal columns resembling giant organ pipes.

Located near the northeastern coast of the island, Dettifoss is one of several waterfalls on the Jokulsa a Fjollum. The source of this river, approximately 30 miles (50 kilometers) to the south, is the Vatnajokull, which is the largest glacier in all of Iceland. (*Jokull* is

Continents on the Move

In the early 1900's a German scientist, Alfred Wegener, proposed a theory that revolutionized geological thought. All the continents, he suggested, were once connected in a single supercontinent that gradually broke up as the pieces drifted apart to their present positions.

Most modern geologists accept Wegener's theory with a few modifications. The earth's crust, they believe, consists of a mosaic of segments that are known as tectonic plates. Their movement is generated where molten material wells up along rifts between adjacent plates, solidifies, and becomes part of the ocean floor. (The Mid-Atlantic Ridge, which crosses Iceland, is an example of a rift zone.) As new material is incorporated into the sea floor, the plates are forced apart. Thus the Atlantic Ocean, for instance, is growing wider as the Americas drift away from Europe and Africa.

But the plates cannot grow indefinitely. Where two plates collide, their margins may crumple to form mountain ranges. Elsewhere the edge of one plate may buckle under its neighbor. Accompanied by earthquakes and volcanism, the sinking plate margin is remelted as it is forced down again toward the earth's interior.

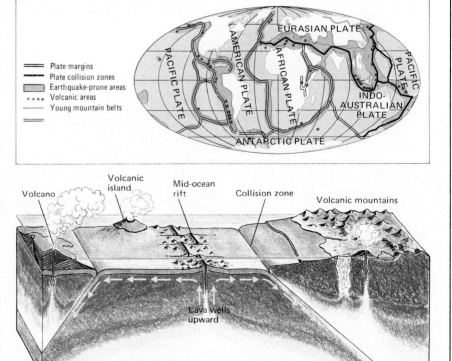

the Icelandic word meaning "glacier.")

But while the river's source is glacial, the waterfall's geological history is rooted in volcanic activity. The entire surface of Iceland, noted for its wealth of volcanoes, earthquakes, hot springs, and other volcanic phenomena, is a relatively young lava plateau. It is in fact an exposed portion of the Mid-Atlantic Ridge, an extraordinarily long submarine range of volcanic peaks that were formed by the up-welling of lava through a gigantic rift between two major plates of the earth's crust. (The island of Surtsey, just south of Iceland, was born of a massive volcanic eruption in 1963.)

Over the past 2 million years, the area around Dettifoss has been covered repeatedly by basaltic lava flows that flooded up through fractures in the earth. As the lava cooled, it contracted and split into prismatic vertical columns like those at the falls. Dettifoss itself and the canyon downstream were formed where the glacier-fed river spills over the edge of one such lava flow. □

Devils Tower

- United States (Wyoming)
- Map: page 10, D–4

The tallest rock formation of its kind in the United States, Devils Tower is an unforgettable landmark, rising like a sentinel above the plain.

Looming above the Belle Fourche River in northeast Wyoming, where pine forests of the Black Hills merge with grasslands of the rolling plains, an imposing, stump-shaped rock formation is visible from as far as 100 miles (160 kilometers) away. Composed of a cluster of long vertical columns that resemble a bundle of organ pipes, Devils Tower rises 865 feet (265 meters) from its wooded base to its flat-topped summit. The base is about 1,000 feet (300 meters) in diameter; the top, 275 feet (85 meters) across.

According to Indian legend, the tower was named for an evil god who used to beat his drums on the summit, creating the roar of thunder and terrifying everyone within earshot. Another legend claims that the fluted markings on the tower's flanks are the work of a giant bear, scratching with his claws as he tried in vain to reach seven maidens stranded on the top. (In more recent times a Hollywood movie

DEVILS TOWER. *Composed of a cluster of fluted columns, the giant monolith was formed when molten material welled upward, then cooled, beneath the surface of the earth.*

depicted the tower as the landing site for a spaceship carrying beings from another world.)

Geologists, however, offer a less poetic—but more convincing—explanation of the monolith's looming presence. According to them, a sea once covered this region. Sediments that settled on its bottom were eventually consolidated into layers of shale, sandstone, gypsum, and limestone—the same kinds of rock that are exposed around the tower's base today. Then about 50 million years ago a mass of molten material from a source deep within the earth oozed upward toward the surface, intruding into the overlying layers of sedimentary rock. Completely enveloped by these older rocks, the molten material slowly cooled and crystallized. As the magma cooled, it also contracted, creating a complicated network of vertical joints, or cracks. These cracks account for the formation of the distinctive polygonal

columns that make up the tower today.

The next step in the process was exposure of the igneous formation that still lay buried beneath the mantle of sedimentary rocks. Over millions of years erosion gradually wore away the softer rock that once covered the much harder intruded formation.

Once it was exposed, erosion began to alter the appearance of the tower itself. Water, seeping into crevices in the rock, expanded when it froze, causing columns to collapse. The remnants of fallen columns make up the aprons of debris, or talus slopes, that ring the base of the tower today.

No columns are known to have fallen recently. But reckoned in human terms, geological processes proceed slowly. In time Devils Tower is likely to disappear completely. In the meantime, however, the tallest rock formation of its kind in the United States will continue to haunt the memories of all who view it. □

Diégo-Suarez Bay

- Madagascar
- Map: page 26, D–4

The sheltered network of deep, tranquil embayments has been a favored haven and port of call for seamen through the ages.

Stretching north to south for nearly 1,000 miles (1,600 kilometers) off the east coast of southern Africa is Madagascar, fourth largest island in the world. From a narrow coastal plain bordering the Indian Ocean the terrain rises abruptly along a series of steep escarpments to a high central plateau, then descends gradually to a broader western coastal plain.

Long noted for its unique plant and animal life (many species native to the island are found nowhere else in the world), Madagascar is also remarkable for the variety of its landscapes. From its fortresslike, nearly impene-

trable Ankarana Plateau and the titanic rock sculptures of its Andringitra Mountains to its palm-studded savannas, forests filled with ebony and rosewood, and steamy coastal lagoons, it is a surprising land filled with endless contrasts.

Among its most impressive natural features is Diégo-Suarez Bay, near the northern tip of the island. Protected by a narrow inlet that shelters it from strong winds blowing in off the Indian Ocean, Diégo-Suarez Bay opens out into a series of arms separated by long ridges and flat-topped plateaus. The bay, including all its arms and inlets, is big: it extends about 12 miles (20 kilometers) from north to south and from east to west. And it is deep: its waters generally average more than 65 feet (20 meters), while the main channel is about 165 feet (50 meters) deep. Remarkably well protected from winds and ocean currents, Diégo-Suarez Bay is considered to be one of the finest natural harbors in the world.

The bay's natural assets were immediately recognized by its first European discoverer, Diogo Diaz, an explorer sailing in 1500 in the service of Portugal's famed Prince Henry the Navigator. A long series of pirates and privateers also found safe haven in the bay between raids on Indian Ocean shipping. (One 17th-century French pirate even tried to found a Republic of Libertalia on its shores.) And to this day the bay remains a major port of call for coastal and overseas shipping.

Geologically, the bay apparently owes its origin to crustal movements that involved the entire island of Madagascar. It is believed that while the interior of the island rose upward over the course of time, its oceanic borders very slowly subsided into the sea. Thus a series of river valleys that once converged near the coast were gradually invaded by the sea. The drowned river valleys, in turn, formed the multiple arms of Diégo-Suarez Bay as it appears today. □

DIÉGO-SUAREZ BAY. *Invaded by the sea as Madagascar's coastline slowly sank, a series of drowned river valleys forms the sheltered bay.*

DIOSSO AMPHITHEATER. *Soft sandstones tinted by oxidized metals are being eroded so vigorously that plants are scarcely able to take root on the constantly crumbling slopes.*

Diosso Amphitheater

● Congo
● Map: page 26, A–3

Gnawed away by erosion, a broad, multicolored gap scars a range of cliffs that overlook the Atlantic Ocean.

North of the bustling port city of Pointe-Noire in the People's Republic of the Congo on the western coast of Africa, the rather narrow coastal plain ends abruptly in a cliff at the edge of a plateau. Averaging about 165 feet (50 meters) in height, the cliff has been deeply eroded into jagged ridges and deep gullies, all tinted with a spectacular rainbow of colors that range from white and yellow to red and even lavender tones.

In the Diosso Amphitheater, the most impressive section, erosion has indented the cliff with a broad, bowl-like gap about 0.6 mile (1 kilometer) long and 1,600 feet (500 meters) deep. The arc of the indentation in the edge of the plateau is not one continuous curve, however. Separated by sharp, knifelike ridges are many smaller secondary amphitheaters within the larger one, creating a more or less scalloped effect. (Somewhat similar erosional amphitheaters, as these features are called, can be seen inland in the Congo's Batéké Plateaus, as well as to the north in Gabon's Bam Bam Amphitheaters.)

The sandstone cliffs that make up the edge of the plateau are fairly soft, porous sedimentary deposits that were laid down about 2 to 3 million years ago as deltas and in the placid water of lagoons. Rather coarse-grained at the bottom, the sediments are finer near the top of the formation, where there are also beds rich with iron deposits.

Uplift of the formation, as well as marked changes in sea level over the past 2 million years, has led to the erosion of the cliffs and the amphitheater. When worldwide sea levels rose as a result of the melting of huge ice-age glaciers, ocean waves attacked the cliffs directly, gnawing away at their bases and causing the collapse of overlying rock layers. At other times rainwater streaming off the edge of the plateau resulted in the gully erosion of the cliffs.

This type of stream erosion continues today. But another force is also at work. Because the sandy formation is quite porous, rainwater soaks into it like a sponge and emerges at the base of the cliff as active springs. As water flows out of the springs, it causes local cave-ins of the overlying rock. The running water rapidly removes the fallen debris, and the cliff continues to retreat. Thus the entire amphitheater is steadily growing wider and deeper.

Because the iron-bearing sediments at the top of the cliffs erode very evenly, the amphitheater's rim is much less jagged than the lower slopes. Yet here too the abundant flow of water has a pronounced effect: it distributes oxidized metals from the rim throughout the formation, producing the wide variety of colors that make the amphitheater so attractive. □

Djerid, Chott

● Tunisia
● Map: page 24, D–2

Flooded in winter and caked with salts in summer, the gigantic desert lagoon is a perpetually changing spectacle.

South of the Atlas Mountains in west-central Tunisia is a broad lowland salt lagoon, the Chott Djerid. In Arabic its name means "Lagoon of the Land of Palms," perhaps because of the palm groves that flourish in bordering oases such as Nefta and Tozeur. But the lagoon itself, which extends more than 60 miles (100 kilometers) from east to west, is a huge, infertile salt plain.

Flooded during winter, the basin is blindingly white in summer as the sun glares down on the salts that encrust the dried-out surface. The heat waves shimmer across the basin, producing mirages that suggest nearby palm groves and pools of water where in reality there are none.

The Djerid basin is the largest in a series of similar salty swamps that extend westward across Tunisia and into Algeria. The easternmost, Chott el Fedjedj, reaches to within 15 miles (25 kilometers) of the coast of the Mediterranean. And in fact the ancients believed that all the basins were once connected to form an inland sea known as the Gulf of the Tritons.

Modern data, however, prove that no connection with the Mediterranean Sea ever existed. Although some of the basins extend below sea level, the bottom of the Chott Djerid stands about 50 to 65 feet (15 to 20 meters) above sea level. Geologists now be-

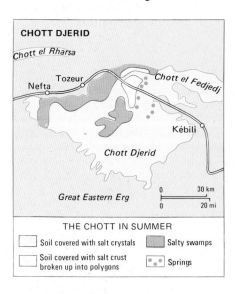

THE CHOTT IN SUMMER

☐ Soil covered with salt crystals   ▨ Salty swamps

☐ Soil covered with salt crust broken up into polygons   ⣿ Springs

CHOTT DJERID. *Ringed by low banks of clay, a spring opens like an eye on the salt-encrusted basin that has been scoured out by the wind.*

lieve that the basins occupy portions of a troughlike downwarping of the earth's crust that extends more or less east to west between the Atlas Mountains and the flat interior plains and plateaus of the Sahara.

The basins themselves have been hollowed out over the past 2 million years by strong winds blowing down from the Atlas Mountains. When the seasonal salt lakes dry out completely, the winds sweep up the salts and other sediments and carry them away across the desert, gradually deepening the depressions. Even extremely fine particles of clay, instead of settling out to form a hard crust as they do when freshwater lakes dry out, coalesce into loose clusters that can be blown away in the swirling dust.

Local rainfall is insufficient to account for the seasonal flooding of the basin, which lasts from October to March. Even after most of the water has evaporated in spring and summer, the underlying beds remain saturated. The lake in fact apparently results from an artesian system. Water from distant sources seeps through the porous underground rocks and emerges on the surface of the basin as the water table rises.

Even in the summer dry season the surface of the salt lagoon is a mosaic of varied forms. Here and there the plain is dotted with springs as much as 16 feet (5 meters) in diameter. In some places the ground is white with solid layers of salt. Elsewhere the crust is patterned by cracks and broken up into salty polygons. Finally there are swamps of very salty water that persist throughout the entire summer. Known as the egg swamps, they are used as springtime nesting sites by brilliant flocks of pink flamingos. ☐

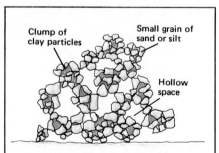

Minute clay particles settle to the bottom as freshwater pools dry out and form hard, pavementlike surfaces. But in extraordinarily salty water such as in Chott Djerid, a process known as flocculation takes place. Instead of forming a hard crust when the lake dries up, the particles of clay join together with each other and with other bits of silt to form loose clusters, resembling grains of sand, that are large enough to be blown away by the wind.

Doda Fallet

- Sweden
- Map: page 16, E–2

In 1796 an upland lake was suddenly transformed into a fertile plain, and a raging river became an empty channel.

Maps of northern Sweden reveal a remarkably uniform drainage pattern. One after another, rivers originate along the mountainous spine of Scandinavia, flow southeastward through long, fingerlike lakes, and finally empty into the Gulf of Bothnia, an arm of the Baltic Sea.

The Indal, a river long renowned for its waterfalls, gorges, and spectacular scenery, conforms to this pattern—but with one significant variation. Along part of its course an abandoned river channel runs parallel to the present-day Indal River. Vegetation partially masks the contours of the steep-sided, rocky ravine, but it is obvious that a rushing river carved the wild gorge. Long, placid pools of water still fill the deepest basins in the ghost streambed. Labyrinths of abandoned channels are only partially colonized by plants. Projecting rocky ledges hint of the rapids that once flowed across them. Here and there along the empty channel are potholes carved in the bedrock by stones that were trapped in swirling whirlpools. And finally there are the remains of a major cataract, the Doda Fallet, or "Dead Falls," for which the place is named.

The story of this remarkable phantom gorge began about 10,000 years ago as the last ice age was coming to an end. Relieved of a tremendous weight as the glaciers melted, the earth's crust slowly began to rebound. Courses of streams were shifted, and rushing meltwater scoured out deep new river channels. Flowing out from the retreating glaciers in this area were two parallel streams, the Doda Fallet and the present-day Indal River.

Meanwhile, the retreating glaciers were also depositing boulders and rock fragments that had been transported by the ice. Upstream from the Doda Fallet this debris formed a dam, blocking the Indal's present course and holding back a great reservoir of meltwater known as Lake Ragunda.

For thousands of years, the water escaped from the lake by way of a smaller unobstructed channel and flowed seaward through the gorge now known as the Doda Fallet. Then in the 1790's man entered the picture. A trench was dug across the dam of glacial debris in order to facilitate the floating of logs to lumber mills downstream. Disaster resulted. During a high-water stage in 1796, a torrent of water flowing through the man-made channel completely swept away the dam of glacial debris. Within a matter of hours Lake Ragunda was emptied, its bed transformed into a fertile plain.

Ever since, the Indal River has been following its present course through the flood-carved opening. The former outlet of the lake, left high and dry, remains today as the phantom gorge of the Doda Fallet—a remarkable natural museum of rock forms that were carved by a vanished river. □

DODA FALLET. *Placid pools in deeper portions of the channel are all that remain of a once-wild river raging through a gorge.*

Dolomites

- Italy
- Map: page 17, E–4

The Dolomites are made of dolomite, the rocky remnants of coral reefs that thrived in ancient shallow seas.

The Dolomites' claim to fame is not great height: the tallest peak in this part of the Italian Alps, Monte Marmolada, reaches up only 10,964 feet (3,342 meters). What makes the Dolomites memorable is their incredibly bold contours, with stark, sheer-walled massifs rising straight up from gently inclined lower slopes.

The contrast is especially striking in winter, when snow blankets the valleys and slopes but not the somber walls of stone. Looming against the horizon are massive rock formations that resemble needles, spires, castles, and fortresses. Saw-toothed ridges tower over distant valleys, while vertical walls rise straight up for 3,300 feet (1,000 meters) and more.

The dramatic contours of the Dolomites attract rock climbers from all parts of the world. Intersecting the mountains are a variety of well-marked trails for every level of expertise. Some of them, accessible by chair lift or cable car, are equipped with built-in handholds, ladders, and other safety features. But a few trails, especially in the Brenta (the rugged southwestern part of the range), are more challenging. Winding across glaciers, they require the use of ice axes, crampons, and other specialized mountaineering equipment.

A visitor trekking across a glacier in the Dolomites may find it hard to believe that the mountains originated in a warm, shallow sea. Some 200 million years ago water covered the region, and a coral reef developed atop much older beds of shale and marl (a clayey rock). Over the millennia the coral was compressed into a distinctive type of limestone that contains magnesium. Known as dolomite, it was named after the 18th-century French geologist Déodat Dolomieu, who first described the rock. Dolomite occurs elsewhere in the Alps and in many other places around the globe, including parts of the American Midwest and some places in the Appalachian Mountains.

During a period of mountain building that began 65 million years ago, the Dolomites were uplifted along

with the rest of the Alps. Many believe that the Alps formed as a result of the movement of continents—specifically when two great landmasses, Africa and Europe, collided and their margins were heaved upward into crumpled mountainous relief.

Even as the mountains were rising,

the forces of erosion began their work of wearing down. Valleys developed where the softer, more easily eroded shale and marl were exposed. The harder dolomite, in contrast, wore away much more slowly. As a result, great masses of dolomite remain more or less intact, forming the stark massifs

DOLOMITES. *Jagged massifs rise above gentler slopes, providing hikers with a choice of easy trails or dizzying mountain climbs.*

that now typify this part of the Alps.

The human history of the Dolomites is as intriguing as the landscape itself. Ruled by Rome for hundreds of years, the mountain people developed their own version of Latin—a language called Ladin that is still spoken by some of the residents. Eventually the region became part of Austria, and German took over as the official language—until the area was ceded to Italy at the end of World War I. As a result, many of the mountain features now bear both Italian and German names. Torre Undici is also called Elferturm (both names mean "Eleventh Tower"), Croda Rossa is Rotwand ("Red Wall"), and Val Sasso Vecchio and Altensteintal both refer to the same "Old Stone Valley." But by whatever names, the formations all contribute to the scenic beauty that makes the Dolomites a popular tourist resort around the year. □

Drach Caves

- Spain
- Map: page 17, D–5

Subterranean lakes mirror the beauty of fantastic formations within the depths of these Majorcan caves.

The island of Majorca, off the Spanish coast in the Mediterranean, is a popular tourist resort. Noted for its rocky shores and mountain scenery, the island also boasts a natural wonder underfoot—the Drach Caves.

Located near the east coast of the island with their entrance just above sea level, the caves owe their special beauty in part to connections with the sea. The series of four magnificently embellished chambers, which extend over a distance of 2.5 miles (4 kilometers), were probably dissolved from the enveloping limestone during past ice ages, when the sea level was lower than today. As the glaciers melted and sea levels rose again, water from the Mediterranean seeped into lower levels of the caves through openings dissolved in the limestone.

As a result the caves include a number of subterranean lakes. Mirrored in the lakes—and redoubling the impact—are reflections of myriads of stalactites, stalagmites, sculptured columns, and other cave formations. □

DRAGON GATE. *Liberated from the confines of the narrow gorge, the silt-laden Yellow River widens to a broad, calm stream as it continues on its seaward course across the plains.*

DRACH CAVES. *Like the frosting on cakes, undulating draperies of flowstone embellish stout stalagmites rising from the floor of a chamber in the Majorcan cavern.*

Dragon Gate

- China
- Map: page 19, M–5

High cliffs hem in the flow of the world's muddiest river on its errant journey toward the Yellow Sea.

The Hwang Ho, or the Yellow River, the second longest in China, takes a roundabout course to the sea. From its source in the Tibetan highlands to its outlet on an arm of the Yellow Sea, it flows some 3,000 miles (4,800 kilometers) across northern China. But about midway to the sea its eastward course is interrupted by a major detour, an enormous northward loop that adds hundreds of miles to its length.

In the area of Lanchow in northwest China, the Yellow River turns suddenly toward the north for about 550 miles (900 kilometers). Making another sharp turn, the river then flows sluggishly eastward for some 150 miles (240 kilometers) across desert plains. Finally it turns again and flows almost due south for about 450 miles (700 kilometers) before resuming its eastward journey toward the sea.

The north-to-south sector of the loop is one of the most picturesque along the river's course. Here the Yellow River flows through the heart of the Shansi Loess Plain, made up of thick, windblown deposits of yellowish silt. Easily eroded, the silt accounts for the river's name and helps make it the muddiest river in the world.

Along much of the river's southward course, it flows swiftly across rapids and through deep, steep-sided, narrow gorges. The most famous is the defile known as the Dragon Gate. Hemmed in by steep cliffs for a distance of about 12 miles (20 kilometers), the mighty river narrows to as few as 50 feet (15 meters) across. Then suddenly the gorge ends, the river abruptly broadens, and it resumes its leisurely journey toward the sea. □

Drakensberg

- Lesotho—South Africa
- Map: page 26, B–6

Resembling an impregnable fortress, sheer volcanic cliffs and craggy crests tower above the undulating coastal lowlands of southern Africa.

Fringing most of the coast of southern Africa is a narrow lowland plain that extends from its Atlantic shores around the Cape of Good Hope and north along the border of the Indian Ocean. And all along the southern perimeter of the continent, not far inland from this coastal plain, the terrain rises abruptly in a zone of cliffs and mountains that mark the edge of a broad, basinlike interior plateau.

The most impressive of all these mountainous barriers is the so-called Great Escarpment along the eastern edge of the plateau. Extending southward from Zimbabwe more or less parallel to the coast of the Indian Ocean, the escarpment's highest, most dramatic sector is known as the Drakensberg, the "Mountain of the Dragon." According to several accounts, the mountains were named for legendary flying, fire-breathing lizards that once lurked among its peaks. Others claim the mountains were so named because their craggy summits resemble the profile of a dragon's back.

The highest section of the Drakensberg is centered in Lesotho, an independent republic completely surrounded by South Africa. From South Africa's Transvaal into Cape Province, the range runs northeast to southwest for 700 miles (1,125 kilometers).

The tallest peak in the range, Thabana Ntlenyana in Lesotho, is 11,425 feet (3,482 meters) high. (The native name of this, the highest peak in all of southern Africa, oddly enough simply means "Nice Little Mountain.") Among the many other peaks exceeding 10,000 feet (3,000 meters) are

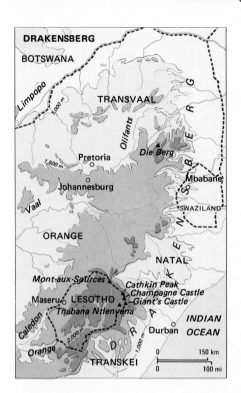

DRAKENSBERG. *Beyond peaceful cultivated plains, the imposing ramparts of the Drakensberg form the eastern boundary of a high plateau.*

DRAKENSBERG. *Torrential rains from the Indian Ocean have carved the mountains into jagged peaks separated by deep valleys and ravines.*

Champagne Castle, Giant's Castle, and Mont-aux-Sources ("Mountain of the Springs"). Other summits, not as high but with equally descriptive names, include Cathedral Peak, the Pyramid, the Bell, the Sentinel, and Rhino Horn, while another especially jagged ridge is known by a native term meaning "Place of the Little Horns."

But altitude alone does not account for the dramatic beauty of the Drakensberg. What makes the range truly breathtaking is the way the high rim of the plateau drops off to the east in nearly vertical escarpments. In some places the mountain wall plunges directly down for about 1,000 feet (300 meters). Then it continues downward in a series of broken steps for another 3,000 feet (900 meters) or so before giving way to rolling grasslands that slope eastward to the coast.

As might be expected, these variations in topography result from differences in rock structure. The under-lying foundation of the Drakensberg is a thick series of almost horizontal sandstones that were deposited between 180 and 260 million years ago. One member of the formation, known as the Cave Sandstone, is especially remarkable. Attacked by wind and water, it has been carved into a series of magnificent caves and rock shelters. And the caves are especially famous as one of the finest natural art galleries in the world: on their walls prehistoric Bushmen produced paintings by the thousands, all noted for their fine coloring and superb artistry.

The cliffs towering above this sandstone foundation, in contrast, are composed of basaltic lava flows. Beginning about 150 million years ago, lava began welling up through fissures in the rock and spreading out in horizontal layers over enormous areas. As one lava flow cooled, another fissure opened up and more molten material oozed up to the surface, sometimes forming beds as much as 165 feet (50 meters) thick. By the time this ancient series of fireworks came to an end, the sandstones were capped by a basalt plateau that in places is as much as 4,500 feet (1,370 meters) thick.

Then the weather took over and began carving its masterpiece. Even today fierce storms blowing in off the Indian Ocean drop about 80 inches (2,000 millimeters) of precipitation per year on the Drakensberg, the rocky spine of southern Africa. From the top of the plateau long rivers, especially the Orange, begin their leisurely flow westward to the Atlantic. But to the east much shorter rivers plunge rapidly downward to the Indian Ocean. Filled with rapids and waterfalls, they are the cutting tools that have dissected the volcanic rampart with the deep valleys and gorges that account for the magnificent scenery abounding along the full length of the Drakensberg Range. □

Dry Falls

- United States (Washington)
- Map: page 10, D–4

Fire, ice, and water all played vital roles in creating this dried-up waterfall that once was larger and far more powerful than Niagara.

The landscape of southeastern Washington is unique—an immense lava plateau scarred by countless coulees, or dried river channels, carved long ago by running water. Largest of all is Grand Coulee, a channel once occupied by the Columbia River. Extending southwest from the river's present course, it is about 1 mile (1.6 kilometers) wide and lined by cliffs up to 1,000 feet (300 meters) high.

Grand Coulee's most spectacular feature is Dry Falls, the remnant of a vanished cataract that would dwarf Niagara Falls. Extending across the riverbed is a curving wall of cliffs 3.5 miles (5.6 kilometers) long and over 400 feet (120 meters) high—many times the width of Niagara and more than twice as high.

Formation of the plateau started about 20 million years ago. Over several million years great fissures opened repeatedly in the earth's crust and spewed out floods of lava. By the time the eruptions ended, the region was covered by layers of volcanic rock up to 6,000 feet (1,800 meters) thick. And as the lava accumulated, the Columbia River was forced to flow around the northern edge of the plateau—the same route it follows today.

Diversion of the river from this ancestral course took place during the most recent ice age. As continental glaciers advanced across the region, they dammed the river's channel near the northern end of Grand Coulee. When the great glaciers eventually retreated, floods of meltwater raged south across the plateau, scouring out the many coulees that characterize the area. The major drainage route, however, was Grand Coulee. Racing down the channel, floodwaters enlarged the riverbed and plucked out chunks of rock to form the cliffs at Dry Falls.

When the ice retreated far enough north to reopen the Columbia's original channel, it was as if a spigot had been turned off. The river returned to its present course, and Grand Coulee was left high and dry, with the falls a mere reminder of the torrents that once roared across the precipice. □

DUNAJEC GORGES. *Following a zigzag course between forested slopes and steep limestone cliffs, the Dunajec has carved deep, narrow gorges through the Pieniny Mountains.*

Dunajec Gorges

- Czechoslovakia—Poland
- Map: page 17, F–4

Rafting down the winding river, visitors are rewarded with breathtaking views at every turn.

The Dunajec is not a very long river. It is formed by the union of the Czarny (Black) Dunajec and the Bialy (White) Dunajec, two streams that originate in northeastern Czechoslovakia in the Tatra Mountains, the highest range of the Carpathians. From this beginning it covers a distance of only about 155 miles (250 kilometers) before flowing into the Vistula northeast of Cracow, Poland. Yet the river is noted for its scenic beauty, especially along its upper reaches.

Most impressive of all is the sector where the Dunajec forms the border between Czechoslovakia and Poland. Following a tortuous course, the river is hemmed in by a series of spectacular gorges as it winds through the Pieniny Mountains. Covered by forests of evergreens and beeches and capped by rocky crags, the mountains reach elevations of 3,000 feet (900 meters) and more. (The highest peak, known as the Three Crowns, is 3,222 feet, or 982 meters, high.) Within the gorge itself, the river narrows in places to as few as 50 feet (15 meters) across as it flows between limestone cliffs and abrupt slopes more than 1,000 feet (300 meters) high.

The river's winding course, as much as the depth of the gorges, contributes to the wild scenic beauty. In one place overlooked by the Three Crowns, for example, it meanders in a giant loop about 6 miles (10 kilometers) long; yet the straight-line distance from the beginning to the end of the loop is only about 2 miles (3 kilometers).

The course of the Dunajec River had already been established by the time the mountains were formed. As the land rose slowly upward, the river incised its channel deeper and deeper into the limestone formations, carving the steep, winding gorges that can be seen today.

The traditional—and exciting—way of exploring the gorges is aboard rafts made of planks and hewn logs that have been lashed together to form picturesque but sturdy craft. Piloted by skilled local boatmen, the rafts hurtle through the Dunajec Gorges at an astonishingly fast rate of speed. As they zigzag around the bends, visitors are rewarded with striking new vistas at every turn.

Parts of the Pieniny Mountains on both sides of the river have been set aside as Polish and Czechoslovak national parks. In addition to the scenic splendor of the mountains and gorges, the parks are noted for their unusually varied plant and animal life. Of special interest are the Polish larch, the Pieniny aster, and a wealth of other rare plants that survive in this small area and are found nowhere else in the entire world. □

Eisriesenwelt

- Austria
- Map: page 17, E–4

Eisriesenwelt—the "world of the ice giants"—is an appropriate name for the largest ice cave in the world.

Much of the interior of this cave system high in the Austrian Alps is filled with the fanciful forms of stalactites and stalagmites similar to those found in other caves. But here the contours seem to be more fluid, the colors more translucent. The reason? In this case the underground formations are composed not of minerals but of ice. In fact Eisriesenwelt, the largest cave system in Austria, is also the largest permanently ice-filled cave in the entire world.

The caves were formed millions of years ago at a time when the climate of Europe was much warmer than today. Mildly acidic water flowing through cracks in the beds of limestone that form much of this part of the Alps gradually dissolved the rock and enlarged the openings to form the present labyrinth of interconnected passageways and chambers.

Now that the climate is cooler, precipitation in the area remains fairly high, and rainwater still seeps into the cave through cracks and porous areas in the limestone. Since the temperature in the cave remains at or near freezing all year round, water dripping from the ceiling solidifies into immense icicles, similar to stalactites. Drops falling to the floor freeze, to form spirelike stalagmites. In some places ice stalactites and stalagmites have joined into large floor-to-ceiling fluted pillars. Elsewhere remarkably beautiful frozen ramparts, cascades, domes, towers, colonnades, draperies, needles, and even curious ice formations that resemble fur all contribute to the fairyland atmosphere of the underground chambers. Although the temperature rises slightly in summer, it does not become warm enough to melt much of the ice, and the formations remain year after year.

The mysteries of Eisriesenwelt were not discovered until 1879. Subsequent exploration revealed that the cave system extends over a total distance of some 26 miles (42 kilometers). Now developed for tourism, the cave, with its entrance perched 3,300 feet (1,000 meters) above the valley floor, is accessible by cable car. Beyond the entrance visitors discover an artfully illuminated, shimmering fantasyland of ice sculptures on a mammoth scale. □

EISRIESENWELT. *In the frigid depths of the Austrian cave, dripping water has frozen into fanciful forms resembling giant sculptures.*

Elbrus, Mount

- U.S.S.R.
- Map: page 18, F–4

The highest peak in the Caucasus— and in all of Europe—is a youthful volcanic cone atop an ancient base.

Dramatically overshadowing all its neighboring peaks in the Caucasus, the rugged mountain barrier extending from the Black Sea to the Caspian, is Mount Elbrus. Its characteristic double cone, perpetually mantled by a blanket of ice and snow, culminates at 18,481 feet (5,633 meters) above sea level, making it the highest mountain in the Caucasus and in all of Europe.

The underlying core of Mount Elbrus consists of ancient folded basement rock that was formed about 250 million years ago. But the bulk of the mountain, towering more than 5,000 feet (1,500 meters) above its neighbors, is a geologically youthful volcanic cone that began forming only 2.5 million years ago. Although the volcano is now dormant, it was active as recently as 1,500 years ago. And the mountain still retains volcanic characteristics: its eastern slopes are dotted with fumaroles—vents that emit sulfurous gases and steam.

The majestic, snowy summit, an imposing sight from any angle, is also a mecca for mountain climbers and skiers. From hotels and camps located in the beautiful coniferous forests that cover the lower slopes, visitors set out year round to explore this major outdoor-sports area of the Caucasus.   □

Elgon, Mount

- Kenya—Uganda
- Map: page 26, C–2

Towering above the plains and plateaus of East Africa is one of the world's highest volcanoes.

The immense, gently sloping hulk of Mount Elgon, rising high astride the border of Kenya and Uganda just north of Lake Victoria, is not a perfect volcanic cone such as Japan's Fujiyama or Mexico's Popocatepetl. Yet for sheer size it ranks among the major volcanoes of the world. Its broad base, up to 50 miles (80 kilometers) across, covers an area of 1,250 square miles (3,200 square kilometers). Its giant crater is 5 miles (8 kilometers) in di-

MOUNT ELBRUS. *Completely dominating its surroundings, the mountain's majestic, snow-covered volcanic crest towers high above the neighboring granitic peaks of the Caucasus.*

ameter and about 2,000 feet (600 meters) deep. And the highest point on the rim of the crater, known as Wagagai, reaches 14,177 feet (4,321 meters), making Mount Elgon one of the highest volcanoes in the world.

The mountain is just one of a series of volcanoes of various sizes rising above the high plateaus that border East Africa's great Rift Valley. (Notable examples along the eastern edge of the Rift Valley include Mount Kenya and Mount Kilimanjaro.) Eruptions along this great fracture zone in the earth's crust began more than 250 million years ago, and in some places volcanic activity continues to this day. Mount Elgon, however, is extinct: the last time it erupted was more than 3 million years ago.

Since that time the immense accumulations of volcanic ash and cinders have decomposed to form deep, rich soil. Precipitation is also ample. (Two rivers flowing down the slopes have

their sources in the marshy crater.) As a result the lower slopes of the mountain are quite densely populated, and farming flourishes, especially in the western valleys. Coffee and tea are major sources of income, while other crops include bananas, sorghum, millet, and corn.

A somewhat hazardous but extremely scenic highway—from Kitale, Kenya, to Mbale, Uganda—makes a giant loop around the flanks of Mount Elgon, providing spectacular mountain views. Hiking trails also lead to the summit. (Still dusted occasionally by snow, the higher elevations show signs of glaciation in the past.) In addition, portions of the slopes in Kenya are preserved in a national park where the varied wildlife ranges from elephants to elands. The high altitudes are also noted for their giant plant life, similar to that found in the Ruwenzori Range, the famed "Mountains of the Moon."   □

Emi Koussi

● Chad
● Map: page 25, E–4

The highest point in the Sahara was formed—and then partially destroyed—by the forces of volcanism.

Deserts usually evoke visions of shimmering sand dunes or bleak, windswept plains. Yet many of them also encompass lofty mountain ranges. Among the most impressive landscapes in the Sahara, for instance, is the Tibesti, a rugged expanse of volcanic peaks and sandstone massifs in the south-central part of the desert. Perhaps the most spectacular spot of all is Emi Koussi, near the southern border of the Tibesti in the north of Chad. The remains of a huge extinct volcano that reaches 11,204 feet (3,415 meters), it is the highest point in the entire Sahara.

Even more impressive, however, is the fact that the peak once was much higher than at present. Today the mountain flanks slope gradually upward on all sides, then drop off very abruptly in a jagged ring of cliffs encircling a broad central depression about 12 miles (20 kilometers) in diameter and more than 3,000 feet (900 meters) deep. (The name Emi Koussi is applied to both the highest point on the rim of the depression and the volcanic structure as a whole.) Like the basin occupied by Crater Lake in Oregon, the saucerlike depression is a caldera, caused by the collapse of the former mountaintop.

Emi Koussi came to life about 5 million years ago at the same time that many other volcanoes in the region became active. At times it erupted in violent explosions, but more often molten lava welled up from its vent in steady flows that poured down the mountainsides. Enough volcanic debris eventually accumulated to form a huge cone-shaped—but now van-

Craters and Calderas

Although craters are often thought to be characteristic volcanic features, some volcanoes lack craters and some craters are not volcanic in origin. Very fluid lava that wells up through fissures in plateau regions or through cracks in the sides of volcanoes, for instance, does not result in craters. And craterlike hollows such as Arizona's Meteor Crater were produced by the impact of meteorites.

Typical volcanic craters are steep-sided, bowl- or funnel-shaped openings at the tops of volcanic cones. Some are formed by the accumulation of ejected debris around a volcanic vent. Some are formed by explosions when bursts of lava shoot up from the vent. Others are formed by the collapse of the roof of the underlying magma chamber.

Calderas are the products of similar forces but are much larger in scale. Sometimes exceeding 12 miles (20 kilometers) in diameter, these broad, shallow basins result from destruction of the entire tops of volcanic cones. The most spectacular calderas are formed after violent explosions. When Indonesia's famous Krakatoa literally blew its top in 1883, the sound was heard 2,000 miles (3,200 kilometers) away. Oftener, however, calderas form less dramatically: because of their weight, the accumulations of material in volcanic cones simply collapse into the void of the partially emptied magma chamber below.

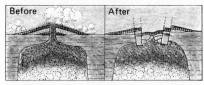

Explosion calderas form when violent eruptions expel much of the lava from the magma chamber beneath a volcano and blast huge amounts of rock from the top of the volcanic cone, causing it to cave in.

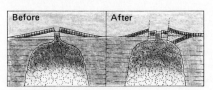

Collapse calderas result from long, slow, repeated eruptions of vast amounts of volcanic material. Eventually the massive top of the volcanic cone collapses into the partially empty magma chamber.

Some calderas are caused when a magma chamber enlarges near the earth's surface without producing an eruption. In time the roof of the chamber becomes so weakened that it collapses.

ished—peak whose dimensions can only be imagined. By that time, however, the flow of lava from beneath the earth's crust had so weakened the volcano's foundations that the top of the mountain collapsed on itself. The result was the huge saucerlike caldera that remains today.

The colossal cave-in did not mean an end to volcanic activity. Even as the center of the caldera was collapsing, lava continued to rise up and pour out through gaps along its rim. Flowing down the mountain slopes, this lava hardened into erosion-resistant rivers of rock that help preserve the

majestic contours of Emi Koussi.

Mountain building on a considerably smaller scale also continued within the caldera itself. Scattered across its floor are a number of low volcanic peaks built up by subsequent eruptions that partially filled the basin with ashes, cinders, and other debris.

Visitors standing on the rim and gazing into the vast caldera below can easily imagine the tumultuous forces that created this unusual volcano. But perhaps the best reminders of Emi Koussi's fiery past are the hot springs that still bubble forth at Yi-Yerra on the mountain's southern slopes. □

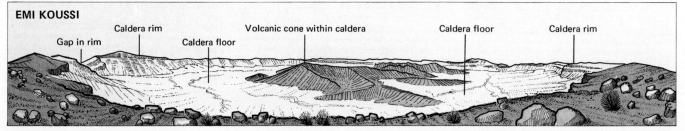

EMI KOUSSI

Gap in rim · Caldera rim · Caldera floor · Volcanic cone within caldera · Caldera floor · Caldera rim

Bleak but enormous, Emi Koussi's basinlike caldera is about 12 miles (20 kilometers) in diameter and more than 3,000 feet (900 meters) deep. As the top of the ancient volcano collapsed to form the caldera, *lava continued to well upward and escaped through gaps in the caldera's rim of jagged cliffs. Subsequent eruptions produced several minor volcanic cones within the caldera.*

ENNEDI PLATEAU. *Reared up like ancient battlements, sandstone cliffs on the plateau overlook barren valleys where few plants survive.*

Ennedi Plateau

- Chad
- Map: page 25, F–4

Dramatically eroded cliffs and gorges in the isolated upland are relics of times when the climate in the Sahara was much wetter than it is today.

Among the many uplands scattered across the Sahara is the Ennedi Plateau, located near the southeastern fringes of the desert in northern Chad. Although it is by no means the highest Saharan plateau (its highest point is only 4,756 feet, or 1,450 meters, above sea level), it is extremely picturesque. Composed of deeply dissected sandstone formations lying on top of ancient granite, the plateau covers an area of about 23,000 square miles (60,000 square kilometers).

The plateau is most impressive if approached from the southwest. One after another, the traveler passes by a succession of sheer escarpments. From the top of each row of cliffs the surface slopes gradually downward, then rises abruptly in the next wall of cliffs, forming a more or less sawtooth profile. Here and there isolated buttes rise as much as 325 feet (100 meters) above their surroundings, adding dramatic accents to the scenery. Within the tableland the sandstone has been dissected by valleys and ravines, while many of the scarps and ridges have been eroded into massifs that resemble battlements and fortresses.

Like the Ahaggar Mountains in the central Sahara, the Ennedi Plateau is underlain by granite formations more than 1 billion years old. And as in the Ahaggar, this ancient basement rock was worn down to a peneplain (a nearly flat eroded surface) by about 600 million years ago. Then, 400 to 500 million years ago, the sandstone that makes up most of the plateau was deposited on the peneplain.

The beautifully eroded landscape that remains today, however, resulted from much more recent events in the earth's history. Within the last 100 million years the surface of the plateau domed upward, while adjacent areas of the earth's surface warped downward. The once-flat surface was then subjected to renewed erosion.

The great width and depth of many of the gorges that intersect the plateau are evidence that the climate at times in the past was much wetter than today. Riverbeds that are now dry channels once were filled with raging torrents. Armed with sand grains worn from the surface of the rocks, the rushing waters became strong abrasive forces able to grind away the less resistant sandstone layers. In one valley a rocky ledge is all that remains of what once must have been a particularly beautiful waterfall. Elsewhere, in a narrow gorge, the base of a former cataract is marked by a large kettle hole, a caldronlike hollow in the rock created by stones and debris whirling in the eddy at the foot of the waterfall.

Even today the Ennedi is not completely dry; summer rainfall amounts to 8 inches (200 millimeters) and more in many places. Because the sandstone that makes up the plateau is porous, much of the water is able to seep into cracks in the rock. There it accumulates in underground reservoirs, then reemerges on the surface in numerous springs and water holes. Thus, long after the rains have passed, permanent water sources are available in many places in the plateau. Besides supporting patches of richly varied plant life, the springs provide water supplies for several thousand nomadic shepherds who inhabit the plateau. □

MOUNT EREBUS. *Towering above a perpetually frozen landscape, the volcano continues to emit jets of steam into the frigid Antarctic air.*

Erebus, Mount

- Antarctica
- Map: page 9

The only active volcano in Antarctica hurls a daily cannonade of lava "bombs" from its glaciated summit.

As head of a British expedition to Antarctica from 1839 to 1843, James Clark Ross made a number of important discoveries. Probing the frozen continent south of New Zealand, he charted an arm of the Pacific now known as the Ross Sea. At the southern margin of the sea he found an impassable barrier, an extraordinary vertical wall of ice bordering the Ross Ice Shelf. (Almost completely filling an indentation in the southern conti-nent, the great mass of ice covers an area about the size of France.) And near one end of the ice shelf he discovered an island (now called Ross Island) capped by two towering, ice-covered volcanoes.

Ross named the mountains in honor of his ships, the *Erebus* and the *Terror*. The smaller of the two, Mount Terror (10,750 feet, or 3,277 meters), is inactive; the other, Mount Erebus (13,202 feet, or 4,024 meters), remains active to this day. Elsewhere on Antarctica there are many extinct volcanoes that probably were active within the past 10,000 years or so, and geyser activity of volcanic origin has been noted in a few other places. But only Mount Erebus remains in active eruption, providing a unique spectacle of fire and ice in the coldest region on earth.

The volcano's crater, emerging from a sheath of ice, is about 2,600 feet (800 meters) in diameter. Cupped within the crater is a lava lake, a bubbling pool of fluid molten lava. Near the margins are several minor cones that erupt two or three times a day, hurling "bombs" of cooling lava through the air. Geysers also are active near the rim of the crater. Found where steam escapes from subterranean pockets, their vents are ringed by high tower-like walls of ice. Elsewhere the escaping gases have hollowed out intriguing ice caves.

Although Mount Erebus was first climbed in 1908, it remains difficult to approach. Even so, scientists continue to scale its flanks in attempts to unravel some of the unsolved mysteries of Antarctica. □

Etna, Mount

- Italy
- Map: page 17, E–5

No one knows the number of times Mount Etna, the most famous volcano in Italy, has erupted—and it still shows no signs of stopping.

Viewed from the Gulf of Catania off the east coast of Sicily, the gently sloping profile of Mount Etna is deceptive in its simplicity. The broad, often snowcapped cone is not only the highest and one of the oldest active volcanoes in Europe; it is also one of the most complex. Ever since its birth about 2½ million years ago, the volcano has had more than one active center of eruption. Today hundreds of secondary cones and craters dot its slopes, and in 1979 a new opening began emitting lava, ash, and smoke.

Mount Etna's highest point at present is about 10,700 feet (3,260 meters) above sea level, but its height varies with time. A century ago the summit

was more than 165 feet (50 meters) higher than it is today. Some 93 miles (150 kilometers) in circumference, the tremendous heap of volcanic debris covers an area about half the size of Rhode Island.

The first eruptions of Mount Etna took place beneath the sea. Still more volcanoes formed as upheavals in the earth's crust lifted the mountain's foundation of sedimentary rock above sea level. The structure seen today was built up by two major ancestral volcanoes, one of which ultimately reached about the same height as the present summit.

Weakened by repeated eruptions, however, the top of each of these volcanoes eventually caved in on itself, leaving a very large saucer-shaped depression known as a caldera. But the mountain building had not yet ended. Renewed eruptions filled in the calderas and rebuilt the uppermost cone to its present height. Even today, intermittent activity suggests that the complex, fascinating mountain will continue to grow and change. □

MOUNT ETNA. *Vapor wreathes the peak, as seen from an ancient theater. The Greek poet Aeschylus, who once lived in Sicily, wrote of a major eruption in 475 B.C.*

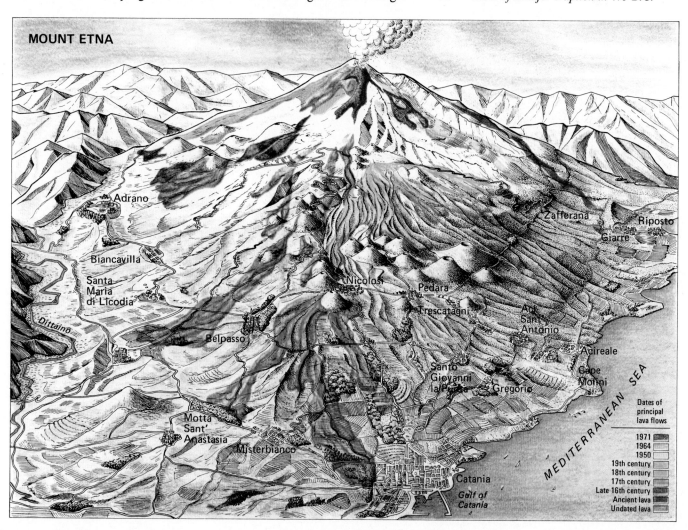

MOUNT ETNA

Adrano
Biancavilla
Santa Maria di Licodia
Dittaino
Belpasso
Nicolosi
Pedara
Trescatagni
Aci Sant' Antonio
Zafferana
Giarre
Riposto
Acireale
Cape Molini
Motta Sant' Anastasia
Misterbianco
Santo Giovanni la Punta
Gregorio
Catania
Gulf of Catania
MEDITERRANEAN SEA

Dates of principal lava flows

1971
1964
1950
19th century
18th century
17th century
Late 16th century
Ancient lava
Undated lava

Étretat, Cliffs of

- France
- Map: page 17, D–4

The cliffs of chalk overlooking the English Channel have inspired generations of artists and writers.

Just north of the port of Le Havre at the mouth of the Seine is the little town of Étretat. Once a tranquil fishing village, it is now an elegant resort noted for its splendid coastline. On both sides of town the scalloped shores of the English Channel are bordered by vertical cliffs up to 300 feet (90 meters) high. Here and there headlands have been undercut to form arches, while offshore one spire known as L'Aiguille—"the Needle"—rises 230 feet (70 meters) above the sea.

Capped by reddish-brown clay deposits, the cliffs are composed of chalk (a very soft type of limestone) that was formed at the same time as the famous white cliffs at Dover on the opposite side of the Channel. Wave erosion carved the cliffs, and surf breaking at their bases continues to alter their contours today. Armed with stones and pebbles, the surging water gradually enlarges crevices in the soft rock to form hollows and caves. With their foundations weakened, sections of the cliffs then collapse, and the debris is washed away by the sea.

The result is a sea-carved coastline of exceptional beauty, with towering cliffs, narrow headlands, coves, and fragile arches. Described by Guy de Maupassant and painted by Claude Monet, the cliffs are celebrated for the subtle variations in color and the interplay of light and shadow that result from differing lighting conditions. □

CLIFFS OF ÉTRETAT. *Whipped up by storms, the tranquil sea at times becomes a powerful cutting tool that undermines the cliffs and reshapes their picturesque contours.*

Everest, Mount

- China—Nepal
- Map: page 20, C–2

The highest point on the planet was formed millions of years ago in a massive collision of continents.

For many years the highest mountain in the world was thought to be much lower than it actually is. Its existence in the northernmost range of the Himalayas had been known for countless decades by local mountaineers, but the peak was almost completely hidden by the nearby summits, which appeared taller. While reviewing old data in 1852, a British surveyor discovered that the mountain was actu-

MOUNT EVEREST. *The mountain's jagged, ice-carved summit looms against the sky above the debris-covered surface of a massive glacier.*

ally higher than any of its neighbors.

The peak was known on maps simply as XV until 1865, when it was named in honor of Sir George Everest, a former surveyor general of India. Almost another century passed before its precise height was determined, however: earlier readings had been thrown off by the effect of the mountain's own gravitational force, by the changing snow levels on the mountain, and by the bending of light rays by the atmosphere during sightings. Eventually, with modern equipment, the height was established as 29,028 feet (8,848 meters); and even this measurement may prove in time to be slightly inaccurate.

Like much of the rest of the Himalayas, Mount Everest was thrust up

millions of years ago when movements in the earth's crust caused the Indian subcontinent to collide with Asia. Deep layers of rock were folded and refolded, creating great peaks. Further modeling by the erosive action of wind, rain, snow, and ice—especially in the form of glaciers—honed the peak to its present contours.

Several large glaciers still occupy the rugged valleys radiating from the mountaintop. Because of extremely low temperatures, the vast snowfields on the mountain's upper slopes do not compact into ice, as do most other deep mountain snowfields. The glaciers around Mount Everest are fed mainly by avalanches, which occur frequently enough to keep the glaciers creeping slowly but steadily down-

slope. Thick sheets of ice extend far down the surrounding valleys.

The peak itself is often covered with snow or obscured by clouds during the summer monsoon season, but during the winter it may be swept free of snow by frequent gale-force winds. And it is virtually devoid of any signs of life. In addition to the fierce winds, temperatures in this extremely inhospitable environment are nearly always below freezing. Since the mountain extends about two-thirds of the way through the earth's atmosphere, moreover, little oxygen is available in the thin air on the mountaintop.

Even so, Mount Everest has been an irresistible lure to mountain climbers ever since its preeminent height was known. In 1921 the Dalai Lama, the

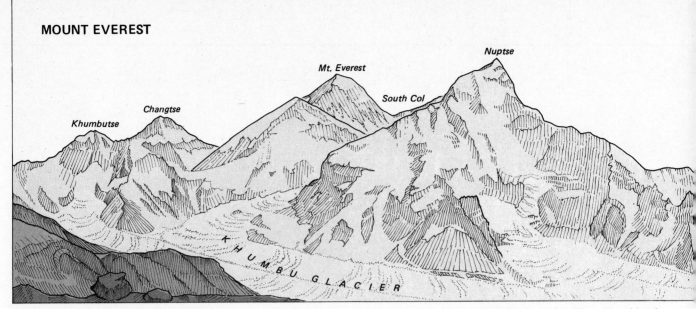

MOUNT EVEREST

Khumbutse

Changtse

Mt. Everest

South Col

Nuptse

KHUMBU GLACIER

A panoramic drawing shows Mount Everest, in the distance, and neighboring peaks of the Great Himalayas on the China-Nepal border as seen from the northwest. The red line on the map (right) indicates the approximate limits of the panorama.

ruler of Tibet, first allowed climbers access to the northern ridge. The British Mallory expedition, in the first attempt to scale the peak, reached an elevation of 22,900 feet (6,980 meters). The next year seven porters died in another futile attempt by Mallory to reach the top. A third expedition, in 1924, reached 28,126 feet (8,573 meters); and Mallory and another climber, Andrew Irvine, continued upward, "going strong for the top." As a fellow expedition member watched through binoculars, both men disappeared in the mist and were never seen again. Nine years later one of their ice axes was found, rusted and buried in the snow about 1,000 feet (300 meters) below the summit. But no one knows if they ever reached the top.

After many more attempts to scale Everest, another British expedition struck out from its base camp in 1953 accompanied by experienced Sherpa mountaineers. Late in May two of the party's strongest climbers, Edmund Hillary, a New Zealander, and the Sherpa Tenzing Norkay, set out alone for the summit with oxygen-breathing equipment strapped to their backs. Chipping steps in the ice, Hillary began to wonder how long the two could keep up what he called "the grim struggle." At last, on May 29, he was surprised to see a narrow ridge leading to the snowy summit. "A few more whacks of the ice ax," he later wrote, "and we stood on top." Men had conquered the highest mountain in the world. □

Everglades

- United States (Florida)
- Map: page 11, E–6

Part prairie, part jungle, and part flowing water, Florida's "river of grass" is an unmatched paradise.

Much of the lower part of the Florida peninsula, from Lake Okeechobee south to Florida Bay, forms the bed of one of the most unusual rivers in the world. Extremely broad, shallow, and covered by a film of water flowing almost imperceptibly toward the sea, the "river" covers some 4,000 square miles (10,500 square kilometers)—an area about twice the size of Delaware. Although the region is dotted with small wooded islands and fringed by mangrove swamps along the coast, most of it is a vast waterlogged prairie laced with a maze of ponds and open channels. Native Americans called it Pa-hay-okee, the "grassy river"; modern man calls it the Everglades.

The region, like the rest of the Florida peninsula, is underlain by a foundation of ancient volcanic and metamorphic rock. Submerged time and again beneath the sea over the course of tens of millions of years, the basement rock was covered by layer upon layer of sediments (mostly the remains of marine animals) that were compacted into limestone.

The most recent changes in sea level resulted from the repeated advances and retreats of continental glaciers

during the Ice Age. When the glaciers advanced, large amounts of water were locked up in the form of ice, and sea levels all around the world were lowered. When the glaciers retreated, meltwater raised sea levels.

With the last retreat of the glaciers, the Florida peninsula assumed more or less its present contours about 6,000 years ago. The southern part of the state now resembles a broad, shallow limestone trough, bounded by a low ridge along the Atlantic Coast and a slight rise in elevation along the Gulf Coast. The entire intervening depression, moreover, is tilted slightly toward the south.

This trough forms the bed of the Everglades, sometimes known as the "river of grass." The water supply that feeds it is the 60 inches (1,500 millimeters) or more of rain that falls each year on Florida. Runoff water from as far away as the central part of the state, well to the north of Lake Okeechobee, is funneled southward across the Everglades as it flows slowly toward the sea.

Because of the Everglades' wetness and flatness (the highest "hills" measure only about 10 feet, or 3 meters), slight differences in elevation result in profound changes in scenery. Low coastal areas where fresh water mingles with the sea are covered by dense, tangled forests of mangroves. Inland, shallow freshwater ponds often support stands of immense bald cypress trees, which, like the mangroves, are adapted for growing with their roots

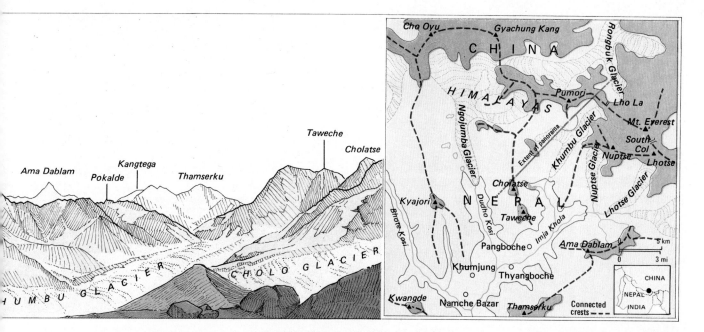

permanently submerged under water.

Islands of higher ground, in contrast, support entirely different sorts of trees. Some are covered by pine groves. Others, known locally as bayheads, rise as low mounds of bays, hollies, and other types of trees found throughout the southeastern states. Most impressive of all are the so-called hammocks—junglelike forests that include many tropical species of trees, their branches tufted with dense growths of orchids, ferns, bromeliads, and other exotic air plants.

But most of the Everglades is overgrown with prairies of sawgrass, a type of sedge named for the serrated edges of its tall grasslike leaves. Covered by a film of water for at least part of the year, these flat, seemingly endless expanses of rippling sawgrass are interrupted only by sloughs (natural drainage channels of open water), ponds (some of them created by alligators wallowing in the mucky soil), and here and there low islands of trees.

The most remarkable feature of the Everglades, however, is the spectacular concentrations of wildlife that flourishes there—particularly in the southernmost sector, which has been set aside as Everglades National Park. The most conspicuous residents there are birds—some 300 species in all—including spoonbills, herons, egrets, pelicans, anhingas, ibises, and scores more. Other creatures range from otters to alligators, turtles, and tree frogs. Like the vegetation, all depend on the steady flow of life-giving water that streams slowly southward across Florida's unique river of grass. ☐

EVERGLADES. *Here and there, low islands of palmettos and other trees punctuate the sodden, prairielike expanses of sawgrass that cover much of Everglades National Park.*

143

LAKE EYRE. *Cupped in a basin amid barren desert plains, the lake is covered from time to time by a shimmering film of salty water.*

Eyre, Lake

- Australia
- Map: page 22, D–4

Appearing and disappearing like a strange mirage, the lake in the Australian desert fills with water only after infrequent rainstorms.

Surrounded by a number of smaller ephemeral salt lakes, Lake Eyre is fed by the intermittent flow of rivers that drain a huge, arid Australian desert basin.

Australia's largest lake, and one of the largest in the world, is also one of the strangest. More often than not its bed is completely dry—a desolate expanse of mud covered with a crust of salt that one observer likened to "a vast white prostrate giant." Only after rare floods is its basin even partially filled with water. Since its discovery in 1840, in fact, Lake Eyre has been completely filled only twice. And both times, within a couple of years, its basin was bone-dry once again.

The lake covers an area of about 3,600 square miles (9,300 square kilometers), making it roughly half the size of North America's Lake Ontario. It is divided into two unequal segments—Lake Eyre North and much smaller Lake Eyre South—connected by a narrow corridor known as the Goyder Channel. With its bottom extending as far as 39 feet (12 meters) below sea level, it occupies the lowest part of a huge inland drainage basin with no outlet to the sea. (The lake's total drainage basin of about 500,000 square miles, or 1,300,000 square kilometers, is nearly twice the size of Texas.) The drainage basin was created by a downwarping of the earth's crust, while the lake itself was subsequently deepened by wind erosion.

The reasons for the ephemeral nature of Lake Eyre are fairly simple. Though vast, its drainage basin occupies one of the hottest, driest parts of Australia's great interior desert—the island-continent's so-called hot red center. Rainfall averages a meager 5 inches (125 millimeters) per year. The potential evaporation rate in the hot, dry air, in contrast, is up to 120 inches (3,050 millimeters) per year. Thus runoff water flowing down major tributaries such as the Diamantina and Cooper rivers usually vanishes before it even reaches Lake Eyre. For a good part of the time their channels are simply dry riverbeds snaking between desert dunes.

Only after extraordinarily intense rainfall—sometimes in distant parts of the drainage basin—does the lake become even partially covered by a film of water. Before long (often within a few days or weeks) the water evaporates again, and dissolved salts that were washed in from the surrounding areas are deposited once more on the surface. (The thickest crusts of salt—up to 15 inches, or 40 centimeters—are found in low-lying Madigan Gulf and Belt Bay.)

An exception occurred in 1949–50, when torrential rains filled the lake to depths of nearly 13 feet (4 meters) for the first time in recorded history. By 1952, however, the lake was completely dry. In 1974 the lake was filled once again, this time to depths of up to 20 feet (6 meters). And once again evaporation began to drain Australia's largest and most elusive lake. □

F

Fachoda Falls

- French Polynesia
- Map: page 9

On an idyllic tropical island, a slender plume of water leaps across the face of a mossy lava ledge.

FACHODA FALLS. *In a secluded valley high on a forested mountainside, the glistening waterfall cascades into a natural bathing pool hollowed out by the falling water.*

Although the South Pacific island of Tahiti covers only 400 square miles (1,000 square kilometers), it abounds in rivers and waterfalls. The exposed, much-eroded tips of two adjoining volcanoes that rise 7,333 feet (2,235 meters) above the sea, the island is drenched by up to 100 inches (2,550 millimeters) of rain per year. Hence the luxuriant vegetation that covers the rugged slopes. And hence the many rivers that radiate from the central peaks, tumbling down steep valleys and across the edges of lava beds in rapids and cascades.

Among the most impressive of all Tahiti's cataracts is Fachoda Falls on the Fautaua River near the capital, Papeete. Located in an exceptionally idyllic setting, the falls are just upstream from a shallow natural bathing pool, the Bain Loti. Beyond the pool the narrow valley is enclosed by a semicircular cliff, where the plume of water cascades down for a total distance of 1,000 feet (300 meters). Especially after heavy rains, the ribbon of water leaps down the cliff in a single sparkling jet of silvery spray. □

Fingal's Cave

- United Kingdom (Scotland)
- Map: page 16, C–3

This remarkable grotto seems to resound with music as the swirling sea rushes through its depths.

Staffa is just a little island in northwestern Scotland, a projection of rock dwarfed by larger neighbors in the Hebrides islands such as the Isle of Skye. Yet in few places on earth are there such spectacular seaswept caves, each with walls made of long, angular, astonishingly symmetrical columns of volcanic rock.

Fingal's Cave, named for a legendary third-century giant who defended the islands against seaborne raiders, is the most famous of these marine grottoes. Its sides, its roof, and its submerged floor are all composed of column after column of gray-black basalt; some of these pillars have five sides, most have six, few have more. The roof of the cave rises 60 feet (18 meters) above the sea; the cavern itself

FINGAL'S CAVE. *Dramatic pillars of basalt line the entrance to the famous Scottish cavern, testimony to the power of volcanoes and the relentless fury of the sea.*

CERRO FITZ ROY. *Sheer-walled and majestic, the massive peak (center) is a supreme challenge to mountaineers; it was not scaled until 1952.*

stretches back into the coastal cliff for more than 200 feet (60 meters).

Surging back into the depths of the opening, seawater seems to sing or chant out with a rhythmic harmony. In fact the sound inspired both the Gaelic name of the cave (Llaimh binn, which means "Cave of Music") and the famous 1830 *Hebrides Overture* by the celebrated German composer Felix Mendelssohn.

Like the other Hebridean islands, Staffa was once the scene of intense volcanic activity, which brought large amounts of molten basalt to the surface. Upon cooling, the basalt contracted and split into the long prism-like shapes we see today.

Similar basaltic columns can be seen in other Staffa grottoes. (In some of them the columns are twisted into weird convoluted shapes.) Even more impressive than these is the famous Giant's Causeway, an extraordinary grouping of steplike columns some 75 miles (120 kilometers) across the sea in Northern Ireland. ☐

Fitz Roy, Cerro

- Argentina—Chile
- Map: page 15, B–7

The awesome granite spire crowns a cluster of some of the most distinctive peaks in the Andes.

Rearing up against the sky near the southernmost tip of South America is a cluster of sheer-walled granite needles, pinnacles, and spires. Although this, the Fitz Roy Massif, is by no means the highest mountain group in the Andes, it is certainly among the most dramatic. Towering above permanent ice fields near their base, the jagged summits culminate at 11,073 feet (3,375 meters) in the massive tower known as Cerro Fitz Roy.

The mountains' magnificent contours, however, are frequently hidden from view. Lashed by fierce winds and exposed to freezing temperatures even during midsummer, the summits are often hidden in clouds. The peaks, in fact, were long thought to be volcanoes, and the clouds, steam from eruptions.

Yet the mountains, which now rise so high above the Argentine pampas to the east, actually began their existence far underground. Hundreds of millions of years ago, a mass of molten material welled upward into overlying rock layers, then cooled and hardened into granite. Subsequent uplift and removal of the overlying rocks by erosion gradually exposed the intruded mass of granite, known as a batholith.

In the process of cooling and uplift, the batholith developed a series of intersecting, nearly vertical cracks or fractures. The unique pinnacles and spires that now crown the massif resulted in part from movements along these fractures. Erosion, especially by long cycles of repeated freezing and thawing during the recent ice ages, further accentuated the mountains' contours. And even today, in this frigid region, glaciers continue to gnaw away at the massif. ☐

Formentor, Cape

- Spain
- Map: page 17, D–5

On the Mediterranean island of Majorca, a rugged mountain range ends abruptly in a spectacularly beautiful limestone headland.

At the northeastern tip of Majorca, largest of the Balearic Islands, a picturesque peninsula juts boldly into the azure Mediterranean. According to many seasoned travelers, it encompasses some of the most beautiful seascapes in the world. In some places the cape's weathered limestone cliffs plunge straight down to the crashing sea. Elsewhere the cliffs border narrow golden beaches, while in still other places scented pine forests cover gentler slopes from the cape's mountainous backbone to the water's edge.

The Northern Sierra, the mountain chain that terminates at Cape Formentor, forms a barrier all along Majorca's northern coast. The mountains are composed mostly of limestone that formed on the bottom of the ancestral Mediterranean some 250 million years ago. The gradual collision of two of the immense plates that make up the earth's crust—those comprising southern Europe and northern Africa—elevated the sedimentary beds far above sea level about 40 million years ago. Later crustal movements separated the Balearic Islands from the mainland and from each other and then submerged them once again. Subsequent shifts in the earth's crust approximately 5 million years ago raised the islands to more or less their present heights.

More recently two forces have altered the contours of Majorca—and Cape Formentor. The island has been slowly subsiding, and at the same time sea levels have risen because of the melting of continental glaciers at the end of the last ice age. The result on Majorca is what geologists call a drowned coastline. Waves now lap at the faces of cliffs that once stood above sea level, and the ocean has invaded once-dry valleys to form picturesque, fjordlike inlets known as rias.

Despite these changes, Cape Formentor still rises dramatically above the sea. Near its tip a lighthouse stands atop a cliff about 690 feet (210 meters) high. It is an excellent vantage point for viewing the cape, the slopes and whitewashed villages inland on Majorca, and on a clear day the neighboring island of Minorca some 25 miles (40 kilometers) to the east across the blue Mediterranean. □

CAPE FORMENTOR. *Majorca's craggy, pine-dotted peninsula seems to grasp at the placid Mediterranean with lofty limestone fingers.*

Fouta Djallon

- Guinea
- Map: page 24, B–4

Three of West Africa's major rivers originate in the dramatic highlands of the Fouta Djallon.

Not far from the Atlantic shores of Guinea, on the great bulge of West Africa, the low coastal plain gives way abruptly to a broad inland plateau. This highland massif, known as the Fouta Djallon, covers an area of some 30,000 square miles (78,000 square kilometers) and is the most prominent upland in West Africa.

It is not especially high. The average elevation is only about 3,000 feet (900 meters), and the highest point, Mount Loura, reaches up only 4,970 feet (1,515 meters). Even so, the Fouta Djallon landscape is extraordinarily dramatic.

Composed of thick sandstone formations that overlie ancient granitic basement rock, the massif is crisscrossed by a dense network of streams and rivers. Vigorous erosion has resulted in a multitude of deep canyons and broad valleys, which in many places are bordered by steep escarpments. Often turning at nearly right angles, the rivers have deeply dissected the great massif and carved it up into a series of broad tablelands that tower majestically above the intervening valleys.

In addition to a number of short rivers that rush directly west into the Atlantic, the Fouta Djallon gives rise to the three major rivers of western Africa. The Senegal and Gambia rivers flow northward across rolling terrain toward the Atlantic. Still other headwater streams find their way into the great Niger (the continent's third longest river), which flows inland across West Africa in a long, broad arc before finally emptying into the Gulf of Guinea. □

FOUTA DJALLON. *A network of rushing rivers has carved the West African massif into a series of picturesque plateaus and towering uplands capped with sheer sandstone cliffs.*

Franz Josef Glacier

- New Zealand
- Map: page 23, H–6

Like a living thing, the glacier's snout alternately advances and retreats over the course of time.

Beyond a narrow strip of coastal lowland along the western shores of New Zealand's South Island, a towering wall of mountains rears against the sky. The Southern Alps, as they are called, include the highest peak in New Zealand, Mount Cook, which reaches 12,349 feet (3,764 meters).

Because of abundant precipitation throughout the year, the mountains are capped with eternal ice and snow, and glaciers stream down their sides. The lower slopes, in striking contrast, are cloaked with luxuriant fern-filled subtropical rain forests.

To preserve a portion of this magnificent alpine scenery, Westland National Park was established on the mountains' western slopes. A superb blend of mountains, forests, lakes, rivers, and sparkling waterfalls, the park is also famous for its so-called twin glaciers, the Fox Glacier and the Franz Josef Glacier. (The Franz Josef was named by an explorer-geologist in honor of the emperor of his native Austria-Hungary.)

Though the Fox Glacier is slightly longer, the Franz Josef is more dramatic in its steep descent. It is also very accessible, with a road leading almost up to its snout. And of all New Zealand's glaciers, it has been the most thoroughly studied because of the pulsing rhythms of its periodic advances and retreats.

The glacier originates in snowfields perched on the mountain slopes at an elevation of about 8,850 feet (2,700 meters). A tongue of ice about 1,600 feet (500 meters) wide, it descends downslope for some 7 miles (11 kilometers) to a terminus about 1,000 feet (300 meters) above sea level.

The movement of the ice mass as it grinds down through its deep, U-shaped valley is quite rapid. Scientists have monitored its progress, but the most dramatic evidence of its downslope movement came about by accident. In November 1943 an airplane crashed on the glacier and was buried in the ice at a distance of 2.2 miles (3.5 kilometers) from its snout. Six years

Frasassi Caves

- Italy
- Map: page 17, E–4

These splendid caverns, halfway up the Italian "boot," are among the country's most beautiful.

Even the approach to the Frasassi Caves is picturesque. The road winding inland from Italy's Adriatic coast just north of Ancona follows the valley of the Esino River through a verdant landscape of gently rolling hills. But as it approaches the foothills of the Apennines, the scene changes quite dramatically. Suddenly the road is hemmed in by the towering walls of the Gola di Frasassi—the Frasassi Gorge. Flowing into the Esino is another river, the Sentito, which has carved an even narrower canyon.

A change in the underlying rocks accounts for this abrupt change in scenery. Downstream the Esino flows among hills formed of soft shales. In the gorges it has carved its route downward through massive limestone formations. And it is in these limestone formations that the Frasassi Caves are found.

The region is an example of what geologists call a karst landscape—a limestone terrain that has been modeled by the dissolving action of slightly acidic groundwater. Karst regions usually include caves, such as those at Mammoth Cave in Kentucky, as well as sinkholes, disappearing rivers, and underground streams.

Also typical of karst regions is the development of cave formations, and the Frasassi Caves are no exception. Throughout the contorted network of passageways and chambers, the interconnected system of caverns is beautifully adorned with stalactites and stalagmites of all imaginable shapes and sizes. In some places large curtainlike formations are so thin that artificial lights shine through them as they would through frosted glass. Other formations resemble alabaster, beautifully colored in rainbow hues. Built up over the course of centuries, these features, known as speleothems, were formed as the minerals dissolved in slowly dripping water were redeposited within the caves.

Perhaps the most startling portion of the Frasassi Caves is the Grotta delle Nottole, the "Cave of the Bats"; it is named for the many colonies of bats that inhabit it. But the most

FRANZ JOSEF GLACIER. *Perpetually renewed by snowfall on the mountaintop, the long narrow tongue of ice plunges abruptly down the western slopes of Mount Cook.*

and four months later the wreckage reappeared at the snout. The velocity of the ice flow in the interior of the glacier was thus found to be an astonishing 5 feet (1.5 meters) per day.

Just as impressive have been the alternating advances and retreats of the glacier's snout over the course of time. Anyone approaching the Franz Josef is sure to notice a group of large so-called *roches moutonées* in the Waiho River Valley downstream from its snout. These streamlined humpbacked, glacier-carved rock outcrops are definite evidence that the glacier

once extended much farther down the mountain than it does today.

Its retreat up the mountain has not been a steady one, however. From time to time its snout has advanced very dramatically, only to lose ground again later on. Beginning in 1965, for example, the glacier grew steadily over the course of 22 months, and its snout moved downslope a total of about 1,300 feet (400 meters). But over the long term its movement has been upslope. Since 1894 the Franz Josef Glacier has retreated a total of some 8,200 feet (2,500 meters). □

149

FRASASSI CAVES. *Delicately colored, fantastically shaped stalactites and stalagmites adorn these caves on the eastern slopes of Italy's ruggedly scenic Apennine Mountains.*

Fraser River Canyon

- Canada (British Columbia)
- Map: page 10, C–3

An otherwise peaceable river becomes a raging torrent when it plunges through the canyon on its way from the Rockies to the sea.

The Fraser River is a placid, meandering stream as it flows out of the Canadian Rockies and starts on its long, circuitous course to the Pacific Ocean. Not far from its mouth, however, the river undergoes a dramatic change of character. Picking up speed, it is transformed into a roiling, turbulent mass of water as it plunges down the long, winding, steep-sided gorge it has carved through the Coast Mountains.

The Fraser River Canyon extends more or less north to south for about 100 miles (160 kilometers) through southwestern British Columbia. It begins just south of the town of Lillooet and ends at Yale, about 40 miles (65 kilometers) north of the U.S.-Canadian border. Beyond the canyon the river turns abruptly west, then resumes its leisurely pace, and finally empties into the sea a short distance south of the city of Vancouver.

Nothing in the upper reaches of the Fraser, where it emerges from the Rocky Mountains and flows quietly across the interior plateau of British

beautiful by far is the Grotta Grande del Vento, the "Great Cave of the Wind." Several of its chambers are immense—each one large enough to hold a cathedral. And many of them have been enhanced by magnificent lighting effects. Especially notable are the Sala delle Candeline, the "Room of the Candles," with its alabasterlike stalagmites, and the Sala dell'Infinito, the "Room of the Infinite," where massive, elaborately decorated columns appear to support the ceiling.

In all, the Great Cave of the Wind includes about 8 miles (13 kilometers) of long passageways. Surprisingly, this crown jewel of the Frasassi Caves was not discovered until 1971. One of its major features, the so-called Abisso Ancona or Ancona Abyss, was named in honor of the speleologists (cave explorers) from Ancona who first discovered this splendid sector of the Frasassi Caves. □

FRASER RIVER CANYON. *Deep in the canyon, the river rushes through the narrows at Hells Gate. Each year millions of salmon brave these waters to reach their spawning grounds.*

Columbia, suggests the wildness of the canyon that is to come. The chasm itself follows the line of an ancient fault (a major fracture in the bedrock) that dates back some 50 million years. As the surface of the land rose slowly in the coastal ranges, the river carved its channel ever deeper along this zone of weakness until it had carved the awesomely rugged canyon that remains today.

Along most of its length the canyon is hemmed in by steep, lofty cliffs. In some places mountains as much as 3,000 feet (900 meters) high rise up virtually from the water's edge. And the river hurtles along, in one observer's words, "frantically tearing its way in foaming whirls." At Hells Gate, where a landslide narrowed the river to a width of only 120 feet (37 meters), the water rushes by at a rate of 25 feet (8 meters) per second.

The surrounding landscape changes dramatically from one end of the canyon to the other. The northern end lies in a semiarid region where sagebrush flourishes in the hot, dry summer climate. Farther south, in contrast, rainfall is heavy, and the canyon is bordered by seemingly endless forests.

The full course of the river was first traced in 1808 by a party headed by the explorer and fur trader Simon Fraser, whose name the river still bears. Struggling through the treacherous canyon, the explorers found the Hells Gate section, in particular, to be especially challenging. "We had to pass," wrote Fraser, "where no human being should venture."

For the next half-century the river was used only by fur trappers and Indians. Then in 1857 gold was discovered along its banks just south of Yale, and a furious rush was on. Yale's population climbed to 20,000, and a narrow track called the Cariboo Road was blasted out of the canyon walls. At one spot the road builders flung a suspension bridge across the deep gorge—the first such span in western North America.

By the late 1860's, after $100 million in gold had been taken out of the area, the bonanza ran thin, and homesteaders began to replace miners on the Cariboo Road. Today two railroads as well as the Trans-Canada Highway wind through the tortuous canyon, running on beds that have been carved into the canyon walls above the river. Otherwise the Fraser River Canyon remains as wild and untamed as ever. ☐

Frauenmauer Cavern

- Austria
- Map: page 17, E–4

A limestone cave perched high in the Austrian Alps is only one part of a much larger labyrinth of dark subterranean passageways.

Local residents of the Hochschwab Alps in central Austria have known about Frauenmauer Cavern for a long time. They even use it as a shortcut through the mountain from Eisenerz to the nearby village of Tragöss—despite the sinister legends of women being turned into stone within its depths. The cave's name, in fact, means "wall of the women."

Like caves in other limestone regions throughout the world, Frauenmauer Cavern was hollowed out by slightly acidic water. Seeping through cracks in the rock, the water gradually dissolved the limestone and formed the network of passageways. Even today, water trickles down and sometimes freezes into immense icicles.

For years spelunkers, or cave explorers, suspected that Frauenmauer Cavern might be connected to other large caves in the area. Before World War II they discovered a link between it and the nearby Bärenlocheishöhle ("Bear's Den Ice Cave"). In 1961 yet another link was found: an opening in the floor of Frauenmauer Cavern plunges downward to Tropfsteinhöhle ("Dripstone Cave"), another cave system at a lower level within the limestone massif. In all, the interconnected network of caves is thought to include about 6 miles (10 kilometers) of passages. But it remains possible that further exploration will reveal still other openings, perhaps at even deeper levels beneath the surface. ☐

FRAUENMAUER CAVERN. *At almost every turn, visitors to this Alpine cave encounter mammoth icicles or ghostly forms that local legend claims are women turned to stone.*

Fuego, Montañas del

- Spain (Canary Islands)
- Map: page 24, B–3

On the so-called Mountains of Fire, active and extinct craters pockmark a stark moonscape of ashes, cinders, and lava fields.

Lanzarote, the easternmost of the Canary Islands, lies only about 75 miles (120 kilometers) off the coast of Morocco in northwestern Africa. Swept by hot, dry Saharan winds, some parts of the island have a rather African look, with palm groves, oases, and desertlike areas. But much of it looks more like the surface of the moon.

The most forbidding area, in the southwestern part of the island, is known as the Montañas del Fuego, "the Mountains of Fire." Scattered over some 75 square miles (200 square kilometers) are more than 300 volcanic cones. Some are extinct, others erupt from time to time, and all are virtually devoid of vegetation.

Like the rest of the Canary Islands, the Azores, and the nearby island of Madeira, Lanzarote was built up by eruptions of submarine volcanoes. In Lanzarote, however, the process of creation seems to be still under way. Major eruptions between 1730 and 1736 and again in 1824 covered large areas with lava and cinders. In some places black basaltic lava flows have

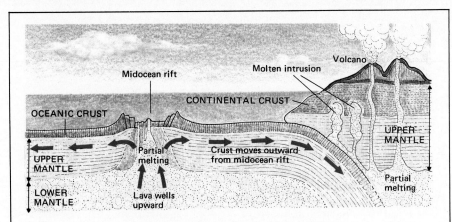

Volcanoes and the Spreading of the Ocean Floor

Some volcanoes result from movements of the oceanic crust. Along midocean rifts, molten material wells up from the mantle and is incorporated in the crust. As the oceanic crust gradually spreads out from the rift in opposite directions like giant conveyor belts (red arrows), this new material is constantly added. Where the spreading ocean floor comes into contact with an island chain, such as Japan, or a continent, it is sucked back (subducted), plunging down into the mantle. Stresses at such subduction zones cause the melting of the crust and upper mantle. This results in volcanoes when the lava escapes through fissures to the earth's surface.

solidified into intricately twisted ropy patterns. Elsewhere great expanses of cinders and ash are strewn with explosively ejected boulders known as volcanic bombs. And even today some of the craters emit jets of steam and periodically spew out fiery ash.

But the most startling evidence of continuing volcanism lies directly underfoot. In some parts of the Mountains of Fire, the soil temperature is as high as 285° F (140° C), while 20 inches (50 centimeters) below the surface it is as hot as 570° F (300° C). In such places it is possible to cook an egg or boil water in just a few minutes.

Despite an arid climate, farmers manage to raise crops in Lanzarote's mineral-rich volcanic soil. Grapes are planted in funnel-shaped pits so that their roots can reach underground moisture while the vines are protected from drying winds. Grains and other crops are grown on layers of fertile cinders that help conserve the moisture from infrequent showers. □

MONTAÑAS DEL FUEGO. *Numerous volcanic cones composed of accumulations of cinders and ash dot this desolate, still-active volcanic area.*

FUJIYAMA. *A splendid sight in every season, the tallest mountain in Japan has inspired generations of painters and poets.*

Fujiyama

- Japan
- Map: page 19, O–5

Famed for its nearly perfect symmetry, Fujiyama lies atop the remains of older volcanoes.

Among the world's most symmetrical volcanic cones, Fujiyama has always been dear to the hearts of the Japanese people. Lovely when viewed from any angle and at every season of the year, its soaring profile provides a continually changing spectacle. For centuries poets have sung its praises, and painters have striven to capture the beauty of its form. Tourists come by the tens of thousands to relax in the nearby resorts and to make the long pilgrimage to the top.

Located about 60 miles (100 kilometers) from Tokyo on the southern coast of Honshu, Fujiyama is impres-

sive for its size as well as its beauty. Rising from a plain that is not much above sea level, the slopes of the highest mountain in Japan taper up to a height of 12,388 feet (3,776 meters). Its base, nearly circular in form, is about 25 miles (40 kilometers) in diameter. The mountain culminates in a crater 2,300 feet (700 meters) wide.

According to legend, Fujiyama first appeared in 286 B.C., when the surface of the earth opened up and formed Lake Biwa, the largest lake in Japan; material displaced from this enormous trench, in turn, was piled up to form the mountain. In fact Fujiyama is what geologists call a stratovolcano. It was built up of alternating layers of molten lava flows and explosively ejected cinders, ash, and pellets of lava.

The apparent simplicity of Fujiyama's slopes actually masks a rather complex history. Buried beneath the imposing mass are remnants of much

older volcanoes that had been eroded before they were buried by outpourings from present-day Fujiyama. The craters of two of them—massive Old Fuji and smaller Komi-Take—are partially exposed on Fujiyama's slopes.

Fujiyama itself has a long recorded history of activity, with major eruptions known from as far back as A.D. 800. The most recent eruption, in 1707, covered the land as far away as Tokyo with volcanic ash and cinders. But today the mountain seems peaceful and serene. Venerated as a dwelling place of the gods, it continues to inspire all who view its majestic form.□

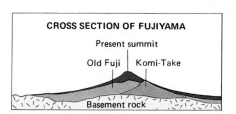

CROSS SECTION OF FUJIYAMA

153

G

Ganges Delta

- Bangladesh—India
- Map: page 20, D–2

Floods caused by fearsome storms sometimes threaten the inhabitants of the largest delta in the world.

To the Hindus of India the Ganges is a sacred river, and there are many holy sites along its banks. But to the inhabitants of the river's heavily populated delta in the Indian state of West Bengal and the neighboring Moslem nation of Bangladesh, its significance is more mundane and practical. Sediments deposited by the river's recurrent floods make the delta's land extremely fertile and provide the basis for their livelihood—agriculture.

As a result of an annual rainfall that ranges from 60 to 100 inches (1,500 to 2,500 millimeters), the extent of the seasonal flooding that occurs on the Ganges delta is quite extraordinary. During the spring (April through June) floods and the summer (June to October) monsoon season, the entire delta becomes a virtual lake, interrupted here and there by islands of slightly higher ground. During the dry season, in contrast, it is a picturesque tapestry of green fields and rice paddies speckled with innumerable ponds and accented with houses nestled in groves of bamboo, mangoes, and coconut palms. At one time the entire delta was densely forested, but now it is heavily cultivated to support the ever-growing population. The one remaining forested area is the Sundarbans region on the southern edge of the delta.

The river, which is approximately 1,550 miles (2,500 kilometers) long, flows out of the Himalayas near the Chinese border and continues, generally southwestward, through northern India. Then, in the Indian state of West Bengal, just before entering Bangladesh, it begins splitting up into the many distributary streams that flow across the delta. The most important distributary is the Hooghly River, which flows south from the apex of the delta past the city of Calcutta and into the Bay of Bengal. The Ganges itself

GANGES DELTA. *During the flood season much of the land is covered by water. Houses are built on high mounds of mud to keep them dry, and transportation is mainly by boat.*

flows into Bangladesh, where it receives the waters of the Brahmaputra, known in its lower reaches as the Jamuna. The combined Jamuna and Ganges form a new river, called the Padma, which finally empties into the Bay of Bengal.

The entire delta region extends for about 250 miles (400 kilometers) from north to south and about 200 miles (320 kilometers) from west to east, making it the largest delta in the world. Yet it is highly unstable. As the Ganges flows across the vast lowland

plains that make up much of its drainage basin of some 615,000 square miles (1.6 million square kilometers), it carries enormous quantities of sediments, then drops them again in the delta or as it enters the sea. Its total sediment load—some 2.6 billion tons (2.4 billion metric tons) per year—is greater than that carried by any other river. And it is these sediments that keep enlarging the delta and extending it in the direction of the sea.

At the same time the courses of distributaries flowing across the delta

Deltas: Changing Landforms at the Mouths of Rivers

A delta is an accumulation of sediment deposited at the mouth of a river in the sea or a lake. When the sediment-laden river reaches the sea, the velocity of its flow decreases abruptly, and the sediment is deposited on the ocean floor. There it accumulates to form low-lying, often marshy lands that gradually extend farther and farther out from shore.

Over the course of time, sediment partially blocks the main river channel, causing it to spill over its banks and branch out into numerous distributaries, which flow their separate ways to the sea.

Some of the distributaries, in turn, may become clogged with sediment, forcing new channels to form and gradually changing the shape of the delta.

Typically fan-shaped deltas like that of the Nile usually form on the coasts of shallow seas, especially where the tidal action is too weak to erode the deposits. Other rivers, such as the Amazon and the Ganges, carry such large amounts of sediment that they have created immense, extremely complex deltas even though they are confronted with strong tides, wave action, and currents.

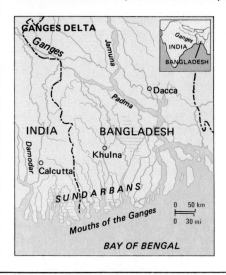

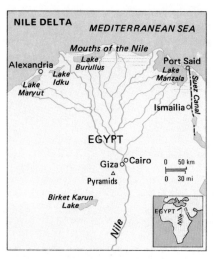

are gradually shifting eastward as a result of a slow tilting of the earth's crust. In the western section of the delta, many former river channels have become clogged with mud and are now inactive. But to the east the distributaries of the Ganges keep carving out new channels and forming new lands. The terrain is also continually being shifted around by monsoon storms.

Sediments deposited by the annual floods make the land highly fertile, and the delta is covered with a multitude of small farms. But the same natural forces that improve the land also threaten its inhabitants. During the monsoon season powerful low-pressure cyclonic storms often swirl up from the Bay of Bengal and sweep across the already submerged delta. When this happens, the sea level rises and offshore winds of up to 100 miles (160 kilometers) per hour drive salt water back up the estuaries, deepening and churning the flood. Homes, crops, and livestock disappear, and there is often a fearsome loss of life. In 1970 the storm struck with unusual force and brought death to 250,000 people. Undeterred, the survivors returned, and the next year were once again cultivating the delta. □

Gauthiot Falls

● Chad
● Map: page 24, E–5

Slowly but surely, the waterfall on a remote central African plain is migrating imperceptibly upstream.

Although not impressive for their size, volume of flow, or surroundings, Gauthiot Falls are unusual because of what might be described as their strategic location. Situated about midway along the course of the Mayo-Kebbi River in southern Chad, they form a series of cascades that tumble down for a total of about 55 feet (17 meters) through a shallow gorge that winds across a nearly flat plain.

Downstream from Gauthiot Falls the Mayo-Kebbi flows into the Benue River, a tributary of the Niger, which ultimately empties into the Atlantic Ocean. Upstream from the falls the Mayo-Kebbi has its source in a series of lakes and marshes on an immense, nearly level plain. Covered with water during the brief summer rainy season, the plain is so flat that there are no well-defined streambeds. Some of the water drains westward into the Mayo-Kebbi; some of it flows

northward into the Logone River, which empties into Lake Chad. (Like Utah's Great Salt Lake, Lake Chad lies at the heart of an enclosed drainage basin with no outlet to the sea.)

It is this poorly defined divide between the drainage systems of the Mayo-Kebbi and Logone rivers that accounts for the strategic importance of Gauthiot Falls. Like all waterfalls, Gauthiot Falls are slowly but surely eroding their way upstream. Niagara Falls, for example, are moving upstream at a rate of up to 3 feet (1 meter) per year, and geologists estimate that in about 25,000 years the falls will reach the shores of Lake Erie and drain it completely.

Filled with abrasive loads of sand and gravel, especially during the rainy season, the waters of the Mayo-Kebbi are gradually moving Gauthiot Falls closer and closer to the source of the river. Eventually, geologists speculate, Gauthiot Falls will eat their way far enough upstream to capture the entire flow of the Logone River. When that happens, the Logone's waters will be diverted from Lake Chad into the Atlantic Ocean, causing Lake Chad to shrink drastically. But as in the case of Niagara, this event is probably thousands of years away. □

Gavarnie, Cirque de

● France
● Map: page 17, D–4

The huge natural amphitheater perched high in the Pyrenees was created by Ice Age glaciers.

High on the slopes of the Pyrenees, the rugged mountain range that forms the boundary between France and Spain, is an awesome spectacle that Victor Hugo described as "the Colosseum of nature." Gouged into the mountain flanks is a cirque (an immense bowllike, glacier-carved amphitheater) of truly colossal proportions—the Cirque de Gavarnie.

More or less horseshoe-shaped in form, the great gap in the mountainside is about 2 miles (3 kilometers) wide and is bounded by sheer rocky walls that rise more than 5,000 feet (1,500 meters) above the amphitheater's rubble-strewn floor. Along the rim a series of snowcapped peaks juts up like the battlements of some giant citadel. And plunging down the walls in spring and summer are a number of tremendous waterfalls. One of them, the Grande Cascade, is the second highest waterfall in Europe: it descends in several steps for a total distance of 1,384 feet (422 meters).

The rim of the cirque forms not only an international boundary but a key watershed as well. On the Spanish side are the headwaters of the Ebro River, which flows into the Mediterranean. On the French side the waters of the Grande Cascade and several other waterfalls eventually flow into the Adour River, which empties into the Bay of Biscay on the Atlantic.

Between the peaks along the rim are a number of deep clefts, or passes. The most dramatic is the sheer-walled Brèche-de-Roland, or Roland's Pass, at 9,200 feet (2,800 meters). According to legend it was carved by the sword of Roland, the famous warrior nephew of the emperor Charlemagne.

The Cirque de Gavarnie is not the only formation of its kind in the Pyrenees; a number of lesser cirques scar the sides of mountains. But it is certainly the most spectacular. Like cirques everywhere, it is a product of glacial erosion. As glaciers creep slowly down mountain valleys, the grinding masses of ice tend to pluck out chunks of bedrock at the heads of the valleys, creating characteristic bowllike indentations.

The immense size of the Cirque de Gavarnie resulted from repeated cycles of glaciation over the past 2 million years or so. With each glacial period the rock was polished and scoured out at the head of an ancient river valley. During the warm interglacial periods, water infiltrated the rock and chiseled out parallel ravines and gullies. Then the glaciers returned, plucking out the rock between the ravines and steepening the slopes until the cirque reached its present enormous size.

Today the upper reaches of the Cirque de Gavarnie provide a haven for a great many rare plants and animals, which are protected by national parks on both sides of the Pyrenees. Martagon lilies, the so-called orchids of the Pyrenees, grow in profusion in the area's pine forests, while out on the icy slopes saxifrages and tiny cushions of alpine flowers cling tenaciously to crevices in the rocks. And up on the heights graceful, antelopelike chamois are glimpsed from time to time leaping among the crags. ☐

CIRQUE DE GAVARNIE. *Patched with snow and streaked with slender waterfalls, the rugged walls of the semicircular hollow in the mountainsides tower high above its floor.*

Geiranger Fjord

- Norway
- Map: page 16, D–2

Sheer walls, shimmering cascades, and snowy plateaus all enhance the beauty of this magnificent fjord.

Hidden away in the heart of Norway's fjord country, about 45 miles (70 kilometers) inland from the coast, is the Geiranger Fjord. An upper arm of the branching Stor Fjord system, it is not especially large—only about 9 miles (15 kilometers) long. Yet many consider it to be the most beautiful of all Norwegian fjords. A narrow cleft winding between snowcapped peaks and plateaus, its sheer rocky walls are laced with ribbonlike waterfalls and reflected in the mirrorlike water below.

Like all fjords, this splendid inland arm of the sea is the result of Ice Age glaciation. Time and again over the past 2 million years, much of Scandinavia was covered by a massive ice cap. As more and more snow and ice accumulated in the interior ice mass, glaciers streamed outward from its edges. Flowing slowly toward the sea through former river valleys, the glaciers gouged them out to form deep, narrow, steep-walled, characteristically U-shaped troughs.

Because so much water was frozen in continental ice caps, sea levels during glacial periods were much lower than today, and the bottoms of fjords lie far below present-day sea level. When the ice caps finally melted, ocean levels rose, seawater flooded into the glacier-carved troughs, and fjords were created all along the mountainous coasts of Norway, New Zealand, and other places.

In Geiranger Fjord, which curves in between picturesque snow-covered highlands, sheer cliffs as much as 1,300 feet (400 meters) high drop straight down to the water's edge. (The water, in turn, is up to 960 feet, or 290 meters, deep.) Cruise ships ply Geiranger Fjord's placid waters, providing spectacular views of the Bridal Veil, the multiple cascades of the Seven Sisters, and the many other waterfalls that plummet down the cliffs along the way. Equally impressive is the vista from Mount Dalsnibba, a vantage point nearly 5,000 feet (1,500 meters) high at the head of the fjord, overlooking the full sweep of this majestic, glacier-carved valley that has been invaded by the sea. □

GEIRANGER FJORD. *Melting snow on surrounding peaks and plateaus feeds the majestic, ribbonlike waterfalls that plunge down sheer walls along this placid inland arm of the sea.*

Geysers, Valley of the

- U.S.S.R.
- Map: page 19, Q–3

In a remote valley of Siberia, geysers erupt from the earth with a mysterious primeval rhythm.

Just west of the Aleutian Islands, the Kamchatka Peninsula juts southward from the Siberian mainland. Like most of the lands bordering the Pacific Ocean, it is a volcanically active region. Of its total of 125 volcanoes, 22 continue to erupt. And like many volcanic regions, it boasts a wealth of geysers and hot springs.

The most impressive display is in the Valley of the Geysers, which was not discovered until 1941. Some 20 geysers are scattered throughout the narrow valley, and about a dozen of them give especially notable performances: at regular intervals (from 10 minutes to 5½ hours) they erupt jets of near-boiling water and steam.

The largest one, named First Born, erupts hourly. It emits columns of water up to 40 feet (12 meters) high and spews out clouds of steam and spray that reach up 500 feet (150 meters). Throughout the valley the geysers periodically erupt, then die down, with a similar rhythm. □

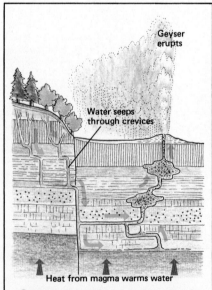

Geysers occur where magma, or molten rock, lies near the earth's surface. When water seeps underground, it is heated in fissures in the hot rock and erupts as geysers as a result of periodic buildups of steam pressure.

GHAR PARAU. *Hidden in the galleries of the remote Iranian cave are elaborate dripstone formations that resulted from the crystallization of minerals in seeping groundwater.*

Ghar Parau

- Iran
- Map: page 18, F–5

Unknown and unexplored until 1971, Asia's deepest cave penetrates a mountain range in western Iran.

The Zagros Mountains in western Iran are tall—up to 15,000 feet (4,400 meters)—and include a lot of limestone. They are just the sort of setting, a group of British speleologists, or cave explorers, concluded, that might conceal a truly deep undiscovered cave. Perhaps even the deepest cave in the world.

In August 1971, on a barren limestone massif nearly 6,600 feet (2,000 meters) above the surrounding plain, the explorers found just what they were looking for: the entrance to what appeared to be a large cave. Day after day they penetrated farther into the opening, descending deeper into the unknown. The cave, they gradually realized, resembles a giant staircase curving step by step into the depths of the mountain.

Progress into the abyss was seldom easy. The team had to climb over fallen boulders, crawl through mud in low places, and squeeze through narrow slots. They gave landmarks along the way such names as the Greasy Slab, the Muddy Squeeze, and the Corkscrew. With all the skill of mountain climbers they had to descend smooth-walled, chimneylike shafts, including one that they named the Shahanshah, with a sheer vertical drop of 138 feet (42 meters).

But there were also rewards. In places the narrow passageway opens out into grottoes and spacious galleries. Strangely beautiful stalactites, stalagmites, and other dripstone formations decorate many of the chambers and passageways. And by the time the explorers had to give up the search, they realized that they had discovered a very deep cave indeed. They had descended 2,434 feet (742 meters) below the surface of the earth.

The following summer the explorers returned, better equipped and anxious to learn what lay beyond. But they were doomed to disappointment. Not far beyond the area they had already explored, the cave comes to an abrupt dead end, with the passageway completely blocked by water. Even so, they had made an important discovery. With a total depth of 2,464 feet (751 meters), Ghar Parau is the deepest cave in Asia. And no one knows what may lie beyond its flooded end. □

Ghats, Western

- India
- Map: page 20, B–3

Along the west coast of India a formidable mountain barrier rises abruptly above the Arabian Sea.

The Western Ghats rise like an immense step along most of the western edge of the Indian peninsula. Stretching from the Tapti River north of Bombay almost to Cape Comorin at India's southern tip, the abrupt mountain range is about 1,000 miles (1,600 kilometers) long. And along the entire length of this gigantic "seawall" there is only one major break, a breach some 20 miles (30 kilometers) wide at Palghat Gap in the southern part of the range.

The Western Ghats are most impressive when viewed from the narrow, fertile coastal plain that separates them from the Arabian Sea. Forbidding slopes rise like a wall to elevations that average between 3,000 and 5,000 feet (900 and 1,500 meters). The loftiest point in peninsular India, Anai Mudi, near the southern end of the range, reaches up 8,841 feet (2,695 meters). To the east, in contrast, the mountains slope gradually downward to a gently rolling interior plateau.

The magnificent mountain wall was created by violent disturbances in the earth's crust. Some 200 million years ago the Indian peninsula was a part of Pangaea, a supercontinent that encompassed all the earth's major landmasses. Upheavals in the earth's surface split the supercontinent apart, and what is now India began drifting north until it collided with Asia, causing the massive Himalayan upheaval.

About 60 million years ago a gigantic fault zone developed along the western edge of the Indian peninsula. Enormous quantities of basaltic lava welled up through fissures in the bedrock. At the same time, the entire western edge of the Indian subcontinent was uplifted above the coastal plain and tilted slightly to the east. The result was the craggy escarpments of the Western Ghats, which mark one of the longest and best-defined fault zones in the world. The concurrent tilting of the subcontinent, in turn, accounts for its curious drainage system: several major rivers—such as the Cauvery, the Krishna, and the Godavari—rise in the Western Ghats not far from the Arabian Sea but then flow eastward all the way across the subcontinent before emptying into the Bay of Bengal.

The annual monsoon rains that fill the rivers are also influenced by the presence of the Western Ghats. During late spring warm, moist winds sweep inland from the Arabian Sea. The mountain barrier forces the air masses up to higher, cooler altitudes where the moisture condenses to produce the torrential rains that continue from June to October.

Though transportation within the mountains is difficult, the Western Ghats have become popular because of their splendid scenery and generally pleasant climate. The high annual rainfall has produced majestic forests on the slopes. The inland plateaus, in turn, are a picturesque patchwork of well-tended farms. Tourists who stay in the Western Ghats after the onset of the monsoon may get wet, but they are also rewarded by the sight of mountain streams leaping to life as mist-shrouded waterfalls. □

The supercontinent of Pangaea split apart 200 million years ago, and India began moving slowly north toward Asia.

WESTERN GHATS. *Rock outcrops, weathered to smoothly sculpted forms by torrential monsoon rains, punctuate the crags along much of India's wall-like western mountain chain.*

GIANT'S CAUSEWAY. *Formed by the slow cooling of a lava flow, then quarried by the waves, the rock columns rise like giant organ pipes.*

Giant's Causeway

- United Kingdom (Northern Ireland)
- Map: page 16, C–3

A spectacular mass of basaltic columns resembles the handiwork of a bygone race of giants.

The entire coast of County Antrim in Northern Ireland is noted for its scenic beauty. Towering cliffs, dramatic headlands, fine beaches, and sea caves that echo with the sounds of crashing surf all vie for attention. But for most visitors the highlight of the coast is the strange assemblage of rocks known as the Giant's Causeway.

Extending out to sea like a highway to nowhere, it is a large mass of some 40,000 polygonal rock columns, level in places and rising elsewhere like steps up to 20 feet (6 meters) or more above the water. The formation, backed by high cliffs, includes three sections known as the Grand Causeway, the Middle Causeway, and the Little Causeway. It is in the Middle Causeway that the symmetry of the rock columns is most pronounced. Some of them have 4, 5, 8, or even 10 sides, but the majority are perfect hexagons ranging from 15 to 20 inches (38 to 50 centimeters) in diameter. Viewed from above, the columns look exactly like paving stones, all neatly fitted into place.

How was this remarkable feature formed? Someone once suggested that it is a petrified bamboo forest, but Irish folklore has a more colorful explanation. According to the tale, the Irish giant Finn Mac Cool was bent on fighting his Scottish counterpart Finn Gall. Driving the columns into place one by one, he eventually completed a causeway to Scotland. (There are in fact similar rock columns on the Scottish Isle of Staffa 75 miles, or 120 kilometers, away near Fingal's Cave.) Wearied by his task, Mac Cool then went home to rest.

In the meantime Finn Gall crossed over to Ireland to have a look at his foe. Startled when he saw the sleeping giant, he was even more alarmed when Mac Cool's wife shrewdly told him that the slumbering hulk was not her husband but her baby. If that's the child, thought Finn Gall, how big can the father be? Alarmed, he fled back to Scotland, destroying the causeway in his wake. And to this day, only its two ends remain, battered by the sea.

Geologists have a less fanciful explanation for the causeway's origin, but even they must invoke forces of gigantic proportions. Some 50 million years ago, violent disturbances in the earth's crust resulted in widespread volcanic activity throughout the British Isles. In the vicinity of Giant's Causeway great fissures opened, and flow after flow of basaltic lava welled up to the surface.

The columns of rock that make up the Giant's Causeway are one of the most dramatic results of these lava flows. There the molten lava cooled at a slow, very even rate. And as it cooled, the lava gradually contracted, forming prismatic patterns in the cooling rock. As cooling and shrinkage continued, the cracks on the surface extended through the entire lava mass to form a network of vertical joints separating the flat-sided basaltic columns.

The sea completed the shaping of the Giant's Causeway. Battered ceaselessly by waves, the prismatic pillars of rock were broken off at various heights to form the causeway's uneven, steplike surface. Among the results are such picturesquely named features as the Giant's Well, the Chimney Tops, and the Wishing Chair. Similar assemblages of basaltic columns are found in many other places, but few can rival the precise geometry of those making up the Giant's Causeway. □

How Volcanism Creates Surface Landforms

Rock types vary in their resistance to erosion. Lavas, for instance, form some of the world's most resistant rocks, while sedimentary rocks are more easily worn away by water, wind, ice, and other agents of erosion. In areas that include both kinds of rock, the sedimentary rocks are worn away first to form valleys and flatlands; the more resistant volcanic rocks remain as prominent landscape features.

A surface lava flow, for example, might fill a stream valley. As the surrounding rock was worn away, it would remain as the erosion-resistant cap rock protecting an elevated mesa (a large flat-topped remnant of a former land surface).

Underground intrusions of molten magma, in turn, result in a variety of volcanic structures. A sill is a horizontal sheetlike intrusion of volcanic rock between layers of preexisting rock. A dike, in contrast, is a vertical sheetlike intrusion. A neck is an intrusion forming a vertical column of ancient lava, a former volcanic feeder pipe. A plug is a small cylindrical lava intrusion that did not break through to the surface. When the surrounding layers of softer rock are worn away, these volcanic structures remain to form hills, ridges, and other prominent topographical features.

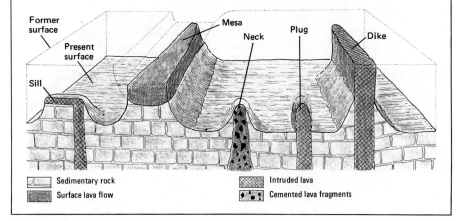

Former surface
Present surface
Sill
Mesa
Neck
Plug
Dike

☐ Sedimentary rock
☐ Surface lava flow
☐ Intruded lava
☐ Cemented lava fragments

Giessbach Falls

- Switzerland
- Map: page 17, D–4

A small stream in the Bernese Alps cascades down a series of rocky terraces on the way to its final destination, the Lake of Brienz.

The Bernese Alps in central Switzerland abound with scenic splendors—among them the Jungfrau, the Aletsch Glacier, and the Lake of Brienz. Another wonder, on a smaller scale but still impressive, is Giessbach Falls. A pristine alpine stream, the Giessbach hurtles down a mountainside through narrow gorges in a steplike series of foaming cascades. Over a distance of only 4 miles (7 kilometers), it drops for a total of approximately 1,300 feet (400 meters).

The falls were carved in layers of sedimentary rocks 180 million years old that were doubled over on themselves in a series of tight folds when

GIESSBACH FALLS. *Hemmed in by wooded gorges, an alpine stream leaps down one of many rocky ledges that interrupt its course.*

the Alps were being formed. Erosion of less resistant rock layers in the folds resulted in the giant rocky steps and terraces where the water leaps down in dramatic torrents.

Beyond the falls, the Giessbach enters into the Lake of Brienz. With the constant roar of the falls in the background, this deep, shimmering lake, bounded on one shore by chalets and orchards and on the other by dense forests, is the center of a resort area popular with vacationers.   □

Golden Gate Highlands National Park

● South Africa
● Map: page 26, B–5

Small but superbly scenic, the South African park is also a haven for a great variety of wildlife.

Among the most beautiful of South Africa's many national parks is this relatively small one atop the towering Drakensberg range at the edge of the country's broad interior plateau. Named for the colorful sandstone cliffs that flank its entrance, the park encompasses some 15 square miles (40 square kilometers) of superb scenery.

The multicolored sandstones that account for much of the park's beauty were formed about 180 million years ago, then capped in many places by layers of basaltic rock. Ravaged by erosion, the sandstones have since been sculpted into massive, fortress-like cliffs and bluffs that are especially striking when autumn turns the park's foliage to a blaze of contrasting colors.

In addition to picturesque landscapes, the park is notable for its abundance of richly varied wildlife. Elands, wildebeests, zebras, and other game animals are often seen there, as well as a wealth of birds.   □

Grand Canyon

● United States (Arizona)
● Map: page 10, D–5

The great chasm represents a gigantic slice through time. Layer by layer, rocks in the canyon walls reveal the history of the earth.

Sightseers gasp when they see it: nothing can prepare them for such an awesome sight. The Grand Canyon, carved by the Colorado River across northwestern Arizona, is almost unimaginably huge—277 miles (446 kilometers) long, up to 18 miles (29 kilometers) wide, and about 1 mile (1.6 kilometers) deep.

It is also incredibly beautiful. In addition to the main gorge through which the river flows, there is a complicated network of side canyons, ravines, towers, buttes, ledges, and gigantic rock formations. Their colors range from black and tan to russet, dusky pink, and creamy white. As sun and clouds pass overhead, light and shadow play upon the rocks, em-

GOLDEN GATE HIGHLANDS. *Deeply eroded, multihued sandstone bluffs accentuate the dramatic beauty of this region of pristine mountain highlands in southern Africa.*

GRAND CANYON. *Constantly shifting light and shadow create an ever-changing spectacle of form and color in the grandest of all canyons.*

phasizing different forms and changing the colors of the rocks from one moment to the next.

The most spectacular portions of the canyon are included in Grand Canyon National Park. Most visitors to this park would probably agree with explorer John Wesley Powell, who called the canyon "the most sublime spectacle on the earth."

But the great chasm is more than just a thing of beauty. The rocks exposed in its walls also reveal a giant slice through time. At the very bottom are the dark schist and granite walls of the inner gorge, through which the river flows today. About 2 billion years old, they are the deeply buried remains of two generations of mountains that were uplifted and then leveled by the forces of erosion.

By about 600 million years ago the surface of these ancient basement rocks had been worn down to a nearly flat plain. Then prehistoric seas began to rise and fall across this land. Layer upon layer, the various kinds of sedimentary rock that make up the canyon walls were deposited on the surface.

Sandy beach deposits were cemented into sandstone, as were gigantic wind-blown desert dunes that once covered the area. Mud was compacted into shale, and the remains of tiny sea creatures were transformed into thick layers of limestone.

The youngest rocks at the top of the canyon walls are limestones about 200 million years old. Yet even they do not represent the end of the story. At one time they were covered by thick layers of still younger rocks—rocks that in most of the area of the canyon have been eroded away.

Just as the rocks from the bottom of the canyon to the top record the passage of time, the fossils they contain record the appearance on earth of increasingly complex forms of life. The oldest fossils in the canyon are the remains of primitive sea plants. In successively higher and hence younger rock layers are found the fossils of crablike trilobites, primitive fish, insects, ferns, and reptiles.

Oddly enough, this chasm whose rocks span such an immense period of time was carved fairly recently. Less than 10 million years ago the Colorado River flowed gently across a level plain. Then stresses in the earth's crust caused the entire region to dome slowly upward. One theory proposes that as the land rose higher, erosion by the river kept pace with the uplift, and the Colorado etched its course ever deeper into the rocks. At the same time landslides, flash floods, ice, and other forces of erosion widened the canyon and carved its infinitely varied rock formations.

Although it seems immutable, the majestic canyon has never stopped changing. Today Glen Canyon Dam, upstream from the national park, has drastically reduced the flow of the Colorado, and now the river is eroding the Grand Canyon at a much slower rate. Major storms wash more debris from the walls; plant roots grow into crevices; rocks split off and come crashing down. A few million years ago there was no Grand Canyon. And scientists predict that within a few million years more, this stupendous cleft in the earth's surface will be totally unlike the canyon of today. □

Grand Teton National Park

- United States (Wyoming)
- Map: page 10, D–4

From valley floor to sawtooth summits, the park is famous for unsurpassed mountain scenery.

In northwestern Wyoming, just a short distance south of Yellowstone National Park, is another national park encompassing some of the most spectacular scenery in the Rocky Mountains. The more accessible lowland portion of Grand Teton National Park is a broad green valley known as Jackson Hole. Studded with shimmering lakes and accented by great looping curves of the aptly named Snake River, the valley is serenely beautiful.

But the added ingredient making the scenery truly majestic is the rugged Teton Range, rising like a wall to the west of the valley. No foothills mask the abrupt ascent of the mountain slopes. In some places the jagged, snow-patched summits tower more than 6,600 feet (2,000 meters) above the valley floor. The range, about 40 miles (65 kilometers) long and 10 to 15 miles (16 to 24 kilometers) wide, was named for its three most prominent peaks, which French-Canadian fur traders called *les trois tetons*—"the three breasts." The highest summit of all is Grand Teton (13,770 feet, or 4,197 meters), a majestic pinnacle reared against the sky.

The somber gray rock that makes up the Tetons (primarily gneiss and schist) is ancient basement rock at least 2½ billion years old—among the oldest rock exposed anywhere on earth. The mountains themselves, in contrast, are extremely youthful; they began to form a mere 10 million or so years ago. They are, moreover, classic examples of what geologists call fault-block mountains.

The process of mountain building began when a great north-south fracture, or fault, developed in the earth's crust. This was followed by a titanic displacement of the two blocks of the earth's crust on opposite sides of the fault. Over a long period of time, probably in a series of tremendous jolts accompanied by violent earthquakes, land to the west of the fault rose upward to create the mountain range. At the same time, rock to the east of the fault dropped downward to

form the floor of Jackson Hole. Hence the dramatic contrast in elevations within the park: in Jackson Hole the valley floor slopes gradually downward to the west; then suddenly, along the fault line, the mountain barrier rises abruptly like a wall.

Even as the Tetons were being uplifted, the forces of erosion were at work altering their contours. Swiftly flowing streams, rockslides, and avalanches all did their destructive work, chiseling away the rock to form the Tetons' striking sawtooth profile.

During the past 250,000 years several periods of intense mountain glaciation further sculpted the craggy peaks. During cold periods snow accumulated in mountain valleys and compacted into ice to form glaciers. Creeping downslope, the massive rivers of debris-laden ice polished the

GRAND TETON NATIONAL PARK. *Mountains of many ever-changing moods, the majestic Tetons at times seem to glow with radiant colors.*

mountainsides, scooped out cirques (bowllike amphitheaters) at canyon heads, gouged out deep U-shaped valleys, and polished valley bottoms.

During warm interglacial periods the ice melted and deposited vast amounts of rock and debris on the floor of Jackson Hole. As the glaciers receded, they also left terminal moraines (damlike barriers of debris) that enclose the jewellike lakes strung out along the foot of the mountains.

Although the Tetons may appear to be a completed masterpiece, the violence that attended their creation has never really ended. The earth's crust continues to move along the fault. (The floor of Jackson Hole is estimated to have fallen about 150 feet, or 45 meters, over the past 15,000 years.) A dozen or so small glaciers reappeared about 4,000 years ago and re-

main on the Tetons as mementos of the Ice Age. Rockslides roar down the slopes with surprising frequency. And spring runoff from heavy winter snows and torrential summer cloudbursts transform otherwise placid streams into powerful erosive forces. Thus, like all mountains, these majestic peaks that so delight visitors today are slowly but surely being transformed into something quite different. □

Great Lakes

- Canada—United States
- Map: page 11, E–4

Though their shorelines have gradually receded, these inland seas remain one of the world's most important reservoirs of fresh water.

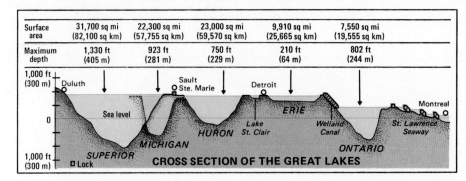

Surface area	31,700 sq mi (82,100 sq km)	22,300 sq mi (57,755 sq km)	23,000 sq mi (59,570 sq km)	9,910 sq mi (25,665 sq km)	7,550 sq mi (19,555 sq km)
Maximum depth	1,330 ft (405 m)	923 ft (281 m)	750 ft (229 m)	210 ft (64 m)	802 ft (244 m)

CROSS SECTION OF THE GREAT LAKES

Stretched out along the U.S.–Canadian border is the vast interconnected chain of the five Great Lakes. From Lake Superior, the largest and westernmost, to Lake Ontario, the smallest and farthest east, with Lakes Michigan, Huron, and Erie in between, they cover a total area of 94,460 square miles (244,650 square kilometers)—the largest expanse of fresh water in the world. Lake Superior alone, with an area of 31,700 square miles (82,100 square kilometers), is the world's largest single freshwater lake.

The lakes, which served as an important avenue for exploration of the interior of North America, remain a vital inland transportation route. Great cities—Chicago, Detroit, Cleveland, Toronto, and others—have grown up on their shores. Yet the lakes are also used for sports and recreation, and many parks and wilderness areas have been created along their shores.

Besides being immense, the Great Lakes are also relatively young: their present shapes and sizes were finally established only 10,000 years ago. The agents that hollowed out their basins were the continental glaciers of the Ice Age. Advancing and retreating several times over the past 2 million years, the crushing loads of ice scoured out preexisting valleys and lowlands and gradually broadened as well as deepened them.

With the final retreat of the glaciers, beginning about 15,000 years ago, meltwater was trapped behind broad damlike barriers of glacial deposits. Huge ancestral lakes were formed, with their shorelines at much higher levels than the present lakes'. As the glacial ice ebbed northward, exposing lower lands, drainage patterns shifted and the lakes shrank. (Many former shorelines can be detected around the lakes, revealing their former levels.) Drainage to the sea, which originally had been via the Mississippi Valley, also changed. Lake water at one time entered the Atlantic by way of the Mohawk and Hudson valleys before finding its present outlet to the sea through the St. Lawrence River.

Today the lakeshores occasionally tremble with minor earthquakes as the earth's crust, relieved of its burden of ice, gradually rebounds upward. But the process of creation has ended. For the past few thousand years the contours of the lakes have remained essentially unchanged. □

GREAT LAKES. *Reeds along the shore of Lake Michigan bend before a summer breeze. In winter the lakes often freeze over completely.*

GREAT SALT LAKE. *The shores of Utah's famous lake, crisscrossed by meandering waterways, advance and retreat, depending on rainfall.*

Great Salt Lake

- United States (Utah)
- Map: page 10, D–4

The largest salt lake in the Western Hemisphere contains so many dissolved minerals that bathers find it difficult to sink—or even swim.

"You can no more sink [in Great Salt Lake] than in a claybank," Horace Greeley observed. He exaggerated little: the lake's briny water, in some places nearly eight times saltier than seawater, buoys up bathers so that their heads and shoulders remain above water. Even swimming in it is difficult.

As impressive as it is today, however, Great Salt Lake is but a remnant of an ancient lake that once extended from Utah into Nevada and Idaho. This ancestral lake, which geologists call Lake Bonneville, occupied some 20,000 square miles (52,000 square kilometers) and was about 20 times the size of the present lake. Former shorelines can still be detected as step-

like terraces on surrounding mountainsides. The highest of these old shores is about 1,000 feet (300 meters) above the lake's present level.

Lake Bonneville was a product of the immense glaciers that covered much of North America during the Ice Age. As the climate slowly warmed, meltwater from the glaciers filled the natural depression until, in time, Lake Bonneville overflowed into the Pacific by way of the present-day Snake and Columbia river valleys.

With the final retreat of the glaciers, the climate became still warmer—and drier. Evaporation from the ancestral lake eventually exceeded the flow of water coming in, and the lake shrank. (Depending on climatic changes, the lake continues to vary dramatically in size and depth from year to year.) Besides shrinking the size of the lake, the evaporation also concentrated the salts and other minerals that were dissolved in its waters.

Today three major rivers flow into the lake, but none flows out: water leaves only by evaporation. Scientists estimate that more than 3 million tons

(2.7 million metric tons) of salts are added to the lake each year. And it is these dissolved salts that make the lake's waters much heavier than seawater—and swimmers so much more buoyant. Despite the high concentration of salts, a surprising variety of life thrives in the lake, from bacteria and brine shrimp to large waterfowl.

Every year thousands of tons of table salt, potassium sulfate, and other valuable minerals are harvested from the lake. In a complex process that involves pumping the water through a series of shallow ponds, the brine is left to evaporate under the burning desert sun. When the water is gone, the various minerals are scooped up and processed.

Similar solar drying forms the vast Bonneville Salt Flats to the west of the lake. Although wet for much of the year, this remnant of the ancestral lake dries out during the hot summer months and forms a surface so hard that it is used as an automobile race course. Thus land speed records have been made—and broken—on what was once the bottom of a lake. □

GREAT WESTERN ERG. *Beyond the palms of a little oasis at the eastern edge of the erg, swirling sand dunes extend from horizon to horizon.*

Great Western Erg

- Algeria
- Map: page 24, C–2

Although the formidable Sahara appears to be stable, the surface sand is in constant motion. Great dunes creep slowly across the desert, sometimes in large V-shaped groups like earthbound flocks of geese.

Very few people would expect to find beauty in this bleak sea of sand near the northern border of the Sahara, one of the hottest, driest places on earth. When the sun is high in the cloudless sky, Saharan temperatures may soar far above 100° F (38° C). Rains come for only a few hours a year, and in some years not at all.

Yet for all its harshness, the Great Western Erg has an unquestionable beauty. The erg (from an Arabic word meaning "great sand dune area") is typical of the picture most people conjure up when they think of a desert—a seemingly endless sea of gigantic golden sand dunes rolling dramatically toward the horizon. Although this and other ergs symbolize the Sahara, however, they actually cover only about one-fifth of its surface: much of the rest is covered by vast,

How Barchans Travel With the Wind

Dunes are most frequently found in dry desert regions free of vegetation, where sand grains are easily picked up and carried by the wind, and where strong winds constantly blow in the same direction. The most active dunes (found in American, African, and Asian deserts) are called barchans. Because of their horseshoe shape, with their horns pointing in the direction in which the wind is blowing, barchans are sometimes called crescent dunes. They travel as far as 66 to 100 feet (20 to 30 meters) in a year—the big barchans move more quickly—and can even cross barriers. (They change direction in the lee of the obstruction.) In open areas large groups of barchans frequently travel in V formations like flocks of migrating geese.

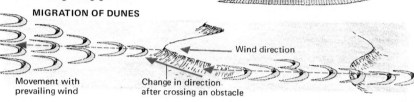

BARCHAN

Direction of movement ◄

MIGRATION OF DUNES

Wind direction

Movement with prevailing wind

Change in direction after crossing an obstacle

monotonous rock and gravel plains.

The Great Western Erg, one of the largest in the Sahara, lies in a natural depression in northern Algeria. Bounded on the north by the Atlas Mountains and on the south by the Tademaït Plateau, it covers an area of more than 30,000 square miles (78,000 square kilometers).

And everywhere there is sand, driven by the wind into an array of patterns that range from surface ripple marks to towering dunes as much as 400 feet (120 meters) high. In some places the dunes form long curving ridges, while elsewhere the sand has accumulated into seemingly endless straight, parallel dunes separated by broad open troughs. There are highly mobile, crescent-shaped dunes known as barchans, as well as large, complex clusters of dunes that have been sculpted by the wind into huge merging pyramids.

Wind, the force that modeled all these intricate forms, sometimes rages across the Sahara with furious intensity. Especially violent storms at times whirl up thick clouds of airborne sand and dust that blot out the light of the sun. Many Saharan legends tell of caravans and even oases disappearing in such storms without a trace. Nor are their effects strictly local. The storm winds sometimes carry Saharan dust all the way across the Mediterranean into Europe. After a particularly violent sandstorm in Algeria in 1947, red desert dust, mixed with snow, turned parts of the Swiss Alps pink.

But it is the ever-present, less violent trade winds sweeping across the desert that do the major work of reshaping the dunes. Frequently they stir up a knee-deep layer of windborne sand that moves across the surface in a golden haze. Above this layer of mobile sand grains the air is almost entirely free of sand.

The sand does not actually become fully airborne. Most of it moves by being bounced along on the ground by the wind. The smaller and lighter the grains of sand, the higher and farther they bounce. Grains of sand that are too heavy to leave the ground are bumped along as they are hit by the bouncing sand grains. Thus the surface patterns on the dunes are constantly being shifted, and the dunes themselves are moved forward by the winds—in the case of barchans, as far as 100 feet (30 meters) per year.

Where did all the sand come from in the first place? It was not carried in on the wind from distant places, nor was it, as was once believed, provided by some ancient Saharan sea that long ago dried up. In fact the sand for the most part was washed down by rivers from the nearby Atlas Mountains.

Over the past 2 to 3 million years the Saharan climate has alternated between wet and dry periods. During each wet period, streams and rivers from the mountains extended their courses farther and farther into the desert, where they deposited their loads of eroded sand and other kinds of sediment. During dry periods the wind took over, modeling characteristic desert landforms.

Ever since the last wet period ended about 4,000 years ago, the Saharan climate has remained very dry. Active streams no longer penetrate the region, and development of the desert has resumed—even while our ancestors watched. Basins that once were filled with water slowly dried out. Where cattle had once grazed, only a few spiny shrubs and hardy grasses were able to survive. And even today, as the climate remains dry, the desert continues to advance. ☐

Greenland

- Denmark
- Map: page 8

The largest island in the world is almost completely blanketed by a permanent cap of ice and snow.

Harsh, forbidding, and almost completely buried beneath a cap of perpetual ice and snow, Greenland is the largest island in the world. From north to south it is 1,660 miles (2,670 kilometers) long—about equal to the distance between New York City and Denver, Colorado—while at its widest point it spans a distance of about 750 miles (1,200 kilometers). Its total area (840,000 square miles, or 2,175,600 square kilometers) is more than three times the size of Texas. And its rugged coastline, deeply indented by fjords and inlets, totals some 25,000 miles (40,000 kilometers)—just about equal to the circumference of the earth at the equator.

Much of the great wedge-shaped island, which is actually a part of Denmark, lies north of the Arctic Circle. (Its northernmost tip is less than 500 miles, or 800 kilometers, from the North Pole.) In this frigid arctic environment, approximately 85 percent of the island's surface is covered by a permanent ice cap. Averaging 5,000 feet (1,500 meters) in thickness, the ice cap in some places is as much as 14,000 feet (4,300 meters) thick and includes about 10 percent of all the ice in the world. Only a relatively narrow coastal strip and scattered nunataks (isolated mountain peaks that project above the surrounding ice) are free of a permanent cover of ice and snow.

GREENLAND. *Streaked with eroded rock debris, glaciers stream through gaps in the coastal mountains as they journey toward the sea.*

The Greenland ice cap, in fact, is the second largest in the world, exceeded only by the massive ice cap that covers Antarctica.

The bedrock beneath the ice is an eastern extension of the Canadian Shield, the expanse of ancient granitic rock that makes up much of Canada's vast interior lowland plain. The surface of the bedrock is far from even. In some places it lies below sea level, while elsewhere it rises up to form high mountain ranges. (The highest peak in Greenland, Mount Gunnbjorn in the eastern coastal range,

reaches 12,139 feet, or 3,700 meters.) In overall contours the land surface beneath the ice is more or less saucer-shaped, with a central depression bordered by mountain ranges.

Snow falls on Greenland in every month of the year, and annual precipitation is substantially heavier in the south than in the northern part of the island, which is relatively arid. Since the temperature of the inland ice mass averages only 10° F (–12° C) even in July, very little is lost by melting. Instead, the snow continues to accumulate, gradually compressing into ice.

The ice, moreover, is constantly on the move: the great weight of the accumulating ice and snow causes it to spread slowly outward toward the edges of the ice cap. Nearing the sea, the ice is gradually forced through gaps between the coastal mountains in the form of glaciers. Some of the glaciers, however, move quite swiftly. One of the biggest, the Jakobshavn Glacier on the western coast of Greenland, advances at the relatively rapid rate of approximately 100 feet (30 meters) per day.

Once the glaciers reach the sea, they break up into tremendous icebergs that crash into the water with a roar and slowly drift away. In all, some 10,000 to 15,000 icebergs are calved by Greenland's glaciers each year; they dump perhaps as much as 125 cubic miles (520 cubic kilometers) of ice into the sea. (It was an iceberg calved by a Greenland glacier that sank the *Titanic* in 1912, and Greenland icebergs remain a menace to North Atlantic shipping to this day.) Thus the snow that falls on Greenland slowly but surely finds its way to the sea, where it melts and returns to the never-ending water cycle—perhaps to fall once again on Greenland. □

Grossglockner

- Austria
- Map: page 17, E–4

The highest mountain in Austria continues to grow taller, while its glaciers grow smaller and smaller.

Snaking across the Hohe Tauern, a lofty range of the Eastern Alps in southern Austria, is one of the highest—and most spectacular—mountain roads in the entire world. Known as the Grossglockner-Hochalpenstrasse (Grossglockner–High Alpine Highway), it provides breathtaking views of craggy, snowcapped peaks, glaciers, and sweeping mountain slopes at every hairpin turn and strategically situated parking area.

Among the most impressive sights along this scenic route is the magnificent angular summit of Grossglockner—at 12,460 feet (3,798 meters), the highest mountain in all of Austria. And it is still growing: geologists have calculated that the entire Hohe Tauern range is rising at a rate of about .04 inch (1 millimeter) per year.

The best view of the snowy summit

GROSSGLOCKNER. *Glaciers both large and small give rise to numerous streams that lace the slopes of the massive Austrian mountain.*

rising above the neighboring peaks can be seen from a spur road leading off the main highway. There, from a scenic overlook, motorists can also get a close-up view of the renowned Pasterze Glacier, an awesome river of ice shattered by deep crevasses. About 6 miles (10 kilometers) long, it is the largest of several glaciers streaming down the sides of Grossglockner. Although it has diminished substantially in size over the last century, the Pasterze remains the largest glacier in the Eastern Alps. □

Guatavita, Lake

- Colombia
- Map: page 14, B–2

This sacred Andean lake is both a geological enigma and the source of the ancient legend of Eldorado.

Guatavita is a small gem of a lake perched high in the Andes not far from Bogotá, the capital of Colombia. Hemmed in by steep slopes, it is about 325 feet (100 meters) deep and 1,300 feet (400 meters) in diameter—and its basin is almost perfectly round. A scenic and scientific curiosity, the lake attracts tourists, geologists, and treasure seekers alike.

The treasure hunters are lured by tales of great wealth to be found in its depths. To the Chibcha Indians, who inhabited the region centuries ago, Lake Guatavita was a sacred spot.

According to legend, their chieftain used to cover himself with gold dust in an annual ceremony; he would then jump into the lake to wash off the gold while his subjects cast emeralds and other riches into the water as offerings to the gods. Only a few gems and broken ceramics have ever been retrieved from the lake, but the fascination of El Dorado, the Gilded Man, lives on. The tale, in fact, grew into the legend of Eldorado, a fabulous land of gold that lured Spanish conquistadores into vain searches to far reaches of the Americas.

Just as elusive as the quest for Eldorado has been the search for an explanation of the lake's origin. To some, its perfectly round shape suggests that it is a meteor crater. Yet the area shows no traces of iron or nickel, which are found in most meteorites. Nor have any of the surrounding rocks been metamorphosed by the intense heat and pressure that would have accompanied impact by a meteorite. Others have suggested that the basin may be a volcanic crater, though no volcanic rock has ever been found in the area. (Some craters, however, are created by explosions of volcanic gases without ejecting lava.) Still others have theorized that the basin resulted from the solution of a subterranean salt formation. But again, no conclusive evidence has been produced to support this theory. Whatever its origin, however, the lovely Andean lake is a natural wonder that continues to delight all visitors. □

Gunnison, Black Canyon of the

- United States (Colorado)
- Map: page 10, D–5

Deep and narrow, with its floor often obscured by dark shadows, the mighty river-carved chasm at times appears to be a bottomless abyss.

Some other canyons may be narrower, deeper, or steeper-walled. But few anywhere in the world can rival the Black Canyon of the Gunnison for the combination of all three qualities: in places this gloomy, sheer-walled gash in the face of the earth is deeper than it is wide.

In the most spectacular segment of the gorge, which has been preserved as a national monument, the depth ranges from 1,730 to 2,700 feet (525 to 825 meters). At its narrowest point, the canyon is only 1,100 feet (335 meters) wide at its rim and tapers down to a mere 40 feet (12 meters) across at the bottom. Hemmed in by somber gray, nearly vertical and even overhanging walls, the depths of the chasm are lost in shadow much of the time—hence the name Black Canyon.

The canyon extends for 53 miles (85 kilometers) about midway along the course of the Gunnison River in western Colorado. In places the cliffs that bound it are a truly dizzying spectacle. One of them, the Painted Wall, drops almost straight down for 2,250 feet

BLACK CANYON OF THE GUNNISON. *Armed with boulders and debris, the river carved the canyon into ancient, erosion-resistant bedrock.*

(685 meters) from the canyon's rim to the river's edge. Just as Captain John Gunnison, who explored the region in 1853, wisely skirted the canyon that is the river's most impressive feature, most visitors today are content to view the spectacle from scenic overlooks on the rim. Only the hardiest hikers and most experienced rock climbers venture down into its depths, where fallen boulders as big as houses litter the canyon floor.

The rocks exposed in the canyon walls are mainly extraordinarily hard, erosion-resistant schist, gneiss, and granite that were formed more than 1 billion years ago. But while the rocks are very ancient, the canyon itself is quite young, geologically speaking. The raging waters of the Gunnison River carved this stupendous chasm over the course of the past 2 million years or so.

How did the river manage to carve a canyon in such erosion-resistant rock? The explanation is based on events that occurred far back in time. Many millions of years ago, layers of sedimentary rock were deposited on the flat, eroded surface of the ancient bedrock. The sedimentary rock, in turn, was partially eroded away and then was covered by a layer of soft volcanic rock.

Flowing over these easily eroded sedimentary and volcanic rocks, the Gunnison River firmly established its course across the landscape and cut its way downward to the basement rock. Since the river by then was too firmly entrenched to change its course, it had no alternative but to continue cutting its way downward into the bedrock.

It was mainly the river's large volume of flow and very steep gradient through the canyon that enabled it to carve so deep a trench through such resistant rock. (The Gunnison drops an average of 95 feet per mile, or 18 meters per kilometer, through the monument.) Armed with rock debris, the raging river was a powerful cutting tool capable of carving the steep-walled chasm and lowering its bed more rapidly than other forces could widen the canyon.

Today dams upstream have slowed the river's flow and moderated the effects of seasonal floods. Even so, it is doubtful that the Gunnison will ever be a gentle stream. The rate of erosion may have been slowed, but it has not been stopped. □

Hammam-Meskoutine

- Algeria
- Map: page 24, D–2

At the so-called Baths of the Damned, the rocky cones and columns deposited by mineral hot springs have inspired an Arabic legend of a forbidden wedding procession that was condemned by the heavens and turned into stone.

In a picturesque little valley not far from the market town of Guelma in northeastern Algeria is one of the most famous hot-spring resorts in the country. Noted for its dramatic rock formations, the valley has attracted arthritics and curious tourists ever since the days of the Roman Empire.

Legend explains the origin of the name Hammam-Meskoutine, Arabic for "Baths of the Damned." According to the story, a man once took his own sister as his bride. As the incestuous couple moved up the valley with their wedding procession, the skies suddenly opened and the entire party was struck by a bolt of thunder. This curse from above instantly turned everyone to stone. Even the participants' billowing robes were frozen in place.

Water surges up from 10 different hot springs in the valley, sending up dense clouds of steam visible from afar. The water is so hot—temperatures are as high as 208° F (98° C)—that visitors can amuse themselves by boiling eggs in the many channels that zigzag over the bedrock.

The water, moreover, is saturated with calcium carbonate, iron, and other dissolved minerals. As the flowing water cools, the minerals are deposited on the surface (mainly in the form of the carbonate rock known as travertine) to make up the fanciful formations at Hammam-Meskoutine.

Approaching the hot springs, visitors first see a series of conical, intricately modeled formations ranging in color from snowy white to rich ocher. (This is the cursed "wedding procession.") Farther on is a spectacular ca-

HAMMAM-MESKOUTINE. *Like a frozen waterfall, multicolored draperies of travertine spill from the edge of a steaming hot spring.*

thedrallike formation where iridescent geyser pools are edged with multi-colored draperies of rock. A thousand rills of boiling water rush across the surface, and steam condenses overhead to fall again in veils of mist.

The mineral-rich, slightly radioactive waters of Hammam-Meskoutine have long been regarded as beneficial to people suffering from rheumatism, arthritis, and other ailments. The Romans built installations here and called the place Aquae Thibilitanae, the "Waters of Thibilis." (The imposing ruins at the Roman colony of Thibilis can still be seen nearby.) And although most people prefer to use the more modern facilities that have been built in recent years, some of the Roman baths at Hammam-Meskoutine are still in use today. ☐

Han, Grotto of

- Belgium
- Map: page 17, D–3

Plunging into an abyss, a Belgian river disappears beneath the ground, flows through a labyrinth of caves, then reappears at the surface.

The Lesse is a lovely river that meanders northward toward the Meuse in the Ardennes region of southeastern Belgium. A pleasant stream, it is bordered in places by steep limestone cliffs and overlooked here and there by fine old castles.

Not far from the village of Han-sur-Lesse, however, it undergoes an abrupt change in course and character. At a great bend in the river, its water plunges with a roar into a sinkhole, the Belvaux abyss. After an uncharted course beneath the limestone hills, the river eventually reaches the labyrinth of water-carved chambers and galleries known as the Grotto of Han. Streaming through the cave, the river finally emerges again at the surface and then continues on its journey toward the sea.

The course of the Lesse has not always been the same as it is today. Near the Belvaux abyss are two more sinkholes, now high and dry, where the river used to flow into the limestone formation. Downcutting of the riverbed has led to the abandonment of these former underground channels and the opening of the newer sinkhole at the Belvaux abyss.

Visitors enter the cave through one of the openings of the former, now-dry channels above the present river. After exploring these dry, abandoned passageways, now lavishly decorated with cave formations, they proceed to lower levels along the present-day underground course of the Lesse, then finally exit from the cave by boat.

Among the highlights of the trip are an aptly named chamber, La Merveilleuse ("The Marvelous"), and a cluster of four smaller ones called Les Mystérieuses ("The Mysterious"), all of them bristling with stalactites and stalagmites. Another chamber, the Alhambra, has two splendid floor-to-ceiling columns that are 10 feet (3 meters) in circumference. Most impressive of all is La Salle du Dôme ("The Hall of the Dome"), a magnificent chamber about 500 feet (150 meters) across that has a spectacular vaulted ceiling 417 feet (127 meters)

GROTTO OF HAN. *Colorful stalactites, columns, and stalagmites of all shapes and sizes decorate the chambers and passageways of the most famous cave in Belgium.*

high. Formed in part by a massive cave-in of the ceiling, the chamber is littered with a chaotic heap of enormous boulders.

Beyond the Hall of the Dome, visitors continue their journey down the Lesse by boat to the point where the river reemerges at the surface. The exit is spectacular. Visitors never fail to be impressed as the boat slips from the black stillness of the cave into the blinding blaze of daylight.

Modern exploration of the cave began in earnest in 1771 and continues to the present. (The first stairs and walkways for guided tours were installed in the mid-18th century.) But the cave has been known to local inhabitants for a much longer time. In the village of Han-sur-Lesse, the Museum of the Subterranean World exhibits ancient relics that have been retrieved from the river and found along its banks. Among them are Bronze Age artifacts that date from about 500 B.C., which seem to indicate that both the river and the grotto had a religious significance for local residents in times long past. ☐

HARZ. *Chaotic heaps of smoothly rounded granite boulders crown the crests and ridges of the German mountains, completely dwarfing surrounding forests of fragrant evergreens.*

Harz

- East Germany—West Germany
- Map: page 17, E–3

Rugged peaks, gentle slopes, misty bogs, and verdant forests contribute to the mountains' aura of romance.

The Harz massif, the most northerly mountain range in the German central highlands, is a romantically beautiful place. Its deep ravines, rocky crags, dark forests, and swirling mists have inspired a rich folklore, including splendid myths and tales of fairies and witches that have found their way into many serious works of German literature. Even Goethe, Germany's greatest poet, dramatized a Harz legend (that of *Walpurgisnacht,* the Witches' Sabbath) in *Faust,* his masterpiece.

Trending from the northwest to the southeast across the border of West and East Germany, the Harz rises dramatically from the vast North German plain to heights of more than 3,000 feet (900 meters). It is a compact range, only about 60 miles (100 kilometers) long and 20 miles (32 kilometers) wide. Even so, it is an impressive sight, jutting up abruptly from lowlands that stretch all the way north to Denmark and the seacoasts.

In the northern and northwestern part of this range—the Oberharz, or the Upper Harz—the mountains are rugged and wild, bounded by steep slopes that drop down to the plain. In the western part of the Oberharz the mountains rise in a series of stepped plateaus, or terraces, cut by numerous valleys. The slopes are interrupted everywhere by outcrops of granite boulders and quartzite ridges. Large peat bogs occupy the valleys and even some slopes, and marsh gas flickers over them in a ghostly fashion. The lower slopes are forested with spruce and fir, but on higher slopes the woods give way to grassy moors. The highest crags are bare and windswept, lashed by violent storms that veil them in rain and fog.

The highest mountain in the Oberharz and in all of northern Germany is the Brocken, at 3,747 feet (1,142 meters). It was on its slopes, in East Germany, that Goethe's Faust witnessed the witches' revels on *Walpurgisnacht.*

Another illusion, seen there to this day, is the "Brocken Specter," caused by a trick of the mist. A traveler standing on the summit when the sun is low and a cloud cover hangs below the peak may see his own shadow, hugely magnified, on the surface of the clouds.

In the Unterharz, or the Lower Harz, to the south and east, the land slopes down more gradually. This is a region of gentler mountains, where small farms are scattered through the forests of beech, oak, and walnut trees.

The varied contours of the Harz reflect a long, active geological history. The original mountain-building episode occurred some 250 million years ago. As layers of sedimentary rock were being uplifted, massive amounts of granite and quartzite were intruded deep beneath the surface. This ancestral mountain range has been completely reshaped by repeated cycles of erosion and renewed uplift. So much overlying material has been removed that the intrusions of granite and quartzite, once buried far below the surface, are now exposed in the dome of the Brocken and in the immense boulders found in many high areas.

During one period of uplift, a great block of the earth's crust was thrust high above the surrounding surface between two faults. The cliffs in the northern part of the Harz mark one edge of this upthrust block, which is known as a horst. In the Harz, however, the drama of legend vies with the drama of topography to attract and hold the attention of the visitor.   □

Hatteras, Cape

- United States (North Carolina)
- Map: page 11, F–5

Part of a chain of golden sandspits, the cape and nearby islands are a battleground between land and sea.

Anyone who climbs the 268 steps to the top of Cape Hatteras Lighthouse, the tallest on the Atlantic Coast of the United States, can easily see why the nearby shoals have been called the Graveyard of the Atlantic. Two great ocean currents collide offshore—the warm Gulf Stream flowing north and a cold countercurrent flowing south—over a treacherous, ever-shifting expanse of sandy shallows known as Diamond Shoals. The combination of tumultuous waves, foamy whitecaps,

CAPE HATTERAS. *Near the cape, Hatteras Island is little more than a sandbar—a fragile barrier at the mercy of storm-tossed waves.*

dangerous currents, and shallow water, as well as the dense fogs and raging storms generated by the mixing of cold and warm waters, has claimed at least 500 ships, from wooden galleons to the *Monitor* of Civil War fame and modern merchantmen.

Cape Hatteras itself is the major promontory on Hatteras Island, one of a chain of barrier islands that stretch almost unbroken for nearly 200 miles (320 kilometers) off the coast of North Carolina. Known collectively as the Outer Banks, they are a series of slender sandspits that barely project above the sea. Nowhere more than 2½ miles (4 kilometers) wide, for long stretches they are not much more than 1,200 feet (365 meters) across. Yet in places the islands lie more than 25 miles (40 kilometers) off the mainland coast, forming a fragile barrier between crashing Atlantic surf and the shallow, placid waters of Pamlico and other lagoonlike sounds.

Resting on a deeply buried foundation of granite and thick layers of sediment on the continental shelf, the islands came into being as the Ice Age drew to a close about 10,000 years ago. As glaciers melted far to the north, sea levels rose all around the world. In this area the sea flooded lowlands behind the former coastline, creating Pamlico and the other sounds. The sand of what had once been coastal dunes meanwhile was shifted and reshifted to form the barrier islands.

The islands are far from stable. During severe storms the sea frequently breaches the narrow sandbars, creating inlets where there were none before. Coastal currents, in turn, sometimes shift the sand and seal off inlets between adjacent islands. Even the contours of Cape Hatteras itself are constantly being altered by waves and currents.

But the sea, aided by the wind, piles sand up as well as washes it away. On Bodie Island, just north of Hatteras, wind and waves have created the highest sand dune on the Atlantic coast of the United States—Jockey's Ridge, at 138 feet (42 meters). Nearby is another famous dune, Kill Devil Hill, where the Wright brothers flew their first airplane in 1903.

The ever-shifting Outer Banks are probably temporary. In time, the Atlantic may wipe away these strips of sand forever. In the meantime, visitors will continue to enjoy the miles of pristine beaches that have been preserved at Cape Hatteras and Cape Lookout National Seashores. □

Helgoland

- West Germany
- Map: page 16, D–3

The tiny island's red sandstone cliffs rise dramatically above the turbulent waters of the North Sea.

Helgoland has had a tempestuous history, both geologically and politically. Located in the North Sea about 45 miles (70 kilometers) from the mouth of Germany's Elbe River, it has endured fierce storms and devastating wars, which have eaten away at its shores and destroyed parts of the island itself. Today Helgoland consists of two parts: the island proper and a sandy satellite islet called Düne. At one time both were part of a single, much larger island. The main island includes the low-lying Unterland and the Oberland, a high area bounded by sandstone cliffs that rise about 200 feet (60 meters) above the sea.

The island is underlain by a series of sedimentary rock layers that slope down sharply toward the southeast. The lowermost layer is limestone that was formed some 250 million years ago. Next come three slightly younger layers of sandstone topped by a second limestone formation about 100 million years old. Finally there is a chalk layer, about 80 million years old, and very recent deposits of sand.

Throughout its history erosion has been altering the contours of Helgoland. About 20,000 years ago Ice Age glaciers planed down the sloping surface of the Oberland, transforming it into a flat plateau. When the ice melted, the sea level rose and stormy waters of the North Sea began gnawing away at the island's shores. As recently as the 17th century the island was partially covered by the upper limestone bed, which no longer projects above the sea. At times the waves cut into the sandstone cliffs, isolating towerlike sea stacks and then grinding them down to eroded debris. Today only one sea stack remains, a picturesque formation known as Hengst ("The Stallion").

Over the years man has joined nature in damaging the island. In the 17th and 18th centuries miners removed much of the accessible limestone. Military fortifications that were built in World War II were blown up after the war; in the process part of the southeastern end of the island was reduced to rubble. Further damage occurred when Helgoland was used as a target for bombing practice.

More recently the island has become a resort. A massive seawall along the north shore protects the cliffs from assault by the waves and slows further erosion. Thus, though greatly reduced in size, Helgoland has survived the attacks of both nature and man. □

CROSS SECTION OF HELGOLAND

Northwest — Southeast

Hengst — Oberland — Düne

- ▨ Lower limestone bed
- ▧ Lower sandstone bed
- ▨ Middle sandstone bed
- ▨ Upper sandstone bed
- ▨ Upper limestone bed
- ▨ Chalk
- ▨ Sand

Helgoland is underlain by thin beds of sedimentary rock that slope steeply to the southeast. Moving from northwest to southeast, each successive bed is younger.

Helmcken Falls

- Canada (British Columbia)
- Map: page 10, D–3

In a pristine mountain wilderness, a foaming cascade plunges over a rugged cliff in a single awesome leap.

Situated in the Cariboo Mountains of southeastern British Columbia, Canada's westernmost province, is Wells Gray Provincial Park, a primitive wilderness tract of breathtaking natural beauty. Its varied scenic attractions include lofty mountain peaks, glaciers, extinct volcanoes, lava flows, dense coniferous forests, and alpine meadows filled with wildflowers. But most of all it is a kingdom of wild cascades, crashing waterfalls, and roiling rapids. Nowhere in the park is the visitor far from the muffled sound of some great cataract.

Highest and noblest of the park's 12 major waterfalls is Helmcken Falls. One of six great cascades on the Murtle River, it plummets 450 feet (137 meters) in one thundering torrent to a plunge pool filled with broken rocks and churning white water.

Underlying the rivers and lakes of the park is a base of extremely old rock. Most of it was formed between 600 and 800 million years ago; the rest is 350 to 550 million years old. In the millions of years since these layers of ancient rock were deposited, they were complexly folded, uplifted, and gradually reshaped by erosion. And then came the Ice Age glaciers of the past 2 million years, which enlarged the park's valleys and scooped out the elongated basins of several large lakes that glisten in the wilderness today.

In a number of places, however, the ice failed to erode the hard-rock thresholds lying across the valleys. These became the cliffs and ledges over which the rivers presently plunge in spectacular cascades, including the precipice at Helmcken Falls.

Today the park is filled with a variety of wildlife. Mule deer, moose, and caribou are plentiful, as are many smaller animals such as beavers and wolverines. Grizzly bears and mountain goats are found in the northern mountains, and the park's rivers are famed for their abundance of trout. Plentiful wildlife and superb scenery make Wells Gray Park popular with hikers, while its network of lakes and rushing waterways makes it a paradise for expert canoeists. □

Hienghene Bay

- New Caledonia
- Map: page 23, G–4

Bizarre rocky islets stand guard over the entrance to the bay on a lush island in the South Pacific.

In 1774 Captain James Cook, the British explorer, discovered the large island of New Caledonia to the east of Australia. Although he did not enter Hienghene Bay on the island's northeast coast, he undoubtedly noticed the many rocky islets scattered across its surface. Missionaries, impressed by their odd shapes, later gave them such descriptive names as the Sphinx and the Towers of Notre Dame.

The islets are eroded remnants of a rock formation that once covered the entire area of Hienghene Bay. Composed of limestone that was raised above the sea less than 40 million years ago, the rocks were partially altered by the heat and pressure that accompanied the uplift. In places the original limestone was replaced by hard masses of silica. Exposed to erosion, the softer limestone was then worn away, leaving the more resistant rock to stand as separate islands.

Some of the islets are riddled with caves and topped by craggy summits. Rising high above the sea, the islands continue to attract the attention of all who visit this lovely coastline. ☐

HELMCKEN FALLS. *With a thundering roar, the waters of the Murtle River plunge into the rocky pool below, carving an ever-deepening hollow in the face of the cliff.*

Himalayas

- Asia
- Map: page 20, C–2

Forbidding and at the same time inspiring, the snow-covered peaks of the highest mountain range in the world are reared against the sky like an immense impenetrable barrier.

The local people long ago named the mountains *himalaya*—Sanskrit for "abode of the snow." Few descriptions are better drawn. The Himalayas are the highest mountains in the world, with more than 30 peaks rising to heights of 24,000 feet (7,300 meters) or more. These majestic summits tower over tiers of lower ranges and reach far above the level of perpetual snow. Many of the permanent snowfields, one of the range's most distinctive features, give rise to immense glaciers as well as some of the mightiest rivers in Asia, including the Ganges, Indus, and Brahmaputra.

The Himalayas are actually a series of three parallel ranges marked by jutting, snowcapped peaks, deeply eroded river gorges, and immense valleys, many of which were carved by slowly creeping glaciers. The ranges sweep almost without interruption in a great northwest-to-southeast crescent some 1,500 miles (2,400 kilometers) long between the Tibetan Plateau and the Indo-Gangetic Plain of northern India. They touch parts of India, Nepal, Pakistan, Bhutan, Sikkim, and China, and cover an area comparable to that of France.

The southernmost range, the Siwalik Hills, has a maximum altitude of about 5,000 feet (1,500 meters) and is indented by many flat-floored valleys called *duns*. The middle range, the Lesser Himalayas, varies in altitude from about 7,000 to 15,000 feet (2,100 to 4,600 meters) and is crossed by valleys whose floors lie some 3,000 feet (900 meters) above sea level. One of them, the Vale of Kashmir, is considered to be one of the most picturesque mountain valleys in the world.

The awesome spine of the mountains is the Great Himalayas. The most northerly range, it is a lofty, rugged chain reaching high above the line of continual snow. Its spectacular peaks include many of the highest in the world—Mount Everest, the highest point on earth, at 29,028 feet, or 8,848 meters; Kanchenjunga, the third highest; and many more. (The second highest mountain, K2 or Mount

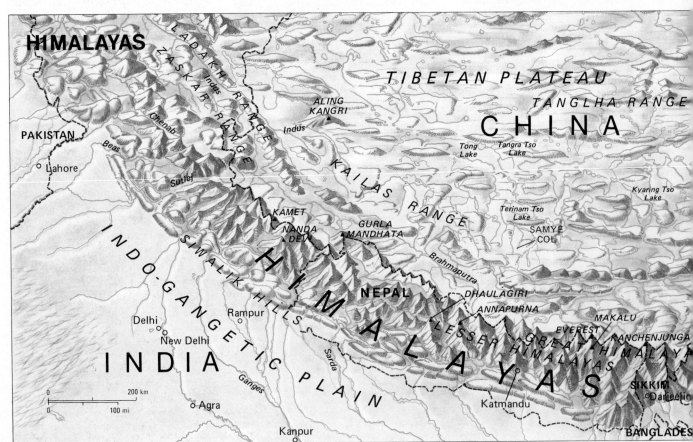

HIMALAYAS. *The snow on many of the peaks collects and compacts to form immense glaciers, which melt and feed the region's rivers.*

Godwin Austen, is in the Karakoram Range, sometimes considered a fourth range of the Himalayas.) Nine of the 14 highest mountains on earth are in Nepal, where the Great Himalayas reach their maximum heights.

Surprisingly, much of the "rooftop of the world" was formed beneath the sea millions of years ago. An ancient ocean named the Tethys Sea, after a figure in Greek mythology, once lay roughly where the Himalayas are now. Rivers entering the sea carried in debris from the surrounding land, and marine animals died and contributed their skeletons to the sediments accumulating on the ocean floor. Eventually the sediments piled up in beds as much as 6 miles (10 kilometers) thick and were compacted into limestone, shale, and several other kinds of sedimentary rock.

Some 200 million years ago most of the earth's landmasses were united in a single supercontinent called Pangaea. About 135 million years ago Pangaea began breaking up, and various sections of it, so-called tectonic plates, began drifting in different directions, moved by pressures from deep within the earth.

The plate forming the Indian subcontinent moved slowly toward the Asian mainland, and finally, about 65 million years ago, the two started to collide. The force of the collision wrinkled and folded the sedimentary rock layers of the former Tethys Sea, but in this case the wrinkles were of colossal size. The process was somewhat similar to two pieces of ice colliding on a frozen river and pushing up a rim of shattered ice at the point of the collision. In many places the heat and pressure of the collision melted the sedimentary rocks and changed them into gneisses, schists, and other metamorphic rocks.

As the Himalayas rose, they were attacked by the elements—wind, rain, snow, and extremes in temperature. During the ice ages great glaciers sculpted the mountains, sharpening peaks and deepening valleys. During warm interglacial periods, meltwater from the glaciers cut deep chasms and carried immense loads of sand and gravel downhill.

Today we see the results of all these forces acting over the course of millions of years. Each step in the history of the Himalayas can be read in the mountains' rock layers, terraced valleys, and scarred cliffs.

And the story has not yet ended, for the Himalayas are still growing. Before the British expedition climbed Mount Everest in 1953, a geologist studying the growth of the mountains jokingly told the mountaineers that they had better hurry to the top before Everest grew any higher. More seriously, the continuing upheaval of the mountains sometimes produces landslides that claim the lives and property of mountain dwellers.

Although geologists have been trying for some time to calculate the Himalayas' growth rate, the task is complicated, since accurate calculation of their height in the past is difficult. One estimate is that they have risen more than 4,000 feet (1,200 meters) in the past 1½ million years.

At present, geologists believe, the mountains are probably rising at a rate of about 3 to 4 inches (8 to 10 centimeters) per year. But while the pressures pushing the Himalayas up are still at work, so too are the forces wearing them down. In fact most of the mountains' upward movement is continually erased by erosion. Thus geologists believe that the net growth of the Himalayas amounts to only 1 to 2 inches (2.5 to 5 centimeters) over the course of a century. □

Hindu Kush

- Afghanistan—Pakistan
- Map: page 18, I–5

Bleak and austere, the massive range of rugged mountain peaks stands astride an age-old route of conquest.

For thousands of years travelers have been awed by the towering, rocky walls of the Hindu Kush. A chain of massive peaks some 600 miles (1,000 kilometers) long, it sweeps in a great arc from central Afghanistan across the top of Pakistan, where it merges with the rugged highlands of the Pamirs and the mighty Karakoram range. One of the highest mountain systems in the world, the Hindu Kush includes more than 20 peaks that exceed 23,000 feet (7,000 meters). The tallest summit, in the eastern and highest part of the range, is Tirich Mir, at 25,263 feet (7,700 meters).

Through the millennia the mountainous wall of the Hindu Kush has been both a barrier and a gateway to mankind: standing astride one of history's great routes of commerce and conquest, its high mountain passes have been crossed by countless merchants and warriors in search of the riches on the other side. As long ago as 328 B.C., Alexander the Great strug-

gled across the Hindu Kush with an army of 32,000 men. In A.D. 1220 Genghis Khan crossed the mountains with his conquering horde, and later in that century Marco Polo traversed the range on his way to the fabled Orient. Still later the Mongol Tamerlane and his descendant Babur also crossed the mountains as they sought to extend their empires.

Today the Hindu Kush is somewhat more accessible to travelers. Roads penetrate parts of the range, and several tunnels have been built beneath key mountain passes. The scenery that visitors discover is remarkably austere. Forests flourish in lowland valleys. But at higher elevations there is little more than scattered shrubs and occasional grassy meadows to mask the stark contours of rugged, rock-strewn slopes.

Although glaciers still cling to the highest mountainsides in the eastern part of the range, they are mere remnants of much more extensive ice caps that once covered the Hindu Kush. Among the many evidences of past glaciation are sharply chiseled, pyramidal peaks similar to the Swiss "horns," glistening lakes held back by dams of glacial debris, and grassy, U-shaped, glacier-sculpted valleys, which are often dotted in summer with

Cross Section of the Himalaya Region

The varied and complexly deformed rocks of the Himalayas reveal the story of a massive collision of continents. Geologists believe that the crustal plate of ancient basement rock that now underlies the Indian subcontinent drifted north over a long period and collided with the Asian continent 65 million years ago. When the two masses met, the leading edge of the Indian plate was forced down under the edge of the Asian plate. At the same time, layers of sedimentary rock that had formed at the bottom of a sea that once lay between the two crustal plates were folded, heaved up, and even overturned as the paroxysm continued over millions of years. Pockets of magma welled up from beneath the earth's crust, cooling and hardening to form intrusions of granitic rock. The great heat and pressure that accompanied the collision also transformed some of the sedimentary rock into metamorphic rock. Today the long mountain range marks the line where two landmasses were joined into one.

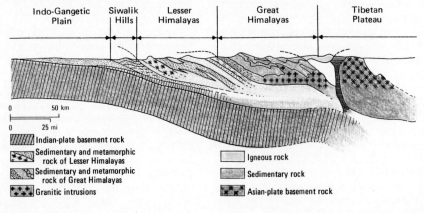

Indo-Gangetic Plain | Siwalik Hills | Lesser Himalayas | Great Himalayas | Tibetan Plateau

0   50 km
0   25 mi

- Indian-plate basement rock
- Sedimentary and metamorphic rock of Lesser Himalayas
- Sedimentary and metamorphic rock of Great Himalayas
- Granitic intrusions
- Igneous rock
- Sedimentary rock
- Asian-plate basement rock

HINDU KUSH. *Widely scattered plants and dusty grasslands relieve the austerity of bare, rocky slopes in the heart of Afghanistan's remote and ancient mountain range.*

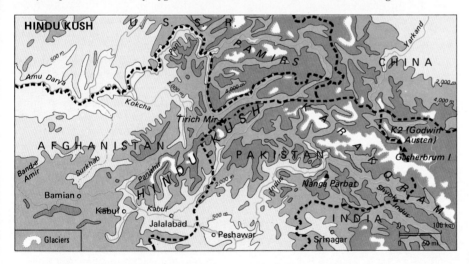

Hölloch Cave

● Switzerland
● Map: page 17, D–4

More than a century of exploration has proved this complex grotto to be the longest cave system in Europe.

When its first explorer entered this forbidding cavern (the name means "hellhole" in German) in 1875, he could hardly have guessed that more than a century later its exploration would still be incomplete. Beyond his first tentative probe there was a truly astonishing undiscovered maze of tunnels, chambers, and underground springs dissolved at several levels in the limestone formation in central Switzerland.

Additional exploration took place around the turn of the century, but it was not until the 1950's that speleologists (cave explorers) began in earnest to unravel the secrets of Hölloch Cave. By 1954 about 30 miles (50 kilometers) of passageways had been surveyed. Probes continued year by year until in 1968 more than 60 miles (100 kilometers) of tunnels were known, making Hölloch the longest mapped cave system in the world at that time. (It has since been surpassed by Mammoth Cave in Kentucky.) By 1976 the cave was found to be approximately 80 miles (130 kilometers) long—the longest cave system in Europe. And parts of it have yet to be explored.

Today visitors can tour a portion of the cave near its entrance. But the dark depths beyond remain the realm of expert speleologists. □

HÖLLOCH CAVE. *The immense Alpine cave has few stalactites or stalagmites, but those it does contain are exceptionally formed. Some resemble slender alabaster tapers.*

the tentlike yurts of nomadic herders.

Geologists are not certain how old the mountains are, since they developed in stages over a long period of time. The first mountain-building episode probably occurred at least 400 million years ago, with further folding and uplift taking place about 250 million years ago, and again about 40 million years ago. Still further uplift has continued within the past 5 million years, elevating the complexly folded peaks of the Hindu Kush to their tremendous heights. Frequent,

often powerful earthquakes in parts of the range, moreover, indicate that the mountains are still growing.

Though the Hindu Kush has been known to geographers since antiquity, it remains sparsely populated and little touched by the rest of the world. Now, however, the mountains are believed to contain considerable mineral wealth. (Rich deposits of the gemstone lapis lazuli have been prized for centuries.) Perhaps the Hindu Kush will not much longer be able to resist the intrusion of the modern world. □

Holmslands Klit

- Denmark
- Map: page 16, D–3

A belt of dunes built up by the wind and waves completely blocks the entrance to a coastal lagoon.

About midway along the west coast of Denmark, a long narrow spit of land separates the placid waters of a broad shallow lagoon from the storm-tossed waters of the North Sea. Known as Holmslands Klit, the barrier is about 20 miles (32 kilometers) long and little more than 1 mile (1.6 kilometers) wide. This natural levee, covered with huge billowing dunes that rise up to 80 feet (25 meters) in height, was built up of masses of sand that was carried in by waves and currents and then modeled by the wind.

At one time a narrow channel at the southern end of Holmslands Klit connected the lagoon (which is actually called the Ringkobing Fjord) with the sea, but constantly shifting sand eventually clogged the opening. In order to alleviate coastal flooding after storms (several rivers drain into the lagoon), an artificial channel was cut across the barrier earlier in this century. Now seawater flows into the lagoon whenever the tide is high, while fresh water from the rivers flows out to sea whenever the tide recedes.

A road runs the entire length of Holmslands Klit, permitting easy exploration of the sandy barrier. Part of the area has been set aside for recreation and to preserve a portion of this unique coastal landscape. Also nearby is Tipperne Reserve, the largest bird sanctuary in Denmark. □

CAPE HORN. *The somber, eroded headland at the tip of a small island, Isla Hornos, is exposed to violent storms that batter the southernmost extremity of Tierra del Fuego.*

Horn, Cape

- Chile
- Map: page 15, C–8

Even in modern ships, "rounding the Horn" is often a perilous journey past forbidding, gale-swept shores.

Few places on earth are associated with such tales of violence and drama as is this inoffensive-looking headland on an island lying off the southern tip of South America. The promontory, known to seamen the world over simply as "the Horn," faces the great westerly winds of the Southern Hemisphere and watches over one of the world's most perilous maritime routes.

Although the cape is actually a rocky headland on Isla Hornos, an island about 70 miles (110 kilometers) south of Tierra del Fuego, it is considered the southernmost extremity of South America. No point on any continent lies closer to Antarctica. Its somber, shaly cliffs have been lashed for centuries by fierce storms and crashing seas and long ago were honed down by Ice Age glaciers.

For years mariners believed that the Strait of Magellan was the only passage through a continent that was thought to extend to the South Pole. In 1616, however, Willem van Schouten, a Dutch seaman, discovered the more southerly route around the cape, and he named it Hoorn after his father's birthplace in Holland.

Following the California gold rush in 1849, countless clipper ships braved the Horn's savage gales rather than navigate the shorter but even more treacherous Strait of Magellan. Traffic declined after the opening of the Panama Canal in 1914. But today supertankers too big for the canal are once again "rounding the Horn." □

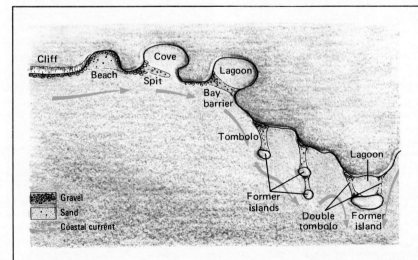

Coastal Barriers Built by Shifting Sands

Beaches change from storm to storm and from season to season as waves and coastal currents constantly rearrange the materials that make them up. When migrating sand reaches a coastal indentation such as a bay, it may be deposited in the form of a spit—a sand barrier that reaches only part of the way across the opening. Eventually the spit may extend all the way across the indentation, as at Holmslands Klit, forming a structure called a bay barrier and transforming the bay into a lagoon. Or the sand barrier may link a rocky island to the mainland, forming a so-called tombolo. In some places coastal currents flowing in opposite directions may build up a double tombolo: twin barriers enclosing a small lagoon.

Hudson River

- United States (New Jersey—New York)
- Map: page 11, F–4

From source to sea, a sparkling mountain stream is transformed into a major avenue of commerce.

In 1609, when Henry Hudson sailed his *Half Moon* up the river that now bears his name, he thought for a time he had discovered the long-sought-after Northwest Passage—a sea route that was believed to cut across North America, connecting Europe with the riches of the Orient. He had good reason for hoping he had discovered a strait between the Atlantic and Pacific oceans. Sailing north for about 150 miles (240 kilometers) to the present site of Albany, New York, he felt the twice-daily ebb and flow of Atlantic tides. (Even at Albany the average daily tidal range is about 5 feet, or 1.5 meters.) But just a little farther north he discovered that the great river becomes too shallow for navigation, and he abandoned his search.

The Hudson is far from a giant among the rivers of the world. From source to sea it travels only about 315 miles (500 kilometers). Yet its beauty, which inspired a whole generation of landscape painters, has often been compared to that of the Rhine.

The river rises in Lake Tear of the Clouds, a glacial tarn on the flanks of Mount Marcy, the highest peak in New York State. For the first third of its course the Hudson is a typical mountain stream, foaming across waterfalls and rapids as it winds down forested slopes of the Adirondacks. At Hudson Falls, north of its confluence with the Mohawk, its major tributary, the river turns abruptly south. From there to its mouth in New York Bay, the Hudson continues on an almost due-south course.

By the time it reaches Albany the river has fallen nearly to sea level. Hence the penetration of tides so far inland. With a barely perceptible gradient, the lower half of the river is a tidal estuary, a long narrow arm of the sea. Broad and deep, it is also a major shipping channel navigable by ocean-going vessels.

South of Albany the Hudson flows through a broad picturesque valley, bordered on the east by the Taconic Mountains and on the west by the gently rolling summits of the Catskills. South of Newburgh the channel is

HUDSON RIVER. *About 200 million years ago lava oozed from deep within the earth and hardened into columns to form the Palisades, which tower over the Hudson near its mouth.*

abruptly constricted as the river proceeds between the ancient metamorphic peaks of the Hudson Highlands. Then even more abruptly the river broadens again to its greatest width: from shore to shore this stretch, known as the Tappan Zee, is about 3.5 miles (5.6 kilometers) across.

The lower course of the river is a place of great contrasts. On the west bank the river is hemmed in by the towering cliffs of the Palisades. As much as 550 feet (170 meters) high, the cliffs are the edge of a sheet of once-molten rock that was intruded as a fluid mass between layers of sedimentary rock. Cracking as it cooled, the extremely hard traprock split into the stockadelike columns that account for much of the beauty of the Palisades. On the east bank of the river, in striking contrast, are the man-made towers

that form the skyline of Manhattan.

The river does not end at New York Bay, however. Beyond its mouth a deep, steep-sided submarine canyon extends across the ocean floor for about 150 miles (240 kilometers). It was carved during the Ice Age, when great glaciers ground down the ancestral Hudson Valley, scouring out and deepening its channel. (In the Highlands the channel was ground down to 800 feet, or 245 meters, below sea level but has since been largely refilled by sediment.) With sea levels lowered because so much water was frozen in continental ice sheets, meltwater from the glaciers carved the canyon across the continental shelf. Then at the end of the Ice Age about 10,000 years ago, sea levels rose again and drowned the Hudson's mighty offshore canyon beneath restless Atlantic waves. □

HUNLEN FALLS. *After flowing through calm glacial lakes and dense green forests, the waters of the Hunlen River descend with one glorious leap into the rocky gorge far below.*

Hunlen Falls

- Canada (British Columbia)
- Map: page 10, C–3

Near the end of its short course, the Hunlen River plunges over a sheer precipice that is nearly seven times the height of famed Niagara Falls.

Hidden away in the Coast Mountains of western British Columbia is a vast untamed wilderness nearly twice the size of Delaware—Tweedsmuir Provincial Park. Among the many scenic attractions in this wildly beautiful landscape are glacier-clad mountain peaks, deep canyons, dense evergreen forests, fish-filled lakes and streams, and broad rolling meadows that are luxuriantly carpeted in spring and summer with brilliant displays of alpine wildflowers.

But the park's crowning glory is Hunlen Falls, one of the highest waterfalls in North America. Plunging in a single uninterrupted leap down the face of a cliff into a narrow rocky gorge, the water drops for a total of approximately 1,200 feet (365 meters) —almost seven times the height of Niagara Falls.

The falls occur on the Hunlen River just north of its confluence with the Atnarko River in the southern part of the park. Though the river is short (its total course is less than 20 miles, or 32 kilometers), the volume of its flow is substantial. Fed by runoff from glaciers and winter snows on the nearby mountains, it streams across a heavily forested plateau. Mule deer and bears can be seen along its banks, and moose frequent the marshy shores of the chain of glacial lakes that interrupt the river's course. (Visitors to the area find that the lakes are ideal for flatwater canoeing.)

The Hunlen makes its formidable leap just a short distance beyond its outlet from Turner Lake, the last lake in the chain. Hurtling over the precipice, the placid lake water is suddenly transformed into a seething sheet of foam and spray.

To reach the falls, visitors must hike a trail about 10 miles (16 kilometers) long from the only highway passing through the park. The hike is worth the effort, however. At the end of the trail, visitors are rewarded with the view of Hunlen Falls, still unspoiled and looking much as it did centuries ago when only Indians roamed this breathtakingly beautiful region. ☐

Ichang Gorges

● China
● Map: page 19, M–5

Deep and swift, the Yangtze surges through a series of spectacular gorges as it journeys toward the sea.

China's great river, the Yangtze, is one of many moods. From its source in the Tibetan highlands to its outlet on the East China Sea, it flows past craggy mountains, through bustling cities, and across fertile plains. One of its most scenic sectors, however, is found where the Yangtze passes from the province of Szechwan into Hupeh. Over a distance of about 125 miles (200 kilometers), the Yangtze passes through a series of three long gorges just upstream from the city of Ichang, for which the giant clefts are named.

Narrow, deep, and steep-sided, the gorges have been carved into thick limestone formations. In places the canyon walls rise almost straight up from the water's edge for as much as 2,000 feet (600 meters). Elsewhere they slope up less abruptly and have been eroded into fantastic towers. Ferns and many other shade-loving plants grow among the crags and niches, adding a surprising note of beauty to the somber depths where sunshine rarely penetrates.

A few million years ago there were no gorges here, nor even highlands. The Yangtze then flowed over a level plain. As the plain was gradually uplifted, the river etched its course into the rising surface, eroding its bed downward as quickly as the land rose.

In areas of softer rock between the gorges, the river carved a broad channel up to 2,000 feet (600 meters) across. In the more resistant limestone formations where it carved the gorges, the river narrows to only about 500 feet (150 meters) across. Because the volume of water flowing through the narrows is the same as that flowing through wider sections of the river, its depth increases abruptly in the gorges. In some places, in fact, the channel is as much as 600 feet (180 meters) deep, making the Yangtze the deepest river in the world. □

IGUASSÚ FALLS. *Veil upon veil of falling water cascades over the cliffs in a junglelike setting, filling an otherwise peaceful paradise with the sound of rolling thunder.*

Iguassú Falls

● Argentina—Brazil
● Map: page 15, D–5

White waters, emerald forests, and multicolored birds and flowers are all part of the spectacle at one of the finest waterfalls in the entire world.

From its source in the Serra do Mar, not far from the Atlantic coast, the Rio Iguassú flows westward for about 820 miles (1,320 kilometers) across southern Brazil. Gathering tributaries, the river grows steadily in volume as it meanders across the uplands of the Paraná Plateau. And step by step it makes its way toward sea level, tumbling over some 70 waterfalls that interrupt its course. One of them, Ñacunday Falls, has a drop of 131 feet (40 meters)—nearly that of Niagara Falls.

But the river takes its grandest leap just a short distance above its confluence with the Paraná, where the Iguassú forms the boundary between Argentina and Brazil. Plunging at last off the edge of the plateau, the river thunders down in what one observer likened to the "awesome spectacle of an ocean pouring into an abyss."

Strung out along the rim of a crescent-shaped cliff about 2½ miles (4 kilometers) long is a series of some 275 individual cascades and waterfalls separated by rocky, densely wooded islets. Some of the cascades plummet straight down for 269 feet (82 meters) into the gorge below. Others are interrupted by ledges and send up clouds of mist and spray, creating a dazzling display of rainbows.

The falls, which would be memorable in any setting, are made all the more beautiful by their lush surroundings. The luxuriant forests are filled with bamboos, palms, and delicate tree ferns. Brilliantly feathered parrots and macaws flit through the foliage, competing for attention with the exotic blooms of wild orchids, begonias, and bromeliads.

National parks have been established on both the Argentine and Brazilian sides of the falls. Visitors can view the spectacle from scenic overlooks, from helicopters, and even from catwalks that lead directly over the thundering cataracts.

The falls are at their best during the rainy season from November to March. The flow slows down during the rest of the year—sometimes drastically. In May and June of 1978 the falls dried up completely for 28 days, the first time such a thing had happened since 1934. But normally Iguassú is a dependable, ever-changing spectacle throughout the year. □

ILLAMPU. *In sharp contrast to the somber Altiplano at their foot, snowcapped Andean peaks glisten majestically against a cloudless sky.*

Illampu

- Bolivia
- Map: page 14, C–4

A massive mountain burdened with glaciers and crowned with twin peaks is among the highest in Bolivia.

South America's great mountain system, the Andes, divides into two major ranges where it crosses Bolivia. To the east is the Cordillera Oriental (Eastern Range) and to the west is the Cordillera Occidental (Western Range). Connecting the two ranges is the Altiplano, a high plateau that is itself approximately 12,000 feet (3,650 meters) above sea level.

Lake Titicaca, the highest navigable lake in the world, is cupped in a depression in the northern part of the Altiplano. And off to the east, forming a magnificent backdrop for the glistening lake and windswept heights, is the imposing angular profile of Illampu, the highest mountain in Bolivia's Cordillera Oriental. Massive, steep-sided, and permanently covered with ice and snow, it culminates in two named summits: Illampu to the north (21,276 feet, or 6,485 meters) and Ancohuma to the south (21,489 feet, or 6,550 meters). Covered with glaciers down to an altitude of about 15,500 feet (4,725 meters), the snow-white massif juts up majestically above the Altiplano.

Illampu began to form about 20 million years ago. While the earth's crust was being folded and uplifted, a mass of molten material welled upward into the overlying layers of ancient sedimentary rock, then cooled and hardened to form the granitic heart of the mountain. Further uplift took place when the entire massif was forced upward between giant faults, or fractures in the earth's crust. Subsequent erosion and intense glaciation wore away much of the sedimentary rock and carved the mountain into its present form—a majestic, forbidding, and awesome sight. □

Illimani

- Bolivia
- Map: page 14, C–4

Austerely snow-clad, the "Glistening Falcon" of the Bolivian Andes looms high above the city of La Paz.

Southeast of La Paz, the capital of Bolivia, Illimani's three glacier-covered crests loom against the horizon. An object of both fear and veneration, the brooding Andean massif has long been known to local inhabitants as the "Glistening Falcon."

At 21,184 feet (6,457 meters), Illimani is merely the second highest mountain (after Illampu) in Bolivia's Cordillera Oriental (Eastern Range). Yet its unusual setting makes it exceptionally impressive. Surging abruptly above rugged foothills at the edge of the Altiplano, or High Plain, the mountain seems to be resting on a vast pedestal. Deep valleys scar its flanks, and to the north a broad pass separates it almost completely from other nearby mountains.

Two violent upheavals of the earth's crust gave birth to the Glistening Falcon. In the first episode, which probably began some 20 million years ago, ancient sedimentary rock layers in the area were drastically folded and uplifted. At the same time a mass of molten material known as a batholith welled up into the overlying strata and later hardened into granitic rock.

A long period of erosion followed, until about 2 million years ago the massif moved upward again along a fault line to its present elevation. Four successive periods of glaciation then honed the mountain's contours.

Glaciers still descend to about 5,400 feet (1,650 meters) below Illimani's summits. Lower slopes are covered with grasslands and in places with scattered remnants of forests. Cacao, coffee, and sugarcane are cultivated in some of the fertile valleys.

Although Illimani is only about 200 miles (320 kilometers) from the Pacific Ocean, the rain and snowfall on its slopes take a roundabout journey to the sea. Flowing into the La Paz River, a headwater of the Amazon, most of its streams drain ultimately into the Atlantic Ocean on the opposite coast of South America. □

Irazú

- Costa Rica
- Map: page 13, D–3

Visitors to the Central American volcano enjoy a rare spectacle: the view from the top encompasses both the Atlantic and Pacific oceans.

With its flanks sloping up to an elevation of 11,260 feet (3,432 meters), Irazú is the highest peak in Costa Rica's Cordillera Central. The volcano, located about 20 miles (32 kilometers) from the capital city of San José, is also a popular tourist destination. A paved road winds up the forested mountainside all the way to the rim of Irazú's crater.

At times visitors to the summit see only the top of a sea of clouds far below, completely masking the landscape in all directions. But when the clouds rise, they enjoy the rare spectacle of viewing two oceans at the same time. Off to the east of this high vantage point on the Central American isthmus is the Caribbean Sea, which is an arm of the Atlantic Ocean; to the west are the blue waters of the Pacific Ocean.

Though quiescent at present, Irazú has not always been so. From March 1963 to February 1965, the volcano erupted almost constantly, spewing sulfurous fumes and clouds of gritty ash over the entire country. When it rained, large accumulations of ash came roaring down the slopes in huge mud slides.

While the eruption was not fatal, it caused severe crop damage and was a constant annoyance to residents of the nearby cities of Cartago and San José. Fine windblown dust seemed to settle everywhere. The cities were constantly shrouded in a grayish, choking haze and at times were swept by clouds of acrid smoke. Residents took to wearing bandannas, goggles, and even gas masks whenever they ventured into the streets.

As eruptions continued, the walls of Irazú's crater caved in repeatedly in recurring landslides. By the time the volcano quieted down, the diameter of the crater had increased from 660 feet (200 meters) to 1,720 feet (525 meters).

Today the volcano is dormant once again. And again tourists venture to Irazú's summit to peer into the gaping crater and to enjoy the view of two oceans from the top. □

Iskar Gorges

- Bulgaria
- Map: page 17, F–4

Whether by train or by car, an excursion through the zigzag gorges offers ever-changing scenic views.

The Iskar Gorges are the chief pass through the Balkan Mountains, which stretch in an almost unbroken line across northern Bulgaria. About 45 miles (70 kilometers) in length, the winding gorges are particularly noted for their varied colors and picturesque rocky walls.

The gorges were carved by rushing waters of the Iskar River, a north-flowing tributary of the Danube. Incised into complexly folded layers of limestone and sandstone, the walls are by turns snowy white, ashen gray, and varied shades of red. In one place they rise almost straight up for about 1,000 feet (300 meters). Elsewhere they are topped by fantastic crags and towers. And in one spot a Vauclusian spring bubbles up from a limestone cave on the canyon wall. □

IRAZÚ. *Quiescent again after erupting constantly for two years in the 1960's, the volcano still emits jets of noxious fumes from vents in its broad lake-filled crater.*

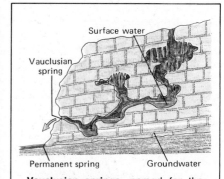

Vauclusian springs, named for the Fontaine-de-Vaucluse in France, are springs in limestone terrain where water emerges under pressure by way of an upward-sloping channel.

ITABIRITO. *Beneath the mountain's jagged summit, broken boulders have taken on a rusty patina, the result of their high content of hematite, an important type of iron ore.*

Itabirito

- Brazil
- Map: page 14, E–5

In a region rich in minerals, a rugged mountain peak is made up of rock composed of almost pure iron.

To the north of Rio de Janeiro, in the Brazilian highlands, is the sprawling state of Minas Gerais. The name means "General Mines," and for good reason. Ever since gold was discovered there in the 1690's, and then diamonds in 1729, prospectors have scoured its streams and rumpled mountains in search of mineral wealth. Aquamarines have been found in Minas Gerais, as well as amethysts, topazes, and other semiprecious stones. Its hills have yielded rich lodes of bauxite, manganese, nickel, molybdenum, and other valuable ores.

But today the region is most famous for its extensive deposits of iron ore. The magnificent rugged highlands to the south and southeast of the capital city of Belo Horizonte are so rich in the metal, in fact, that the region is sometimes known as "the Iron Rectangle." Entire mountains are made up of a type of metamorphic rock composed of the mineral hematite, which may contain as much as 70 percent iron. The land itself looks as if it has been splashed with iron rust, just as it does in other iron-rich, red-earth regions of the world. The total reserves of high-grade ore here are in fact among the largest on earth.

Among the many nearly solid iron mountains in the area, one of the most characteristic is the peak known as Itabirito. Travelers going from Belo Horizonte to the former capital of Ouro Prêto can hardly fail to notice its striking profile dominating the hills and deeply eroded intervening valleys. Part of a sawtooth ridge of peaks, it rises like a strange, stark beacon. More or less cone-shaped, it is formed of barren rocky walls that drop precipitously from the craggy summit.

Like the neighboring ridges topped by jagged triangular crests, the one on which Itabirito stands is the mere root of an ancient folded mountain. Attacked by the forces of erosion over the course of 2 billion years, the mountains have been almost completely destroyed; only their metamorphic cores remain.

And now man has entered the picture. Using explosives and power machinery, miners are stripping away the easily excavated ore of the Iron Rectangle and shipping it off to blast furnaces. Even Itabirito, like other nearby peaks, is slowly being whittled away. Before long it is possible that this age-old landmark will disappear completely. □

The Three Types of Rocks

Depending on their origin, the rocks that make up the earth's crust are classed as igneous, sedimentary, and metamorphic rocks. Igneous rocks form when magma, the earth's molten inner material, cools and hardens. Magma that is extruded onto the surface of the earth is called lava, which cools and hardens quickly to form various kinds of so-called extrusive igneous rocks. Some examples include obsidian (a glasslike volcanic rock), pumice (such as the pumice stones sold in drugstores), and basalt (a dark, fine-grained volcanic rock). Intrusive igneous rocks, in contrast, form when magma hardens without ever reaching the surface; cooling slowly, the magma solidifies into coarse-grained crystalline rocks (such as granite).

Sedimentary rocks are produced when layers of water- or wind-borne materials are consolidated into stone. They may be composed of fragments eroded from older, preexisting rocks (such as sandstone and shale), of the remains of plants or animals (such as coal and certain types of limestone), and of minerals that were once dissolved in water (such as rock salt and gypsum). Characteristically deposited in horizontal layers, sedimentary rocks often include fossils of plants and animals that lived when the rocks were being formed.

Metamorphic rocks, like those that make up much of the Brazilian highlands, result from the transformation of other types of rocks. Subjected to intense heat and pressure by such forces as mountain-building movements or simply by being buried at great depths, they are changed in structure, texture, and appearance. Granite may be metamorphosed into gneiss, limestone into marble, and shale into slate. Metamorphic rocks, in turn, may be altered over time into still other types of metamorphic rock.

J

Jean-Bernard Cave

- France
- Map: page 17, D–4

First discovered in 1963, this subterranean wonderland of tunnels, chambers, and underground rivers has proved to be the second deepest cavern in all the world.

JEAN-BERNARD CAVE. *In the dark, silent depths of the cavern, slender stalactites and other fragile cave formations decorate the complex maze of winding passageways.*

Hidden in a limestone massif in the Alpine foothills south of Lake Geneva is a vast cave system that was completely unknown to the world before 1963. Like other limestone caves, it was formed by the dissolving action of slightly acidic groundwater as it drained through cracks and crevices in the rock.

Five known entrances to Jean-Bernard Cave are perched at various levels on the slopes. The vertical distance between the highest and lowest entrances is approximately 1,000 feet (300 meters). Beyond them lies a complicated labyrinth of narrow winding tunnels, shafts, chambers, and galleries, many of which are adorned with delicate stalactites and other cave formations. A number of underground rivers course through the network, splashing eerily in the darkness, while other tunnels at higher elevations are now completely dry.

Exploration of the cave began almost immediately with its discovery in 1963. By 1969 a group of spelunkers (cave explorers) had descended to a depth of 2,044 feet (623 meters) below the uppermost entrance. There they were stopped by a siphon, a U-shaped tunnel completely filled with water, and exploration of the cave temporarily ceased.

The subsequent discovery of another entrance to the cave revived the interest of spelunkers. Probing new tunnels into the labyrinth, they managed to bypass the siphon and descended to a new depth of 3,077 feet (938 meters), where a mass of fallen rocks blocked their progress.

Removal of the rocks in 1976 permitted the group to descend to yet another siphon at a depth of 4,259 feet (1,298 meters). So it was that Jean-Bernard Cave was revealed to be the deepest limestone cave in the Alps and the second deepest cave in the entire world. It is exceeded only by Pierre-Saint-Martin Cavern on the French side of the Pyrenees Mountains, which has a maximum depth of 4,364 feet (1,330 meters). □

How Seeping Water Carves Limestone Caves and Decorates Them With Mineral Deposits

Slowly seeping water is the agent that carves limestone caves. When rainwater percolates through the soil, it becomes charged with carbon dioxide, forming a mild acid capable of dissolving limestone. Making its way through cracks and crevices in the rock, it gradually enlarges them to form sinkholes opening to the surface, vertical shafts and chimneys, horizontal galleries, and even large chambers. Rockfalls from the ceiling sometimes help enlarge the openings. After thousands of years, limestone formations frequently become honeycombed with complex labyrinths of interconnected chambers and galleries.

Seeping water is also the agent that decorates caves with elaborate formations. As it erodes the limestone, it becomes saturated with dissolved minerals. Dripping from the ceiling or flowing in thin films across the walls, the water evaporates and the minerals are redeposited on the surface. Stalactites grow down from the ceiling, and stalagmites grow up from the floor; the two sometimes meet to form columns. Draperies, flowstone terraces, and numerous other formations create an enchanting subterranean world in limestone caves.

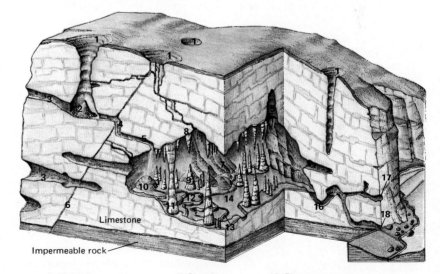

1. Sinkhole	7. Chamber	13. Flowstone terrace
2. Rockfall	8. Stalactite	14. Underground lake
3. Gallery	9. Stalagmite	15. Chimney
4. Vertical shaft	10. Dome	16. Siphon
5. Underground stream	11. Column	17. Former resurgence (spring)
6. Fault	12. Pool	18. Active resurgence (spring)

Jeita Cave

- Lebanon
- Map: page 18, E–5

An accidental discovery led in time to the exploration of one of the largest cave systems in all of Asia.

During a hunting trip in the 1830's, an American named Thompson stopped to rest in the shade at the entrance to a small cave about 10 miles (16 kilometers) northeast of Beirut. Hearing what he thought was the sound of running water, he crept into the opening and found himself at the edge of a large underground lake. Just how large it might be Thompson could only imagine: when he fired his rifle into the darkness, the sound reverberated like rolling thunder.

Serious exploration of the mysterious grotto did not begin until 1873, when a group of men returned with a small boat. Water was flowing into the lake via an underground river. The overflow, in turn, emerged at a large nearby spring, the source of Nahr el Kalb ("The Dog River"), which supplies Beirut with drinking water. Tracing the course of the underground river, the explorers penetrated some 3,300 feet (1,000 meters) upstream, where they were stopped by Hell's Rapids, a treacherous underground waterfall.

Exploration continued well into this century, with each expedition reveal-

JEITA CAVE. *Dripstone draperies cover the walls in parts of the immense Lebanese labyrinth. Certain other formations, when strummed, produce rich musical tones.*

ing more of the labyrinth. (Diving equipment had to be used to pass through tunnels completely filled with water.) Today Jeita Cave is known to include more than five miles (eight kilometers) of passageways, making it one of the largest cave systems in Asia.

It is also among the most beautiful. Dry passageways where the underground river at one time flowed are now filled with fantastic displays of cave formations, including stalactites, stalagmites, rippled travertine draperies, multicolored columns, and numerous other deposits of dripstone. Visitors can tour illuminated portions of the cave on foot and by boat. They can also attend concerts in an immense natural underground auditorium that is noted for its exceptional acoustics. ☐

Jenolan Caves

- Australia
- Map: page 23, F–5

Wonders abound on the surface as well as underground at one of the most spectacular caves in Australia.

According to local stories, Jenolan Caves were first discovered in 1841 by searchers hunting for a notorious highwayman who used them as a hideout. Situated in the Blue Mountains about 70 miles (110 kilometers) west of Sydney, they are now the most famous underground tourist attraction in Australia.

The caves, which began to form about 500,000 years ago, are eroded into thick beds of limestone and marble. A maze of intersecting tunnels and immense chambers, the caves are decorated throughout with dazzling displays of intricately sculpted cave formations. Some are sparkling white; others have been tinted orange, yellow, and reddish-brown by traces of iron in the seeping water that formed them. Parts of the caves are artificially illuminated, while other areas are lighted by shafts of sunlight that angle down through natural windowlike openings in the ceilings.

Just as interesting as the caves themselves is the aboveground area, preserved as a nature sanctuary. Wallabies, wombats, and spiny anteaters all can be seen there. Black swans swim on a nearby lake, and lyrebirds and satin bowerbirds are sometimes glimpsed along the trails. ☐

Jewel Cave

- United States (South Dakota)
- Map: page 10, D–4

The underground labyrinth, lined with glittering mineral crystals, is an exquisite natural treasure chest.

About 1900, two men traveling in the rugged Hell Canyon in the Black Hills region of South Dakota were attracted by the strange whistling of wind from a hole partway up on the canyon wall. Enlarging the opening, the men discovered that it was the entrance to a cave. An even bigger surprise awaited them when their eyes grew accustomed to the dim light: the walls of the cave were heavily encrusted with thick layers of jewellike crystals of the mineral calcite.

The men filed a claim to the area, calling it Jewel Lode, and began to mine the shimmering crystals. In their spare time they explored the cavern, which came to be known as Jewel Cave, and found that many of the chambers and passageways were lined with similar crystals and an astonishing variety of other beautiful cave formations.

The federal government compensated the men for improvements to the cave and in 1908 created Jewel Cave National Monument. More than 60 miles (100 kilometers) of passageways have so far been explored, making Jewel Cave one of the largest cave systems in the world.

As in other limestone caverns, the underground passageways at Jewel Cave developed when slightly acidic groundwater dissolved the limestone as it seeped through cracks and fissures in the rock. The water that filled the passages, moreover, became saturated with dissolved minerals, which were redeposited on the walls in the form of crystals of amazing beauty and variety. Much of this jewellike adornment is called dogtooth spar because the pointed crystals resemble large canine teeth. In places the layers of crystals on the walls are 7 inches (18 centimeters) thick.

The water has since drained from the cave, and many other formations have been deposited on the walls. In addition to stalactites and stalagmites, some of the more unusual decorations include clusters of needlelike mineral crystals known as frostwork, bunches of knobby nodules called popcorn, and flowerlike growths of gypsum

JEWEL CAVE. *An amazing variety of rare formations abounds here, including delicately beautiful tangled strands of gypsum that are found in a few remote areas of the cave.*

crystals. Among the rarest are strange bubblelike formations with paper-thin walls that are found at Jewel Cave and nowhere else in the world.

The wind often whistles through the entrance and some of the passageways at Jewel Cave. It is apparently caused by differences in atmospheric pressure, with the air moving from areas of higher to lower pressure. □

Jigokudani Hot Springs

- Japan
- Map: page 19, P–4

One look into this old but not entirely extinct volcanic crater is enough to explain the reason for its name—the Valley of Hell.

Japan, a land of earthquakes and volcanoes, has long been renowned for its hot-spring resorts. One of them, tucked away in a densely wooded valley on the northernmost island of Hokkaido, is the famous Noboribetsu Spa. Behind the main hotel a broad slope leads up to the rim of an old volcanic crater about 1¼ miles (2 kilometers) in circumference and 325 feet (100 meters) deep. Hidden inside the crater is an unearthly spectacle, Jigokudani Hot Springs.

The desolate, tormented appearance of the place vividly conveys the meaning of its name: "the Valley of Hell." On the crater's slopes and floor are numerous domelike hillocks, their

fractured surfaces painted in garish combinations of ocher, yellow, and red. Through the openings in the surface a multitude of hot springs hiss and bubble incessantly, churning with boiling water and scalding mud.

Erupting here and there amid the small geysers are solfataras, which emit violent bursts of steam and sulfurous gases. One of the solfataras, now extinct and dried out, bristles weirdly with a cluster of stunted, shriveled bamboos. And cupped in a low point on the crater floor is a dead lake of sulfurous water fed by emissions of the hot springs.

The crater is never free from the sounds of hissing vapors, growling springs, and rumblings from deep underground. As a result, many of its volcanic orifices bear such descriptive names as the Kettle, the Cannon, and the Tiger. □

Jostedal Glacier

- Norway
- Map: page 16, D–2

The largest ice field in Europe is a mere relic of vast glaciers that once covered much of the region.

Perched high on a mountainous plateau in southern Norway is a glistening white expanse of permanent ice and snow, a mecca for hardy hikers who delight in trekking across it on foot or on skis. Known as the Jostedal Glacier, it is located northeast of the famed Sogne Fjord on a tableland that averages some 4,750 feet (1,450 meters) above sea level.

The central ice cap, which is believed to be more than 1,000 feet (300 meters) thick, is fringed by about 25 glacial tongues that radiate downward into the surrounding valleys. No high mountains rise above the Jostedal; its sole source of replenishment is frequent and abundant snowfall nourished by a steady flow of moist air from the Atlantic Ocean. A single peak, the Lodalskapa, at 6,834 feet (2,083 meters), is the only bit of land that projects above the flat, frigid expanse of 315 square miles (815 square kilometers) of ice and snow.

The Jostedal is one of the few surviving remnants of a vast continental ice cap that retreated northward and all but disappeared at the end of the last ice age about 10,000 years ago. Since then the glacier and its branches have shrunk and expanded in response to climatic changes. They enlarged considerably during the 18th century but began to shrink around 1930; they have been expanding again since 1960. □

JIGOKUDANI HOT SPRINGS. *Clouds of suffocating vapors and multicolored sulfurous deposits contribute to the unearthly spectacle at this famous Japanese hot-spring resort.*

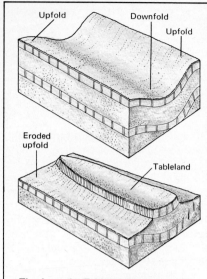

The Jugurtha Tableland is an example of inverted relief. It was formed when gently folded rock layers were eroded in such a way that a downfold (valley bottom) remained as the top of a tableland after the surrounding upfolds had been worn away.

Jugurtha Tableland

● Tunisia
● Map: page 24, D–2

Once the bottom of a valley, an imposing natural fortress now looms high above the surrounding plain.

Soaring some 2,000 feet (600 meters) above the plain of ez-Zghalma in western Tunisia is a great rampartlike butte known as the Jugurtha Tableland. Rimmed by near-vertical cliffs, the almost flat-topped formation is about 5,000 feet (1,500 meters) long and 1,600 feet (500 meters) wide.

The tableland, which resembles a fortress, was long ago recognized as a virtually invincible stronghold. In the second century B.C., Jugurtha, king of the ancient North African kingdom of Numidia, adapted it for use as a citadel in his war against Rome. Even today the uppermost cliffs bear traces of 180 steps his men had to chisel into the sheer rock to gain access to the top of the tableland.

Capped by a protective layer of hard limestone over softer shaly formations, the tableland came into existence as the surrounding hills were worn away by erosion. Eventually the former valley bottom was transformed into the highest point in the area—a reversal of roles that geologists describe as "inverted relief." □

Jungfrau, Mönch, and Eiger

● Switzerland
● Map: page 17, D–4

Renowned for their perfect beauty and challenging slopes, the trio of Alpine peaks is a mecca for both sightseers and mountain climbers.

Although the Jungfrau, at 13,653 feet (4,161 meters), is not the Alps' loftiest mountain—that honor is reserved for Mont Blanc—it is among the most beloved. Along with its sister peaks, the Mönch, at 13,468 feet (4,105 meters), and the Eiger, at 13,036 feet (3,973 meters), in Switzerland's Bernese Alps, it embraces some of the finest winter sports and mountaineering terrain in the world.

But above all the three mountains are renowned for their unsurpassed beauty. Each seems perfectly sculpted, especially the Jungfrau, whose gleaming slopes inspired one admirer to describe it as the "loveliest of snow-mountains."

The central mountain bastion of Switzerland, the Bernese Alps consist mainly of granite and metamorphic rocks that are extremely resistant to erosion. Overlying these crystalline rocks is a series of sedimentary formations that in places have been buckled up and contorted into overturned folds. Subsequently scoured by glaciers, the mountains are now marked by deep valleys, knife-edged ridges, and steep walls that rise abruptly above the lower slopes.

Most dramatic of all the precipices is the dizzying north face of the Eiger, which rises almost straight up for nearly 1 mile (1.6 kilometers). Although the Eiger's south side is relatively easy to climb, its north face defied mountaineers until 1935, and it remains one of the world's most formidable ascents. Similarly, the taller Jungfrau was first ascended from its eastern side in 1811, but not until 1865 was its far steeper northwestern face conquered by two Englishmen.

Today the summits are far more easily accessible to visitors: an unusual cog railway climbs to the Jungfraujoch, a pass at 11,412 feet (3,478 meters) between the Jungfrau and the Mönch. One of the highest railways in Europe, it travels through a tunnel that burrows right through the rocky mountain slopes. Along the way passengers can look out through rock "windows" that have been cut in the Eiger's north face.

But the best views come at the end of the ride. From the top the panorama encompasses much of northern Switzerland and stretches south to the Italian Alps. Nearer at hand are the pristine summits of the Mönch and Jungfrau, while curving down the southern slopes is the Aletsch Glacier—at 15 miles, or 24 kilometers, the longest in the Alps. □

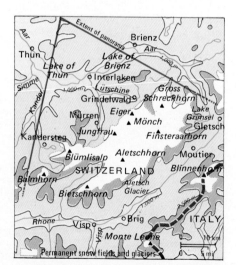

The Jungfrau and a number of its neighboring peaks in Switzerland's Bernese Alps are shown in a panoramic view (right) that encompasses the full sweep of their dramatic northward-facing slopes. The red lines on the map (above) indicate the scope of the view.

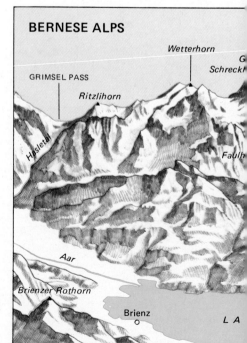

JUNGFRAU, MÖNCH, AND EIGER. *The steep ramparts of the Eiger (left) and the Jungfrau (right) frame the central mass of the Mönch.*

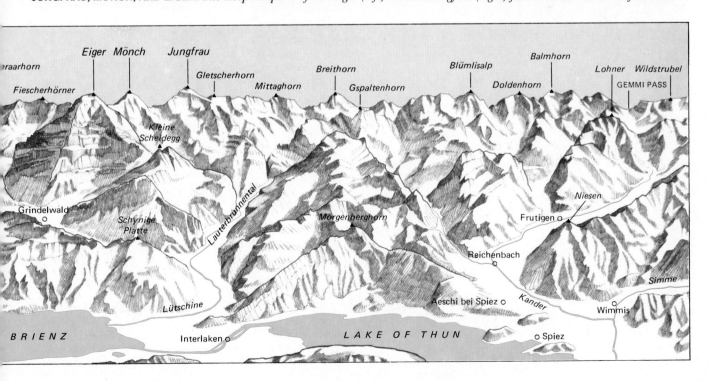

Kaieteur Falls

- Guyana
- Map: page 14, D–2

In a lush jungle setting, an awesome wall of water falls over the edge of a remote South American plateau.

Extending from western Guyana into Venezuela and northern Brazil is a high sandstone plateau bounded in places by steep cliffs. Fed by abundant rainfall in this equatorial region, rivers meander across the undulating surface of the plateau, then drop off the edge in rapids and waterfalls.

Among the most impressive are Kaieteur Falls on the Potaro River. From its source in the Pakaraima Mountains near the Brazilian border, the Potaro flows in a great curve across the rolling plateau. About 60 miles (100 kilometers) upstream from its junction with the Essequibo River, which flows north into the Atlantic at Guyana's capital city of Georgetown, the Potaro plunges abruptly over a sheer cliff.

The result is one of the most beautiful waterfalls in South America. Bordered by lush green forests, the river at the top of the cliff is more than 300 feet (90 meters) wide. Suddenly it plunges over the edge of the escarpment as a solid wall of water that crashes with a deafening roar into the gorge far below. With its total uninterrupted drop of 741 feet (226 meters), the cascade is about four times the height of North America's Niagara Falls.

For generations the seething torrent was known only to local Indians, who called it Kai Tuk. The first European to view the spectacle was C. Barrington Brown, a British geologist who was exploring the area in 1870. Today Kaieteur Falls are the focal point of Guyana's only national park.

Accessible by air from Georgetown and by a more arduous land-and-water route, the park would be a notable preserve even without the falls. Dense tropical forests intermingling with grassy savannas flourish in the warm, moist tropical climate. Lush and primeval, they are filled with a wealth of exotic wildlife. Capuchin, howler, and spider monkeys are all found in the park. Other mammals include anteaters, sloths, armadillos, ocelots, peccaries, jaguars, and dozens more. Among the area's varied bird life are parrots, macaws, toucans, tanagers, eagles, and a host of other colorful species.

But above all visitors come to the park to see the falls. With the Potaro River constantly being replenished by abundant rainfall, Kaieteur Falls flow at full force throughout the year. At any time a special thrill awaits visitors who make the difficult climb to the top of the escarpment. If one stands at the brink of the falls, the view of the water hurtling endlessly into the depths of the gorge below is an almost overwhelming spectacle. □

KAIETEUR FALLS. *Frequently swollen by heavy rainfall, Guyana's Potaro River plunges over the edge of a precipice into the deep gorge it has eroded downstream from the falls.*

Kailas Range

- China
- Map: page 20, C–1

North of the vast Himalayan system, the remote Asian range is considered to be a holy place in both the Hindu and Tibetan Buddhist traditions.

Situated to the north of the main ranges of the Himalayas in the Tibetan province of China is the remote and rugged Kailas Range. Austere and windswept, with its highest peaks eternally capped by ice and snow, the range has been associated since time immemorial with the religion and the mythology of the region.

The highest and most revered of all the peaks in the range is Mount Kailas, an immense pyramidal mass that reaches an altitude of 22,028 feet (6,714 meters). According to the traditions of Hinduism, Mount Kailas is the sacred abode of the great god Shiva and his beautiful consort Parvati. Tibetan Buddhists, in turn, identify the peak with Mount Sumeru, which they venerate as the center of the universe. A roadway up the mountain permits access for the many pilgrims who come to worship there.

Spread out to the south of Mount Kailas are two splendid lakes that are also considered sacred. One of them, crescent-shaped Rakas Tal, is honored as a symbol of the night; the other, Manasarowar, is consecrated to the powers of the sun. (At 14,950 feet, or 4,557 meters, above sea level, Manasarowar is also the highest freshwater lake on earth.) In addition, three of the sacred rivers of India (the Indus, Brahmaputra, and Sutlej) originate on the slopes of the Kailas Range.

Like the rest of the Himalayas, these venerable peaks were created by a titanic collision of continents. About 65 million years ago the northward-drifting crustal plate that makes up the Indian subcontinent crashed into the plate underlying the rest of Asia. In the ensuing upheaval the main ranges of the Himalayas were thrust upward, and the Tibetan Plateau—which includes the Kailas Range—was raised to enormous heights. Erosion by glaciers and running water then took over, honing down the peaks, carving out deep gorges, and chiseling the mountains into their present majestic contours. □

Kalambo Falls

- Tanzania—Zambia
- Map: page 26, C–3

Near the end of its short course, the Kalambo River hurtles over the brink of an escarpment, forming one of the highest waterfalls in Africa.

As the Kalambo River meanders lazily southward across an upland in western Tanzania, it gives no hint of the spectacle that lies ahead. Near the end of its short course the river turns toward the west, forming the border of Tanzania and Zambia just upstream from its outlet near the southern tip of Lake Tanganyika.

It is in this sector that the river leaps suddenly to life. Plunging over the edge of a precipice, its waters drop in a single uninterrupted cascade for a total of 704 feet (215 meters)—about twice the height of Africa's much better known Victoria Falls. Kalambo Falls, in fact, are one of the highest waterfalls on the entire continent.

EL-KANTARA. *Reduced to a trickle except after occasional storms, the river nevertheless has flowed long and powerfully enough to carve a gorge through the limestone barrier.*

(The highest, South Africa's Tugela Falls, drops 3,110 feet, or 948 meters, in a series of five cascades, including one unbroken leap of 1,350 feet, or 411 meters.)

The grandeur of the waterfall varies with the time of year. During the local rainy season from November to April, the width of the river at the top of the falls swells to about 100 feet (30 meters), and the water falls in torrents. During the dry season, in contrast, the falls are reduced to a slender, graceful ribbon of water less than 10 feet (3 meters) across at the top. Beyond the falls the river flows through two narrow gorges before finally emptying into Lake Tanganyika.

Like the lake itself, the falls resulted from the formation of a system of "rift valleys" in East Africa that began about 25 million years ago. Great stresses within the earth created a series of parallel fractures in its crust. Blocks of the crust dropped downward between the fractures as the land rose up on either side.

The ultimate consequence was a system of very long, narrow rift valleys that are bounded by steep escarpments. Lake Tanganyika, with its bottom extending well below sea level, occupies the lowest part of the western arm of the Rift Valley, while the falls were formed where the Kalambo River plunges over the escarpment on the eastern edge of the valley. □

Kantara, El-

- Algeria
- Map: page 24, D–2

A narrow gorge through a limestone ridge has served since antiquity as a gateway to the Sahara Desert.

Nearly 2,000 years ago Roman soldiers of the Third Augustan Legion dubbed the gorge Calceus Herculis —"Hercules' Shoe," or more loosely "Hercules' Kick." It was an apt description of the deep cleft that runs through a limestone ridge on the northern fringes of the Algerian Sahara. Scarcely 130 feet (40 meters) wide and hemmed in by steep walls reaching up to 400 feet (120 meters) in height, it does look as though it might have been hewn by the foot of the legendary hero famed for his superhuman strength.

In reality, the gorge was eroded in the ridge by the river Wadi El-Kantara. Though easily forded today, the river flowed much more powerfully in wetter climates of the past.

The fact that the Romans went to the trouble to build an arched bridge (its remains are visible to this day) across the river attests to the importance of this natural gateway to the desert. Through it passed one of the few reliable routes for caravans and military supplies traveling between the Mediterranean Sea 125 miles (200 kilometers) to the north and the desert oasis at Biskra, about 25 miles (40 kilometers) to the south. Even today a modern highway and railroad faithfully retrace the ancient Roman road through El-Kantara.

The place was named El-Kantara—"the bridge"—by Arab conquerors. Apparently they were less impressed by the gorge or the picturesque oasis at its southern end than they were by this sophisticated example of Roman engineering.

By any name, however, El-Kantara has long been known for its beauty and surprising contrasts. In the second century A.D. the bridge was guarded by a detachment of Syrian archers from Palmyra who are said to have planted the first date palms in the region. Centuries later, in 1854, a battalion of French troops marching to Biskra were so startled to find a large palm grove at the oasis at the end of the gorge that they sounded a fanfare in spontaneous delight. More recently a French writer and artist, Eugène Fromentin, found that the scene had changed very little: "After crossing the bridge and going a hundred steps into the gorge, you come down a steep slope to a charming village irrigated by a deep stream and buried in a forest of 25,000 date palms. You are now in the Sahara."

Passage through the gorge is memorable at any time of year. The rocky walls on either side seem to glow with the warm colors of the desert—every shade of ocher, tinted with a patina of gold and amber that changes in intensity with the season and the time of day. And contrasting with these hues at the end of the gorge is the most beautiful of all desert colors—the rich, eternally welcome greenery of a palm-filled oasis. □

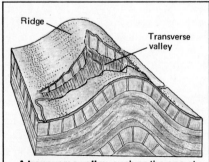

A transverse valley, such as the one at El-Kantara, is a narrow gorge that has been eroded at right angles across an otherwise continuous ridge.

KARAKORAM. *The towering central massif of the second highest mountain range in the world is a chaotic array of bleak, craggy peaks composed primarily of gneiss and granite.*

Karakoram

- India—Pakistan
- Map: page 20, B–1

An almost impenetrable wilderness of gigantic mountain peaks, the Karakoram is crowned by K2, the world's second highest peak.

One of the most formidable mountain ranges in the world, the Karakoram rises as an immense, nearly impenetrable barrier to the north and west of the even more formidable Himalayas. About 300 miles (500 kilometers) long and 150 miles (250 kilometers) wide, the range sweeps from northwest to southeast across northern Pakistan and India and extends into Afghanistan, the U.S.S.R., and China. To the north, near the Afghanistan border, the Karakoram merges with the towering peaks of the Hindu Kush and the Pamirs; to the south it is separated from the Himalayas by the valley of the Indus.

A chaotic realm of craggy, snow-covered peaks, precipitous slopes, and gigantic glaciers, the Karakoram is the second highest mountain range in the world. (It is exceeded only by the Himalayas, of which it is sometimes considered a part.) The average height of the range is about 20,000 feet (6,100 meters), and it includes 18 peaks that rise to more than 25,000 feet (7,600 meters). Even its passes are higher than most mountains; one major pass near the southeastern end of the range lies about 18,000 feet (5,500 meters) above sea level.

The highest peak in the entire Karakoram system is a majestic summit that is known simply as K2. (It is occasionally called Mount Godwin Austen, after a British scientist who surveyed it in the 1860's.) Surpassed only by Mount Everest, it is the second highest mountain in the world, with an elevation of 28,250 feet (8,611 meters). The array of towering peaks surrounding it is so vast, however, that its summit cannot be seen from any inhabited area.

The glaciers in the Karakoram are just as awesome as the peaks. A total of some 6,900 square miles (17,900 square kilometers) within the range is permanently covered by glaciers—an area larger than Rhode Island and Connecticut combined. On northern slopes, where the climate is semiarid and snowfall light, the glaciers are shorter and occur at higher altitudes. But on southern slopes, where monsoons sweep in from the Indian Ocean and bring more plentiful precipitation, there are some of the longest valley glaciers in the world. They sometimes descend all the way down to elevations where the slopes are covered by subtropical forests.

Fed by frequent avalanches that come roaring down the extraordinarily steep slopes, the glaciers of the Karakoram sometimes advance with astonishing bursts of speed. In 1904, for example, the Hasanabad Glacier surged downslope more than 4 miles (7 kilometers) in just two months at the incredible rate of about 16 feet (5 meters) per hour.

These sudden advances occasionally result in catastrophic floods. Several times in the last 100 years, the Chongkumdam Glacier blocked the flow of the Shyok River completely, causing water to accumulate behind it in a vast lake. Each time, when the water finally broke through the dam of ice, a devastating flood of water, mud, rocks, and ice swept down the slope, destroying everything in its path.

The mountains are composed of a central core of crystalline rocks, primarily a remarkably pale granite and gneiss. To the south this core is bordered by a zone of schist crossed by many intrusions of volcanic rock. To the north it is flanked by a belt of sedimentary rock. The entire mass began to be uplifted about 65 million years ago, at about the same time the Himalayas were formed. Since then the mountains have been attacked and altered in form by floods, earthquakes, avalanches, and repeated cycles of glaciation. Even so, the Karakoram remains among the highest and steepest mountains in the world.

It is no doubt because of their relative inaccessibility, their steepness, and the hazards involved in climbing them that the high peaks of the Karakoram have remained one of the great challenges to mountaineers. K2, in fact, was long thought to be unclimbable. During the first half of the 20th century, many parties tried—and failed—to reach its summit, often with disastrous results.

It was not until 1954 that two Italians, Lino Lacedelli and Achille Compagnoni, assisted by some 500 native porters, finally succeeded in scaling its summit. But though man has at last managed to climb K2, he will never subdue the awesome wilderness of that great mountain and its towering neighbors in the Karakoram. □

Kara-Kum

- U.S.S.R.
- Map: page 18, G–4

Irrigation projects and discoveries of oil and natural gas are bringing changes to the sandy wastes and sere uplands of the great Asian desert.

Stretching across much of the Soviet Turkmen Republic between the Caspian Sea and the Amu Darya River is a vast and inhospitable desert, the Kara-Kum. (The name, based on a Turkic word, means "black sands," and refers to the dark soil that underlies much of the desert.) To the north the Kara-Kum is bounded by arid uplands of the Ust-Urt plateau, and to the south it is bordered by the Kopet-Dagh and other mountain ranges.

Approximately 115,000 square miles (300,000 square kilometers) in area, about the size of Arizona, the desert has an enormous variety of distinctive features. In the north are immense, seemingly endless stony plateaus, interrupted here and there by shallow, wind-eroded hollows. This upland is bordered on the south by a steep escarpment that marks an ancient, now-abandoned course of the Amu Darya River.

Farther south is a more typically sandy desert. In some places, especially along watercourses, there are actively moving, crescent-shaped barchan dunes as much as 250 feet (75 meters) high. But most of the dunes and sand ridges are held in place by a sparse cover of plants that are able to withstand the arid climate.

With annual rainfall averaging less than 6 inches (150 millimeters), most streams die out in the sandy wastes, and shallow temporary pools soon dry up. Yet the desert is not without life. Large flocks of sheep graze on the meager desert vegetation. In addition, the Kara-Kum Canal, completed in 1958, now brings water from the Amu Darya River to southern portions of the Kara-Kum. As a result, industry flourishes at Ashkhabad and other population centers, and the cultivation of irrigated crops, especially cotton, has been greatly expanded. Proposed extension of the canal all the way to the Caspian Sea undoubtedly will result in even more extensive irrigation projects. And recent discoveries of both oil and natural gas deposits bode still further changes in the future for the otherwise harsh Kara-Kum. □

Kashmir, Vale of

- India
- Map: page 20, B–1

Once the resort of Mogul emperors, a remote mountain valley nestled high in the Himalayas has long been noted for its exceptional beauty.

The Vale of Kashmir, a jewellike mountain valley in the Indian state of Jammu and Kashmir, has been celebrated since ancient times for its magnificent setting and idyllic beauty. Perched at an elevation of 5,300 feet (1,600 meters), the vale is a vast oval basin about 85 miles (135 kilometers) long and 20 miles (32 kilometers) wide. Hemming it in is an almost unbroken wall of jagged, snowcapped peaks ranging from 12,000 to 16,000 feet (3,650 to 4,875 meters). To the northeast are the lofty summits of the main ranges of the Himalayas; to the southwest, the rugged peaks of the Pir Panjal Range.

Irrigated by melting snows on the surrounding mountains, the vale is a matchless mixture of luxuriant vegetation and sparkling water. Meandering through the heart of the valley is the Jhelum River, bordered by marshes, terraced rice paddies, and verdant fields. Scattered everywhere are lovely lakes, their surfaces spangled with the exotic blooms of lotuses and water lilies. Above all there are the gardens—Shalimar, Shahi, Nishat, and others—that were planted more than three centuries ago when the vale was the resort of Mogul emperors.

According to an ancient chronicle of the kings of Kashmir, the *Rajatarangini,* the vale once lay at the bottom of an immense lake. The lake, moreover, was the realm of the evil demon Jalodbhava. Though the gods wanted to destroy him, Jalodbhava was invin-

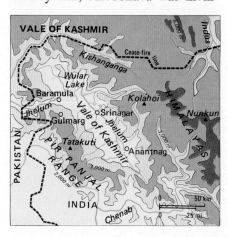

cible as long as he remained in the water. The problem was solved by the king and holy man Kashyapa, a grandson of the great Brahma, creator of the universe. With a thrust of his magic sword he cut a notch into the mountains near Baramula. In a single stroke the lake was drained, the demon was vanquished, and the beautiful valley was born.

And in fact the Vale of Kashmir once was submerged beneath a large lake. The depression itself was formed by folding of the earth's hard crust, which produced a long, narrow, steep-sided trough in the area. Over the ensuing millennia, torrents rushing down from the surrounding uplands gradually filled the depression with thick layers of sediment and debris. (The deposits in places are as much as 2,300 feet, or 700 meters, thick.) Fossils found in upper layers—fine sediments of mud and clay—indicate that the basin once was occupied by an extensive, rather shallow lake in a time when the climate was very hot and humid.

During the past 2 million years, glaciers also played a large role in filling in the basin. As Ice Age glaciers advanced and subsequently retreated in the nearby mountains, their meltwater carried additional loads of sediment into the valley. Eventually the lake disappeared completely, leaving behind only the meandering Jhelum River, the bird-filled marshes, and the few small lakes that remain today.

One legacy of the vanished lake is the fertile alluvial soil that fills the valley and produces rich yields of rice, corn, fruits, and vegetables. But the vale's most valuable resource is its exceptional beauty. Each year tourists come from all over the world to lodge in ornately decorated houseboats, to go sightseeing in gondolalike *shikaras,* and to enjoy the princely gardens and the sky-blue lakes that mirror snow-crowned mountain peaks. Above all they come to find the feeling of tranquillity and isolation from the cares of the world that pervades the remote, most romantic of mountain valleys nestled among towering Himalayan summits. □

VALE OF KASHMIR. *Pack animals are still a common means of transportation on mountain slopes fringing the secluded Himalayan valley.*

Katwe Craters

- Uganda
- Map: page 26, B–3

In a beautiful region of East Africa, an idyllic pastoral landscape was created by violent volcanic activity.

Uganda's Ruwenzori National Park, once known as Queen Elizabeth National Park, is a place of exceptional beauty. Forming the western backdrop are glistening, snowcapped peaks of the Ruwenzori, the fabled Mountains of the Moon. Spread out at their foot are broad grasslands and savannas dotted with glimmering blue lakes and populated by enormous numbers

KATWE CRATERS. *A peaceful, lake-filled volcanic crater in the foreground is backed by the bowllike depressions of a series of adjoining craters in the distance.*

of waterbucks, buffaloes, topis, and other grazing animals.

Though peaceful—even idyllic—today, the park has been the scene of violent events in the past. For one thing, it is located in the western branch of Africa's Rift Valley system. The valley was formed millions of years ago when, in a great paroxysm of the earth's crust, a block of the basement rock fell between two more or less parallel fault lines.

More recently, volcanic activity in the valley has testified to the continuing instability of the area. Among the most unusual of all the volcanic features are the Katwe Craters, a spectacular grouping of bowllike depressions that pockmark the landscape near the village of Katwe. More than 50 in number, they are stretched out over a distance of about 12 miles (20 kilometers).

No lava welled up from these openings to accumulate in typical cone-shaped volcanic mountains. Instead, the craters were formed one by one in a series of violent explosions within the last 1 million years. Heaping up accumulations of ash and cinders, the craters overlap and even enclose each other. The resultant depressions are up to 2 miles (3 kilometers) in diameter and 325 feet (100 meters) in depth.

When the explosions ended, the area no doubt was as barren as a moonscape. Today, in contrast, lakes are cupped in many of the depressions, while others are carpeted with grasses that nourish placid herds of grazing animals. □

Kef Toghobeit Cave

- Morocco
- Map: page 24, C–2

The deepest cave in Africa was first discovered in 1959—and only a portion of it has ever been explored.

In 1959 the mouth of a major limestone cave was discovered in the Rif, a rugged mountain chain in the north of Morocco. Named Kef Toghobeit Cave, it opens at an altitude of 5,580 feet (1,700 meters) near the summit of Djebel Bou Halla.

Over the next few years several expeditions penetrated deeper into the abyss. Exploration stopped in 1970, when the probers were blocked by water-filled passageways. But, even so, they had reached a level 2,300 feet (700 meters) below the point of entry, proving that Kef Toghobeit is the deepest cave in Africa and one of the deepest in the world.

And it is now known that the labyrinth extends much farther beneath the surface. Dye placed in the water at the limit of exploration reappeared two days later at a spring more than 2 miles (3 kilometers) away and about 2,790 feet (850 meters) farther down the mountainside. The volume of water per second emerging from the spring, moreover, was about 150 times greater than where the dye was introduced. Thus it is clear that the known portion of Kef Toghobeit Cave is only a small part of a much larger system of caves. □

MOUNT KENYA. *Beneath the craggy, snowcapped summit, giant groundsels and other rare plants grow on the glacier-carved volcanic slopes.*

Kenya, Mount

- Kenya
- Map: page 26, C–3

Though its original, much higher summit has long since been lost to erosion, the peak is still a giant among the mountains of Africa.

Sacred to the Kikuyu people of East Africa, who regard it as the dwelling place of their god Ngai, Mount Kenya is a massive volcanic mountain that rises to an elevation of 17,058 feet (5,199 meters). Although it is located just south of the equator, its summit is so lofty that the upper slopes are mantled with a dozen or so glistening white glaciers. Mount Kenya, in fact, is the second highest peak in Africa, exceeded only by Kilimanjaro.

One of the mountain's most distinctive features is the rocky peak shaped like a huge jagged tooth that forms its summit. Its presence is explained by deep erosion of the original volcanic cone, whose crest was at least 3,300 feet (1,000 meters) higher than the present summit. The rocky crag is actually a volcanic neck, a plug of extremely hard rock that solidified deep down in the original volcano's vent. When the softer surrounding rock was

eroded away, only the resistant plug remained.

The mountain was formed by three separate phases of volcanic activity that occurred between 2½ and 3 million years ago. Its origin was probably linked to vigorous stresses and structural changes taking place along the great Rift Valley, a tremendous cleft in the earth's crust that extends from Syria through the Red Sea and down across East Africa.

Mount Kenya's present-day glaciers are relics of the last ice age, which ended some 10,000 years ago. Like other high African peaks, it was then covered by massive tongues of ice that carved deep glacial valleys and other characteristic ice-sculpted landforms.

It is in the high glacial valleys, covered by boggy moorlands, that a number of Mount Kenya's most unusual plants are found. (Some of these are seen nowhere else in the world.) Decorating the slopes are strange-looking giant groundsels and giant lobelias, tree-sized versions of plants whose near relatives are familiar wildflowers. Elsewhere on the mountain there are dense thickets of bamboo, lush rain forests, and a rich variety of other plant and animal life, much of which has been preserved in Mount Kenya National Park. □

Kilimanjaro

- Tanzania
- Map: page 26, C–3

Really three volcanoes in one, the soaring profile of the highest mountain in Africa was built up by a complex series of eruptions.

Rising majestically above the plains of Tanzania near the Kenyan border is the towering, snow-covered summit of Kilimanjaro. With a maximum elevation of 19,340 feet (5,895 meters) above sea level, it is the highest as well as the most celebrated mountain in Africa. Its profile is all the more impressive since it stands in splendid isolation, with no adjoining peaks to detract from its beauty. Looming some 16,000 feet (4,900 meters) above the plains that spread out from its base, it dominates its surroundings.

Massive and complex, Kilimanjaro covers an area about 60 miles (100 kilometers) long and 40 miles (65 kilometers) wide. It is composed of not one but three separate volcanoes that began erupting within the last 2 million years; their lava fields overlapped and partially obliterated each other. At the center is the culminating massif named Kibo, flanked by the lower summits of Mawenzi to the east and Shira to the west.

Shira, the oldest and most eroded of the three, was once much higher than it is today. Following a violent, explosive eruption, its summit collapsed and then was further reduced by erosion. It now forms a plateau that only reaches 12,395 feet (3,778 meters).

Mawenzi, the second oldest of the summits, appears from a distance to be nothing more than a bulge on the side of Kibo. Yet it is a well-defined rocky peak that reaches 17,564 feet (5,354 meters). Linked to Kibo by a saddle about 7 miles (11 kilometers) long, its craggy, deeply eroded summit is bounded by high, steep cliffs.

Kibo, the central and highest part of the Kilimanjaro complex, was built up during several eruptive cycles. From the plains its summit looks like a gently rounded, snowcapped dome. In fact it is topped by a caldera, a broad, basinlike depression about 1¼ miles (2 kilometers) in diameter that was formed by the collapse of a once much higher summit. Within the caldera subsequent eruptions built up a second volcanic cone with a crater some

2,950 feet (900 meters) across. And this in turn is partially filled by a cinder cone that was built up by a third eruption.

Because of its great height, Kilimanjaro influences its own weather. Winds blowing in from the Indian Ocean are deflected upward by the slopes and drop their moisture as rain and snow. The result is a variety of vegetation zones that contrast dramatically with the savanna grasses and the semidesert scrub on the surrounding plains. The lower slopes were probably once forested but have now been cleared for the cultivation of coffee, corn, and other crops. This is followed by a belt of tropical rain forest, which extends up to about 9,800 feet (3,000 meters). The forest in turn gives way to grasslands and moorlands, which, at about 14,500 feet (4,400 meters), are replaced by high-altitude desert where little more than lichens can survive. Finally, at the highest elevations, there is the zone of permanent ice and snow that is responsible for the name Kilimanjaro, which in Swahili means "the mountain that glitters." □

How the Permanent Snow Line Varies With Latitude

Location	Latitude	Altitude
Franz Josef Land	80°N	165 ft (50 m)
Iceland	65°N	3,300 ft (1,000 m)
Altai Mountains	49°N	7,200 ft (2,200 m)
Western Alps	46°N	9,500 ft (2,900 m)
Himalayas	28°–33°N	16,400 ft (5,000 m)
Kilimanjaro	3°S	15,100 ft (4,600 m)
Aconcagua	33°S	13,100 ft (4,000 m)
Southern Andes	45°S	3,900 ft (1,200 m)
Tierra del Fuego	54°S	3,300 ft (1,000 m)
Antarctica	66°S	Sea level

KILIMANJARO. *Towering over game-filled plains of northern Tanzania is the eternally snowcapped summit of the highest peak in Africa.*

Killarney, Lakes of

- Ireland
- Map: page 16, C–3

Famed for their pristine beauty, three Irish lakes bask in a climate with a curiously tropical touch.

Tucked among the green hills of Kerry, near the southwestern tip of Ireland, are the lovely sky-blue Lakes of Killarney. Though they are situated only about 65 feet (20 meters) above sea level, the lakes have a distinctly alpine look. Rising steeply all around

them are rugged mountain slopes, including those of nearby Macgillycuddy's Reeks, which is the highest range in Ireland.

The lowest and largest of the lakes, Lough Leane, is dotted with wooded islands—among them Innisfallen, where the ruins of an abbey that was founded about A.D. 600 can still be seen. Just to the south, separated from Lough Leane by a small peninsula, is Muckross, or Middle Lake. Beyond it, at the end of a winding channel about 2½ miles (4 kilometers) long, lies the Upper Lake, which is considered by many of the visitors to the area to be

the most picturesque of all of them.

The lakes, in contrast to the surrounding sandstone mountains, are cupped in limestone troughs. Their basins were formed in part by solution of the limestone but are primarily the results of glaciation. During the last ice age, great fingers of ice forced their way through gaps in the nearby mountains. Grinding over the bedrock, they scoured out the depression that became the basin of the Upper Lake and deposited heaps of glacial debris that eventually dammed up the Middle and Lower lakes.

Most traces of the Ice Age have long

LAKES OF KILLARNEY. *A creation of bygone glaciers, the chain of three lakes is kept full by runoff from the surrounding mountains.*

since vanished; sheltered from cold winds by the surrounding hills, the lowlands around the lakes are now noted for their exceptionally mild climate. Lush forests are filled with hollies, oaks, birches, and mountain ash, interspersed with lavish plantings of rhododendrons, azaleas, and magnolias. The arbutus shrub, a species common along the shores of the Mediterranean, flourishes throughout the area. And gardens are filled with camellias, hydrangeas, groves of bamboo, and a wealth of tropical and subtropical plants and shrubs. □

Kimberley Mines

- South Africa
- Map: page 26, B–5

A cluster of African mines has yielded untold wealth in one of the greatest of treasures—diamonds.

The city of Kimberley in the heart of South Africa is known as "the diamond capital of the world"—and with good reason. Located within a radius of less than five miles (eight kilometers) around the city are five of the most famous diamond mines in the entire world: the Kimberley, De Beers, Wesselton, Dutoitspan, and Bultfontein mines.

According to one story, the rush for diamonds began in 1869, when a local farmer discovered a few of the precious stones while tilling his fields. Another tale claims that a child found one of the gems while playing. Whatever the case, the chance find triggered a frantic search for diamonds. Over the years untold wealth has been extracted from the mines, and South Africa has led the world in diamond production ever since.

The most impressive monument to all this activity is the Kimberley Mine. Although the other mines are still being actively worked, the Kimberley ceased operation in 1915 and is now preserved as an open-air museum. Located within the city limits of Kimberley, it is affectionately referred to as the Big Hole.

And that is exactly what it is: the largest man-made excavation in the world. From an observation platform suspended over the edge, visitors look down into a gaping hole that is nearly 1 mile (1.6 kilometers) in circumference and covers an area of about 37 acres (15 hectares). The depth of the

How Diamonds Are Formed and Reach the Surface

Diamonds are made up of carbon—the very same material that makes up graphite, the "lead" in common lead pencils. In the case of diamonds, however, the carbon atoms are far more tightly packed and much more strongly bonded together than they are in graphite, resulting in the hardest substance found in nature.

Diamonds are formed under intense pressure (between 50,000 and 1 million times normal atmospheric pressure) and extraordinarily high temperatures (up to 3800° F, or 2100° C). And although diamonds have been produced artificially by man, the necessary strong pressure and high temperature are also found naturally at great depths within the earth's mantle. The mantle is the layer of partially molten material that is found between the outer crust of the earth and the core.

It is here, at depths of at least 60 miles (100 kilometers) beneath the surface, that diamonds are formed by nature. They reach the surface by way of intrusive structures known as diamond pipes. The cylindrical pipes allow molten material from the mantle to penetrate the earth's crust, where it cools and solidifies into the rock kimberlite. Diamonds that originally formed deep below the surface are thus found throughout the pipe, where they can be extracted by mining operations. In addition to those in southern Africa, important diamond pipes have been discovered in Brazil, India, and a few other widely scattered places.

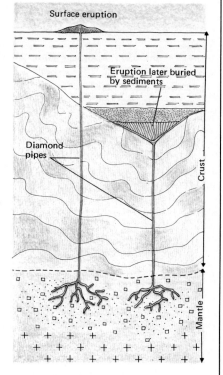

	Igneous rock
	Kimberlite
	Diamond-bearing mantle material
	Other mantle material

open pit is some 1,300 feet (400 meters), while shafts from the bottom lead down to a depth of about 4,000 feet (1,200 meters).

In the years that the mine was in operation, it yielded a total of about 14.5 million carats of diamonds. Yet to secure that many gems—about 3 tons, or 2.7 metric tons—nearly 25 million tons, or 22.7 million metric tons, of rock were removed from the pit.

The rock that contains the diamonds is unique. The mines are located in geological formations called diamond pipes. Formed of narrow funnels or cylindrical intrusions of molten material from deep within the earth, they are somewhat similar to the feeder pipes that supply molten lava to active volcanoes.

In fact geologists regard diamond pipes as the remains of ancient volcanoes that probably erupted some 70 million to 130 million years ago. Subsequent erosion removed most of the evidence of any volcanic cones, leaving the diamond-laden pipes awaiting discovery.

The diamond-bearing rock is referred to, appropriately, as kimberlite, and the pipes are sometimes called kimberlite pipes. Kimberlite in the upper part of the pipes is exposed to weathering and deteriorates into a soft substance that miners call "yellow ground." Diamonds in yellow ground are easily washed out and are often found far from their sources. (Sands and gravels in the Namib Desert far to the west of any mines, for example, contain rich placer deposits of diamonds.) Deeper down in the pipes, where the kimberlite is protected from weathering, it is much harder and blue in color. This "blue ground" is mined, crushed, and then screened to separate the diamonds.

Aside from its commercial worth, scientists value the rock kimberlite because it contains substances that originated in a layer of molten material deep beneath the earth's crust. By studying kimberlite, they hope to unravel secrets of a region within the earth itself that man so far has been unable to reach. □

Kinnekulle

- Sweden
- Map: page 16, E–3

In an area the botanist Linnaeus called "lovelier than any other in Sweden," a massive flat-topped mountain delights all who see it.

Rising to a height of 1,004 feet (306 meters), the massive flat-topped profile of Kinnekulle dominates the horizon of a lake-filled lowland region of southern Sweden. Hikers, skiers, and lovers of rare wildflowers all come to enjoy the spectacular views from its slopes and summit.

About 8½ miles (14 kilometers) long and 4 miles (7 kilometers) wide at the top, Kinnekulle, like a number of smaller flat-topped mountains in the area, is actually the remnant of a once much larger plateau. It rests on a foundation of ancient crystalline rock that long ago was worn down to a nearly flat plain.

About 550 million years ago, the basement rock was submerged beneath the sea. There it was covered by thick layers of sedimentary rock that had formed from sand, mud, and the remains of marine animals that were deposited on the floor of the ocean.

The area was then uplifted above the sea again, and about 200 million years ago molten lava forced its way into the sedimentary rock. Spreading out between the layers in sheetlike formations, the lava cooled and hardened into diabase.

The old plateau has been subjected to the forces of erosion ever since that time, and most of the relatively soft sedimentary rock has been worn away completely. Only where it is protected by a hard, erosion-resistant cap of diabase has it remained intact, forming Kinnekulle and the neighboring mesalike mountains. ☐

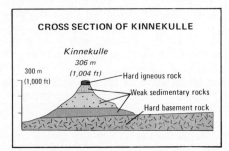

CROSS SECTION OF KINNEKULLE

Kinnekulle
306 m
(1,004 ft)
300 m
(1,000 ft)
Hard igneous rock
Weak sedimentary rocks
Hard basement rock

Kinnekulle is a remnant of a once-extensive plateau. It survived because the erosion-resistant cap of igneous rock protected the weaker rocks beneath it from erosion.

Kivu, Lake

- Rwanda—Zaire
- Map: page 26, B–3

Bordered by volcanoes that created it and still mold its shoreline, an exquisite lake ornaments an arm of the great Rift Valley in Africa.

Considered by many to be the most beautiful lake on the continent, Kivu is one of a series of lakes strung together like pearls along the western branch of Africa's Rift Valley. It is the product of a particularly unusual sequence of geological events that gave it its great depth, created its dramatically indented shoreline, and even reversed the direction in which water flows from it to the sea.

Bordered by Zaire on the west and Rwanda on the east, the island-dotted lake is about 55 miles (90 kilometers) long and 30 miles (50 kilometers) wide. With an average depth of 722 feet (220 meters), it reaches a maximum of 1,558 feet (475 meters).

The Rift Valley in which the lake lies began to take its present form about 25 million years ago. At that time two more or less parallel bands of faults developed in the African Shield, the billion-year-old granitic basement rock that underlies the continent. In a long series of violent upheavals, the land surfaces on both sides of the faults rose upward until they reached heights of 8,200 to 9,800 feet (2,500 to 3,000 meters) above sea level. At the same time the land between the faults gradually subsided. (The surface of Lake Kivu is only about 4,800 feet, or 1,460 meters, above the sea.)

The end result of these movements was the Rift Valley, a long, narrow trench in the earth's crust reaching northwestward from Lake Tanganyika. Subsequent erosion rounded off the sharp edges of the escarpments rimming the Rift Valley, while streams flowing off the edges of the adjacent

LAKE KIVU. *Occupying part of the Rift Valley, a giant fracture in the earth's crust, the African lake is noted for its verdant islands and picturesquely indented shorelines.*

plateaus carved deep valleys back into the cliffs.

Until about 1 million years ago, water from the present site of Lake Kivu drained north through the Rift Valley and emptied into the Mediterranean by way of the Nile River. The situation changed radically when the Virunga group of volcanoes began to erupt just north of the lake. Accumulating lava flows gradually built up a high barrier that blocked the northward flow of water and backed it up to form Lake Kivu. The rising water invaded former river valleys draining into the lake, creating the deep fjordlike bays along its shores.

Finally the water rose enough to begin spilling over uplands at the south end of the lake, creating a new drainage pattern. Lake Kivu's overflow now moves south by way of the Ruzizi River into Lake Tanganyika. Tanganyika in turn drains into the Congo River, which flows across Africa and into the Atlantic. ☐

LAKE KIVU. *The processes that created the lake have by no means ended: nearby volcanoes are still active and continue to alter its shorelines with solidified lava flows.*

Koko Nor

- China
- Map: page 19, L–5

An Asian salt lake has two names, one Chinese, the other Mongolian. But both agree on the color of its water—as blue as the sky above.

Koko Nor, a shimmering expanse of salty blue water, lies at the heart of a vast plateau about 10,000 feet (3,000 meters) above sea level in west-central China. Hemmed in by rolling mountain ranges to the north and higher snowcapped peaks to the south, the plateau is an enclosed drainage basin with no outlet to the sea. Streams running down the mountainsides simply end in the many lakes and ponds that dot the basin. There their waters evaporate in the relatively dry climate, leaving behind the dissolved salts and other minerals that were washed down from the slopes.

As a result, most of the lakes are true salt lakes, with a salt content of more than 3.5 percent. Under cloudless skies most of the year, some of them at times dry out completely, leaving their beds encrusted with salt deposits. The sun glinting off their surfaces then gives the impression that the entire region has been blanketed by a light snowfall.

The largest salt lake in the basin, and in all of Central Asia, is Ching Hai

itself—or Koko Nor, to use its better-known Mongolian name. (Both terms, roughly translated, mean "sky-blue sea.") The size of the lake varies with the seasons and from year to year, depending on changes in the rates of inflow and evaporation. At present its maximum size averages about 65 miles (105 kilometers) long by 40 miles (65 kilometers) wide, with a surface area of approximately 2,300 square miles (6,000 square kilometers). At times the area shrinks by about one-third, to 1,600 square miles (4,150 square kilometers).

Shrinkage in the past has been even more drastic. Terraces on surrounding slopes mark the levels of former shorelines. They indicate that with the melting of continental glaciers at the close of the last ice age, Koko Nor had a maximum depth of nearly 165 feet (50 meters), compared to 125 feet (38 meters) today.

Although the water is too salty to drink, carp and a few other fish thrive in Koko Nor. In the past the surrounding area was sparsely populated, chiefly by nomadic Mongols on the north shore and Tibetans to the south. More recently, discoveries of oil in the basin have led to growing industrialization. But the region's greatest resource remains what it had always been in the past—salt. Estimated reserves in the entire Koko Nor region are large enough to meet China's needs for the next 8,000 years. ☐

Königssee

- West Germany
- Map: page 17, E–4

A jewel of a lake in a magnificent mountain setting is hemmed in by rugged slopes that rise almost straight up from the water's edge.

Königssee, the "Lake of the King," is not large by any means. In the Bavarian Alps in West Germany, just south of the famous resort of Berchtesgaden, it is only about 5 miles (8 kilometers) long and nowhere much more than 1 mile (1.6 kilometers) wide.

Yet many travelers consider it to be one of the most beautiful lakes in the country. Occupying a long, narrow trench in a seemingly impenetrable mountain barrier, the Königssee is almost completely surrounded by precipitous mountain slopes. Some are forested; others are bare limestone cliffs that plunge straight down to the water's edge. Tranquil and crystal clear, the lake shimmers like a rare gem in a setting of massive mountain bastions. Most visitors tour the lake by boat. The more adventurous hike on the many trails that wind across the surrounding mountains and provide spectacular views of the region.

The highest peak in the area is the Watzmann, at 8,901 feet (2,713 meters). From its jagged summit an almost vertical wall drops down for nearly 6,600 feet (2,000 meters). On a delta extending into the lake at its foot, in charming contrast, is a little onion-domed chapel dedicated to Saint Bartholomew. Not far away is the Malerwinkel, or "Painter's Corner," a quiet bay with beautiful views across the Königssee. Forming the backdrop at the southern end of the lake is the Steinernes Meer, the "Stony Sea," a mass of limestone forming a high plateau crowned by the pyramidal crest of the Schönfeldspitze.

Long, narrow, and bordered by steep mountain slopes, the lake reminds many visitors of the Norwegian fjords; like them, its basin, which reaches a depth of 617 feet (188 meters), was scooped out by Ice Age glaciers. Grinding slowly down the mountain valley, a massive, debris-laden river of ice gradually deepened the trench now occupied by the lake. Other evidences of glaciation can be seen in the ice-carved cirques (large amphitheaterlike basins) that scar the flanks of the Watzmann, the Hoher Göll, and other nearby mountains.

Most of the glaciers that created this remarkable scenery have long since disappeared. But not all of them. To the west of the Königssee, on the upper slopes of the Hochkalter (8,553 feet, or 2,607 meters) is the Blaueis ("Blue Ice") Glacier, the northernmost glacier in the Alps. □

KÖNIGSSEE. *Occupying a long, narrow, glacier-carved basin, the Bavarian lake is almost completely surrounded by steep mountain slopes.*

Kotor, Gulf of

- Yugoslavia
- Map: page 17, E–4

Subsiding land and rising seas along the Adriatic coast have created a sinuous series of hidden inland bays.

The entrance to the Gulf of Kotor, on the Adriatic coast southeast of the port city of Dubrovnik, is not especially impressive. From the sea it appears to be little more than a gap between low-lying hills backed by taller mountains inland. But beyond the entrance of the gulf, like a well-kept secret, lies one of the finest harbors on the coast: a maze of narrow, interconnected, deepwater bays hemmed in by abrupt mountain slopes.

At the end of one of the innermost bays is the town of Kotor, huddled on a narrow lowland at the foot of the Lovcen. And winding up the looming massif—it rises to 5,737 feet, or 1,749

meters—is a road composed of a succession of hairpin turns. With every bend the intrepid traveler is presented with new and sweeping views of the entire gulf.

Looking down across the network of sheltered bays, visitors can easily understand why the gulf has been valued since antiquity for its maritime and strategic importance. Kotor itself was founded as an outpost of the Roman Empire, and the gulf was controlled in turn by Turks, Venetians, and various other nationalities.

Today the gulf still has important naval facilities, and several of the towns along its shores are centers of light industry. But because of its natural beauty, mild climate, and many architectural and artistic treasures, it is also a popular vacation resort. In contrast to the stark fringing mountains, which are hot in summer and cold in winter, the lowlands around the gulf enjoy a mild Mediterranean climate. Cactuses, palms, and citrus trees, in

addition to other subtropical plants, enhance the beauty of charming towns dating from the Middle Ages.

The configuration of the bays making up the Gulf of Kotor is quite unusual. The gulf essentially is composed of two long, narrow, water-filled valleys that lie between a series of highlands paralleling the seacoast. A breach in the first row of hills forms the entrance from the sea to the first flooded valley. A break in the second line of hills forms the channel that leads to the second flooded valley. The gulf thus is shaped more or less like a giant letter H lying on its side parallel to the coast.

How did this extraordinarily sheltered system of waterways come into being? The process began about 200 million years ago, when the area lay beneath the sea and thick deposits of limestone were formed on the ocean floor. Subsequently uplifted above the sea, the crust was subjected to stresses about 40 million years ago that com-

GULF OF KOTOR. *Stark, eroded limestone ridges hem in narrow valleys that have been invaded by long, winding arms of the sea.*

pressed it into a series of corrugated folds parallel to the seacoast. The upfolds eventually became parallel rows of mountain ridges; the downfolds became intervening valleys.

All might have remained dry land except for rivers that were already present when the folding began. As the folds were slowly uplifted, these antecedent streams eroded steep valleys across the rising ridges, carving water gaps as they maintained their courses toward the sea.

In more recent times the entire coastal zone of Yugoslavia has been subsiding very slowly into the sea, as evidenced by frequent earthquakes throughout the area. In addition, at the end of the last ice age sea levels rose all around the world. As a result, the sea was able to invade the water gaps, flooding once-dry interior valleys and creating the fjordlike waterways of the Gulf of Kotor.   □

Yugoslavia's Distinctive Drowned Coastline

The Gulf of Kotor is a special type of drowned coastline. Over a long period, layers of sedimentary rock were compressed into a series of folds running parallel to the coast. Upfolds formed mountain ridges; downfolds formed valleys. As the mountains rose, rivers carved water gaps across the ridges.

The land later subsided and the sea level rose, enabling water to invade the gaps and "drown" the valleys. The result is a pattern of long headlands, bays, and islands that run parallel to the coast. Along the coast of Maine, in contrast, the drowned valleys and intervening ridges are at an angle to the shore. As a result, rocky headlands and offshore islands (the exposed tops of submerged ridges) point out to sea.

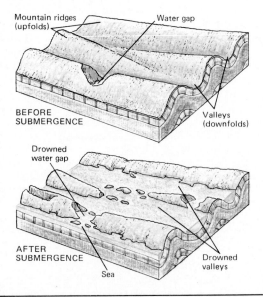

Krakatoa

- Indonesia
- Map: page 21, E–5

In 1883 the remote volcanic island erupted with one of the most powerful explosions in recent history.

Before 1883 the name Krakatoa (or Krakatau in Indonesian) was known chiefly to fishermen and others familiar with the waters between the islands of Java and Sumatra. There, rising some 2,700 feet (820 meters) above the Sunda Strait, was a picturesque volcanic island that had lain dormant for generations. Everything changed in the summer of 1883, when Krakatoa came to life with a ferocity that made its name familiar around the world.

The origins of the drama date back about 1 million years, when a large volcanic cone first rose on the site. A subsequent eruption virtually destroyed the old volcano, leaving only a caldera (a basin-shaped depression much larger than a normal crater) and several islets where segments of the caldera's rim projected above the sea.

Over the millennia, recurrent volcanic activity gradually enlarged one of the islets, forming the island known as Krakatoa. Following the last recorded eruption in 1681, Krakatoa lay dormant for two centuries. To all appearances it was just one more beautiful South Sea island—remote, uninhabited, and densely covered with lush tropical vegetation.

The great drama began to unfold on May 20, 1883. With a roar heard 125 miles (200 kilometers) away, Krakatoa sent a violent burst of steam, ash, and cinders flying high in the sky. But that first eruption was only a prelude. Intermittent activity continued for three months, until the afternoon of August 26, when a series of extraordinarily violent explosions began. By the following morning huge tidal waves, or tsunamis, were being launched by the eruptions and underwater collapses of the volcano.

The final paroxysm occurred at 10 a.m. on August 27, when Krakatoa was shattered by one of the most colossal explosions ever recorded. It was heard as far away as central Australia, some 2,200 miles (3,540 kilometers) across the sea. Almost instantly a gigantic black column of steam and ash rose perhaps 50 miles (80 kilometers) in the air, blotting out the sun for miles around. Within half an hour, tidal waves more than 100 feet (30 meters) high began swamping the shores of Java and Sumatra and drowned an estimated 36,000 people.

By August 28 the reservoir of magma, or molten rock, beneath Krakatoa was exhausted, and the violence came to an end. Some 4.5 cubic miles (19 cubic kilometers) of rock debris had been ejected; most of Krakatoa had collapsed into the empty magma chamber, leaving a caldera about 4 miles (6.5 kilometers) wide and extending 900 feet (275 meters) beneath the sea. In the aftermath of the eruption, a windblown layer of fine ash encircled the globe and caused unnaturally brilliant sunsets around the world for more than a year.

There was no further activity until 1927, when a new cinder cone appeared on the floor of the caldera. Named Anak Krakatoa, "Child of Krakatoa," the cone remained under water until a fresh eruption in 1952 thrust it above the surface. Anak has since grown to a height of more than 500 feet (150 meters) above the water and remains active—evidence that a new long-term cycle of volcanism may have begun. ☐

KRAKATOA. *Clouds of sulfurous steam rise lazily from young volcanic islets—gentle reminders of violent forces still active far below.*

KWEILIN KARST. *Reflected in the placid water of a river, rank upon rank of strangely eroded limestone hills fill the countryside around the Chinese city of Kweilin.*

Kweilin Karst

- China
- Map: page 21, F–2

Reminiscent of Chinese landscape paintings, which in fact they have often inspired, the array of domelike limestone pinnacles and towers forms a setting like no other on earth.

For generations the unearthly beauty of the hills surrounding the city of Kweilin, in southern China, has inspired the imagination of poets and landscape painters. Stretching off in all directions as far as the eye can see, their ethereal, otherworldly profiles are poised against the horizon. Neatly spaced and separated by winding ravines, the steep-sided conical hills rise to heights of 325 feet (100 meters) and more. The gigantic rocky domes, stained with variegated ocher tones, are penetrated by caves within and channeled on the outside by vertical flutings. Trees cling precariously to some, their branches overgrown with orchids and entwined with garlands of vines, adding the perfect finishing touch to their romantic beauty.

Geologists, in their turn, find these fantastic hills exciting because they are among the world's most spectacular examples of tower karst. (Karst refers to the distinctive landforms —caves, underground streams, sinkholes, and the like—that develop in limestone regions.) The Kweilin karst is part of a much larger karst region extending across south-central China and into northern Vietnam.

Throughout the region the erosive agent that has sculpted this fantastic landscape is abundant rainfall charged with acids absorbed from the air as well as from decaying vegetation. Seeping into openings in thick deposits of limestone, the mildly acid solution dissolves the rock and gradually enlarges the openings to form complex networks of tunnels, caves, and sinkholes. In warm, humid tropical regions, such as this part of southern China, the solution processes are greatly accelerated and often produce spectacular results.

In the Kweilin region, thick layers of limestone were formed beneath an ancient sea, uplifted above sea level, and then worn down to a flat plain. Already riddled with dissolved openings, the land was then uplifted again. In the process all the previously existing channels in the rock were deepened, and weakened roofs above them collapsed. Then eventually nothing was left except for the individual freestanding peaks and towers composed of the more resistant parts of the limestone formation. □

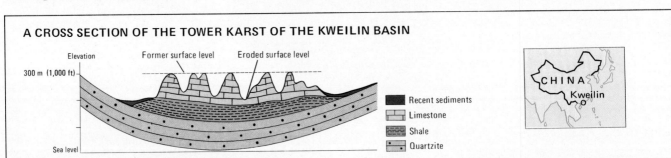

A CROSS SECTION OF THE TOWER KARST OF THE KWEILIN BASIN

Elevation

300 m (1,000 ft)

Former surface level   Eroded surface level

Sea level

- Recent sediments
- Limestone
- Shale
- Quartzite

CHINA
Kweilin

About 300 million years ago the limestone deposits of the Kweilin basin were formed beneath the sea on a base of shale and quartzite. The area was later uplifted above the sea in the form of a shallow basin, and erosion planed the top of the limestone down to a flat surface. Further uplift then occurred, permitting deep dissection of the limestone by karst processes until only tall towers remained.

L

Laacher See

- West Germany
- Map: page 17, D–3

Where volcanoes once erupted, a medieval abbey now is mirrored on the surface of a tranquil lake.

The haunting beauty of the Eifel plateau, an upland on the west bank of the Rhine to the south of Bonn, results from a pleasing blend of the forces of nature and the works of man. Scattered across the countryside are romantic old castles, many now in ruins; nestled among the wooded hills are many dark and brooding lakes, their tranquil surfaces mirroring the sky.

Though still and peaceful now, the area was once the scene of violent volcanism. Many of the hills, their distinctive profiles masked by trees, are really ash cones that were built up by volcanoes. And the lakes, known as maars, are the circular water-filled craters of extinct volcanoes.

The largest and most picturesque of all the maars is the Laacher See, with a surface area of 1.3 square miles (3.4 square kilometers) and a depth of 174 feet (53 meters). Cupped in the bottom of a rounded basin, it is fringed by wooded slopes that rise up to a ring of irregular basalt outcrops about 325 feet (100 meters) above water level.

The lake was formed by two stages of volcanic activity. In the first, eruptions built up the surrounding ring of basalt outcrops. In the second stage, which took place only about 11,000 years ago, two adjacent overlapping craters were formed by violent explosions of pumice and ash. Hence the shape of the lake today: an oval slightly narrowed at its center.

But the special beauty and fame of the Laacher See results from human endeavor. Sheltered on the wooded slopes near the edge of the water is the Benedictine church and abbey of Maria Laach, begun in 1093 and completed in 1220. Crowned by six towers, it is one of the Rhineland's finest examples of Romanesque architecture. Today the site is part of a reserve designed to protect both its esthetic and unusual geological heritage. □

LA PAZ RIVER. *Over the centuries, water rushing down steep slopes of the Andes in the La Paz valley carved the maze of rugged spires that make up the Valley of the Moon.*

Laichau Canyon

- Vietnam
- Map: page 20, E–2

Flowing through jungles, the Black River cuts a straight and narrow course across an impressive obstacle.

Like the other major rivers of northern Vietnam, the Song Bo, or Black River, rises in the highlands of Yunnan Province in southern China. Fed by abundant monsoon rains, it foams over many powerful rapids and passes through a number of gorges as it surges southeastward toward the sea.

The most impressive sector is near the town of Laichau just south of the Chinese border. For a stretch of about 9 miles (15 kilometers), the river slices its way through a limestone massif that rises high above the surrounding countryside. Hemmed in by vertical walls up to 2,600 feet (800 meters) high, the canyon is so deep and narrow that the bottom is perpetually dim and often as dark as night. Joined by two equally impressive side canyons, the Laichau Canyon is among the most spectacular gorges in this part of the world. □

La Paz River

- Bolivia
- Map: page 14, C–4

High in the Andes, a headwater of the Amazon winds across stark but strangely varied terrain.

Although it is only about 100 miles (160 kilometers) long, the Río de la Paz passes through a variety of contrasting and picturesque landscapes. From its source on a snowcapped Andean peak, the river slices through a deep, wide canyon that shelters the capital city of La Paz and then continues on between weirdly eroded plateaus and gorges along both banks.

The river rises on the slopes of the Chacaltaya, a peak in the Cordillera Oriental (the great eastern range of the Andes) overlooking the eastern shore of Lake Titicaca. Formed by the merger of two headstreams, the Choqueyapu and the Chuquiaguillo, the La Paz flows southward for about 10 miles (16 kilometers) before plunging into the canyon that encloses the city of La Paz. The river then curves gently to the northeast as it spills down the eastern slopes of the Andes, where its waters eventually flow into those of the Beni, one of the major tributaries of the Amazon.

Along its upper course the La Paz flows across the Altiplano, the high, arid plateau between the eastern and western ranges of the Andes. Although the sunshine there is often brilliant, the Altiplano can be bitterly cold. Once the sun dips behind the western mountains, the temperature drops sharply, and chill winds whip across the bleak boulders and sparse grasses of the high plain. It was to escape the harsh conditions on the highlands that the Spaniards chose the broad, amphitheaterlike basin in the river's upper valley when they founded the city of La Paz in 1548.

Although nestled within a valley, La Paz is still the highest major city in the world, with an average elevation of about 12,000 feet (3,650 meters). Denver, Colorado, famed as the mile-high city, in contrast, is less than half as high above sea level. La Paz has a few long, broad avenues near river level, but most of the streets climb steeply up the surrounding slopes. It is in fact possible for residents to climb or descend some 3,000 feet (900 meters) without ever leaving town.

Downstream from the city the river passes through many oddly eroded landscapes, which are made all the more impressive by their backdrop of towering Andean peaks such as Illimani and Illampu. In places the valley walls are slashed by deep, winding gorges called *quebradas*. Elsewhere the mountain slopes have been eroded into strange earth pyramids, pinnacles, and spires. One, the Devil's Tooth, overlooks the river from a high cliff. The stark spire is the core of erosion-resistant rock that once filled the vent of an ancient volcano.

The strangest of all the landscapes in the La Paz basin is found just a short drive from the capital city. Known as Valle de la Luna (the "Valley of the Moon"), it is an area of desertlike badlands that contrast vividly with the plantings of hardy eucalyptus trees along the river. Stretching off in all directions is a maze of weirdly eroded spires and columns deeply dissected by narrow ravines. Composed of sedimentary deposits capped in places by harder volcanic rock, the eerie forms were carved by water rushing down from nearby highlands. The scene is so impressive that the Valley of the Moon remains a perennially popular destination for sightseers from La Paz. □

LARDERELLO HOT SPRINGS. *Once shunned by local peasants as evil entities, the region's spurting steam jets have now been harnessed to generate electricity.*

Larderello Hot Springs

- Italy
- Map: page 17, E–4

The hot springs that inspired Dante's vision of Inferno now spin the turbines of great generators.

Visitors exploring the treasures of Florence seldom bother to travel some 40 miles (65 kilometers) southwestward to the little village of Larderello in the hills of Tuscany. Yet here too there is an attraction of unusual interest: it was at Larderello that geothermal energy was first—and still is—harnessed for the production of electricity.

The mineral-rich hot springs clustered around Larderello and several nearby towns have been known for centuries. The sight of superheated jets of steam spurting as much as 165 feet (50 meters) into the air is thought to have inspired Dante's memorable vision of Inferno.

The *soffioni,* or natural steam jets, are caused by a pocket of magma (molten rock) that long ago welled upward into the earth's crust. Trapped quite near the surface beneath overlying layers of sedimentary rock, the molten material continuously sends up jets of superheated steam with temperatures that reach as high as 375° F (190° C).

Although the steam originally escaped through natural fissures in the rock, it has been harnessed for in-dustry since early in this century. Wells averaging between 500 and 1,500 feet (150 and 450 meters) in depth have been drilled through the rock to underground pockets of steam. Escaping to the surface under high pressure, the steam is then piped across the countryside to huge steam-turbine generators and chemical plants. (Rich in minerals and gases, the steam is also an important source of boric acid, liquid ammonia, and other products.)

The result is a seldom achieved objective—a dependable, nonpolluting source of electricity. Much of the area's electrical power is supplied without need for giant dams and reservoirs, without the despoliation of strip mining and unsightly piles of coal, without oil tankers or storage depots, and without an industry-blackened countryside. The only "smoke" escaping from the power plants is steam that originated deep within the earth. ☐

Ledenika Cave

- Bulgaria
- Map: page 17, F–4

When winter comes, glistening icicles mingle with the clusters of delicate stalactites that hang from the ceiling of this Balkan cave.

First explored around the turn of the century and open to visitors since 1961, Ledenika Cave in northwestern Bulgaria is one of the most popular natural attractions in the Balkan Mountains. From a nearby tourist chalet on the surface, visitors descend a flight of stone stairs leading into the mouth of the cave.

Beyond the entrance they find a series of chambers, all artificially illuminated and decorated with fine displays of cave formations. The largest room, known as the Great Temple, has a ceiling 50 feet (15 meters) high. But the richest display of stalactites and stalagmites is in the grotto called the Concert Chamber. In winter the spectacle is enhanced by enormous icicles that form on the ceilings of the cave. The icicles in fact are responsible for the name Ledenika, which is derived from a word meaning "glacier."

Beyond the areas that have been developed for tourism, the windings of Ledenika's passageways remain generally unknown. Located in an extensive limestone region, the cave apparently is only part of a much more extensive subterranean labyrinth. Although direct links with other nearby caves have yet to be established, it seems likely that future exploration will prove that most of them are in fact interconnected. ☐

LARDERELLO HOT SPRINGS. *A wraith of scorching steam escaping from a fissure in the earth is just one of many* soffioni *(natural steam jets) in the Larderello area.*

LEDENIKA CAVE. *In the depths of the Bulgarian cavern, dripstone draperies and delicate stalactites contrast with the massive forms of elaborate, domelike stalagmites.*

LENA RIVER. *With the violence of its annual summer flood ended, the Lena flows placidly across the seemingly endless Siberian plains, its uneven banks lined with reedy marshes.*

Lena River

- U.S.S.R.
- Map: page 19, N–1

Frozen solid during the bitter Siberian winter, the river is transformed in spring into a violently surging flood.

Flowing across the great vastness of eastern Siberia through thick forests and across trackless tundra, the Lena River assumes a number of differing personalities on its circuitous journey toward the Arctic Ocean. One of the longest rivers in the world, it travels 2,648 miles (4,262 kilometers) from its source in southern Siberia to its delta north of the Arctic Circle, where it empties into the Laptev Sea.

The Lena (its name means "big river" in Yakut, a Siberian dialect) rises in the mountains west of Lake Baikal. Setting out on a northeastward course, it passes through rugged countryside bounded by sheer cliffs that enclose deep gorges. The river begins to change noticeably in character about one-third of the way on its journey to the sea, beyond its junction with the Vitim, one of the largest of its many tributaries. Growing steadily wider and deeper, it approaches the mouth of the Olekma River through a broad valley flanked by gentle, heavily wooded slopes.

Beyond the Olekma the valley narrows again and is hemmed in by towering rocky crags. At Yakutsk the Lena curves toward the northwest and is joined by another major tributary, the Aldan. Separating into several branches interspersed with countless islands and marshes, the river suddenly broadens to as much as 9 miles (15 kilometers) wide.

The Lena eventually crosses the Arctic Circle and enters the final stage of its journey. For more than 400 miles (650 kilometers) it courses northward across the flat, inhospitable arctic tundra, where even during the brief summer the soil remains permanently frozen beneath a shallow surface layer. At last it empties into the Laptev Sea, flowing at an average rate of 550,000 cubic feet (15,500 cubic meters) per second, or almost 100 cubic miles (420 cubic kilometers) per year.

Governed by the extreme contrasts in Siberia's weather, however, the river's flow is far from evenly distributed throughout the year. In the course of its long travels the Lena passes through three distinct climatic zones: cool and temperate in the Baikal area, milder but often rainy around the Aldan basin, then dry and bitterly cold to the north.

Winter near the Arctic Circle begins in September; by October much of the surface of the Lena River is already icebound and remains frozen for almost eight months. The ice thickens as the temperatures continue to drop. (The *average* January reading at Yakutsk is –45° F, or –43° C.) By late winter long stretches of the river are frozen solid from top to bottom.

But then, toward the end of May, the Siberian spring abruptly returns, compressing into just a few weeks a process that elsewhere would take months. By early June temperatures north of Yakutsk reach as high as 68° F (20° C). The ice breaks up, plants burst into life—and floodwaters are suddenly unleashed across the Yakutsk plain. In a violent surge, tremendous blocks of ice are hurtled northward on the current, uprooting trees in their path and crashing into the riverbanks. By mid-June the Lena River pours into the Laptev Sea at a torrential rate, its flow 65 times greater than it was in April.

Throughout July and into August much of the Yakutsk plain remains submerged, the frozen subsoil unable to absorb the overflow. By September the flood subsides and cold weather returns. The delta freezes over, and by late October ice once again covers the Lena as far south as Yakutsk, locking the great river into the tight grip of yet another long and implacable Siberian winter. □

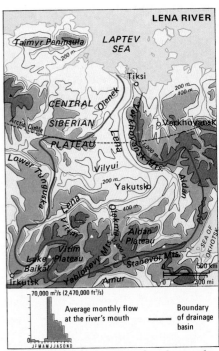

Despite the immense size of its basin, the Lena's flow is reduced to a trickle in winter, when ice blocks its channel. The spring thaw, however, releases it in a torrent.

LEVIATHAN CAVE. *The remote African cavern penetrating a basaltic lava flow is as symmetrical in cross section as a man-made tunnel.*

Leviathan Cave

- Kenya
- Map: page 26, C–3

Although broken into sections by movements of the earth's crust, this remains Africa's longest lava tube.

In southern Kenya, about midway between Nairobi and Mombasa, the Chyulu Range of hills forms a long, low barrier at the edge of the Nyiri Desert. Formed by volcanic eruptions, the hills are penetrated by a tunnellike cavern known as Leviathan Cave.

Shaped like a slightly flattened cylinder, the cave is a fine example of a lava tube. It was formed when the surface of a lava flow cooled and started to harden while it streamed downslope. The core of the lava flow, remaining hotter and more fluid, then drained out from beneath the solidified crust, leaving the tunnellike void.

Partially explored in 1976, Leviathan Cave is known to have originally been a continuous lava tube at least five miles (eight kilometers) in length. Subsequent movements of the earth's crust along fault lines, however, broke the tube into three sections. Even so, its longest sector, a continuous tunnel totaling 1½ miles (2½ kilometers), still ranks as the longest lava tube in all of Africa. □

Lofoi Falls

- Zaire
- Map: page 26, B–4

In a lush unspoiled wilderness, a splendid plume of water spills across the face of a sheer escarpment.

In the extreme southeastern corner of Zaire, an isolated upland, the Kundelungu plateau, rises high above its surroundings. Bounded on the west by sheer escarpments, it overlooks a broad marshy plain some 2,500 feet (750 meters) below, where the Lufira River meanders northward in great looping curves.

Rainfall on the plateau is sparse, totaling only about 40 inches (1,000 millimeters) every year. Even so, a number of rivers originate in the upland. Tumbling over the edge of the plateau in a multitude of cascades and waterfalls, they have carved deep, narrow gorges that grow wider toward the plains.

One such river is the Lofoi. On its short course from the Kundelungu plateau to its junction with the Lufira, it rushes down a deep, densely vegetated valley. Hidden in this pristine setting is the river's most majestic feature, the splendid plume of water known as Lofoi Falls.

Hurtling over the brink of an es-carpment into a broad plunge pool at its foot, the waters of the Lofoi plummet straight down for 1,115 feet (340 meters) in a single uninterrupted leap. Although the river shrinks drastically during the dry season from June to October, the falls remain a breathtaking spectacle for the rest of the year.

Lofoi Falls and the surrounding countryside have been preserved since 1970 as Kundelungu National Park. Vegetation ranges from dense forest on the foothills to savannalike grass-lands on the plateau. The grassy up-lands are especially beautiful at the start of the rainy season, when they are spangled with myriads of multi-colored wildflowers.

The park is also notable for its varied wildlife. Lions and cheetahs roam the hills and plains. Elephants come crashing through the brush. And the herds of grazers include zebras, antelopes, elands, and hartebeests. Frequenting the lowland plains during the dry season, they retreat to the foothills when the rains return.

Although accommodations in the park are limited and the roads are rough, visitors are amply rewarded. In addition to Lofoi Falls and the varied wildlife, one of the highlights of the park is the spectacular views from the highlands across the valley of the Lu-fira River far below. □

The Origins of Lakes

Lakes are formed where some sort of barrier interferes with normal drainage. Some lake basins were scoured out by glaciers that deposited terminal moraines—damlike barriers of debris. Landslides and lava flows can also block river valleys. Other lakes result from a variety of processes.

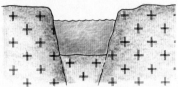

Lakes such as Lake Baikal occupy grabens. Their basins were formed when a portion of the earth's crust fell between faults, or fractures, while the surface rose on either side.

Stresses sometimes cause a downwarping of the earth's crust, forming a broad subsidence basin that becomes filled with water. Africa's Lake Chad lies in such a depression.

Some lakes fill volcanic craters. Even larger basins, called calderas, are formed when the top of a volcano collapses after an eruption. Crater Lake in Oregon is in a caldera.

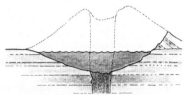

Lakes such as Laacher See in West Germany are known as maars. They occupy small circular basins that were formed by violently explosive volcanic eruptions.

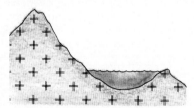

Some mountain lakes, called tarns, fill the basins of cirques—depressions shaped like amphitheaters that were carved by glaciers in the bedrock at the heads of valleys.

Lucerne, Lake of

- Switzerland
- Map: page 17, D–4

Rich in history, the famous Alpine lake is also celebrated for the tranquil beauty of its picturesque setting.

As might be expected of a lake situated in the very heart of Switzerland, the Lake of Lucerne has names in two languages. In French it is the Lac des Quatre-Cantons, the "Lake of the Four Cantons"; in German it is the Vierwaldstättersee, the "Lake of the Four Forest Cantons." It was on the shores of Lake Lucerne, in 1291, that representatives of the four original cantons of Switzerland signed a pact uniting themselves against domination by the Austrian Hapsburgs, thus giving birth to the Swiss Confederation. Rich in historical associations, the lake is also linked with tales of the exploits of the archer William Tell.

Today the lake is most famous as the center of a resort area. Irregular in shape with arms branching off in various directions, it is formed by the convergence of four major river valleys. To the south it is bounded by high peaks of the Alps (the view from Mount Pilatus overlooking the city of Lucerne is legendary); to the north it is fringed by more gently rolling hills. Almost fjordlike in appearance, the lake's winding shorelines are bounded in places by steep, romantic cliffs, lush green forests, and craggy mountain peaks.

The complex contours of the Lake of Lucerne apparently resulted from a combination of events. The general outline of the lake basin was first formed by a gentle subsidence of the earth's crust. Rivers rushing down from the Alps then deepened valleys running into the basin. Finally and most important, Ice Age glaciers converging in the basin scoured out the preexisting river valleys, carving deep basins and partially damming their outlet with moraines (large barriers of eroded debris).

The end result is one of the loveliest lakes in the Alps. Whether viewed from mountaintop overlooks or scenic lakeside highways, it remains an incomparable spectacle. □

LAKE OF LUCERNE. *Hemmed in by craggy limestone mountains, the sinuous shorelines of the placid Alpine lake form a complex series of branching arms and inlets.*

Lurgrotte

- Austria
- Map: page 17, E–4

Experiments have shown that the streams in the limestone cave are part of a complicated drainage system.

Visitors to Lurgrotte, about 10 miles (16 kilometers) to the north of Graz in southeastern Austria, have a choice. They can enter the largest cave in the Eastern Alps at the little market town of Semriach, where the Lur River also enters the cave and disappears into subterranean channels. Or they can enter the cave at Peggau, a few miles to the west, where the Schmelz River emerges from a spring within the cave.

From either end visitors can take guided tours of various lengths to admire the exceptional displays of stalactites and other cave formations. Wandering through passageways and chambers, they discover surprises everywhere. A highlight of the tour is the Big Dome, one of the largest underground chambers in central Europe.

Or visitors can travel the entire length of the cave, entering the world of darkness at either Semriach or Peggau and emerging in daylight at the other end. The total length of the cave is about 3 miles (5 kilometers), and the difference in elevation between the entrances is 720 feet (220 meters).

Scientists long ago surmised that there was a connection between the disappearing Lur River at one end of the cave and the emerging Schmelz at the other. The first attempt to prove the link, in 1894, almost ended in disaster. A flash flood on the Lur trapped the explorers underground for 10 days before they were finally rescued.

In this century experimenters have poured dye into some of the many disappearing streams in the area to trace the underground flow of water. Their findings have yielded some surprises. Most of the water flowing underground from the Lur, they discovered, emerges in springs to the south of Lurgrotte. Most of the flow of the Schmelz, in turn, originates at sources to the north of the cave.

Yet a connection between the two streams does exist. Like most limestone areas, this one is penetrated by a network of underground channels. Experiments have shown that when rainfall is heavy, water backs up in the channels, and the Lur's overflow does indeed escape into the Schmelz. ☐

VALLE DE LA LUNA. *Precariously balanced rock formations and heaps of fallen boulders have been sandblasted by the wind to form an immense natural sculpture garden.*

Luna, Valle de la

- Argentina
- Map: page 15, C–5

As sere and stark as the surface of the moon, the valley at one time was home to exotic animals and plants.

Valle de la Luna, the "Valley of the Moon," is remote, desolate—and beautiful. Hidden among the Andean foothills of northern Argentina, it is a harsh and arid place. Temperatures change abruptly from one extreme to another. The few streams that flow after rare summer storms quickly die out in immense salt-encrusted flats. The only plants able to survive here are a few tenacious spiny shrubs.

The special beauty of the valley results from the array of endlessly varied rock formations. Sharply chiseled boulders are strewn all across the floor, blasted ceaselessly by sand-laden winds. Elsewhere giant fractured stones are piled one atop another in strange natural sculptures that resemble birds, sphinxes, and other bizarre forms.

Yet the valley was not always the inhospitable place it is today. A remarkable variety of fossils have been discovered in its barren rocks. Among them are the remains of giant ferns and reptiles, testifying to times when a more equable climate prevailed in the Valley of the Moon. ☐

Mackenzie Delta

- Canada (Northwest Territories)
- Map: page 10, C–2

Hushed and frozen through the Arctic winter, the great watery delta teems with life in summertime.

From its beginning, the outlet of Great Slave Lake, to its ending in the Arctic Ocean's Beaufort Sea, the Mackenzie River travels 1,070 miles (1,722 kilometers)—a substantial river by any standard. But from its ultimate source, the headwaters of the Finlay River in British Columbia, its mainstream flows a total of 2,635 miles (4,241 kilometers). The Mackenzie is thus the final segment of the second longest river system in North America, exceeded only by the Mississippi-Missouri system.

And like the Mississippi, it enters the sea through an enormous complex delta. Over the eons its waters have deposited layer upon layer of sediment and gradually built up a triangular delta more than 100 miles (160 kilometers) long and about 50 miles

(80 kilometers) wide. At Point Separation, the head of the delta, the river branches into a network of innumerable intertwining channels enclosing a mosaic of islands and countless lakes and ponds.

The delta lies north of the Arctic Circle, and it is completely underlain by permafrost, or permanently frozen ground. Only a few scattered trees protrude above the low-lying tundra vegetation. Here and there domelike pingos (strange hills with cores of ice) punctuate the uniformly flat terrain.

Though locked each year in the seemingly endless Arctic winter, the delta teems with life when spring returns. Muskrats, quiescent through the winter, begin their reproductive cycle. Insects fill the air. Fireweed and other wildflowers burst into bloom. But above all the delta is a haven for migrant birds. Ducks, geese, swans, and other water birds by the tens of thousands converge on the watery wilderness to mate, breed, and depart again when winter returns. □

How a Pingo Eventually Becomes a Pond

A pingo forms when a lens-shaped mass of ice freezes beneath the surface of the tundra and heaves the soil up into a domelike hill. When the ice melts, the soil slides down to form a high-rimmed depression that becomes filled with water.

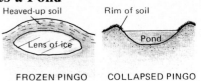

Heaved-up soil / Lens of ice / **FROZEN PINGO**

Rim of soil / Pond / **COLLAPSED PINGO**

MACKENZIE DELTA. *On its vast delta the Mackenzie River breaks up into countless channels interspersed with a maze of ponds and islands.*

LAGO MAGGIORE. *Illuminated by a low-lying sun, the view across the lake is softened by a layer of haze that often permeates the air.*

Maggiore, Lago

- Italy—Switzerland
- Map: page 17, D–4

This gem of a lake combines the scenic splendor of the Alps with the warmth of the Mediterranean.

Hailed by one writer as "the Eden of Italy," Lago Maggiore, or Lake Maggiore, has entranced visitors for centuries with the uncommon beauty of its setting. Spanning the border between Italy and Switzerland, the long narrow ribbon of water is flanked on three sides by thickly wooded foothills of the southern Alps, which rise up steeply from its shores. Sheltered by this natural enclosure against northerly winds, the lake enjoys the warmer climate of the Lombard plain bordering it on the south.

The second largest lake in Italy (after Lake Garda), Lago Maggiore is 34 miles (55 kilometers) long, with an average width of only about 2.5 miles (4 kilometers). Like so many long narrow lakes hemmed in by steep mountain slopes, its contours are a clue to its origin: the deep trench now occupied by the lake was scooped out during the last ice age by an enormous glacial tongue that moved down from valleys to the north. As the climate gradually warmed up and the ice eventually melted, moraines of glacial debris accumulated in tremendous ridges at the snout of the glacier. Today the southern end of the lake is bounded by a natural crescent-shaped dam of glacial deposits.

Lago Maggiore's major river is the Ticino, which enters the lake at its northern end and spills out over the moraine at its southern tip. Other rivers feeding the lake include the Maggia, flowing in from the north, the Toce from the west, and the Tresa, which links Maggiore to Lake Lugano about 9 miles (15 kilometers) to the east. Situated some 636 feet (194 meters) above sea level, the lake's surface is raised an additional 5 feet (1½ meters) by spring rain and melting snow, and again by rain in the fall.

Like many glacier-carved lakes, Lago Maggiore is also very deep: its maximum depth of 1,220 feet (372 meters) extends well below sea level. Because it is so deep, the lake provides excellent habitat for lake trout, grayling, char, and other fish adapted to life in cold water.

To the southwest, Lago Maggiore opens into a wide gulf, Pallanza Bay. At its mouth lie the Borromean Islands, four small picturesque islets that include the celebrated Isola Bella. In the 16th century its owner, an Italian nobleman, built a magnificent palace on Isola Bella and began transforming the entire island into an idyllic garden retreat.

The ambitious project was carried on by several generations of his heirs (the islands, in fact, are still owned by the same family), who produced one of the most beautiful and exotic gardens on earth. The terraced landscape, designed to resemble the contours of a ship, was planted abundantly with orange and lemon trees, cypresses, and other species native to the Mediterranean. In addition, a profusion of rare subtropical trees, shrubs, and flowers were imported from around the world and continue to thrive in the mild climate. □

MALASPINA GLACIER. *Formed by the convergence of several glaciers flowing off the St. Elias Mountains, the great ice sheet spreads across the coastal plain toward the sea.*

Malaspina Glacier

- United States (Alaska)
- Map: page 10, B–2

Between the coastal mountains and the sea lies a dazzling sheet of ice that is larger in area than all the glaciers of the Alps combined.

Along the Gulf of Alaska, where the Alaskan panhandle joins the rest of the state, the St. Elias Mountains rise like a wall against the sky. Deflected upward by the mountainous barrier, moist winds blowing in off the ocean drop an abundance of snow on their craggy summits, and great glaciers stream slowly down their slopes.

The most impressive accumulation of ice, however, lies not on the mountainsides but in the coastal lowlands between the mountains and the sea. Spread out along the shoreline near Yakutat Bay is an enormous fan-shaped lobe of ice, the Malaspina Glacier. Spanning more than 50 miles (80 kilometers) along its front and sloping gently inland about 28 miles (45 kilometers), it is the most extensive ice field in the United States.

The Malaspina is a classic example of a piedmont glacier—one formed at the foot of a mountain by the convergence of a number of other glaciers. Relatively little ice forms on the surface of piedmont glaciers themselves; they are supplied almost completely by the tributary glaciers flowing into them. The Malaspina is fed by the Seward Glacier and about a dozen others that stream through gaps in the St. Elias Mountains.

Filling a basin that extends well below sea level, the Malaspina in places is as much as 2,000 feet (600 meters) thick. It expands and contracts with the passage of time. Occasionally it surges forward in catastrophic advances; at other times losses through melting and evaporation exceed the influx of new ice, and it shrinks. At present the Malaspina covers about 1,500 square miles (3,900 square kilometers)—an area larger than all the glaciers in the Alps combined, and greater in size than the entire state of Rhode Island. □

Malawi, Lake

- East Africa
- Map: page 26, C–4

The mountainous fringes of three countries plunge abruptly into the depths of a vast African lake.

Surrounded by high, rugged peaks and prone to sudden violent storms, Africa's Lake Malawi (also known as Lake Nyasa) is a place of stunning wildness and beauty. With a length of 360 miles (580 kilometers) and a width that ranges from 15 to 50 miles (24 to 80 kilometers), it is the third largest lake on the continent. Only Lakes Victoria and Tanganyika are larger.

Dubbed the Lake of Storms by the famed explorer David Livingstone, for whom the mountains at its north end were named, Lake Malawi often takes on the appearance of an open sea. In turbulent weather its surface swells with ocean-sized waves, and from most vantage points the opposite shore can be seen only on the clearest of days.

The lake lies near the southern end of the Rift Valley, a major cleft in the earth's crust extending across much of East Africa. Its location in the Rift Valley accounts for the lake's great depth—2,316 feet, or 706 meters—and also for the steep slopes along much of its shore, which were thrust upward by faulting as the valley floor subsided between the slopes.

Geologically the lake is very old indeed. Fossil discoveries indicate that a lake existed in the same place as long

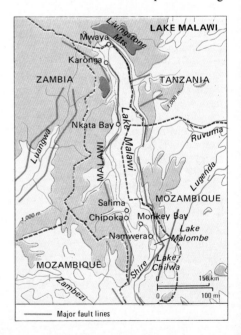

as 120 million years ago, while the ancestor of the present lake began to form 65 million years ago. Traces of former shorelines on surrounding slopes, moreover, reveal that the lake once rose about 1,000 feet (300 meters) above the present water level.

The average elevation of the lake's surface today is 1,535 feet (468 meters) above sea level, although seasonal variations in rainfall cause the level to rise and fall noticeably in the course of a year. Lake Malawi is fed by several rivers but has only one outlet, the Shire River, which flows into the great Zambezi River and eventually empties into the Indian Ocean. □

Maletsunyane Falls

- Lesotho
- Map: page 26, B–5

The roar of the African cascade gives way to an eerie silence when the falls freeze over in winter.

Maletsunyane Falls are located near the center of Lesotho, the tiny nation that is completely surrounded by South Africa. A land of great mountains and steep valleys, it is bounded on the north and east by the massive ramparts of the Drakensberg range. From altitudes of 10,000 feet (3,000 meters) and more, the land slopes to the south and west to elevations of only about 5,000 feet (1,500 meters).

As might be expected, rivers encountering such abrupt changes in altitude over short distances are interrupted by many rapids and waterfalls. Of all the cascades in Lesotho, the most famous is Maletsunyane Falls. Tumbling over a basalt cliff into a deep gorge downstream, the ribbon of water drops 630 feet (192 meters) in a single leap.

Because of the clouds of mist and spray that rise when the falls are flowing at their peak, the place is sometimes called Semonkong, the "Land of Smoke." The falls are also noted for the weird reverberating echoes they generate. According to local legend, the sounds are the wailing of the lost souls who have fallen into the swirling water.

The lamenters' voices are suddenly stilled when winter comes to the frigid highlands. In striking contrast to the noisy torrent of summer, Maletsunyane Falls are then transformed into a silent, twisted tower of ice. □

MALETSUNYANE FALLS. *With a reverberating roar, the Maletsunyane River leaps down a cliff into the deep ravine it has eroded in an ancient basaltic lava flow.*

Mammoth Cave

- United States (Kentucky)
- Map: page 11, E–5

A seemingly endless labyrinth of corridors and chambers makes this the longest cave in the world.

Despite its many underground marvels, the most impressive feature of Mammoth Cave is simply its overwhelming size. Nearly 200 miles (320 kilometers) of passageways have been surveyed (and many more unexplored passages undoubtedly exist), making Mammoth by far the longest cave system in the world.

In some places the passageways enlarge into enormous rooms, including one tall enough to hold a nine-story building. The cave's main corridor, extending west from the Historic entrance, varies in width from 20 to 140 feet (6 to 45 meters) and averages about 40 feet (12 meters) high. The lowest level of cave passages is located 360 feet (110 meters) below the rolling, wooded countryside.

The visitor's first impression, however, is not one of size but of temperature. The cave, located about 85 miles (140 kilometers) south of Louisville in south-central Kentucky, has a year-round temperature of about 54° F (12° C). Despite the constantly high relative humidity (about 87 percent), the cool interior comes as a pleasant surprise in summer, when most people tour the cave. During winter, in contrast, the cave is considerably warmer than the outside air.

As visitors penetrate deeper and deeper into the labyrinth, they gradually realize how truly large it is. One room, the Temple, or Chief City, measures about 540 by 290 feet (165 by 90 meters) and is 125 feet (40 meters) high. Another, the Rotunda, is about 140 feet (45 meters) in diameter and 40 feet (12 meters) high. It contains the remains of equipment that was used to extract saltpeter for the manufacture of gunpowder during the War of 1812.

The cave contains a variety of lakes, rivers, and waterfalls. Echo River, the largest stream, came by its name honestly; shouts reverberate clearly across its water. Flowing at a level of about 360 feet (110 meters) underground, the river is up to 40 feet (12 meters) in width and as much as 25 feet (8 meters) in depth.

Like most limestone caverns, the labyrinth that makes up Mammoth Cave was formed by water. Between 200 and 600 million years ago a shallow sea covered much of the continent, and seashells and oceanic ooze settled to the bottom, where they gradually hardened to form a thick deposit of limestone. Sand, silt, and clay were cemented into a protective overlying layer of sandstone and shale. Slightly acidic groundwater eventually dissolved openings in the limestone after it had been uplifted above sea level.

Water is also responsible for the cave's many impressive natural decorations. Dissolved minerals released from water seeping into the cave have created many fantastically shaped formations, which include some resembling needles, pendants, flowers, and coils, in addition to the more familiar stalactites and stalagmites. Frozen Niagara, a large formation near one of the cave's man-made entrances, does indeed resemble a gigantic motionless cascade of water. Visitors to the cave (protected in a national park) can admire these and other formations on various guided tours.

The process of limestone solution in the cave is still going on. Water entering through cracks and sinkholes and flowing through the underground streams continues bit by bit to dissolve the limestone. Mammoth Cave, as big as it is, is slowly getting bigger. □

MAMMOTH CAVE. *The immensity of the cave's network of underground passages and galleries dwarfs the figures of two explorers, one wearing a brightly lighted miner's lamp.*

Manavgat River

- Turkey
- Map: page 18, E–5

As if by magic, a modest mountain stream grows into a surging river as it flows through a rugged gorge.

At its source the Manavgat is a modest river. It is formed by a few springs bubbling from the earth at an elevation of 4,400 feet (1,350 meters) in the Taurus Mountains, the great chain of high peaks arching halfway across southern Turkey parallel to the Mediterranean coast. Almost immediately the little river enters a series of wild gorges, and over the course of about 30 miles (50 kilometers) descends to the coastal plain, which is only 100 feet (30 meters) above sea level.

No tributaries can be seen entering the Manavgat as it flows through the gorges. Yet as it emerges on the coastal plain and flows south into the Mediterranean, it is a broad swollen river with an average discharge of about 5,500 cubic feet (155 cubic meters) per second.

Where does all the water come from? Cave openings perched on the canyon walls high above river level provide a clue to the mystery. Most are now dry and inactive, but all of them were formed by underground drainage of water in the past. Today numerous underground streams at lower levels emerge on the surface as springs within the gorges, providing the tremendous flow of the Manavgat.

The largest, most impressive spring flows into the river from a gaping cave opening at the base of the high cliffs of Dumanli near the end of the gorges. (*Dumanli* means "the place where there is fog," referring to the misty vapors that often form above the cold water.) The water emerges from the cave in a huge white, frothing cataract that mixes turbulently with the mainstream. Although normally much less, the flow from the Dumanli Spring during January floods sometimes attains a peak of 10,600 cubic feet (300 cubic meters) per second.

Experiments have revealed that the water emerging from springs into the Manavgat originates at many distant sources. By coloring the water of disappearing streams with dye, researchers have traced the courses of underground streams to their reappearance in springs. They have found that in addition to sources in the

MANAVGAT RIVER. *At the base of a high cliff the Dumanli Spring surges from the mouth of a cave and merges with the Manavgat in a frenzy of white water. The spring is the outlet of the largest of many underground streams feeding the rushing mountain river.*

MANAVGAT RIVER. *After leaving the Taurus Mountains, the river flows across the peaceful coastal plain on its way to the Mediterranean.*

Taurus Mountains, some of the Manavgat's water reaches it from large lakes on the Anatolian plateau well to the north of the mountains.

These underground connections exist because the Manavgat River flows through a region where much of the bedrock is limestone. As rain falls to the earth, it absorbs carbon dioxide from the air and from decaying vegetation on the surface. The carbon dioxide turns the water into a mild solution of carbonic acid, which seeps into cracks and crevices in the underlying rock. If the rock is limestone or some other soluble rock such as gypsum, the acidic water dissolves it and carries it away in solution. Eventually the openings in the rock are enlarged into sinkholes, caves, and the channels of underground streams, which often emerge on the surface as springs. Areas in which this process occurs are said to have karst topography, named for a region of spectacularly eroded limestone terrain that is located in Yugoslavia.

The many springs feeding the Manavgat are part of an active karst drainage system; the numerous cave openings higher up on the canyon walls, in contrast, are relics of now abandoned underground streams that flowed when the water table was higher. Few of them have been explored, though one in particular has proved to be exceptional. Known as the Urunlu Cave, it has a long gallery partially filled by a large, dark subterranean lake. (The lake is filled by overflow during the flood season.) Flanking the lake are massive cave formations resembling flowing draperies, including one that rises 150 feet (45 meters) above the water.

The high summits of the Taurus Mountains, the rugged gorges carved by the Manavgat River, the enormous resurgent spring at Dumanli, and the eerily beautiful Urunlu Cave are each and every one a spectacle to behold. Taken together, they form an area of natural wonders with few rivals anywhere in Turkey. □

Mandara Mountains

- Cameroon—Nigeria
- Map: page 24, E-4

Though it has neither lofty summits nor snow-clad slopes, this remote African range is remarkable for the wild beauty of its rough terrain.

The Mandara Mountains are not an extensive range. Straddling the border between Nigeria and Cameroon to the south of Lake Chad, they stretch only about 120 miles (190 kilometers) from north to south and are nowhere much more than about 50 miles (80 kilometers) in width. Nor are the Mandara Mountains especially lofty: their highest point reaches only 4,902 feet (1,494 meters) above sea level.

Yet the mountains are unusually impressive. Bordered in some places by steep escarpments, their weathered peaks rise abruptly to heights of about 3,300 feet (1,000 meters) above the surrounding plains. Like a natural

fortress, the mountain ramparts completely surround a series of elevated inner plateaus. To the east and south the main mountain bastion breaks up into spurs and isolated massifs that extend out across the plain.

The mountains were formed by the uplift of a segment of the crustal plate of ancient basement rock underlying the continent of Africa. During those times when the climate was much wetter than it is today, a dense network of rushing rivers gradually widened and deepened fractures that developed in the bedrock as it was uplifted, carving the massif into fantastically varied rugged terrain.

But the most spectacular landscape features resulted from volcanic activity. Volcanoes erupted in many places, spilling lava on the surface of the ancient basement rock and building up isolated mountain peaks. Erosion then stripped away most of the lava, leaving only the cores of extremely erosion-resistant rock that plugged the vents of the dying volcanoes. Today these so-called volcanic necks stand as isolated needlelike spires rising as much as 650 feet (200 meters) above their surroundings.

The special beauty of the Mandara Mountains, however, results as much from the works of man as the forces of nature. Despite the steep slopes and the rugged terrain, humans long have lived in the mountains, which stand as an easily defended natural stronghold against any enemies that approach from the plains.

The mountains are inhabited primarily by Kirdi people, whose way of life has become perfectly attuned to their rugged environment. In order to cultivate millet on the steep slopes, they have built terraces to hold back the soil. Using bricks that they have made from sun-dried mud as well as taking advantage of natural outcrops of rock, they have built retaining walls up to 6 feet (1.8 meters) high that rise tier upon tier like great staircases up the sides of the hills.

Their settlements blend just as naturally with the landscape. Clustered on ridges, along the slopes, and at the foot of mountains are groups of small round huts made of dried mud and local stone and capped with steeply pointed conical roofs. These roofs are thatched with millet stems, which quickly take on the shiny, grayish tint of the surrounding rocks.

Thus a rugged, harsh, and wild countryside has been gentled by the hand of man. Living in complete harmony with their environment, the modern practitioners of an age-old mountain way of life provide a sense of scale and add a humanizing influence to an awesomely majestic setting deep in Africa. □

MANDARA MOUNTAINS. *Like towering sentinels, weathered pinnacles of volcanic rock stand guard over dry, eroded hills and valleys.*

MANDING MOUNTAINS. *The sandstone cliffs and crags were sculpted by running water in times when the region's climate was much wetter.*

Manding Mountains

- Mali
- Map: page 24, B–4

Over the millennia the forces of erosion have carved these remote African mountains into fantastic ramparts and legendary figures.

Near the upper reaches of the Niger River in the western part of Mali, the Manding Mountains rise dramatically above their surroundings. Bordered in places by sheer escarpments up to 1,000 feet (300 meters) high, the great sandstone plateau has been cut up into isolated buttes and eroded into fanciful formations that have inspired many legends.

On the side of one butte, for example, is a cluster of rocky crags with strangely human forms. Resembling a seated woman surrounded by several other figures, the formation is known as the Butte of the Stubborn Woman. It is said to have come into being when a young woman set out in search of her lost husband. On the way, though,

she apparently had second thoughts about her mission, sat down on the spot, and refused to go any farther. As punishment for her rebelliousness, the woman and all her companions were immediately turned to stone.

The petrified search party is just one of many natural stone sculptures in the Manding Mountains. Others range in form from legendary figures to the ruined towers and battlements of lost strongholds.

The mountains are underlain by crystalline bedrock that is more than 1 billion years old. Composed mainly of granite, gneiss, and schist, this core of ancient rock was long ago worn down by erosion. Thick deposits of sandstone, covered in places by layers of basaltic rock, then formed on top of the old eroded surface.

Over the millennia great stresses and shifts in the earth's crust produced numerous cracks and fractures in the enormous, flat-topped mass of sandstone. It was along these lines of weakness that the forces of erosion were able to carve the mountains to their present distinctive form. In by-

gone eras when the region's climate was much wetter than it is today, rushing rivers incised their valleys deeply into the sandstone plateau.

As a result the mountains now stand in the form of isolated buttes that are bounded in places by steep cliffs and rocky crags. Some of the buttes are flat-topped; others have round summits. Many rise to heights of as much as 2,600 feet (800 meters). Relentlessly attacked by running water and landslides, the buttes have been carved over many years into monumental sculptural forms.

Erosion also created many caves in the sandstone buttes. In prehistoric times local inhabitants are believed to have conducted their harvest rituals in many of the caves. Today the Manding Mountains are of growing interest for tourism. In addition to visiting the prehistoric cave sites, rock climbing and hunting are popular pastimes. The highlands, covered by a crust of reddish soil that supports extensive grasslands, also provide a pleasing contrast with the wooded savanna that surrounds them. □

Mandraka Falls

- Madagascar
- Map: page 26, D–4

In the midst of a luxuriant green forest, a seething cascade of foam hurtles across a granite barrier.

Although not especially high—their total drop is only about 100 feet, or 30 meters—Mandraka Falls are noted for the beauty of their picturesque setting. Flowing through a lush green primeval forest, the Mandraka River spills suddenly across a granite ledge in a foaming cascade, then continues on its eastward course. Located only about 40 miles (65 kilometers) from Madagascar's capital, Tananarive, the falls are an especially popular destination for holiday outings.

Like the many other waterfalls in eastern Madagascar, Mandraka Falls owe their existence to a combination of topography and climate. Running from north to south for nearly the full length of the island, like a massive rocky spine, is a ridge of highlands and mountains. From the heights the land slopes down gradually to the west in a series of plateaus and plains. To the east the surface drops abruptly to the narrow coastal plain in a steplike series of escarpments 1,000 to 2,000 feet (300 to 600 meters) high.

The steep mountainous wall, known as the Great Cliff or the Cliff of Angavo, is impassable in many places. But besides being a barrier to transportation, it is almost a climatic barrier. Moist trade winds that sweep in constantly from the Indian Ocean are deflected upward by the wall of mountains. Cooled as it rises, the moisture in the air condenses and falls on the highlands in frequent storms and showers throughout the year. As a result many short torrential rivers rise in the highlands and flow eastward toward the coast, with their courses interrupted by frequent waterfalls and cascades.

In the area of Mandraka Falls, erosion has gradually worn away much of the soft metamorphic rock along a mountain slope. Here and there as the soft rock was worn away, however, beds of much harder granite were exposed. One of these erosion-resistant outcrops interrupts the course of the Mandraka River. Leaping suddenly over its edge, the river forms the foaming, splashing, and never-ending spectacle of Mandraka Falls. ☐

MANDRAKA FALLS. *One of many waterfalls in the eastern part of Madagascar, the foaming torrent is fed by abundant rainfall blown in off the Indian Ocean by ceaseless trade winds.*

Mardalsfoss

- Norway
- Map: page 16, D–2

One of Europe's loftiest waterfalls provides a dramatic focal point as it tumbles down a sheer cliff in a breathtaking Norwegian landscape that was carved by Ice Age glaciers.

In a land where splendid scenery is taken almost for granted, the region of Norway sometimes known as "the top of the fjord country" has long been celebrated for its exceptional beauty. Slicing in from the Atlantic coast are Sogne Fjord, the longest in Norway, Geiranger Fjord, often considered to be the most beautiful, and many other glacially carved inlets of the sea. And

spilling down from the heights are rapids and waterfalls by the thousands, many of them tumbling over sheer cliffs in ribbonlike cascades.

The tallest of all the falls in Norway, and one of the highest in Europe, is Mardalsfoss. (*Foss* means "waterfall" in Norwegian.) To reach the falls, the visitor must travel to the end of a branch of Romsdal Fjord, then take a

MARDALSFOSS. *Reflected in the calm blue water of Eikesdal Lake, the double cascades plunge into a deep, glacier-carved valley.*

boat the full length of Eikesdal Lake, about '? miles (20 kilometers) long, in the deep glacial valley at the head of the fjord.

The effort is amply rewarded when the double cascades of Mardalsfoss finally come into view. From an indentation in the high granite ridge that encloses the valley, near the very end of the lake, Mardalsfoss plummets down in a powerful column of glistening white water. Hurtling past a sheer vertical span of rock, the water hits a ledge that diverts its flow and hides it briefly from view. It reappears farther down as two foaming streams meet and form a second cascade that plunges into a cleft in the forest below. The upper and lower falls drop for a total of 2,150 feet (655 meters), making Mardalsfoss one of the world's highest waterfalls.

Like most of the region's spectacular landscape features, Mardalsfoss owes its existence to the great glaciers that covered the area several times over the past 2 million years or so. Grinding seaward from ice caps that covered interior plateaus, major gla-

ciers scooped out deep, steep-sided valleys that were later invaded by the sea to form the fjords. Smaller tributary glaciers flowing into the major ones were much less powerful erosive agents, and so were not able to scour out such deep valleys. When the glaciers melted, the bottoms of the tributary valleys were perched high on the steep walls of the major valleys.

Mardalsfoss emerges from one of these so-called hanging valleys and spills into the much deeper trench now occupied by Eikesdal Lake and the Romsdal Fjord. In fact, many of the world's loveliest waterfalls cascade from hanging valleys, including several of the plumelike falls in California's Yosemite National Park.

The waters of Mardalsfoss, derived chiefly from heavy winter snowfall on a high interior plateau, approach the escarpment along a narrow channel dotted with lakes. The flow accelerates with the spring thaw and reaches a peak in June. Then for a brief period the volume is so great that from the lake below, Mardalsfoss appears to be a single uninterrupted cascade. □

Marismas, Las

● Spain
● Map: page 17, C–5

Sometimes wet, sometimes dry, the silt-choked delta of a Spanish river is a matchless sanctuary for wildlife.

Las Marismas ("The Marshes"), at the mouth of the Guadalquivir River in southwestern Spain, is one of the finest wilderness areas in southern Europe. Behind a belt of coastal dunes is a vast mosaic of land and water: low-lying islands, ponds, and seasonally flooded marshland crisscrossed by countless river channels.

Comparatively unscathed by civilization, Las Marismas is also one of Europe's finest havens for wildlife. Deer, lynx, and wild boar roam the dunes and marshes. Vultures and rare imperial eagles circle overhead. Flamingos, herons, and spoonbills wade in the wetlands, and in winter ducks and geese by the thousands converge on the flooded plains.

Las Marismas was not always as it is

LAS MARISMAS. *Cut off from the sea by a barrier of dunes, the delta of the Guadalquivir is a complex maze of marshland and water.*

today. Just a few thousand years ago the Guadalquivir entered the Atlantic through an open gulf. The action of coastal currents and waves gradually built a line of barrier beaches and dunes across the entrance to the bay, transforming it into a lagoon. As recently as the days of the Roman Empire the river's outlet was called Lacus (Lake) Lagustinus. Siltation by the river completed the transformation, filling the lagoon with thick deposits of sediment.

Today the barrier of wind-sculpted dunes extends about 45 miles (70 kilometers) along the coast. Known as Arenas Gordas, the "fat sands," they are crossed only by the main channel of the river at their southern end. Inland there are pine forests, savannalike plains dotted with gnarled cork oaks, and finally the seemingly limitless expanse of marshland. Portions of all these habitats have been preserved in Coto Doñana National Park.

Far from static, Las Marismas varies dramatically from season to season. In summer the marshes dry out almost completely, leaving parched mud flats to bake beneath the sun. The autumn rains, and later the spring snowmelt on inland mountains, bring the marshes back to life. The wetlands are flooded once again. Wildflowers burst into bloom. And the birds for which the area is especially famous seem to throng everywhere. □

Mascún Gorge

- Spain
- Map: page 17, C–4

Attacked by the forces of erosion, the limestone gorge is filled with an array of strange rock formations.

The high limestone plateaus of the Sierra de Guara, a range of the Pyrenees in northeastern Spain, conceal a number of natural curiosities. But none can rival the Mascún Gorge. Hidden in its depths is an astonishing variety of strangely eroded rock formations: slender towers, needles, and spires, enormous arches and natural bridges, and massive fortresslike bastions topped by craggy ramparts.

The strangely sculpted rock formations result from the structure of the local limestone, which tends to waste away in lens-shaped masses. In many places the walls of the gorge are pocked by immense, honeycomblike hollows. Where a spur of rock projects

MASCÚN GORGE. *Sculpted by erosion, a castlelike monolith topped by towering stone spires stands guard over the wild mountain gorge.*

LAKE MASHU. *The product of volcanic activity, the tranquil lake is bordered (on the right) by a small explosion crater.*

from the canyon walls, the hollows sometimes become deep enough to penetrate all the way through the rock wall and form windowlike openings. The windows in turn enlarge to form natural arches. When the tops of the arches collapse, nothing remains but the sides, in the form of bristling pinnacles and spires.

Although wild and unpopulated, the gorge is quite easily accessible. From the little village of Rodellar, perched on the rim near the mouth of the gorge, a road winds down to the canyon floor. The ravine is best explored during summer, when the Río Mascún dries out completely. Visitors can simply wander along the rocky riverbed as it winds in and out between steep cliffs.

The lower part of the gorge is the most picturesque. The first major feature to be seen is the Fuente Mascún, a powerful spring supplied by subterranean streams. Overlooking the spring are Las Ventanas ("The Windows"), a pair of natural arches that are each about 130 feet (40 meters) wide and 50 feet (15 meters) high.

A little farther upstream is the Candle, a towering monolith nearly 400 feet (120 meters) high. Just beyond is the Citadel, a great fortresslike massif topped by rocky pinnacles and ramparts. Nearby, an imposing cluster of tall, slender stone needles rises in front of a double arch resembling a camel's back. Continuing on between intricately honeycombed cliffs, the lower gorge ends in a great chaos of fallen boulders.

The canyon begins to narrow in the middle gorge. At every turn of the river visitors are greeted by new views of stone needles jutting from ledges on the canyon walls. At one point a natural bridge spans the entire canyon.

In the upper gorge the walls close in to form a narrow, winding cleft in the rock. Hemmed in by sheer cliffs more than 325 feet (100 meters) high, the gorge in places is scarcely 3 feet (1 meter) wide. Virtually impassable here, the riverbed is scarred by giant potholes and steep ledges that form cascades. The upper gorge, in fact, was never thoroughly explored until 1956—and then only with the help of cave exploration equipment. Beyond the many falls and rapids near its head, the gorge finally ends at the top of the limestone plateau. □

Mashu, Lake

- Japan
- Map: page 19, P-4

One of the most transparent lakes in the world, it is noted for its calm beauty and solitary grandeur.

Lake Mashu in Akan National Park is among the most scenic and beloved sites on the island of Hokkaido. Bordered by steep forested slopes and having no inlet or outlet, it is tranquil, aloof, and serenely beautiful.

Like a number of other lakes in the park, it occupies a caldera—a huge craterlike depression caused by the collapse of a volcano into its empty magma chamber. (An island in the center of the lake was built up by a later eruption.) Covering an area of 8 square miles (20 square kilometers), the more or less crescent-shaped lake reaches a maximum depth of 695 feet (212 meters).

Practically devoid of life, Lake Mashu is notable for the remarkable clarity of its water. Objects are clearly visible at a depth of 135 feet (41 meters) below the surface. □

MATAKIL FALLS. *After dropping over a sheer sandstone cliff, the waters of the Koumbala River seethe through a jumble of fallen boulders.*

Matakil Falls

- Central African Republic
- Map: page 25, F–5

Partially obscured by a wall of dense tropical forest, a remote African river makes a dazzling plunge off the edge of a vast sandstone plateau.

The Central African Republic is located near the very heart of Africa, tucked between Chad and Sudan to the north and Zaire to the south. Here and there the country's gently rolling plains give way to isolated uplands, including in the north a vast sandstone plateau. A major watershed, this large tableland gives rise to a number of rivers: a few that flow eastward and drain into the Nile; several that flow southward into major tributaries of the Congo; and still others that flow northward toward the Chari River, which empties into Lake Chad.

One of the rivers flowing to the north is the Koumbala. Interrupted here and there by minor cascades and rapids, it makes a major leap at Matakil Falls. Reaching an escarpment at the edge of the plateau, its waters plummet down for a total drop of about 200 feet (60 meters).

Although not exceptionally high, the falls are an impressive sight. Their flow diminishes in the dry season, but in the wet months several plumes of water spill over the brink of the precipice. Over the course of centuries, huge angular boulders have fallen from the cliff and litter the riverbed at the foot of the falls; beyond them the water spills down in several smaller cascades.

The finishing touch is provided by the lush riverside forest that frames the entire scene. The rampant growth of trees and tropical vines offers a refreshing contrast in a region that is covered mainly by grasslands. □

Matmata Range

- Tunisia
- Map: page 24, D–2

A desolate-looking chain of hills at the edge of the desert provides a surprisingly comfortable home for a small but industrious society.

Arching some 70 miles (110 kilometers) southeastward from the town of Matmata in southern Tunisia, the Matmata Range has long been a bastion of sedentary life in an otherwise nomadic part of the world. For centuries members of an ancient tribe have lived there as troglodytes, or cave dwellers, in elaborate shelters dug into the region's thick deposits of dense, ocher-colored soil.

Deep, man-made pits up to 25 feet (7½ meters) in diameter dot the countryside. From these central "courtyards" (which are sometimes complete

MATMATA RANGE. *Caves are easily dug in the thick, compacted beds of wind-deposited soil that covers large areas in the Tunisian hills.*

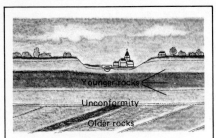

An unconformity occurs when a layer of sedimentary rock is deposited on top of older rocks that were worn down and partially removed during a previous period of erosion. When the older layers lie at an angle to the younger layers, the break is called an angular unconformity.

with palms and other trees), underground chambers have been hollowed out to serve as living quarters, granaries, and even livestock shelters. There the residents can live protected from both the blistering summer sun and the cool winter nights.

A combination of factors makes possible this settled, year-round way of life in a predominantly desert region. Besides being easily excavated, the soil is fertile enough for the cultivation of barley, olives, figs, and dates. Annual rainfall on the hills, moreover, averages from 8 to 12 inches (200 to 300 millimeters)—about twice as much as on the lowland between the hills and the Mediterranean coast to the east.

The jagged line of hills rises suddenly to heights of about 1,600 feet (500 meters) above the coastal lowland at their foot. They are composed of a thick layer of limestone that was formed about 80 million years ago on the eroded surface of much older underlying rocks. (Such a break in the sequence of rock formation, when some of the older rock was worn away before the younger rock was deposited, is called an unconformity.)

The basic contours of the Matmata Range were established about 45 million years ago, when crustal movements created a long, slightly curving fold in the limestone. The eastern edge of the fold drops down abruptly to the coastal lowland in cliffs and steep slopes. To the west the hills slope down gradually toward the Sahara. Stream erosion then cut up the fold into hills and valleys and in places carved deep gorges in the limestone crust.

But it was much more recently that the region acquired its most distinctive feature: the thick deposits of wind-

borne soil, known as loess, that cover it in many places. During the last 250,000 years, violent winds blowing in from the southwest carried immense quantities of fine-grained sand and silt into the area. Slowed down by the hills, the winds dropped their loads of airborne sediment in sheltered spots, especially where there was vegetation to hold it in place.

Today the loess deposits among the hills are as much as 65 feet (20 meters) thick, making possible the unusual society that has endured there for hundreds of years. In order to slow down erosion of the rich soil and retain the rainwater, each valley is protected by damlike walls built across the streambed. Behind them the olive and fig trees continue to thrive, as they have for centuries. □

MATSUSHIMA BAY. *Once dry land, the bay was invaded by the sea, enabling waves to attack the volcanic rock and carve the picturesque archipelago of hundreds of islands.*

Matsushima Bay

- Japan
- Map: page 19, P–5

Land and water intermingle in the island-studded bay, creating a seascape of great beauty and charm.

Matsushima Bay does not appear to be especially impressive on maps: it is just a small indentation on the Pacific coast of northern Honshu, the main island of Japan. Viewing it in person, however, is an unforgettable experience. The bay, in fact, is one of Japan's foremost scenic attractions.

Scattered across its surface like an abandoned fleet of ships are hundreds of islands and islets of every shape and size imaginable. Wildflowers grow in

Matterhorn

- Italy—Switzerland
- Map: page 17, D-4

Soaring high above its surroundings, the austere pyramidal peak is one of the world's best-known mountains.

The French call it Mont Cervin; the Italians, Monte Cervino. Among German- and English-speaking people, in turn, it is known as the Matterhorn. But by whatever name, to countless admirers from around the world it is the mountain of mountains, the Alp par excellence.

Straddling the border between Italy and Switzerland in the Pennine Alps, the Matterhorn, at 14,691 feet (4,478 meters), is not the highest peak in Europe. But its stark, sharply sculpted, pyramidal summit has made it unquestionably one of the most famous mountains in the world. Its four nearly identical triangular faces, separated by four jagged ridges, have a geometric purity that is unique. Viewed from any angle, its distinctive profile rising high against the sky is an incredibly breathtaking sight. Dark gray and austere during the summer and glistening brilliantly beneath a mantle of snow in winter, it has been called "the most noble rock of Europe."

As with other very high peaks in the Alps, the summit of the Matterhorn is composed of extremely hard, erosion-resistant crystalline rock that was produced deep beneath the surface. Uplifted when the Alps came into being some 40 million years ago, this very hard core was subsequently stripped of thick overlying layers of softer, younger rock formations. Exposed at last on the surface, the crystalline bedrock itself was then subjected to the forces of erosion.

Weathering, running water, and alternate freezing and thawing each played a role in shaping the Matterhorn's majestic summit. But the master sculptors that carved its steep, massive walls were the great Ice Age glaciers that blanketed the Alps within the past 2 million years. Plucking out chunks of bedrock as they slowly ground down the mountain slopes in various directions, the powerful glaciers chiseled out the neatly faceted sides of the almost perfectly pyramidal mountain crest.

Because of its abrupt, forbidding slopes, the Matterhorn long defied the efforts of mountain climbers. The first

the scanty soil and lilies scent the air, but the islands' crowning glory is their pine trees. (*Matsushima* means "pine-covered island" in Japanese.) Resembling delicate bonsai on bases of solid rock, the beautiful islands have been praised time and again by generations of Japanese poets.

Most of the islands are uninhabited, though a few are decorated with Buddhist temples and shrines. The names of some of the islands are enigmatic (Question and Answer); others are symbolic (The Entrance of Buddha into Paradise). Little bridges link many of the islets with each other and with the shore, and boat tours are also available for viewing the sights of Matsushima Bay.

At one time the area now occupied by the bay was an expanse of volcanic rock that had been worn down to a nearly flat surface. Submerged for a time beneath the sea, it reemerged about 250,000 years ago. Running water and other forces of erosion then took over, deeply dissecting the surface and cutting it up into countless hills and valleys. With the melting of huge glaciers at the end of the last ice age about 10,000 years ago, sea levels rose all around the world. Water once again invaded the bay, and waves began attacking the islands. Undercutting their sides, the waves carved the steep cliffs, jagged spurs, caves, and tunnels that fringe the infinitely varied islands.

Today the archipelago forms a barrier protecting the bay from the full onslaught of Pacific storms. Viewed in sunshine or moonlight, through a veil of mist or falling snow, the islands reflected in the tranquil waters of Matsushima Bay are a never-ending source of delight. □

MATTERHORN. *Renowned for the striking symmetry of its form, the soaring summit is breathtaking from any vantage point.*

successful ascent was not completed until July 1865, when a team headed by the English mountaineer Edward Whymper reached the top by way of a ridge on the Swiss side. Just three days later an Italian team led by Giovanni Carrel scaled the summit by traversing a ridge on the Italian side.

Although other parts of the mountain remained unclimbed until much later—the south face was not conquered until 1931—the exploits of Carrel and Whymper soon transformed the previously quite isolated region around the Matterhorn. Zermatt on the Swiss side, in particular, became a popular gathering place for hikers, mountain climbers, and more recently, winter sports enthusiasts. With the development of other resort centers, sightseers and skiers can travel well up on the slopes of the Matterhorn by means of railways, tramways, and other types of lifts.

Indeed, even the summit—once a challenge reserved only for the most experienced climbers—is now quite easily accessible to amateurs. The ridge route pioneered by Whymper has since been equipped with footholds and cables to help tourists over the difficult spots. On clear summer days, as many as 200 enthusiasts have been known to meet the challenge successfully.

On their way to the top, however, they pass a memorial erected on the spot where four of Whymper's companions fell to their deaths during their descent from the summit. It is a grim reminder of a fact that veteran Zermatt guides are quick to point out: even today the mountain is not without dangers. Devastating storms can move in swiftly, and this most familiar of peaks can suddenly be transformed into the implacable, perilous Matterhorn of old. □

Mauna Loa

- United States (Hawaii)
- Map: page 9

Born of a rift in the ocean floor, Hawaii's fiery giant is the largest active volcano in all the world.

The Hawaiian Islands extend in a great arc for about 1,600 miles (2,600 kilometers) across the central Pacific Ocean. Including more than 100 islands and islets, they are actually the exposed tips of one of the world's greatest mountain ranges. All the islands are volcanic in origin: they were formed as lava oozed up through a giant rift in the earth's crust and built up a chain of enormous peaks.

The easternmost island, Hawaii, is also the largest and the youngest of the group. Composed of the summits of five overlapping volcanoes, Hawaii rises to its highest point on the crater rim of Mauna Kea, at 13,976 feet (4,260 meters). From its base on the ocean floor, however, the island of Hawaii is the exposed top of a mountain more than 30,000 feet (9,150 meters) high—higher than Mount Everest, at 29,028 feet (8,848 meters).

Although Mauna Kea and two of the other volcanoes that make up the island are apparently extinct, their neighbors Mauna Loa and Kilauea are very much alive. Mauna Loa, with its summit rising 13,680 feet (4,170 meters) above sea level, is in fact the largest active volcano in the world.

Mauna Loa is what geologists term a shield volcano. In contrast to the steep-sided symmetrical cones of such classic volcanoes as Japan's Fujiyama or Mount Shasta in California, its summit is a broad, gently sloping dome resembling an inverted saucer. Steep cones similar to Fujiyama's are formed of very viscous lava that congeals soon after it is erupted. Mauna Loa's lava is extremely fluid, due to its low content of silica and gases and its very high temperature. Usually about 2000° F (1100° C) when it erupts, the lava often flows 20 miles (32 kilometers) or more before it cools and hardens. Spreading out in broad sheets like melted tar, layer upon layer of lava flows have accumulated to form Mauna Loa's domelike profile.

Mauna Loa is extremely active. It erupts on an average of about once every 3½ years. At that rate of growth, geologists estimate that it could have been formed within the last 1 million years. Although individual lava flows are usually only about 10 feet (3 meters) thick, the volcano has been built up of a total accumulation of some 10,000 cubic miles (41,700 cubic kilometers) of lava.

At the summit of Mauna Loa is a huge oval crater about 3 miles (5 kilometers) long, 1½ miles (2½ kilometers) wide, and 600 feet (185 meters) deep. Called Mokuaweoweo, it merges at each end with a large satellite crater. All three are actually calderas—big depressions resembling craters that were formed by subsidence of the mountain's summit.

In addition to outpourings from the central caldera, Mauna Loa often erupts from long fissures that open on the slopes. At the beginning of a fissure eruption, molten lava spurts from the opening in an almost unbroken line of low fountains, which occasionally reach a height of 50 feet (15 meters). This spectacular display, known as "the curtain of fire," usually lasts less than a day.

Activity then slows down at the ends of the fissure and becomes concentrated in the middle section, where jets of lava may spurt as high as 800 feet (245 meters). In the 1959 eruption of Kilauea, noted for its much more violent activity, however, one lava fountain shot 1,900 feet (580 meters) into the air—a record for Hawaii.

As the eruption continues, clouds of yellowish gas billow high above the lava founts. Bits of fine debris—pumice and so-called Pele's hair, which is actually filaments of volcanic glass—rain down on the surrounding countryside. And for several weeks or even months, floods of lava pour down the mountainsides. Traveling at speeds of up to 25 miles (40 kilometers) per hour, the lava flows sometimes reach the sea. One of the largest flows from Mauna Loa in recent times occurred in 1950, releasing an estimated 600 million cubic yards (460 million cubic meters) of lava over a time span of 23 days—enough to pave a four-lane highway reaching 4½ times around the earth.

Such lava flows can be extremely devastating, destroying forests, entire villages, homes, and everything else in their paths. As a result, both Mauna Loa and Kilauea have been studied continuously since 1912; the present Hawaiian Volcanic Observatory is located on the rim of Kilauea's caldera. Seismographs and other instruments constantly monitor underground activity so that eruptions can be predicted quite accurately.

The two volcanoes are also among the world's finest showcases of the awesome power of volcanic activity. As such they are the central attraction of Hawaii Volcanoes National Park, one of the few places on earth where visitors can drive right up to the rim and peer down into the crater of an active volcano. □

MAUNA LOA. *After streaming down the volcano's gentle slopes, a once-molten flow of fluid lava cooled and hardened to form a contorted mass of solid rock.*

Mayon, Mount

- Philippines
- Map: page 21, G–3

Celebrated as one of the world's rare perfect volcanic cones, Mayon conceals a sometimes explosive temper beneath its classic profile.

Located near the southeastern tip of Luzon, the principal island of the Philippines, Mount Mayon presides in lordly splendor over the surrounding lowlands. From a base not much above sea level, its slopes rise up to form an almost perfectly symmetrical cone 7,943 feet (2,421 meters) high. Sinuous, lazy wisps of steam escape from its summit, which towers over Albay Gulf like a welcoming beacon.

One of 10 active volcanoes in the Philippines, Mount Mayon is a superb example of what geologists call a stratovolcano. Its slopes were built up of layers (strata) of lava alternating with layers of explosively ejected cinders and other material. Such a structure often results in a particularly graceful, symmetrical volcanic cone.

Mount Mayon's slopes rise up from a broad, nearly circular base about 80 miles (130 kilometers) in circumference. The crater is also circular but quite small, with a diameter of only 1,600 feet (500 meters) and a maximum depth of 325 feet (100 meters).

Nurtured by abundant rainfall and fertile volcanic soil, dense vegetation and abaca (Manila hemp) plantations thrive on the northern and western slopes. In contrast, the eastern and southern flanks are nearly devoid of plant life. Scarred by deep gullies and ravines, they bear witness to the sometimes violent episodes in the history of Mount Mayon.

Although most often benign, the volcanic activity of the mountain has hardly ceased since the 1700's, when an eruption was first chronicled by Franciscan priests in the area. The worst eruption took place in February 1814 when, following a night of earth tremors, a violent explosion sent a billow of smoke and dust high in the sky. A scorching cloud of superheated volcanic gas swept down the south slope, and a wave of mud and lava streamed across the plain, leveling everything in its path. More than 1,200 lives were lost in the disaster, and the town of Cagsawa, about 10 miles (16 kilometers) to the south, was utterly destroyed. Today only the steeple of the church and a few rooftops project above the avalanche of volcanic material that buried the town.

Similar though less deadly eruptions occurred in 1897 and 1968, and many other minor eruptions have taken place. But most of the time the mountain is quiescent, the centerpiece of Mayon Volcano National Park. □

McKinley, Mount

- United States (Alaska)
- Map: page 10, B–2

The shimmering, snow-clad summit of the highest peak in North America completely dominates the wilderness reservation that bears its name.

Soaring to a height of 20,320 feet (6,194 meters), Mount McKinley is the overwhelming giant of the Alaska Range, a crescent-shaped chain of mountains that parallel the Pacific coast in south-central Alaska. Named in 1896 for the 25th U.S. president, it was long known to Indians of the region as Denali, "The High One."

Mount McKinley actually has not one summit but two, the southern peak rising about 850 feet (260 meters) higher than its companion a short distance to the north. Like much of the Alaska Range, the mountain is composed chiefly of erosion-resistant granite that was uplifted more than 60 million years ago. This granite mass and the folded sedimentary and metamorphic rocks that make up the rest of the range were sculpted to their present contours by great glaciers that blanketed the region during the past 2 million years.

Although the last ice age ended some 10,000 years ago, glacial periods have recurred intermittently ever

MOUNT MAYON. *Quiet but still active, its slopes scarred by past eruptions, Mayon releases a stream of vapor into the Pacific trade winds.*

MOUNT McKINLEY. *The rugged, snow-capped mountain, reflected in the waters of Wonder Lake, looms high above its surroundings.*

since, and at present about a dozen glaciers are active on the mountainsides. One of the largest, the Muldrow Glacier, flows east, then to the north, for a total of 35 miles (55 kilometers) on Mount McKinley's northern flank.

The region's climate is well suited to glacial growth. Mount McKinley lies only about 250 miles (400 kilometers) south of the Arctic Circle, and in winter the temperature in the area often falls to –58°F (–50°C). Even in summer, when temperatures at its foot near 80°F (27°C), McKinley's summit remains shrouded in endless winter, with daytime readings rarely exceeding 10°F (–12°C). Thus the snow persists year-round and continues to feed glaciers radiating from the summit.

Much of Mount McKinley's grandeur results from the fact that it rises so dramatically above its surroundings. Mount Everest, the world's highest mountain, for instance, is nearly lost among its enormous neighbors in the Himalayas. Mount McKinley's summit, in contrast, towers nearly 17,000 feet (5,180 meters) over the adjacent lowlands—one of the greatest elevation contrasts of any mountain in the entire world.

Since 1917 much of the mountain and the lowlands to the north of it have been set aside as Mount McKinley National Park. With an area of 3,000 square miles (7,775 square kilometers), it is half again as large as Delaware and second in size only to Yellowstone among the country's national parks.

Its boundaries enclose a wilderness not only of high peaks and glaciers, but also of lakes, streams, forests, and above timberline an expanse of alpine tundra covered by mosses, lichens, and dwarf shrubs. The reserve is also home to a tremendous variety of wildlife, including such species as grizzly bears, wolves, Dall sheep, and herds of caribou that migrate each year across the tundra. □

Permafrost and Patterned Ground

In areas that are underlain by permafrost (permanently frozen ground), such as much of the area around Mount McKinley, the surface of the soil sometimes develops curiously geometric patterns. Alternate freezing and thawing of the surface layer results in this phenomenon, known as patterned ground. Repeated expansion and contraction of the soil forces loose rocks to the top and arranges them in many-sided patterns, or polygons, on the surface. On steep slopes this layer tends to slide downhill when it thaws, distorting the polygons into a striated pattern called striped soil.

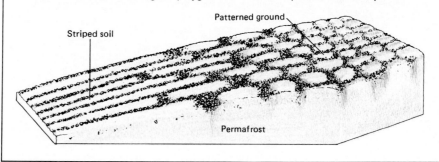

241

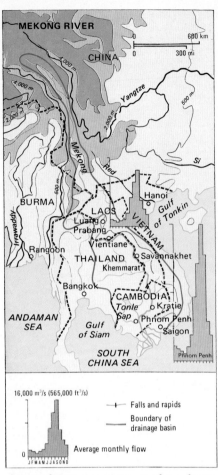

MEKONG RIVER

CHINA

Yangtze

Mekong

Red

Si

BURMA

Irrawaddy

Hanoi

Gulf of Tonkin

LAOS

Luang Prabang

VIETNAM

Rangoon

Vientiane

Savannakhet

THAILAND

Khemmarat

Bangkok

CAMBODIA

Tonle Sap

Kratie

Phnom Penh

Saigon

ANDAMAN SEA

Gulf of Siam

SOUTH CHINA SEA

Phnom Penh

16,000 m³/s (565,000 ft³/s)

—+— Falls and rapids

Boundary of drainage basin

Average monthly flow

J F M A M J J A S O N D

Seasonal monsoon rains produce drastic fluctuations in the river's volume of flow.

Mekong River

- Southeast Asia
- Map: page 21, E–3

A restless, untamed giant, the river swells and shrinks dramatically with the changing of the seasons.

The greatest river of Southeast Asia rises as a rushing mountain stream in the Tibetan highlands of China and flows the full length of the Indochina Peninsula before emptying into the South China Sea. Along its course of about 2,600 miles (4,200 kilometers), the Mekong changes notably in character. From its source in the Tanglha Range in Tibet, at an elevation of more than 16,000 feet (5,000 meters), the river flows through narrow rugged gorges as it rushes southward across China. A typical mountain stream, its Chinese name in this sector means "Turbulent River."

The Mekong's middle course begins where it first touches on the border of Thailand and continues all the way into the north of Cambodia. Still hemmed in at times by mountains, the river zigzags erratically southeastward. In places it flows through narrow gorges; elsewhere it broadens as it streams across undulating plains. Interrupted repeatedly by churning rapids, the middle course is suited only to local navigation.

As it enters Cambodia, the Mekong finally assumes the character of a lowland river—a broad, lazy, silt-laden giant clogged with islands and congested with river traffic. At Phnom Penh the river divides in two, and then as it enters Vietnam, divides again and again as it crosses its vast swampy delta and merges with the sea.

Although it is fed in part by snowmelt on the mountains, most of the Mekong's flow is derived from heavy monsoon rains. The rainfall, however, is very unevenly distributed between a wet summer season and a dry winter season. As a result the volume of the river varies dramatically, slowing to a trickle in early spring and swelling to a mighty torrent at the end of summer.

Fortunately the Mekong's floods are tempered by a natural flow regulator. At Phnom Penh, a branch of the river connects it with an enormous lake, the Tonle Sap. During the flood season some of the Mekong's overflow streams north into the Tonle Sap. During the dry season the flow reverses, and water drains back into the Mekong. But until man-made flood-control basins are built, the Mekong River will remain an untamed giant that fluctuates drastically from season to season. □

MEKONG RIVER. *For the millions living along its banks, the mighty river provides fish, a thoroughfare for boats, and water for crops.*

Melnik Badlands

- Bulgaria
- Map: page 17, F–4

A little town in Bulgaria is noted for its magnificent architecture, its fine wines—and its strange setting.

A high cliff rises behind the town of Melnik in southwestern Bulgaria, completely barren and furrowed by deep ravines and jagged ridges. As striking as it is, however, it is only one of several strange landforms in the area. Elsewhere steep-sided, flat-topped hills up to 325 feet (100 meters) high rise in splendid isolation. The slopes of entire valleys have been cut up into desolate badlands, named for the famous area located in South Dakota. In some places the gullied badlands include hundreds of curious chimneylike spires, where boulders protected parts of the knife-edged ridges from further erosion.

All the forms resulted from rapid erosion following heavy rains. The local hills are composed of thick deposits of sand, clay, and boulders that accumulated at the bottom of a bygone lake. Later exposed as dry land, these soft deposits were easily eroded into the gullied badlands and isolated buttes that remain today. □

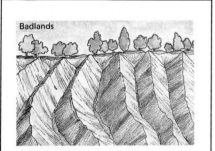

Severe erosion from torrential rains sometimes dissects slopes into barren badlands characterized by deep ravines that are separated by sharp ridges *(top)*. Where boulders protect the ridges from further erosion, tall spires known as earth chimneys are sometimes formed *(bottom)*.

MELNIK BADLANDS. *Attacked by running water after heavy rains, many slopes in the area have been carved up into deep gullies, sharp ridges, and slender chimneylike spires.*

Merapi, Mount

- Indonesia
- Map: page 21, F–5

The destroyer of an entire kingdom nearly a millennium ago, this restless volcano still ranks as one of the most dangerous—and feared—in the world.

The lush, fertile islands of Indonesia are studded with an amazing total of 128 active volcanoes—far more than in any other nation. Near the very center of Java, rising 9,551 feet (2,911 meters) above sea level, is Mount Merapi, the most active of them all.

The mountain's history of violence dates back at least to the year 1006, when a huge explosion demolished Merapi's entire summit and destroyed the ancient kingdom of Mataram. It was on the ruins of the old cone that the present mountain subsequently rose to carry on its lethal tradition.

Since the 1820's alone, Merapi has erupted with deadly results at least 23 times. One of the worst catastrophes occurred in 1930, when a cloud of superheated gases and volcanic ash surged rapidly down the mountainside, killing 1,300 people and incinerating everything in its path.

A principal reason for the violence of Merapi's eruptions is the consistency of its lava, which is too viscous to flow freely and solidifies almost immediately after surfacing. As a result, the vents become clogged with an increasingly thick, pluglike barrier until eventually enough heat and pressure build up inside them to blow open a new outlet.

To provide advance warning of such disastrous explosions, observers continually monitor Mount Merapi's seismic activity and the temperatures inside its crater. As an added measure of protection, nearby residents have also preserved the age-old ritual of holding an annual feast at the crater's edge, complete with music, dancing, and offerings designed to appease the ancient gods of Merapi. □

Mesa Verde

- United States (Colorado)
- Map: page 10, D–5

Rising like a citadel above its surroundings, the looming tableland sheltered generation after generation of prehistoric Indian peoples.

Mesa Verde, which means "green table" in Spanish, is well named. Covered by forests of juniper and piñon pine, the massive, flat-topped tableland is bounded by steep cliffs that rise about 2,000 feet (600 meters) above the surrounding valleys in southwestern Colorado. Indented by numerous canyons, the huge mesa is some 20 miles (32 kilometers) long and 15 miles (25 kilometers) wide.

Besides being ruggedly beautiful, the mesa formed the ideal setting for a vivid chapter in the human history of the Southwest. On the flat, fertile top of the mesa, Indians—possibly the ancestors of today's Pueblo Indians—

MOUNT MERAPI. *Steam and sulfurous gases rise almost ceaselessly from the barren, jagged summit of this old and still deadly volcano.*

MESA VERDE. *The famous Cliff Palace is the largest of many communal dwellings found in sheltered alcoves in the sandstone cliffs.*

tilled the soil from the first century A.D. until 1300. Toward the end of that time they built large multistoried dwellings in many of the enormous cavelike niches that indent the upper part of the sandstone cliffs.

Encompassing the largest and most elaborate assemblage of Indian ruins in the United States, the region is now protected in Mesa Verde National Park. There visitors can explore the cliff dwellings and admire pottery, jewelry, and other artifacts that trace the development of the Indian culture.

The nature of the rocks that form Mesa Verde helps explain its suitability as a site for human habitation. Over millions of years the area was by turns submerged and raised above the sea. A massive layer of sandstone was deposited on top of a thick layer of shale. The sandstone was then covered by a layer of shale and coal, which in

turn was covered by a second layer of sandstone. Some of the sandstone was deposited on the ocean floor, some as dunes on dry land. The shale and coal were formed in a swampy forest at a time when the area stood well above sea level.

The entire region was uplifted to its present elevation about 60 million years ago, at the same time the Rocky Mountains were formed. Then vigorous stream erosion deepened and widened the surrounding valleys, separating Mesa Verde from other highlands to which it had been connected and then carving the many canyons that now indent the mesa.

The layer of shale and coal sandwiched between the two sandstone formations accounts for the mesa's water supply and hence its suitability to agriculture. Rainfall and meltwater from heavy snow on the mesa are able

to seep into the porous layer of sandstone on the top. Stopped from further seepage by the impermeable barrier of shale and coal, the water remains in the sandstone as a natural underground reservoir.

Emerging here and there along the canyon walls as springs, the underground water probably played a role in forming the cavelike niches high on the surrounding cliffs. By dissolving cement in the sandstone, it loosened individual sand grains and permitted them to be blown away. Water freezing in cracks also helped loosen larger slabs of the rock. The end result was the formation of large shallow caves beneath overhanging rims of sandstone on the mesa's walls. And it was in these sheltering alcoves that the Indians built their vast fortified dwellings during their final century of residence on Mesa Verde. □

METEORA. *Ancient monasteries crown many of the giant rock towers in a rare, harmonious blending of the works of man and nature.*

Meteora

● Greece
● Map: page 17, F–5

In the heart of ancient Thessaly, strange man-made aeries are perched on top of natural bastions of stone.

The little town of Kalambaka lies in a valley at the foot of the Pindus Mountains in Thessaly. Picturesque in itself, the town is all the more impressive for its unusual setting. Rising in the background, just to the north, are three groups of stark, dramatic rock formations shaped like massive columns, towers, and multiturreted fortresses. Known as the Meteora, from a Greek word meaning "high in the air," the giant pillars average about 1,000 feet

(300 meters) in height, while a few tower nearly 1,800 feet (550 meters) above the valley floor. And perched atop many of these seemingly inaccessible rocky crags is a series of ancient monasteries that blend so well with their foundations that they seem to be natural extensions of the rocks.

The rocky pinnacles and towers are the eroded remains of a massive, once-continuous formation of sandstone and conglomerate. Deeply fractured by a network of intersecting vertical cracks, the rocks were attacked by erosion along these lines of weakness. Groundwater was concentrated in the fissures and eventually eroded deep vertical clefts all the way down to the base of the formation, while the unfractured rocky masses remained generally intact.

The monasteries—more than 20 in all—were mostly built in the 14th and 15th centuries by monks seeking refuge from political disputes. Their isolation from the world was nearly complete: the only approach to their man-made aeries was by means of removable ladders and crude lifts made of baskets that were hoisted up by pulleys and ropes.

The sanctuaries remained in use until the 19th century, when they began to fall into decline. Virtually deserted by the monks, the monasteries today are frequented primarily by tourists. (Stairways and ramps have been added to make access easier.) In addition to admiring the fine fresco decorations, visitors enjoy breathtaking views of the surrounding countryside in the Peneus River valley. ☐

Meteor Crater

- United States (Arizona)
- Map: page 10, D-5

Thousands of years ago a meteorite crashed to earth and created this colossal scar on the Arizona desert.

No one knows exactly when Meteor Crater was formed. Estimates of the date of the impact that created it range from 2,000 to 50,000 years ago. But the results of the collision, well preserved in the arid Arizona climate, are unmistakable. The crater is an immense saucer-shaped depression about 4,000 feet (1,200 meters) in diameter and nearly 600 feet (180 meters) deep, encircled by a rim rising more than 150 feet (45 meters) above the desert.

Estimates of the meteorite's size and speed have also varied greatly. One recent theory suggests that the iron-rich mass of material from outer space had a diameter of about 80 feet (25 meters), weighed some 70,000 tons (63,500 metric tons), and was traveling

Meteors and Meteorites

One of the most beautiful sights the night sky has to offer is a shooting star—or better yet, a whole shower of them—streaking briefly but brilliantly across the darkness. The creators of the light are not stars, of course, but meteors—pieces of stone or metal from elsewhere in the solar system that happen to enter the earth's gravitational field. Traveling at speeds of up to 160,000 miles (257,500 kilometers) per hour as they enter the atmosphere, meteors are subjected to intense friction that produces luminous trails and in most cases burns them up well before they reach the earth.

Some meteors are not entirely consumed by the heat, however, and the term "meteorite" is reserved for those remnants that complete the trip to earth. Many shatter on impact, but a few very large meteorites, such as the one that created Meteor Crater, explode like bombs. Surviving specimens, which range up to 60 tons (54 metric tons) in size, have long been of interest to scientists: until the first rocks were brought back from the moon, meteorites were the only available samples of extraterrestrial matter.

9 miles (15 kilometers) per second when it smashed into the earth.

Whatever its size and speed, however, it is clear that the meteorite hit with so much force that it not only shattered but actually created an explosion with a release of energy comparable to that of an atomic bomb. Most of the meteorite and much of the ground it hit were pulverized and vaporized, while rock fragments ranging in size from pebbles to huge boulders

were hurled from the crater and scattered over the surrounding land.

The discovery of two very rare forms of silica in the crater in the early 1960's provided further evidence of the force of the impact. They can be produced artificially only under intense heat and pressure comparable to that found far beneath the earth's crust; here they were produced naturally on the surface by the collision of the meteorite. □

METEOR CRATER. *Buildings on the crater's rim provide a clue to the immensity of the depression and the power of the forces that created it.*

MILFORD SOUND. *A beautiful U-shaped valley that was carved by a tributary glacier enters the main glacial trench of the fjord, which has been invaded by the sea.*

Milford Sound

- New Zealand
- Map: page 23, G–6

Fringed by sharp peaks and towering cascades, the deep fjord indents the coast of New Zealand's South Island.

According to a legend of the Maoris, New Zealand's aboriginal people, the great cleft of Milford Sound was made by a god carving South Island into its present form with an enormous ax. His inexperience showed in the rough shoreline and small islands he inadvertently chipped off the southwest coast. But his skill increased as he moved northward, and on reaching the site of Milford Sound he cleaved the land with a single deft and powerful stroke.

At first sight of this magnificent fjord, even the most hardened skeptic might be tempted to believe the legend. About 2 miles (3 kilometers) wide and 12 miles (20 kilometers) long, Milford Sound is flanked by towering walls that rise abruptly from its clear, deep water. In some places the cliffs are decorated with graceful, windblown waterfalls; elsewhere the luxuriantly forested slopes soar suddenly upward to the level of snowcapped summits. The most remarkable of all the mountains bordering Milford Sound is Mitre Peak, an almost perfect triangle that slopes steeply up from the water's edge to the impressive height of 5,560 feet (1,695 meters).

The geological origins of Milford Sound may have been less poetic than its mythological creation, but they involved forces no less powerful. As recently as 15,000 years ago the entire region was covered by ice so thick and heavy that as it pushed through the valleys carved by earlier glaciers, it gouged out their floors to depths well below sea level. When the ice eventually melted away, rising seawater flooded into the long, narrow trenches to form the series of fjords that indent the island's southwestern coast.

Like the fjords of Scandinavia, Milford Sound is deepest near its head, where the glacial ice was thickest, and shallower at its outlet to the sea. The water at the entrance is only 180 feet (55 meters) deep, while farther inland its depth increases steadily to a maximum of 950 feet (290 meters). The tributary valleys, which were not so deeply carved, enter the main trench of the fjord partway up its walls, providing the settings for the sound's numerous waterfalls.

The entrance to Milford Sound is narrow as well as shallow. Indeed, during his historic explorations of the Pacific in the 1770's, Captain James Cook sailed past on at least two occasions without noticing it. It was not until the 1820's that the sound began to be visited by European whalers and sealers, one of whom named it for its resemblance to Milford Haven, an inlet in Wales.

Another seal hunter, an enterprising Scotsman named Donald Sutherland, became the area's first permanent resident, living initially as a hermit and then as the proprietor of a small but successful hotel. His name was given to nearby Sutherland Falls, which is the highest cataract on the island and among the highest in the entire world, with a breathtaking total drop of 1,904 feet (580 meters).   □

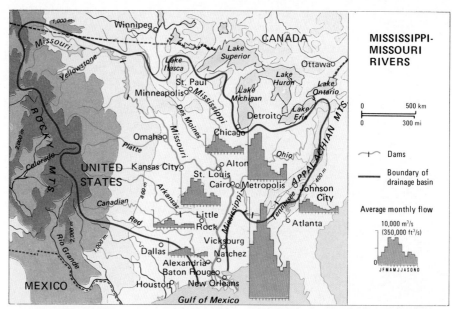

Extending from the Rocky Mountains to the Appalachians, the Mississippi-Missouri's vast drainage basin includes all or part of 31 states and 2 Canadian provinces. Although a network of dams, levees, and other flood-control structures has been built, even they are sometimes unable to contain the flow when the mighty river crests in spring.

Mississippi-Missouri Rivers

- United States
- Map: page 11, E–5

From a source high in the Rocky Mountains to an outlet on the Gulf of Mexico, the combined streams of the two American giants form the third longest river in the world.

Revered by Indians as the Father of Waters, the mighty Mississippi is an anomaly among rivers. It owes its ultimate majesty and power not to its own main trunk but instead to its two principal tributaries, the Missouri and the Ohio.

Although the Mississippi proper is a respectable 2,348 miles (3,779 kilometers) long, the Missouri flows a greater distance—2,466 miles, or 3,969 kilometers—before joining it. The Missouri's drainage basin is also about three times the size of the upper Mississippi's (north of its merger with the Missouri). And it is the Ohio that contributes the most water. Its average discharge amounts to about 260,000 cubic feet (7,350 cubic meters) per second, compared to only about 90,000 cubic feet (2,550 cubic meters) for the upper Mississippi and about 70,000 cubic feet (2,000 cubic meters) for the Missouri.

Acknowledging these contradictions, geographers consider the com-

bined Missouri and lower Mississippi to be the true mainstream of this great river system. With a total length of 3,740 miles (6,020 kilometers), it ranks as the third longest river in the world, exceeded only by the Nile in Africa and the Amazon in South America.

In terms of economic and historical importance, however, the Mississippi-Missouri has few rivals. Its drainage basin extends all the way from the Appalachian Mountains in the east to the Rocky Mountains in the west. Covering an area of 1,244,000 square miles (3,222,000 square kilometers), it takes in the agricultural and industrial heartland of the United States and a bit of Canada as well. The rivers played a crucial role in the country's westward expansion, were responsible for the growth of many of its major cities, and still are important shipping arteries.

The recognized source of the Mississippi (from the Ojibway Indian term *Missi Sipi,* meaning "Great River") is Lake Itasca in northern Minnesota. The lake's name in turn is made up of the central letters of the Latin phrase *veritas caput,* or "true head." In its upper reaches the river flows through lake-filled forests and over a multitude of rapids until it arrives at the Falls of St. Anthony at Minneapolis–St. Paul, where it drops 65 feet (20 meters). From there on it is navigable all the way to the Gulf of Mexico. Continuing south, the river becomes a broad, stately stream lined

by high bluffs nearly to its confluence with the Missouri.

Meanwhile, far to the west in the Rockies, the Missouri is formed by the union of three rivers in western Montana. Flowing across the Great Plains, it picks up so much silt from the surrounding land that it has earned the nickname Big Muddy. (Early settlers described its water as "too thick to drink, too thin to plow.") When the sprawling Missouri joins the Mississippi just north of St. Louis, its yellow, silt-laden water can be seen as a separate stream flowing side by side with the mainstream's sparkling blue water for many miles before they finally mix.

At Cairo, Illinois, the Ohio's copious flow more than doubles the river's volume. From there to the delta it is a meandering, silty giant that is constantly changing its course as it creates new horseshoe bends and cuts across old ones to leave oxbow lakes at its sides. Joined by two more major tributaries, the Arkansas and the Red, the lower part of the river is flanked for long stretches by swampy backwaters.

Finally, near New Orleans, the river begins to flow across the vast marshy lowlands that make up its delta. That giant cone of sediment covers an area of 12,000 square miles (32,000 square kilometers), and even more of it lies under the water of the Gulf of Mexico. Enlarged by an estimated 400 million tons (363 million metric tons) of sediment each year, the delta extends itself toward the sea at an approximate rate

MISSISSIPPI-MISSOURI RIVERS. *Meandering across the plains of Montana, the muddy Missouri is bounded in places by steep, somber cliffs.*

of 6 miles (10 kilometers) per century.

Although the Mississippi-Missouri's discharge is always substantial, it increases drastically in spring as seasonal rains add to the heavy runoff from winter snows. Dams on the tributaries—those in the Tennessee Valley are particularly well known—contain much of the increase. Even so, the river's potential for damage is tremendous. Bursting through the extensive system of levees that have been built all along the main stem, the river occasionally inundates vast areas with disastrous results.

At such times the river's commerce is badly disrupted, as are the lives of riverside residents. Almost the only creatures unaffected are the untold millions of waterfowl and other birds for whom the Mississippi is a special kind of highway—a flyway that helps guide them each year on their seasonal migrations from the Gulf of Mexico through the center of the United States to Canada and then back again. □

Misti, El

● Peru
● Map: page 14, B–4

The ancient Incas once worshiped atop this cone-shaped volcanic peak high on the flank of the Andes.

Three volcanoes rise in a row to the west of the city of Arequipa, high in the Andes in southern Peru. Nevado de Chachani, the farthest to the north, is the highest of the trio, and Nevado de Pichu Pichu, the southernmost, is the lowest peak. But it is El Misti, the central massif, that is by far the most famous. Culminating at an altitude of about 19,150 feet (5,840 meters), it towers more than 7,500 feet (2,300 meters) above the city nestled at its foot.

The beauty of its almost perfectly symmetrical cone has made El Misti one of the most famous landmarks in Peru. It has in fact inspired awe for centuries. Long before any Spaniards arrived in Peru, the native Incas built a temple atop the mountain, which apparently played a role in their religion. Peruvian poetry and legends are also filled with references to the peak.

Although occasional, sometimes severe earthquakes strike the area, El Misti has not erupted for centuries. Only a few fumaroles (vents emitting steam and noxious fumes) in the crater hint at possible volcanic activity.

The local people, however, continue to benefit from past eruptions of El Misti and its neighbors. Much of the surrounding area is covered by thick deposits of lava and volcanic ash. The extremely fertile volcanic soil makes it one of the most productive farming areas in Peru. The people also use a widespread type of volcanic rock for construction. Known locally as *sillar,* it is lightweight and strong yet easily worked with simple tools. Arequipa, Peru's third largest city, in fact is built almost entirely of the pearly white stone, which has earned it the name *la ciudad blanca,* "the white city." □

EL MISTI. *Capped by a faint crown of snow and deeply furrowed by erosion, the volcano towers above the city of Arequipa at its foot.*

CLIFFS OF MOEN. *Towering over the Baltic Sea, the irregular line of cliffs is indented with alcoves where rocks and masses of debris have collapsed in landslides.*

Moen, Cliffs of

● Denmark
● Map: page 16, E–3

Formed of the compacted remains of marine animals, the dazzling cliffs of chalk make up one of the most unusual seacoasts in all of Denmark.

Like most of Denmark, the little island of Moen to the south of Copenhagen is a gently rolling lowland. Toward the eastern end of the island, however, the land slopes up to a high point 469 feet (143 meters) above the Baltic Sea. Just beyond, the surface slopes down again and then drops off abruptly in a line of sheer white cliffs about 4 miles (7 kilometers) long and in many places more than 400 feet (120 meters) high.

Known locally as Moensklint (*klint* means "cliff" in Danish), the rocky precipices are the island's most picturesque attraction. Trails wind through the dense beech forest that grows right to the edge of the cliffs; others lead down through gaps and gullies to the wave-washed beach at their base.

One rocky crag, from which a spring emerges, has been named the Weeper. Another one, noted for the echoes associated with it, is called the Orator. And still another is known as the Queen's Chair. A cluster of beech trees at the top forms the queen's crown, while a waterfall flowing down its side is fancifully considered to be the train of her gown.

The rocks that make up the cliff are composed of chalk (a very soft type of limestone) embedded with bits of flint. The thick beds of chalk were formed of the accumulated remains of marine animals about 70 million years ago and were subsequently uplifted above the sea. During the Ice Age the weight and movement of huge glaciers deformed the upper layers of the chalk and fractured it into enormous blocks. Large quantities of sand, clay, boulders, and other kinds of glacial debris were also deposited on the surface and in gullies between the blocks of chalk.

Undercut by waves, the cliffs are slowly receding as pieces of rock fall down and accumulate at their base in talus slopes. Occasionally the cover of glacial debris also slips down in landslides. Even so, the strikingly white cliffs, capped by verdant forest and reflected in the sea, remain one of the most distinctive stretches of seacoast in all of Denmark. □

The Changing Face of the Cliffs of Moen

The massive layers of chalk that make up the cliffs of Moen undergo slow but constant change. The glacial deposits that cover them slip down in landslides, rocks fall from time to time, and waves undercut the foot of the cliffs, changing their appearance.

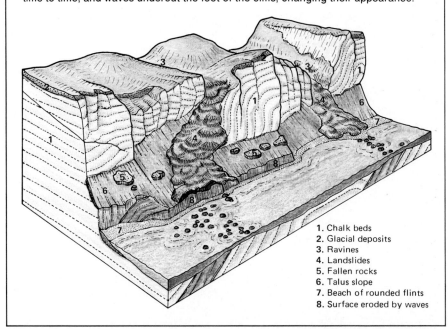

1. Chalk beds
2. Glacial deposits
3. Ravines
4. Landslides
5. Fallen rocks
6. Talus slope
7. Beach of rounded flints
8. Surface eroded by waves

Mont Blanc

- France
- Map: page 17, D–4

Wrapped in a sparkling blanket of ice and snow, the highest mountain in Western Europe towers above the deep valleys surrounding it.

Mont Blanc is part of an enormous Alpine massif that extends about 30 miles (50 kilometers) along the border between France and Italy just south of Switzerland. Scoured time and again by glaciers, the massif is surrounded by deep valleys and has been carved into a bristling array of individually named peaks—Mont Maudit, La Tour Ronde, Dôme du Goûter, Aiguille du Midi, and many more.

A total of 10 peaks in the group are more than 13,100 feet (4,000 meters) high. But the giant of them all is the towering summit of Mont Blanc itself, overlooking the deep Chamonix valley near the southern end of the massif. Reaching a height of 15,771 feet (4,807 meters), it is the highest peak in the Alps and the second highest in all of Europe. (It is exceeded only by Mount Elbrus in the Soviet Caucasus.)

The massif is composed primarily of coarse-grained granite and in places hard crystalline schist. Like the rest of the Alps, it was raised to its present height in a great mountain-building episode that began about 65 million years ago. Uplifted bit by bit over the course of millions of years, the granite massif was fractured in places into great wedge-shaped blocks. These in turn were eroded into the towering rocky pinnacles known as *aiguilles* (French for "needles") that are so common around Mont Blanc.

Much of the sharply chiseled beauty of the mountain and its neighbors was created by the glaciers that covered the Alps several times during the past 2 million years. The Ice Age, in fact, has not entirely ended on Mont Blanc, the "White Mountain." A few minor glaciers persist on the steep slopes on the Italian side of the massif, and several very big ones stream down the French side. The largest is the Mer de Glace ("Sea of Ice"), the second largest glacier in the Alps. At its snout it gives rise to the Arveyron River, which flows into the Arve, the principal river of the mountain group.

Among the best-known mountains in the world, Mont Blanc has been attracting visitors for three centuries.

MONT BLANC. *The great dome of granite, looming high above the craggy peaks that surround it, was carved long ago by massive glaciers—and a few still stream down its flanks.*

Foreigners began to seek it out in the late 17th century, and the stream of admirers has continued ever since. One of them was the English Romantic poet Percy Bysshe Shelley, who visited the Chamonix valley in 1817. Inspired by a view of the mountain from a bridge over the Arve, he wrote an eloquent poem, "Mont Blanc," extolling the beauties of the famous Alpine spot.

Mountain climbers have been especially attracted to Mont Blanc. In 1786 Michel Gabriel Paccard, a French doctor, and Jacques Balmat, his porter, became the first climbers to reach the summit. Many others followed in their footsteps; among them was Henriette d'Angeville, who reached the top in 1838 and thus became the first woman to scale a major mountain anywhere in the world.

Today mountaineers continue to come from afar to face the challenges of Mont Blanc and the neighboring summits. The less ambitious ride cable cars high up on the massif for breathtaking views of the entire ensemble. For their descent they can ski all the way back down to the Chamonix valley. They can even drive right through the mountain barrier by means of a tunnel connecting the Chamonix valley with Italy. □

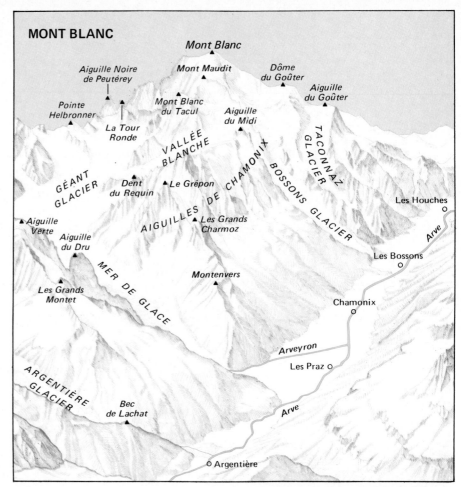

MONT BLANC

MONT BLANC. *Broken by crevasses and darkened by glacial debris, the Mer de Glace slides slowly downward between sharply chiseled peaks.*

MONUMENT VALLEY. *Among the many sandstone remnants rising from the valley floor are the two Mittens (left) and Merrick Butte.*

Monument Valley

- United States (Arizona—Utah)
- Map: page 10, D–5

Towering buttes dot the desert in a landscape that epitomizes the stark beauty of the old Southwest.

Monument Valley, astride the border between northeastern Arizona and southeastern Utah, is a broad expanse of flatlands punctuated by hundreds of towering sandstone pillars, spires, and buttes. Rising to heights of 1,000 feet (300 meters) and more, some of the massive eroded monoliths resemble crumbling castles, ancient temples, and tall skyscrapers, bearing such descriptive names as Castle Rock and the Alhambra. Other formations have more fanciful but equally appropriate names, such as the Mittens, the Setting Hen, and the Bear's Ears. And still others are associated with the local folklore, including Merrick Butte and Mitchell Butte, named for two prospectors who were killed there searching for a silver mine.

Though the monuments stand as isolated buttes and pinnacles today, they once were part of a continuous layer of rock that covered the entire valley. The sheer-walled formations are composed primarily of thick layers of red sandstone atop sloping bases of shale. The sandstone began to form about 250 million years ago, when the area emerged from beneath a shallow sea and was transformed into a desert. Winds blowing in from the north and northeast spread huge quantities of sand across the valley and piled it up into enormous dunes that were eventually compacted into the distinctive red sandstone. The sea invaded the region once again about 200 million years ago. Sediments that accumulated on coastal mud flats and in shallow streambeds formed the thin layers of shale and conglomerate that cap many of the monoliths.

The next chapter in the story began about 70 million years ago, when the earth's crust warped upward in the area in the form of a broad, elongated dome. In the process, internal stresses scored the rock with numerous faults and fractures that were gradually enlarged by the forces of erosion. Running water, windblown sand, and alternate freezing and thawing of ice in cracks and crevices in the rock all took their toll. Bit by bit, much of the rock that once covered the valley was worn away, leaving only the massive, more resistant blocks in the form of freestanding monoliths.

There are also a few remnants of volcanic activity. One of the highest formations in the valley is the metallic-blue spire known as Agathla Peak. Rising 1,255 feet (383 meters) above its base, it is the core of very hard lava that once plugged a volcanic vent.

The final chapter in the history of Monument Valley is yet to be written. Eventually even the remaining monoliths may be leveled by erosion, leaving nothing but a flat plain. In the meantime its austere beauty continues to epitomize the universal image of the great Southwest. (The famous John Wayne movie *Stagecoach* was filmed in Monument Valley.) Seeming to glow in full sunlight, then standing out in stark silhouette as evening shadows creep across the valley floor, the monuments inspire a sense of awe in all who see them. □

255

MOOREA. *Bordered by a placid lagoon, the shoreline remains undisturbed by the waves that break constantly against its barrier reef.*

Moorea

- French Polynesia
- Map: page 9

The dreamlike beauty of this South Pacific island paradise has its origins in a stormy volcanic past.

One of the world's most spectacularly beautiful islands, Moorea has all the ingredients of a classic South Pacific paradise. Crowded with saw-toothed ridges and sharp, deeply eroded peaks that slope gracefully toward the sea, Moorea is covered by lush tropical vegetation that flourishes in the warm, moist environment of the island. Some 25 rivers wind down from the peaks through deep valleys that run seaward in every direction.

Like Tahiti, its larger neighbor 12 miles (20 kilometers) to the southeast, Moorea is one of the Society Islands of French Polynesia, an archipelago governed by France since the 19th century. Generally triangular in shape, Moorea has an area of 50 square miles (130 square kilometers), and its highest peak, Mount Tohivea, rises 3,976 feet (1,212 meters) above the sea. On the northern coast the island's second highest peak, Mount Rotui, is flanked on either side by Moorea's two principal inlets, Cook's Bay and Papetoai Bay, both of which extend about two miles (three kilometers) inland.

As with other nearby Polynesian islands, Moorea is the exposed summit of an ancient volcano. Rising gradually from the ocean floor, the mountain was built up of a complex series of basaltic lava eruptions before it became extinct more than 2 million years ago. Subsequent erosion transformed the island's surface into an intricate pattern of steeply sloping valleys, high jagged peaks, and sharp ridges. The result is a much more mountainous appearance than the relatively modest elevations of the island would normally suggest.

A coral barrier reef that encircles the island almost completely shelters Moorea's shoreline from the open sea. Consequently, much of the island is fringed by white sandy beaches and a narrow, fertile coastal plain, rather than by the abrupt cliffs that would result from constant exposure to ocean waves. The broad, placid lagoon that lies between the island and the coral reef provides a natural haven for a thriving and colorful population of marine life. □

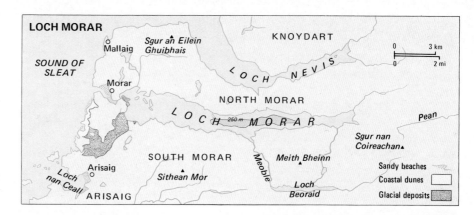

Morar, Loch

- United Kingdom (Scotland)
- Map: page 16, C–3

Carved long ago by grinding glaciers, the long, shimmering loch is the deepest lake in all of the British Isles.

Loch Morar is a long green ribbon of water extending far inland from the picturesque western coast of Scotland. Only a narrow belt of lowlands separates it from the sea, while rugged mountain ridges border it on the north and south. Stretching in an almost straight line from west to east, the lake is about 12 miles (19 kilometers) long but nowhere more than 2 miles (3 kilometers) wide. With a maximum depth of 1,017 feet (310 meters), however, it ranks as the deepest freshwater lake in the British Isles and one of the deepest in Europe.

What made Loch Morar so deep? Like the many long, narrow, fjordlike arms of the sea (also called lochs) that indent the entire northwest coast of Scotland, it is a deep trench that was excavated by Ice Age glaciers. In the case of Loch Morar, a river probably flowed through the valley now occupied by the lake when the Ice Age began. Following the line of an east-west fault (a fracture in the earth's crust), the river gradually widened and deepened its valley—though to nowhere near its present depth.

Eventually, about 2 million years ago, a worldwide cooling of the climate brought about the onset of the Ice Age. More snow fell in winter than was able to melt in the brief cool summer, and it began to accumulate on landmasses in enormous ice caps. Much of the British Isles in time was buried beneath a crushing sheet of ice at least 3,000 feet (900 meters) thick, just as most of Greenland today is completely covered by ice.

The great weight of the accumulating mass of ice and snow forced it to spread outward from the center. Tongues of glacial ice began to stream slowly toward the sea, following the troughs of preexisting river valleys. As the boulder- and debris-laden ice scraped over the bedrock, it gradually deepened the shallow valleys.

The Ice Age was not one continuous episode, however. From time to time the climate warmed sufficiently for the ice caps to disappear completely. Then it turned cold again and the glaciers reappeared. Following the lines of least resistance, new tongues of glacial ice moved along much the same routes as their predecessors, and chiseled deeper and deeper trenches in the valleys. (Many now extend well below sea level.) The result was the numerous long, narrow, fingerlike lakes strewn across the Scottish countryside (Loch Ness is perhaps the most famous); the thousands of smaller glacial lakes called lochans; and the fjordlike inlets that indent the coast where glaciers carved their valleys all the way out to the sea.

It is only by chance that Loch Morar is an inland lake rather than an arm of the sea. Toward the close of the last glacial stage, about 10,000 years ago, the snout of the glacier that carved Loch Morar became stabilized near the present seacoast. The front of the glacier melted at about the same rate that new ice flowed down from the Highlands. As it melted, all the pebbles, sand, and rock debris that had been trapped in the ice were released and built up a thick natural dam in the valley's former outlet to the sea at the southwestern corner of the present lake. When the glacier finally disappeared completely, the surge of meltwater carved a new outlet to the sea: the short river that now spills through a gorge at the northwestern corner of Loch Morar. □

MOSKENESOY. *Jagged mountain peaks, deeply sculpted by glacial erosion, stand guard over the island's picturesque harbors and fjords.*

Moskenesoy

- Norway
- Map: page 16, E–2

This picturesque offshore island offers a fine sampling of Norwegian scenery—jagged mountains, deep fjords, and tiny fishing villages.

The Lofoten Islands and the neighboring Vesteralen group jut southwestward like a peninsula from the northern coast of Norway. Only narrow channels separate the northernmost part of the archipelago from the mainland; and the individual islands, which fit together like the pieces of a jigsaw puzzle, are separated from each other by nothing more than narrow, winding straits. The islands in fact are the exposed tops of a mountain range that was once connected to the mainland, while the channels in between them are glacier-carved valleys that have been flooded by the sea.

The island chain is an unforgettable sight when approached across Vest Fjord, the broad inlet between the mainland and the lower part of the archipelago. A seemingly continuous mountain barrier rising abruptly from the sea to heights of 3,000 feet (900 meters) and more, the jagged rampart is renowned as the Lofoten Wall.

The southernmost of the major islands in the group—and one of the most scenic—is Moskenesoy. About 22 miles (35 kilometers) long and 6 miles (10 kilometers) wide, it is a maze of jagged peaks and promontories intersected by deep fjords and placid coves. Most of the mountains plunge directly into the sea. The only bits of level land are scattered coastal terraces, called strand flats, where picturesque fishing villages nestle at the foot of somber, treeless slopes.

Some of the finest scenery, most visitors agree, is in the vicinity of the village of Reine. The largest settlement on Moskenesoy, Reine is located on a rocky spit projecting into the mouth of Kirke Fjord, a large inlet that almost cuts the island in two. Virtually surrounded by water and backed by rugged mountain peaks, the town has long been a favorite with artists and photographers.

Reine is also a popular starting point for mountain-climbing enthusiasts, who find an enormous challenge in Moskenesoy's spectacularly varied terrain. (The highest peak towers 3,392 feet, or 1,034 meters, directly above the sea.) Covered by a massive ice cap during the Ice Age, the island was deeply dissected by large glaciers that streamed ponderously down the slopes. In addition to carving the deep fjords that indent the coastline, the glaciers plucked the bedrock from the mountainsides and hollowed out deep concave depressions known as cirques. The result is long lines of jagged mountain crests connected by steep, razor-sharp ridges that are a mountaineer's delight.

The island, which is located about 100 miles (160 kilometers) north of the Arctic Circle, is especially beautiful from late May until mid-July, when it is bathed in the warm glow of the midnight sun. For 24 hours a day the disk of the sun remains above the horizon and never sets completely. For several weeks in winter, in contrast, the sun never appears, and the island remains in darkness.

Even then, all the Lofoten Islands are alive with activity. Between January and April, tremendous schools of codfish migrate south from more northern seas to spawn in the shoals and coastal banks around the islands. And fishermen from all along the Norwegian coast converge on the islands to share in the catch.

They do well, however, to avoid the famous Maelstrom, an occasionally dangerous tidal current that sweeps through the strait in between the southern tip of Moskenesoy and the islet of Mosken. Imaginative descriptions by such writers as Jules Verne and Edgar Allan Poe have made the name of this current synonymous with a malevolent whirlpool capable of swallowing entire ships.

In reality small boats can often cross the strait quite safely. But at times a certain combination of wind and tide directions makes it a particularly terrifying hazard to navigation. Another much weaker current benefits the island, however. The warm North Atlantic Drift brings Moskenesoy a remarkably mild climate despite its far northern location, making it a popular vacation place. □

Muir Glacier

- United States (Alaska)
- Map: page 10, C–3

At the end of a remote inlet, great icebergs plunge into the water from a towering wall of glacial ice.

Near the northern end of Alaska's panhandle a long arm of the sea, Glacier Bay, extends about 65 miles (105 kilometers) inland. Here and there along its length, other narrower inlets (actually glacier-carved fjords) branch off in various directions, forming a treelike pattern of channels. And at their heads, many of the inlets end abruptly in massive walls of ice—the snouts of glaciers that stretch from the mountainsides right down to the sea and discharge their excess ice directly into the water. With more than a dozen of these so-called tidewater glaciers in the vicinity, much of the area around the bay is protected as Glacier Bay National Monument, a unit of the National Park System.

Among the most impressive of all these tongues of ice is Muir Glacier, located at the head of an inlet more than 20 miles (32 kilometers) long. Named for the pioneering naturalist John Muir, who visited the area in the late 19th century, it meets the waterline with a glittering wall of ice nearly 200 feet (60 meters) high.

Like the rest of the tidewater glaciers in the area, it is constantly calving icebergs into the sea. As the water undermines the front of the glacier, huge blocks of ice break off and plunge violently into the water. The Muir discharges so many bergs into the sea, in fact, that boats normally can come no closer than two miles (three kilometers) to the wall of ice. Beyond that point the sea is littered with a chaos of heaving blocks of ice.

One of the most striking characteristics of Muir Glacier and many others around the bay is the speed with which they are retreating. In 1794, when Captain George Vancouver explored the area, most of Glacier Bay itself was covered by an enormous sheet of ice that was as much as 4,000 feet (1,200 meters) thick in places. Muir Glacier, in turn, has receded more than 20 miles (32 kilometers) since 1892. At one point it retreated about five miles (eight kilometers) in the course of just 10 years. While glaciers all over Alaska have generally been on the wane in this century—a reflection of a gradual warming of the climate—nowhere else have they receded so rapidly as at Glacier Bay.

As the glaciers retreated, plants quickly moved in to reclaim the newly uncovered land. Mosses and low-growing plants came first, then shrubs and thickets of willows and alders, which in turn were replaced by the advancing ranks of dense evergreens. In time the area may be completely forested—until, perhaps, the climate cools again and the glaciers resume their seaward flow. □

Muldrow Glacier

- United States (Alaska)
- Map: page 10, B–2

In the winter of 1956, a mighty glacier on North America's highest mountain surged suddenly forward in a dramatic, unexplained advance.

The most spectacular sight in Alaska's Mount McKinley National Park is, naturally enough, the snow-covered summit of the great mountain itself. Rising to an altitude of 20,320 feet (6,194 meters), it reigns as the highest mountain in North America.

But it is by no means the only wonder in the park. There are other lofty peaks, including Mount Foraker,

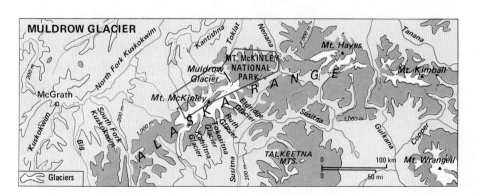

at 17,398 feet (5,303 meters), and no fewer than a dozen active glaciers. One of the largest of these is Muldrow Glacier, which originates on the north slope of Mount McKinley and is an awesome spectacle in its own right.

A great river of ice shattered in places by deep crevasses, Muldrow Glacier covers an area of 150 square miles (400 square kilometers). Fed by descending tongues of the Harper, Traleika, and Brooks glaciers high up on Mount McKinley, the Muldrow flows northeast and then turns rather sharply toward the northwest, with a total length of 35 miles (55 kilometers). The glacier is heavily streaked by dark, ribbonlike bands of rocks and

other eroded debris that have been trapped in the ice and carried along by its flow.

The Muldrow is noteworthy for more than its size, however. Glaciers generally move down through their valleys at a slow, steady pace, their descent governed chiefly by the steepness of the slope and the amount of snow and ice accumulating at higher elevations. During the first half of this century, the Muldrow was essentially stagnant and even receding slightly.

Then in the mid-1950's it became noticeably more active, and in the winter of 1956–57 it underwent a dramatic forward surge, advancing more than 4 miles (6½ kilometers) in a sin-

gle year. In the course of the surge, the upper portion of the glacier became much thinner, with a corresponding increase in thickness at the snout.

Such acceleration in a glacier's rate of movement is usually the result of an earthquake, an avalanche, or a rapid change in climate, but no such cause could explain the Muldrow's sudden advance. Instead, it appears that the steady, year-by-year accumulation of snow and ice in the glacier's upper reaches may at last have grown so great that, like a swollen reservoir bursting through a dam, it suddenly launched the entire ice mass on its rapid descent. But no one knows for sure what caused the sudden surge. □

MULDROW GLACIER. *A sled pulled by a team of huskies seems almost lost on the vast icy wilderness of this massive glacier.*

Nabesna Glacier

- United States (Alaska)
- Map: page 10, B–2

Born in a giant ice field and still fed by a number of tributaries, this Alaskan glacier has nonetheless been retreating for many years.

The Wrangell Mountains are a small but impressive range located in southeastern Alaska not far from Canada's Yukon Territory. About 100 miles (160 kilometers) long and 70 miles (110 kilometers) wide, the range is part of the much larger mountain system that extends in a broad arc across southern Alaska from the panhandle to the Aleutian Islands. Reaching a maximum height of more than 16,000 feet (4,900 meters), the cluster of volcanic peaks forms a natural barrier between the moist, mild coastal climate and the much colder conditions that generally prevail inland.

Because of the perennially heavy snowfall, a vast permanent ice cap has accumulated on the high central peaks of the range. The long narrow tongues of valley glaciers radiate in all directions from the ice cap, including such giants as the Nizina and Kennicott glaciers on the southern slopes. The major glacier flowing down the mountains' northern flanks is the Nabesna, which extends about 20 miles (32 kilometers) below the main snowfield. Fed by several tributary glaciers, it streams downslope through a broad U-shaped valley and is on the average three miles (five kilometers) wide.

First explored in the early 19th century, the glacier has been undergoing a long though not continuous retreat ever since. There have been brief intermittent periods of growth, but the overall trend toward decline has been unmistakable, especially since the early 1900's. Indeed, glacial deposits left farther down in the valley indicate that the Nabesna Glacier at one time was actually more than twice as long as it is today.

As the glacier melts, its runoff water gives rise to the northward-flowing Nabesna River. Like many other Alaskan rivers that flow from glaciers, the upper reaches of the Nabesna are a so-called braided stream. Flowing down a slight gradient across old glacial deposits and gravel that has been washed out from the melting front of the ice, it divides and rejoins in a multitude of shallow channels separated by low, elongated sand and gravel bars. The result is a network of interwoven channels that form a pattern much like the strands woven into a braid. Farther downstream the Nabesna joins the Tanana River, which in turn flows northwest into central Alaska's main waterway, the Yukon.   □

Nanga Parbat

- Pakistan
- Map: page 18, I–5

Among the highest mountains in the world, this stark Himalayan peak is also one of the most treacherous.

Nanga Parbat, whose name means "naked mountain," stands near the western end of the Himalayas in the north of Pakistan. Also known locally as Diamir, meaning "king of the mountains," it is an impressive peak by any standard. Its southern wall rises steeply for about 15,000 feet (4,600 meters) above the valley at its base. The north face soars even more dramatically for about 23,000 feet (7,000 meters) over the great bend of the Indus River. With its summit reaching 26,660 feet (8,126 meters) above sea level, Nanga Parbat is in fact one of the highest mountains in the world.

Composed primarily of a granite-like rock called gneiss, the rocky tower of Nanga Parbat is covered on all sides by massive glaciers. All are remarkable for their speed: the advance of the Rakhiot Glacier on the northern flank has been measured at almost 8 feet (2½ meters) per day. The rapidly moving ice triggers numerous avalanches. Justifiably feared, the roaring cascades of ice have been likened by local inhabitants to demonlike snow serpents. Landslides also are frequent on the mountain's steep slopes. A particularly disastrous one in 1840 disrupted the flow of the Indus River and caused a catastrophic flood.

Because it is quite easily accessible, Nanga Parbat was the first of the very high peaks of the Himalayas to tempt mountain climbers. But because of its sheer slopes, ice, and landslides, it has also proved to be one of the most treacherous. The first attempt to scale it, in 1895, ended in the death of three climbers. The second attempt was not made until 1932, and was also unsuccessful. Still more climbers were killed on expeditions in 1934, 1937, and 1950. It was not until 1953 that the German climber Herman M. Buhl finally reached the top of the mountain. Since that time, all sides of Nanga Parbat, including the formidable south wall, have been conquered. But the mountain over the years has exacted a fearful toll in human lives.   □

Narmada River

- India
- Map: page 20, B–2

A sacred river surges through a snow-white gorge, inspiring all who contemplate its tranquil beauty.

Second only to the Ganges among the sacred rivers of India, the Narmada is believed by Hindus to have sprung from the body of the god Siva. The devout purify themselves by walking from the river's mouth to its source about 800 miles (1,300 kilometers) away and then returning on the opposite bank. The pilgrimage symbolizes the journey of a legendary king whose

NARMADA RIVER. *The Indian river plunges over many waterfalls on its journey to the Arabian Sea. Fed by monsoon rains, its flow drops drastically during the dry season.*

sails turned from black to white as his boat descended the river.

Originating in the Maikala Range in central India, the Narmada is one of the few rivers on the Indian peninsula that flow to the west. (Most rise in the Western Ghats and flow eastward.) Passing through a valley bounded by the sandstone hills of the Vindhya Range on the north and the Satpura Range on the south, the Narmada finally empties into the Gulf of Cambay. Since time immemorial it has served as a link between the Arabian Sea and the Ganges Valley.

The most scenic spot on the Narmada is the so-called Marble Rocks, just downstream from the city of Jabalpur on the river's upper course. After leaping over a waterfall about 50 feet (15 meters) high, the river narrows dramatically as it surges through a majestic limestone gorge hemmed in by walls more than 100 feet (30 meters) high. The gorge is only about 1¼ miles (2 kilometers) long. Yet it is so beautiful that it is said that if the emperor Shah Jahan had only seen it, he would have chosen it as the site for the Taj Mahal. □

Nefta

- Tunisia
- Map: page 24, D–2

Once an important way station for desert caravans, the oasis known in Roman times as Nepte remains a welcome sight for weary travelers.

Encircled by ocher-colored hills on the edge of a vast salt lagoon, the desert oasis of Nefta in western Tunisia is considered by many to be the most beautiful in northern Africa. The oasis itself is a broad, roughly triangular basin where bubbling springs nourish groves of tens of thousands of date palms, as well as oranges, lemons, apricots, pomegranates, and a variety of other crops. Scattered among the palms and spread out on the margins are the picturesque tawny brick buildings of the town of Nefta, noted for the beauty of its many mosques and Moslem shrines. The finest views of the town, which at sunset glows with tints of orange, lavender, and rose, are from a nearby hilltop vantage point known as the Belvedere.

In striking contrast to the luxuriant greenery of the oasis is the desolate expanse of the Chott Djerid stretching off to the south and east. Covered by a shallow, shimmering lake in winter, the chott dries out almost completely in summer. A few marshes persist, but most of the basin is transformed into a glistening, salt-encrusted plain that bakes beneath the summer sun.

The seasonal flooding of the chott results not from sparse local rainfall but from a rise in the water table. Water from far away seeps through underlying layers of porous rock and emerges at the surface when the rocks are saturated, then subsides when the dry season returns.

These same saturated rock layers are the source of the water that bubbles up from the numerous artesian springs at Nefta. Supplemented in recent years by drilled wells, the spring water is distributed throughout the oasis by a network of irrigation channels, sluices, and earthen dams. And there on the Sahara's northern fringes it nourishes a basin brimming with rich vegetation, just as it has down through the centuries. □

NEFTA. *Surrounded by terraced slopes, the dense palm grove at the Tunisian oasis is nourished by water that pours from artesian springs.*

NEGEV. *Reminiscent of a temple, the Columns of Amram have been eroded from the sandstone of the Red Canyon in the southern Negev.*

Negev

- Israel
- Map: page 18, E–5

*The remarkable Israeli desert is
as rich in topographical diversity
as it is in historical importance.*

Few places on the globe have been the scene of more intense historical dramas than the land now called Israel, for thousands of years a crossroads for the civilizations of three continents. Nearly half of this unique area is occupied by the Negev, a desolate, southward-pointing triangle of land with an ample history of its own. Some 4,000 years ago, according to the Bible, the Hebrew patriarchs Abraham, Isaac, and Jacob lived at Beer-

sheba, now the Negev's principal city. Moses led the Israelites through the Negev after the exodus from Egypt, and King Solomon's copper mines were located near its southern tip.

During biblical times and for some centuries thereafter, much of the Negev was not the desert that is seen today. Despite a general scarcity of rain (its name comes from a Hebrew word meaning "dry"), the soil was fertile and, with proper planting and cultivation, capable of producing an abundance of crops. The people of Judaea tilled the land for generations, and when Nabataeans from Jordan began to settle there in the first century B.C., they developed so successful an agricultural system that the Negev became a major source of grain for the Roman Empire.

It was not until the seventh century A.D., when the climate became drier, that most of the Negev's permanent settlements were abandoned and the land reverted to desert conditions. So it remained until the mid-20th century, when the founding of modern Israel brought about a new determination to "make the desert bloom."

Geographically, the Negev encompasses some 4,700 square miles (12,200 square kilometers). Its northern border extends for about 60 miles (100 kilometers) east from the Mediterranean to the Dead Sea. A natural boundary is formed on the east by the Wadi Araba, a perennially dry riverbed that stretches more than 100 miles (160 kilometers) south from the Dead Sea to the Gulf of Aqaba. The Dead Sea and the Wadi Araba both lie in the

NEGEV. *Patterns of hard and soft rock, brought into sharp relief by centuries of intense erosion, are illuminated by a low-lying sun to create a stark, hauntingly beautiful landscape.*

Rift Valley, an enormous elongated trench in the earth's crust that begins in Syria, runs southward through the Red Sea, and reaches far down into Africa. The Negev is bounded on the west by the Sinai Peninsula and narrows southward to the Gulf of Aqaba. There, around the port of Elath, Israel's southernmost city, the Negev comes almost to a point, with its southern tip only about 6 miles (10 kilometers) wide.

Heavily dissected by wadis, the region has been compressed into a series

Eroded depression

Former
land surface

Eroded depressions at the tops of ridges are known as *makhteshim* in the Negev. Hollowed out by rivers (most of them now dry) that flowed along the axis of upward folds in the earth's crust, many of these craterlike basins are extremely large, deep, and remarkably symmetrical in outline.

of folds that run northeast to southwest, creating an undulating pattern of uplands and valleys. To the north the landscape is one of rolling hills, with enough rainfall—as much as 12 inches, or 305 millimeters, in some years—to make it the most arable part of the Negev.

Farther south in the central Negev, elevations rise to more than 3,000 feet (900 meters). The most striking features of this area are the elongated, craterlike depressions (called *makhteshim* in Hebrew) that have been eroded in the tops of many ridges. The largest, Makhtesh Ramon, is 23 miles (37 kilometers) long and as much as 5 miles (8 kilometers) wide. Hollowed out of the upward folds in the terrain, some of these remarkable basins have depths of more than 1,000 feet (300 meters) and steep inner walls that reveal progressively older layers of rock.

Still farther south is the Paran Plateau, a desolate rocky expanse that has frequently been likened to the surface of the moon. Finally, at the Negev's southern extremity, rise the Mountains of Elath, merging in the west with the mountains of the Sinai Peninsula. There erosion has sculpted the reddish crests into fantastic shapes, among them some impressive cliffs known as the Pillars of Solomon. □

Neretva Gorges

- Yugoslavia
- Map: page 17, E-4

Slicing through one of Yugoslavia's most rugged ranges, the Neretva River created deep and scenic gorges.

For centuries the Neretva River was both a thoroughfare and a barrier to transportation. The rushing river, which is only about 135 miles (220 kilometers) long, flows in a crescent-shaped course through rugged mountain gorges before entering the Adriatic Sea about 40 miles (65 kilometers) north of Dubrovnik. But while the lower course is navigable and the canyons along the upper course form one of the two main passes through the Dinaric Alps, long stretches of the precipitous gorges were virtually impossible to cross.

Steep-sided and starkly beautiful, the gorges in some places are up to 4,000 feet (1,200 meters) deep. Elsewhere they narrow down to gloomy chasms only 10 feet (3 meters) wide. One of the first attempts to span the river was made in the 15th century, when a wooden suspension bridge was built at Mostar. In 1566 the Turks replaced that with an arched stone bridge that still stands. Other bridges have since been built, and today visitors can admire the gorges' wild beauty from a highway that follows the river for much of its length. □

Nettuno, Grotta di

- Italy (Sardinia)
- Map: page 17, D-4

Partially flooded by the sea, the Cave of Neptune is a wonderland of water and strange cave formations.

Near the northwestern tip of the island of Sardinia, a high, cliff-bound promontory, Cape Caccia, juts into the Mediterranean. Attacked long ago by water that seeped underground and dissolved part of the limestone, the headland is riddled with caves. The most beautiful and famous of them all is the Grotta di Nettuno ("Cave of Neptune"). Named for the god of water, it was partially flooded by the sea when the melting of glaciers at the end of the Ice Age resulted in a world-wide rise in sea level.

Today visitors can enter the cave by

boat through a small opening at sea level or by means of a long flight of stairs carved into the rock from the top of the cape. Beyond the entrance, a small chamber opens into the main cavern, which is filled by a lake of seawater about 400 feet (120 meters) long and up to 165 feet (50 meters) wide. Splendid, pure white stalagmites and columns rise from the tranquil lake amid reflections of stalactites and other cave formations on the walls and ceiling.

Across the lake is the Salla dell' Organo ("Organ Chamber"), with its striking stone "organ pipes." And beyond that, atop a steep slope, is the Palco della Musica ("Music Box"). It offers a fine vantage point for admiring the broad expanse of the lake and its fantastic array of formations. □

NGORONGORO CRATER. *Ringed by steep gullied slopes, the huge bowllike depression is partially filled by a large saline lake that attracts enormous flocks of birds.*

GROTTA DI NETTUNO. *Stalactites, draperies, and other intricately formed cave formations decorate the dim, silent, watery chambers of Sardinia's famous Cave of Neptune.*

Ngorongoro Crater

● Tanzania
● Map: page 26, C–3

Famed for its wealth of wildlife, the "crater" was produced by the collapse of a gigantic mountain.

Ngorongoro Crater, an enormous natural basin in northern Tanzania, is a nearly circular depression with a diameter of some 12 miles (20 kilometers). Steep slopes drop about 2,000 feet (600 meters) from the brink to the grassy plain, lake, and marshes on its floor. A unique natural sanctuary, the bowllike hollow is famous for the variety of wild animals that find refuge in it: great herds of wildebeests, zebras, gazelles, and many more.

The crater owes its existence to the formation of Africa's Rift Valley, an enormous fracture in the earth's crust that began to form about 25 million years ago. In the long period of instability that followed, lava welled up through fissures in the rock and built many volcanoes along the length of the valley.

At one time Ngorongoro was covered by a mountain that rose well above the present rim. Then, a few million years ago, long after the volcano became extinct, a renewed phase of rifting began in the valley. In the process, a circular fracture developed under the mountain. The entire summit collapsed into the empty magma chamber beneath the crust, leaving the gigantic basin (technically classed as a caldera) that is known today as Ngorongoro Crater. □

Niagara Falls

- Canada—United States
- Map: page 11, F–4

The seething spectacle of Niagara—really two falls in one—has few rivals for its dual traits of beauty and sheer overwhelming power.

The Niagara River is not very long. From its source, the outlet of Lake Erie, to its end in Lake Ontario, it flows a total distance of only about 35 miles (55 kilometers). Yet its name is known far and wide. About halfway along its short northward course the river, which carries the overflow of four of the five Great Lakes, plunges over a precipice in the paired cascades of Niagara Falls.

A thunderous, unending roar greets visitors long before the falls come into view. But nothing can quite prepare them for the sight of the two seething sheets of water hurtling into the gorge on either side of Goat Island. To the north of the island is the long, nearly straight line of the American Falls, spanning a distance of about 1,060 feet (325 meters). To the south and west, on the Canadian side of the river, is the gracefully curving arc of Horseshoe Falls, with the length of its crest measuring slightly more than 2,200 feet (670 meters). Both cascades drop a total of 180 feet (55 meters).

Although the falls may seem both

The Birth and Death of Niagara Falls

Niagara Falls began to form at the end of the Ice Age about 10,000 years ago. Carrying the overflow from Lake Erie, the Niagara River spilled over the edge of a high escarpment en route to Lake Ontario and the sea (1). Almost immediately the huge volume of water flowing over the cliff began to erode a gorge by undermining the rock layers that make up the escarpment. Although the rate of erosion undoubtedly varied over the centuries, the falls receded upstream at an average rate of about 3 feet (0.9 meter) per year. Today the falls are located 7 miles (11 kilometers) upstream from their original site at the edge of the escarpment (2). Divided by an island into two separate cascades, the falls most certainly will continue to extend their long gorge upstream. Eventually they will reach Lake Erie and disappear entirely (3). Only furious rapids will remain in the river's rubble-filled gorge. But the disappearance of the falls is not likely to occur soon. Geologists estimate that at least 25,000 years will pass before the Niagara River extends its gorge all the way to Lake Erie.

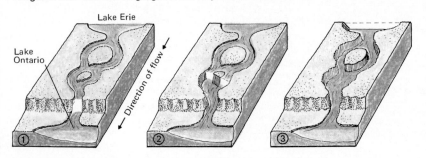

very old and quite unchanging, they actually are neither. Niagara Falls came into being only as the Ice Age drew to a close some 10,000 years ago. As the enormous ice cap that had covered much of northern North America wasted away, the Great Lakes gradually assumed their present form and drainage pattern. The lakes once emptied into the Mississippi River. But as the ice receded to the north, they eventually found their present outlet to the sea by way of Lake Ontario and the St. Lawrence River.

Besides being the easternmost of the Great Lakes, Ontario is also the closest to sea level. About 7 miles (11 kilometers) north of Niagara Falls, the surface of the land drops abruptly in a steep escarpment. And originally it was there that the Niagara River made its breathtaking plunge en route to Lake Ontario.

But the falls did not remain at the edge of the cliff for long. The escarpment is capped by a thick, nearly hor-

NIAGARA FALLS. *To the right of Goat Island, the river spills over the brink of Horseshoe Falls. Only the end of the American Falls is visible.*

izontal layer of extremely hard dolomite (a type of limestone). Beneath the dolomite are layers of shale, sandstone, and other much more easily eroded rocks. As water poured over the precipice, churning up fallen rocks in the riverbed below, the softer underlying layers were worn away, leaving an overhanging cornice of dolomite. But eventually tensions in the dolomite became so great that huge blocks of it came crashing down.

Century by century, as undercutting of the dolomite continued, the falls receded upstream, leaving the deep Niagara Gorge in their wake. It is believed that they reached more or less their present location about 600 years ago, when the obstruction of Goat Island divided them into two separate cataracts.

Because the river is both wider and deeper on the southwestern side of the island, erosion proceeded much more rapidly there, and carved the deep, curving indentation of Horseshoe Falls. (According to one estimate, Horseshoe Falls have receded more than 1,000 feet, or 300 meters, since the French explorer Louis Hennepin first viewed them in 1678.) With less than 10 percent of the river's flow channeled over them, the American Falls are much more stable, forming a long, more or less straight line.

Parks have been established on both sides of Niagara. The best known of several bridges that span the gorge is Rainbow Bridge, just below the falls, which affords fine views of the rainbows that form on the falls' towering clouds of spray. Other favored vantage points include scenic walkways in the parks (the most dramatic views are from the Canadian side), as well as nearby observation towers. The falls can also be inspected from helicopters, but the most unusual views are from boats that ply the turbulent water in the gorge below the falls. The boats have traditionally been named *Maid of the Mist,* commemorating the legend of an Indian girl who is said to have gone over Niagara in a canoe, and whose ghostly image sometimes appears in the spray.

Because the Niagara River drops a total of 326 feet (99 meters) between lakes Erie and Ontario, its huge volume of flow has long been used for generating power. Today water is diverted from the river above the falls and channeled through mammoth ducts to the generating plants downstream. Thus, though few are aware of it, only about half as much water spills over the falls as did in the past.

The lessened flow has slowed the rate of erosion, as have elaborate control structures built above the falls. The cataracts are still receding, although very slowly now, and experts predict that they will remain in their present general location for hundreds of years to come. □

Niger River

- West Africa
- Map: page 24, D–5

The greatest river of West Africa not only ends in a delta but has also created a vast "inland delta" far upstream from its outlet on the sea.

From its source in the Fouta Djallon highlands in Guinea to its outlet on the sea, the Niger River flows a total of 2,600 miles (4,180 kilometers), making it the principal river of West Africa and the third longest on the continent. Its course is a roundabout one, forming a great curve through the heart of West Africa. Originating within 150 miles (240 kilometers) of the Atlantic Ocean, it flows northeastward into Mali, brushes against the southern fringes of the Sahara, and then turns southeastward across Niger and Nigeria to its wide delta on the Atlantic's Gulf of Guinea.

Although the Niger rises at an elevation of nearly 3,000 feet (900 meters), the river makes a quick descent from the Fouta Djallon highlands. The most dramatic plunge occurs after the Niger enters Mali: in a long series of rapids, the river drops down more than 1,000 feet (300

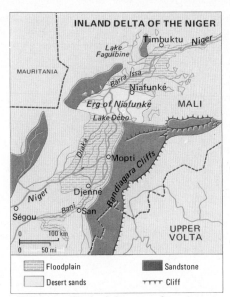

INLAND DELTA OF THE NIGER

About one-third of the way along its seaward course, the Niger branches into a maze of channels where it spills over its banks each year across a deltalike floodplain.

meters) in just 40 miles (65 kilometers).

Beyond that, the river slows down abruptly as it enters the broad flat plain known as the inland delta. A maze of shifting, intertwining channels, lakes, and low sandy islands, the delta covers an area of about 30,000 square miles (77,700 square kilometers) southwest of the fabled town of

Timbuktu. Seasonally inundated by floodwaters originating in the highlands, the delta is a thriving oasis that produces plentiful crops of rice, millet, and cotton.

The Niger's volume of flow is substantially diminished as it leaves the inland delta and the irrigated areas that flank it farther downstream. More than half of its water is lost through seepage into the soil, use by plants, and especially, in this hot, dry region, by evaporation. Gathering tributaries as it curves southeastward across Niger and Nigeria, the river again swells dramatically when it is joined by the Benue about 250 miles (400 kilometers) from the coast.

Doubled in volume by the waters of its major tributary, the Niger then surges almost directly south to its mouth on the Gulf of Guinea. There it branches once again into a multitude of channels as it spreads out over its broad fan-shaped delta. (With an area of approximately 14,000 square miles, or 36,000 square kilometers, the Niger's is the largest delta in Africa.) Although a number of these channels are clogged by sandbars, others are navigable by oceangoing vessels, making the lower course of the so-called Nile of West Africa an important avenue of commerce. ☐

NILE RIVER. *The Blue Nile spills over the Bahar-Dar waterfall in Ethiopia en route to its desert rendezvous with the White Nile.*

NILE RIVER. *Once surrounded by dry land, a rocky island projects from the surface of Lake Nasser, the largest man-made lake in the world.*

Nile River

- East Africa
- Map: page 25, G–2

The longest river in the world—and perhaps the most historic—this unique waterway continues to shape and be shaped by human events.

For thousands of years the people of Egypt revered the Nile as a sacred river. They did not know where it originated, nor what caused its annual flooding. But they did know that without it their civilization might never have come into being. Today the ancient riddles have been solved, but the Nile still retains its age-old power over the human imagination.

With a length of 4,132 miles (6,650 kilometers) from its farthest headstream to the Mediterranean, the Nile is the world's longest river. Its drainage basin, estimated at 1,293,000 square miles (3,349,000 square kilometers), includes parts of nine countries and encompasses about one-tenth of Africa's land area.

Down through the ages, the source of the great river was shrouded in mystery despite many efforts to discover it. The task was complicated, as it turned out, by the fact that the Nile has not one but three major sources, since its northward flow unites the waters of its longest branch, the so-called White Nile, with those of the Blue Nile and the smaller Atbara.

If the ancient Egyptians knew of the Blue Nile and its source, the knowledge was lost. It was not until the 17th century that a Spanish missionary first traced it to its origin: Lake Tana in the highlands of Ethiopia.

The White Nile proved a more difficult problem. In A.D. 150 the Greek astronomer Ptolemy placed its headwaters in a range he called the Mountains of the Moon—a range that has since been identified as the Ruwenzori mountains on the border between Uganda and Zaire. Although Ptolemy was not far from the truth, attempts to confirm his theory were unsuccessful. The mystery remained unsolved until the 19th century, when a series of British expeditions finally discovered the river's ultimate headstream, the Kagera River, which rises in present-day Burundi and flows northeast 250 miles (400 kilometers) into Lake Victoria.

The overflow from the northern end of Lake Victoria, in turn, is the beginning of the White Nile proper. Flowing northward through Lake Kyoga, the White Nile plunges 120 feet (37 meters) over Murchison Falls and begins its rapid descent from the lake plateau to the low flat plains of southern Sudan. Also called Bahr el Jebel in this region, the river slows drastically as it spreads out across a broad marshy area. Aptly known as the Sudd, or "Barrier," it is clogged by papyrus reeds, elephant grass, and other vegetation. The river loses half of its water to seepage and evaporation as it winds slowly across the Sudd.

Slightly replenished by tributaries flowing in from either side, the White Nile eventually escapes from the Sudd and continues its northward journey. Some 500 miles (800 kilometers) farther downstream, the White Nile is joined by the Blue Nile at Khartoum.

Although much shorter than the White Nile, with a length of 850 miles (1,370 kilometers), the Blue Nile carries a far greater and more variable

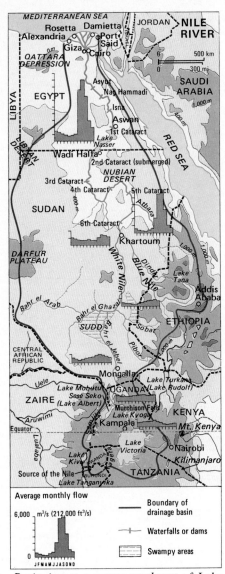

Beginning at a source southwest of Lake Victoria, the Nile drains about one-tenth of the land area of Africa as it flows northward to the Mediterranean Sea.

volume of water. The meager flow of the White Nile at Khartoum changes little from one month to the next. But both the Blue Nile and the Atbara, the latter joining the mainstream 200 miles (320 kilometers) farther north, are swollen dramatically each year by summer rains on the Ethiopian highlands. It is this sudden influx of water that accounts for the annual—and for centuries inexplicable—flooding of the arid lower Nile Valley. North of Khartoum the river, now known simply as the Nile, flows in a broad S-shaped curve some 1,200 miles (1,930 kilometers) long. Flanked by desert, the river in this sector is interrupted by six cataracts numbered in ascending order from north to south.

As the Nile crosses into Egypt north

of the Second Cataract (which is now submerged beneath Lake Nasser), it brings precious moisture to a strip of arable land that continues all the way to Cairo. Hemmed in by desert on both sides, with a maximum width of 20 miles (32 kilometers), this fertile, intensively cultivated swath of green produces much of Egypt's food supply.

The world of the delta begins at Cairo. The Nile delta is, in a sense, the prototype for all others; its roughly triangular shape reminded early geographers of the Greek letter "delta," and they named it accordingly. About 100 miles (160 kilometers) from north to south and as much as 150 miles (240 kilometers) wide, the delta disperses the Nile's water into the sea through a fan-shaped network of shallow channels. The thick layers of silt carried downstream over the years provide the Nile delta with the most fertile soil on the entire continent of Africa.

Like all deltas, the Nile's is in a constant state of change. Its normal evolution, however, has been seriously disrupted since the completion of the Aswan High Dam in 1971. The dam has fulfilled its primary goals of controlling the annual floods and generating much-needed electricity. But in creating Lake Nasser, the world's largest man-made lake, it has also formed a huge sediment trap that greatly decreases the amount of silt reaching the lower valley. As a result, salt water from the Mediterranean has begun to seep into parts of the delta. The reduction in nutrients carried downstream has also depleted the population of some fish species, not only in the Nile but through much of the eastern Mediterranean as well. Thus the ancient river, though partially tamed by modern technology, continues to influence life along its banks and far beyond. □

NILGIRI HILLS. *Rising like a wall across the horizon, the steep hills are well watered by monsoon rains. At their foot is a reservoir that stores the runoff water for irrigation.*

Nilgiri Hills

- India
- Map: page 20, B–3

A mountainous bastion rising high above the coastal plain, the Blue Hills of India have been favored as a resort haven for many generations.

The Nilgiri Hills, also known as the Blue Hills, are a cool refuge from the steamy summer heat of southern India. Part of the Western Ghats, the great mountain barrier that rises like a wall along the western coast of the Indian peninsula, they are a steep-sided, undulating plateau covering an area of about 1,000 square miles (2,600 square kilometers). Rising suddenly from their surroundings, the hills resemble a gigantic natural fortress with deep clefts and gorges dissecting the fringing escarpments.

The hills are composed of a block of ancient basement rock, mainly gneiss, that was long ago eroded down to a nearly flat plain. About 70 million years ago, in response to stresses in the earth's crust, the entire block was thrust upward along faults to its present elevation. The result was a region of rolling hills, which average about 6,600 feet (2,000 meters) above sea level, bordered by steep escarpments.

Despite the seeming inaccessibility of the hills, several roads wind up the densely forested slopes and provide magnificent views of the surrounding countryside. The cool climate and great natural beauty of the uplands long ago attracted Europeans, who established thriving summer resorts and extensive plantations in the hills. One of the oldest and most picturesque resort centers is the city of Ootacamund (also popularly known as "Ooty"), not far from Dodabetta, at 8,648 feet (2,636 meters) the highest point in the hills.

In many places the original forests of teak, bamboo, and blackwood have been replaced by plantations growing tea, coffee, eucalyptus, and cinchona, the tree whose bark yields quinine. Even so, much of the original vegetation remains intact. Because of the high elevation, winds blowing in from the sea drop abundant monsoon rainfall upon the hills and nurture the rampant growth of tropical forests. Abounding in wildlife and laced with streams and waterfalls, the highlands of the Nilgiri Hills amply justify their popularity as a tourist resort. □

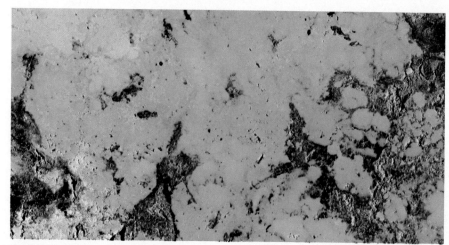

NISHAPUR MINES. *Tinted with various shades of blue-green by the presence of minute amounts of copper, turquoise is typically formed at or near the surface in arid regions.*

Nishapur Mines

- Iran
- Map: page 18, G–5

For thousands of years, the world's most valued turquoise has been extracted from these Iranian mines.

The ancient town of Nishapur in the northwestern corner of Iran is known today chiefly as the home and burial place of Omar Khayyam. But long before the 11th-century mathematician and astronomer wrote the verses of his famous *Rubaiyat*, the town was famous as a source of turquoise. The semiprecious gemstone has been extracted from nearby mines for at least 2,000 years, and even today the mines are celebrated as the source of the finest specimens of the stone found anywhere in the world.

The opaque blue-green gems are typically found at or near the surface of the earth in arid regions such as the American Southwest. At Nishapur the mines are located northwest of the town in the stark foothills of the rugged Binalud Range. Beyond irrigated lowland plains, the sere reddish hills rise toward the mountains amid dazzling white patches of salt flats. And there, in an area of intensely folded sedimentary and volcanic rock layers, four mines continue to yield quantities of the coveted stones.

A phosphate mineral deposited by circulating water, turquoise receives its characteristic color from the presence of small amounts of copper. Although the color may range from blue to a dull greenish gray, the sky-blue specimens are generally the ones that are most highly valued by gemologists.

Typically found in strings of kidney-shaped masses, the stones are also occasionally found in broad veins.

Although the mines at Nishapur are old, those on the Sinai Peninsula are even older. Originally imported to Europe by way of Turkey, the gem gets its name from *pierre turquoise*, a French term that means "Turkish stone." Esteemed since antiquity for its exquisite colors and waxy sheen, turquoise is still highly valued for use as jewelry and in mosaics. □

Nyanga Rapids

- Gabon
- Map: page 24, E–6

Supplied by high equatorial rainfall, a remote African river flows seaward across a series of impressive rapids.

From its source just south of the equator, the Nyanga River meanders southwestward for about 250 miles (400 kilometers) to its outlet on the Atlantic in southern Gabon. The river is noted for its many rapids, especially the impressive series that is found where the Nyanga tumbles down from the highlands to the narrow coastal plain. Over the course of about 20 miles (32 kilometers), the river drops for a total of some 100 feet (30 meters), churning over rocky outcrops in foaming rapids between long stretches of calmer water.

Hemmed in at some places by narrow gorges and bordered by dense equatorial forests, the rapids are difficult to approach. No roads penetrate the dense vegetation to parallel this part of the Nyanga's course. It is pos-

NYANGA RAPIDS. *Low water reveals the rocky outcrops that transform the river into a scene of raging fury when the flow is at its peak.*

sible to descend the river by canoe or rubber raft, but the many jagged, rocky bars that cross the channel make the trip quite hazardous.

The flow of water over the rapids is somewhat variable. Like all of Gabon, the Nyanga's drainage basin receives more than 120 inches (3,000 millimeters) of rainfall each year. But most of it comes between October and May. During the dry months the river's flow abates substantially.

Even so, the year-round flow of water across the rapids is about 10,600 cubic feet (300 cubic meters) per second. Hence they have considerable potential as a site for hydroelectric power generation. But so far no attempts have been made to harness the fury of the Nyanga Rapids. They continue to flow through the steaming, sparsely populated jungle just as they have for centuries, with the roar of their frenzied waters made all the more impressive by the silence of their surroundings. ☐

Nyiragongo

● Zaire
● Map: page 26, B–3

Famed for its crater's now-vanished lake of molten lava, this African volcano remains active to this day.

The Virunga Mountains rise as a formidable barrier across the western arm of Africa's Rift Valley, a major fracture zone in the earth's crust. Located to the north of Lake Kivu, they extend west to east for about 50 miles (80 kilometers) and form part of the water divide between the Nile and Congo rivers. Lake Kivu, in fact, drained northward into the Nile until this chain of volcanic peaks began to form within the past 1 million years.

The highest of the eight major peaks in the group is Karisimbi, at 14,787 feet (4,507 meters). Its snowcapped summit, according to local legend, is the eternal resting place of the souls of

the pure and virtuous. The westernmost peak in the range and the most unusual, however, is Nyiragongo, a stratovolcano that reaches 11,385 feet (3,470 meters) above sea level. In contrast to the legends associated with Karisimbi, Nyiragongo is said to be the place where doomed souls are sent to expiate their sins.

The local people have good reason for viewing Nyiragongo with fear and foreboding. While most of the Virunga volcanoes are dormant or extinct, Nyiragongo and its neighbor, Nyamlagira, are very much alive. The youngest peaks in the group, they began to form only about 20,000 years ago and have been active ever since then. As recently as 1948, a lava flow streamed from a cone on Nyiragongo's flanks and reached all the way to the shores of Lake Kivu about 10 miles (16 kilometers) to the south. And until early 1977 it was one of the few volcanoes in the world with a lake of molten lava in its crater.

The mountain, which is now one of the attractions of Zaire's Virunga National Park, was unknown to the outside world until 1894, when it was first explored by a European. Scientists long suspected that its crater contained a pool of fiery lava: at night the plume of steam rising from its vent glowed with a reddish light. But it was not until 1948 that a scientific expedition actually confirmed the existence of the lava lake.

Much studied ever since, the lake has fluctuated dramatically in size and level over the years. In 1948 it covered an area of about 143,500 square yards (120,000 square meters) at the bottom of a deep, sheer-walled crater some 1¼ miles (2 kilometers) in diameter. By 1953 the level of the lake had subsided by 65 feet (20 meters), and it had shrunk to half its former size.

The lake's surface continued to subside until 1958, when the lava pool was reduced to a mere 22,700 square yards (19,000 square meters). That year, in conjunction with the International Geophysical Year, a scientific team made a daring descent into the crater itself and camped there for a week. Using special equipment, they discovered that the temperature of the lava on the lake's surface varied between 1800° and 2200° F (1000° and 1200° C).

By 1959 the lake had become even smaller. Although calm phases alternated with active ones between 1948 and 1959, observers found that the surface of the lake was never completely quiescent: the lava boiled constantly at two corners of the pool, forming unearthly "fountains" of fire.

A new expedition in 1966 discovered that the situation in the crater had changed radically. The lava pool by then was seething with activity, hurling out lava bombs and sending up bursts of flaming gas. A whole new supply of lava, moreover, had welled up into the pool, raising its level high above what it had been in 1948 and increasing the surface of the lake to about 200,000 square yards (170,000 square meters).

A series of violent eruptions began late in December 1976 and continued through most of January 1977. New cones were built up on Nyiragongo's flanks, and streams of amazingly fluid lava poured down the slopes. By the time this burst of activity had come to an end, the lava lake in the depths of Nyiragongo's crater was drained completely. But what the future may hold in store no one can guess. □

Major Types of Volcanic Mountains

Volcanoes are formed and behave in various ways. Stratovolcanoes are built up of alternating layers of lava and exploded debris. Shield volcanoes are broad domes formed from very fluid lava flows. In pelean volcanoes, the vents become clogged with solidified lava that is eventually blown off in violent explosions. Strombolian volcanoes are constantly active, with periodic explosive eruptions.

Pelean volcano

Stratovolcano

Strombolian volcano

Shield volcano

NYIRAGONGO. *A crust of solidified lava broken by gaping fissures is all that remains of the lake of molten magma that once filled the bottom of the African volcano's deep crater.*

Ob-Irtysh Rivers

- U.S.S.R.
- Map: page 18, H–2

In the heart of western Siberia, the lower Ob and its major tributary, the Irtysh, combine to form one of the longest waterways in the world.

From opposite slopes of the Altai Mountains in central Asia, the Ob and Irtysh rivers set out on apparently separate courses across the vast, seemingly endless expanse of the West Siberian Plain. Far downstream, however, they converge to form the fourth longest river system in the world. From the farthest headstream of the Irtysh to its junction with the Ob, and then on to their combined outlet in Ob Bay, the waterway covers a distance of 3,460 miles (5,568 kilometers).

The sources of both rivers are the numerous massive glaciers and deep lakes located high in the Altai Mountains, which straddle the borders of the Soviet Union, China, and Mongolia. From the northwestern flank of the mountains, the headstreams of the Ob descend rapidly to the great West Siberian Plain, one of the largest—and flattest—lowland areas on the earth. There are great expanses of marshy areas, and none of the hills rise more than 200 feet (60 meters) above the intervening valleys. Parts of the entire region were honed down by the great continental ice cap that covered it during the Ice Age, and deposits of glacial debris are abundant everywhere. The upper Ob itself follows an ancient glacial channel across the plain, sluggish in its flow but invaluable as a transportation artery for the thriving farmlands and manufacturing cities of western Siberia.

Meanwhile, the Irtysh rises on the Altai's southern flank in Chinese territory. Moving west across Lake Zaisan, it descends to the lowlands and meanders slowly to the northwest for a distance of 2,312 miles (3,720 kilome-

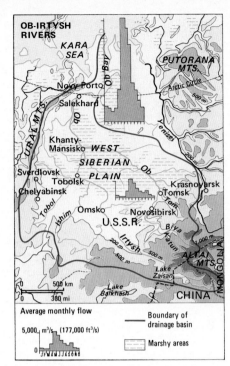

The Ob-Irtysh rivers funnel the runoff from an enormous drainage basin northward into Ob Bay. The combined flow of the two rivers increases quite drastically following the annual spring thaw.

OB-IRTYSH RIVERS. *Near Novosibirsk in southern Siberia, the Ob meanders placidly across a level, sparsely wooded lowland plain.*

OGOOUÉ RAPIDS. *Flanked by rolling hills, the Ogooué splashes over rapids in zones where it crosses outcrops of erosion-resistant rocks.*

ters) before merging with the Ob at Khanty-Mansisk. Like the Ob, it is an important transportation route.

Beyond the confluence of these two main branches, the Ob broadens drastically. In places it is up to 12 miles (19 kilometers) wide, with a network of multiple channels separated by numerous low-lying islands. At one point the river divides into two arms that flow in separate channels for more than 200 miles (320 kilometers) before reuniting.

Finally, at the Arctic Circle, the river comes to an end as it enters Ob Bay. Dropping its heavy load of sediment over the centuries, the Ob has built up a large delta at the head of the bay. Beyond, the long, narrow, and nearly landlocked Ob Bay extends approximately 500 miles (800 kilometers) northward to its outlet on the Arctic Ocean's Kara Sea.

Despite the immensity of its drainage basin, the average year-round flow of the Ob-Irtysh is the least of any river in Siberia. The flow, however, varies considerably with the season. After a low-water stage in late winter, there is a dramatic surge as the spring thaw sends torrents of water to the sea in May and June. The flow then gradually diminishes, to be followed again by the next spring flood. □

Ogooué Rapids

- Gabon
- Map: page 24, E–6

As it leaves the interior highlands in West Africa, the Ogooué River hurtles across foaming rapids on its journey to the Atlantic Ocean.

The Ogooué is the principal river of the West African republic of Gabon. Together with its tributaries, it drains almost the entire country. About 750 miles (1,200 kilometers) in length, the mainstream rises in the Congo's Batéké Plateaus, flows northwestward through densely forested uplands, and then turns southwest toward the Atlantic at Port-Gentil.

Like many West African rivers, the Ogooué raised high hopes among European explorers who hoped it might provide easy access to the continent's mysterious interior. Its broad mouth, clogged by several large islands, was first discovered in 1857. But it was not until about 1880 that Pierre Savorgnan de Brazza succeeded in tracing the river all the way to its source.

The main obstacle was the many foaming rapids that interrupt the middle course of the Ogooué. As he attempted to cross them, de Brazza lost many men in the wild, swirling water when his dugouts were shattered on treacherous rocks beneath the rapids.

Today the river is navigable year round from its mouth to the island town of Lambaréné, made famous by the mission hospital that Albert Schweitzer founded there about 110 miles (175 kilometers) inland. During high-water months it is navigable as far as the town of N'Djolé, about 40 miles (65 kilometers) upstream.

But beyond that point the river surges across innumerable rapids as it courses down from the interior uplands to the coastal plain. For mile after mile between long reaches of calm water, it churns across outcrops of erosion-resistant rock, mainly granite. In one of the most impressive sectors, the Ogooué foams through a narrow, winding gorge known as the Gates of Okanda, named for a tribe that once controlled this area.

It is possible, with the help of an experienced local boatman, to descend the Ogooué Rapids by dugout. In addition to the thrills of white-water boating, the trip is rewarding for the beauty of the surrounding countryside. On the long stretches of calm water that alternate with the rapids, travelers enjoy distant views of the rolling hills of central Gabon. □

Ojo Guareña

- Spain
- Map: page 17, C–4

Spain's longest cave is located in a limestone region honeycombed with sinkholes and subterranean corridors.

Cave explorers so far have penetrated some 30 miles (50 kilometers) of twisting passageways and chambers in the underground network at Ojo Guareña. The labyrinth, located in the Cantabrian Mountains in northern Spain, is thus the longest cave system in the country.

The cave is situated in a limestone formation that is only about 325 feet (100 meters) thick. But because it was extensively fractured by movements of the earth's crust, the limestone is riddled with fissures where water has seeped in and dissolved underground passageways. Indeed, a total of 10 cave openings exists in the immediate area; it is suspected that all are part of the same cave system, although direct links between all of them have not yet been established.

The most convenient entry to Ojo Guareña is through a broad opening known as Palomera Cave. This leads to the principal gallery, where corridors branch off in various directions. At one point visitors can look up and see daylight through a natural skylight 185 feet (56 meters) overhead. □

Old Man of Hoy

- United Kingdom (Scotland)
- Map: page 16, C–3

A "lighthouse" without a light, this towering sandstone monolith rises like a beacon off the northwest coast of the Scottish island of Hoy.

OLD MAN OF HOY. *The lofty sea stack, left standing when the rocks surrounding it were destroyed by crashing surf, will itself eventually succumb to the onslaught of the waves.*

Though not the largest, Hoy is by far the highest of the Orkney Islands, the picturesque archipelago of some 70 islands and islets clustered off the northernmost tip of Scotland. Facing the full fury of storms blowing in from the Atlantic Ocean, the western coasts of most of the islands have been eroded into towering lines of cliffs. The most impressive of all are found on the northwest coast of Hoy: at St. John's Head, one of the highest coastal cliffs in the British Isles, a wall of rock rises almost straight up for 1,141 feet (348 meters) above the crashing surf.

An equally imposing reminder of the erosive power of waves is the nearby sea stack known as the Old Man of Hoy. Only 89 feet (27 meters) across at its widest point, the isolated offshore pinnacle rises to 450 feet (137 meters). Composed of the same delicately tinted horizontal layers of sandstone as the cliffs behind it, the monolith was in fact at one time part of the line of cliffs. An intersecting network of joints (vertical fractures) in the sandstone resulted in the formation of vertical surfaces as the cliffs retreated before the onslaught of the waves. By chance, the erosion-resistant sandstone tower known as the Old Man of Hoy remained standing as the surrounding rocks crumbled away.

Yet it seems certain that the Old Man will also eventually be destroyed. Paintings, drawings, and engravings made in the 19th century show an archlike spur supporting one side of the monolith. But it has since fallen into a pile of debris. Resting on a foundation of hard volcanic rock, the Old Man of Hoy is partly protected from the waves gnawing at its base. But in time it too will disappear. □

The Formation of Inselbergs and Pediments

Inselbergs, or "island mountains," such as the Olgas are isolated masses of rock that rise abruptly above the surrounding terrain. They are typically found in tropical regions where the climate is arid today but has been much wetter at times in the past. During humid periods, weathering caused the rocks to decay unevenly and crumble into tiny fragments, especially around their bases. During dry periods the debris was removed by wind erosion and heavy seasonal storms, resulting in steep-sided, rounded domes that rise sharply above their bases. The gently sloping surface at the base of an inselberg is known as a pediment. It may merge with other pediments to form a broader surface called a pediplain. The angle between the pediment slope and the steep side of the inselberg—usually abrupt and well defined—is called the piedmont angle.

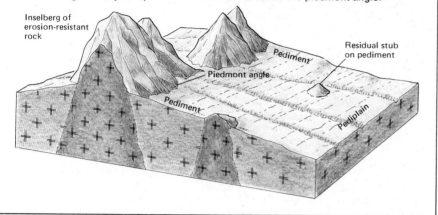

Olga, Mount

- Australia
- Map: page 22, D–4

As if huddled in self-defense, a massive group of domes rises at the center of a vast encircling plain.

In the heart of the central Australian desert, a cluster of massive, hump-backed rocks looms against the horizon. They create a slightly eerie spectacle—some 30 giant, smoothly rounded domes huddled in the midst of a vast empty plain. The highest of the group is Mount Olga, rising some 1,500 feet (460 meters) above its surroundings and 3,507 feet (1,069 meters) above sea level.

Named for the Queen of Spain by the Australian explorer Ernest Giles, who first sighted them in 1872, Mount Olga and its massive companions are known collectively as the Olgas. The group occupies an area of about 11 square miles (28 square kilometers).

MOUNT OLGA. *About 30 of these domed monoliths, known as the Olgas, rise like an archipelago above the central Australian desert.*

From a distance the Olgas at first appear only as a vague, bluish silhouette obscured by haze on the horizon. From closer vantage points, however, the individual rocky masses take form, and their true red and reddish-yellow colors become apparent. Fringed by meager vegetation, they are especially beautiful in spring, when they are set off by a brief but brilliant display of wildflowers.

Along with famed Ayers Rock, located some 20 miles (32 kilometers) to the east, the Olgas are protected in an Australian national park. And like Ayers Rock, they are spectacular examples of what geologists call inselbergs (from a German term meaning "island mountains").

The Olgas are composed of durable conglomerate, which is a type of rock made up of pebbles and boulders that are fused together much like cemented gravel. Formed approximately 400 million years ago, the mass of rock was subsequently uplifted and folded by movements in the earth's crust. It was then subjected to alternating periods of moist and dry climates and was gradually dissected into its present pattern of freestanding domes by wind and water erosion.

Some of the rounded monoliths are separated from their neighbors by nothing more than slotlike ravines; others are set apart by wider, gently sloping surfaces known as pediments. Most are bounded by steep, nearly vertical sides that rise to rounded, domelike summits.

The Olgas were long known to Australia's aborigines as Katajuta, "the mountain with many heads." According to legend, they were created in a primeval "dream time" when ancient deities first gave life and form to the earth, and their mysterious shapes were associated with many tales of supernatural beings. The continual breeze in the so-called Valley of the Winds, for example, was explained as the breath of a sacred serpent that could transform the breeze into a hurricane in order to punish evildoers.

Even today the size and austere beauty of the Olgas can scarcely fail to summon up images of titanic, elemental forces. Indeed, such was the reaction of Ernest Giles. Upon seeing them for the first time, he wrote: "There they have stood as huge memorials from the ancient times of the earth, for ages, countless eons of ages, since creation first had birth." □

Olot Volcanic Field

- Spain
- Map: page 17, D–4

Masked beneath a mantle of forests, many of the hills on this Spanish plain are actually extinct volcanoes.

The city of Olot, near the foot of the Pyrenees in northeastern Spain, is surrounded by a broad undulating plain. Though tranquil today, the region's fertile farmlands and wooded hills were once the site of intense volcanic activity. In all, more than 30 principal volcanic cones loom above their surroundings in the Olot Volcanic Field.

The volcanoes are all quite young. Although the most recent eruption occurred in the 15th century, most were formed about 1 million years ago. Occasional earth tremors continue to testify to the geological instability of the region, however. In 1427 a violent earthquake completely destroyed the city of Olot, while more recent quakes shook the area in 1901 and 1902.

Dense green forests mask the contours of many of the volcanic cones, but the basic forms of most are remarkably well preserved. The largest, Santa Margarita, has a crater some 1,600 feet (500 meters) in diameter. Another, Montescopa, to the north of Olot, has a perfectly preserved crater some 50 feet (15 meters) deep and 325 feet (100 meters) across. It is formed of scoria (volcanic cinders), lapilli (hardened lava droplets), and large fragments of porous lava. Yet another of the volcanoes, Garrinada, is noted for its magnetic properties. The high iron content of its compact bluish lava causes a compass needle to be deflected by up to 4°.

Nearby, several dozen smaller, secondary volcanic cones have been reduced by erosion to form a particularly strange landscape. Elsewhere, erosion of basaltic lava flows has exposed prismatic columnar formations with "organ-pipe" jointing and produced a series of flat-topped, steep-sided mesas. The village of Castellfullit de la Roca is perched at the edge of a cliff atop one of these mesas, overlooking the surrounding plain.

Now that the volcanoes are apparently extinct, residents of the area continue to benefit from their past activity. Watered by abundant rainfall, the fertile volcanic soils of Olot have become rich, productive farmlands. □

OLOT VOLCANIC FIELD. *Once the scene of fiery volcanic activity, the crater of the Santa Margarita volcano now provides a peaceful setting for a humble little country chapel.*

OLYMPUS. *The austere, seemingly unapproachable summit of the mountain was revered by ancient Greeks as the site of the throne of Zeus.*

Olympus

- Greece
- Map: page 17, F–4

Seemingly ageless and unchanging, the highest peak in Greece is one of the world's younger mountains.

The steep slopes of the great massif known as Olympus rise abruptly from the shores of the Aegean Sea in northern Greece. Sometimes covered by snow, the craggy summit culminates in a jagged crest, Mytikas ("The Needle"), at 9,570 feet, or 2,917 meters.

Besides being the highest mountain in Greece, Olympus is one of the most famous in the western world. Since time immemorial its lofty summit has had the power to stir the human imagination. To the ancient Greeks it was the dwelling place of their entire pantheon of gods, and on its heights was perched the throne of Zeus, the mightiest of deities.

Even stripped of the aura of mythology, Olympus remains one of the most beautiful and fascinating of all Mediterranean mountains. The entire massif, about 25 miles (40 kilometers) in length, completely dominates the landscapes of Thessaly to the south and much of Macedonia to the north.

Gently rounded in some places and elsewhere marked by sheer walls and steep ravines, its lower slopes are covered by green forests that give way to barren, windswept heights where snow lingers in the crevices even through the summer.

Although Olympus was long the object of veneration, its geological origins remained an enigma until quite recently. It is now believed that the thick beds of limestone and dolomite that make up the bulk of the mountain accumulated over tens of millions of years at the bottom of a shallow sea. The rocks remained undisturbed until about 65 million years ago, when this part of the world was convulsed by a violent upheaval of the earth's crust. In the process a great mass of gneiss, schist, and serpentine that had formed deep below the surface was displaced and thrust into position on top of the limestone and dolomite.

There was no mountain yet. Until about 2 million years ago the limestone remained hidden beneath the covering of other rocks. Then, in another great upheaval, the entire mass bowed into an arched formation and was broken by many faults as it was thrust up to towering heights.

Erosion then set in and stripped away much of the covering layer of gneiss, schist, and serpentine. (Remnants of this former cover persist only in the foothills that ring the central massif.) Exposed at last, the core of limestone and dolomite was finally carved to its present contours. Thus, although the rocks that form it are very old, Olympus itself came into being only yesterday in terms of the long history of the earth. ☐

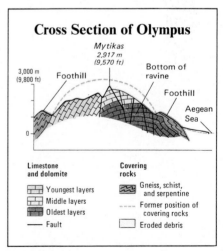

The famous massif of Olympus was formed by the uplift of a mass of limestone and dolomite that was originally covered by a layer of other rocks. Except in the surrounding foothills, these covering rocks have been completely eroded away.

Ombla of Dubrovnik

- Yugoslavia
- Map: page 17, E–4

Water flowing from the mountains through underground channels emerges at this large seaside spring.

For centuries a large spring has bubbled from the base of a limestone cliff near the ancient walled city of Dubrovnik on Yugoslavia's picturesque Dalmatian Coast. The spot was once a favorite haunt of noblemen who built impressive summer villas along the short inlet that carries the overflow from the spring to the Adriatic Sea. But although the spring was widely known for its exceptionally attractive setting, no one could explain the source of its cool, clear water.

Modern-day scientists have used dyes to solve the mystery of the so-called Ombla of Dubrovnik. By adding dyes to rivers where they disappear into sinkholes and noting where the colored water reappears at the surface, they have traced the courses of a number of underground streams in the area. Much of the water supplying the Ombla, they discovered, originates in the Trebisnica River. Flowing through the limestone Dinaric Alps northeast of the city, it is one of the largest disappearing rivers in all the world. Several other rivers disappearing into sinkholes in the mountains far from Dubrovnik have also been found to contribute to the discharge from the Ombla.

The Ombla is a classic example of a resurgent spring, one in which water infiltrating a limestone massif passes through underground channels and reappears at the surface. Supplied by several subterranean sources, its flow is plentiful and dependable at any time of year. ☐

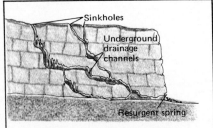

A resurgent spring such as the Ombla of Dubrovnik is the point where surface water reappears after vanishing into sinkholes and draining through underground channels in limestone.

OMETEPE ISLAND. *Deeply furrowed by ravines, the forested slopes of one of the island's two volcanoes are revealed by a break in the clouds that wreathe its lofty summit.*

Ometepe Island

- Nicaragua
- Map: page 13, D–3

The largest island in the largest lake in Central America is made up of the soaring, nearly symmetrical cones of two almost identical volcanoes.

Hundreds of islands dot the tranquil surface of Lake Nicaragua, the largest lake in Central America. (Spanish conquistadores called it Mar Dulce, the "freshwater sea.") But all of them are dwarfed by the soaring profile of Ometepe Island, which is composed of two nearly identical volcanic cones linked by a narrow isthmus.

The larger of the two is the volcano Concepción, in the northwestern part of the island. About 10 miles (16 kilometers) in diameter at the base, its beautifully symmetrical cone slopes up to a crater at 5,282 feet (1,610 meters). To the southeast is its twin peak, Madera. Some 7 miles (11 kilometers) across, Madera's cone reaches 4,015 feet (1,224 meters).

Located in a zone of intense volcanic activity, the two mountains are part of a long chain of volcanoes that were built up over the past 2 million years. (Although Madera is extinct, Concepción still shows signs of intermittent activity.) Indeed, Lake Nicaragua itself is believed to have once been a broad bay of the Pacific that was finally separated from the ocean by a "dam" of volcanic mountains.

The island, inhabited since pre-Columbian times, is now a center for the production of coffee, tobacco, and other crops. But its greatest asset is its exceptional beauty. Even the English pirate Edward Hume, after sacking the lakeside city of Granada, declared that his loot was worth nothing compared to the sight of Ometepe and its lovely setting. ☐

Omo River

- Ethiopia
- Map: page 25, G–5

The remote African river is noted for the fossils of man's ancestors that have been found in its broad valley.

From its source in the central highlands of Ethiopia to its outlet in Lake Turkana (formerly Lake Rudolf) on the Kenya border, the Omo River flows a total of only about 400 miles (650 kilometers). Yet it is one of the truly great wild rivers of the world. Until 1973, no boat had ever traveled the length of its upper course, and it remains to this day a pristine, rarely visited wilderness.

Rising in a mountainous region to the west of Addis Ababa, the Omo River begins its tumultuous descent across long stretches of foaming rapids that are hemmed in by narrow, winding gorges. In places the walls rise almost straight up in breathtaking lines of cliffs. Waterfalls plunge over the brink where tributaries enter the mainstream, and lush green vegetation crowns the heights.

Eventually the canyons give way to rolling hills where primitive tribesmen live as they have for centuries. Hippopotamuses throng in the pools and crocodiles lurk on the banks. At Omo National Park, the river wanders over plains inhabited by a splendid concentration of wildlife ranging from elands and zebras to warthogs and ostriches. Finally the Omo meanders across dry, rough bush before spilling its silty orange-brown water into the green expanse of Lake Turkana.

Though rugged and forbidding, the lower part of the Omo Valley is especially fascinating. Fossil remains of the ancient ancestors of modern man have been found entombed in its thick deposits of sediment and volcanic ash. Up to 1,600 feet (500 meters) thick in places, the sediments accumulated along the shores at a time when Lake Turkana was much larger and deeper than it is today.

The first fossil finds in the area were made by a French expedition in 1901, but the most significant discoveries were made by an international team of archeologists between 1967 and 1975. Their finds ranged from the jawbone of a humanlike individual of the genus *Australopithecus* estimated to be 2½ million years old to the remains of true humans, *Homo sapiens,* more than 100,000 years old. Crude, sharp-edged quartz tools, apparently carried to the site from a deposit several miles away, were found along with the skeletal remains. And as investigations continue, it seems likely that the Omo Valley and other nearby areas will yield even more clues to the ancestry of modern mankind. ☐

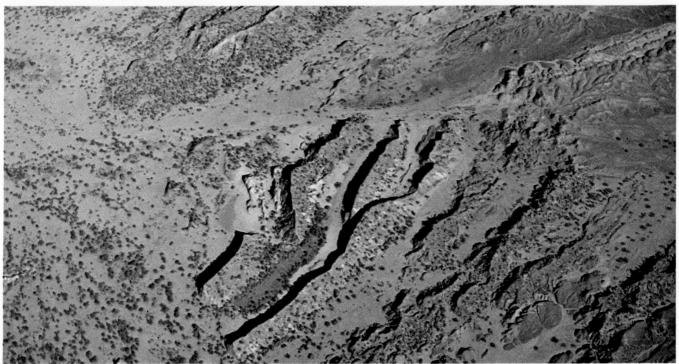

OMO RIVER. *Though arid and inhospitable today, the lower Omo Valley has been the home of man and his ancestors for millions of years.*

Optimists' Cave

- U.S.S.R.
- Map: page 18, D–4

Named by optimists who hoped they had discovered a major cave, this huge labyrinth has proved to be the longest cave in the Soviet Union.

Optimists' Cave is located in the Ukraine in the southwestern U.S.S.R., just a short distance north of the Rumanian border. Exploration of the cave, which was completely unknown before 1966, has led to the revision of one of the basic assumptions of cave science.

Unlike most major cave systems, which are usually formed in limestone, Optimists' Cave was dissolved from a layer of gypsum about 100 feet (30 meters) thick. Since gypsum is so soft (it can be scratched even with a fingernail), scientists long assumed that it was too fragile to support great caverns. They believed that any openings dissolved in gypsum would soon collapse.

Optimists' Cave proved the experts wrong. By 1976 a total of 68 miles (109 kilometers) of passageways had been discovered in the underground labyrinth, making this the longest cave in the U.S.S.R. and one of the longest in the world. And exploration of the cave is not yet complete.

Most of the galleries in the network are about 10 feet (3 meters) wide and 5 feet (1½ meters) high, with flat ceilings. But in places where passageways intersect, some of them are as much as 33 feet (10 meters) high, and the ceilings are in the form of arches. Several chambers, including one that is 260 feet (80 meters) long and 80 feet (25 meters) wide, are among the largest ever found in a gypsum cave.

Because the gypsum bed enclosing Optimists' Cave is capped by a thin layer of limestone, seepage of underground water has decorated parts of the labyrinth with typical calcite cave formations. But the most beautiful are the formations composed of gypsum crystals and tinted in a variety of colors by the presence of mineral salts. Most impressive of all are the cave's many gypsum rosettes—large flower-like clusters of gypsum crystals that have been colored an opaque black by manganese oxide. □

Ordesa Valley

- Spain
- Map: page 17, D–4

Hidden high in the Pyrenees is a glacier-carved masterpiece of sheer cliffs, sparkling cascades, and elegantly geometric rock forms.

The Ordesa Valley is nestled high in the Aragonese Pyrenees, the central section of the mountain chain that separates the Iberian Peninsula from the rest of Europe. Although it is considered today to be one of the most beautiful spots in Spain, it was not discovered until 1820, when a Frenchman exploring the heights of Monte Perdido first noticed the great glacier-carved trench extending off to the west. But the valley was so inaccessible that nearly a century passed before it was mapped in detail.

Since 1918, however, the entire valley has been protected in Ordesa National Park. About 7 miles (11 kilometers) long, it is flanked on both sides by sheer limestone cliffs. Elegantly sculpted rock forms, dense forests, meadows, waterfalls, wildflowers, and rare mountain wildlife all contribute to the park's scenic splendor. No longer isolated and unknown, the valley is often described as "the paradise of the Pyrenees."

Like France's famed Cirque de Gavarnie on the other side of the high ridge that forms the international border to the north of the park, the Ordesa Valley is a fine example of glacier-carved scenery. Where the Río Arazas now tumbles across waterfalls

ORDESA VALLEY. *Sheer limestone cliffs flank the entire length of the remote Spanish valley. Protected as a national park, it attracts visitors from far and wide.*

along the length of the valley, rivers of ice once ground slowly westward.

These glaciers originated on the southwestern flanks of the mountain group known as Las Tres Sorores ("The Three Sisters"). The central peak in the group and the highest in the area is Monte Perdido, at 11,007 feet (3,355 meters). Plucking out the bedrock, the glaciers hollowed out the big basinlike amphitheater, or cirque, known as the Circo de Soaso, that hems in the head of the valley. Then, as they proceeded westward, the glaciers deepened the valley floor and steepened its walls, carving the U-shaped profile that is characteristic of glacial valleys.

Today waterfalls plunge down the walls of the Circo de Soaso, including one known as La Cola de Caballo ("The Horse's Tail"). Merging on the floor of the cirque, the streams form the Río Arazas, which flows west through the heart of the valley. In places its course is interrupted by steplike outcrops of limestone that result in picturesque cascades. Steep lines of cliffs rise to the north and south, backed by fortresslike mountain bastions. All along the way, deciduous forests in the valley give way to coniferous forests on higher slopes, which are replaced in turn by mountain meadows filled with rhododendrons and wildflowers.

The Arazas's brief journey ends at the mouth of the valley, where it flows into the southbound Río Ara. It is there that two great stone ramparts, the cliffs of Mondarruego and Duáscaro, rise to form the majestic natural gateway to the Ordesa Valley.   □

CAPE ORSO. *Attacked by an unusual process known as honeycomb weathering, a great bear-shaped boulder on top of the cape appears to be the creation of a master sculptor.*

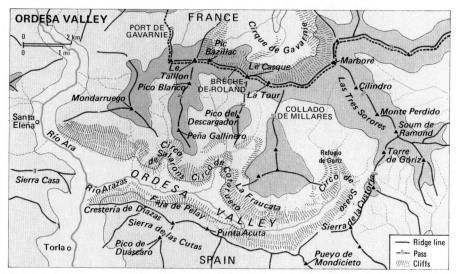

Surrounded on every side by high peaks of the Pyrenees and walled in by nearly vertical cliffs, the Ordesa Valley is an outstanding example of a typical glacier-carved trench.

Orso, Cape

- Italy (Sardinia)
- Map: page 17, D–4

A subtle sculptor—dew condensed from the cool night air—has shaped an amazing stone bear atop this headland on the coast of Sardinia.

Capo d'Orso, the "Cape of the Bear," is a high granite headland near the northeastern tip of the Mediterranean island of Sardinia. The reason for the name is immediately obvious to anyone who climbs the rugged flight of steps to the summit of Cape Orso from the nearby village of Palau. Perched at the top, overlooking a maze of islands in the Strait of Bonifacio, is an astonishingly realistic natural stone sculpture that looks exactly like a huge standing bear. Seeming to gaze across the panorama of land and sea that stretches north to the neighboring French island of Corsica, the great stone bear is a unique attraction on an island that is noted for its variety of scenery.

Both the bear and the deep concave depressions that pock the surfaces of surrounding rocks were long thought to be the result of wind erosion and the corrosive action of salt spray. Today geologists attribute their formation to a process known as honeycomb weathering. The hemispherical pits and cavities that dot the surface of the rock are called tafoni, from a Corsican word meaning "hole" or "hollow." Under ideal conditions, tafoni may grow to the size of caves big enough to hold several people.

This special type of erosion typically takes place in climates that are both warm and dry. It characteristically attacks rocks with a crystalline struc-

ture, such as the granite at Cape Orso.

The erosive agent that carves the tafoni is water, but water in a gentle ephemeral form: the dew that condenses on rock surfaces at night. There it chemically decomposes the rock. On bright sunlit surfaces, the moisture quickly evaporates in the morning and the dissolved minerals are redeposited as a surface crust. But in shaded areas the moisture persists well into the day, loosening tiny fragments of rock that fall off and are blown away.

As the weathering process continues through the centuries, the hollows are gradually enlarged and sometimes assume bizarre forms. Neighboring Corsica, for example, is famous for its well-developed tafoni, and in the coastal desert area of Chile the Rocks of Caldera have been shaped into many grotesque forms. But rarely has the process of honeycomb weathering produced such an instantly recognizable sculptural form as the giant bear standing guard over Cape Orso. □

Oum er Rbia, Forty Springs of the

- Morocco
- Map: page 24, C–2

In a lush North African valley, springs of cool water bubble from the rocks to feed a rushing river.

The Oum er Rbia, the principal river of Morocco, rises high up in the Atlas Mountains in the central part of the country. It flows southwest, then northwest, for 345 miles (555 kilometers) to its outlet on the Atlantic near Casablanca. More regular in its flow than any other Moroccan river, the Oum er Rbia has been dammed in several places for irrigation and power generation. Part of the reason for its dependable flow is to be found near its headwaters. Cool and crystal clear, the river is fed by innumerable springs as it flows through a deep valley filled with forests of cedar that remain lush and refreshing even in the scorching heat of summer.

Although this area is known as Les Quarante Sources ("The Forty Springs") of the Oum er Rbia, the name is probably an understatement, because no one knows precisely the number of springs that nourish the river. Water seems to gush forth everywhere: springs bubble up from shallow pools, pour from crevices in the rock, and spill over the walls of natural terracelike dams. And for almost 12 miles (20 kilometers) downstream, countless other springs and trickles along the banks add to the river's flow.

The origin of all this water is in a limestone basin in the mountains beyond the river's source. As is true of limestone in so many areas, the rock is honeycombed with underground drainage channels. They were formed over tens of thousands of years as surface water seeped in through crevices and dissolved the limestone to form the network of channels.

Water from the sporadic torrential rains and melting snow continues to infiltrate the channels. But eventually it meets a sloping layer of impermeable rock beneath the limestone formation. Channeled along the surface of the impermeable rock, it escapes again to daylight where the rocks outcrop in the valley of the Oum er Rbia. Hence the countless lovely springs that issue from the earth at Les Quarante Sources. □

OUM ER RBIA. *Many of the river's "Forty Springs" spill into terraced pools behind travertine barriers that were built up by deposition of dissolved minerals in the spring water.*

Pamir

- Central Asia
- Map: page 18, I–5

Seldom seen by outsiders, this harsh mountainous region is sometimes described as "the roof of the world."

The remote, rugged region known as the Pamir, or sometimes the Pamirs, is a high, mountainous plateau. Most of it lies in the U.S.S.R., but it also extends across the borders into China and Afghanistan. An austere landscape of steep peaks, knife-edged ridges, and high mountain valleys lashed by violent winds, it is often referred to as "the roof of the world."

Several mountain ranges converge on the tangle of peaks that make up the Pamir. The Kunlun Mountains and the Karakoram Range sweep in from the east and the southeast, the Hindu Kush from the southwest, and the mighty Tien Shan from the northeast. In the Pamir, where they all meet, they form an intricate aggregation of mountains and plateaus, including more than 100 peaks that exceed

20,000 feet (6,100 meters) and immense valleys at elevations of more than 12,000 feet (3,700 meters). The highest peak in the region, and the highest point in the entire U.S.S.R., is Communism Peak, at 24,590 feet (7,495 meters).

The name Pamir is thought to be based on a Persian term meaning "the foot of mountain peaks." This is believed to refer to the broad high-altitude valleys where, despite the harsh climate and scanty vegetation, native Kirghiz people graze their flocks of sheep and goats.

The Pamir is composed of many rocks of various ages. Metamorphic rocks such as gneiss and marble predominate to the north, while farther south there are limestone, sandstone, and other sedimentary rocks. All were uplifted within the past 100 million years and then subjected to intense erosion that steepened the slopes and carved valleys along major fault lines. The most drastic sculpting occurred during the Ice Age, when the entire Pamir was buried beneath an ice cap.

Although the ice cap has long since disappeared, the climate remains very harsh. In winter, temperatures often fall below –58°F (–50°C), and violent winds are commonplace. Snow covers the highest peaks all year round, nourishing more than 1,000 glaciers that persist on the slopes. Among the other phenomena reminiscent of arc-

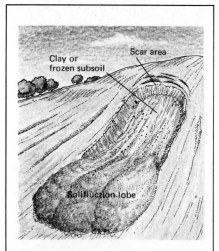

Solifluction is the process by which waterlogged soil slides slowly downhill. It typically occurs in arctic and high-altitude regions, such as the Pamir, when the surface soil thaws in spring and slides downward on underlying clay or frozen subsoil.

tic regions are so-called solifluction lobes—masses of saturated surface soil that slides downslope when it thaws.

The rugged terrain and severe winters make much of the Pamir uninhabitable. Even so, ancient trade routes were forged across it centuries ago. The name of one illustrious traveler who used them is borne today by a mountain dweller native to the Pamir: the Marco Polo sheep. □

PAMIR. *Lines of sharp-edged, glacier-honed peaks rise above broad, flat intervening valleys in this remote mountainous region of Asia.*

Pamukkale

- Turkey
- Map: page 18, D–5

Like a frozen cascade, the stepped terraces of Pamukkale descend the slope of a Turkish mountainside. Romans visited the spot, and tourists still come to admire its beauty.

From a distance the fantastic rock formations of Pamukkale in south-western Turkey resemble a castle built of snow and ice. Tier upon tier, the dazzling white ramparts and parapets descend for more than 300 feet (90 meters) down a rugged mountainside. On closer inspection, however, the steplike series of overlapping basins looks more like a gigantic waterfall petrified by some mysterious, awesome force of nature.

And that in fact is closer to the truth, for the strange rocks of Pamukkale are the improbable handiwork of hot springs. Farther up the mountainside springs bubble from the earth, issuing a stream of water with a temperature of about 110° F (43° C) and a very high concentration of dissolved mineral salts. For longer than anyone can guess, the water has been flowing down the slope, cooling, evaporating, and depositing the dissolved minerals. Bit by bit, the walls of the many-stepped rocky terraces and basins took their present form.

For centuries the spring water has been prized for its therapeutic properties. In ancient times the Romans built a thermal resort, Hierapolis, nearby. Today a modern tourist resort stands on the same spot. □

PAMUKKALE. *Overlapping tiers of snow-white rocky basins adorn a Turkish mountainside. The creation of bubbling hot springs, they were formed of minerals dissolved in the water.*

Papandayan

- Indonesia
- Map: page 21, E–5

Sulfurous fumes and deep rumblings provide constant reminders that this Java volcano is far from extinct.

The Indonesian island of Java fully deserves its reputation as "the land of volcanoes." From one end to the other it is covered by literally dozens of volcanic cones, some active, others apparently extinct.

One of the smoldering giants is Papandayan, with its cone rising some 6,400 feet (1,950 meters) above the adjacent plain. Its eruptive center has changed many times in its long history. At present four major craters can be distinguished, as well as four groups of smaller vents. The largest crater has a diameter of 3,600 feet (1,100 meters). Solfataras (vents emitting sulfurous gas and vapors) are still very active in one of the craters. Temperatures of more than 900°F (480°C) have been recorded in some of these vents.

Papandayan's last major eruption took place in August 1772, when a disastrous explosion annihilated 40 villages, killing thousands. Today the volcano is relatively quiescent. Even so, it remains under surveillance. The continued venting of steam and pungent fumes, as well as the deep rumblings that occasionally shake the mountain, is a grim reminder that Papandayan's inner fires still burn. □

PAPANDAYAN. *In one of the volcano's craters, clouds of scalding fumes and vapors escape from openings among the broken blocks of lava.*

Paricutín

- Mexico
- Map: page 12, B–3

On an afternoon in February 1943, this volcano sprang into being in the middle of a Mexican cornfield.

Earthquakes heralded the birth of the volcano Paricutín. All through the month of February 1943 they grew in numbers and intensity, alarming the residents of the little village of Paricutín, about 200 miles (320 kilometers) west of Mexico City.

The actual birth occurred on the afternoon of February 20 before the eyes of a farmer, Dionisio Pulido, and his family as they worked in their cornfield. For quite some time a small fissure in the field had been slowly growing longer. Suddenly the ground began to shake. The surface of the land around the fissure rose, and a hissing cloud of ashes, smoke, and sulfurous fumes began to pour from the vent. By evening the rising cloud of smoke was visible in Paricutín, and during the night red-hot rocks were seen shooting into the air.

The volcano grew with amazing speed, and geologists from all over the world rushed to the site for the opportunity to study a volcano from its birth. Within 24 hours of the first eruption, the remote Mexican cornfield was covered by a cone of ashes 165 feet (50 meters) high. Before long lava also began to escape from the vent and spread over the surrounding countryside. Within a week Paricutín's cone reached a height of about 500 feet (150 meters).

Activity continued without cease in the weeks that followed. Incandescent rocks were hurled into the air, providing a constant display of fireworks, and ashes from Paricutín fell as far away as Mexico City. By April an advancing lava flow forced the evacuation of Paricutín, and in June another village three miles (five kilometers) from the volcano also had to be abandoned completely.

Particularly violent eruptions occurred in July and August. Then in October a subsidiary vent opened on the side of the main cone and added more lava to the flood. For the next two months or so, Paricutín remained comparatively calm while its off-spring, named Sapichu, continued with violent eruptions. When Sapichu died down, the fireworks resumed in the main cone. By year's end Paricutín had grown to a height of about 900 feet (275 meters).

Intermittent, sometimes explosive eruptions continued in the years that followed. At times huge chunks of rock and lava were hurled from the vent and landed as far as two miles (three kilometers) away. Activity increased notably in 1951, with dozens of explosions occurring daily.

Then, just as suddenly as it had begun, Paricutín's activity abruptly ended. The last lava flow died out on February 25, 1952, just 9 years, 4 days, and 12 hours after the volcano first sprang to life. The rim of its crater by then stood 1,345 feet (410 meters) above the remains of Señor Pulido's cornfield. Its lava flows had covered an area of 10 square miles (25 square kilometers) and had engulfed two villages and hundreds of homes. But the greatest significance of Paricutín was not the destruction it caused. It offered scientists a rare opportunity to study the life of a volcano from its first breath to its last gasp. □

FJORDS OF PATAGONIA. *Chiseled peaks and lingering patches of snow are reminders of the great glaciers that once blanketed the area.*

Patagonia, Fjords of

- Chile
- Map: page 15, B–8

Assaulted by the elements down through the ages, a long expanse of coastline provides a magnificent display of the handiwork of nature.

The mere mention of fjords usually conjures up images of the majestic coast of Norway, scalloped by long, narrow, glacier-carved inlets of the sea that are flanked by steep slopes and snowy peaks. Yet Scandinavia has no monopoly on such landscapes: the coasts of Alaska and New Zealand's South Island, for example, are indented by numerous beautiful fjords.

Equally imposing though less well known is the incredibly complex maze of fjords that ornament the western coast of Patagonia. (European explorers, impressed by the large feet, or *patagones,* of the native inhabitants, named the entire tapering southern tip of South America Patagonia.) Here the high spine of the Andes forms the boundary between Chile and Argentina as it dwindles down to disappear beneath the sea south of the large island of Tierra del Fuego.

To the east of the mountains, in Argentina, broad semiarid plateaus gradually give way to coastal lowlands. The narrow ribbon of land on the Chilean side of the mountains has a totally different look. There the mountains plunge steeply down to the Pacific. All along the coast, land and water intermingle in a convoluted labyrinth of long deep fjords, winding channels, and mazelike clusters of offshore islands.

In this area far south of the equator, the mountaintops are still covered by sizable remnants of the massive ice cap that blanketed the Andes during the Ice Age. Throughout the year, raw, piercing winds whip the surf and carry moisture-laden masses of Pacific air inland. Torrential rains drench the coastal lowlands, and heavy snows constantly replenish the snowfields and glaciers that glisten brilliantly among the sharp peaks. The long white tongues of valley glaciers seem to descend from the clouds themselves, cutting through dark evergreen forests, and in many cases descending right down to sea level. From time to time in this sparsely populated region, the profound silence of a fjord is shattered as a massive iceberg splits from the end of a glacier and crashes into the sea.

Spectacular though they are, however, the glaciers that remain today give only a hint of the awesome rivers of ice that carved the complex network of fjords in Patagonia. During the Ice Age, which ended scarcely 10,000 years ago, glaciers advanced and retreated repeatedly on the slopes of the Andes. And with each advance they scoured deeper and deeper trenches into the bedrock, eventually fashioning the broad U-shaped troughs that distinguish glacial valleys from the V-shaped valleys carved by mountain rivers. By the time the climate warmed and the glaciers began their final retreat, many of the valleys extended hundreds and even thousands of feet below present sea level. The enormous volume of meltwater in turn raised the

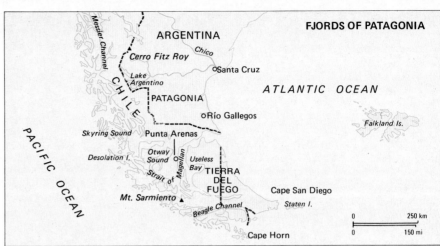

FJORDS OF PATAGONIA

How Valley Glaciers Remodel the Landscape

Valley glaciers form where snow and ice accumulate at valley heads and move downslope to the glacial snouts, where they waste away. They carve cirques (bowllike basins at valley heads) and shape high peaks into horns and arêtes (sharp ridges). Crevasses form as they pass over basins and ridges on the valley floors. Eroded debris is carried downslope as lateral moraines (along the sides) and medial moraines (where two glaciers merge). Glacial snouts leave debris in terminal moraines, and then in recessional moraines as they retreat upslope. Streamlined hills of debris are called drumlins, while boulders dropped far from their origin are called erratics.

1. Valley Head	6. Crevasses	11. Subglacial stream
2. Arête	7. Water pocket	12. Drumlins
3. Accumulation zone	8. Rock basin	13. Recessional moraine
4. Lateral moraine	9. Subglacial ridge	14. Erratics
5. Medial moraine	10. Glacial snout	15. Terminal moraine

level of the oceans all around the world and flooded the glacial trenches with seawater.

So the fjords of Patagonia came into being, carved by the same forces that created the better known but scarcely more spectacular fjords of Norway. Many of them penetrate far inland, with their high, nearly vertical walls decorated here and there by shimmering waterfalls. Elsewhere a grid of smaller channels cuts across the fjords at various angles, creating the complex chain of islands and archipelagoes that stretches along the coast.

The clutter of islands and tortuous channels, compounded by the effects of sudden violent storms, makes the area extraordinarily treacherous for navigation. Many of the vivid place names—Anxious Point, Desolation Island, Port Famine, Useless Bay, and others—are grim reminders of the hardships and tragedies that have been endured there. Yet it is this same mixture of land and sea, swirling mists and snowcapped peaks, that accounts for the harsh grandeur and austere beauty of the fjords of Patagonia. □

Pátzcuaro, Lake

- Mexico
- Map: page 12, B–3

Its tranquil beauty and abundance of fine fish have made this lovely lake a favorite Mexican tourist attraction.

Several lakes dot the high plateau to the northwest of Mexico City. One of the prettiest, most visitors agree, is Lake Pátzcuaro, about 150 miles (240 kilometers) west of the capital. Indeed, its name in the local Tarascan Indian language means "place of delight."

More or less horseshoe-shaped, the lake is about 14 miles (23 kilometers) long and covers an area of 100 square miles (260 square kilometers). Much of the beauty of the lake results from its tranquil setting. Well watered by moist winds blowing in from the Pacific, the gently rolling slopes along the shores are a mosaic of green pasturelands, forests, and cornfields. In the distance, rising high against the sky, are about 20 volcanoes, some of them ancient and deeply eroded, others much younger, with their graceful conical forms still intact. (The famous volcano Paricutín is located about 50 miles, or 80 kilometers, to the west.)

In addition to forming a pleasing background for the lake, the volcanoes are responsible for its very existence.

Like some of the other lakes in the region, Lake Pátzcuaro was formed when massive lava flows from the volcanoes formed a barrier that acted as a natural dam.

But the volcanoes are dormant now, and the area has been inhabited for centuries. The sleepy lakeside village of Tzintzuntzán (the name means "place of the hummingbirds") was the site of the capital of the Tarascan Indians long before the arrival of Europeans. Ruins of some of their distinctive, T-shaped temples can still be seen nearby.

On a slope overlooking the southern shore of the lake is the town of Pátzcuaro. Noted for its 16th-century colonial atmosphere, it is considered one of the most picturesque small towns in Mexico. It is especially lively on market days, when Indians from all around the lake come to offer lacquerware and other goods for sale.

Elsewhere little fishing villages huddle along the shore and on some of the islands that seem to float on the calm blue water. Among the most popular destinations for tourists is the island of Janitzio. In addition to the charming buildings that line its steep cobbled streets, it offers unforgettable views of the mountains and of the lake where fishermen ply the waters in long slim dugouts just as they have for many generations. ☐

Pen-Hir Point

- France
- Map: page 17, C–4

Thousands of years of storms and raging seas have sculpted this point of land overlooking the Atlantic.

The remote and wave-beaten coast of Brittany, the westernmost section of France, is an intricate maze of bays, promontories, and offshore islands. Among the most remarkable promontories is Crozon Peninsula, a tongue of land jutting far out into the Atlantic. Near its tip the peninsula branches into three separate arms, each bordered by high sandstone cliffs.

The central and westernmost prong of the peninsula culminates in Pen-Hir Point. There the land drops away to the sea in jagged, nearly vertical cliffs as much as 230 feet (70 meters) in height. Offshore, eroded remnants of the peninsula project up from the water like the tops of craggy pyramids.

For countless centuries, bombardment by the elements has gnawed away at the rocks and carved their picturesque contours. Tidal fluctuations in this area are among the greatest in Europe. The weather can also be extreme, whipping up storms that lash the land mercilessly, sending mountainous seas against the cliffs.

LAKE PÁTZCUARO. *Distant, gently sloping volcanic peaks overlook the rippled surface of the lake, dammed up by ancient lava flows.*

Perce Rock

- Canada (Quebec)
- Map: page 11, F–4

Like a ship run aground, the famous rock lies just offshore near the tip of Quebec's lovely Gaspé Peninsula.

Just south of the entrance to the St. Lawrence estuary, a great lobe of land, the Gaspé Peninsula, points across the Gulf of St. Lawrence toward Newfoundland. Famed for its extraordinary natural beauty, it is a popular tourist destination. And for most visitors, a highlight of the drive along the road that skirts the entire coastline is the view of Percé Rock.

The great limestone bastion looms like a stranded ship just a short distance offshore from the picturesque fishing village of Percé. Bounded by sheer russet-colored cliffs, the rock is 1,420 feet (433 meters) long. From a height of 288 feet (88 meters) on the landward end, its top slopes down to 160 feet (49 meters) at the offshore end. Striated by deep grooves and indented by alcoves, it is penetrated by one giant wave-carved arch about 60 feet (18 meters) high. (The monolith's name in French, Rocher Percé, means "pierced rock.")

Percé Rock does not stand alone. Just beyond it is a smaller rock, the Obelisk, also pierced by an arch. Standing still farther offshore is the much larger mass of Bonaventure Island. Bounded by cliffs 300 feet (90 meters) high, its top is virtually inaccessible to all but the seabirds that flock there to nest.

The arch that penetrates Percé Rock hints at the origin of all three of these formations. Bonaventure Island, the Obelisk, and Percé Rock are all eroded remnants of the Shickshock Mountains, a northern range of the Appalachians that here dip down into the sea. At one time all three may have been connected to each other and to the mainland as a great promontory extending into the Gulf of St. Lawrence. Attacked by storms and raging seas, the promontory may well have been pierced by many arches that later collapsed, separating the peninsula into a number of islands that later were leveled by erosion. As recently as the 16th century, chroniclers referred to other arches in the vicinity of Percé Rock—arches that have since disappeared.

But as long as they remain standing, Percé Rock and Bonaventure Island will be more than just scenes of beauty. Both are protected as bird sanctuaries. Herring gulls and cormorants are the most numerous nesters on Percé Rock. And among the birds that swarm over Bonaventure Island is the largest colony of gannets in North America. □

PEN-HIR POINT. *Beyond the tip of the wave-carved peninsula, a craggy line of islets seems to be marching out to sea.*

The results of this assault might have been less impressive had the rocks that make up Pen-Hir Point been more uniform. But because of differences in resistance to erosion and because of fractures in the sandstone, nature has shaped the point into a spectacular combination of cliffs, sea caves, and jagged islets. □

PERCÉ ROCK. *Pierced by a wave-carved arch that accounts for its name, the rock is a sanctuary for cormorants, gulls, and other seabirds.*

Petrified Forest

- United States (Arizona)
- Map: page 10, D–5

Transformed by nature's alchemy from wood into stone, the remains of a bygone forest lie gleaming in the sun.

High on a desert plateau in northeastern Arizona there is a landscape of unique and haunting beauty. In an area where the hills themselves are tinted with horizontal bands of color, thousands of gleaming, multicolored logs of solid stone are strewn across the countryside.

This is the famed Petrified Forest, the largest collection of fossilized wood in the world. Protected within the boundaries of Petrified Forest National Park, the logs delight and at the same time puzzle visitors. What are they doing in the middle of a desert with no living tree in sight? How were they changed from wood into stone that is harder than steel?

The riddle of their existence began about 200 million years ago, when the now-elevated plateau was a low, swampy floodplain. Among the vast wealth of plants and animals that flourished in the warm, moist climate were huge cone-bearing trees up to 200 feet (60 meters) tall. Many of those growing on hills to the south of the present park were toppled by storms and carried into the area by heavy floods.

Large numbers of the logs accumulated on the marshy floodplain, where they were eventually covered by thick deposits of mud and sand that later hardened into shale and sandstone. Mixed in with the sediment, moreover, was a great deal of mineral-rich volcanic ash produced by nearby eruptions and scattered over the area by wind and water.

Groundwater seeping through these deposits became saturated with dissolved silica, one of the minerals in the volcanic ash. As the water penetrated the buried logs, the silica was deposited inside individual wood cells. Some of the silica formed clear quartz crystals; much of it, mixed with traces of other minerals, was deposited as jasper, agate, amethyst, and other colorful variants of typical quartz.

Following the burial of the logs, the area was invaded by a shallow sea. Thick deposits of other rocks were formed on the shale and sandstone that enclosed the petrified wood. Then about 70 million years ago the land began to rise in the great upheaval that produced the Rocky Mountains. The water drained away, and erosion began to take its toll.

Layer by layer, the covering rocks were gradually stripped away until the shale and sandstone containing the petrified wood were laid bare on the surface. As the shale and sandstone were also worn away, the ancient logs—by then solid rock—were gradually revealed. Glinting in every color of the rainbow, some of them are more than 100 feet (30 meters) long. Spectacular though the present display of petrified wood may be, however, the drama has not yet ended. Thousands more of the petrified logs no doubt remain hidden beneath the surface, awaiting their turn to be exhumed by the unending work of erosion. □

PETRIFIED FOREST. *Attacked by the forces of erosion, the area's neatly banded layers of rock have been carved into huge gullied domes.*

PETRIFIED FOREST. *Fractured by movements of the earth's crust as the region was uplifted above sea level, some of the ancient logs have been broken into shorter pieces.*

Pierre-Saint-Martin Cavern

- France
- Map: page 17, C–4

A bird offered the first clue to the existence of this labyrinth—the deepest cave system in the world.

But for a bird, the deepest cave system in the world might still be undiscovered. The first hint of its existence came about as two spelunkers probed an area of deeply eroded limestone terrain high in the French Pyrenees not far from the border of Spain. Curious when the bird flew from a small opening at the bottom of a sinkhole, the men tossed a stone into the abyss—and never heard it hit bottom.

Convinced that the hole must be a deep one, they returned to plumb its secrets in 1951. With the help of a winch, one of the explorers was lowered into the opening until he finally reached a large chamber filled with fallen debris. The bird, it turned out, had emerged from the top of a vertical, chimneylike shaft 1,050 feet (320 meters) deep. It is among the deepest cave chimneys in the world.

Subsequent probes of the Pierre-Saint-Martin Cavern continued to offer many surprises. As spelunkers explored the underground river flowing at the bottom of the shaft, they gradually pieced together maps of an elaborate network of subterranean canyons, corridors, and debris-filled chambers, as well as additional openings up to the surface.

One of the biggest discoveries came in 1955, when the explorers chanced upon the underground chamber now known as the Verna. Some 820 feet (250 meters) long and 590 feet (180 meters) wide, the colossal void has a ceiling 490 feet (150 meters) high. It is in fact the second largest cave chamber in the world, exceeded only by Spain's Carlista Cavern.

With each probe, moreover, the explorers established connections with surface openings higher and higher on the mountainside and found tunnels leading farther and farther underground. With the discovery of the Verna, it was realized that the vertical distance between the highest known entrance to the cave and its lowest known depth was 2,460 feet (750 meters). By the early 1960's the known depth of the system was more than 3,300 feet (1,000 meters). New discoveries in 1975 finally established the total depth of the cave at 4,364 feet (1,330 meters), making Pierre-Saint-Martin Cavern the deepest known cave system in the world. And investigators suspect that if connections are found between it and other caves in the area, the total depth may ultimately prove to be even greater. □

PIERRE-SAINT-MARTIN CAVERN. *Dark and slotlike, the entrance to the cave on the deeply eroded limestone surface gives little hint of the magnitude of the subterranean network.*

PILAT DUNES. *Sloping up gently from the Bay of Biscay, the dunes drop steeply on their leeward side. Throngs of tourists visit the dunes for fine views of both land and sea.*

Pilat Dunes

- France
- Map: page 17, C–4

Whipped by Atlantic storms and westerly winds, these untamed sand dunes—the highest in all of Europe—are marching steadily inland.

The coast of southwestern France, south of the Gironde estuary, is bordered by an almost continuous line of sand dunes 150 miles (240 kilometers) long. Constantly remodeled by the wind, the dunes in places have sealed off marshy lagoons; elsewhere they are marching steadily inland and engulfing extensive pine forests.

The most impressive stretch of all, the Pilat Dunes, is found just south of the seaside resort of Arcachon, about midway along the coast. Extending north to south for nearly two miles (three kilometers), they are among the most actively mobile dunes in the area. They are also the highest sand dunes in Europe. Sloping up gently from the Bay of Biscay, then dropping off abruptly to half-buried inland forests, the dunes in places are 325 feet (100 meters) high.

Like other coastal dunes, the Pilat Dunes were created by strong westerly winds blowing inland across a sandy beach. A dune starts to form where an obstacle causes the wind to slow down and drop airborne sand grains on the leeward side of the obstruction. As the pile of sand grows, it becomes a more efficient windbreak. Additional sand is deposited until a sizable dune has been formed.

Unless stabilized by deep-rooted vegetation, the dune migrates inland. The wind blows sand up the windward slope of the dune, then drops it on the steep leeward side. In this way the dune moves slowly forward, burying everything in its path. □

Sand Grains Have Their Own Stories to Tell

Sand grains are tiny fragments of various types of rock. The soft, powdery sand found on many tropical beaches, for example, consists of bits of ground-up coral. Black beaches, in turn, are likely to be lava sand. Most sand grains, however, consist of bits of quartz, which is more resistant to chemical and mechanical erosion.

Just as sand grains are made up of different materials, they also vary in shape and surface texture. A "young" sand grain—one that is freshly eroded from the original rock material—is usually rough and angular. As it is blown about by the wind or rolled about in water, it constantly bumps into other sand grains. Abrasion blunts the sharp angles, and in time this buffeting produces a smoothly rounded shape. A grain of sand, moreover, is shiny or dull, depending on whether it has been transported by wind or water. Waterborne sand from rivers, lakes, and seas tends to be shiny. Windblown sand from dunes and deserts is dull; repeated collisions with other sand grains produce a dull "frosted glass" surface effect.

Microscopic examination of individual sand grains often reveals details of their histories. Angular, shiny sand grains *(left)* are likely to be young and water-transported. In time their coarse edges will be smoothed to form blunt, shiny sand grains *(center)*. Rounded, dull sand grains *(right),* such as those found in the Pilat Dunes, have been rounded in the sea and then dulled as they were blown about by the wind.

Angular, shiny sand grains

Blunt, shiny sand grains

Rounded, dull sand grains

Pinargozu Cave

- Turkey
- Map: page 18, E–5

Swirling waters and gale-force winds long impeded exploration of this subterranean network perched high on Turkey's Central Anatolian Plateau.

Pinargozu Cave is located on the side of a mountain near the western shore of Lake Beysehir, one of several large lakes just north of the Taurus Mountains on the Central Anatolian Plateau. The entrance to the cave is quite readily apparent: a substantial stream of sparkling water, the Devre Su, pours continuously from its mouth.

Even so, the cave, which has proved to be one of the largest in Turkey, long defied the efforts of would-be explorers to probe its underground passageways. Not far from the entrance the cave narrows down to a low arch where the water comes swirling out at a tremendous rate. In addition, a constant wind whistles through the narrow opening at speeds of as much as 60 miles (100 kilometers) per hour—a "whole gale" on the Beaufort Scale.

These barriers were first overcome

PINARGOZU CAVE. *Parts of the cave are decorated with fragile clusters of calcite formations that resemble bursts of frozen fireworks.*

in 1965 by French speleologists. Further exploration has proved the cave to be almost three miles (five kilometers) long. The maximum vertical contrast between the highest and lowest known sections of the cave system is 814 feet (248 meters).

Upstream from the impeding arch near the entrance, a tributary joins the mainstream of the Devre Su. In places the main passage winds around tortuous curves. Other sections are dry galleries decorated with delicate formations. Elsewhere the ceilings open up in high fissures, apparently dissolved along major fractures in the limestone. It is suspected that underground erosion linked a series of formerly separate cavities to create the present cave network.

The surface sources of the Devre Su and its tributary have not yet been found. It is believed that they originate where groundwater seeps into fissures in limestone formations farther up on nearby mountain slopes.

The wind that blows perpetually through the cave is also something of an enigma. It appears to originate in the upper part of a meander in the innermost part of the cave system. But again, its exact source—and even the reason for its existence—are unknown so far.

The cave has not yet been entirely explored. Speleologists hope that future probes will reveal the sources of both the rivers and the wind that courses continuously throughout the cave. But whatever the outcome of their efforts may be, most of them agree that the already known sections of Pinargozu Cave are one of the underground wonders of Turkey. □

Pipi Natural Bridge

- Central African Republic
- Map: page 25, F–5

Now high and dry, the top of this remarkable natural bridge may once have been part of the riverbed.

The Pipi River rises in the northeastern highlands of the Central African Republic. Flowing southward toward the Congo River, it surges through a number of gorges. And within one of the gorges it passes beneath an imposing natural bridge.

Composed of a massive slab of sandstone that spans the gorge, Pipi Natural Bridge is more than just a sight to behold. It also poses some intriguing questions. No one knows exactly how it was formed. But a cou-

PIPI NATURAL BRIDGE. *Vines and other vegetation soften the angular contours of the huge slab of sandstone that forms the bridge.*

ple of odd features in the area suggest interesting possibilities.

Within the gorge the riverbed is scarred by many potholes—caldron-like depressions in the bedrock that were hollowed out by stones whirling in eddies. But there are also remnants of potholes on the walls of the gorge—and even on top of the bridge—more than 30 feet (9 meters) above the present river level. Thus it seems apparent that the river once flowed at a much higher level and the top of the bridge was once part of the river bottom.

Upstream from the bridge, moreover, rocky cornices project from the sides of the gorge, suggesting the remains of the roof of a tunnel that collapsed. And that may be exactly what did happen. At some time in the past, the river may have eroded an underground channel through the rock. (Underground rivers are generally found in limestone, but on rare occasions they develop in sandstone.) Eventually, some geologists suggest, the roof of the underground channel caved in. Only one small section remained intact: the part that forms Pipi Natural Bridge. □

Plata, Río de la

- Argentina—Uruguay
- Map: page 15, D–6

Muddy, silt-laden waters belie the name of the South American estuary known as the River of Silver.

The Río de la Plata ("River of Silver") is a great funnel-shaped indentation on the southeastern coast of South America. It is bordered by Uruguay on the north and Argentina on the south, and the capitals of both countries—Montevideo, Uruguay, and Buenos Aires, Argentina—are located on its shores.

Formed by the union of two great rivers, the Río de la Plata is not really a river at all, but a vast tidal estuary or, in the opinion of some geographers, a gulf of the sea. It is 136 miles (219 kilometers) wide where it opens on the Atlantic. At its head 180 miles (290 kilometers) inland, it narrows down to a mere 30 miles (48 kilometers) across.

There the Uruguay River flows in from the north and the Paraná River from the northwest. The Paraná, the

second longest river in South America, is by far the more important of the two. Rising at distant sources in Brazil, it is 2,485 miles (3,999 kilometers) long. These two rivers, together with their feeder streams, channel the runoff from an area of about 1.5 million square miles (3.9 million square kilometers) into the Río de la Plata. Its drainage basin includes parts of Bolivia, Brazil, Paraguay, Uruguay, and Argentina.

Although early explorers named the river for the many silver ornaments worn by the local Indians, the water itself is anything but silvery. Each year the Paraná and the Uruguay carry an estimated 2 billion cubic feet (57 million cubic meters) of silt into the Río de la Plata, where the muddy water is continuously stirred up by winds and tides.

From various maps made over the past 150 years, it is estimated that the Paraná's enormous delta is advancing into the Río de la Plata at a rate of 230 feet (70 meters) per year. Within the estuary, enormous shoals and shifting sandbars pose problems for navigation. (Even where it enters the sea, the estuary is only 65 feet, or 20 meters, deep.) An artificial channel 130 miles (210 kilometers) long connects Buenos Aires with deepwater areas of the estuary. But with so much sediment being washed in, it must be dredged constantly in order to maintain the minimum depth required for commercial shipping.

The first European to sail into the Río de la Plata was Juan Díaz de Solís, who entered it in 1516 in hopes of discovering a strait connecting the Atlantic and Pacific oceans. Ferdinand Magellan probed it briefly in 1520, and Sebastian Cabot explored it more thoroughly betweeen 1526 and 1529. The first settlement in the vicinity was Santa María del Buen Aire—now known as Buenos Aires—which was founded in 1536. Attacked by Indians soon afterward, it was abandoned and then reestablished in 1580. In the years since, the Río de la Plata and its feeder streams have been developed into South America's most important system of navigable waterways, crucial to the commerce and communications of a large and populous region. □

Plitvice Lakes

- Yugoslavia
- Map: page 17, E–4

Blue-green and crystal clear, this remarkable cluster of mountain lakes is connected by a series of splendid cataracts and foaming waterfalls.

The Plitvice Lakes are the scenic centerpiece of a large national park in the Dinaric Alps in northwestern Yugoslavia. Nestled in a deep, steep-walled limestone valley, the 16 major lakes and many smaller ones form a continuous chain about three miles (five kilometers) long. The lakes descend into the valley in a steplike series, each one contained by a natural stone dam. The streams connecting the lakes spill over the travertine barriers in numerous rapids and waterfalls, including some more than 200 feet (60 meters) high.

The headwaters of the lakes are two small mountain streams that join to form the highest lake, Prosce. The largest lake, Kozjak, covers 205 acres

(85 hectares) and is 150 feet (45 meters) deep. Plunging from one gemlike, blue-green lake to the next, the water makes one final spectacular leap into the canyon of the Korana River and disappears into the forest.

The natural dams that contain this unusual series of lakes are creations of the water that spills over them. Flowing across the limestone terrain upstream from the lakes, the water in the feeder streams becomes heavily saturated with dissolved calcium carbonate. Over a long period of time, algae living on the streambed have caused the dissolved mineral to precipitate, or come out of solution, and build up the travertine barriers.

The resultant chain of lakes is an impressive sight in every season of the year. The foaming waterfalls are at their peak flow following the spring thaw on the mountains. In summer the calm green surfaces of the lakes mirror the dense forests on their shores, and in autumn they contrast with flaming fall foliage. Finally, in winter the dams are covered by spectacular walls of giant icicles. □

RÍO DE LA PLATA. *The Paraná River branches into many channels as it crosses its huge delta at the head of the great estuary.*

Pobitite Kamani

- Bulgaria
- Map: page 17, F–4

Are these pillars the ruined temple of some lost civilization—or the mysterious handiwork of nature?

About 12 miles (20 kilometers) from Varna, the major port on Bulgaria's Black Sea coast, there is a strange landscape that looks exactly like the ruins of some ancient temple. Scattered over an area about 2,600 feet (800 meters) long and 325 feet (100 meters) wide is an array of 300 stone pillars. Some have toppled but most of them remain upright, planted firmly in the sandy soil. The name of the major group, Pobitite Kamani, means "planted stones."

A few of the rock columns resemble teeth with projecting roots, and a couple seem to form a giant gateway. But most of them, neatly spaced and up to 20 feet (6 meters) high, are almost perfectly cylindrical pillars of rock. It is hardly surprising that a Russian archeologist who visited the area in 1892 assumed that they were the ruins of an ancient temple.

Nor are these the only "planted stones" in the area. Nearby there are other clusters of similar rock columns. Some have swollen conical bases; others, capped by pieces of limestone, resemble giant mushrooms. In yet another group there is a huge column some 40 feet (12 meters) in circumference and a pillar that stands 23 feet (7 meters) tall, decorated with limestone formations similar to those found on cave walls.

The cave formations offer a clue to the origin of the strange stone columns

How the Columns of Pobitite Kamani Were Formed

Before there were any "planted stones" at Pobitite Kamani, the land was covered by a layer of limestone resting on a thick deposit of sand, which in turn overlay an impermeable layer of marl and clay *(left)*. Acidic groundwater dissolved the limestone and seeped through fissures into the layer of sand. There the dissolved minerals were redeposited, much as stalactites are formed in caves *(center)*. Finally the limestone disappeared completely and the sand itself was eroded away, gradually exposing the mixed sandstone-limestone columns visible today *(right)*.

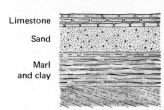

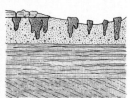

Limestone

Sand

Marl and clay

of Pobitite Kamani. Geologists theorize that they are in effect stalactites that formed in a layer of sand rather than in the open space of a cave. Bit by bit the sand deposit was covered by a layer of limestone. But eventually the limestone was dissolved by groundwater that had filtered down through cracks and fissures into the sand. There the minerals were redeposited, cementing the sand into columns of resistant rock that were eventually exposed by erosion. □

POBITITE KAMANI. *Symmetrical and neatly spaced, the array of stone columns long puzzled archeologists and geologists alike.*

PONT D'ARC. *Once forced to flow around the massive limestone barrier, the Ardèche now glides through the gateway it carved into the rock.*

Pont d'Arc

- France
- Map: page 17, D–4

The lofty archway penetrates a thick limestone wall and remains as a monument to the river that created it.

From its source in the Cévennes, a mountain range in southern France, the Ardèche River follows a scenic, winding course of 70 miles (113 kilometers) to its confluence with the southward-flowing Rhone. Along the way it passes through the Ardèche Canyon, a deeply eroded gorge that is about 20 miles (32 kilometers) long and is hemmed in by craggy limestone cliffs that rise to heights of as much as 1,000 feet (300 meters).

Of all the striking rock formations it passes along the way, the most impressive is the Pont d'Arc, a natural bridge that pierces a massive wall of gray limestone at the head of the canyon. Some 112 feet (34 meters) high and 194 feet (59 meters) wide at water level, the bridge forms a monumental natural gateway to the canyon.

It is believed that in the distant past the river flowed in a meandering curve around the promontory now penetrated by the Pont d'Arc. The bridge itself originated as a minor underground stream that flowed through the wall of limestone. (Underground streams are common in limestone terrain, which is readily dissolved by slightly acidic water.)

The underground channel was very gradually enlarged until, during a flood, the river finally abandoned its original course and began to flow permanently beneath the natural bridge. Continuing solution of the limestone, abrasion by waterborne debris, and undermining by the river then accelerated the process of erosion and enlarged the archway to its present imposing dimensions. □

Popocatepetl

- Mexico
- Map: page 12, C–3

The second highest peak in Mexico still lives up to its ancient Aztec name, meaning "the smoking mountain."

When the Spanish conquistadores under Hernando Cortez invaded Mexico in 1519, they encountered several great volcanoes in the vicinity of present-day Mexico City. Among the most impressive was the snowcapped, symmetrical cone called Popocatepetl by the Aztecs. It is believed that the first ascent of the awesome peak was made by one of Cortez's captains, Diego de Ordaz. His show of bravado evidently was intended to convince the Aztecs that no obstacle could impede the invading army.

According to one account, Ordaz was nearing the summit after a long, hard climb when the volcano began to roar and tremble. Taking shelter under an overhanging rock to escape the clouds of burning ash that fell all around, he then continued undeterred to the top. Even Ordaz was apparently impressed when he peered into the crater and saw a seething mass of incandescent lava boiling "like water in a pot." Upon his return, however, the Aztecs were even more impressed by his daring exploit, and stood in greater awe than ever of the conquering Spaniards.

Today Popocatepetl is the most famous volcano in Mexico. Its graceful snow-white summit rising against the sky is easily visible from Mexico City, about 45 miles (72 kilometers) to the northwest. And despite the difficulties Ordaz may have encountered, it is considered comparatively easy to climb. Those who make it to the top are rewarded with an extraordinary view encompassing nearby volcanic peaks, the distant rooftops of Mexico City, and points far beyond in the Valley of Mexico.

With a maximum height of 17,887 feet (5,452 meters) above sea level, Popocatepetl is not the highest peak in the country. It is exceeded by nearby Pico de Orizaba, also known as Citlaltéptl, which rises to 18,700 feet (5,700 meters). Even so, besides being the second highest peak in Mexico, it ranks as the fifth highest mountain in all of North America.

Technically, Popocatepetl is classified as a stratovolcano: its cone is built up of alternating layers, or strata, of lava flows and explosively ejected cinders. The graceful symmetry of its contours, however, masks a somewhat more complex structure. When the present cone is viewed from the north, it becomes apparent that it was built on the ruins of a much older volcano that grew up over a long period of time and then was partially destroyed by erosion. It was only during the past 2 million years or so that intense volcanic activity resumed and elevated Popocatepetl's summit to its present commanding height.

Thick layers of pumice dating from the end of the Ice Age reveal that violent eruptions continued until as recently as 8,000 years ago. The Aztecs

recorded a series of eruptions in the 14th century, and Spanish chronicles reported 10 more that occurred in the 16th and 17th centuries. Since that time, however, eruptions have been much more intermittent. The most recent sustained outbursts of smoke and gas took place in 1920, but they continued for only a few months.

Even so, Popocatepetl is not completely dormant. Its immense oval crater, nearly 2,000 feet (600 meters) across on its major axis and more than 500 feet (150 meters) deep, is paved with thick deposits of sulfur. Here and there within the crater, numerous vents, known as fumaroles, continue to spout noxious vapors. And from time to time Popocatepetl still sends out great clouds of smoke, thus living up to its ancient Aztec name, which means "the smoking mountain." □

POPOCATEPETL. *The most famous of all Mexican volcanoes is admired for the beauty of its gracefully symmetrical slopes and its sparkling, perpetually snow-covered summit.*

LA PORTADA. *Protected by a firm foundation of erosion-resistant volcanic rock, the huge natural arch withstands the attack of the waves.*

Portada, La

● Chile
● Map: page 15, B–5

Sculpting by the sea creates many fantastic forms, such as this massive arch off Chile's northern coast.

About 12 miles (20 kilometers) north of Antofagasta, the principal city of northern Chile, there is a dramatic stretch of seacoast that is backed by high sandstone cliffs. The Pacific surf pounds endlessly on the beach, enveloping ruggedly eroded rock outcrops in clouds of sea spray.

The most striking of all the rock formations is a huge natural stone arch standing a short distance offshore. Known as La Portada, "The Gateway," its monumental silhouette inevitably evokes images of the great ceremonial arches of Rome and the Arc de Triomphe in Paris.

Composed primarily of the same yellowish sandstone that forms the coastal cliffs, the arch is an eroded remnant of a much-altered coastline. As the relatively soft sandstone cliffs slowly retreated before the onslaught of the waves, the mass of rock that forms the arch was left standing offshore. A substantial foundation of erosion-resistant andesite (a type of volcanic rock) at the bases of the two upright "pillars" of the arch protects them from destruction by the surf. Lime, in turn, has impregnated the uppermost sandstone layers, cementing them and keeping the top of the arch from collapsing.

La Portada and the adjacent coastline are so exceptionally scenic that they are almost always included on sightseeing itineraries from Antofagasta. The beach is also a popular spot for bathing. The mists generated by the cold coastal currents, the dramatic offshore rocks, the cliffs, and the fine sandy beaches result in seascapes of extraordinary beauty—seascapes that contrast refreshingly with the harshness of the great coastal desert that lies just a short distance inland. Also found in the area are a number of ghost towns, settlements that were established to mine the rich deposits of guano left by seabirds on the rocks lying just offshore. Subsequently deserted by the miners, the towns are crumbling to picturesque ruins that are inviting to tourists.   □

PORT CAMPBELL CLIFFS. *As the limestone ramparts retreated before surging seas, isolated pinnacles of rock remained as sea stacks.*

Port Campbell Cliffs

- Australia
- Map: page 22, E–5

The pounding sea has carved this coastline into spectacular headlands, arches, and isolated sea stacks.

The western coast of the Australian state of Victoria is notable for its rocky cliffs and rugged capes. But in the opinion of many visitors, the most beautiful stretch of all is the Port Campbell Cliffs, preserved in Port Campbell National Park. Extending in an unbroken line for 20 miles (32 kilometers), the gold and russet limestone cliffs tower above the sea.

Pounded by stormy surf and fierce breakers, the bases of the cliffs are constantly being hollowed out and undercut, causing the upper sections of the cliffs to collapse into the sea. The result is an extraordinarily irregular series of jagged headlands and narrow, intricate coves.

Many of the headlands are pierced by arches, including one with a double

How the Sea Attacks Cliffs and Causes Them to Retreat

Rocky coasts such as the Port Campbell Cliffs are carved primarily by the mechanical erosion of breaking waves and tidal currents. Usually, however, other processes first weaken the rocks. The salt in seawater attacks them chemically and leads to their disintegration. Surface water seeps into crevices and helps enlarge the openings. In cold climates the water freezes and wedges the rocks apart. Even plants and animals play a role. Certain algae secrete rock-dissolving chemicals, and animals such as sea urchins and certain mollusks bore holes in the rocks.

But breaking waves do the greatest damage. Pounding the rocks with enormous force, the breakers undermine the bases of cliffs. When the water is driven into hollows and fissures in the cliffs, it sometimes causes actual explosions in the rock. And when it retreats, the suction can lead to collapse. Fallen rocks and pebbles are then hurled about by the waves, hitting the cliffs like shrapnel and hastening their breakdown.

The creations of these combined forces include sheer cliffs, headlands, coves, overhangs, caves, and sea stacks. The results, of course, vary from place to place, depending on such factors as the composition of the rocks, their resistance to erosion, whether the rock layers are horizontal or tilted, and the force of the assaulting seas.

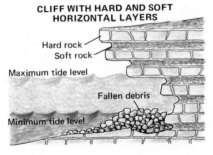

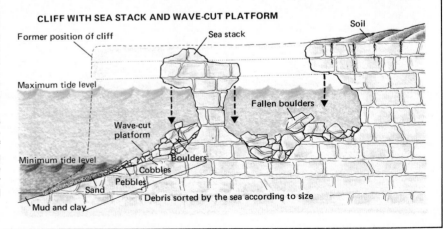

arch known as the London Bridge. Where the tops of arches have collapsed, their offshore supports remain standing as islets and sea stacks of various sizes. Perhaps the most notable of all are the Twelve Apostles, a cluster of craggy pinnacles that rise high above the surf.

One especially remarkable feature is the Great Blowhole. There the sea has carved a tunnel that extends 325 feet (100 meters) inland from the cliffs. At the end of the tunnel the overlying rock collapsed, leaving a huge natural well about 130 feet (40 meters) in diameter. Under favorable conditions, waves surge through the tunnel and emerge through the blowhole with the force of an erupting geyser.

In other places the entire roofs of tunnels have caved in, forming narrow gorges that are gradually widened into canyons. One such is the Loch Ard Canyon, named for a ship that was wrecked on the coast in 1878. Indeed, many ships have foundered on this shoreline, where even the slightest sea swell produces treacherous surf. Despite the hazards to humans, however, the Port Campbell coast is a splendid haven for wildlife: huge colonies of seabirds nest, free from interference, on many of the rocky islets. ☐

Porto, Gulf of

- France (Corsica)
- Map: page 17, D–4

Along the jagged western flank of Corsica, the turquoise waters of the Mediterranean intrude deeply into a red-hued, rockbound coastline.

Lying about 100 miles (160 kilometers) southeast of the mainland of France, the Mediterranean island of Corsica has long been known for the ruggedness and beauty of its terrain. The west coast is particularly striking, with a succession of gulfs and inlets indenting it from one end to the other.

Among the most impressive is the Gulf of Porto, nestled in a setting of steep, jagged mountains midway down the coast. More or less triangular in shape, the gulf is 5 miles (8 kilometers) wide at its mouth and extends some 7 miles (11 kilometers) inland. The gulf is enclosed by a mass of ancient crystalline rock—primarily various types of granite—that was abruptly uplifted about 30 million years ago, at the same time that the western Mediterranean basin was being formed.

Perhaps the most arresting feature of the Gulf of Porto is the radiant combination of colors to be seen there. The blue of the sea contrasts with the varied reddish hues of the rocks that border it, and they in turn contrast with the rich green of the so-called maquis—the dense growth of shrubs that cover the slopes. The colors are made all the more dramatic as the sun gradually alters them throughout the day, creating a different palette from one hour to the next.

Along the gulf's southern shore is a stretch of nearly straight coastline known as the Calanche di Piana. There a line of steep granite cliffs topped by jagged pinnacles and turrets rises as much as 1,300 feet (400 meters) above the water.

The northern shore, in contrast, is scalloped by numerous capes enclosing lesser bays. The profusion of plant life includes oaks, wild olive trees, and an especially dense covering of maquis. In addition to the multihued granite, the cliffs include areas of volcanic rock that issued originally from the nearby Mont Cinto massif. Many of the cliffs on the north coast have been eroded into distinctive columnar forms, and the highest among them rise nearly 2,000 feet (600 meters) above the tranquil blue sea. ☐

GULF OF PORTO. *Over the eons, the sea hollowed out weak areas in the fringing rocks, creating a dramatically indented coastline.*

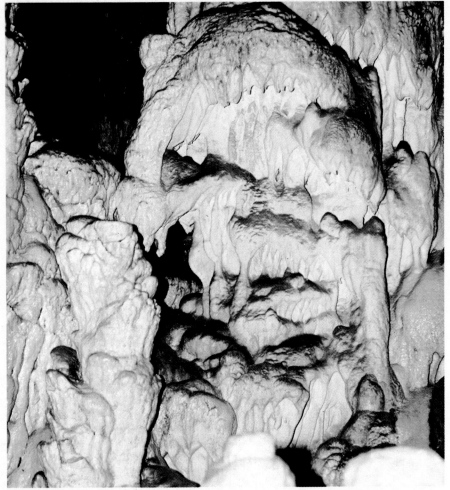

POSTOJNA CAVE. *One of the most famous labyrinths in all of Europe, this Yugoslav cave is noted for its abundance of beautifully shaped and colored mineral decorations.*

Postojna Cave

- Yugoslavia
- Map: page 17, E–4

This labyrinth of corridors and chambers—most of them festooned with elaborate formations—is among the most visited caves in Europe.

Postojna Cave, located in northwestern Yugoslavia just a short distance from Trieste, Italy, is one of the largest and most beautifully decorated caves in Europe. Part of a cave system 13 miles (21 kilometers) long, it contains several chambers more than 100 feet (30 meters) high.

Like other caverns in the world's limestone regions, Postojna Cave was carved by the dissolving action of water, in this case the Pivka River. The river flows above ground for several miles, disappears into the mountain containing the cave, and then reappears on the surface farther downstream. The limestone is about 100 million years old; the cave itself was formed within the last 2 million years.

Postojna Cave has been known to local residents for centuries. Some of the abundant graffiti on the walls dates from the year 1213. In more recent times, the cavern has been the site of some unusual events. During World War I, Russian prisoners of war built a bridge—still used by tourists—

Dripstone and Concretions

Stalactites, stalagmites, and other cave formations are known as dripstone. They form where water seeping through limestone and similar rocks becomes saturated with dissolved minerals. When the water enters the open air in a cave, the minerals are deposited as pure calcite crystals. The dripping water at first creates a hollow tube that slowly increases in length. Water running down the outside of the tube then thickens the walls to form a stalactite. Water dripping to the floor, in turn, deposits the upward-growing cone of a stalagmite. Eventually the two may meet and form a column.

Concretions are also formed by the deposition of dissolved minerals. Composed of calcite, pyrite, silica, and various other materials, they accumulate in small cavities in sedimentary rock. Spherulites are globular masses of crystals radiating from a common center. Concretions with deep mineral-filled cracks are known as septaria. Irregularly shaped flint nodules commonly form in chalk deposits. Cave pearls are an exception: they form in depressions on cave floors, where constant movement keeps them from becoming attached to the surface.

Water infiltrating through limestone ceiling

FORMATION OF STALACTITES AND STALAGMITES

Dripping water

Calcite tube

Formation of a stalactite

Formation of a stalagmite

Mound of calcite

Walls thickened by additional layers of calcite

Stalactite ⎫
Stalagmite ⎬ unite to form a column

Calcite crystal

SOME TYPICAL CONCRETIONS

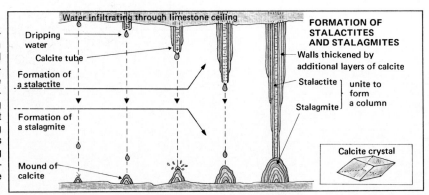

Spherulite   Septaria   Flint nodule   Cave pearls

across a deep chasm within the cave. During World War II, German troops used part of the cave as an ammunition dump, which was blown up by Partisan forces. The explosion destroyed most of the stalactites and stalagmites near the cave's mouth and blackened the walls with smoke.

Today visitors by the tens of thousands tour Postojna Cave each year. Traveling through part of the labyrinth on a narrow-gauge electric railway, they marvel at the cave's fantastic array of dripstone formations: stalactites, stalagmites, flowstone draperies, canopies, and pillarlike structures, all with their natural colors enhanced by dramatic lighting.

Among the most awesome sights in Postojna Cave is a great vaulted chamber known as the Concert Hall where Toscanini himself once conducted. Encompassing some 30,000 square feet (2,800 square meters), the vast room can accommodate 10,000 visitors beneath its soaring roof. □

Prachov Rocks

- Czechoslovakia
- Map: page 17, E–3

In a quiet, secluded forest, the forces of erosion have worked together to create a hauntingly beautiful exhibit of very realistic stone sculptures.

In the north of Czechoslovakia, about 45 miles (70 kilometers) northeast of Prague, lies a scenic region known as the Cesky Raj, the "Bohemian Paradise." Heavily forested, the area is celebrated equally for its historic sites and its natural beauty. Of particular interest are its clusters of rock formations hidden deep in dense forests.

The most elaborate of these are the Prachov Rocks, sculpted in a small plateau of sandstone that was formed more than 60 million years ago. Attacked by the forces of erosion, the coarse sandstone has been carved into a labyrinth of narrow valleys and ravines that wind among the fantastically shaped rocks. Some have the appearance of ruined buildings, while others look like humans and animals, motionless but seemingly poised for action. The variety and vividness of these natural sculptures are reflected in the names they have inspired, from the Leaning Tower and the Devil's Kitchen to the Monk, the Elephant, and the Eagle. □

PRAIA DA ROCHA. *On the sun-drenched Algarve coast, erosion by the sea left numerous massive rocks standing offshore as the irregular line of cliffs retreated slowly inland.*

Praia da Rocha

- Portugal
- Map: page 17, C–5

Bizarre rock formations sculpted by the sea punctuate the golden beaches of Portugal's picturesque Algarve.

Russet and yellow rock formations stand like tall sentinels all along the beaches of the Algarve, the sunny resort region washed by the waters of the Atlantic in southern Portugal. Among the most dramatic are those at Praia da Rocha, where the golden sands are dotted with odd shapes bearing such names as the Three Bears and the Two Brothers.

The Algarve's mild climate—the almonds are already in bloom in January—is ensured by a mountain barrier that blocks out cold northerly winds. The unusual coastline, in turn, is testimony to the power of the sea, which has gnawed away at the thick layer of limestone that underlies the countryside. In places the cliffs are tall and gaunt, plunging straight down to the sea. Elsewhere the coast is lined by long, broad beaches backed by lower cliffs and studded with picturesque eroded rocks.

Like the neighboring towns, Praia da Rocha is perched atop a cliff and surrounded by groves of oaks and fruit trees. But its most alluring attraction is the weird rock shapes that punctuate the beaches below. Fancifully likened to pediments, castles, pyramids, and domes, all are eroded remnants of the cliffs, which have gradually retreated before constant attack by the surf. In many places the cliffs are indented by caves and grottoes—some accessible only by boat—where mats of seaweed are heaved about by the waves and shafts of sunlight are reflected intermittently along the reddish walls. Blessed with an incomparable setting and an equable climate, Praia da Rocha has for good reason become one of the most popular resort centers in the entire Algarve. □

PUENTE DEL INCA. *High in the Argentine Andes, the immense natural bridge spans a stream flowing from mineral-rich hot springs that were frequented by the ancient Incas.*

Puente del Inca

- Argentina
- Map: page 15, C–6

This unusual natural bridge is in part the creation of the hot spring waters that now flow beneath it.

High in the Andes at the southern foot of Aconcagua, the highest peak in the Western Hemisphere, is the little hot-spring resort of Puente del Inca. The area has been known since the days of the Incas for the curative powers of the mineral-rich waters that bubble from its trio of hot springs. Today it is equally famous for the monumental natural bridge that spans the stream issuing from the springs.

Glaciers played a role in creating the "Incan Bridge." During the Ice Age, massive glaciers surged down the mountain valley and, as they retreated, littered its floor with thick deposits of eroded debris. Later, land-slides and floods also added to the accumulation.

The thermal springs also helped create the bridge. The water that flows from them is so rich in dissolved minerals that it "petrifies" objects thrown in by tourists by encrusting them with a colorful layer of minerals. In much the same way, the spring waters have "petrified" the thick deposits of debris on the valley floor. Impregnating the upper layers, they have cemented the rocks, pebbles, and smaller particles into a solid mass.

At a time when the climate was wetter than today, a powerful river began to flow down the valley. Cutting a channel through the least cemented lower layers of debris, the river gradually enlarged the opening and in time created the natural bridge. Still growing in width with each flood and increasing in height due to collapses of the underside of the arch, Puente del Inca will possibly be destroyed entirely one day. □

Puys Volcanic Chain

- France
- Map: page 17, D–4

This chain of extinct volcanoes, stretching across the countryside in a row of hills and peaks, includes the youngest mountains in France.

The Puys Volcanic Chain in south-central France is among the most unusual mountain ranges in the entire country. Stretching north to south for about 25 miles (40 kilometers) just west of the industrial city of Clermont-Ferrand, it consists of a series of 60 volcanic cones. Some have been partially destroyed by erosion, but most remain virtually intact.

Besides being quite picturesque, the range is very young. The volcanic activity that created it began within the last 2 million years, and eruptions continued until about 10,000 years

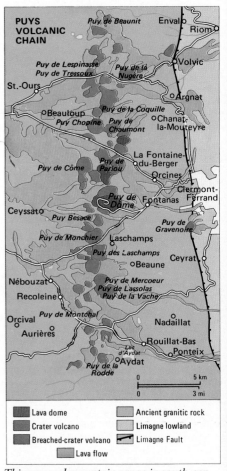

This unusual mountain range in south-central France stretches from north to south for some 25 miles (40 kilometers) and includes the remains of about 60 volcanoes.

ago. Some of these peaks are thus the youngest mountains in France. Although the volcanoes are quiescent now, the many hot springs in the area provide evidence that the pockets of molten magma that produced the mountains still lie quite close to the surface of the earth.

While the cones themselves are not especially lofty, part of their beauty results from the region's marked contrasts in elevation. To the east of the range in the vicinity of Clermont-Ferrand, the earth's crust has been broken by an immense north-south fracture known as the Limagne Fault. To the east of the fault is a gently rolling fertile lowland averaging about 1,150 feet (350 meters) above sea level. To the west of the fault the surface rises abruptly to an ancient eroded upland of granitic rock 2,300 to 2,600 feet (700 to 800 meters) above the sea. And atop the platform of granite, like the icing on a cake, is the multitude of volcanic cones, with great lava flows spreading out in all directions. Many of the peaks (*puy* means "peak" in the local dialect) rise to heights of 4,000 feet (1,200 meters) and more.

The highest summit of all, the Puy de Dôme, reaches a maximum elevation of 4,806 feet (1,465 meters). Once crowned by a temple dedicated to the god Mercury, its flat top today can be reached by a winding road. It is a fine vantage point for viewing the entire range from north to south.

Most of the cones were produced by Strombolian-type eruptions (named for the famous Italian volcano Stromboli). Volcanoes of this sort are in a constant state of activity, interrupted periodically by explosive eruptions of gas and cinders. The explosions are not terribly dangerous, however, since most of the erupted material falls back into the crater.

Many of the Strombolian cones in the chain have well-defined craters at their summits. Some, as a result of the periodic explosions, have secondary craters nested within the main craters. Still others have breached craters: their rims are interrupted by gaps where lava broke through the walls and poured down the slopes. The lava flows, which followed the contours of preexisting valleys, are most extensive to the west of the range. To the east, however, some especially long lava flows extended all the way to the Limagne Fault and spilled into the adjoining lowland.

Puy de Dôme and a few other volcanoes in the chain differ from their neighbors; they were produced by pelean-type eruptions, named for Mount Pelée on the Caribbean island of Martinique. In this type of volcano, violent, extremely destructive explosions alternate with long quiet periods. Following an explosion, extraordinarily viscous lava solidifies in the volcanic vent and forms a plug. Eventually, enough pressure builds up in the magma chamber below to blast away the plug—and even the entire mountaintop—in a gigantic explosion of fiery gas and ash. Viscous lava then wells up, rapidly solidifies, and once again clogs the vent, beginning the cycle anew.

Although the Puys Volcanic Chain has witnessed such violent episodes in the past, today all is peaceful and serene. Pasturelands, shrubs, and even extensive forests mask the undulating contours of the cones with a dense mantle of greenery. Flocks of sheep graze on rocky lava flows, and tourists come to marvel at the beauty of this unique landscape. □

PUYS VOLCANIC CHAIN. *Scarcely altered by erosion, the smooth slopes and summit craters of many of the cones remain virtually intact.*

Raabjerg Mile Dunes

- Denmark
- Map: page 16, E–3

This wild, windswept stretch of sand is the only area of shifting dunes on the coast of the Jutland peninsula.

The Raabjerg Mile Dunes are located just to the southwest of the busy fishing port and resort center of Skagen at the northernmost tip of Denmark's Jutland peninsula. Billowing across the landscape like waves on a stormy sea, they are the only major stretch of shifting sand dunes in the country.

All along the rest of the western coast of Jutland, there is an almost continuous belt of dunes, in places up to 6 miles (10 kilometers) wide. And in the past they too were continually on the move, shifting inland before the steady, occasionally violent westerly winds that blow in off the North Sea. But most of them have been stabilized by plantings of coniferous trees and deep-rooted grasses that anchor the sand in place.

Only at Raabjerg Mile do the dunes continue their relentless inland march. Ever since the turn of the century, this one stretch of dunes has been protected by the government as a showcase of the power of untrammeled wind and sand, and as a reminder of what the other coastal dunes used to be like. Covering an area of about 250 acres (100 hectares), the clean white dunes of Raabjerg Mile in some places are more than 65 feet (20 meters) high. And they are moving steadily eastward at a rate of 13 to 26 feet (4 to 8 meters) per year.

Nearby, just south of Skagen, the so-called Church in the Sand provides a striking example of the results of marching dunes. Built in the 13th century, it was threatened late in the 17th century by an advancing dune. For nearly 100 years attempts were made to halt the movement of the constantly shifting sand that seemed certain to engulf the church. But in the end the wind and sand won the battle. The church was finally abandoned in 1795, and today only the top of its bell tower projects forlornly above the all-encompassing dunes. □

RAABJERG MILE DUNES. *Despite a cover of grasses, the dunes are moving steadily inland before winds blowing in off the North Sea.*

RABBITKETTLE HOT SPRINGS. *Tier upon tier, shimmering pools descend the slopes of the dome of minerals left by hot spring water.*

Rabbitkettle Hot Springs

- Canada (Northwest Territories)
- Map: page 10, C–2

Mineral-rich water gushing from the earth has built a huge staircase of pools in the remote Canadian wilds.

The remote and beautiful valley of Canada's South Nahanni River has inspired more than its share of legends. Tales of murdered prospectors and other dark, mysterious events are commemorated in such place names as Broken Skull River, Deadmen Valley, and the Funeral Range.

On a less ominous note, there long were persistent rumors of tropical valleys as well, true Edens hidden among the mountains where snow never fell. Such tales no doubt were inspired by the area's many thermal springs, including the most spectacular of all, Rabbitkettle Hot Springs.

Perched on the bank beside a meander in the Rabbitkettle River, a tributary of the South Nahanni, they are an unbelievable sight. A broad, nearly circular dome of rock some 225 feet (69 meters) in diameter rises to a height of 90 feet (27 meters). From a central pool at the top, water spills down the sides through a succession of terraced pools, each bounded by a curving wall of rock about 12 inches (30 centimeters) high. Ranging in color from yellowish-white to gray, the huge natural fountain stands out in stunning contrast to the dense spruce forests that surround it.

The water that wells up into the summit pool is pleasantly warm, since its temperature reaches about 70° F (21° C). But in this limestone region it is saturated with dissolved calcium carbonate and other minerals. As the water flows in a thin film over irregularities on the surface, the dissolved minerals are precipitated from the water and then deposited as layers of rock—in this case a fragile type of travertine known as tufa.

Despite its look of timelessness, the elaborately terraced structure is relatively young. During the Ice Age, which ended a mere 10,000 years ago, the entire region was blanketed by a continent-wide ice cap; any similar mound of rock that might have existed on the spot before that time would have been completely destroyed. But ever since the glaciers retreated, the hot springs have been bubbling to the surface and depositing their burden of dissolved minerals.

Even now the mound is constantly though imperceptibly changing. In time individual pools become filled with rock, the water spills over their edges, and new tiers of damlike barriers are formed.

Rabbitkettle Hot Springs have been protected as part of Canada's Nahanni National Park since 1972. Other attractions in the area include glacial lakes, snow-covered mountain peaks, pristine forests, deep caves, and dark canyons filled with the deafening roar of foaming white-water rapids. And vying with Rabbitkettle Hot Springs for honors as the prime scenic attraction in the park are the towering twin cascades of Virginia Falls hurtling into a wilderness chasm. □

RAINBOW BRIDGE. *Once a spur of solid rock, the sandstone was undercut by a stream, and the opening was enlarged to form the bridge.*

Rainbow Bridge

- United States (Utah)
- Map: page 10, D–5

The world's largest natural bridge, according to legend, was formed when a rainbow turned into stone.

Despite its awesome size, Rainbow Bridge was long unknown to anyone but the local Paiute and Navajo Indians. And not even many of them had seen it, for it is hidden away in a narrow canyon in the south of Utah amid some of the wildest country in the United States. It was not until 1909 that a party of white men, guided by two Indians, made the grueling trek through rocky wastelands and winding canyons to find it.

Like everyone who has viewed it since, the men were overwhelmed by what they saw. The largest formation of its kind in the world, Rainbow Bridge spans a distance of 275 feet (84 meters). From its base to its top, the bridge towers to a height of 290 feet (88 meters)—as high as the Capitol in Washington, D.C. The sandstone at the top of the arch is 42 feet (13 meters) thick—the equivalent of a 3-story building. And the top of the bridge, with a width of 33 feet (10 meters), is as wide as a highway.

Rainbow Bridge is not just huge, however; it is also extremely beautiful. Theodore Roosevelt went so far as to declare it the world's greatest natural wonder. When the late afternoon sun strikes the pinkish sandstone streaked with variegated reds and browns, the effect is especially impressive. Visitors then can understand why the Indians named it Rainbow-Turned-to-Stone.

How Rock Fins Are Transformed Into Natural Arches

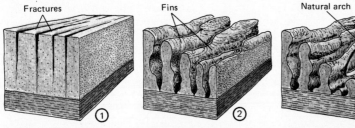

Rainbow Bridge was formed when a meandering stream cut an opening through the base of a projecting spur of rock. Many natural arches in the area are similar in appearance but were formed in a different way. As the surface of the land domed upward, deep fractures developed in the rock. Running water and chemical weathering deepened and widened these openings, in the process creating narrow fins of rock. Weathering agents then cut through the fins, producing holes that were gradually enlarged to form the long, graceful spans of natural arches.

MOUNT RAINIER. *Perpetually capped by ice and snow, the mountain has one of the most extensive glacial systems of any U.S. peak.*

The bridge is carved in a layer of sandstone that was originally deposited as windblown dunes, and it rests on a foundation of much harder sandstone. It began to take shape some 60 million years ago, when the entire Colorado Plateau started to dome slowly but steadily upward. As the land arched up, a river that flowed across the surface in broad, meandering loops carved a canyon deeper and deeper in the rock. According to one theory, at the site of the bridge it flowed in a tight curve around a thin projecting spur of rock. Eventually the river carved an opening through the base of the spur. Another theory suggests that the archway developed by rapid heating and cooling of the canyon walls in the desert climate. Bit by bit the opening was enlarged to form today's monumental span.

Rainbow Bridge has been protected as a national monument since 1910. Until recently it could be reached only over a long, difficult trail. With the creation of Lake Powell, however, it is now easily accessible by boat.   □

Rainier, Mount

- United States (Washington)
- Map: page 10, C–4

Once even loftier than it is today, the snowcapped volcano is still the highest peak in the Cascade Range.

The British explorer George Vancouver made the first written reference to Mount Rainier as he sailed through Puget Sound on May 8, 1792. Describing it simply as a "round snowy mountain," he named the great massif for Peter Rainier, a friend and fellow navigator in the British Navy.

Today the most famous landmark in the Pacific Northwest is the focal point of Mount Rainier National Park. Its gleaming summit, at 14,410 feet (4,392 meters), is all the more impressive since it rises nearly 8,000 feet (2,400 meters) above any neighboring peaks. Though often veiled in clouds and mist, on clear days the massive glacier-covered mountain is visible from 100 miles (160 kilometers) away.

The peak is noted for its richly varied plant and animal life. Mountain goats are often seen on rugged, precipitous slopes. Black-tailed deer and bears also are common. But the most conspicuous animals are marmots, chipmunks, Clark's nutcrackers, and Oregon jays.

The lower slopes are mantled by dense coniferous forests typical of the humid Pacific Northwest. At higher elevations the forests give way to extensive alpine meadows dotted with scattered clumps of trees. Here visitors enjoy the annual spectacle of blossoming wildflowers. As melting snow retreats up the slopes each spring and summer, glacier lilies, lupines, monkey flowers, and many others carpet the meadows with a profusion of color.

Beyond is the realm of eternal ice and snow. Radiating from Rainier's summit like the arms of an octopus is a total of 27 named glaciers and a number of minor ones. Covering some 35 square miles (90 square kilometers), they constitute the largest single-peak glacial system in the United

States south of Alaska. The largest, the Emmons Glacier, is about 4 miles (6.4 kilometers) long and 1 mile (1.6 kilometers) wide. Deep cirques, glacier-carved valleys, and sharp ridges on the slopes testify to much more extensive glaciation during the Ice Age.

Far younger than the neighboring peaks in the Cascade Range, Mount Rainier is a volcano that sprang to life within the last 1 million years. Escaping through a weak spot in the earth's crust, successive lava flows and later explosions of rock debris gradually built up the great mountain that towers so high above its surroundings. And in fact, judging from the angles of lava flows on opposite sides of the summit, geologists speculate that Mount Rainier may once have been at least 1,000 feet (300 meters) higher than it is today. The former summit, they believe, was probably destroyed by a combination of explosions, land-slides, and mudflows.

Although the most recent eruptions of Mount Rainier—minor explosions of pumice—occurred more than 100 years ago, the volcano is not entirely dormant. Steam issuing from vents in the two summit craters has melted a system of caves and tunnels in the ice and snow that fill the basins—vivid proof that Mount Rainier's inner fires are burning still. ☐

Rakov Skocjan

- Yugoslavia
- Map: page 17, E–4

In the depths of a sheer-walled valley, a disappearing river reappears briefly at the surface.

The Rak River, also known as the Reka, rises in the limestone uplands of northwestern Yugoslavia. It eventually empties into the Gulf of Trieste at the northern tip of the Adriatic Sea. Along much of its lower course, however, the river is invisible. About 30 miles (48 kilometers) from its source, the Rak flows into a hole and disappears underground. From there to its emergence near the Adriatic coast, the river is visible from the surface at only one place.

Near the picturesque little village of Skocjan, the land drops off abruptly into a small, steep-walled valley known as the Rakov Skocjan. Unlike most valleys, it is enclosed by sheer cliffs at both ends as well as along its sides, some of them as much as 1,000 feet (300 meters) high. And there, rushing along the bottom of this great trench, is the Rak River. It emerges from the mouth of a cave at the head of the valley, plunges down a waterfall into a lake, and then disappears once

again into a sinkhole near the foot of the valley. The Rak does not surface again until it has nearly reached the sea, where, having crossed into Italy, it is known as the Timavo.

At one time even the Rakov Skocjan sector of the Rak was not visible from the surface. The great chasm through which it flows was formed by the collapse of the ceilings of two adjoining underground caverns. These broad, sheer-walled depressions, known as collapse dolines, are common features in limestone areas where slightly acidic groundwater has dissolved large cavities in the rock. The larger of the two dolines forming the Rakov Skocjan, the Velika doline, is about 1,600 feet (500 meters) in diameter and has an average depth of about 500 feet (150 meters).

Because of its great beauty and scientific interest, the area is protected in a Yugoslav national park. Trails and stairways thread along the cliffs, and in several places bridges span the seething river. Visitors can also explore part of the cave at the head of the valley and a longer sector of the river's subterranean course beyond the foot of the valley. In addition to a long underground pool called Charon's Lake, the lower caves contain very impressive displays of stalactites and stalagmites. But some of the finest views of the Rakov Skocjan and the surrounding countryside are from vantage points at the top of the encircling cliffs. ☐

Red Deer Badlands

- Canada (Alberta)
- Map: page 10, D–3

Dinosaurs once roamed in a swampy, subtropical lowland that time has transformed into a great expanse of barren, dramatically eroded rocks.

For about 200 miles (320 kilometers) along its course across the south of Alberta, the Red Deer River flows through the heart of one of Canada's rich wheat-growing regions. Only the occasional silhouettes of grain elevators and oil-drilling rigs interrupt the monotony of the grainfields that extend from horizon to horizon.

Within the river's valley, however, is a scene of striking contrasts. About 1 mile (1.6 kilometers) wide and 400 feet (120 meters) deep, the valley has been eroded into a spectacular display of

RAKOV SKOCJAN. *The foaming waters of the Rak River emerge from the darkness of a slotlike cave into a deep, sheer-walled canyon created by the collapse of a cave's ceiling.*

RED DEER BADLANDS. *Protected by caps of hard sandstone, some of the massive rock formations rise high above their surroundings.*

badlands, so named for their resemblance to the gullied landscapes of the Badlands of South Dakota.

As barren and inhospitable as their name suggests, the Red Deer Badlands nevertheless have an undeniable beauty. Composed primarily of varicolored sandstone and shale, the terraced slopes are deeply furrowed by grooves and gullies. Among the array of endlessly varied rock formations are steep-sided buttes that rise starkly above the valley floor. Huge broken blocks litter the slopes where projecting ledges have been undercut by erosion. Most striking of all are the strange conical formations known as hoodoos. Topped by protective rocky caps, they reach upward in ghostly clusters, some of them grotesque, others as slender and delicate as the spires of a majestic cathedral.

The rocks now exposed in the badlands began to form about 80 million years ago. At that time the area was part of a low-lying marshy delta at the edge of a shallow sea that extended across the center of North America. Over the course of the next few million years it was alternately submerged and elevated above the sea several times. Thick deposits of mud and sand accumulated on the delta and were eventually consolidated into layers of shale and sandstone. Finally the shrinking sea drained away, and the area became dry land. Then about 60 million years ago, during the same series of upheavals that created the Rocky Mountains, the region was uplifted to its present elevation high above sea level.

Erosion then set in and began to strip away the rock layers. It was especially severe as the Ice Age drew to a close and huge amounts of meltwater came sluicing down the valley. But the process continues even today. Though the climate is semiarid—precipitation amounts to only about 12 inches, or 300 millimeters, per year—much of the rainfall comes in torrential summer downpours. With little vegetation to slow the runoff, these brief but intense floods gnaw away at the softer layers of rock. Slopes are carved into complex networks of gullies and ridges, while areas protected by layers of erosion-resistant rock remain standing as buttes and hoodoos.

Erosion has also uncovered fossils that reveal that the climate on the vanished delta was very different from what it is today. Lush vegetation flourished in the warm, wet, subtropical lowland, and it was inhabited by dinosaurs of many species. In all, the remains of some 320 of the giant reptiles have been uncovered in the valley. Some of the finest fossil specimens can be seen where they were found in Dinosaur Provincial Park.   □

Rhine River

- Northern Europe
- Map: page 16, D–3

Immortalized by poets and musicians, the strategically located, legendary river changes from Alpine torrent to scenic waterway to busy highway carrying Western Europe's commerce.

The Rhine is far from longest among the major rivers of the world. From its mountain source in Switzerland to its outlet on the North Sea, it flows a total of only 820 miles (1,320 kilometers)—less than half the length of the Danube. And its drainage basin of 85,000 square miles (220,000 square kilometers) is only slightly larger than the state of Kansas.

Yet few rivers can compare with the Rhine for its combined aura of history and romance. Valued since Roman times for its strategic location, it was for centuries both a source of international friction and a major avenue for commerce and migration. To this day it remains the busiest waterway in the world. At the same time, the extraordinary beauty of its valley, populated by mythical heroes and death-dealing Sirens, has been a constant source of inspiration to poets and musicians.

Much of the Rhine's unique personality results from its varied nature. Seemingly made up of several radically different rivers linked together at random, it changes repeatedly in character as it makes its way from the mountains to the sea.

At its source the river belies its name, which is based on the word *rein*, meaning "pure" or "clear" in both ancient Celtic and modern German. Its two headstreams, the Vorder Rhein

Although the headwaters of the Rhine reach flood stage during the summer, downstream tributaries are at their highest during the winter, ensuring a dependable flow in the lower river all year round.

and the Hinter Rhein, rise high in the Swiss Alps. Fed by glaciers and melting snow, they are clouded, turbulent torrents that unite at the town of Reichenau to form the Rhine proper.

Heading northward, with its muddy waters constrained by dikes to prevent flooding, the upper Rhine flows past the orchards and meadowlands of Liechtenstein and Austria. Its current slows dramatically as it enters the calm expanse of the Lake of Constance on the border between Switzerland and West Germany. The vast accumulations of mud and silt settle to the bottom, and when the river emerges from the opposite end of the lake it is truly *rein*—pure and clean.

Following a westerly course, the river reverts to its Alpine character as it plunges over the picturesque Falls of the Rhine near Schaffhausen, Switzerland. Though only about 65 feet (20 meters) high, the falls are famous for the beauty of their multiple thundering cascades.

As it continues westward along the border between Switzerland and West Germany, a number of Alpine tributaries join the Rhine, most notably the Aar. By the time it reaches Basel, the Rhine has traveled some 230 miles (370 kilometers) and descended near-

RHINE RIVER. *Near its source high in the Alps of eastern Switzerland, the youthful Rhine is a rushing mountain torrent fed by the runoff of melting snowfields and glaciers.*

RHINE RIVER. *Clogged with islands and hemmed in by steep wooded slopes, the river flows majestically through its famous scenic gorge.*

ly 7,000 feet (2,100 meters) from its mountain source. From that point to the sea its waters will drop only 800 feet (250 meters) more.

At Basel the river turns abruptly to the north and passes through a broad valley. A trench formed by the collapse of a segment of the earth's crust, the valley is bounded by France's Vosges Mountains on the west and by the rugged uplands of West Germany's Black Forest on the opposite side. Once shallow and meandering, this section of the river has been greatly altered by canals and dredged channels, so that the Rhine is now navigable by barges from Basel all the way to the North Sea.

Beyond the border with France, two major tributaries, the Neckar and the Main, enter the Rhine and help stabilize its flow. While its Alpine sources reach flood stage in early summer, tributaries in the lower basin have their greatest flow in winter. The result is a balanced year-round flow that facilitates navigation.

One of the many legends of the Rhine is associated with this sector of the river; the city of Worms on the west bank was the setting for the *Nibelungenlied.* The epic poem, with its tales of treachery and treasure buried

in the Rhine, was the inspiration for Richard Wagner's *Ring* operas.

The river's most romantic stretch, however, begins at Bingen. Deflected to the west by the Taunus Mountains, then turning north again, the Rhine enters a narrow winding gorge that continues all the way to Bonn, some 90 miles (145 kilometers) to the north. Terraced vineyards flourish on the sunny slopes, and castles, once the seats of warring medieval lords, crown the hilltops.

Rocky outcrops in the gorge have always complicated the task of river pilots, but none so much as the famed Lorelei, a cliff 433 feet (132 meters) high. According to legend, a beautiful Siren used to sit atop the rock and, with her seductive singing, lure sailors to their deaths in the treacherous currents swirling at its base. Farther down, near Bonn, are the Siebengebirge, the "Seven Mountains," said to have been dropped from the shovels of giants as they excavated the riverbed. It was on one of them, the Drachenfels, or "Dragon's Rock," that the Wagnerian hero Siegfried slew his mythical dragon.

Downstream from Bonn, West Germany's capital, the Rhine undergoes another transformation. Leaving the

mountains once and for all, it widens considerably as it flows sluggishly across the coastal plain. Passing Cologne, the river flows by Düsseldorf and the Ruhr, the great coal-mining and steel-manufacturing regions. By this time the river is not *rein* at all, but its polluted channel does carry a formidable amount of river traffic.

The changeable river makes its final alteration as it leaves West Germany and passes into its delta in the Netherlands. There it divides into two major channels, the Lek and the Waal, as well as a number of minor ones. (Bridges over the branches at Nijmegen and Arnhem were the focus of two important battles in World War II.) A network of canals connects the delta with nearby cities such as Amsterdam, but the Rhine's principal seaport is Rotterdam, which ranks as one of the world's major deep-sea ports.

In recent years the Dutch have begun to build enormous dams across some of the Rhine's lower branches in an effort to exclude seawater from the delta. When this system is completed, it will no doubt bring still further changes to the restless Rhine, which for so long and so dramatically has influenced and in turn been influenced by mankind. □

RHUMEL GORGE. *Vertical cliffs of the canyon carved by the Rhumel River form the natural ramparts of the ancient city of Constantine.*

Rhumel Gorge

- Algeria
- Map: page 24, D–2

Part of the "moat" surrounding a great natural fortress, the gorge has witnessed centuries of history.

The ancient city of Constantine in northeastern Algeria is noted for its magnificent setting. Perched atop a high limestone bluff, the Rock of Constantine, it is nearly encircled by steep cliffs. On the east and north the city is bounded by the Rhumel Gorge, a dizzying chasm carved by the Rhumel River on its short course from an interior plateau to the Mediterranean. On the west the bluff is bordered by still more cliffs, carved by a tributary of the Rhumel. Only a narrow, ramplike neck of land on the southwest connects the Rock of Constantine with the adjoining hills.

Thus cut off from its surroundings, the rock is a remarkable natural fortress, and its strategic value has been recognized since antiquity. In prehistoric times humans lived in some of the many caves that pock the walls of the Rhumel Gorge. By the third century B.C., the bluff was occupied by Cirta, the flourishing principal city of

the Numidian kingdom. Conquered by the Romans, Cirta was destroyed in a civil war in A.D. 311 and then rebuilt by the Roman emperor Constantine the Great and renamed in his honor. Taken over in turn by the Arabs, Turks, and French, all of whom left their mark on it, Constantine remains the largest inland city in Algeria.

The Rock of Constantine is no longer isolated from its surroundings. A number of bridges now span the Rhumel Gorge, which in places narrows to only 15 feet (4.6 meters) across. One of them occupies the same site as a bridge that was built by the Romans. Far below—parts of the canyon are as much as 700 feet (215 meters) deep—the river in several places passes under natural bridges that have been eroded in the limestone massif. As it leaves the gorge the river plunges down in a series of waterfalls, where its power has been harnessed in a hydroelectric generation plant.

Fine views of the Rhumel Gorge are available from the bridges and from roads that cling to the edges of the cliffs. One of them is named Boulevard de l'Abîme ("Boulevard of the Abyss"). Other points of interest in the city include Roman ruins, the old native quarter, Moorish palaces, and a number of ancient mosques. □

Ribeira Caves

- Brazil
- Map: page 15, E–5

A tropical river system weaves its way through a maze of canyons, caves, and disappearing streams.

The Ribeira River rises on the southern flanks of the Serra Paranapiacaba, a short mountain range not far from the Atlantic in southern Brazil. Flowing more or less eastward for about 200 miles (320 kilometers), it passes through a region of dense tropical forests before emptying into the sea.

All along the way it is joined by tributaries that have strikingly irregular drainage patterns. Flowing above the ground one moment and then under the ground the next, their unpredictable and sometimes untraceable courses include complicated networks of caves, springs, sinkholes, and subterranean channels. Streams plunge underground on adjoining plateaus, reappear as springs at the heads of canyons, then after short courses on the surface disappear again.

Landscapes of this sort are known to geologists as karst topography, named for the Karst region of northwestern Yugoslavia, where such features are especially well developed. They occur chiefly in limestone terrain, which is easily dissolved by slightly acidic groundwater.

Though less famous than some of its Yugoslav counterparts, the Ribeira's drainage basin offers a particularly striking example of the kinds of water circulation that can develop in a karst region. One of the Ribeira's tributaries, the Rio Alambari, for instance, is fed by a stream that disappears into a sinkhole on a nearby plateau and emerges at a spring. Flowing down its valley, the Alambari in turn disappears into a cave, crosses a beautifully decorated chamber, and then descends through a passage that leads out into a neighboring valley. Another river in the area has an even more convoluted course: it plunges into a sinkhole, flows through an underground channel, emerges briefly on the surface, disappears into a second sinkhole, and after another underground passage makes its final exit into daylight.

As with other karst landscapes, the Ribeira's drainage basin is notable for its many caves, including some of huge dimensions. One, the Casa de Pedra, is 500 feet (150 meters) high. Some of the Ribeira Caves are easily accessible to exploration; others remain little known and visited. In addition to the beauty of their mysteriously disappearing underground streams, many of the caves are exceptional for their displays of stalactites, stalagmites, and other types of dripstone deposits. □

Rift Valley

- East Africa—Southwest Asia
- Map: page 26

The awesome intercontinental cleft is evidence of the titanic forces that have altered the face of the earth.

The Rift Valley, sometimes known as the Great Rift Valley, is a gigantic trenchlike fracture in the earth's crust. It extends from northern Syria across East Africa to southern Mozambique —a total distance of about 4,800 miles (7,700 kilometers). Averaging 25 to 35 miles (40 to 55 kilometers) in width, it is typically bounded by high cliffs or tiers of cliffs that in places rise thousands of feet above the valley floor. The floor itself varies in elevation from far below sea level in the Dead Sea to 6,000 feet (1,800 meters) above the sea in Kenya. The overall contours of the Rift Valley can be traced on any map by noting the many bodies of water cupped in the depression. Its northern extremity is marked by the Jordan River valley, the Dead Sea, and the Gulf of Aqaba. Beyond that the great cleft is occupied by the Red Sea, with a branch extending east through the Gulf of Aden.

The Rift Valley enters Africa in the broad, fan-shaped Danakil Depression, an area of intense heat and barren salt flats reaching some 400 feet (120 meters) below sea level. The valley floor rises to much higher elevations as it bisects Ethiopia and, in

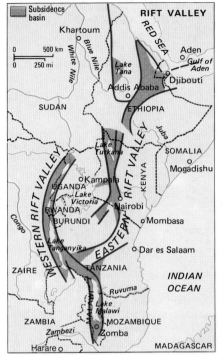

The two arms of the Rift Valley are among the most conspicuous topographic features in East Africa. The red lines indicate major fault zones bordering collapsed sections of the earth's crust that make up the valley.

northern Kenya, contains the waters of Lake Turkana. Continuing across Tanzania and Malawi into Mozambique, the southern part of the Rift Valley is occupied by long, narrow Lake Malawi.

To the north of the lake the valley divides in two, with the Western Rift Valley branching away from the main Eastern Rift Valley. Curving northward along the border of Zaire, the Western Rift Valley contains a conspicuous chain of large lakes, including Lake Tanganyika and Lake Kivu.

Most geologists explain the origin of the Rift Valley in terms of the concept of continental drift. This theory suggests that the earth's crust is made up of a number of rigid plates drifting about on the earth's molten interior. In some places the plates have collided, producing great mountain ranges; in other places they are drifting apart. While most plates move apart at the ocean floor, in the Rift Valley they are pulling apart the land. In the north the Arabian Plate is drifting away from the African Plate, and in the south the African Plate is breaking up into a number of subplates.

It is generally believed that the process began when an upflow of heat caused the earth's crust to bulge upward in an arch. The actual rifting

RIBEIRA CAVES. *A variety of complex dripstone formations decorates a chamber in the Caverna do Diabo, the "Devil's Cave," one of the many caverns in the Ribeira River valley.*

began some 25 million years ago, when parallel lines of faults developed along the top of the arch, until the keystone of the arch finally collapsed between the faults and formed a series of huge depressions.

The process of subsidence occurred in repeated stages and is probably still under way today. In some areas a number of faults developed on each side of the Rift Valley, so that it is bordered by a steplike sequence of cliffs rather than a single high escarpment. A great deal of volcanic activity, which continues to this day, was also associated with the rifting. In some places the bottom of the trench has been obscured by huge floods of lava that welled up through the faults and filled in much of the valley floor. Elsewhere lava flows formed the barriers that dammed up lakes. When viewed atop a bordering escarpment, the Rift Valley is an awesome reminder of the tremendous forces that have shaped the face of the earth.   □

Riglos, Los Mallos de

● Spain
● Map: page 17, C–4

The huge rock towers—by-products of the birth of the Pyrenees—were sculpted from stone that was formed as the mountains came into being.

In the foothills of the Pyrenees in northern Spain, three clusters of tremendous rock towers rise abruptly from the valley of the Gállego River. Known as Los Mallos de Riglos (*mallos* means "mallets"), many of the giant monoliths culminate more than 1,000 feet (300 meters) above the valley floor. The westernmost group of towers overlooks the river like massive silent sentinels. But the highest and most spectacular by far is the central group, which completely dwarfs the village of Riglos huddled at its base.

The austerely furrowed rock masses are by-products of the creation of the Pyrenees. Even as the mountain range was being uplifted to its present elevation, the forces of erosion were gnawing away its slowly rising summits. Streams washing down from the heights deposited a deltalike cone of smoothly rounded pebbles in the Riglos area. Cemented together by sandy limestone, the pebbles over a period of time were compacted into a thick mass of reddish-colored conglomerate rock.

Erosion then began to attack the conglomerate. Ravines developed between the three groups of towers, landslides deepened the gaps, and cracks and fissures in the rock were widened to form the outlines of each group of hulking monoliths. Completely dominating their surroundings, Los Mallos de Riglos remain as testimony to the gradually changing contours of the landscape along the southern flanks of the Pyrenees.   □

RIFT VALLEY. *Beneath a somber sky, outcrops of volcanic rock interrupt the general flatness of a section of the valley floor in Kenya.*

Rio de Janeiro

- Brazil
- Map: page 15, E–5

Sandy beaches and unique sugar loaf mountains surround a sparkling bay to form an incomparable setting.

Rio de Janeiro, at the mouth of Guanabara Bay, is universally acknowledged to have one of the most spectacular settings of any city in the world. On all sides the steep slopes of domelike, emerald-green mountains plunge down almost to the edge of the bay and the sea. The city itself spreads out in every direction through narrow valleys between the ancient granite massifs. And on the oceanfront, rows of skyscrapers line the long, crescent-shaped beaches such as the famed Copacabana and Ipanema.

Standing like a sentinel at the entrance to the bay is the city's best-known landmark, Pão de Açúcar, or Sugar Loaf Mountain. Its rounded summit, accessible by cable car, towers 1,296 feet (395 meters) over the bay. The neighboring crest of Corcovado, the "Hunchback," at 2,310 feet (704 meters), affords even more sweeping views of the city, mountains, beaches, and bay.

The city's name, meaning "River of January," originated with Portuguese

LOS MALLOS DE RIGLOS. *Towering over terraced orchards and the little village of Riglos, the clustered monoliths were carved from a deltalike deposit of pebbles and rock debris.*

RIO DE JANEIRO. *The smoothly rounded dome of Sugar Loaf Mountain at the entrance to Guanabara Bay is a famous landmark.*

The Formation of Sugar Loaf Mountains and Rock Domes

Rio de Janeiro's Sugar Loaf Mountain is an extreme example of a rock dome. Barren, steep-sided, smoothly rounded formations of this sort most commonly develop in massifs of granite and other very hard crystalline rock that have not been broken up by faults. They are primarily the result of exfoliation, a process that splits the outer layers away from the underlying rock, often in great curved slabs that resemble the layers of an onion. The slabs are loosened in part by chemical disintegration of the rock. Strong temperature contrasts between day and night also play a role in loosening the surface slabs; alternate heating and cooling causes them to expand and contract at a different rate from the inner core of rock. One by one, the layers flake off and disintegrate, leaving a smoothly rounded dome that projects high above its surroundings.

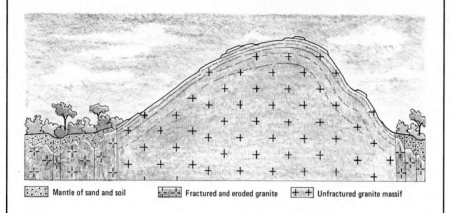

Mantle of sand and soil   Fractured and eroded granite   Unfractured granite massif

explorers who sailed into the entrance to the bay on January 1, 1502, and mistook it for the mouth of a river. Had they sailed in farther, they would have discovered their error, for Guanabara Bay is one of the largest and safest natural harbors in the world. Beyond the entrance, which is only about 1 mile (1.6 kilometers) across, the bay opens into a broad, island-dotted expanse of water some 18 miles (29 kilometers) long and as much as 12 miles (19 kilometers) wide.

Actually a so-called drowned valley, the bay was inundated by rising seas when vast continental ice caps melted at the end of the Ice Age. Although its shoreline was originally rocky and irregular, it is being smoothed out by erosion and sedimentation. Extensive landfill and reclamation projects have also altered the contours of the bay.

More than most cities', Rio de Janeiro's growth has been governed by topography. Hemmed in between the mountains and the sea, it spread out along the coast and expanded far inland by following the random contours of the valleys. (In many places, tunnels penetrate the mountains to connect nearby points in the city that would otherwise be nearly inaccessible.) Despite extensive slums that cling precariously to the mountainsides, the city matches the grandeur of its setting. □

Rio Grande

- Mexico—United States
- Map: page 11, E–6

Rich in history and folklore, the great river flows through landscapes of stark and startling beauty.

The Rio Grande rises at an altitude of more than 12,000 feet (3,650 meters) in the San Juan Mountains in southwestern Colorado. From its source near the Continental Divide, it flows some 1,885 miles (3,034 kilometers) to its outlet on the Gulf of Mexico, making it the fifth longest river in North America. Its drainage basin of 170,000 square miles (440,000 square kilometers) is more than three times the size of Illinois.

Fed by melting snowfields, the Rio Grande at first rushes down steep, densely forested mountain slopes. As it passes into New Mexico and flows south across the center of the state, it enters a canyon 70 miles (113 kilometers) long and up to 800 feet (244 meters) deep. Along its middle course it flows through a semiarid region of piñons, junipers, and sagebrush that gradually gives way to a desert zone dotted with cactus, mesquite, and other drought-resistant plants.

The river turns southeastward when it reaches Texas and for the rest of its length marks the U.S.–Mexican border. Forming a great loop in the Big Bend region of West Texas, the Rio Grande passes through an area of gaunt mountains and hidden valleys. There the river has carved three spectacular, sheer-walled canyons, one of them 1,700 feet (518 meters) deep. The U.S. side of the Big Bend, once the lair of outlaws, is now a national park.

Below the Big Bend the Rio Grande enters the coastal plain, where its silty waters change course frequently. After traversing a lush, subtropical region famous for its truck farms and citrus groves, the river empties into the Gulf of Mexico.

The Rio Grande's flow is extremely variable. Melting snow brings high water to the upper course in late spring, but rainfall in the lower basin is sparse and unpredictable. In some areas, so much water is withdrawn for irrigation that the river often slows to a trickle or even dries up completely. Even so, long stretches of the Rio Grande still justify its name, which means "the big river." □

Rocher de Sel

- Algeria
- Map: page 24, D–2

On an African plateau, a mountain of salt has managed to withstand the relentless attacks of water erosion.

Near the market town of Djelfa, just north of the high peaks of the Saharan Atlas in northern Algeria, a strange whitish dome bulges conspicuously above the surrounding plateau. Some 5,000 feet (1,500 meters) in diameter and 350 feet (105 meters) high, its glistening summit is visible from afar.

Its name, Rocher de Sel, is French for "rock of salt," and that is exactly what it is: an entire mountain of common salt mixed with clay. Its surface is hard and barren, devoid of vegetation except in a few depressions where enough soil has accumulated to support a sparse cover of hardy grasses.

A number of similar formations, some of them even larger than Rocher de Sel, exist elsewhere in Algeria,

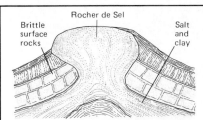

Rocher de Sel was formed when the earth's crust buckled up in a fold, and a buried layer of salt and clay burst through more brittle overlying rocks.

Morocco, and other parts of the world. Although geologists know how the domes came into being, they are less certain of why the salt was not dissolved and washed away long ago.

Rocher de Sel is part of a layer of salt and clay that was once buried beneath the surface. As stresses in the earth's crust caused the surface to arch upward in a fold, the relatively pliant layer of salt and clay ruptured the more brittle overlying rock layers and burst through to the surface.

The resulting dome bears the marks of prolonged water erosion, both on the surface and internally. The summit is smooth and rounded, while the slopes are scarred by networks of ravines and furrows. Inside the dome, rainwater seeping through joints and crevices has dissolved a labyrinth of narrow, twisting channels. Some lead to dead ends, closed off by mud slides; others are interconnected, forming an irregular drainage system that guides rainwater to a few saline springs at the edges of the dome.

Despite its susceptibility to erosion, however, Rocher de Sel remains basically intact. One theory accounts for this by suggesting that the light local rainfall simply runs off or is absorbed by the clay before it can dissolve much of the salt. Another suggests that the folding of the rock is still under way; new salt bulges upward as fast as the surface is worn away. But it seems more likely that any water penetrating the dome soon becomes a brine so saturated with salt that it cannot dissolve any more. Hence the durability of Rocher de Sel. □

ROCHER DE SEL. *Though deeply gullied on the surface and riddled by channels within, the massive salt dome remains basically intact.*

ROCKY MOUNTAINS

ROCKY MOUNTAINS. *Peyto Lake in Canada's Banff National Park is fed by a melting glacier that persists among the high mountain peaks.*

Rocky Mountains

- Canada—United States
- Map: page 10

Thrust upward from an ancient sea, the great mountain rampart forms the spine of western North America.

The Rocky Mountains, which extend from Alaska to New Mexico, are part of the great mountain system that continues all the way down the western part of the Americas to Cape Horn at the southern tip of Chile. The northernmost range of the Rockies, the Brooks Range, spans all of northern Alaska and merges in the east with the various ranges of the Canadian Rockies. South of the United States border, the mountain chain continues into Idaho, western Montana, Wyoming, Utah, Colorado, and New Mexico. Farther south the Rockies merge finally with the Sierra Madre Oriental in Mexico. From Alaska to New Mexico the chain is approximately 3,100 miles (5,000 kilometers) long.

The eastern border of the Rockies is clearly defined. From Alberta to New Mexico the mountain ramparts rise as an abrupt wall above the Great Plains, which slope away to the east. The western edge of the Rockies, bounded by a series of high plateaus and basins, is less obvious. From north to south these highlands include the interior plateaus of British Columbia, the Columbia Plateau in the northwestern United States, the Great Basin (itself a rugged mountainous region), and the Colorado Plateau. These uplands in turn are bordered on the west by the high peaks of the Cascade Range and the Sierra Nevada, which give way to the Coast Ranges immediately parallel to the Pacific Coast.

The highest summits of the Rockies are concentrated in Colorado, where about 50 peaks exceed 14,000 feet (4,300 meters). The highest of all is Mount Elbert, to the southwest of Denver, at 14,431 feet (4,399 meters); the highest peak in the Canadian Rockies is Mount Robson, at 12,972 feet (3,954 meters).

From north to south the rugged mountain spine forms North America's Continental Divide. Waters on the western side flow to the Pacific Ocean, those on the eastern side to the Arctic and Atlantic oceans. Canadian rivers such as the Peace and Athabasca flow to the Arctic Ocean by way of the Mackenzie River. Other great rivers rising on the eastern slopes of the Rockies, including the Missouri, Yellowstone, and Rio Grande, empty eventually into the Gulf of Mexico, an arm of the Atlantic. Among the major Pacific-bound rivers are the Yukon, Columbia, and Colorado.

The great mountain range that now separates the flow between oceans had its own origins at the bottom of a shallow sea. At one time a long troughlike basin extended all the way across western North America from the Gulf of Mexico to the Arctic Ocean. Over tens of millions of years debris was washed into the sea that

ROCKY MOUNTAINS. *An autumn snowfall enhances the beauty of a glacier-carved range of the Rockies in western Colorado.*

occupied the basin, where it accumulated in thick deposits of sandstone, limestone, shale, and other sedimentary rocks.

Then, about 60 million years ago, a long series of upheavals occurred that elevated the rocks above the sea and transformed them into mountains. A great variety of mountain-building processes was involved. Many of the individual ranges, which tend to be oriented from north to south, are the result of pressures that caused the earth's crust to buckle up in elongated folds. Erosion subsequently stripped away the cover of sedimentary rock on the top of the folds, exposing the core of ancient crystalline basement rock. On the mountain flanks, the once-horizontal sedimentary rocks remain in steeply tilted layers.

Elsewhere great blocks of the earth's crust were thrust up along major faults. Among the most spectacular examples of such fault-block mountains are the Tetons in Wyoming. As the mountains moved up on the west side of this fault, the floor of Jackson Hole dropped down on the east side. Today the sheer mountain wall towers as much as 6,600 feet (2,000 meters) above the valley floor.

Mountains of the Lewis Range in Glacier National Park in northern Montana, in contrast, are the result of an overthrust fault. There a huge block of the earth's crust slid eastward for a total distance of about 35 miles (55 kilometers) over the top of an adjacent block of the crust. As a result, ancient basement rock there rests on top of much younger sedimentary rock layers. Most of the mountains of Idaho, in turn, are eroded in a giant batholith. In that area a huge mass of molten material from the earth's interior welled up into the overlying rock layers, ultimately cooling and hardening into a mountain core of massive granitic rock.

Volcanism also played a role in building the Rockies. The San Juan Mountains of western Colorado and New Mexico were formed by a long series of volcanic eruptions. Farther north the Yellowstone Plateau was built up by repeated lava flows. The area's abundance of geysers and hot springs provides evidence that even today molten material lies not very far beneath the surface. Much of the Rockies' mineral wealth is also the result of igneous activity; silver, gold, and other metals are found in dikes or veins of once-molten rock that was injected into the earth's crust.

The Rockies took their present form after a final period of uplift that ended about 2 million years ago. The master sculptors were the glaciers of the Ice Age that scoured the slopes, creating bowllike cirques, sparkling lakes, jagged mountain crests, and U-shaped glacial valleys. Glaciers still persist on many of the peaks, especially in the northern part of the range. Among the most impressive remnants of the Ice Age is the Columbia Icefield in the Canadian Rockies, straddling the Continental Divide and covering 120 square miles (310 square kilometers).

Despite their varied origins, the far-flung ranges of the Rocky Mountains, most visitors agree, share one common attribute: extraordinary beauty. With large areas of pristine wilderness protected in national parks and other sanctuaries, it is probable that their beauty will remain intact for generations to come. □

Roraima, Mount

- Northern South America
- Map: page 14, C–2

This steep, flat-topped mountain is the highest point in the remote wilds of South America's Guiana Highlands.

The Guiana Highlands are an area of mountainous uplands that extend some 1,200 miles (1,900 kilometers) across northern South America. Composed of plateaus of ancient crystalline basement rock overlaid by massive sandstone and lava formations, the remote, sparsely populated region forms the drainage divide between the Orinoco and Amazon river basins.

The entire area has been dissected by erosion into a number of mountain ranges and enormous isolated flat-topped plateaus. The highest point in the Guiana Highlands is Mount Roraima, at 9,219 feet (2,810 meters). Located where the borders of Venezuela, Guyana, and Brazil converge, it is a large table mountain some 9 miles (15 kilometers) long and 3 miles (5 kilometers) wide. Most of the reddish sandstone massif lies within the borders of Venezuela.

Flat-topped and bordered by steep slopes, Mount Roraima towers high above the surrounding grasslands and luxuriant tropical forests at its base. Frequently obscured by clouds, the rather barren mountaintop is well watered by frequent rainfalls. Multitudes of streams cascade down Mount Roraima in all directions, some bound for the Orinoco River to the north, some headed toward the Amazon basin to the south, and still others flowing northeastward to the coastal lowlands of Guyana. Nearly all of them are interrupted by impressive waterfalls where they spill over the edges of sheer cliffs.

Because of its remoteness and inaccessibility, Mount Roraima is little known to the outside world. No one had even climbed to its top until 1884. Indeed, the entire Guiana Highlands remain one of the world's least developed areas. Spanish conquistadores once thought the uplands might be the site of El Dorado, a land of unimaginable wealth, but they had little success in penetrating the rugged wilderness. In more recent times substantial deposits of gold and diamonds have been mined in the highlands, and other mineral discoveries may lead to the region's eventual development. □

MOUNT RORAIMA. *On the mountain itself and throughout the Guiana Highlands, rivers and streams form spectacular waterfalls where they spill over the edges of high plateaus.*

ROSS ICE SHELF. *Responding to stresses in the ice, gigantic icebergs regularly break from the edge of the shelf and drift off to sea.*

Ross Ice Shelf

- Antarctica
- Map: page 9

On the frozen margin of the frozen continent, an enormous floating shelf of ice extends far out into the sea.

In 1841 the British explorer James Clark Ross approached Antarctica in an attempt to reach the South Magnetic Pole. Sailing into the Ross Sea, an arm of the Pacific later named in his honor, he was halted by an impenetrable barrier. Stretching from horizon to horizon were the sheer cliffs of a solid wall of ice.

Although Ross sailed along the barrier for several days, he could find no break in it that would enable him to sail farther south. For in fact there are no breaks. The explorer had discovered the northern edge of the Ross Ice Shelf, an enormous floating raft of ice that completely fills a huge embayment on the coast of Antarctica.

The seaward edge of the shelf is a solid line of ice cliffs some 500 miles (800 kilometers) long and as much as 200 feet (60 meters) high. Beyond this wall-like margin, the gently rolling surface of the ice shelf extends about 600 miles (965 kilometers) toward the south, where it is connected to the shoreline at the edge of the continent. By far the largest of several ice shelves that fringe Antarctica, the Ross Ice Shelf covers a total of about 200,000 square miles (520,000 square kilometers)—an area nearly the size of Texas.

Although the seaward edge of the ice shelf extended much farther north during the Ice Age, its position has been relatively stable during historic times. The great ice platform is far from static, however. Fissures develop in the ice, causing huge tabular icebergs to break off and drift northward across the sea. The bergs are commonly 20 to 30 miles (32 to 48 kilometers) in length, and some of them are even larger.

Despite losses to icebergs and melting, the margin of the shelf is not receding, since it is constantly replenished by new ice. Some of the ice is contributed by glaciers that spill down through gaps in the coastal mountains, and some is added as seawater freezes on the bottom of the platform. But the major source of growth is snow that falls on the surface of the shelf and is gradually compacted into ice. The sheer weight of the enormously thick layer of ice causes it to spread outward in much the same manner as continental ice caps. In some places the ice is moving seaward at a rate of about 6 feet (1.8 meters) per day. Thus the Ross Ice Shelf is like a gigantic conveyor belt, calving icebergs into the sea at more or less the same rate that new ice is being added to it.

Ironically, although the ice shelf was a barrier to Ross, it became the launching point for many later Antarctic expeditions. Roald Amundsen, the first to reach the South Pole, Robert Falcon Scott, the second to do so, and many others approached the interior of the continent by way of the Ross Ice Shelf. Today the United States and New Zealand maintain research stations on McMurdo Sound at the western end of the shelf, an area that is even visited occasionally by tourist ships. □

Rügen

- East Germany
- Map: page 16, E–3

This island, noted for its contorted shape and cliffs of chalk, was once a cluster of several separate islands.

Separated from the mainland by a narrow channel, Rügen lies off the northern coast of East Germany in the Baltic Sea. With an area of about 360 square miles (930 square kilometers), it is the largest East German island.

Rügen is noted for the extraordinary complexity of its coastline. Peninsulas appear to radiate in all directions, enclosing small coves, bays, and convoluted channels. The island's profile, moreover, slopes up dramatically from lowlands on the west to lines of sheer sea-carved chalk cliffs that tower high above the sea on the east.

The island's strange shape is explained by an unusual sequence of events. At one time it was not just one island but a small archipelago. The group of islands was formed by the fracturing and tilting of the chalk formation from the tremendous weight of Ice Age glaciers. The glaciers then deposited boulders and debris on top of the chalk as they retreated to the north. (Many of the boulders were erected as monuments by Neolithic inhabitants of the island.) When the sea level rose at the end of the Ice Age, waves began rearranging the glacial deposits. Gradually, interconnecting spits of sand and gravel were built up between the islands, knitting the little archipelago into the single picturesque island of Rügen. □

Rumoka

- Zaire
- Map: page 26, B–3

Small and seemingly dormant, this African volcano posed a problem when it last erupted in 1912 and 1913.

Rumoka is one of the smaller volcanoes that make up the Virunga Mountains, directly north of Africa's Lake Kivu. Despite its small size, Rumoka's one known eruption posed a problem that continues to puzzle geologists today.

In December 1912 Rumoka began to expel streams of gray-black lava, and the lava flows continued until March 1913. There was nothing unusual about Rumoka's eruption. But observers were quite surprised when on February 13, 1913, a much larger neighboring volcano, Nyamlagira, suddenly exploded with a massive simultaneous eruption.

Differences in the composition of the lava that flowed from the two volcanoes proved that it could not have come from the same magma reservoir. Yet it seems clear that Nyamlagira's eruption was in some way influenced by Rumoka's activity. But no one has been able to explain how the one volcano's eruption might have triggered an explosive blast by its gigantic neighbor. ☐

Ruwenzori

- Uganda—Zaire
- Map: page 26, C–2

This snowcapped mountain range, hidden by clouds much of the time, long remained a tantalizing myth.

In the second century A.D. the Greek geographer Ptolemy drew a map that identified the mysterious source of the Nile as "the Mountains of the Moon," a range he believed rose more than 2,000 miles (3,200 kilometers) south of the river's outlet on the Mediterranean. He was wrong about the source of the Nile, but some 17 centuries later he was proved to be right about the mountains' existence. In the 1880's the famed explorer Henry Morton Stanley sighted an impressive, hitherto unknown range about 150 miles (240 kilometers) west of Lake Victoria—almost exactly where Ptolemy's ancient map said the Mountains of the Moon would be found.

Vivid though the old name was, however, Stanley favored the African name for the lofty, often cloud-covered range: Ruwenzori, "the Rainmaker." The mountains' multitude of streams, fed by some 75 inches (1,900 millimeters) of precipitation per year, turned out not to be the ultimate source of the Nile. But they do contribute to its flow—and from higher elevations than any other tributaries.

Running roughly north to south along the border between Uganda and Zaire, the Ruwenzori has six summits that rise to more than 15,000 feet (4,600 meters) above sea level. The highest of them all is Mount Margherita, with an elevation of 16,763 feet (5,109 meters). Surrounded by clusters of smaller peaks, the major summits rise along the crest of the range, which has an overall length of about 75 miles (120 kilometers) and a width of 30 miles (48 kilometers).

Though situated just north of the equator, the Ruwenzori is capped by a perpetual cover of ice and snow, with several valley glaciers at higher elevations. It also has an extremely lush rain forest at altitudes between 10,000 and 14,000 feet (3,000 and 4,300 meters). There the slopes are covered by mosses, lichens, and a profusion of tree-sized giant lobelias, groundsels, and other flowering plants.

Unlike many of the region's other major mountains, the Ruwenzori is not volcanic in origin. It is composed of a block of ancient crystalline basement rock that was thrust upward rather recently in geologic terms, possibly within the last 2 million years or so. The cause of the uplift is not entirely clear, but it seems likely that it was related to the massive faulting and subsidence that resulted in the creation of the adjacent Rift Valley. ☐

RUWENZORI. *Temporarily freed of its usual covering of clouds, the massive mountain range rises high above the grassy plains of Uganda.*

S

Saana Mountain

- Finland
- Map: page 16, F–2

Though isolated today, this majestic Finnish mountain at one time was connected to ranges far to the west.

Far to the north of the Arctic Circle in Finnish Lapland, isolated mountains here and there loom high above their surroundings. Stark and barren, they rise like islands above seemingly endless expanses of birch and evergreen forests that are dotted with countless lakes, bogs, and marshes.

Among the most impressive of all is Saana Mountain (also known as Saanatunturi), located in the northwesternmost corner of Finland where its border touches on both Sweden and Norway. Once revered as a sacred mountain by the local Lapp population, Saana Mountain has a striking streamlined profile that resembles the overturned hull of a ship or a huge wave surging up from the forested lowlands.

Reaching a maximum elevation of 3,376 feet (1,029 meters) above sea level, the mountain's barren, rocky summit stands some 1,600 feet (500 meters) above its base. Hikers who climb the long winding trail that leads to the top are rewarded with sweeping views of the entire area. Stretching off to the southeast is a whole series of lakes, including, along the Swedish border, Lake Kilpisjarvi, sometimes called "the pearl of Lapland." To the northeast a number of other high, barren plateaus create a scene of stark grandeur. And off toward the west are the snowy summits of the mountains of Sweden and Norway. The views are especially beautiful when autumn tints the lowland forests with vivid colors and on the long summer nights of this land of the midnight sun.

The rocks of Saanatunturi are the same types of schist and gneiss that make up the long chain of mountains extending all the way down the western coast of Scandinavia. And in fact Saana Mountain, like the other isolated summits nearby, is an outlying remnant of that mountain chain. When the mountains were being uplifted, an enormous mass of rock was thrust eastward over the ancient basement rock of northern Scandinavia, where it formed a high plateau. Attacked by eons of erosion—especially during the Ice Age—the former plateau was worn down until only the most resistant rock masses remained as isolated mountains towering above otherwise nearly flat plains. □

Sable Island

- Canada (Nova Scotia)
- Map: page 11, F–4

Off the coast of Nova Scotia, this slender, treacherous crescent of sand is migrating gradually to the east.

Long known to sailors as "the Graveyard of the Atlantic," Sable Island lies about 100 miles (160 kilometers) east of Nova Scotia. Some 20 miles (32 kilometers) long but scarcely 1 mile (1.6 kilometers) wide, it is ringed by hidden sandbars and often obscured by fog, a fatal combination that has resulted in hundreds of shipwrecks over the years. The entire island, in fact, is nothing more than the exposed tip of a huge accumulation of sand on the continental shelf. Only a thin mantle of vegetation prevents it from being eroded out of existence. As it is, waves continually wear down its western tip and add new deposits of sand at the opposite end, causing the island to move gradually toward the east. The western end has retreated approximately 6 miles (10 kilometers) in the last two centuries.

Desolate though it appears, however, Sable Island provides a home for a small but hardy breed of wild horses and a resting ground for seals. It is also the world's only known nesting area for the little Ipswich sparrow. □

Saguenay River

- Canada (Quebec)
- Map: page 11, F–4

Part river and part fjord, the great Canadian waterway courses between sheer cliffs of awesome majesty.

The Saguenay River rises at Lake St. John in southern Quebec and empties into the St. Lawrence about 120 miles (190 kilometers) northeast of the city of Quebec. Although its course is short—the total length of the Saguenay is only about 105 miles, or 170 kilometers—the river has two distinct personalities. Along the upper third of its course it is a turbulent river that churns across rapids as it plunges headlong toward sea level. For the rest of its length it is a fjord, hemmed in by steep cliffs as it completes its journey in a deep glacier-carved trench.

Lake St. John, the river's source, is a nearly circular basin covering almost

SAANA MOUNTAIN. *The Finnish mountain's imposing streamlined summit rises like an island above the boulder fields, bogs, and forests of far northern Lapland.*

SAGUENAY RIVER. *Flowing through a flooded glacial valley, the river narrows as it joins the seemingly limitless expanse of the St. Lawrence.*

390,000 square miles (1 million square kilometers). Its maximum depth is about 325 feet (100 meters). Supplied by several rivers flowing down from the rugged Laurentian highlands, it stills their waters only briefly. On its eastern shore the Saguenay escapes through two channels that soon unite, and begins its swift descent.

By the time it reaches Chicoutimi at the head of the fjord, the river has dropped about 300 feet (90 meters) and is virtually at sea level. No longer the fierce torrent that it used to be, the upper Saguenay has been tamed by a number of dams and now supplies electricity for the area's major industries, huge aluminum refineries and pulp and paper mills.

From Chicoutimi to its junction with the St. Lawrence at Tadoussac some 70 miles (115 kilometers) downstream, the Saguenay flows through a deep trough that extends far below sea level. In all likelihood, before the Ice Age an earlier river followed much the same course through a modest water-eroded valley. Then a glacier advanced down the ancestral river valley, scouring away the ancient bedrock and carving a characteristically U-shaped glacial trench that averages

about 1 mile (1.6 kilometers) in width.

Today the water in the Saguenay's fjord has an average depth of about 800 feet (245 meters); in one place it is 912 feet (278 meters) deep. And along much of its length the fjord is flanked by sheer ash-gray cliffs. They reach their highest point at the twin promontories of Cape Trinity and Cape Eternity, where walls of rock loom 1,150 feet (350 meters) above the water—and extend nearly as far beneath the surface.

Salt water reaches all the way to the head of the fjord, and the maximum tidal range is 20 feet (6 meters). When the high tides of the St. Lawrence estuary rush into the fjord—they travel its full length in just 45 minutes—the swirling water smashing against the rocky shores is an awesome spectacle. In an earlier era, iron mooring rings were anchored in the cliffs so that smaller craft could tie up safely until the violent, unpredictable currents calmed down.

But now excursion boats ply the waters of the fjord. In addition to majestic scenery, attractions of the cruises include opportunities to watch snowy white beluga whales romping in the inky waters of the Saguenay. □

How Fjords Were Formed

Fjords are long, relatively narrow glacier-carved arms of the sea. Deep and steep-sided, they often extend far inland along mountainous seacoasts that were scarred by massive glaciers during the Ice Age. In addition to the well-known fjords of Norway, some impressive examples can also be seen along the coasts of Iceland, Labrador, Alaska, New Zealand, Chile, and in a few other places.

Most fjords are believed to have been formed in ancient, preexisting river valleys. As massive tongues of ice moved slowly seaward from inland ice caps, the glaciers scoured the bedrock and carved deep U-shaped trenches that extend far below present-day sea level. Norway's Sogne Fjord, for example, is more than 4,000 feet (1,200 meters) deep. The deepest parts of fjords are usually found well inland, where the erosive power of the thick tongues of ice was greatest. Near their mouths, where the ice was thinner, the bedrock was cut less deeply and the fjords are shallower.

When the glaciers retreated at the end of the Ice Age, the meltwater caused a worldwide rise in sea level. Salt water invaded the deep glacial valleys, resulting in fjords of great beauty along many coastlines.

SAHAND. *Some of the volcano's slopes are nearly devoid of vegetation and have been deeply scarred by gullies. But the mountain's overall contours remain virtually intact.*

Sahand

- Iran
- Map: page 18, F–5

This very young volcano, almost untouched by time and erosion, towers above an Iranian plateau.

Sahand is one of several large volcanoes that dot the high plateaus of the Azerbaijan region in northwestern Iran. Located about 30 miles (48 kilometers) southeast of Tabriz, it is part of a volcanic zone that extends into eastern Turkey and includes another famous volcano, Mount Ararat.

Soaring some 6,600 feet (2,000 meters) above the surrounding area, Sahand's massive cone-shaped profile is crowned by twin summits. The higher of the two culminates at 12,172 feet (3,710 meters) above sea level, the other at 11,611 feet (3,539 meters).

Some of Sahand's slopes are ravaged by gullies, and a number of deep valleys radiate from the top. During the Ice Age small glaciers gouged basins on its flanks. But basically the mountain has been little altered by erosion: besides being in an extremely arid region, it is a very young volcano.

Earlier volcanoes rose in the area some 50 million years ago, then were largely leveled by erosion. About 2 million years ago, a new phase of upheavals began. Great blocks of the earth's crust shifted up, down, and sideways along faults, and masses of volcanic material were erupted onto the surface. It was then that Sahand and the other volcanoes of the region were born. Although Sahand is now extinct, a few of its neighbors are still active. Frequent earthquakes in the area are further evidence that the earth's crust there is still in flux.

In spite of the region's aridity, numerous springs support flourishing farms and orchards on Sahand's lower slopes. Streams flowing down from the mountain also provide part of the water supply in Tabriz. Even so, the mountain is not the island of greenery it once was. Most of the forests of oak and juniper that used to grow on its slopes have been cut down or destroyed by overgrazing.   □

St. John River

- Canada—United States
- Map: page 11, F–4

A beautiful river ends its journey from the Maine woods to the sea in a stretch of foaming rapids that seem to defy the laws of gravity.

The St. John River rises in a pond in the remote, roadless wilderness of northwest Maine and ends 418 miles (673 kilometers) downstream in the Bay of Fundy in New Brunswick. Along the way the river undergoes a complete change in personality.

For the first 100 miles (160 kilometers) of its course, the St. John is a true wilderness river. Flowing northeastward toward Canada, it is hemmed in by dense forests and interrupted by long stretches of rapids. No roads approach it in this far corner of Maine. The only traffic intruding on the solitude is the canoes of white-water boating enthusiasts.

As it approaches Canada, the St. John enters a broad U-shaped curve and for the next 80 miles (130 kilometers) forms the international boundary. Roads now follow its course; at Edmundston, New Brunswick, the St. John is joined by the Trans-Canada Highway, which parallels the river almost all the way to the coast.

At Grand Falls the river descends nearly 80 feet (25 meters) in a very dramatic cascade. Now a completely Canadian river, it flows south across New Brunswick through a broad and beautiful pastoral valley. Forests still line the banks, but there are also rich farmlands and picturesque villages. Numerous islands, marshes, and baylike branches all add to the tranquil beauty of the lower St. John.

The river's journey ends at the city of St. John on the Bay of Fundy. It is there, just upstream from its mouth, that the river undergoes its final transformation. Twice daily at the famed Reversing Falls, seawater rushes inland and climbs some 17 feet (5 meters) *up* a span of rapids. Soon the flow reverses, and the river resumes its normal descent down the rapids toward the sea. The cause of the Reversing Falls is the phenomenal tides in the Bay of Fundy, which fluctuate as much as 50 feet (15 meters) per day. With each incoming high tide, a wall of water is funneled into the river's mouth and actually flows upstream across the rapids.   □

ST. JOHN RIVER. *Before making its final descent to the Bay of Fundy, the swollen river inundates a floodplain in New Brunswick.*

St. Lucia

- Windward Islands
- Map: page 14, C–1

Twin conical peaks and bubbling sulfur springs are vivid reminders of this tropical island's volcanic past.

St. Lucia is in the Windward Islands group of the West Indies—the great island chain that runs eastward past Florida and then curves southward almost to the coast of South America. It is not a large island. Its total area is only about 240 square miles (620 square kilometers). But it is a place of extraordinary beauty. High mountains green with dense tropical forests give way to lowland plantations and quaint seaside villages. Palm-lined, powdery beaches on the east coast overlook the deep blue Atlantic Ocean; those on the west coast are lapped by the tranquil turquoise Caribbean Sea.

Like many of the West Indian islands, St. Lucia is volcanic in origin. Its highest summit, Morne Gimie, towers 3,145 feet (959 meters) above sea level. But the island's most distinctive feature is a pair of almost perfectly cone-shaped peaks that rise straight up from the water's edge on the southwest coast, where they are separated by only a small bay. The larger of the two, the Gros Piton ("Big Peak"), juts up 2,619 feet (798 meters) from the sea—about twice the height of the Empire State Building in New York City. Its neighbor, the Petit Piton ("Little Peak"), culminates at 2,461 feet (750 meters).

The Pitons are exceptional examples of volcanic plugs, essentially the solidified cores of now-vanished volcanoes. When the volcanoes ceased erupting, the molten magma in their vents cooled and formed masses of extremely hard rock. In time the forces of erosion stripped away the ash and cinders that once covered the plugs, leaving only the huge sharp cores of rock that now loom abruptly above the sea.

Nearby is another vestige of St. Lucia's fiery past. Outside the town of Soufrière (the name means "sulfur mine"), a former volcanic crater still shows signs of life; the basin is a veritable caldron of boiling, hissing, malodorous sulfur springs. Harmless but nevertheless awe-inspiring, this scene of inferno is one of the most popular attractions on an otherwise Eden-like tropical isle. □

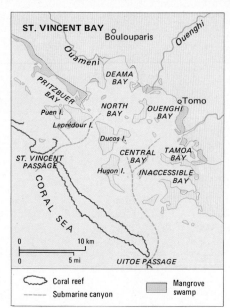

Isolated from the Coral Sea by a barrier reef, St. Vincent Bay is crossed by submarine canyons that were carved by rivers at a time when the present-day bay was dry land.

St. Vincent Bay

- New Caledonia
- Map: page 23, G–4

Skirted by mangrove swamps and sandy beaches, a tranquil lagoon indents the coast of a Pacific island.

The mountainous island of New Caledonia, located in the Pacific Ocean some 750 miles (1,200 kilometers) east of Australia, is almost completely surrounded by a coral barrier reef—one of the longest in the world. Here and there gaps in the barrier permit passage from the open sea to placid lagoons inside the reef.

Among the largest and loveliest of these sheltered inlets is St. Vincent Bay on the southwest coast. Dotted with islands and fringed by mangrove swamps and sandy beaches, it ranges from 15 to 50 feet (5 to 15 meters) in depth.

A number of submarine canyons traverse the floor of the bay, evidence that it was once dry land. They were carved during the Ice Age, when so much of the world's water supply was locked up in continental ice caps that the sea level everywhere dropped substantially. Rushing across the exposed surface of the bay, now-vanished rivers eroded deep valleys in the shale and sandstone that form the basin's floor. When the ice melted, the sea rose and flooded the bay, creating today's harmonious blend of land and water. □

Salpausselka and the Lake Region

- Finland
- Map: page 16, F–2

Rows of rampartlike ridges span the south of Finland and overlook a rolling heartland that is filled with a labyrinth of crystal-clear lakes.

Among the most striking and distinctive landscape features of southern Finland is a long double line of rampartlike ridges that span the entire country. Rising as much as 260 feet (80 meters) above their flat surroundings, the more or less parallel lines of hills extend some 300 miles (500 kilometers) from northeast to southwest. The tops of the ridges, which in places are up to 2½ miles (4 kilometers) wide, form a sort of natural causeway; for long distances they are used as the roadbed for a major highway and a railroad line. One part is even flat and wide enough to serve as an airfield.

The ridges, known as the Salpausselka, also provide superb vantage points for viewing Finland's Lake Region, which stretches off to the north. From horizon to horizon the flat terrain is a mosaic of blue and green—lakes by the thousands, of every size and shape imaginable, are dotted with islands and encircled by dense, dark evergreen forests. Lake Saimaa, considered the largest, is actually an interconnected network of more than 100 smaller lakes. Most of the lakes, in fact, are linked by rivers and canals, forming a vast and beautiful inland waterway system.

SALPAUSSELKA AND THE LAKE REGION. *Countless glacier-carved lakes form a maze of interconnected waterways across the forested heart of southern Finland.*

Salton Sea

- United States (California)
- Map: page 10, D–5

Born of a catastrophic flood, this oasis in the desert is now a popular recreation area and wildlife refuge.

The Salton Sea, a large saline lake in southernmost California, owes its existence in part to nature and in part to man. Over the course of its long and varied history, it has been by turns an arm of the ocean, a landlocked lake, a dry, sunbaked salt flat, and a salty lake once more.

Some 30 miles (48 kilometers) long and 10 miles (16 kilometers) wide, the lake occupies the lowest part of a vast depression that extends 287 feet (88 meters) below sea level. The surface of the lake itself is about 230 feet (70 meters) below the sea.

At one time the entire basin that contains the lake was the northern end of the Gulf of California, which lies between the Mexican mainland and Baja California. But eventually the Colorado River's huge delta grew into a damlike barrier across the upper gulf. With little inflow of fresh water, the resultant lake gradually dried out as the water evaporated under the scorching desert sun. In historic times all that remained of the bygone lake was an expanse of white salt-encrusted flats known as the Salton Sink.

From time to time, shifting channels of the lower Colorado flooded the sink, creating short-lived lakes that soon evaporated. But in 1905 the river broke through a levee built for an irrigation project and began to flow into the basin in torrents. By the time the gap was repaired two years later, the newborn Salton Sea was a lake about 40 miles (65 kilometers) long and 90 feet (27 meters) deep.

In the following decades, the Salton Sea shrank substantially as evaporation lowered the water level. Today, however, its level has become more or less stabilized. Stretching off to the northwest are the rich farmlands of the Coachella Valley and to the southeast, the Imperial Valley, both heavily irrigated with water channeled in from the Colorado. Thus, with the aid of man, runoff from irrigation projects is about equal to losses through evaporation. And the Salton Sea has become both a popular recreation area and a haven in the desert for multitudes of waterfowl.   □

The Lake Region, an increasingly popular vacation area, is at its best in the haunting twilight of long summer evenings, when the fringing forests are reflected in the tranquil waters. But even in winter, when the lakes are locked beneath a cover of ice and snow, the region has a stark and somber beauty all its own.

At one time it was thought that the Salpausselka ridges act as a natural dam and so account for the profusion of lakes that dot the region. In fact the origins of the lakes and ridges are quite different, though both are products of the Ice Age. The lake basins for the most part were created as the glaciers advanced; the ridges, as they retreated.

During the Ice Age, continental ice caps advanced several times across the ancient gneiss and granite bedrock of Scandinavia. With each advance the crushing mass of ice, laden with debris and boulders, scoured the surface of the land and gouged shallow depressions in the bedrock. The hollows in time became the basins of the region's many lakes.

Some of the lakes and marshes are different, however; they are contained by natural dams of glacial debris: long, narrow mounds of gravel, sand, and pebbles that snake across the country-side. Generally about 100 feet (30 meters) high and often many miles long, these natural levees, known as eskers, sometimes form the margins of lakes and marshes. The winding belts of debris mark the courses of streams that flowed through or under the ice. Long thought to be streambed deposits, eskers are now believed by some scientists to be chains of deltas deposited at the mouths of tunnels where streams emerged from the receding front of the glacier.

The Salpausselka ridges are also products of glacial retreat. Basically they are a pair of so-called terminal moraines, deposited when the Ice Age drew to a close about 10,000 years ago. Each of the two lines of ridges marks a pause in the glacial retreat: a period when the ice was melting along the glacial front at about the same rate that new ice was advancing from the north. As the ice melted, all the rock debris trapped in it accumulated in a great mound along the front of the glacier. After the southern line of ridges had been deposited, the climate warmed up and the glacier retreated about 15 miles (25 kilometers) toward the north. The glacier then "stalled" again, and the second line of terminal moraines was formed before the ice cap went into its final retreat.   □

Salzkammergut

● Austria
● Map: page 17, E–4

Rich salt mines once made this area a jealously guarded possession of Austria's kings. Today fine scenery makes it a year-round vacation resort.

The Salzkammergut is a region of the northern Alps located to the east of Salzburg in north-central Austria. Its name, meaning "property of the salt administration," refers to the area's huge underground deposits of salt, once a government monopoly. But today the Salzkammergut, sometimes called "the Switzerland of Austria," is best known for its breathtaking scenery. Rugged, snowcapped mountains, dense forests, and splashing waterfalls are accented by an abundance of serenely beautiful mountain lakes.

The focal point of the Salzkammergut is the town of Bad Ischl, a noted mineral springs resort about 28 miles (45 kilometers) southeast of Salzburg. Frequented by Emperor Franz Josef I, Bad Ischl was for a time a center of fashionable life, and it remains the region's major tourist hub.

To the north of Bad Ischl the land descends toward the Danube valley across forested limestone mountains interspersed with broad valleys. The largest lakes of the region are found there, cupped within glacier-carved trenches. One of them, the Attersee, is the largest lake located entirely in Austria. The nearby summit of the Schafberg affords spectacular views of both the Attersee and the Alpine foothills far below. Farther to the east is the equally majestic Traunsee, the country's deepest lake.

The lakes to the south of Bad Ischl tend to be smaller and wedged between the steep limestone slopes of towering massifs. The most celebrated of them all is the picturesque Hallstättersee, nestled at the foot of the Dachstein Massif. With a maximum elevation of 9,826 feet (2,995 meters), the Dachstein is both the southern boundary and the highest mountain mass of the Salzkammergut.

The rugged grandeur of the mountains is the product of a complex variety of geological forces. The region's once-horizontal layers of limestone, dolomite, and shale have been folded, faulted, and in some places thrust horizontally for long distances over other rock layers. And all have been subjected to intense glaciation.

Underlying most of the region are thick deposits of salt mixed with varying amounts of clay, gypsum, and anhydrite. Trace impurities color the salt red and gray. At mining centers such as Bad Ischl, where the salt formation reaches the surface, the salt is extracted by dissolving it and pumping the brine to evaporation works.

One brine conduit built in 1607 is still in use. But even that is a relatively recent development in the history of the Salzkammergut. Humans have utilized the salt deposits for about 4,500 years, and underground mines date back more than 2,500 years. The ancient mining town of Hallstatt was the site of an Iron Age settlement, while an even older Stone Age settlement at Mondsee has yielded the remains of lake dwellings estimated to be some 5,000 years old. ☐

San Andreas Fault

● United States (California)
● Map: page 10, C–5

The long, ominous scar across the California landscape is a perpetual reminder of the awesome movements of the earth's ever-restless crust.

One of the most intensively studied geological features in North America—and one of the most dangerous—is the San Andreas Fault in California. Nearly 700 miles (1,125 kilometers) long, it cuts into the Pacific coast to the north of San Francisco and runs southeast into Mexico at the head of the Gulf of California.

The earth's surface, of course, is broken by a multitude of faults—fractures along which segments of the earth's crust have moved in opposite directions. What makes the San Andreas Fault especially notable is not only its great length but also its particular nature. Most faults are breaks in once-continuous rock formations; the San Andreas Fault, in contrast, forms the boundary between two different sections of the earth's crust.

As recent geological studies have made clear, the world's continents and oceans rest not on a single inflexible shell, as was long assumed, but on 12 enormous individual plates that are continually in motion. Averaging some 60 miles (100 kilometers) in thickness, these immense slabs of rock drift about on the fluid upper layer of the earth's mantle, perpetually jostling one another as pressures from deep within the planet guide their slow

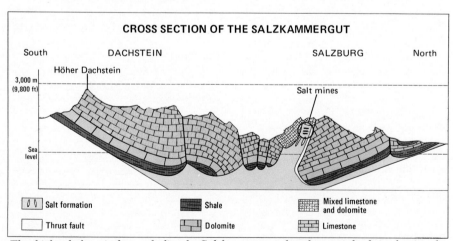

CROSS SECTION OF THE SALZKAMMERGUT

South   DACHSTEIN   SALZBURG   North

Höher Dachstein

3,000 m (9,800 ft)

Salt mines

Sea level

| Salt formation | Shale | Mixed limestone and dolomite |
| Thrust fault | Dolomite | Limestone |

The thick salt deposit that underlies the Salzkammergut played a crucial role in shaping the terrain. During the uplift of the Alps, the highly plastic salt formation acted as a lubricant when the harder upper rock layers were thrust across each other. Mines are located where salt was squeezed up to the surface in the process.

migrations. The massive earthquakes unleashed as adjoining crustal plates grind against each other are the obvious consequences of this jostling.

As it happens, the San Andreas Fault represents just such a junction. It marks part of the boundary where the crustal plate underlying North America abuts the one beneath the Pacific Ocean. All the land west of the fault, including Los Angeles, San Diego, and other population centers, actually lies on the Pacific plate; all the land east of the fault is part of the American plate.

In some areas of the world, drifting crustal plates have met each other in massive head-on collisions resulting in the formation of great mountain ranges. For example, when the northward-drifting Indian subcontinent collided with the Eurasian plate, the surface of the earth was heaved up to form the Himalayas.

In the case of the San Andreas Fault, the adjoining crustal plates are not on a direct collision course. Their movement, rather, is primarily a sideswiping one. The two plates grind laboriously past each other as they have for millions of years, with the Pacific plate drifting inexorably northwestward and the American plate toward the southeast. A winery building near Hollister, southeast of San Francisco, offers especially graphic evidence of this motion. Unwittingly built directly astride the fault, the structure is being pulled apart at the rate of ½ inch (1¼ centimeters) per year.

Movement of this sort does not occur simultaneously along the entire length of the fault. Nor is it by any means a smooth or regular process. The San Andreas Fault, for one thing, is flanked by dozens of smaller local fractures that branch off in complex patterns. In some places the opposing edges creep past each other uneventfully, moving as much as 2½ inches (6 centimeters) per year. Such localized movements serve as a kind of safety valve, permitting the regular release of energy in the form of barely perceptible tremors.

Elsewhere, however, the two sides become locked together for varying periods of time. They are unable to move until enough pressure has built up to release them with a sudden surge of motion—in other words, an earthquake. And in fact earthquakes occur quite often along the San Andreas network, most of them so small that they cause little or no damage.

But occasionally a portion of the fault remains locked in place for a dangerously long time and is subjected to strains that build steadily until the two sides finally burst past each other in a violent release of pent-up energy. Such was the cause of the 1906 San Francisco earthquake, when the ground along the fault moved as much as 20 feet (6 meters) within a matter of minutes.

A major concern today is the likelihood of another large-scale earthquake in the near future. While most of the tension between the American and Pacific plates is safely released through minor tremors, certain sections of the San Andreas Fault have not registered any movement in years. And every day that the plates remain locked in place, a bit more energy is being stored up against the inevitable moment when they will break free of each other. The question, thus, is not whether there will be a major earthquake, but when. Predictions vary, but there seems to be little doubt that it will take place within 50 years, and possibly much sooner.

The story, of course, will not end with that sudden violent release of energy. Pressures will then build up again, only to be released again, time after time into the indefinite future. Indeed, scientists estimate that present-day Los Angeles, riding on the northward-bound Pacific plate, will reach the latitude of San Francisco about 10 million years from now. And in about 50 million years it will have migrated all the way north to the Aleutian Islands. □

SAN ANDREAS FAULT. *An aerial view provides a striking portrait of the long, deep fracture where two great sections of the earth's crust abut and move fitfully past each other.*

SANTORIN. *Sheer cliffs on the island's rugged coast are actually the remains of a gigantic collapsed volcanic crater.*

Santorin

- Greece
- Map: page 17, F–5

A group of stark volcanic islands in the eastern Mediterranean marks the site of a cataclysm that engulfed a civilization some 3,500 years ago.

Santorin (also known as Santorini and Thera) is the major island of a small archipelago in the Aegean Sea. Some 12 miles (20 kilometers) long and 3 miles (5 kilometers) wide, it is shaped like a crescent. Together with two smaller sister islands, it nearly encircles a broad oval bay with two barren islets at the center.

Named for its patron, Saint Irene,

Santorin seems the essence of peace and tranquillity today. Only the starkness of its contours provides a hint of the island's tumultuous past. Rising straight up from the deep water of the bay is a line of cliffs as much as 1,000 feet (300 meters) high. Composed of layer upon layer of volcanic rock, the cliffs are topped in many places by a thick deposit of gleaming white volcanic ash that looks almost like snow.

Santorin and the neighboring islands, in fact, are the shattered remnants of an ancient volcano—one that erupted with a cataclysmic blast some 3,500 years ago and in the process changed the course of history. Prior to the eruption, which occurred about 1500 B.C., the most powerful and cultivated people in the eastern Mediter-

ranean were the Minoans, who ruled from the island of Crete some 70 miles (110 kilometers) to the south of Santorin. The Minoan era suddenly ended about the same time that Santorin exploded. And, many experts believe, the demise of their civilization was a direct result of the eruption.

Before the explosion, a single island rose from the sea where the archipelago rings the bay today. Dominating the island was a volcano perhaps 3,000 feet (900 meters) high, with at least one Minoan settlement on the surrounding lowlands. Classical accounts took note of the volcano's long history of furious eruptions: according to Greek mythology, as Jason and the Argonauts sailed past Santorin, they were showered with rocks hurled by a

over the island and the surrounding sea. Earthquakes then followed as the shattered mountaintop collapsed into the empty magma chamber below, and finally seawater rushed into the void. The resultant caldera—the present-day bay surrounded by the islands—is filled with water to depths of 1,200 feet (365 meters) and more.

While wiping out all life on Santorin, the explosion spread layers of hot destructive ash on neighboring islands, including Crete. Its most lethal effect, however, came in the form of tidal waves generated by the earthquakes that accompanied the collapse of the crater. Racing toward Crete, they caused catastrophic floods that are believed to have destroyed the Minoan world. The tidal waves and dust clouds probably reached as far as Egypt and could well have been among the "plagues" mentioned in Exodus. So widespread were the repercussions that the destruction of Santorin is thought to be one source of the ancient Greek legend of the lost "continent" of Atlantis.

Centuries after the blowout, Santorin was resettled by people from mainland Greece. Eruptions had not ceased, however, nor have they to this day. Subsequent upheavals shaped the present contours of the island group and created additional islets in the center of the bay. Called the Kaimenes or Burnt Islands, they are notable for their many vents that still emit nauseating sulfurous fumes. Eruptions accompanied by tremors have continued into modern times, including a particularly destructive earthquake in 1956.

In recent years archeologists have discovered even more fascinating evidence of the great eruption of 3,500 years ago. Digging through layers of ash near Akrotiri on Santorin's south shore, they have unearthed the remains of a prosperous Minoan city that was totally buried by the eruption in 1500 B.C., much as Pompeii was buried by the eruption of Vesuvius in the first century A.D. Bit by bit scientists have uncovered buildings, streets, furniture, and other artifacts of a vanished civilization. Most impressive by far are a number of large frescoes, now painstakingly restored, which are among the finest known from the Minoan era. From these and from the many everyday objects that have been unearthed, experts are piecing together a picture of life on Santorin long ago, before it was so brutally overwhelmed by fire from the deep. □

giant with streams of liquid flowing from his feet.

The actual eruption of 1500 B.C., however, was far more awesome than any mythological giant. In a series of violent explosions, the volcano blew its top with a force that rivals the famous 1883 eruption of the Indonesian volcano Krakatoa. Time and again clouds of gas, fragmented lava, ash, and pumice were hurled as high as 20 miles (32 kilometers) into the sky. Huge rocks were thrown a mile or more from the volcano's vent. Showers of pumice and ash poured down on the island, burying it under a deep layer of volcanic debris.

By the time the explosion ended, some 15 cubic miles (65 cubic kilometers) of material had been scattered

Sarisariñama Plateau

- Venezuela
- Map: page 14, C–2

A remote tropical plateau is pierced by two extraordinary pits so large that forests flourish in the dim depths beneath their overhanging cliffs.

In his novel *The Lost World*, Sir Arthur Conan Doyle described an imaginary plateau bounded by giant vertical cliffs. The famed British author's description of this pristine setting may well have been inspired by accounts of a contemporary expedition into the remote wilds of southern Venezuela. There, in the basin of the Río Caura, a tributary of the Orinoco, the explorers encountered not one but several such isolated plateaus looming high above their surroundings.

One of them, the Sarisariñama Plateau, has proved to be particularly intriguing. Covering an area of 300 square miles (775 square kilometers), it juts up abruptly above the region's seemingly endless jungles. Because of its inaccessibility, the upland was seen by few outsiders other than pilots who occasionally flew over it.

In 1954 strange reports began to circulate about the Sarisariñama Plateau: some of the pilots had noticed that it was penetrated by two gigantic well-like shafts. It was not until the 1960's that a coordinated effort was launched to survey and photograph these enigmatic openings. The results confirmed the existence of two enormous, nearly circular sinkholes near the northern edge of the plateau. But they posed a puzzling geological question. How could they possibly have been formed?

Sinkholes, even very large ones, are no novelty to geologists. There are numerous examples all around the world of so-called karst landscapes, typified by such features as sinkholes, caves, and underground streams. But they are almost always found in limestone and other types of rock that can be dissolved by groundwater.

And there was the heart of the puzzle, for the Sarisariñama Plateau is not made up of limestone. It is composed of hard, compact formations of sandstone and quartzite. Geologists had never before encountered examples of karst-type erosion in rocks of this sort. Clearly they would have to examine

SARISARIÑAMA PLATEAU. *An aerial view provides some idea of the immensity of the sinkholes that penetrate the sandstone plateau in the midst of a vast impenetrable jungle.*

Saxonian Switzerland

- East Germany
- Map: page 17, E–3

In the East German state of Saxony, a river valley flanked by dramatic sandstone cliffs and towers is filled with scenes of Alpine beauty.

the site firsthand if they hoped to understand it.

Early in 1974 a team of 30 investigators was airlifted to the plateau, where they set up camp at the very brink of the larger opening. It proved to have a diameter of 1,215 feet (370 meters) and a depth of 1,030 feet (314 meters). Investigation of the interior revealed that the cylindrical shaft widens slightly at the bottom, where an entire forest flourishes amid huge jumbles of sandstone blocks. Violent blasts of air escaping from crevices between the fallen rocks suggest that they may cover the entrance to a major cave system in the plateau. Named the Humboldt Abyss (in honor of Alexander von Humboldt, the first scientist to explore the region), this phenomenal sinkhole is among the largest known to have been created by karst-type erosion.

Not far away, the second opening, named the Martel Sinkhole, is smaller but nonetheless impressive. At its bottom, which is also covered by dense jungle vegetation, an unexplored passageway plunges down toward the interior of the plateau.

In 1976 another expedition returned to study the two extraordinary cavities, as well as a third one that had been discovered on the plateau. Their origin remains an enigma, however, since scientists have yet to explain how such sinkholes could develop in sandstone. One theory suggests that they resulted from the collapse of cave ceilings that had been weakened by an unusual, extremely localized erosion process. Considering the enormous amount of rain that falls on the pla-

teau—as much as 110 inches (2,800 millimeters) per year—and the presence of major faults in the massif, this seems the most plausible explanation.

In any event, exploration of the Sarisariñama Plateau has barely begun. What is already known about it has proved to be extraordinarily provocative; what lies ahead promises to be even more so. ☐

South of Dresden in the East German state of Saxony, the historic Elbe flows from Czechoslovakia into a deep valley lined with dense forests and meticulously cultivated fields. Towering above the lowlands on both sides of the river is a region of high plateaus that have been carved into a series of craggy cliffs and jagged, fantastically varied rock formations. Inspired by their wild and romantic beauty, 19th-century visitors named the entire area Saxonian Switzerland.

The rocky towers are not mountains, and they are certainly not Swiss, but the name has endured for more than a century. And tourists continue to come and marvel at the monumental forms of the natural rock sculptures that so beautifully embellish the

SAXONIAN SWITZERLAND. *Rising high above the Elbe River, a cluster of sandstone bastions provides visitors with sweeping, panoramic views of the East German countryside.*

landscapes of Saxonian Switzerland.

On all sides, columns, towers, turrets, and flat-topped buttes are bordered by sheer cliffs and separated by deep gorges and ravines. Some of the rocky bastions stand alone; others rise in clusters like the skyscrapers of some fantastic city.

The rock formations were eroded from thick layers of sandstone that were deposited some 80 million years ago on the floor of an inland sea. Subsequently uplifted, the rocks were fractured by networks of intersecting cracks that broke them up into more or less rectangular blocks. Running water, alternate freezing and thawing, chemical weathering, and other agents of erosion then began their ceaseless attack, gradually deepening and widening the crevices.

Floodwaters on the Elbe in time carved a deep valley: the river enters East Germany through an impressive gorge some 4 miles (6½ kilometers) long. Meanwhile the sandstone highlands on either side of the river were dissected into the stout bastions and clustered towers that remain standing like tireless sentinels above the German countryside. □

SCARISOARA CAVE. *Gradually lengthened by the slow dripping of water from overhead, ice stalagmites embellish the dim, silent depths of the Rumanian ice cave.*

Scarisoara Cave

- Rumania
- Map: page 17, F–4

The cold air of countless winters filled this unusual Carpathian cave with masses of ice, creating a subterranean polar landscape.

Scarisoara Cave is located in the Apuseni Mountains, a range of the great Carpathian mountain system in the northwest of Rumania. With their abundance of limestone, the Apusenis are particularly notable for their numerous caves, sinkholes, underground rivers, and other so-called karst cavities. And just as in other limestone regions, most of the caves are decorated with impressive displays of stalactites and stalagmites formed by the deposition of dissolved minerals on the caverns' ceilings and floors.

Scarisoara Cave, in contrast, is decorated almost entirely with ice. Within its frigid depths there are thick masses of ice, some of them thousands of years old, as well as glittering arrays of icicles and ice stalagmites. Scarisoara is in fact considered one of the most spectacular ice caves in the world. It contains an estimated total of 65,000 cubic yards (50,000 cubic meters) of ice, with the deposits in some places as much as 65 feet (20 meters) thick.

The cave's only known entrance is a sinkhole on a plateau some 3,600 feet (1,100 meters) above sea level. From the surface the well-like shaft plunges straight down for about 165 feet (50 meters). At the bottom it opens out into the cave's two main chambers, the Great Hall and the Church. Additional chambers and passageways extend the labyrinth to a maximum depth of 394 feet (120 meters) below the surface.

Both the Great Hall and the Church are filled with massive accumulations of ice, including, in the Great Hall, a cliff of ice some 60 feet (18 meters) high that overlooks the so-called Pool of Ice. The Church is especially notable for its clusters of ice stalagmites, built up by the slow dripping of water from overhead. A number of the frozen columns are as much as 6 feet (1.8 meters) in height.

The vast amount of ice that remains permanently frozen in Scarisoara results primarily from the shape and location of the cavern. The deep vertical sinkhole that forms its entrance acts as a trap for cold winter air. Since cold air is heavier than warm air, it invariably flows downslope. When a refrigerator door is opened, for example, the cold air inside spills out at the bottom of the door. In the case of the cave, masses of cold air sink down the shaft and fill the chambers, and they remain there until they are displaced by even colder and therefore heavier air masses.

Most of the ice in Scarisoara Cave was formed thousands of years ago, when the climate was colder than today, and has been preserved in this natural underground refrigerator ever since. Analysis of pollen grains that were trapped in the ice as it was being formed indicates that the lowest layers are about 3,000 years old. Other studies conducted since scientists first began to investigate Scarisoara in 1921 reveal that the total amount of ice in the cave has decreased somewhat in the intervening years, probably as a result of a general warming of the climate throughout the world. Tourists are permitted to visit the cave, but its lowest portions have been set aside as a scientific reservation where studies can continue to be conducted to probe more of the cavern's secrets. □

SEMOIS RIVER. *Flowing between flat, grass-covered deposits of alluvial soil, the river has carved its circuitous course through the gently rolling hills of the Forest of Ardennes.*

Scilly Islands

- United Kingdom (England)
- Map: page 16, C–4

Rolling moorland, golden fields of flowers, and a picturesque but perilous coastline distinguish England's isolated Scilly Islands.

Once a haven for smugglers and pirates, the Scilly Islands are located some 25 miles (40 kilometers) off the coast of Land's End at the southwestern tip of England. Only 5 of the 150 or so rocks and islets in the group are inhabited, and the land area of the entire archipelago is a mere 6.3 square miles (16.3 square kilometers).

The islands are the exposed surface of a deeply eroded mass of granite. In many places the bedrock is covered by dunes and ridges of white sand that was formed by the decomposition of the granite. Bounded by rocky shores and surrounded by dangerous shoals, the islands have been the site of many shipwrecks.

Although the islands lie nearly as far north as the southern end of Hudson Bay, the warm waters of the North Atlantic Drift bring them a mild year-round climate. Even in the coldest winter months, the average temperature remains about 45° F (7° C). As a result, subtropical plants flourish there, and flowers are one of the Scilly Islands' main products. □

Semois River

- Belgium—France
- Map: page 17, D–4

Winding its way through the historic Forest of Ardennes, this beautiful meandering river evokes the mood of simpler and more pastoral times.

The short but picturesque Semois River (also called the Semoy) rises in southern Belgium near the border of Luxembourg. Flowing westward across Belgium, it passes into France, where it soon merges with the northward-flowing Meuse—a total distance of only 110 miles (177 kilometers).

Along the way it winds through a deep, narrow valley carved into the forested uplands of the Ardennes plateau. The special beauty of the river results from its extraordinarily meandering course. Bounded by steep slopes that rise as much as 650 feet (200 meters) above the river, the Semois is a seemingly endless series of extremely broad, looping curves.

In some places the loops enclose flat, peninsulalike terraces of rich alluvial soil. Villages huddle on some of these lowlands; others are devoted to farming, especially tobacco culture. Elsewhere towns are perched on the plateau above the valley, overlooking sweeping panoramas of this lovely, historic countryside that has thus far escaped industrial development. □

Seychelles

- Indian Ocean
- Map: page 9

High mountain peaks and balmy coral islets abound in this far-flung island group in the Indian Ocean.

The Seychelles are scattered across the Indian Ocean about 1,000 miles (1,600 kilometers) east of the historic African port of Mombasa, Kenya. Located just south of the equator, they are noted for their lush tropical beauty and their flourishing production of spices and oils for fragrant perfumes.

Of the 85 or so islands that make up the group, about 40 are mountainous masses of granite that rise steeply from the sea. The rest are low-lying coral islets. Small fishing villages are stretched out along the narrow coastal lowlands of the granitic islands. Inland they are dominated by rugged chains of forested mountain peaks. The highest crest, Morne Seychellois on Mahé, the largest of the islands, reaches 2,993 feet (912 meters) above the sea. The fertile soil in the lowlands supports plantations devoted to the production of coconuts, vanilla beans, cinnamon, and patchouli oil, a popular perfume essence.

The coral islands are flat, sandy, and much smaller than the granitic islands. They were once covered by thick layers of guano, most of which has been mined for fertilizer. Coconuts remain the major crop. The coral islands are also notable for their fringing reefs, inhabited by a wealth of colorful fish and other kinds of exotic marine life.

The granitic islands of the Seychelles were long a puzzle to geologists, since oceanic islands are generally either volcanic or coralline in origin. The ancient granitic rocks of the Seychelles, in contrast, are of the same type that underlies the continents, and there are no traces of volcanic activity. It is now believed that the islands and the undersea platform beneath them were once attached to Madagascar and were torn away by the restless shifting of the earth's crustal plates.

Among the unusual native wildlife are such rarities as the Praslin black parrot and the giant land tortoise. One of the strangest plants is the *coco de mer,* a palm that produces bizarre double coconuts weighing as much as 40 pounds (18 kilograms). □

Shansi Loess Region

- China
- Map: page 21, F–1

A fertile layer of windblown silt gave northern China its nickname, "The Land of the Yellow Earth."

Everything is yellow. The hills, the roads, the fields, the water of the rivers and brooks are yellow ... even the atmosphere is seldom free from a yellow haze." It was thus that the geologist Baron Ferdinand von Richthofen (the father of Germany's World War I flying ace) described the extraordinary landscape of Shansi Province in north-central China in the 1870's. The scene remains much the same today.

The Shansi Loess Region is just a part of a much more extensive area of similar landscapes in the middle part of the Yellow River basin in northern China. Its distinctive look results from deep deposits of a yellow loosely packed, fertile type of soil known as loess. The name, derived from a German word meaning "to loosen," was originally applied to a similar soil in the Rhine Valley. Great quantities of loess are also found in the Mississippi Valley, Central Asia, and many other areas. But in few places in the world is it so deep and widespread as in this part of China.

SHANSI LOESS REGION. *Neatly cultivated terraces—and even caves for the farmers' dwellings—have been carved in the massive deposits of fine-grained windblown soil.*

Besides being highly fertile, this fine-grained type of soil also holds together well enough to form vertical cliffs and support the roofs of caves. In the Shansi region, in fact, farmers have traditionally lived in caves beneath their fields. An unexpected result is the sight of plumes of smoke rising from their hearth fires and escaping through shafts dug in their grainfields overhead.

Loess is also susceptible to severe erosion. The Shansi Loess Region is crisscrossed by networks of deep gullies and ravines that grow in length and depth with each rainfall. Ultimately the eroded soil is carried into the Yellow River, making its water even yellower. The Yellow carries so much sediment, derived for the most part from the loess region, that it is the muddiest river in the world.

The loess itself consists of extremely fine-grained particles of quartz, mica, feldspar, calcite, and other materials, mixed with clay dust. At one time it was believed that all loess originated as strictly windblown deposits of these silty particles. Many geologists now believe, however, that other processes were also involved. Water, for example, probably played a significant role in both rearranging and weathering the material.

Whatever the case may be, it is agreed that the loess accumulated over at least the last 3 million years. The deposits in the Shansi region, which in places are hundreds of feet deep, were probably blown in from the Ordos and Gobi deserts, situated just to the northwest. Similarly, the loess of the American Midwest consists of deposits blown in from regions where finely scoured glacial debris was freed by the melting of the continental ice cap during the Ice Age. □

The Loess Landscapes of Northern China

The deep, widespread loess deposits of the Shansi area are far from simple uniform accumulations of windblown silt. The cross section of the region (*below*) shows how the contours of the underlying bedrock are almost completely masked by debris and severely eroded loess deposits of various ages. Nor does a single loess deposit remain unchanged over the course of time. The soil profile (*right*) shows how a deposit evolves: calcite in surface layers is dissolved by seeping water and then redeposited as a cementing agent at greater depths.

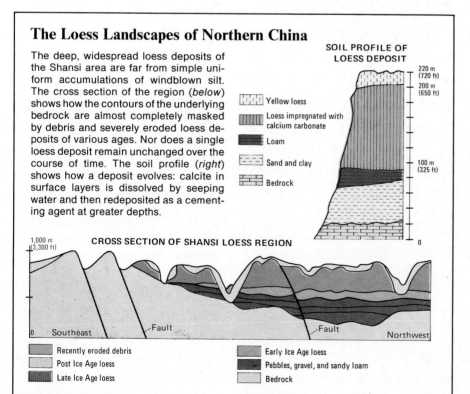

SOIL PROFILE OF LOESS DEPOSIT

- Yellow loess
- Loess impregnated with calcium carbonate
- Loam
- Sand and clay
- Bedrock

220 m (720 ft)
200 m (650 ft)
100 m (325 ft)
0

CROSS SECTION OF SHANSI LOESS REGION

1,000 m (3,300 ft)
0 Southeast
Fault
Fault
Northwest

- Recently eroded debris
- Post Ice Age loess
- Late Ice Age loess
- Early Ice Age loess
- Pebbles, gravel, and sandy loam
- Bedrock

Shatt al Arab

- Iran—Iraq
- Map: page 18, F–5

A river created by the merging of two far more famous waterways still nurtures a way of life that has changed little since ancient times.

The Shatt al Arab is formed by the confluence of two great rivers, the Tigris and the Euphrates, in southeastern Iraq. Flowing southeastward for some 120 miles (190 kilometers) across a region of marshlands and lakes, it forms a portion of the border between Iran and Iraq before it eventually empties at the head of the Persian Gulf.

The waterways that form the Shatt al Arab figured prominently in the earliest chapters of recorded history. Nourishing the eastern half of the Fertile Crescent, which stretched from the Persian Gulf to the Nile delta, the waters of the Tigris and Euphrates gave life to the first civilizations of ancient Mesopotamia. (The name is Greek, meaning "between the rivers.") Among the cities that flourished along their courses were Nineveh on the banks of the Tigris and Babylon on the

Euphrates. Indeed, the area where the two rivers converge is believed by some biblical scholars to have been the site of the Garden of Eden.

Today, as in antiquity, the flow of both the Tigris and the Euphrates is greatly diminished by the time they merge, due to diversions for irrigation and losses to evaporation in the hot, dry climate. Downstream from their confluence at Al Qurna, Iraq, however, the Shatt al Arab is augmented by the Karun, a long and winding river that originates in the Zagros Mountains in Iran. The Shatt al Arab is also influenced by the tides on the Persian Gulf. They keep its water deep enough to make the port of Basra, which is more than 60 miles (95 kilometers) inland from the coast, easily accessible to oceangoing vessels.

The lower course of the Shatt al Arab is actually the principal channel of a complex delta that is extending seaward at a rate of two miles (three kilometers) per century. Some of the channels have been dammed in recent years to regulate the river's flow. Even so, vast marshlands remain all along the lower course, as do a number of large lakes such as the shallow expanse of Hor al Hammar.

Even to this day, the myriad lakes

and marshes provide a refuge for a way of life dating back to antiquity. The local inhabitants, representing a mixture of cultures, rely on date palms and other crops. But above all they depend on the giant reeds that flourish in the marshes. Growing up to 20 feet (6 meters) in height, the reeds provide food for the people and their livestock as well as fuel and material for woven goods. The reeds are also the basic material used for the construction of houses and the indispensable reed boats, which are made in the same way that they have been for countless generations. □

SHATT AL ARAB. *Lined by dense groves of date palms, the river flows across a delta formed from the sediment of the Tigris and Euphrates.*

Ship Rock Peak

- United States (New Mexico)
- Map: page 10, D–5

A commanding landmark visible from far across the New Mexican plains, this craggy volcanic peak is sacred to the Navajo Indians.

Located on the Navajo Indian Reservation in the northwestern corner of New Mexico, the pointed summit of Ship Rock Peak is a famous landmark that completely dominates its surroundings. The great mass of dark volcanic rock, bounded by nearly vertical cliffs and crowned with jagged pinnacles and spires, towers 1,400 feet (425 meters) above the otherwise featureless plains.

To 19th-century pioneers its craggy profile was reminiscent of a ship under full sail. To the Navajos it is Sa-bit-tai, "The Rock With Wings." Among their many legends concerning this sacred rock is one that explains its origin on the plains. Besieged by enemies in a distant land, the Indians took refuge on the rock and prayed for help from their gods. In time the crags became wings, and the rock rose into the air and soared to its present location.

In actuality, Ship Rock Peak is a classic example of a volcanic neck. It was formed when a plug of molten lava cooled and then solidified in the vent of a volcano. The various forces of erosion eventually stripped away the surrounding accumulation of volcanic material until only this core of much more resistant rock remained standing.　　□

Sigri, Petrified Forest of

- Greece
- Map: page 17, F–5

On a lush Aegean isle, an arid array of fossilized trees remains as mute testimony to the devastating effects of a bygone cataclysm.

The island of Lesbos, birthplace of the ancient Greek poet Sappho and the philosopher Theophrastus, has a long-established place in the history of the eastern Mediterranean. Located just off the coast of Turkey in the Aegean Sea, it has been prized since earliest times both for its strategic lo-

PETRIFIED FOREST OF SIGRI. *Like a prehistoric stone monument, a fossilized log juts from the deposits of volcanic ash and lava that buried a forest millions of years ago.*

cation and its rich, productive soil. In one corner of Lesbos, however, there is a landscape that shows few signs of life or fertility: the dry and desolate Petrified Forest of Sigri.

The first scientific observations of the area were made by a French geologist late in the 19th century. Traveling across the southern part of the island, he passed through a lush region of olive groves, vineyards, and wheat fields interspersed with forests of pine and chestnuts. But as he continued on to the northwest, near the little fishing port of Sigri he came upon a scene that stood in startling contrast.

Spreading off in all directions was a barren moonscape of solidified lava flows and mounds of volcanic ash. And protruding from the surface were a great number of ocher, red, and black tree trunks, petrified and seemingly charred: some were still standing, while others had fallen as if struck by bolts of lightning.

In fact these trees were struck by a force that was much more powerful than lightning. Sometime between 2 million and 20 million years ago a tropical climate prevailed in this part of the world. Northwestern Lesbos

was dominated by a very large, apparently extinct volcano, its slopes covered by flourishing groves of palms and pine trees.

Then suddenly and without warning, the volcano exploded. Waves of white-hot ash poured down its slopes like avalanches, completely devastating and engulfing everything in their paths. Buried before the trees had a chance to catch fire, the forest was smothered beneath a blanket of ash and lava that in some places was more than 325 feet (100 meters) thick.

The petrifaction took place over the ensuing millennia as water seeped down through the volcanic deposits and carried dissolved silica to the buried trees. Cell by cell, the wood was infiltrated and replaced by the silica until the original structure of each tree had been duplicated in stone.

Once the transformation had been completed, it remained only for the slow erosive action of wind and water to strip away the overlying deposits of volcanic debris and reveal the fossilized logs below. So the relics of an ancient cataclysm were preserved, and so they stand today in an eerie display of varied forms and colors.　　□

Simpson Desert

- Australia
- Map: page 22, D–4

Unending ridges of deep red sand corrugate the surface of this desert in the great Australian Outback.

The Simpson Desert is located near the very center of Australia in the vast, sparsely populated heartland known as the great Outback. Stretching to the northwest from the usually dry basin of Lake Eyre to the foothills of the Macdonnell Ranges, it covers an area of some 56,000 square miles (145,000 square kilometers).

So harsh and inhospitable that it was shunned by even the hardy ab-origines, the Simpson Desert (also known as the Arunta Desert) long defied the probes of explorers. It was not until 1939, in fact, that the first successful crossing was made by Cecil Thomas Madigan, who named the desert in honor of a former president of a local geographical society.

The major obstacle to exploration—and the most impressive distinguishing feature of the Simpson Desert—is the seemingly endless succession of long, parallel sand ridges that traverse it. The dunes, heaped up long ago by the wind, extend from the northwest to the southeast in straight, unbroken ridges up to 180 miles (290 kilometers) long. Rising to heights of 100 feet (30 meters) and more, they are separated by troughs that average about 1,000 feet (300 meters) in width. The corrugated pattern of ridges and troughs, when viewed from the air, has been likened to a field plowed by giants. Viewing them from ground level, an early explorer compared them to the waves of a monstrous sea.

The dunes are also notable for their color, which is particularly beautiful at dawn, when the flaming orange-red of their crests contrasts with inky shadows in the troughs. The color, in effect, results from common rust; each grain of sand is coated with a thin film of iron oxide, a characteristic product of weathering in dry climates.

Rainfall in the desert, sparse and erratically distributed throughout the year, amounts to only about 6 to 8 inches (150 to 200 millimeters) an-

SIMPSON DESERT. *Following infrequent rainfall, a carpet of lush green vegetation comes to life in the dune-ribbed Australian desert.*

nually. Temperature contrasts compound the harshness of the climate. The thermometer often soars above 100° F (38° C) by day and falls below freezing at night.

Even so, the desert is far from lifeless. Low shrubs and clumps of hardy spinifex grass survive on the steep slopes of the dunes and anchor the sand in place. And after infrequent rains the desert is completely transformed. Short-lived plants then sprout and burst into bloom, covering the land with a carpet of flower-spangled greenery. Birds flock in and insects abound, as does the year-round population of lizards and small mammals that escape the sun by burrowing beneath the sand and emerging at night to forage. □

SINOIA CAVES. *In the dim recesses of the cave system, eroded in a dolomite massif, a deep, calm lake reflects the images of stalactites hanging from a vaulted ceiling.*

Sinoia Caves

- Zimbabwe
- Map: page 26, C–4

Sunlight filtering into these African caves illuminates an underground lake with a kaleidoscope of colors.

Sinoia Caves are the focal point and main attraction of a small national park near the village of Sinoia, located about 60 miles (100 kilometers) northwest of Harare on the main highway to Zambia. Eroded in a massif of dolomite, a carbonate rock that can be dissolved over time by slightly acidic groundwater, the caves actually consist of a series of sinkholes that open to the surface and are linked to one another by a network of natural underground corridors. Running in several directions, the passageways converge on a larger central sinkhole. And at its bottom is the deep, dark, mysterious expanse of Sleeping Lake.

Although they are frequented by tourists today, the caves have known stormy times in the past. The African name for the spot, which means "hole of the fallen," commemorates an especially grim episode in the history of tribal warfare. Around 1830 the Angonni, a tribe that was migrating from the south, passed through the area, made a surprise attack on the local people, and disposed of their victims by throwing them into the abyss.

But such thoughts are far from the minds of present-day visitors as they descend a flight of steps to an overlook that commands a breathtaking view of Sleeping Lake. Overhead the ceiling of the cave is decorated with an array of delicate stalactites built up over the centuries from minerals deposited by dripping water. Below is the calm blue surface of the lake, illuminated by sunlight that filters in through the cave's entrance. Throughout the day, the ever-changing colors and intensity of the light are reflected on the stalactites, resulting in an eerily beautiful interplay of ghostly shapes and fleeting shadows. The effect is at its best at midday, when the sun beams in and creates an amazing display of colors and contrasts. □

ISLE OF SKYE. *The jagged summits of the Cuillin Hills, the highest peaks on the island, rise far above the lowland lochs and moors.*

Skye, Isle of

- United Kingdom (Scotland)
- Map: page 16, C–3

A misty, mountainous Scottish isle is famed for its coastal cliffs and its magnificently varied landscape.

The Isle of Skye, the largest of the Inner Hebrides off the west coast of Scotland, is a mecca for both mountain climbers and geologists. Climbers are attracted by an array of some of the most spectacular and challenging peaks in the British Isles, geologists by the island's dramatic evidence of both volcanic action and severe glaciation.

The rocks responsible for the fantastically varied scenery on Skye were formed some 50 million years ago, at a time of widespread volcanic upheav-

als throughout the British Isles. Massive intrusions of igneous rock welled up to form the island's two mountain ranges. Extensive lava flows in turn created broad undulating plateaus that in many places end abruptly at the sea in towering cliffs. Within the past 1 million years, both types of formations were scoured by Ice Age glaciers to their present contours. The end result, in addition to striking contrasts in elevation, was an incredibly indented coast. Although Skye is only about 50 miles (80 kilometers) long, its coastline totals nearly 1,000 miles (1,600 kilometers), and no point on the island is more than 5 miles (8 kilometers) from the sea.

The higher of Skye's two mountain ranges, the Cuillin Hills, is made up mainly of gabbro, a dark, coarse-grained igneous rock. Water erosion,

weathering, and glaciation have dissected the gabbro into lines of sharp peaks, saw-toothed ridges, and steep slopes indented by many glacier-carved cirques. One of these deep basins contains a lake with its bottom reaching 100 feet (30 meters) below sea level. Twenty of the Cuillin Hills exceed 3,000 feet (900 meters) in elevation, and the highest one, Sgurr Alasdair, reaches 3,309 feet (1,009 meters).

The neighboring range, the Red Hills, in contrast, is formed of granite. Not as hard as gabbro, the granite has been eroded into smoother and more gently rounded summits. Pink granite sand and gravel on the slopes account for the Red Hills' color. The highest peaks in the group rise to about 2,500 feet (750 meters).

The island's basaltic lava flows, in turn, form broad undulating plateaus

Sleeping Bear Dunes

- United States (Michigan)
- Map: page 11, E–4

A splendid dune field, protected in a national lakeshore, overlooks the shining expanse of Lake Michigan.

In the northern part of Michigan's Lower Peninsula, a remote and lovely stretch of shoreline overlooks the chill, clear waters of Lake Michigan. Over a distance of some 30 miles (48 kilometers), the scalloped lakeshore is bounded by steep bluffs capped by a billowing sea of sand that extends far inland from the lake. High points, towering as much as 450 feet (135 meters) above Lake Michigan, provide sweeping panoramas of the inland sea to the west and the dunes and lake-studded forests to the east.

These, the Sleeping Bear Dunes, were named by Chippewa Indians for one great forested sandhill that suggested the form of a bear in deep repose. According to legend, the bear and two cubs once tried to swim across Lake Michigan. While still far from shore, the cubs grew tired and sank beneath the waves, but the mother swam on and lay down onshore to await their arrival. And there she remains, for she was transformed into Sleeping Bear Dune, and her cubs became the two Manitou Islands some 14 miles (23 kilometers) offshore.

In reality, Sleeping Bear and the rest of the dunes along the lake are relics of the Ice Age. Advancing several times across this area, continental ice caps left a deep deposit of sand and gravel along the present shoreline when they retreated. This so-called moraine, averaging 300 feet (90 meters) in height, forms the bluffs that tower above the lake. Winds sweeping in across Lake Michigan then began their ceaseless attack on the bluffs. Plucking fine sand grains from the mixed glacial debris as they were deflected upward, the winds carried the sand to the top of the bluffs and dropped it in the form of dunes. The actual dunes are thus like the icing on a cake—a thin layer of windblown sand atop a thick glacial deposit.

The process, moreover, is unending, as anyone standing on top of the bluffs soon realizes. Sand is constantly carried up from below, and while many of the dunes have been stabilized by vegetation, others are moving steadily inland before the wind's assault. □

Slieve League

- Ireland
- Map: page 16, C–3

Assaults by the sea and by glacial ice have carved the contrasting precipices on this Irish mountain.

The northern shore of Donegal Bay in far northwestern Ireland is notable for its wild and magnificent scenery. The highest point on the coast, and one of the most starkly dramatic, is the great, more or less flat-topped peak known as Slieve League. On its south side, a long stretch of rugged cliffs plunges straight down to the surf. On its north side, steep slopes drop down to the interior of County Donegal.

Slieve League's treeless summit is nearly 2,000 feet (600 meters) above the sea. Accessible from a road that leads partway up the mountain, it affords superb views of Donegal Bay and the Irish coast and countryside. In addition, visitors can gaze far to the west for great distances across the Atlantic Ocean.

The seaside cliffs of Slieve League, among the most impressive in Ireland, average some 800 feet (250 meters) in height and extend about 2 miles (3 kilometers) along the coast. Composed primarily of gleaming white quartzite, they have been stained yellow and pink in places by feldspar and iron impurities in the rock. The long assault by the waves has undermined the rock along intersecting networks of joints and fractures, resulting in stark, angular facets on the face of the slowly retreating line of cliffs.

The steep precipices on the mountain's northern flanks, in contrast, are the creations of Ice Age glaciers, which left their mark in many parts of Ireland. There the side of the mountain is scarred by a large cirque, a broad basinlike valley that was formed at the head of a glacier. As snow and ice accumulated on the mountainside and the glacier made its slow descent, chunks of bedrock were plucked from the slope to form the steep-sided hollow that remains today.

Unlike the white seaside cliffs, the dark outcrops in the cirque are schist, a coarse-grained metamorphic rock. The soil, fairly rich in lime, and the sheltered location make the cirque a refuge for a number of typically alpine plants that would not be able to survive on the constantly windblown summit or coastal cliffs. □

and moorland, interrupted here and there by flat-topped hills and giant terraces. One such cliff forms a continuous escarpment nearly 20 miles (32 kilometers) in length, overlooking broad lowlands at its base. An isolated pinnacle in front of the cliff, a survivor of past landslides, is known as the Old Man of Storr and is a famous landmark for sailors.

Elsewhere the plateaus terminate in gigantic coastal cliffs and headlands. Dunvegan Head, among the most imposing of all the promontories, rises straight up from the sea for 1,028 feet (313 meters). On the shores of Loch Dunvegan, the inlet beyond the head, stands Dunvegan Castle, the ancestral home of the Macleod clan. Dating from the ninth century, it is said to be the oldest continually occupied dwelling in Scotland. □

SLOVENSKY RAJ. *Adorned with eerie formations of permanent ice, Dobsina Cave is one of many caverns in the limestone plateau.*

Slovensky Raj

- Czechoslovakia
- Map: page 17, F–4

A lovely plateau crisscrossed by a network of dizzying chasms provides a fine display of nature's artistry.

In the Slovak Ore Mountains of eastern Czechoslovakia, a broad, heavily forested plateau bears the vividly descriptive name of Slovensky Raj, the "Slovak Paradise." Some 55 square miles (140 square kilometers) in area, the limestone and dolomite plateau is crisscrossed by an intricate network of spectacularly deep and remarkably narrow canyons. A number of them are no more than 3 feet (1 meter) wide at the bottom, yet they are hemmed in by cliffs as much as 1,000 feet (300 meters) high.

Spring-fed streams course along the bottoms of the canyons, leaping down waterfalls and swirling in giant potholes. Ladders and bridges have been installed to facilitate visits down to the depths of some of the canyons. A superb example of so-called karst erosion, the plateau is also honeycombed with caves and an endless variety of sinkholes, blind valleys, disappearing streams, and other features that make Slovensky Raj a landscape of rare and enchanting beauty. □

How Distinctive Landforms Develop in Limestone Regions

The complex, highly irregular surface of a landscape such as Slovensky Raj results from the particular chemical effects of groundwater on layers of limestone, dolomite, and similar rocks. When the water contains a slight amount of carbon dioxide, it becomes a very mild acid that is capable of dissolving the limestone and carving out a variety of distinctive landscape features. Geologists term this process "karst erosion," after the Karst region of northwest Yugoslavia, where the resultant landforms are especially well developed. Caves and subterranean streams are typical underground features. Common surface landforms, illustrated below, originate where zones of weakness in the limestone are gradually broadened and deepened until a layer of impermeable rock is reached. In addition to solution, the corrosive effect of running water, alternate freezing and thawing, and collapse of the rock all play a role.

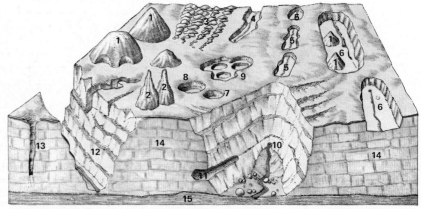

1. Residual limestone hill
2. Residual limestone tower
3. Lapies (deeply grooved surface rock)
4. Blind valley with disappearing stream
5. Window (collapsed tunnel exposing underground stream)
6. Polje (large flat-bottomed depression, often of great length)
7. Sinkhole (saucer-shaped depression into which a stream may disappear)
8. Doline (hollow formed by erosion and collapse)
9. Uvala (a compound doline)
10. Resurgent stream
11. Rock cavity exposed by erosion
12. Canyon
13. Chimney
14. Limestone
15. Impermeable rock

Snake River

- United States
- Map: page 10, D–4

This wild and scenic waterway of the Pacific Northwest has carved the deepest gorge in all of North America.

Originating in Yellowstone National Park in northwestern Wyoming, the Snake River flows in a broad arc across southern Idaho, turns north along the boundary of Idaho and Oregon, and finally loops down into Washington, where it joins the mighty Columbia River. Its total length is 1,038 miles (1,671 kilometers).

The Snake descends rapidly from its source near the Continental Divide in the Rocky Mountains and is already a substantial river as it flows southward across Jackson Hole at the foot of the towering Teton Range. Turning westward into Idaho, it leaves the mountains behind and enters an entirely different landscape. For much of the rest of its course it traverses a vast lava plateau, built up by repeated outpourings of volcanic rock some 20 million years ago.

Subsequent erosion and glaciation have produced a varied landscape of high plains, immense fields of volcanic rubble, and ever-deepening gorges. The fertile volcanic soil of the Snake River Plain in Idaho yields an abundant potato crop. But more typically the river cuts a wild and spectacular course through desolate country. Here and there dams slow down its progress; elsewhere the river leaps across gigantic waterfalls. At the Thousand Springs near Twin Falls, a multitude of underground streams emerge from the porous volcanic rock and then cascade down the walls of the river's deep gorge.

But the most impressive scenery lies downstream where the river turns north along the border between Idaho and Oregon. For a distance of some 125 miles (200 kilometers), the Snake passes through the awesome cleft of Hell's Canyon, the deepest gorge in North America. More than 1 mile (1.6 kilometers) deep for long stretches, Hell's Canyon has a maximum depth of 7,900 feet (2,407 meters). Leaving the canyon, the river finally turns to the west into Washington and merges with the Columbia River, which empties into the Pacific. □

SNAKE RIVER. *At the foot of the majestic Teton Range, the river has carved a meandering course through deep deposits of glacial debris.*

Sniezna Cave

- Poland
- Map: page 17, F–4

*The secrets of this great abyss—one
of the deepest caves in the world—
have yet to be completely unraveled.*

More than 200 caves are known to
exist in the limestone massifs of the
Tatra Mountains, which straddle the
border of Poland and Czechoslovakia
to the south of Cracow. Probably the
most impressive is Sniezna Cave. (Its
Polish name means "abyss of snow.")
Although it was only recently discovered and has not yet been completely
explored, it ranks as the deepest cave
in Eastern Europe and one of the
deepest in the world.

The cave's highest known entrance
is perched on a mountainside at an
elevation of 6,020 feet (1,835 meters).
From this level a number of winding
tunnels descend to a large gallery
1,300 feet (400 meters) below the
surface. Sloping gradually downward
into the mountain, the gallery comes
to an abrupt end at 2,467 feet (752
meters) below the surface, where it is
blocked by a siphon—a U-shaped tunnel filled with water.

In 1972 speleologists equipped with
diving gear managed to penetrate the
siphon. Beyond this obstacle they discovered yet another gallery descending still deeper into the mountain.
Continuing exploration of this gallery
has proceeded to a depth of 2,569 feet
(783 meters) below the surface, and it
is believed that Sniezna Cave may
eventually prove to be even deeper. □

Soborom Hot Springs

- Chad
- Map: page 24, E–3

*In a mountain valley in the Sahara,
bubbling hot springs and geysers
testify to a violent volcanic history.*

Soborom Hot Springs are located in
a valley high in the Tibesti Massif
in northwestern Chad. The rugged
mountain range, born of a violent volcanic upheaval some 5 million years
ago, includes the jagged summit of
Emi Koussi, the highest point in the
Sahara. For the most part the volcanic
fires have long been stilled, but at

SOBOROM HOT SPRINGS. *In a valley hemmed in by ancient eroded lava flows, the trickling
water from numerous hot springs has encrusted the surface with colorful mineral deposits.*

Soborom and a few other hot springs,
vestiges of this fiery past linger on.

The many hot springs, geysers, and
fumaroles at Soborom attest to the
presence of a pocket of molten rock
that remains quite close to the surface
of the earth. Lava is no longer being
expelled on the valley floor; only
gases, steam, and hot water escape
from the holes and fissures in the
earth's crust. The fumaroles are vents
emitting noxious sulfurous fumes. In
the hot springs, water filled with gas
bubbles gurgles constantly to the surface. Its temperature ranges from a
lukewarm 70° F (21° C) to a scalding
198° F (92° C). The gradual buildup
and sudden release of subterranean
pressure causes the geysers to erupt
intermittently with jets of hot water

and steam. Elsewhere pools of hot
mud sputter with escaping gases.

Besides being hot, the extraordinarily acid water is laden with sulfates,
salts, ammonia, iron oxides, and other
types of impurities. Some of these res-
idues have been deposited in cone-
shaped mounds around the vents of
the geysers. Others tint the surfaces of
ancient lava flows with brilliant hues
where the overflowing water trickles
across the valley floor. Colors range
from the brilliant white of salt crystals
and yellow in sulfur deposits to varying shades of red and gray in the
slippery mud. Because of their high
mineral content, the thermal waters
are also valued by local people for
their curative powers, especially for
the treatment of rheumatism. □

Sof Omar Cave

- Ethiopia
- Map: page 25, H–5

Remote and only recently explored, this Ethiopian cave ranks among the longest caverns in all of Africa.

Located in an isolated region of the Ethiopian highlands, Sof Omar Cave was first explored in detail in 1973. With some 9 miles (15 kilometers) of passageways, it proved to be one of the longest caves in Africa.

A river enters Sof Omar through an opening in the face of a limestone cliff and flows in broad meandering curves through the cave's extensive galleries. Heavy loads of sand and gravel are washed into the cave and deposited in bars and banks all along the river's subterranean course. Far from filling up the cave, however, the debris contributes to its enlargement. Violent floods periodically flush out the sand and gravel, which erode the channel by mechanical abrasion. □

Sogne Fjord

- Norway
- Map: page 16, D–2

Norway's longest, deepest fjord is also cherished as one of the most beautiful valleys in all the world.

Sogne Fjord, a long, narrow arm of the North Sea, penetrates far into the Norwegian coast some 45 miles (70 kilometers) north of Bergen. Known as the King of the Fjords, it is both the longest and the deepest of the many similar inlets that indent the west coast of Norway. From its mouth to the town of Skjolden at the end of its longest branch, Luster Fjord, the great waterway is 127 miles (204 kilometers) long. And in places the water in Sogne Fjord reaches a maximum depth of 4,291 feet (1,308 meters).

Famous for its scenic beauty, the fjord is most easily explored from the excursion boats that ply its tranquil waters. The main branch of the fjord, which averages about 3 miles (5 kilo-

meters) in width, extends almost due east into high plateau and mountain country, where steep slopes and snow-capped peaks rise straight up from the water's edge.

In many places waterfalls plummet down the cliffs in foaming cascades. Elsewhere the deltas built up by incoming rivers provide the sites for age-old settlements. Picturesque villages and innumerable farms along the banks provide a pastoral atmosphere that contrasts with the dramatic sweep of the mountain slopes. Neat, well-tended fields are separated by stone fences and highlighted by dwellings painted in bright primary colors. In spring the meadows burst with wildflowers, and blossoming fruit trees in countless orchards perfume the air.

The most spectacular scenery begins in the vicinity of Balestrand, where the first of several arms, Fjaerlands Fjord, branches off to the north of the main channel. Long and narrow, it reaches some 15 miles (25 kilometers) into the mountains, where its

SOGNE FJORD. *Beyond the hamlet at the head of an arm of the main fjord, the typically U-shaped, glacier-carved valley continues far inland.*

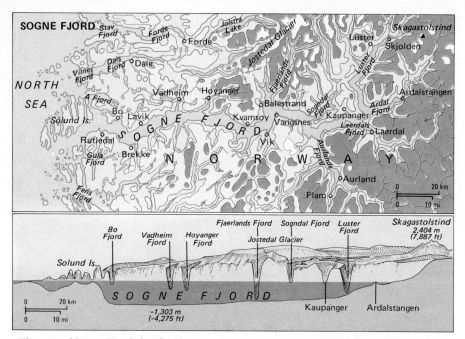

SOGNE FJORD

NORTH SEA

NORWAY

The map of Sogne Fjord clarifies the branching pattern of the glacially deepened former river valleys that make up the main fjord and its several arms. The cutaway diagram along the main axis of the fjord reveals the startling height and steepness of the cliffs along their walls, which extend far below present sea level.

Soos Springs

- Czechoslovakia
- Map: page 17, E–3

An immense bog alive with bubbling springs and jets of carbon dioxide provides a hint of more violent forces that once shook this region.

headwaters are fed by runoff from Jostedal Glacier, the largest permanent ice field in Europe.

The next major branch, Sogndal Fjord, also extends off to the north. On the opposite shore Aurlands Fjord branches off to the south and is itself divided into two arms. At the head of the fjord is the small village of Flam, where an electric rail line, its coaches safeguarded by five separate braking systems, breathtakingly zigzags nearly 3,000 feet (900 meters) up a steep mountainside.

Still farther inland is the short but picturesque Laerdals Fjord, noted for the wooden 12th-century church in the town at its head. The next branch, Ardal Fjord, is given over to industry. On its banks is one of the largest aluminum plants in all of Norway, powered by water that pours down from an upland lake by way of a tunnel bored through solid rock.

And finally, at the head of Sogne Fjord, its longest arm, Luster Fjord, branches off on a winding northward course. Broader and less steep-walled than some of the other branches, it extends some 30 miles (50 kilometers) into mountainous uplands, where it too receives meltwater from the massive Jostedal Glacier.

The glacier, a mass of ice thought to be more than 1,000 feet (300 meters) thick, is but a remnant of the immense ice cap that blanketed the entire re-

gion several times during the Ice Age. And it was tongues of ice spilling down to the sea from the ice cap that so deeply carved the fjords on the Norwegian coast.

Grinding seaward through a preexisting network of river valleys, the glaciers scoured out deep, steep-sided trenches. Tributary glaciers carved the many present-day branches of Sogne Fjord. Where the tributary glaciers merged, their combined mass scooped out the main trunk of this great fjord.

But the true magnitude of this awesome cleft is only partially apparent to visitors. From the edge of the fjord, sheer cliffs rise to elevations of 3,000 feet (900 meters) and more. Below water level, the cliffs plunge down in places for an additional 4,000 feet (1,200 meters). The total depth of this immense glacier-carved trench is thus even greater than that of the Grand Canyon of the Colorado River in Arizona, which on the average is about 1 mile (1.6 kilometers) deep.

The depth of Sogne Fjord is not uniform throughout. Just like other fjords, its bottom rises abruptly near its mouth. There, where the glacier thinned out at the edge of the sea, it lost much of its power to excavate the bedrock. But farther inland, the fjord that extends so far below sea level is awesome testimony to the erosive force of the bygone rivers of ice that sculpted the coast of Norway. □

In a government-protected nature reserve near the westernmost corner of Czechoslovakia, the Soos Springs create a landscape unlike any other in Europe. Filling the basin of an ancient lake bed is a vast bog comprising an estimated 250 million cubic feet (7 million cubic meters) of peat. Penetrating this thick, brownish accumulation of partially decayed plant remains are a number of so-called bog geysers—vents through which muddy mineral-laden water bubbles up to the surface.

These unusual cold springs are animated by carbon dioxide gas that escapes through cracks and fissures that developed in the underlying bedrock some 2 million years ago, at a time when volcanic activity occurred throughout the region. During periods of dryness these vents or openings (known as mofettes) arc free of water, but the gas continues to escape, often with enough force to create a distinctive hissing or whistling noise. □

SOOS SPRINGS. *Patches of mineral salts carried up by carbonated spring water encrust the surface of the peat bog that fills an ancient lake bed in western Czechoslovakia.*

Soufrière

- France (Guadeloupe)
- Map: page 14, C–1

Ever since the time of Columbus, this Caribbean volcano has hinted of continued unrest within its depths.

Soufrière forms the high point of the French island of Guadeloupe, about 375 miles (600 kilometers) north of Venezuela in the Caribbean Sea. Its slopes, covered by a lush tropical rain forest, rise to a summit 4,813 feet (1,467 meters) above the sea.

Ever since Columbus explored this part of the Caribbean in 1493, Soufrière (its name means "sulfur mine" in French) has rested fitfully. From time to time minor eruptions occurred, and down through the decades numerous vents and small craters near the summit continued to emit sulfurous fumes. Even so, most dismissed it as an essentially dormant volcano.

In the summer of 1976, however, Soufrière proved how deceptive a "sleeping" volcano can be. For several months earth tremors in the vicinity had been hinting of growing unrest beneath the earth's crust. Then, instead of the usual sulfurous fumes, summit vents began issuing clouds of ash and steam. Authorities began to fear that a major eruption might be near. Recalling the disastrous explosion of Mount Pelée on the nearby island of Martinique in 1902, when an entire city was destroyed within minutes, they ordered the evacuation of 72,000 residents from the area.

The culminating blast came on August 30, 1976. Clouds of ash and steam were blown high up into the sky, and masses of boiling mud and lava poured from the vents. Although less violent than some observers had predicted, the eruption nevertheless was severe. Two scientists were injured, but because of the evacuation there were no fatalities. Even so, islanders no doubt glance at Soufrière from time to time and wonder when their sleeping giant may once again grow restless. □

Spectrum Range

- Canada (British Columbia)
- Map: page 10, C–3

A multicolored range of volcanic peaks is a prime feature of a park deep in the Canadian wilderness.

The Spectrum Range—remote, rugged, and also mysteriously beautiful—is hidden away in northwestern British Columbia not far from the Alaskan border. Except for prospectors and geologists, few visitors have witnessed the spectacle of the mountains' multicolored slopes. Although the range is protected in Mount Edziza Provincial Park, no roads traverse the area; the peaks are accessible only on foot or by helicopter. Even so, all who make the difficult trek into this genuine wilderness area are rewarded with an unforgettable experience.

The major mountain of this unusual volcanic area is nearby Mount Edziza, rising to an elevation of 9,143 feet (2,787 meters) and topped by a snow-filled crater about 2 miles (3 kilometers) in diameter. Though only about 1 million years old, the volcano has erupted often enough to build up an enormous surrounding plateau of cinders and lava some 5,000 feet (1,500 meters) thick. (*Edziza* is an Indian word meaning "cinders.") Not far away, more recent eruptions have produced many symmetrical cinder cones on the surface of the plateau.

To the south of Mount Edziza are the main ramparts of the Spectrum Range, older peaks created by volcanic activity that began some 4 million years ago. Because of their greater age, they have been far more deeply eroded than Edziza by repeated glaciation. Numerous cirques (deep hollows excavated at the heads of valley glaciers) indent the mountainsides. In many places sharp-edged ridges, known as arêtes, form the boundary between cirques.

But the most striking feature of the Spectrum Range, and the reason for its name, is the rich array of colors that tint the mountainsides. Vivid combinations of red, yellow, orange, and mauve, caused by magma combining with mineral salts, have stained the rocks with multicolored stripes. Except for stunted trees in the lower valleys, no vegetation masks the rainbow hues of the slopes. Glinting in the sunlight of the brief northern summer, the Spectrums are among the world's most unusual mountain ranges. □

SPECTRUM RANGE. *The volcanic slopes, streaked with vivid hues, have been deeply scarred by the repeated advances of mountain glaciers.*

SPITSBERGEN. *A pale light touches a coastal inlet, heralding the return of summer, when the Arctic island will suddenly teem with life.*

Spitsbergen

- Norway
- Map: page 18, C–1

This remote Arctic island, about the size of Switzerland, was sculpted by Ice Age glaciers, and even now is locked under a thick cover of ice.

Spitsbergen is the largest island in the Svalbard archipelago, located some 400 miles (640 kilometers) north of the Norwegian mainland in the Arctic Ocean. The Vikings first discovered the bleak and frozen island group in 1194 and gave it the forbidding name of Svalbard, meaning "cold coast." Subsequently forgotten, the islands were rediscovered by the Dutch explorer Willem Barents in 1596. Impressed by their jagged profiles, he named the archipelago Spitsbergen, land of the "pointed peaks."

Whalers soon converged upon the area, followed in turn by hunters and fur trappers. Then the islands drifted back into obscurity until their extensive coal deposits began to be exploited at the turn of this century. To

this day, coal mining remains the islands' principal industry. (Svalbard's administrative center, Longyear City on Spitsbergen, was named for an American who began mining operations there in 1906.)

Although parts of Spitsbergen are bordered by broad coastal flatlands, the rugged, mountainous interior has more than enough pointed peaks to justify its name. Composed of intensely folded and faulted rocks of many kinds, the highest of the peaks culminates 5,633 feet (1,717 meters) above the sea.

The mountains' sharply chiseled crests and ridges are ample testimony to the severe glaciation that affected them during the Ice Age, as are the many fjords that indent the island's tortuous coastline. Even now, some 60 percent of Svalbard's land area is covered by glaciers and permanent snowfields. In many places the glaciers stream down to the coastal lowlands and calve icebergs directly into the sea, which itself is clogged with drifting ice for several months of the year.

The warm waters of the North Atlantic Drift (a branch of the Gulf

Stream) have a moderating effect on Spitsbergen's climate. Even so, because of its far northern location, the entire archipelago is indeed a land of frozen coasts, especially in midwinter, when temperatures plummet to –40° F (–40° C), and the sun provides only an eerie glow at noon.

From April to August, by contrast, the daylight hours are long (in midsummer the sun does not set at all), and temperatures reach as high as 50° F (10° C). Surface ice melts, the upper layers of the frozen ground thaw, and harbors are opened to shipping. In a brief but spectacular display, carpets of colorful wildflowers burst into bloom. The year-round residents—polar bears, reindeer, and arctic foxes—are suddenly outnumbered by millions of migratory birds. Eiders, geese, gulls, and terns converge on the boggy tundra, where they feast on swarms of insects, while auks and guillemots nest on the rocky cliffs and fish along the coasts. Then the sun begins to dip beneath the horizon again, and before long Spitsbergen is locked once more beneath the frozen silence of winter. □

STAUBBACH FALLS. *Tumbling over a cliff into a deep glacial valley, the water of the falls is transformed into a dazzling veil of spray.*

Staubbach Falls

- Switzerland
- Map: page 17, D–4

High in the Alps, one shimmering cascade stands out among a score of others pouring into the same valley.

To the south of Interlaken on the fringe of the Bernese Alps in south-central Switzerland, a mountain valley known as the Lauterbrunnental is regarded by many as the epitome of Alpine scenery. The Jungfrau and other lofty summits rise in the distance, while nearer at hand the broad, deep valley is flanked by cliffs up to 1,500 feet (450 meters) high. Cattle graze in the green pastures, and fine old chalets dot the valley floor.

The finishing touch is provided by the 20 or so cascades that spill over the edges of the cliffs and plummet to the valley far below. Among the loveliest of all is Staubbach Falls, with a drop of nearly 1,000 feet (300 meters). The name, which means "spray stream," is particularly appropriate because the Staubbach's shimmering flow of water is transformed into billowing clouds of mist by the time it finally reaches the floor of the valley.

Like the other cascades in the Lauterbrunnental, Staubbach Falls is a creation of the Ice Age. When glacial ice deepened the main valley, tributary streams were left perched high atop the flanking cliffs. □

Stockholm Archipelago

- Sweden
- Map: page 16, E–3

A haven for boaters, artists, and summer vacationers, this labyrinth of land and sea is a creation of the ice cap that once blanketed Scandinavia.

The Stockholm Archipelago is a maze of rocky islands and islets in the Baltic Sea just off the coast of Sweden's capital. Extending from north to south over a distance of about 80 miles (125 kilometers), the islands are infinitely varied in size and shape and number in the thousands.

This idyllic labyrinth of land and water, besides being serenely beautiful, is a classic example of a glacier-carved landscape that is very slowly

STOCKHOLM ARCHIPELAGO. *Although forests thrive on larger islands near the coast, the low-lying outermost islets support little more than a sparse cover of heather and wildflowers.*

emerging from the sea. During the Ice Age, which ended only about 10,000 years ago, all of Scandinavia was covered by an immense ice cap. Advancing across the region, the ice honed down the ancient gneiss and granite bedrock, smoothing and rounding the high spots and gouging out deep, narrow channels along fractures and other zones of weakness in the rock. The unimaginable weight of this enormous ice cap also caused the earth's crust to warp downward. And so it was that by the end of the Ice Age, the rocks that form the archipelago had been depressed well below present-day sea level.

When the ice at last retreated to the north, vast quantities of meltwater resulted in a general rise in sea level. As water flooded into the Baltic, the area where the archipelago now stands was submerged beneath the sea. Waves and tides removed any debris that had

The Slowly Changing Levels of Land and Sea

The relative levels of sea and land have changed many times. Vertical movements of the earth's crust can raise or lower whole sections of a coastline. And the basins of the oceans themselves slowly change in capacity as a result of shifts in the earth's great crustal plates.

Glacial ages are another major factor in the changing of sea levels. During the last Ice Age, for example, so much water was locked up in vast continental ice caps that sea levels all around the world were 300 to 500 feet (90 to 150 meters) lower than they are today. If all the remaining ice caps on Antarctica, Greenland, and elsewhere were to melt, moreover, it is estimated that the level of the sea would rise an additional 200 feet (60 meters), causing the flooding of many densely populated coastal regions.

been deposited by the retreating ice sheet, leaving only bare rock.

Relieved of the great weight of the ice, the crustal rocks then began a very slow rebound and gradually rose above the water. One by one, the islands emerged from the sea. And the process is continuing even to this day: in fact it is estimated that the archipelago is rising at a rate of 18 inches (46 centimeters) per century. As a result of this ongoing uplift, the sizes and shapes of the islands are slowly changing, as is the depth of the water in the channels between them.

The islands nearest the coast—the first to emerge from the sea—are the largest and highest. Farther offshore they decrease in size and elevation; the outermost islets are low rocks that barely protrude above the sea. Tranquil and unspoiled despite their proximity to Stockholm, the islands are a popular haven for vacationers seeking an escape from city life.   □

Stone Mountain

- United States (Georgia)
- Map: page 11, E–5

The great monolith towering so high above its surroundings at one time was buried deep beneath the surface.

Looming above the rolling Georgia uplands some 15 miles (24 kilometers) east of Atlanta is the region's largest exposed mass of granite: the great gray monolith known as Stone Mountain. With no other mountains in the immediate area, it has inevitably attracted attention since the days of the Indians. A broad oval dome of rock about 1½ miles (2.4 kilometers) long, it rises 825 feet (251 meters) above its surroundings and 1,686 feet (514 meters) above sea level.

It was probably the Creek Indians who built the breast-high stone wall that once surrounded the mountain's barren summit. The first Europeans to see Stone Mountain are believed to have been Spaniards on an expedition led by Captain Juan Pardo in 1567. Pardo reported that the mountain glistened in the sun like crystal, and the land around it was littered with diamonds and rubies. Harassed by Indians, he was unable to examine the "gems," which were actually quartz crystals.

In more recent times the rock's north face has been embellished by a monumental sculpture. Commemorating the Civil War Confederate heroes Jefferson Davis, Robert E. Lee, and Stonewall Jackson, the carving is 190 feet (58 meters) wide and 90 feet (27 meters) high.

The great dome is actually the exposed tip of a much larger mass of rock. It was formed when a pocket of molten magma forced its way up from the earth's interior into overlying rock layers. The magma never reached the

STONE MOUNTAIN. *Except for mosses, lichens, and a scattering of trees, the mountain's granite slopes are virtually devoid of vegetation.*

surface. It was intruded into a now-vanished range of the Appalachian mountain system, where it cooled beneath an insulating blanket of older rock layers estimated to have been some 10,000 feet (3,000 meters) thick.

The Stone Mountain massif was formed about 300 million years ago. While intrusion of the magma took place over a relatively short time, it took 100 million years or so for the molten material to cool and then solidify into an extremely hard, erosion-resistant rock.

Even as the granite was solidifying, the softer overlying rocks were being worn away. Eventually the massif's tip was exposed on the surface. Erosion of the covering rocks continued until the looming granite hulk achieved its present height above its surroundings. And as erosion of the rocks around its base goes on, Stone Mountain eventually will loom even higher above its surroundings. □

STORA SJOFALLET. *The waters of Sweden's Lule River accumulate in the basin of a lake scooped out by Ice Age glaciers, then escape by spilling over an erosion-resistant sill of rock.*

Stora Sjofallet

- Sweden
- Map: page 16, E–2

In a wilderness north of the Arctic Circle, an icy, foaming waterfall connects two fingerlike glacial lakes.

Stora Sjofallet, or the "Great Lake Falls," is an icy cascade on the upper course of the Lule River in northern Sweden's Lapland. Streaming southeastward to its outlet on the Gulf of Bothnia, the river courses down a broad glacier-carved valley through a series of long, narrow, fingerlike lakes.

The falls form the link between two of the lakes. Spilling over a steplike sill of ancient, erosion-resistant bedrock that acts as a natural dam for the upper lake, the water plunges down to the lower lake in a powerful, foaming torrent. The total drop is 131 feet (40 meters).

Other falls that interrupt the course of the Lule farther downstream have been harnessed for power generation. But Stora Sjofallet remains pristine, the focal point of a national park. Combined with two adjacent reserves, it makes up the largest wild area in Europe. Best explored on foot, the area presents untrammeled vistas of superb arctic scenery—rugged mountains, some with glaciers still active on their slopes; broad expanses of tundra; and the glistening, icy lakes. For less ambitious explorers, boat trips up the Lule's chain of lakes are also available, including stops at Stora Sjofallet's thunderous cascade. □

Strokkur

- Iceland
- Map: page 16, A–2

In a land where abundant geothermal energy is used for heating and power generation, this geyser continues to amaze with its regular eruptions.

STROKKUR. *Just as the Icelandic geyser is about to erupt, the water in its basin heaves up into a dome that bursts into a spectacular jet of steam and boiling water.*

Ever since medieval times, Iceland has been famous for its many hot springs and geysers. Indeed, the name of the most spectacular of them all, the Geysir, or "Gusher," is the basis for the English word for all such intermittently erupting hot springs.

Although the Geysir's performance has become less impressive in recent times, dozens of other hot springs continue to bubble and spurt in the same thermal area in southwestern Iceland. Among the most active and predictable in the group, located in a valley at the foot of a range of volcanic mountains, is Strokkur, the "Churn." Every 4 to 10 minutes it shoots a jet of boiling water as high as 100 feet (30 meters) into the sky.

Fluctuations in the water level in its basin herald each eruption. As the turbulence increases, the surface of the water heaves up into a dome, then explodes into a column of steam and water droplets. The clouds of vapor blow away on the breeze, but the water falls back to the basin to contribute to the next eruption.

The abundance of geysers is due to Iceland's geological history. A relatively young basaltic lava plateau, the island is part of the Mid-Atlantic Ridge, the boundary between two of the earth's great crustal plates. In this volcanically active zone, molten magma lies close to the earth's surface, where it heats underground water and powers its periodic eruptive escapes through fissures in the crust. □

Stromboli

- Italy
- Map: page 17, E–5

The glow of its endless eruptions reflected against the nighttime sky has earned this volcano the title "Lighthouse of the Mediterranean."

Stromboli, which rises from the Tyrrhenian Sea to the north of Sicily, forms the northernmost of the Lipari Islands. Erupting virtually without cease since the dawn of recorded history, it is among the most predictable of all volcanoes. Every 15 to 45 minutes or so, its summit lava pool emits clouds of vapor and hurls clots of incandescent lava high into the sky.

Stromboli's eruptions are generally so mild, however, that the farms and villages of the island are rarely threatened. The amazing regularity of its outbursts, in fact, has made the volcano a tourist attraction. From a vantage point on the rim, it is possible to look down into the restless, fiery crater.

Although the volcano rises to a height of only 3,038 feet (926 meters) above the sea, Stromboli is deceptive. From its base on the ocean floor, its cone is actually some 10,400 feet (3,170

STROMBOLI. *A wisp of vapor rises above the Sciara del Fuoco, a long, steep slope built up of erupted debris that escaped through a wide breach in the rim of the crater.*

lapsed, or perhaps subsided. Ever since then, any volcanic debris that escaped from the crater has poured through the opening down a huge, steep slope known as the Sciara del Fuoco. This feature may account for Stromboli's gentle nature. Whereas many volcanoes periodically become clogged with their own debris, Stromboli's vent remains clear.

On rare occasions, however, even Stromboli becomes burdened with debris. Villagers who are accustomed to the volcano's continual thundering and shaking grow fearful only when the noises stop. For when the volcano is silent, it means the pressure is building up for a major explosion.

In 1930, for example, after a long period of inactivity, the island was convulsed by a gigantic shudder that caused a tsunami, or seismic tidal wave. In the explosion that followed, a mushroom cloud rose two miles (three kilometers) above the summit, and enormous blocks of debris were hurled high into the sky. Another great blast took place in 1954, but in general Stromboli remains predictable. It is its silence that warns of danger. □

Surtsey

- Iceland
- Map: page 16, A–2

On November 14, 1963, at about 7:00 a.m., a volcanic island rose out of the North Atlantic, spewing forth fire, ash, and clouds of smoke.

When the crew of a fishing vessel off the coast of Iceland sighted smoke one November morning in 1963, the captain assumed that a ship was on fire. He radioed for help, then headed toward the stricken vessel to render assistance. As the fishermen neared, the true nature of the explosion became clear: a volcano was breaking through the surface of the sea. Within hours, columns of smoke rose 12,000 feet (3,650 meters) into the air.

In the days, weeks, and months that followed, reporters and scientists came from all over the world to study the birth of this newest volcanic island. Their small aircraft and ships were pelted by a rain of vapor, ash, and volcanic bombs (lumps of partially solidified lava). In less than a month there was enough land for a daring team of French reporters to go ashore briefly. The island, located 6 miles (10

meters) high—nearly equal to nearby Mount Etna, the highest volcano in all of Europe.

The first submarine eruptions that produced Stromboli began about 2 million years ago. Eventually its cone burst through the surface of the sea and grew to its present size. Today the continually active pool of lava in its crater characteristically cools until a crust begins to form on the surface. Gases then accumulate until the pressure is great enough to blast off the crust with a small explosion. Based on their famous Italian counterpart, all volcanoes exhibiting this pattern of moderate but continuous explosions are called Strombolian volcanoes.

At some point in the distant past, one side of Stromboli's crater col-

SURTSEY. *Though seemingly devoid of life, the volcanic island was colonized by plants within months of the first eruptions that created it.*

kilometers) off the southern coast of Iceland, was named Surtsey in honor of Surtr, the god of fire in Norse mythology.

Surtsey erupted from a submarine mountain chain called the Mid-Atlantic Ridge, which takes a zigzag path from north to south along the floor of the Atlantic Ocean. The ridge marks the boundary between two crustal plates—vast segments of the earth's crust. In this region, as the plates spread slowly apart, molten rock from the upper mantle welled up to the surface, producing the volcano.

The initial submarine eruptions occurred beneath some 425 feet (130 meters) of seawater. The hot lava, coming in contact with cold water, cooled to form an accumulation of porous, ashy material and pillow lavas (bulbous lumps with glassy skins). Surtsey rests on a table-shaped platform of such debris.

As the vent neared the surface, the volcano began to erupt explosively. The water vaporized, sending up dense white clouds of steam along with plumes of black ash and cinders. Eventually outpourings of fluid lava began to flood down over the ash and cinder deposits. With the piling up of this more resistant material, a shield developed, and Surtsey became a per-

manent island that ultimately rose to a height of 568 feet (173 meters) above the sea.

After three years, its eruptive force spent, Surtsey measured a mere 1 square mile (2.6 square kilometers) in area. Even so, the first seeds and sprouting plants had been discovered within months of the island's birth, either carried in on the wind or else dropped by birds. Scientists are following the colonization of the island, recording all new species of plants and animals as they arrive. And they are patiently monitoring the island itself, watching constantly for any signs of renewed volcanic activity. □

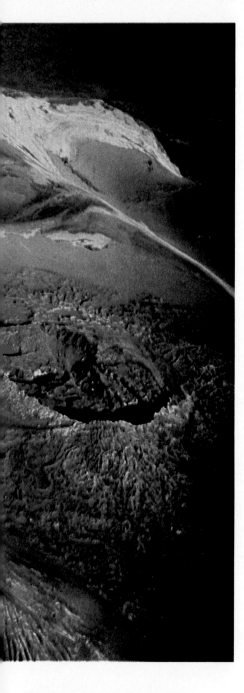

Sutherland Falls

- New Zealand
- Map: page 23, G–6

A remote mountainous corner of a Pacific island is the setting for one of the world's loftiest waterfalls.

SUTHERLAND FALLS. *Formed by the overflow from Lake Quill, which is fed by heavy rainfall and melting snow, the falls plunge in a triple cascade to the wooded valley far below.*

Hidden away in the mountains of New Zealand's South Island, Sutherland Falls quickly came to world attention after their discovery late in the 19th century by a Scottish settler named Donald Sutherland. On the strength of his claim that the plume of water dropped more than 3,300 feet (1,000 meters), the falls were thought for years to be the highest in the world.

Later surveys proved Sutherland's estimate to be considerably inflated. Even so, his falls rank among the loftiest anywhere, with a total drop of 1,904 feet (580 meters) in a triple span interrupted by two ledges. The water issues from bowl-shaped Lake Quill, named for an adventurer who made the first ascent of the sheer rock wall in 1890 and discovered the lake at the top. Modern visitors can hike into the remote area or, more simply, fly in with light aircraft for spectacular aerial views of the falls. □

Tafraoute

- Morocco
- Map: page 24, C–3

A tiny village surrounded by huge rock formations is at its best in spring, when blossoming almonds enhance the grandeur of the scene.

The village of Tafraoute, some 50 miles (80 kilometers) from the Atlantic coast in southern Morocco, lies amid some of the most picturesque scenery in the Anti-Atlas Mountains. Towering above the town to the west is a massive ridge of pinkish-brown quartzite known as Djebel Lekest, the "amethyst mountain," noted for the shimmering interplay of light and shadow on its slopes. And rising in the background are gigantic rock formations with chaotic heaps of boulders. Pleasant oases nestle in some of the valleys amid fields of barley and almond groves. The scene is especially beautiful in spring, when the almonds come into bloom.

The pinkish granite of the rock piles was formed more than 1 billion years ago, when a mass of molten magma forced its way up into even older overlying rocks. Erosion has long since worn away the older rocks that once covered the granite; exposed at the surface, the granite itself is now being sculpted by wind, water, and chemical weathering. Attacking and enlarging joints and fractures in the rock, they have carved it into walls, pillars, flattish domes, and precariously balanced clusters of boulders. □

TAFRAOUTE. *Like the ruins of an ancient city, huge boulders and debris from rockslides are strewn around a core of erosion-carved granite.*

TAGBALADOUGOU FALLS. *At the uppermost of the falls' three cascades, a misty curtain of water begins its descent to the plains far below.*

Tagbaladougou Falls

- Upper Volta
- Map: page 24, C–4

Along the upper course of the Comoé River in western Africa, a tributary stream plunges from a high plateau in a beautiful three-tiered cascade.

In the generally flat terrain of the small West African country of Upper Volta, the Banfora Cliffs are a conspicuous landscape feature. Forming the boundary of a sandstone plateau in the southwestern part of the coun-

try, they rise some 500 feet (150 meters) above the plain at their base. Several gorges indent the face of the cliffs, all of them carved by tributaries of the Comoé River as they spill off the top of the plateau. Descending to the plain, the courses of all the rivers are inevitably interrupted by rapids and waterfalls.

Among the loveliest are the Tagbaladougou Falls, especially during the rainy season from June to September, when the flow of water is at its peak. The falls are actually a series of three well-defined cascades, each somewhat different as a result of differences in the thick layers of sandstone that make up the plateau.

At the upper falls, pictured here, a broad span of water spills over the hard cap rock of the plateau. The second falls, about 325 feet (100 meters) downstream, in contrast, is a classic plumelike cascade. With a drop of about 100 feet (30 meters), the water falls into a narrow cleft eroded in a much softer layer of sandstone.

The river broadens again at the lowest falls, where the water drops over an outcrop of quartzite, a hard variety of sandstone that has resisted erosion well. Beyond the falls the river joins the Comoé, which meanders southward some 475 miles (765 kilometers) across the Ivory Coast to its outlet on the Gulf of Guinea. □

365

Taka Sinkhole

- Greece
- Map: page 17, F–5

Local legend long ago explained the mystery of what happens to the water that disappears into this abyss.

The Taka Sinkhole takes its name from Lake Taka, which is cupped at the bottom of a basin ringed by hills near the heart of the Peloponnesus, Greece's famous southern peninsula. The sinkhole, an opening 6½ feet (2 meters) in diameter, is eroded in the flank of one of the fringing hills. At times of high water, the overflow from the lake pours into the sinkhole and disappears. After a long underground journey, the water reappears in a spring at the village of Koniditza some 15 miles (25 kilometers) to the south.

Subterranean streams and sinkholes, common features of limestone regions around the world, have frequently been a mystery to local people. But apparently the residents of this area long ago unraveled the puzzle of the disappearing waters of the Taka Sinkhole.

According to local legend, a shepherd boy once lost his flute in the hole. When his mother found it floating in the spring at Koniditza, the boy decided to take advantage of the hidden channel to keep his family's larder filled. Whenever they needed food, he dropped a stolen sheep into the hole and later recovered it from the spring at Koniditza. And that, scientists have proved, is exactly where the water from the Taka Sinkhole reappears. □

Talari Gorges

- Mali
- Map: page 24, B–4

The Senegal River in West Africa begins its journey to the Atlantic in a region of splendid waterfalls and constricted sandstone gorges.

The Senegal River is formed approximately 650 miles (1,050 kilometers) upstream from its outlet on the Atlantic by the union of two other streams. At Bafoulabé, "the Meeting of the Waters," in southwestern Mali, the Bafing ("Black") River joins the Bakoy ("White") River to form the northwestward-flowing Senegal.

Almost immediately the youthful river glides easily across a former barrier to its progress. Just a short distance downstream from Bafoulabé it passes through the steep-walled trench of the Talari Gorges, carved in a thick deposit of ancient reddish sandstone that was formed some 600 million years ago.

In contrast to the river's broad, sluggish lower course, its flow here is constricted in a narrow channel about 325 feet (100 meters) wide and as much as 100 feet (30 meters) deep. On each side of the river a steep, boulder-strewn slope rises about 165 feet (50 meters). At the top there is a broad ledge, and then a sheer cliff that rises up another 100 feet (30 meters). The warm reddish tones and stark contours of the rock both contribute to the beauty of the scene. Also in the vicinity are a number of rapids and waterfalls, most notably those at Gouina and Felou, where the river makes abrupt leaps of 50 feet (15 meters) on its descent to the sea. □

Tandil Rocks

- Argentina
- Map: page 15, D–6

This amazing array of intricately eroded rocks includes a fallen giant that used to waver in the wind.

The Sierra del Tandil, a long, low range of granite hills, rises above the flat and fertile plains of the Argentine pampas some 200 miles (320 kilometers) south of Buenos Aires. In places the contours of the hills have been altered by quarries. (Much of the granite was used for construction in Buenos Aires.) Elsewhere the natural forces of erosion have sculpted the rocks into sentinels, columns, and a variety of other forms.

One of the most unusual, the Piedra Movediza de Tandil ("Trembling Rock of Tandil"), long attracted the attention of visitors. A giant balancing rock perched atop a steep bluff, it wavered when the wind blew and could easily be pushed by hand. But it never fell. According to local legend, a team of 1,000 horses once tried—and failed—to dislodge the rock.

Then in 1912 the seemingly impossible happened: the famous rock tumbled from its rocky pedestal. Although it is only a memory now, its many oddly shaped neighbors remain popular tourist attractions. □

Tanganyika, Lake

- East Africa
- Map: page 26, C–3

The second deepest lake in the world, exceeded only by Lake Baikal in the U.S.S.R., is also notable for its great age and exceptional beauty.

Lake Tanganyika, with a maximum depth of 4,710 feet (1,436 meters), fills a long, narrow trough in the western arm of Africa's Rift Valley. Besides being the second deepest, it is the longest lake in the world, stretching 410 miles (660 kilometers) from north to south. Its width varies between 10 and 45 miles (16 and 72 kilometers). Bordered on both sides by steep slopes that rise to elevations of up to 9,000 feet (2,750 meters), the trench descends more than 2,000 feet (600 meters) below sea level.

LAKE TANGANYIKA. *Stirred up by the winds, the whitecapped waters of this spectacularly beautiful lake are often as blue as a tropical sea.*

The trough began to form some 25 million years ago as part of the formation of the great Rift Valley. The lake basin is actually a graben, a landform in which a block of the earth's crust has dropped down between blocks that rose up on either side. A chain of similar graben lakes traces much of the path of the Rift Valley from the Red Sea in the north all the way south to Mozambique.

Lake Tanganyika's drainage basin is quite small. The only major rivers flowing into it are the Ruzizi (an outlet of Lake Kivu to the north) and the Malagarasi, which flows in from Tanzania (formerly Tanganyika) to the east. The sole outlet, the Lukuga on the west shore, is a tributary of the Congo, which curves all the way across the continent and empties into the Atlantic Ocean.

Navigable throughout, the lake is an important trade route between the bordering countries. It also supports a thriving fishing industry, with a catch sufficient for local needs and export as well.

About 75 percent of the lake's fish species are endemic: they are found in Lake Tanganyika and nowhere else in the world. The abundance of endemic species is further evidence of the antiquity of the lake and its long isolation from other bodies of water, for it takes millions of years for new species to develop.

Tourism is still in its infancy, but the attractions are many. Apart from its sheer beauty, the lake is rich with wildlife, including multitudes of birds and astonishing numbers of hippopotamuses and crocodiles. Herds of elephants roam through surrounding forests, as do troops of chimpanzees and an occasional elusive leopard. □

TANGE GHARU. *Snaking through tunnels and around hairpin curves, a highway parallels the Kabul River as it passes through the gorge.*

Tange Gharu

- Afghanistan
- Map: page 18, H–5

On its tumultuous descent from the highlands, the Kabul River passes through a dramatic limestone gorge.

From its source in the mountainous highlands of northeastern Afghanistan, the Kabul River flows eastward past the ancient capital city of Kabul. Continuing its descent just north of the historic Khyber Pass, the Kabul drains into Pakistan, where it finally merges with the Indus River.

A traditional avenue of conquest, the Kabul valley was the route used by Alexander the Great when he invaded India in 327 B.C. Present-day travelers following in his footsteps can make the descent much more easily: a modern highway links Kabul with Peshawar, Pakistan, via the river valley.

The most spectacular segment of the route by far is just east of the city of Kabul, where the highway passes through the gorge of Tange Gharu. Traversing a series of tunnels bored into solid rock and winding around many breathtaking hairpin turns, the road descends some 2,300 feet (700 meters) over the course of just 9 miles (15 kilometers). On both sides, the stark, blue-gray limestone cliffs that tower high above the road and river-bed echo sonorously with the roar of countless rapids and waterfalls.

Although the thick layers of limestone that make up the walls of the gorge were formed some 250 million years ago, Tange Gharu itself came into being within the past 2 million years. Geologists theorize that, at least in the upper reaches of the gorge, the river at one time may have flowed in an underground channel through the limestone. A subsequent collapse of the tunnel's roof there may have resulted in the deep ravine.

But the major architect of the defile was a mountain-building episode that folded and uplifted the limestone beds to their present elevation. Proceeding on a tumultuous course down the rocky mountainside, the river increased its erosive power. In a relatively short period of time, the deep, spectacular gorge was chiseled into the surface of the rock. Although irrigation projects have partially depleted the river's flow, it remains a powerful cutting tool, ever altering the contours of the gorge. □

TANNOGOU FALLS. *Hemmed in by a fringe of forest, the African falls tumble from the edge of a high plateau. The flow is at its fullest during the May to September rainy season.*

Tannogou Falls

- Benin
- Map: page 24, D–4

In a remote corner of West Africa, a gentle river leaps to life as it spills over an abrupt escarpment.

The terrain of the West African nation of Benin (formerly Dahomey) consists mainly of flat plains and plateaus that rise gently northward from the Gulf of Guinea. The highest elevations—about 2,100 feet (640 meters)—are reached in the Atakora Range in the northwestern part of the country. Although not especially high, the range is nevertheless impressive, for it completely dominates the plains around it. Its western edge, in particular, is bordered by escarpments up to 650 feet (200 meters) high.

The range is actually a high plateau composed of a compact, resistant formation of quartzite more than 1 billion years old. A number of rivers lined by narrow ribbons of forest meander across the grasslands on the top of the plateau. At the edge they make their descent to the plains by way of rapids and waterfalls through narrow gorges eroded in the rock.

The most celebrated of the many cascades is Tannogou Falls, named for a village nestled at the foot of the Atakora's western escarpment. There a river plunges off the plateau in a picturesque double leap. At the larger upper falls, a veil of water spills into a broad basin enclosed by steep walls. After rushing across a stretch of rapids broken up by immense boulders, the water descends the second cascade, and then it continues peacefully on toward the plains. □

TASSILI N'AJJER. *Running water in a now-vanished underground stream carved the narrow curved base of this complex sandstone pillar.*

Tassili n'Ajjer

- Algeria
- Map: page 24, D–3

These sandstone plateaus seem like crumbling ruins, but rock paintings recall a bygone era when the land was green and game was abundant.

The Tassili n'Ajjer, located near the very heart of the Sahara in southeastern Algeria, is a series of magnificent sandstone plateaus so remote and rugged that they have not yet been fully explored. Described without exaggeration as "the domain of the fantastic," this austerely beautiful region has been sculpted into checkerboards of massive stone towers, astonishingly deep and narrow ravines, massive arches, and great bastions of rock as big as cathedrals.

The Tassili plateaus are primarily composed of sandstone that was deposited on the eroded, nearly flat West African Shield. (Estimated to be 2 billion years old, the shield is a vast expanse of basement rock that underlies much of the Sahara.) Repeated inundations of the shield by rivers, seas, and melting ice caps brought in the sediment that was consolidated into the sandstone formations.

The Tassili actually consists of two more or less parallel plateaus, the Inner Tassili and the Outer Tassili. They extend from the northwest to the southeast just north of the Ahaggar Mountains.

The Inner Tassili, the older and higher of the two, is composed of sandstone that was formed some 450 million years ago. Its southern margin is marked by a wall of cliffs and steep slopes. From the bottom of a lowland depression that separates the Tassili from the Ahaggar, the surface of the land rises abruptly in a great step up to 1,300 feet (400 meters) high. In some places, sheer cliffs define the southern margin of the plateau. Elsewhere it resembles a giant stairway, while in other places the cliffs are masked and softened by continuous aprons of talus (sloping heaps of fallen debris).

From the top of the cliffs, the surface of the Inner Tassili slopes gradually downward to the north and ends at a second depression. Eroded from thick deposits of shale that were laid down 420 million years ago, the relatively gentle contours of the depression allow easy passage.

North of the depression another wall of cliffs rises to the summit of the Outer Tassili. Like the Inner Tassili, its surface slopes gradually down to the north. The rocks that form the plateau are sandstone and shale that were deposited 380 million years ago.

The masses of sediment that ultimately formed both of the plateaus were washed in from an area much farther to the south long before the uplift of the intervening barrier of the Ahaggar Mountains. Some of the sediment was deposited on coastal plains by running rivers, some at times when the region was inundated by a shallow sea. Scientists have also established that parts of the Sahara were once covered by an ice cap. Thus, astonishingly, many traces of glacial debris are incorporated into the rocks throughout this hot, dry land.

Because sandstone is a brittle rock that responds to stresses by cracking rather than bending, the plateaus were long ago crisscrossed by networks of vertical fractures. At times when the climate was much wetter than today, running water and chemical weathering worked together to deepen and enlarge these fractures, cutting up the plateaus into fantastic rock formations. Great clusters of columns and massive bastions were left standing on the surface. Water rushing through channels at the bottom of the fractures opened up grottoes, arches, and tunnels. And many of the fractures were ultimately transformed into dizzying ravines hundreds of feet deep but only a few feet wide.

One of the most arresting features of the Tassili n'Ajjer is the desert varnish that stains many of the rocks. Ranging in color from dull red to black, the varnish is a thin layer of metallic oxides dissolved from the rocks themselves and deposited on the surface. In many places the desert varnish, which has been undisturbed for thousands of years, gives the rocks the appearance of scorched ruins.

Yet another remarkable feature of the Tassili plateaus is the abundance of astonishingly beautiful prehistoric rock paintings that adorn many of the cliffs and cave walls. The oldest of the paintings depict a hunting people who lived in the region as early as 5000 B.C. The animals they stalked—antelopes, elephants, leopards, ostriches, and many others—are evidence that plant life then must have been quite plentiful. Later paintings, superimposed on the hunters' art, indicate a great change in the way of life. Instead of hunters stalking game, they portray herdsmen tending cattle and other domesticated animals.

In time the herdsmen vanished as well. As the climate gradually became warmer and drier, much of the vegetation disappeared, as did the animals that depended on it. Eventually camels and goats were the only domesticated animals that could endure the harsh conditions. The mouflon, a species of wild mountain sheep, is the last survivor of the large wild mammals shown in the rock paintings. The humans adapted to the desert by taking up a nomadic way of life.

Although in many places the Tassili looks like a burned-out fortress, a few hardy species of plants and animals

Erosion Formed the Surrealistic Landscape of the Tassili

The strange landforms of the Tassili n'Ajjer result from the specific characteristics of sandstone, the plateaus' predominant rock. Because sandstone tends to be quite brittle, under stress it is easily broken up by intersecting networks of vertical cracks and joints. For millions of years, when the climate of the Tassili was much wetter than today, running water attacked the sandstone along these joints, carrying off bits of the rock and leaving jagged forms behind. The diagrams below show how a surface channel and an underground channel can gradually be enlarged and ultimately joined, as a fracture in the rock between them is widened by erosion. Many of the deep, narrow ravines in the Tassili were formed in this way. Dual erosion of this sort also resulted in the formation of stout pillars that seem to totter on narrow bases.

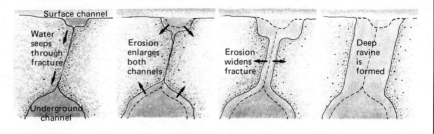

TASSILI N'AJJER. *In past eras, when the climate was much wetter, vigorous erosion sculpted the fantastic rock formations on the plateaus.*

continue to exist, sustained by the meager irregular rainfall and by the presence of chains of small water holes called *gueltas.* Stands of gnarled and stunted Mediterranean cypresses still survive in a few isolated valleys. More plentiful are the oleanders, thorny acacias, and several kinds of wild-flowers. Lizards and scorpions skitter across sandy patches, while vipers bury themselves, awaiting prey. Insects include dragonflies and even some lovely butterflies.

The *gueltas* are populated by fish, frogs, shrimps, and mollusks. Crag martins usually live nearby, building their mud nests on the overhanging rocks. But the most surprising inhabitant discovered on the plateaus was a species of dwarf crocodile. Found in modern times but believed to be extinct now, it was the last holdover from ancient times, when the Tassili was lush and green. □

Teide, Pico de

- Spain (Canary Islands)
- Map: page 24, B–3

Soaring high above the sea, this solitary volcano has been a beacon to seafarers since ancient times.

Approaching Spain's Canary Islands off the coast of West Africa by sea or by air, the traveler first glimpses sometimes snowcapped Pico de Teide —a memorable sight. The summit of the great volcanic peak, soaring 12,198 feet (3,718 meters) above the sea, is the highest point on all Spanish territory, and indeed in the entire Atlantic Ocean. Known to seafarers since remotest antiquity, it was regarded as a welcoming beacon by those early sailors who dared venture beyond the Strait of Gibraltar out into the open Atlantic.

The volcano, which makes up the entire island of Tenerife (the name means "mountain of snow"), was once even higher than it is today. Like the rest of the Canaries, Tenerife was formed by a succession of lava flows that welled up through a fissure in the ocean floor. It is believed that a buildup of pressure from gases trapped in the original volcano eventually resulted in a tremendous explosion, followed by the collapse of the summit into the core of the mountain.

The result was a caldera—a huge, oval, craterlike depression on the top of the mountain 10 miles (16 kilometers) long and 7 miles (11 kilometers) wide. High up on the mountainsides, steep ridges known as Las Cañadas mark the rim of this giant basin. Millions of years later, renewed eruptions built up a succession of new volcanic cones within the caldera, including the magnificent Pico de Teide. And even today fumaroles (vents emitting sulfurous fumes) in the caldera hint of the possibility of volcanic activity continuing long into the future.

The mountaintop, protected in the 50 square miles (130 square kilometers) of Teide National Park, is accessible by roads leading to Las Cañadas, and from there by cable cars to the slopes of Pico de Teide. Visitors can observe a variety of volcanic phenomena in the stark caldera, including the steaming fumaroles, sulfur deposits, chaotic flows of red and black lava, and shimmering bits of obsidian, a type of volcanic glass.

Hikers can also follow a trail to the very summit of Pico de Teide. Offering spectacular views of both sunrise and sunset, it is also a superb vantage point for viewing the entire Canary archipelago, seemingly adrift on the restless sea. They may also find a hardy bluish-violet gillyflower growing not far away, its delicate hues recalling the color of the volcano looming against the sky at dusk. □

PICO DE TEIDE. *The young volcanic cone rises from the caldera of a much older volcano whose summit was destroyed by a gigantic explosion.*

Tengger

- Indonesia
- Map: page 21, F–5

Volcanoes within the remains of an older volcano are the highlights of this lunar landscape in Java.

The long, narrow Indonesian island of Java is dotted from end to end with volcanoes, some of them active but most of them extinct. Among the most unusual relics of Java's stormy volcanic past is the Tengger, a great oval-shaped depression in the highlands near the eastern tip of the island. A barren moonscape also known as the Sea of Sand, the enormous basin is approximately 5½ miles (9 kilometers) long and 4½ miles (7 kilometers) wide.

According to legend, an ugly ogre, in a futile attempt to win the hand of a beautiful princess, scooped out the hollow with nothing more than half a coconut shell. But failing to complete the task in the allotted time, he finally died of heartbreak.

In reality, the Tengger marks the site of a now-vanished volcano that rose on the spot some 2 million years ago. When it was completed, the great weight of the mountain caused its summit to collapse into the partially empty magma chamber beneath it. And so the basin, technically described as a caldera, was formed.

But even then volcanic activity did not come to an end. Subsequent eruptions produced a trio of new volcanic cones within the confines of the caldera: Mount Bromo ("The Fire"), Mount Widodaren ("The Bride"), and Mount Batok ("The Cup").

The symmetrical cone of Bromo, corrugated by neatly spaced ravines, is definitely the most impressive of the three. It rises approximately 650 feet (200 meters) above the floor of the caldera. It is also the only one that is still active, spewing out occasional but relatively harmless eruptions of ash and volcanic debris.

Tourists visit the area to experience the strangeness of the scene and view the spectacle of sunrise from the caldera's rim. The local people also celebrate Buddha's birthday with an annual predawn ceremony held on the summit of Mount Bromo. □

TENGGER. *The youthful cone of Mount Bromo, its slopes furrowed by deep ravines, dwarfs the procession of visitors trailing past its base.*

A few days later, satisfied that the Indians had suffered enough, Bochica suddenly appeared atop the arch of a rainbow. With a wave of his magical golden wand, he opened a cleft in the rocky barriers surrounding the highlands and drained the flooded plain. Thus, to the relief and joy of the repentant Chibchas, Tequendama Falls were born.

And in fact geologists believe that several million years ago the Bogotá plain was indeed the bottom of a large lake. Although the plain today is some 8,500 feet (2,600 meters) above sea level, it was then in a hot and humid lowland. In the course of the uplift of the Andes, the lake was eventually drained as the water escaped through a break in the enclosing rocks and began its tumultuous descent toward the sea.

Unfortunately, Tequendama Falls are no longer quite the spectacle they were in the days of the Chibchas. Polluted by wastes from chemical factories upstream, the waters of the Río Bogotá have lost their sparkling clarity. Diverted to a nearby hydroelectric plant, moreover, the river's flow is often reduced to a trickle. But whenever the channel is swollen by heavy rains, the falls become an impressive sight once again. □

Terres de Couleurs

- Mauritius
- Map: page 9

On a remote volcanic island already ablaze with colors and contrasts, an area of multicolored soil provides an especially unusual visual treat.

A onetime colony of France and then England, the island-nation of Mauritius rises from the Indian Ocean some 500 miles (800 kilometers) east of Madagascar. On most maps it appears as little more than a speck, for it is only 38 miles (61 kilometers) long and 29 miles (47 kilometers) wide.

Within that compact area, however, it includes a striking array of scenes and colors. Outcrops of black basaltic lava on the high central plateau contrast with the brilliant white of fossil coral reefs and the deep green of forests and sugarcane fields. Even the soil is tinted with a surprising variety of hues.

The most colorful area of all, near Tamarin Bay on the island's southwest

TEQUENDAMA FALLS. *In times of peak flow, veils of mist rise from the thundering torrent as the Río Bogotá plunges off the edge of an upland plateau high in the Andes.*

Tequendama Falls

- Colombia
- Map: page 14, B–2

An old Indian legend comes close to the truth in explaining the origin of this splendid Andean waterfall.

Tequendama Falls are located on the Río Bogotá (also known as the Funza), about 20 miles (32 kilometers) west of the capital city of Bogotá. Upstream from the falls the river meanders across the fertile, mountain-rimmed plateau surrounding the city. Then, narrowing into a rocky, forested gorge, the river suddenly plunges over a precipice into a huge bowllike amphi-theater walled in by sandstone cliffs. The river's total drop is nearly 500 feet (150 meters).

Just as tourists today make the trip from Bogotá to see the falls, Spanish noblemen as early as the 17th century traveled out to witness the spectacle. And even earlier the Chibcha Indians who once inhabited the area apparently were fascinated by the falls, for they made them the subject of one of their legends.

According to their story, one of their gods, Bochica, once became outraged by crimes committed by the proud and warlike Indians. As punishment, he caused all the rivers in the region to overflow and flood the high plains surrounding present-day Bogotá.

TERRES DE COULEURS. *At the edge of a tropical forest, colorful volcanic soil on the gullied slopes is tinted by its content of metallic oxides.*

coast, is known as Terres de Couleurs; its name, retained from the days of French rule, means "colored earth." Rapid runoff from heavy rainfall has resulted in intense erosion, stripping the slopes of vegetation and furrowing them with gullies. The exposed soil, a clayey mixture, is rich in metallic oxides, especially iron and manganese, which have colored the earth with a spectrum of hues. In addition to red and russet, the colors range from yellow to purplish tones, all blended together in a seemingly endless variety of combinations.

The colored soil is a product of the island's volcanic past. Mauritius is actually the remnant of a giant volcano that once towered high above the sea. An explosive eruption blew away its upper structure, leaving a huge crater known as a caldera. Renewed lava flows then filled in the caldera to form the island's central plateau. Rapid erosion of the lava produced the fine, silty particles that were deposited on the lower slopes, and their high metallic content resulted in the splendid variety of hues. □

Tibesti Soda Lake

● Chad
● Map: page 24, E–3

Glistening white beds of carbonate salts on the floor of an enormous explosion crater are the last vestiges of a long, violent volcanic history.

The Tibesti Massif in northwestern Chad is the highest mountain range in the Sahara. Born of volcanic activity that began 5 million years ago, it abounds in rugged volcanic peaks, impressive calderas and craters, and bubbling hot springs that offer evidence that in places magma is still quite near the surface.

One of the most impressive relics of the region's volcanic past is a huge craterlike depression known variously as the Trou au Natron or the Doon Orei. Reminiscent of a gigantic open pit mine, it is about 5 miles (8 kilometers) in diameter and 3,300 feet (1,000 meters) deep. A sparkling crust of carbonate salts—the so-called soda lake—covers much of the bottom of the pit,

its snow-white color accentuated by several small black scoria cones that rise to heights of approximately 325 feet (100 meters).

The crater is unusual not only for its size, but also because eruptions here did not build up a cone of debris. And unlike other craters of such imposing dimensions (technically known as calderas), the collapse of the earth's crust into an empty magma chamber does not seem to have played a role in its formation. Instead, scientists believe that it was created entirely by a succession of three colossal explosions, each of which progressively deepened the enormous pit. The blasts were of such a powerful nature that chunks of debris 6½ cubic yards (5 cubic meters) in size were hurled over distances of 6 miles (10 kilometers).

Today there is little volcanic activity—only small vents that emit gases and hot springs that issue streams of mineral-laden water. Beneath the Saharan sun, the water soon evaporates and the minerals remain behind, adding to the blinding white crust that covers much of the floor. □

TIBESTI SODA LAKE. *Recent minor eruptions created the small volcanic cones on the mineral-encrusted floor of the gigantic Saharan crater.*

Tien Shan

- China—U.S.S.R.
- Map: page 18, I–4

The glittering, perpetually snowy summits of this great range in Asia inspired its ancient Chinese name, which means "celestial mountains."

One of the great mountain systems of the world, the Tien Shan stretches all the way from the heart of the Sinkiang region of western China southwestward along the Chinese-Soviet border toward the Pamir. Its total length is about 1,800 miles (2,900 kilometers).

A complex system of high parallel mountain ridges separated by long valleys and deep depressions, the Tien Shan is remarkable for its dramatic elevation contrasts. The highest point, Pobeda Peak, is 24,406 feet (7,439 meters) above sea level; to the east, within Sinkiang, the great basin of the Turfan Depression, the lowest point in central Asia, descends to 505 feet (154 meters) below sea level. The combination of severely eroded high peaks and alpine valleys, snowfields and summer streams, makes the Tien Shan one of the most picturesque mountain ranges in all of Asia.

The Tien Shan is formed primarily of ancient crystalline rocks overlaid in many places by younger sedimentary rocks of various ages. The major elevation of the range took place in a great mountain-building episode that occurred between 300 and 400 million years ago. But continuing renewal of the uplift has occurred periodically ever since then, and even today the mountains are being quite actively uplifted.

For the most part the high mountain ridges of the Tien Shan are formations

When the Earth Cracks: Faults, Horsts, and Grabens

Faults are fractures in the earth's crust along which the rocks on either side have moved. In some cases, such as along California's famous San Andreas Fault, the slippage, or displacement of the rocks, is mainly horizontal. In other cases the movement is primarily vertical, which results in much more dramatic and conspicuous landscape features. In a so-called normal fault *(below, left)*, a block of the earth's crust has moved downward relative to the adjoining block. (Originally their surfaces were flush.) In a reverse fault *(below, right)*, one block has moved upward past the facing block and may even have actually overthrust it.

Among the most arresting of all fault formations are horsts and grabens *(below, center)*. A horst is a ridgelike block of rock that was thrust upward between parallel faults. The high ridges of the Tien Shan are exceptionally massive examples of horsts. A graben (from the German word meaning "trench"), in contrast, is a long narrow trough that was formed when a block of crustal rock slipped downward in relation to the adjoining rocks. Death Valley in California is a graben; East Africa's famous Rift Valley, in turn, is an extremely long series of interconnected grabens. Bounded by steep cliffs known as fault scarps, horsts and grabens are unmistakable landforms.

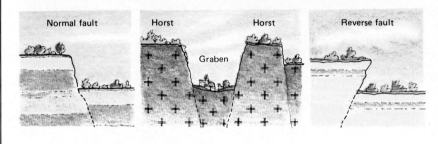

known as horsts: great blocks of the earth's crust that were thrust up between parallel faults. Many of the intervening basins such as the Ili Depression, in contrast, are gigantic grabens: blocks of the crust that subsided between faults. One such depression is occupied by the Issyk-Kul, one of the world's largest mountain lakes. Its remarkably clear water reaches a maximum depth of 2,303 feet (702 meters).

Still other depressions between the mountains have been filled in by debris eroded from the higher slopes, including thick deposits of loess, a fine-grained yellowish silt that was blown in by the wind, and conglomer-

ate rocks. Sudden earth tremors also unleash rockslides that send loose fragments plunging down the mountainsides to pile up in the valleys. The yellow and red of these younger deposits and the brilliant green of the alpine valleys stand out in vivid contrast to the stark white and gray rock of the surrounding massifs.

Though bordered on both the north and the south by great desert basins, the Tien Shan itself is banded with varied zones of vegetation. The semidesert foothills give way at higher elevations to extensive steppe landscapes where drought-tolerant grasses predominate. These in turn are interspersed with mixed forests and alpine meadows on higher slopes. Beyond the snowline the peaks are capped by permanent ice and snow, including numerous active glaciers.

Drainage from the Tien Shan has little moderating effect on the adjacent deserts, but the waters are sufficient to make the land hospitable to shepherds. The mountain rivers also sustain a chain of oases on the lower slopes. They were once important stops on the ancient route by which the Chinese first made contact with the western world. Today the Tien Shan is important for its mineral wealth, which includes deposits of iron, lead, zinc, and copper, as well as petroleum and coal. □

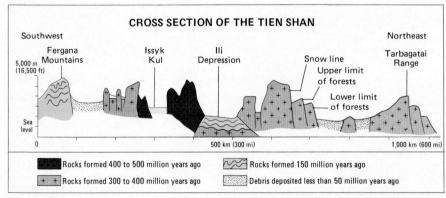

A slice across the Tien Shan reveals the positions of the rocks of various ages that make up the mountains. Vertical movements of the formations along faults have resulted in the immense contrasts in elevation that characterize the rugged range.

TIEN SHAN. *The massive snowcapped mountain barrier, reared high against the sky, is the source of the water that irrigates the verdant lowland basins in the foothills.*

Timpanogos, Mount

- United States (Utah)
- Map: page 10, D–4

Chief of the lofty peaks of the rugged Wasatch Range, this massive snowcapped mountain reaches skyward above a sunbaked desert.

The Wasatch Range of the Rocky Mountains, extending north to south for some 250 miles (400 kilometers) across northern Utah, towers steeply above the Great Salt Lake in the valley just to the west. Of the many peaks in the range over 11,000 feet (3,350 meters), the highest is Mount Timpanogos: its snowy summit stands 12,008 feet (3,660 meters) above sea level and more than 6,000 feet (1,800 meters) above the desert valley to the west. The mountain's Indian name is believed to mean "rock river."

Like the rest of the range, Mount Timpanogos was formed when a tre-mendous block of the earth's crust was tilted sharply upward along a great north-to-south fault line. Erosion then chiseled the rock into a jagged line of peaks. The western slopes of the range along the fault are steep and abrupt; the eastern slopes, much gentler.

The best known feature of Mount Timpanogos is a series of three small but exquisite caves on its northwest-ern shoulder. Created long ago when groundwater dissolved many cavities in the mountain's thick limestone for-mations, the caves are lined with deli-cate filigrees of translucent white crys-tals that sparkle like precious jewels. In addition to massive stalactites and stalagmites, there are fragile soda-straw stalactites, unusual contorted formations known as helictites, and many natural reflecting pools. Origi-nally separate, the three caves are now connected by short man-made tunnels and are accessible to the public as the focal point of Timpanogos Cave National Monument. □

Tinajani Canyon

- Peru
- Map: page 14, B–4

An eerie, otherworldly atmosphere pervades this remote and craggy canyon where stone sentinels guard ancient Indian burial grounds.

Tinajani Canyon, not far from Lake Titicaca in southern Peru, is a rugged gash in the foothills of the Western Cordillera of the Andes. A haven of silence and solitude, it offers a star-tling contrast to the broad expanses of the Altiplano, the high, windswept plain east of the mountain rampart.

Hemmed in by steep walls up to 650 feet (200 meters) high, the branching gorge is dotted with rocky towers and enormous, precariously perched formations that resemble primitive sculpture. Ancient Indian tombs are nestled in rock shelters, adding to the strangeness of the atmosphere. Many of these rounded adobe structures con-tain human bones and crudely fash-ioned funerary offerings.

No one knows exactly how the can-yon got its name. *Tinaja* is a Spanish word meaning "large earthen jar." But it is uncertain whether the corruption of the term refers to the rounded tombs or the rock sculptures.

The reddish cliffs and rock forma-tions at Tinajani were eroded from thick deposits of sandstone and con-glomerate, a type of rock composed of pebbles cemented together in finer material. Millions of years ago, fol-lowing a major uplift of the Andes, rapid erosion of the peaks resulted in a deltalike accumulation of debris that was consolidated into rock layers at their foot. The mixture of rock types in the conglomerate is testimony to the Andes' complex history: the pebbles include bits of granite, limestone, and various types of volcanic rock that were eroded from the mountains.

Near the entrance to the canyon there is also evidence of the particu-larly devastating volcanoes that once wracked much of southwestern Peru. The soft, chalklike layers of volcanic tuff exposed there were formed when clouds of incandescent volcanic ash rained down on the land. (Embedded in the tuff are splinters of wood that were burned by the fiery ash.)

The rugged gorges and the curious sculptural forms at Tinajani were not produced by the mild erosive forces of today (only a meager stream passes

TINAJANI CANYON. *Although many of the massive reddish rock formations in the Andean canyon resemble primitive sculptures, they were produced by the natural forces of erosion.*

Tinkisso Falls

- Guinea
- Map: page 24, B–4

Unable to wear down the barriers in its path, a West African river spills over them in splendid cascades.

The Tinkisso River, a tributary of the upper Niger, rises in the southern foothills of Guinea's Fouta Djallon highlands. Flowing to the northeast for about 250 miles (400 kilometers), it passes through a rugged savanna landscape punctuated by mesas that tower over the lower hills and valleys.

Especially along its upper course, the Tinkisso spills over numerous outcrops of the region's ancient gneiss and granite bedrock. The outcrops are extremely hard and resistant to erosion. The river, moreover, carries mainly silt and sand but few rocks or pebbles, and so has been unable to wear them down significantly.

As a result, the Tinkisso's upper course is interrupted by many rapids and waterfalls where it flows across these durable barriers. At the largest of these obstructions, Tinkisso Falls, the river splits into a shimmering series of cascades 230 feet (70 meters) wide and 150 feet (45 meters) high. The display is at its best during the rainy season, when there is a tenfold increase in the river's flow. □

Titicaca, Lake

- Bolivia—Peru
- Map: page 14, C–4

South America's second largest lake and the highest navigable lake in all the world is also the legendary birthplace of the Incan civilization.

Lake Titicaca is cupped in a depression in the Altiplano ("High Plain") between the Eastern and the Western Cordilleras of the Andes on the border of Bolivia and Peru. With an elevation of some 12,500 feet (3,800 meters), it is so high above sea level that the inhabitants of the region actually differ physically from people living at lower altitudes. The local Aymaran, Quechuan, and Uran Indians have larger lungs, hearts, and spleens and many more red blood corpuscles than the majority of humans. These physical adaptations enable them to survive in the thin, oxygen-poor air.

through the canyon now). At the end of a great glacial episode between 10,000 and 20,000 years ago, meltwater from retreating glaciers poured down the mountainsides in great torrents. Racing across the foothills, they carved out the branching gorges and left the stranded towers and colonnades behind.

Fierce winds of the region provided the finishing touches. Laden with bits of debris, they etched the fine surface details on the cliffs and monoliths. And they continue their work today: the solitude of the canyon is constantly accentuated by the sound of the wind whistling through the sparse tufts of grass on the canyon floor. □

LAKE TITICACA. *The immense lake is perched high above sea level on the Altiplano, the upland plateau between parallel ranges of the Andes.*

The lake's total area of 3,200 square miles (8,300 square kilometers) makes Titicaca the second largest lake in South America. (Lake Maracaibo in Venezuela is larger.) Stretching some 120 miles (190 kilometers) from northwest to southeast, it is nearly 50 miles (80 kilometers) across at its widest point, and its maximum depth is approximately 900 feet (275 meters).

Traces of former shorelines ringing its basin reveal that Lake Titicaca was even larger in the past. At the end of the Ice Age, torrents of meltwater from the huge ice cap that once blanketed the Andes poured into a virtual inland sea known as Lake Ballivian. Its shoreline was about 150 feet (45 meters) above the present lake level.

Even today the water level varies by as much as 16 feet (5 meters) from season to season and from year to year. The lake is fed by rainfall and meltwater from glaciers on the towering peaks that border the Altiplano. Only about 10 percent of the inflow escapes through the lake's single outlet, however; the rest is lost through evaporation caused by intense sunshine and strong winds.

Lake Titicaca is an important commercial waterway, with steamers regularly plying its waters. The shoreline is dotted with settlements, as are most of the islands in the lake. An Indian people, the Uros, dwell on the lake itself: they live on reed rafts constructed of totora, a reedlike papyrus that grows in the shallows. Clinging to an ancient way of life, they depend on the lake for fish.

The past is deeply revered throughout the region, where everyone knows the legend of "the Children of the Sun." For it was from the lake, on Isla de Titicaca, that the Sun God sent forth the man and woman who long ago founded the Inca Empire. □

LAKE TOBA. *Steep cliffs furrowed by erosion mark the perimeter of the immense caldera now partially filled by the lovely Indonesian lake.*

Toba, Lake

- Indonesia
- Map: page 20, D–4

Born of a gigantic explosion, the tranquil mountain lake has now become a popular vacation resort.

Lake Toba is hidden away in the mountains near the northwestern tip of the Indonesian island of Sumatra. Surrounded by steep cliffs and half filled by mountainous Samosir Island, it is one of the few resort centers on Sumatra. In addition to water sports and excursions into the nearby rain forests and plantations, visitors are attracted by the customs and architecture of the local Batak people.

More or less oval, the lake is about 55 miles (90 kilometers) long and has an area of 448 square miles (1,160 square kilometers). Calm and inviting in a lush tropical setting, its serene beauty belies the extraordinary vio-

lence of the events that produced it.

Indonesia is one of the most volcanically active areas in the world. In the vicinity of Lake Toba, eruptions over the last 5 million years have completely blanketed the bedrock beneath thick deposits of lava and ash.

But it was a major cataclysm about 60,000 years ago that formed the basin now occupied by the lake. Lake Toba's parent volcano erupted with a massive explosion that expelled some 475 cubic miles (2,000 cubic kilometers) of debris. Layers of pumice up to 2,000 feet (600 meters) deep were deposited around the volcano, and windborne ash fell as far away as India.

With so much material removed, the roof of the volcano's magma chamber caved in and formed the gigantic craterlike depression (known as a caldera) that is now the lake basin. Renewed eruptions on the floor of the caldera then built up the mountainous cone of Samosir Island, looming high above the placid waters of the lake. □

Todos los Santos, Lake

- Chile
- Map: page 15, B–7

This exquisite mountain lake is encircled by snow-clad volcanoes in a lush primeval forest region.

Lake Todos los Santos—"All Saints Lake"—is far from the largest body of water in the lake district of south-central Chile. But it is generally regarded as one of the most beautiful. Some 50 square miles (130 square kilometers) in area, it is bounded by densely forested slopes and guarded on every side by snowcapped volcanoes.

In the 19th century, German colonists, apparently impressed by the sometimes greenish tint of the water, named it Lake Esmeralda—"Emerald Lake." But it has since regained the original name bestowed by Jesuit mis-

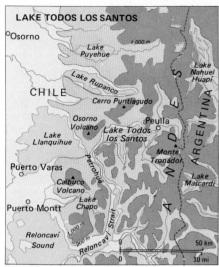

LAKE TODOS LOS SANTOS

plied the glaciers that ground down their slopes. As recently as 20,000 years ago, the lake basin was filled by an immense glacier that extended westward between the Osorno and Calbuco volcanoes. It ended in a large lobe in the foothill area, where it scooped out the vast depression now occupied by Lake Llanquihue.

When the Ice Age came to an end some 10,000 years ago, there was no Lake Todos los Santos. Rivers simply streamed down the broad glacial valley and emptied into Lake Llanquihue. Renewed eruptions of the Osorno and Calbuco volcanoes then built up a barrier across the lower part of the valley, forming the dam that now contains the waters of the lake.

Today, instead of flowing westward into Lake Llanquihue, the overflow from Todos los Santos flows southward via the Río Petrohué. First it breaks over basaltic colonnades—outpourings of the Osorno Volcano—in a fantastic sequence of falls and gorges. Farther downstream, diverted again by deposits of ash and debris from Calbuco Volcano, the river continues southeast through a valley to its outlet on Reloncaví Strait.

Throughout the area, lush woodlands greatly enhance the beauty of the mountain-girt lake. As dense as they are varied, the forests provide a feeling of remoteness and solitude that adds to the special aura of tranquillity surrounding Lake Todos los Santos.☐

sionaries at a time when it lay on the supposed route to the City of the Caesars, a fabulous but fictitious center of great wealth that was sought by generations of adventurers.

The highest of the volcanoes that ring the lake is Monte Tronador. Rising near the Argentine border on the main axis of the Andes to the east of the lake, its icy summit towers over the surrounding forests at an altitude of 11,200 feet (3,415 meters) above sea level. It is meltwater from Monte Tronador's glaciers, filled with finely scoured rock debris, that accounts for the lake's greenish color.

Cerro Puntiagudo, another extinct volcano, rises to the north of the lake. Still covered by permanent ice and snow on its upper slopes, in the past it was carved by even more extensive glaciers that chiseled its summit into a razor-edged pyramid.

Dominating the western horizon is the majestic profile of the Osorno Volcano, which towers over the lake to an elevation of 8,725 feet (2,659 meters) above the sea. Finally, farther away to the southwest, overlooking the lake's outlet, Río Petrohué, is the Calbuco Volcano. Lower than its neighbors but more massive, it has a level summit that drops off into an enormous crater.

The imposing complex of glaciated volcanoes surrounding Lake Todos los Santos is a silent reminder of its origins, for the lake's basin is simply a glacier-carved valley that was subsequently dammed by lava flows. During the last 2 million years, the western flanks of the Andes were repeatedly subjected to intense glaciation. With humid winds blowing in continuously from the Pacific, enormous amounts of snow fell on the mountains and sup-

LAKE TODOS LOS SANTOS. *Hemmed in by a ring of volcanoes, the sparkling Andean lake fills a valley that was scooped out by Ice Age glaciers and then dammed up by lava flows.*

TODRA GORGES. *Two people standing at the bend in the river give a hint of the size of these deep, narrow mountain chasms.*

Todra Gorges

- Morocco
- Map: page 24, C–2

Usually dry but sometimes in flood, a small Moroccan river continues to enlarge these limestone gorges.

The Todra Gorges on the southern flanks of the High Atlas Mountains are among the most beautiful in North Africa. Deeply incised in a limestone formation, the narrow chasms are in some places hemmed in by cliffs up to 1,300 feet (400 meters) high.

A traditional travel route for local nomads, the gorges are now traversed by a road frequented by tourists. Paralleling the river that created the gorges and fording it in many places, the route offers spectacular views of the ocher cliffs.

The trip can be hazardous. The Todra is a seasonal river, dry for most of the year. But after one of the area's infrequent rains, it can become a raging torrent, forcing travelers to abandon their vehicles and scramble to safety on rocky ledges.　　　　□

Toluca, Nevado de

- Mexico
- Map: page 12, C–3

Although much reduced from its former size, this peak remains among the highest volcanoes in Mexico.

The imposing, snowcapped summit of Nevado de Toluca, some 40 miles (65 kilometers) southwest of Mexico City, rises to a height of 14,977 feet (4,565 meters) above sea level. From the top, the Pacific Ocean is dimly visible on the horizon, while nearer at hand, within the crater, there are two smaller bodies of water, the Lake of the Sun and the Lake of the Moon. Rising near the center of the crater is a strange rocky dome known as El Ombligo ("The Navel").

Riddled by explosive eruptions and erosion, the volcano was originally much higher than it is today. It is believed that, prior to a cataclysmic blast some 25,000 years ago, the cone rivaled that of the famous Popocatepetl, which rises nearly 3,000 feet (900 meters) higher than the present sum-

mit of Nevado de Toluca. The explosion, besides blowing off the top of the cone, generated massive mudflows, known as lahars, which sent great avalanches of debris hurtling down the slopes.

After a dormant period of about 500 years, a second, relatively minor eruption did little more than deposit layers of pumice on the east and northeast sides of the mountain. Then a long period of erosion ended very abruptly some 11,500 years ago with two more violent blasts that further reduced the size of the cone. The volcano belched out enormous quantities of pumice that showered down over some 650 square miles (1,700 square kilometers) of the surrounding countryside.

Eruptions finally ceased when a plug of dark gray lava solidified in the volcano's vent, forming the little dome of El Ombligo. For a time fumaroles continued to deposit sulfur in the crater, but eventually they too died out. Ever since, Nevado de Toluca has slumbered beneath the Mexican sun, a magnificent volcanic ruin that is gradually succumbing to the relentless forces of erosion.　　　　□

NEVADO DE TOLUCA. *Great past explosions and ongoing assaults by the forces of erosion have slowly pared down this Mexican volcano.*

Tonle Sap

- Cambodia
- Map: page 20, E–3

The largest freshwater lake in all of Southeast Asia is alternately filled and drained each year by the flow of a unique reversing river.

The Tonle Sap in west-central Cambodia is not an especially impressive lake during the annual dry season, which lasts from December until May. Month by month, it gradually shrinks when its waters drain southeastward some 80 miles (130 kilometers) via the Tonle Sap River to its junction with the great Mekong at Phnom Penh. By late spring the lake is little more than a reed-filled swamp crisscrossed here and there by channels of deeper water.

When the monsoon season begins in June, the Mekong is suddenly swollen to a raging torrent. But not all of its water escapes to the sea. At Phnom Penh, at the head of the Mekong's vast delta, much of the river's overflow is diverted into the Tonle Sap River. For the next several months, currents in the river flow upstream instead of down and empty into the Tonle Sap. (The lake basin, once a gulf of the sea, was separated from the ocean by the growth of the Mekong delta.)

From a dry-season low of 3 feet (0.9 meter), the depth of the water in the Tonle Sap increases to 45 feet (14 meters), and the area of the lake quadruples to 4,000 square miles (10,350 square kilometers)—the largest freshwater lake in Southeast Asia. And then the dry season returns and the lake begins to shrink once again.

The Tonle Sap thus acts as a natural flood-control reservoir for the Mekong. But it is also something more; its extraordinary annual fluctuations traditionally have governed every aspect of life in the region. As the waters rise, vast tracts of scrubland and tropical forest are flooded, providing exceptionally good breeding and feeding grounds for hordes of fish, especially carp. When the waters recede, the fish become stranded and are easily caught in shallow pools, providing an important food resource. (The lake has long been regarded as one of the world's richest freshwater fishing grounds.) The ebbing waters also leave behind a layer of silt that enriches the seasonally flooded soil, which for generations has been used for the cultivation of rice. □

Topolnitsa Cave

- Rumania
- Map: page 17, F–4

Beneath a rural landscape of neatly cultivated fields lies a network of tunnels, vaulted chambers, chasms, and subterranean waterways.

Flowing southward toward the Danube in southwestern Rumania, the Topolnitsa River crosses the meadows and rich farmlands of the Mehedintsi Plateau. Suddenly it plunges beneath a rocky overhang some 165 feet (50 meters) high and disappears into the earth. It is not seen again until it emerges at the foot of a hill farther downstream.

In the course of its hidden journey, the river traverses the mysterious labyrinth of Topolnitsa Cave, a far-reaching network of underground chambers and passageways. One of the largest cave systems in the country, it includes more than 10 miles (16 kilometers) of tunnels on several levels beneath the ground. Hollowed out of a layer of ancient limestone, some of the tunnels are still being actively eroded by running water, while others are now completely dry.

The complex system of passageways within the cave, some of them as much as 130 feet (40 meters) high, includes a veritable museum of underground rock formations. Throughout the labyrinth there are numerous chasms, deep sinkholes, water-filled channels, chambers littered with debris left by erosion and cave-ins, and springs bubbling from openings in the rock.

Among the most memorable sections of the cave is Racovitsa Gallery, named for a pioneering Rumanian cave explorer. A broad corridor some 6,600 feet (2,000 meters) long, it has a virtual forest of slender stalagmites rising from its rubble-strewn floor. Overhead the high, arched ceiling is covered with graceful stone draperies and a bristling array of stalactites.

The cave is also notable for the presence of fractured cave formations in various areas. Explorers have discovered thick columns broken into pieces and stalagmites split neatly into fragments. There are even whole sections of roofs tilted so far from their original positions that their stalactites point horizontally—apparently the result of earthquakes that have shaken these dim and silent vaults over the centuries. □

Torcal
de Antequera

- Spain
- Map: page 17, C–5

High in the mountains of southern Spain, an array of strangely sculpted rocks is the exposed remnant of a collapsed labyrinth of onetime caves.

Torcal de Antequera is a limestone plateau in the mountains about 20 miles (32 kilometers) north of the port city of Málaga on the Mediterranean Sea. All across the surface of the plateau, strangely eroded rock formations suggest the ruins of an ancient city. Oddly realistic sculptural forms and huge bastions that resemble ruins are separated by labyrinths of alleys and rubble-strewn trenches.

No city ever rose on this site, however; the "ruins" in fact are typical remnants of erosion in a limestone landscape. The limestone here, more than 2,000 feet (600 meters) thick, was long ago broken up by vertical and horizontal fractures. At a time when the water table was higher than it is today, underground streams coursed through the fractures. The water dissolved the limestone and gradually enlarged the openings into a maze of galleries and chambers. Eventually the roofs of the tunnels caved in, forming the trenches—the streets and plazas of the ruined city.

The process has not yet ended. Ever since they were exposed, the rocky bastions that were left standing between the trenches have been attacked by wind and weather, which have gradually softened and reshaped their contours.

Meanwhile the water continues to work its way through the limestone that makes up the plateau. Seeping through fractures at lower levels beneath the eroded surface, it is carving out new networks of channels, chasms, and caves. In time the ceilings may once again collapse, thereby revealing another, presently hidden underground landscape.

But that is not likely to happen for quite a long time. For centuries to come, visitors will be able to wander among these monumental limestone formations, which are accented here and there by sparse, deep green vegetation. The scene is especially beautiful in spring and fall, when clusters of wildflowers come into bloom. □

TORCAL DE ANTEQUERA. *Formed initially by underground streams, this majestic stone sculpture was further refined by wind and weather after being exposed on the surface.*

Tritriva, Lake

- Madagascar
- Map: page 26, D-4

In the heart of highlands that once were shaken by volcanic activity, a placid blue lake lies nestled at the very center of a broad, deep crater.

The island of Madagascar, located some 250 miles (400 kilometers) off the coast of southern Africa in the Indian Ocean, has a history of volcanic activity. Manifestations of past eruptions are especially well preserved in the volcanic highlands south of the capital city, Tananarive. In addition to ancient lava deposits, steaming hot springs, and the characteristic shapes of ash and cinder cones, there are even a number of so-called nested cones—volcanoes that are topped by craters within craters.

Rising in the midst of these highlands is the extinct Tritriva Volcano, with its summit 6,600 feet (2,000 meters) above sea level. Visitors who

LAKE TRITRIVA. *The small crater lake is surrounded by slopes made up of debris that was expelled in a violent eruption of the volcano.*

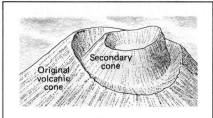

Nested cones, which are also known as nested craters, result when renewed eruptions by a volcano eventually build up a second, smaller cone within the confines of the volcano's original summit crater.

Tronador, Monte

● Argentina—Chile
● Map: page 15, B–7

With a deafening roar, ice avalanches from time to time come crashing down the cliffs of this ancient and deeply eroded Andean volcanic peak.

The "thundering mountain," Monte Tronador, is one of the great snow-capped peaks that punctuate the sky-line of the southern Andes. Straddling the border between Argentina and Chile, the ancient volcano reaches a maximum elevation of about 11,200 feet (3,400 meters)—nearly 6,600 feet (2,000 meters) above the beautiful surrounding landscape of deep, glacier-carved valleys, dense forests, and countless sparkling lakes.

A stratovolcano formed of alternating layers of ash and lava, the mountain has been greatly denuded by erosion. Near the top there are broad mesalike plateaus surmounted by a number of volcanic necks (plugs of extremely hard lava that solidified in volcanic vents and then were exposed when softer debris on the surrounding slopes was eroded away).

Just as the mountain was severely glaciated during the Ice Age, it continues to be altered by glacial ice today. Moist winds blowing in from the Pacific drop heavy loads of snow on Monte Tronador, especially on the western slopes, nurturing a great number of glacial tongues that radiate from the summit.

Some of them proceed downslope through normal glacial valleys, but three of the glaciers are fed by periodic avalanches of ice. From time to time, parts of the ice caps on the high plateaus break off and come crashing down the bordering cliffs into the valleys lying far below. It was the thundering din caused by these occasional ice falls that gave Monte Tronador its name. □

climb to the top are rewarded with views of Lake Tritriva, nestled peacefully at the center of the crater more than 165 feet (50 meters) below the rim. About 650 feet (200 meters) long, the oval lake is encircled by the broad, fertile slopes of the crater, which was formed by a violent eruption that long ago blew off the original summit of the volcano. □

MONTE TRONADOR. *Broken up into sharp peaks and littered with eroded volcanic debris, a massive glacier grinds down the mountainside.*

TROU AUX CERFS. *The small lake at the bottom of this explosion crater is ringed by greenery that flourishes on the combination of rich volcanic soil and heavy rainfall.*

Turfan Depression

- China
- Map: page 19, J-4

Despite extreme temperatures and little rainfall, the lowest point in China is a flourishing green oasis.

The Turfan Depression, at the eastern end of the Tien Shan Mountains in western China, is all the more impressive for its setting. Descending to 505 feet (154 meters) below sea level, it is bordered on the north by snow-clad peaks that rise to heights of 16,500 feet (5,000 meters) and more.

The depression was formed when a block of the earth's crust slipped down between parallel faults. Cupped in the deepest part of the basin is swampy, salt-encrusted Lake Aiting. The Hwo Shan (Fire Mountains), noted for their flaming red color, stretch across the northern part of the basin. To the east are the Sha Shan (Sand Mountains), overlooking a sea of dunes.

Rainfall in the depression is scarcely 1 inch (25 millimeters) per year, and temperatures range from well below freezing to summer highs of 130° F (54° C). Despite the harsh climate, the basin has been inhabited since before the time of Christ. Turfan is a flourishing city, and much of the basin is checkered with vineyards, farms, and orchards noted for their production of grains, fruits, nuts, and especially seedless grapes.

All are sustained by snowmelt from the nearby mountains, which soaks into the soil on the lower slopes. Some of the water emerges from springs. But most of it is tapped for irrigation by an age-old system of subterranean canals dug into the slopes to guide the groundwater to the surface. □

Trou aux Cerfs

- Mauritius
- Map: page 9

A jewellike lake is cupped within this highland crater, which was formed by an explosive volcanic eruption.

The little island-nation of Mauritius is located some 500 miles (800 kilometers) east of Madagascar in the Indian Ocean. Volcanic in nature, it was formed in two stages. The summit of the volcano that originally marked the spot was blown off in a great explosion, leaving a huge, craterlike depression technically known as a caldera. Renewed eruptions then filled in this immense basin, forming the island's central plateau.

The Trou aux Cerfs, the "Hole of the Deer," near the heart of the central highland, is a product of the second phase of volcanism. An explosion crater with a small lake cupped in its bottom, it was formed less than 2 million years ago.

Today the island's volcanoes have been stilled, and tourists can drive around the crater's rim. The imported deer that once drank in the little lake have disappeared, as have the extinct flightless dodoes, the island's most famous native inhabitants. But the views from the rim remain as impressive as ever. Besides the densely vegetated crater, they encompass the full sweep of the lush green island and the azure sea beyond. □

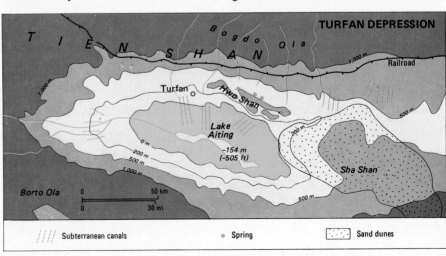

Urgup Cones

- Turkey
- Map: page 18, E–5

Countless rocky towers, pyramids, and cones create a strange yet lovely landscape in central Turkey.

Travelers are usually startled as they approach the village of Urgup, some 140 miles (225 kilometers) southeast of the capital city of Ankara in central Turkey. For miles around in this part of the ancient region of Cappadocia, the land is studded with strange rocky pyramids, cones, towers, and bulbous formations that resemble mushrooms. Some stand alone; others rise in dense clusters. And most are of imposing dimensions, rising to heights of 100 feet (30 meters) and more.

On closer inspection, visitors are even more surprised to discover that many of the Urgup Cones are inhabited. From the 4th to the 13th century, early Christians in the area found refuge in these fantastic citadels by hacking caves into the soft rock for use as living quarters and places of worship. More than 300 churches have been discovered so far, ranging from simple chapels to sizable sanctuaries decorated with elaborate frescoes. In some places there are whole villages of interconnected cave dwellings. Even today many of the grottoes, carved out at several levels in the cones and towers, serve as homes for Turkish peasants who till their fields and orchards nearby.

The cones are the eroded remnants of a once-continuous plateau composed of layers of rocks of various kinds. Some 8 million years ago this part of Turkey was the center of a region of prolonged volcanic activity. Clouds of ash and dust from many volcanic vents showered down on the land and eventually were consolidated into thick beds of soft whitish rock known as tuff.

At times the eruptions produced somewhat coarser debris that was cemented together to form patches of cindery rock called breccia. Still other eruptions poured out liquid flows of basaltic lava. Finally, in calm periods between the eruptions, lakes covered the region and layers of limestone formed on their bottoms. Thus the soft deposits of tuff alternate with and in many places are capped by layers of harder, more resistant rock.

In times when the climate was wetter than today, runoff draining north toward the Kizil Irmak (the major river of the area) and west toward a large salt lake began to dissect the surface of the plateau. Rushing streams cut quickly down into the soft tuff, creating intricate networks of narrow ravines. The eventual result was a deeply gullied landscape similar to the famous Badlands located in South Dakota.

As erosion continued, intersecting ravines in places left portions of the badlands standing as isolated conical towers. Elsewhere caps of ignimbrite (hard, crystallized tuff) protected the softer tuff below, which resulted in the formation of stout earth pyramids. Where the tuff was mixed with patches of cinders, the cinders in time were completely destroyed by weathering, leaving the surfaces pockmarked with veritable honeycombs of hollows. The end product of all these processes was a unique and varied landscape that continues to amaze and delight all who see it. □

URGUP CONES. *The fanciful cones and towers are the eroded remnants of a plateau of solid rock that once covered the entire area.*

Vaihiria, Lake

- French Polynesia
- Map: page 9

Dreamlike in its beauty, a tranquil lake is hidden in the rugged interior of a storied South Pacific island.

The lush green volcanic island of Tahiti covers an area of some 400 square miles (1,000 square kilometers) in the heart of the South Pacific. The population has always been concentrated along the coast, since the island's interior is rugged and mountainous, with sharp, knifelike ridges separated by steep ravines.

Yet the remarkably unspoiled interior also harbors some of the island's most beautiful scenery. The vegetation is wild and luxuriant, and the valleys are drained by networks of lovely streams, roaring waterfalls, and small secluded lakes—among them exquisite Lake Vaihiria.

Accessible by a footpath from Tahiti's southern coast, the lake is hidden away in a valley approximately 1,450 feet (440 meters) above sea level. About 2,000 feet (600 meters) in length and 500 feet (150 meters) wide, its tranquil surface mirrors the jagged and densely forested slopes that rise abruptly from the water's edge. Besides being extremely beautiful, the cool, stream-fed lake provides a haven for a variety of rare aquatic plants and animals. □

Valle Encantado

- Argentina
- Map: page 15, B–7

This stark Andean valley contrasts dramatically with its surroundings in a region noted for its sparkling blue lakes and dense green forestland.

The "Enchanted Valley," Valle Encantado, was carved by the Limay River, the outlet of Lake Nahuel Huapi in the eastern foothills of the Andes. The lake, with an area of 250 square miles (650 square kilometers), is the focal point of Nahuel Huapí National Park, the oldest in Argentina. Dotted with tiny islands and fringed by scalloped shorelines, it is a popular resort area. Lining the horizon are high, snow-clad Andean peaks, including the lofty summit of Monte Tronador, or the

LAKE VAIHIRIA. *Lush tropical vegetation covers the steep slopes around the lake, which fills a valley that was dammed up by a lava flow.*

VALLE ENCANTADO. *In the arid eastern foothills of the Andes, only a few hardy plants mask the stark contours of the Enchanted Valley.*

"thundering mountain," named for the great avalanches of ice that sometimes roar down its steep slopes. At lower elevations, rivers, lakes, and waterfalls provide sparkling accents in an area that is famous mainly for its dense, primeval forests.

The Limay River, flowing northeastward from the lake toward the pampas, passes through a startlingly different landscape. There, on the leeward side of the Andes, where rainfall is scant, only a few scattered trees and shrubs manage to survive on the slopes of the Valle Encantado. Instead, the valley is studded with thickets of stark, rocky pinnacles, domes, and fanciful towers.

The rocks in the valley—some volcanic, others sedimentary—were modeled by long periods of erosion. Deposits of tuff, a soft rock formed from volcanic ash, contrast with the angular contours of hard outcrops of basalt, the products of ancient lava flows. In many places there are strangely sculpted formations of sandstone and conglomerate—rocks that were formed long ago on the beds of vanished lakes and rivers. Towering on all sides in the Enchanted Valley, these sculptures in stone create the impression of a frozen, timeless world that has been immobilized by a spell. □

Valley of Ten Thousand Smokes

● United States (Alaska)
● Map: page 10, B–3

Born of a frightful explosion, the remote Alaskan valley shows signs that renewed eruptions could once again alter the face of the land.

The Valley of Ten Thousand Smokes, in Katmai National Monument in southwestern Alaska, did not exist before June 1912. It came into being when the area was wracked by one of the most violent volcanic outbursts ever recorded. Following several days of earthquakes, Novarupta Volcano exploded with a roar. Clouds of hot ash and pumice were blasted into the sky, and avalanches of fiery debris hurtled down the slopes.

By the time the eruption ended, more than 40 square miles (100 square kilometers) of land were blanketed

beneath ash and pumice up to 300 feet (90 meters) deep. Deposits up to 1 foot (0.3 meter) deep showered down over some 3,000 square miles (7,800 square kilometers).

The full extent of the devastation was not realized until 1916, when an expedition finally penetrated the remote wilderness valley. The discoverers found that the volcanic fires had not yet been stilled. All across the valley floor, countless fumaroles were sending forth plumes of scalding-hot smoke—hence the valley's name.

Today most of the fumaroles have ceased smoking. Here and there a few plants have begun to colonize the deposits of debris, which are now furrowed by ravines. But the valley remains an awesome reminder of the violence that created it. And the occasional eruptions of neighboring peaks are reminders that this starkly beautiful landscape could once again be changed completely. □

Vatnajokull

● Iceland
● Map: page 16, B–2

Heat from the volcanic fires beneath this enormous glacier sometimes unleashes sudden, catastrophic floods.

Iceland, although not nearly as frigid as its name implies, still is covered by substantial remnants of the ice cap that blanketed the entire island during the Ice Age. The glaciers, known as jokuls, cover approximately 11 percent of the island's surface and occur in the form of enormous ice caps surrounded by numerous glacial tongues that radiate in all directions.

The largest of the jokuls by far is Vatnajokull, the "Water Glacier," near the coast in the southeastern part of the island. With a total area of approximately 3,200 square miles (8,300 square kilometers), it is larger than all the glaciers of Europe combined. The ice on the average is more than 3,000 feet (900 meters) thick, and its volume is estimated to total nearly 500 cubic miles (2,100 cubic kilometers).

Like glaciers elsewhere, Vatnajokull is supplied by heavy snowfalls on its surface. Oozing out from its central ice cap are numerous tongues of ice that move at the rate of some 6,000 feet (1,800 meters) per year. As they descend to lower elevations, the meltwater from their snouts gives rise to

a number of the most important rivers in Iceland.

Vatnajokull differs from most other glaciers in one important respect, however. Iceland is entirely volcanic in origin, and its internal fires, far from being stilled, continue to play a crucial role in Vatnajokull's activities.

The glacier sprawls over the surface of a tremendous lava plateau, including one projecting volcanic peak called Hekla that, at 6,952 feet (2,119 meters), is the highest point in all of Iceland. But it is the many other volcanoes buried *beneath* the ice that make Vatnajokull such an unusual and sometimes very threatening glacier. When the volcanoes erupt, the intense heat causes the rapid melting of enormous quantities of the glacial ice. The result is occasional but devastating floods known as jokulhlaups.

The melting of the ice causes huge pockets of water to develop beneath the glacier. (Hence the name "Water Glacier.") Eventually the weakened ice gives way, like a dam bursting, and releases a catastrophic flood of meltwater, giant chunks of ice, boulders, and other debris. Surging across the countryside at speeds of up to 60 miles (100 kilometers) per hour, the jokulhlaups sweep along the houses, barns, livestock, and everything else in their paths. One such flood in 1934 released more than 3½ cubic miles (15 cubic kilometers) of water in the course of just a few days.

As the floods subside, their loads of gravel, sand, and boulders are deposited on sandurs—broad plains of mixed glacial debris. The detritus in rivers resulting from the normal melting of the glacier also contributes to the buildup of the sandurs. But the jokulhlaups drop so much debris that they often clog streambeds, causing rivers to alter their courses, and sometimes radically change the contours of the land.

The fascinating phenomenon of the jokulhlaup has been especially well studied in a rather remote area on the western part of Vatnajokull. Past volcanic eruptions in that vicinity have proved to be quite predictable, occurring at intervals of every 10 years or so. Scientists in that area have had unparalleled opportunities to study the effects of the combination of two of the earth's most powerful natural forces, volcanism and glaciation. There they are striving to unravel the mysteries of Iceland's sometimes deadly combination of fire and ice. □

VATNAJOKULL. *At the snout of one of the glacial tongues radiating from the main ice field, disintegration of the glacier results in a chaos of partially melted blocks of ice.*

FONTAINE DE VAUCLUSE. *After uncharted journeys beneath the surrounding limestone hills and plateaus, water emerges from the famous spring in a frenzy of thundering torrents.*

Vaucluse, Fontaine de

- France
- Map: page 17, D–4

This famous spring, celebrated long ago by the poet Petrarch, remains an awesome and beautiful spectacle.

The Fontaine de Vaucluse, famous for its size and picturesque setting, is located about 15 miles (25 kilometers) east of Avignon in the southeast of France. The name Vaucluse, from the Latin *vallis clausa,* meaning "closed valley," aptly describes the setting: the spring's emerald-green water wells up from a basin beneath overhanging crags at the head of a valley hemmed in by limestone cliffs.

The surge of water from the basin, which is the source of the Sorgue River, is most impressive when it reaches its peak flow in spring. Welling up over the accumulation of fallen boulders and debris that form the edge of the pool, the water cascades downslope in a thunderous waterfall that echoes off the surrounding walls. The maximum flow from the spring—some 5,300 cubic feet, or 150 cubic meters, per second—is equal to the average flow of the Seine at Paris and is thought to be the highest for any limestone cave in the world.

At the low-water stage, in contrast, the spectacle is diminished to a trickle. The water level in the basin drops dramatically, and as few as 140 cubic feet (4 cubic meters) of water per second seep through openings among the fallen debris.

The water issuing from the spring is the overflow from a large underground reservoir that receives the subsurface drainage from perhaps 775 square miles (2,000 square kilometers) of the surrounding limestone plateaus and hills. Plunging into caves and sinkholes, the water from numerous disappearing streams flows through a network of channels in the rock, eventually to emerge again at the Fontaine de Vaucluse.

There the water escapes under pressure through a lengthy tunnel that slopes steeply upward through the limestone to the basin of the spring. In honor of this outstanding example of the phenomenon, all springs in which the water flows out under pressure through an ascending feeder channel are known as vauclusian springs. □

VENICE LAGOON. *Intricate networks of drainage ditches are among the many man-made changes that have altered the nature of the lagoon.*

Venice Lagoon

- Italy
- Map: page 17, E–4

Sinking of the land and tampering by man have combined to endanger the existence of this unique lagoon.

The lovely city of Venice rises like a mirage at the center of a vast lagoon—a protected expanse of shallow, brackish water—at the head of the Adriatic Sea in northern Italy. The seaward margin of the lagoon is formed by a line of long, low, narrow barrier islands, the *lidi,* famous for their resorts and sandy beaches. Here and there the *lidi* are broken by *porti,* channels through which both ships and tides are able to pass.

Behind this fragile coastal barrier is the lagoon itself, about 30 miles (50 kilometers) long and on the average some 7 miles (11 kilometers) wide. Innumerable islands dot the lagoon; Venice alone is built on a cluster of 118 of them. In addition to broad expanses of shallow water, the lagoon includes extensive mud flats, known as *barene,*

interlaced with mazes of winding canals and channels.

For centuries the lagoon has acted as a buffer protecting Venice from ravage by the sea. But in recent times many forces have conspired to change the lagoon and threaten the existence of Venice itself. First and oldest of the problems is subsidence. From the time the earliest inhabitants drove wooden piles into the muddy islands, forming the foundation of present-day Venice, until today, the land has been sinking. Movements of the earth's crust, the compacting of the mud at the bottom of the lagoon, and the pumping out of well water have all played a role. At present the city is sinking at the rate of 12 inches (30 centimeters) per century.

Human tampering has also interfered with the delicate balance that once prevailed in the lagoon. Extensive landfill and dredging projects have altered its contours. Large areas have been diked off for fish farms. Deep shipping channels have been dug, permitting high tides to sweep much more rapidly through the *porti* and into the lagoon. Pollution in turn has killed much of the vegetation that

once covered the *barene* and acted to slow down the flow of incoming tides.

Finally there is the problem of the tides themselves. Throughout most of the Mediterranean, tidal fluctuations are negligible. But at the head of the Adriatic they can be substantial, especially when strong southerly winds sweep up across its basin, piling the water up before them. At such times tides of up to 2 feet (0.6 meter) pound the *lidi* and sweep into the lagoon.

Occasionally, when heavy rains are combined with extraordinarily high tides, the result is catastrophic flooding. And with the many changes in the lagoon, such floods are increasing in frequency. All too often the famous Piazza San Marco is turned into a reflecting pool, and the basilica and the Doge's Palace are invaded by lapping waves.

Many schemes have been proposed to correct the problem, including the building of huge floodgates across the *porti* that can be raised at times of *acqua alti*—the dreaded "high water." Clearly, drastic steps must be taken if the lagoon, and Venice itself, are to be saved from destruction. □

VERDON GORGE. *Bounded by rugged slopes, the Verdon River winds through the dizzying canyon it has carved through a limestone massif.*

Verdon Gorge

- France
- Map: page 17, D–4

Along its short but superbly scenic course, the Verdon River passes through one of the most spectacular and accessible gorges in Europe.

Rising in the mountains of Provence in southeastern France, the Verdon River flows south and then west for about 120 miles (200 kilometers) before merging with the Durance River, a tributary of the lower Rhone. All along the way it passes through a region of varied and beautiful scenery.

The most spectacular sector by far is on the river's middle course, where it rushes through the Verdon Gorge, the longest and deepest canyon in France. Over a distance of about 12 miles (20 kilometers), the river is hemmed in by slopes that rise precipitously from the water's edge. In places the canyon walls are only 650 feet (200 meters) apart. The rugged gash through the limestone plateau has a maximum depth of 2,300 feet (700 meters).

The gorge is easily accessible to tourists. A modern highway known as the Corniche Sublime parallels one rim of the canyon for its entire length, and another road clings to the edge of the chasm on the opposite side. Several scenic overlooks along the way provide breathtaking views of the river winding in and out between the rugged slopes far below. For experienced hikers, there is also a trail leading into the depths of the canyon.

The gorge is deeply incised into a thick series of limestone formations. It is generally assumed that the river, fed primarily by snowmelt in the mountains at its source, etched its course ever deeper into the rock as the land was slowly being uplifted. The limestone in the area, however, is honeycombed with subterranean passageways, sinkholes, and caves. Some have suggested that the Verdon itself may once have been an underground river, and that the canyon may have been formed, at least in part, by the collapse of the cave ceiling over the riverbed. But whatever its origins, the Verdon Gorge remains to this day an awesome spectacle. □

How Surface Streams Carve Scenic Canyons

The Verdon Gorge, like the Grand Canyon and other great chasms, is the result of long periods of river erosion. In many cases the river establishes a meandering course across a flat plain. Uplift or tilting of the land may then cause the river to flow more rapidly and carve a deeper channel.

The speed of erosion depends upon the steepness of the slope and the volume of the river. In limestone regions, deepening of the canyon is sometimes accelerated by the presence of underground channels, which are exposed as their roofs give way. Arches may also develop where the river carves a new channel through a projecting spur of rock.

The resultant canyons are often very beautiful. Arches, dry channels high on the canyon walls, and projecting ledges of harder rock all add variety to the scene, as do the differing colors and compositions of the rock layers exposed as the river carves its ever-deepening gorge.

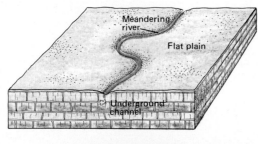

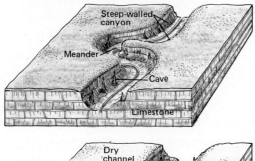

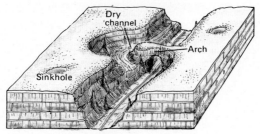

Vesuvius

- Italy
- Map: page 17, E–4

Famed for burying Pompeii, this volcano has been ominously quiet for years. Scientists fear that a major explosion may be overdue.

Vesuvius, one of the most celebrated volcanoes in the world, rises majestically beside the Bay of Naples in southern Italy. Despite a long and continuing history of destructive eruptions, it is best known for its first recorded explosion: the great cataclysm in A.D. 79 that destroyed the nearby cities of Pompeii, Herculaneum, and Stabiae.

A long series of earthquakes preceded the eruption. Then on the night of August 24 the volcano exploded. (An eyewitness description by the Roman statesman Pliny the Younger is considered the oldest document in the science of volcanology.) Fiery clouds of ash and cinders were hurled high in the sky and then rained down on the countryside. When the eruption ended, Pompeii, a flourishing city of 20,000 inhabitants, was buried beneath a thick deposit of ash and cindery pumice, as was Stabiae. Herculaneum, in turn, was engulfed by a mudflow of water-soaked volcanic ash.

Forgotten for centuries, these entombed cities were rediscovered about 1600 and have been excavated bit by bit ever since. Today they are unique museums preserving a moment frozen in time. Wandering on the streets of Pompeii, visitors can experience something of life in Roman times.

Vesuvius, the only currently active volcano on the European mainland, is just one in a chain of volcanoes along the west coast of Italy. The nearby island of Ischia, for example, is a volcano that last erupted in 1302. And the so-called Phlegraean Fields, on the outskirts of Naples, are a cluster of about 20 craters, including one, Monte Nuovo, that was formed by an eruption in 1538.

The Vesuvius that we know today is far different from the volcano that formed the backdrop for ancient Pompeii. The product of a long, complex history, the precursor of modern Vesuvius was a broad, flat-topped mountain. Much of the older volcano was destroyed in the course of the eruption of A.D. 79, and the cone of present-day Vesuvius was gradual-

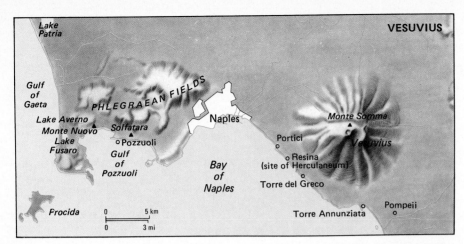

VESUVIUS

ly built up in its collapsed crater.

The remains of the older volcano now form the high, crescent-shaped ridge known as Monte Somma that partially encircles the younger cone of Vesuvius. The highest point on Monte Somma is 3,714 feet (1,132 meters) above the sea. The highest point on the cone of Vesuvius stands at about 4,000 feet (1,200 meters). The height of the summit varies substantially—sometimes by hundreds of feet—following each major eruption.

Although Vesuvius had apparently been dormant for centuries prior to the explosion of A.D. 79, it has been

VESUVIUS. *The volcano looming over the Bay of Naples includes a high encircling ridge* (left) *that is the remnant of an even older volcano.*

active repeatedly ever since. From the time of the disastrous eruption of 1631, when several villages were destroyed, the volcano has displayed a more or less regular cycle of activity. Quiescent periods last an average of 7 years, followed by 20 to 30 years of minor activity confined to the crater. The cycle then ends with a paroxysmal explosion, and a renewed period of dormancy begins. Vesuvius reached its greatest recorded height, 4,338 feet (1,322 meters), just before the eruption of 1906. The last major eruption was in 1944, and scientists fear that another may be overdue. □

VESUVIUS. *Sulfurous fumes rising from the high, snow-fringed summit crater are grim reminders that the volcano that long ago destroyed Pompeii could erupt again at any time.*

Victoria, Lake

- East Africa
- Map: page 26, C–3

The world's second largest freshwater lake, Victoria is exceeded in size by North America's Lake Superior.

Located in the highlands of East Africa, Lake Victoria was unknown to the outside world until 1858, when it was discovered by the British explorer John Speke. The lake was originally known as Ukerewe (which is still the name of its largest island), but Speke renamed it Victoria in honor of the queen of England. Although Speke believed he had found the source of the Nile, the river's ultimate source today is considered to be the Kagera River, which rises in the Burundi highlands farther to the south and flows into Lake Victoria.

The lake was created by massive movements of the earth's crust that resulted in the formation of the eastern and western branches of the Rift Valley. As the trenchlike rifts opened up, the plateau between them sagged in the center, forming the broad, shallow basin occupied by the lake.

Bounded on the north and east by Uganda and Kenya and on the south by Tanzania, the lake covers some 26,500 square miles (68,600 square kilometers)—an area nearly equal to the state of Maine. The shores are so deeply indented with bays and inlets

that its coastline totals more than 2,000 miles (3,200 kilometers). Hundreds of islands rise above the water, ranging from tiny specks to large, densely populated Ukerewe Island in the south.

The many shallows along the shores and around the islands provide superb breeding conditions for fish, and fish are a staple in the diet of the several million inhabitants of the area. In addition to shipping on the lake, agriculture is important in the local economy, especially the production of cotton, coffee, sugar, and corn. At the outlet of this vast inland sea, the Owen Falls Dam harnesses Victoria's waters as they flow north toward the Nile. □

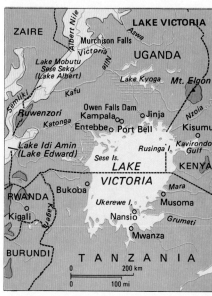

Victoria Falls

- Zambia—Zimbabwe
- Map: page 26, B–4

Just as impressive as this great waterfall is the unique chasm that its rushing waters have created.

Like generations of natives before him and countless tourists ever since, the British explorer David Livingstone became aware of Victoria Falls long before he ever saw them. On November 16, 1855, the first European to witness the awesome cataract was canoeing down the Zambezi River, which forms the boundary between present-day Zambia to the north and Zimbabwe to the south. Far ahead on the horizon he saw plumes of vapor rising like smoke in the sky.

This cloud of spray, which is sent up as the river plunges over the brink of a cliff with a deafening roar, in fact, inspired the natives' name for the waterfall: Mosi-oa-tunya, "the smoke that thunders." The curtain of mist, rising 1,000 feet (300 meters) in the air, is sometimes visible from 25 miles (40 kilometers) away.

But the real surprise came when Livingstone landed on an island that interrupts the line of falls and peered down into the abyss. The explorer, who named the falls in honor of his queen, later described them as "the most wonderful sight I had witnessed in Africa." Plummeting over a cliff at one of the widest spots on the river, the never-ending wall of water spans more than 5,500 feet (1,675 meters). The total drop is approximately 350 feet (107 meters).

But the most unusual feature of the falls is the chasm into which the water spills. There is no broad open valley downstream. Instead, just 250 feet (75 meters) from the line of cliffs that form the falls, the chasm is enclosed by an equally lofty facing wall of cliffs. The only outlet from this narrow, slotlike chasm is a channel a mere 200 feet (60 meters) wide that breaches the downstream barrier of cliffs.

The entire flow of the Zambezi River—some 270,000 cubic feet (7,650 cubic meters) per second in flood season—is funneled through this narrow cleft as it continues on its journey downstream. Beyond this short outlet gorge, the Zambezi is hemmed in by a sheer-walled canyon that zigzags downstream in abrupt hairpin turns for some 45 miles (70 kilometers).

Deep fractures in the bedrock account for the tortuous contours of the canyon. In this area the Zambezi flows across a plateau formed of layers of sandstone and massive basaltic lava flows. Over the course of time the rock was broken up by an intersecting network of deep vertical fractures that cross each other at sharp angles.

Since the fractures are lines of weakness, they are quite easily enlarged by erosion. The "zigs" and "zags" of the lower canyon are simply intersecting fractures that were opened by erosion as the falls migrated upstream to their present posi-

tion. The slotlike chasm at the foot of the falls, in turn, was formed by the erosion of a fracture that intersects the river's course at a right angle.

In time, however, it too will be transformed into an abrupt turn in the upper canyon. At one end of the long line of falls there is a tumultuous cas-cade known as the Devil's Cataract. Here the water is beginning the up-stream erosion of yet another fracture that crosses the river at a sharp angle. As this new sector of the canyon is enlarged, the entire flow of the river will spill over its edge into the newly created abyss, and the old line of falls will ultimately be left high and dry.

But that change is far in the future. In the meantime generations of tour-ists will continue to enjoy close-up views of Victoria Falls from a unique vantage point—atop the facing wall of cliffs that parallel the long line of the waterfall. □

VICTORIA FALLS. *Vantage points all along the facing wall of cliffs provide spectacular views of the magnificent African waterfall.*

Vikos Canyon

- Greece
- Map: page 17, E–5

Even in a land well known for its striking landscapes, this rugged canyon stands out for wild beauty.

The Tymphe, a limestone massif in the Pindus mountain range in north-western Greece, is notable for its stark and rugged scenery. The wild gorges of the Aoos River form its northern border, while Vikos Canyon slices across the heart of the mountain mass. A chasm with towering, nearly vertical walls, it was carved into a startlingly white formation of extremely fine-grained limestone. The sparsity of vegetation on the precipitous slopes and the surrounding peaks accentuates the austere beauty of the awesome chasm.

Vikos Canyon is the creation of the northward-flowing Voidomatis River, a tributary of the Aoos. But it was obviously carved at a time when the climate was wetter and the river much more vigorous. Today the Voidomatis is a meager trickle until its flow is swelled by a large spring near the northern end of the canyon.

The river, moreover, must have been in existence before the Tymphe massif was uplifted to its present elevation. The mountain mass slopes generally upward from south to north, reaching a high point of 8,192 feet (2,497 meters) on a peak called Gamela near its northern edge. At the head of the canyon the walls are only about 1,300 feet (400 meters) high. But farther

VIKOS CANYON. *The whiteness of its sheer limestone cliffs—and Greece's famous bright sunshine—accentuate the stark and rugged grandeur of this remote mountain canyon.*

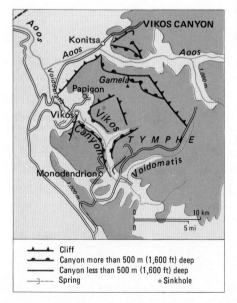

downstream, to the north, the walls soar to a maximum height of nearly 4,000 feet (1,200 meters) above the floor of the canyon.

Thus it is clear that the river had established its course long before the limestone massif was tilted upward along the faults marked by steep cliffs near its northern margins. Even as the land was being uplifted in the north, the river maintained its northward course. By eroding its bed ever deeper as the limestone was tilted upward, the river created the great cleft that now traverses the massif.

The interior of the Tymphe is so remote and rugged that the only farms and villages in the area are scattered along its margins. Even so, Vikos Canyon is accessible by roads leading to both ends. Visitors who venture into its depths are rewarded with the opportunity to glimpse a majestic mountain landscape that even to this day remains virtually untouched by modern civilization. □

Virginia Falls

- Canada (Northwest Territories)
- Map: page 10, C–2

This thundering double cascade is the crowning glory of one of Canada's finest wilderness rivers.

The South Nahanni River rises in the mountains of Canada's Northwest Territories and meanders southeastward for about 375 miles (600 kilometers) before joining the Liard, a tributary of the mighty Mackenzie. Along the way it passes through such a splendid and varied wilderness that it is protected as the focal point of Nahanni National Park.

In the course of its short journey, the river descends some 3,000 feet (900 meters) in elevation. For much of the way, as a result, the South Nahanni hurtles across boulder-strewn rapids, which make it a favorite with white-water canoeing enthusiasts.

But the South Nahanni makes its single most spectacular leap at Virginia Falls near the lower part of its middle course. Flowing across a wide, densely forested valley, the river is suddenly divided in two by a massive limestone pinnacle projecting from its bed. Just beyond, the double cascade of Virginia Falls plunges over a precipice into a seething caldron of spray 316 feet (96 meters) below. The face of the descending wall of water covers an area of 4 acres (1.6 hectares).

At the falls the river undergoes a marked change in personality. Upstream it follows a lazy serpentine course through a glacier-carved valley framed by snowcapped peaks. A famed attraction in the upper valley is Rabbitkettle Hot Springs, which issue an endless stream of warm water in this cold northern setting.

Farther downstream the South Nahanni becomes a turbulent wilderness river. First it turns abruptly through a very narrow passage known as Figure Eight Rapids. Violently swirling whirlpools make this the river's most treacherous stretch of water.

Beyond, the South Nahanni begins its descent through the trio of wild gorges that constrict its lower course. The uppermost, known as the Third Canyon, is 19 miles (30 kilometers) long and as much as 4,000 feet (1,200 meters) deep. At one point the river makes a breathtaking hairpin turn between sheer cliffs 1,510 feet (460 meters) high. It then passes in turn through the Second Canyon and the First Canyon, equally spectacular chasms bounded by towering cliffs. Finally, as it nears its end, its fury spent, it splits into a multitude of channels before flowing into the Liard and then into the Mackenzie. □

VIRGINIA FALLS. *The seething double cascade of the Canadian waterfall plunges from a precipice nearly twice the height of Niagara.*

Virgin Islands National Park

- United States (Virgin Islands)
- Map: page 11, F–7

Small but marvelously scenic, this island park preserves the essence of an unspoiled West Indian paradise.

St. John, the smallest of the principal U.S. Virgin Islands, has also been called the loveliest of them all. An enchanting blend of land and water, the little Caribbean island is famous for its ruggedly beautiful, forested interior, its deeply indented coastline fringed by long crescents of white sandy beaches, and offshore, crystal-clear tropical seas that ripple across myriads of colorful coral reefs.

Ever since 1956, about two-thirds of the island—some 9,500 acres, or 3,850 hectares—have been protected within the boundaries of Virgin Islands National Park. Since the sea is an integral part of the character of any West Indian island, 5,650 acres (2,300 hectares) of the surrounding waters are also included in the park.

Most visitors are attracted first and foremost by the park's superb seashores. Some 40 sizable bays indent St. John's coastline, each with a personality of its own. Offshore, visitors can don snorkels to explore the island's innumerable coral reefs, teeming with brilliantly colored tropical fish and an amazing variety of other marine life. At Trunk Bay, a marked underwater nature trail introduces snorkelers to the intricacies of reef ecology. Besides protecting the shoreline from erosion by breaking the force of incoming ocean swells, the reefs are the source of the beaches' basic building material: pulverized coral sand.

The park's inland areas also offer ample rewards. Roads and trails wind through the rugged hills, which are composed primarily of volcanic rock. There visitors can explore the park's dense mantle of subtropical forest, the picturesque ruins of sugar plantations that once flourished on the island, and even petroglyphs that were carved in the rocks by local Indians long before Christopher Columbus sailed among the Virgin Islands in 1493. And from the island's high point, Bordeaux Mountain, at 1,277 feet (389 meters), visitors can enjoy breathtaking views of the entire ensemble of the land and tranquil, island-dotted sea. □

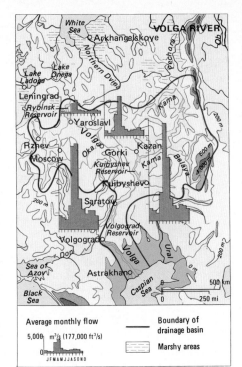

The Volga funnels the entire runoff from its vast drainage basin into the landlocked Caspian Sea. The river's peak flow is in spring, following the annual thaw.

Volga River

- U.S.S.R.
- Map: page 18, F–4

Once feared for its annual floods, Europe's longest river has been harnessed for power generation.

The majestic Volga, the longest river in Europe, rises in marshy forests northwest of Moscow. It flows 2,293 miles (3,690 kilometers) across the steppes and semidesert regions before it finally empties into the landlocked Caspian Sea. From a source at an altitude of only 748 feet (228 meters), it gradually descends to an elevation of 92 feet (28 meters) below sea level at its outlet on the Caspian. The river's drainage basin, which covers 525,000 square miles (1,360,000 square kilometers), includes about one-third of the Soviet Union's territory in Europe and approximately one-fourth of the country's population.

Once an untamed river feared for its annual flooding, the Volga has been transformed by huge dams and hydroelectric projects into a chain of tremendous reservoirs connected by navigable stretches of river. Canals link the Volga not only to the Baltic and White seas to the west and north, but also to the Mediterranean (by way

of the Black Sea) in the south. Thus, spanning the entire continent and linking forested northern regions to key grain-producing and industrial areas, the Volga is a crucial transportation artery. Two out of three tons of freight shipped by water in the Soviet Union are carried on the far-flung Volga River system.

Flowing through small lakes and marshes near its source, the river meanders southeast past Rzhev, then turns northeastward to bypass Moscow in an enormous curve. A canal, however, links Moscow to the river, making the capital a major port city. A short distance downstream, the Volga enters its first major impoundment, the Rybinsk Reservoir. With an area of 1,770 square miles (4,585 square kilometers), it was once the largest manmade lake in the world.

Turning southeastward, the river receives the Oka, its principal right-bank tributary, as it flows past Gorki. At Kazan, the Volga enters the largest of its artificial lakes, the mammoth Kuibyshev Reservoir. Covering 2,500 square miles (6,500 square kilometers), the reservoir is larger than the entire state of Delaware. Here the Volga also receives its main left-bank tributary, the Kama, which rises 1,262 miles (2,031 kilometers) to the northeast in the Ural Mountains.

Flowing southward now, the Volga enters the last of its big reservoirs, Volgograd. Just below the reservoir is the city of Volgograd, formerly named Stalingrad. During World War II it was the site of a decisive battle that ended in defeat for the invading Nazi forces. Below Volgograd Reservoir a canal leads west and links the entire Volga system to the Don River and the Black Sea. It is here also that the Volga begins its descent below sea level into the landlocked basin occupied by the Caspian Sea.

Although much has been done to harness the power of the Volga, some things do not change. The Volga basin, like the interiors of all continents, is subject to seasonal extremes in temperature. In winter the entire river freezes over. Then summer returns with an abrupt transition: an intense thaw is followed by a drastic rise in the river's volume of flow. Because of the many dams that have been built, the spring floods are no longer the recurrent threat that they were in the past. Even so, man has by no means entirely tamed the force of the Russians' beloved "Mother Volga." □

Voringfoss

- Norway
- Map: page 16, D–2

The music of composer Edvard Grieg was inspired in part by the region surrounding this splendid waterfall.

The spectacularly beautiful waterfall known as Voringfoss is one of the many tourist attractions in the fjord country of Norway. (*Foss* means "waterfall" in Norwegian.) The cascade is almost completely hidden away in a river valley about 7 miles (11 kilometers) beyond the head of Eidfjord, one of the many branches of lovely Hardanger Fjord, which angles inland south of the city of Bergen.

Near the edge of a high plateau, the Bjoreia River plunges into a narrow gorge, spilling downward in plumes of rushing water for a total drop of 535 feet (163 meters). Beyond the falls the water continues downslope and finally flows into the deep, glacier-carved trench of Eidfjord. The falls are most impressive during spring and summer, when the river is swollen by the melting of winter snow and a large glacier that lingers on the highlands of Hardanger Plateau.

Generally, a waterfall spilling into the head of a closed canyon is the product of gradual upstream erosion of the bedrock by the river that forms the cascade. Voringfoss, however, is a creation of the Ice Age, when all of Scandinavia was blanketed by an enormous ice cap. (Jostedal Glacier, not far to the north, is the largest remnant of the great ice cap existing on the continent of Europe.)

Yet the canyon below the falls is not simply an ice-carved trench. The gorge traces the line of a fracture in the ancient metamorphic rock that makes up the plateau. And glaciers grinding down the slope did indeed slightly enlarge this weak area in the extremely erosion-resistant rock.

But the major excavator of the trench was a torrential, debris-laden river that escaped from beneath the glacier as the ice cap melted at the end of the Ice Age. Flowing rapidly and under intense pressure within a narrow channel along the fracture in the bedrock, it carved the deep, steep-walled canyon and, churning round and round in a whirlpool, formed the cul-de-sac where Voringfoss spills into the gorge today.

Spectacular views of the falls are

VORINGFOSS. *The force of the plunging water produces a perpetual mist at the foot of the waterfall. Rainbows often appear when the sun strikes the mist at just the right angle.*

available to tourists traveling on the road that winds down from the plateau to Eidfjord. Downstream from the falls, visitors enter a countryside dotted with charming villages and farms that has long been a popular vacation retreat. The richest orchard district in Norway, it is breathtakingly beautiful in spring, when the land is adrift in the pink and white blossoms of the fruit trees.

Among the most famous visitors to the area was composer Edvard Grieg, who had a small log cabin on Hardanger Fjord. Summer after summer he returned to revel in the splendid views of steep forested slopes and distant mountains. Many music lovers find in his compositions a perfect reflection of this majestic land. On overcast days the mood of the countryside is brooding, even ominous. But in clear weather the colors are dazzling, and the vistas seem endless. □

Waddenzee

- Netherlands
- Map: page 16, D–3

This shallow saltwater gulf is the site of a centuries-old struggle between the land and invading sea.

The Waddenzee is a long, shallow arm of the North Sea. It extends along the northern coast of the Netherlands between the mainland and the West Frisian Islands—an area where the distinction between land and sea has never been clear-cut. The waters of the Waddenzee ebb away almost completely at low tide, revealing broad sand flats interlaced with channels.

At one time the bordering islands formed a continuous barrier, and the Waddenzee was part of a large freshwater lake. Storms in the 13th century then broke through the barrier and transformed the lake into a shallow saltwater gulf called the Zuider Zee.

Efforts have been made since the Middle Ages to reclaim the land by draining the salty expanses of the Zuider Zee and protecting them with high dikes or embankments. These polders, as the reclaimed tracts are called, have an obvious importance to a country as small and densely populated as the Netherlands.

In the 1930's a dike about 20 miles (32 kilometers) long was built across

WADDENZEE. *In this half land, half water habitat, natural drainage channels snake across silt that has accumulated in the shallows.*

the Zuider Zee, separating its northern portion, the Waddenzee, from the southern part, which was transformed into the large freshwater lake now known as the Ijsselmeer.

The Ijsselmeer's size has since been greatly reduced by the creation of several polders. When the last of these, the Markerwaard polder, is finally completed, nearly 900 square miles (2,330 square kilometers) of arable land will have been reclaimed.

Similar schemes have been proposed for draining the Waddenzee. Such plans have raised serious questions, however, since the Waddenzee is not only an area of great beauty but also an important wildlife refuge. At the peak of the migration season, it provides sanctuary for as many as half a million water birds at a time. □

Waimangu Hot Springs

- New Zealand
- Map: page 23, H–5

Once the site of the world's most powerful geyser, these hot springs are still an impressive spectacle.

Waimangu Hot Springs, in the northern part of New Zealand's North Island, are a prime attraction in one of the world's great thermal areas. In this unstable, volcanically active region, astonishing numbers of geysers, hot springs, and boiling mud pots are visible evidence that pockets of molten magma lie perilously close to the surface of the earth. And at Waimangu, the destruction of old features and the creation of new ones even within the past century are reminders that renewed upheavals could occur at just about any time.

Throughout most of the 19th century, Waimangu was especially famous for its dazzling White and Pink terraces, often called the most beautiful formations of their kind in the world. The White Terrace was the larger of the two. A fan-shaped array of tiered pools that sloped down a hillside like a giant alabaster staircase, it covered an area of 7½ acres (3 hectares). A geyser that erupted periodically from a large pool at the top of the slope provided the basic building material for this fantastic structure: dissolved minerals that were precipitated from the water to form the damlike barriers contain-

WAIMANGU HOT SPRINGS. *Varicolored mineral deposits encrust the surfaces of volcanic rocks where steaming water spills from one of this thermal area's numerous hot springs.*

WAIMANGU HOT SPRINGS. *Water that was heated in the depths of the earth rises to the surface and fills this steaming pool in the basin of an extinct volcanic crater.*

ing the individual pools. The celebrated Pink Terrace covered only about five acres (two hectares), but was even more striking because of the contrast between its pools of azure water and their salmon-rose walls.

All this beauty was destroyed on June 10, 1886, when suddenly and without warning the nearby, supposedly extinct volcano, Tarawera Mountain, exploded with a roar that could be heard hundreds of miles away. A huge fissure opened on the mountainside as 22 vents spewed out incandescent lava, and ash and debris showered down over an area of about 6,000 square miles (15,500 square kilometers). By the time the violence ended, several villages had been destroyed and the famous terraces were completely obliterated.

Their loss was considered a national disaster. Yet hot springs continued to bubble in the area and geysers continued to spout. And then in 1900, as if in compensation for the loss of the beloved terraces, a new geyser began to spout—one that soon dwarfed all the others. Indeed, for a time the Waimangu Geyser was the most powerful in the world. At roughly 34-hour intervals, it blasted jets of mud, steam, and scalding-hot water up to heights

of as much as 1,500 feet (450 meters).

But it too proved to be a passing thing. By 1904 the Waimangu Geyser's eruptions became feeble and intermittent, and since 1908 it has been completely extinct.

In 1917 another volcanic eruption destroyed a nearby hotel and left another great scar on the landscape. Its crater, known as the Waimangu Caldron, is now filled by a lake of boiling water some 10 acres (4 hectares) in area. Looming over the lake is a bank of red-streaked, steaming cliffs known

as the Cathedral Rocks. Ruamoko's Throat, a brilliant turquoise-blue lake in a crater produced by the 1886 eruption, is also bordered by scarlet cliffs.

In fact there are patches of astonishing colors throughout the area, all of them the residue of thermal upheavals. The water that emerges on the surface in hot springs and geysers is heated as it passes through rocky subterranean channels near the hidden pocket of magma. There it also becomes heavily saturated with dissolved minerals that are carried to the surface and deposited in thin, multicolored crusts. The differing mineral content of the water results in various hues—the yellow of sulfur deposits, for example, and the red of iron oxides.

Although there have been no major upheavals in recent years, Waimangu Hot Springs are still in turmoil. Visitors to the area pass in turn by the steaming basins of hot springs filled with water near the boiling point and geysers that periodically send fountains of scalding water high into the air. In ponds filled with burning-hot mud, bubbles of gas rise fitfully to the surface and burst in small, sputtering explosions. Plumes of gas and steam emanate from volcanolike cones of hardened mud, and jets of nauseous sulfurous fumes rise hissing from fissures in the earth.

On all sides, the residue of minerals cast up by the never-ending thermal activity adorns the steaming ground with stark textures and vivid colors. Visitors contemplating this eerie, otherworldly scene are reminded that the restless landscape of Waimangu Hot Springs is in a perpetual state of flux. At just about any time, an unexpected outburst could change it completely once again. □

Why Hot Springs Bubble and Geysers Erupt

Hot springs and geysers like those in New Zealand result from a combination of ample groundwater, a source of heat, and suitable escape routes to the surface. They occur in volcanic areas where reservoirs of molten or slowly cooling magma lie close to the surface and have heated the covering rocks. The water is heated as it seeps through fissures in the rocks, and if it has an unobstructed passage to the surface, it bubbles up continuously in the pool of a hot spring.

Geysers are characterized by intermittent explosive eruptions of steam and hot water. As the long, usually constricted tube of a geyser fills with water, the water is heated from contact with the hot rocks. But it does not boil immediately, since an increase in pressure—caused by the weight of the water higher up in the tube—raises the boiling point of a liquid. Eventually even this elevated boiling point is reached, and some of the water vaporizes into steam, which causes water to spill from the top of the tube. The resultant decrease in pressure lowers the boiling point of the water at the bottom of the tube, which immediately turns into superheated steam. Expanding as it vaporizes, the steam expels the entire column of water in an explosive eruption. Water then refills the tube, and the cycle of periodic eruptions begins once again.

Whakarewarewa Thermal Area

- New Zealand
- Map: page 23, H–5

A hidden reservoir of boiling water regulates the pulse and power of this stunning array of gushing geysers.

Like southwestern Iceland and Yellowstone National Park in the United States, New Zealand's North Island is well known for its abundance of hot springs and geysers. Of the several hot-spring areas in the northern part of the island, a perennial favorite with visitors is the Whakarewarewa Thermal Area. Although it includes a number of hot springs and perpetually boiling mud pots, the main attraction is spectacular geyser displays.

The so-called Geyser Flat is a group of seven geysers that erupt from an extensive silica terrace. The terrace was formed from minerals that were dissolved in the steaming water. Another cluster of geysers, the Prince of Wales Feathers, sends up jets of spray to heights of 40 feet (12 meters).

Here too is found Pohutu. (Its name means "splashing.") The largest geyser now active in New Zealand, it produces fountains up to 100 feet (30 meters) high. Pohutu is quite unpredictable, however. In 1926 it erupted 613 times, but from April 1932 until June 1934 it did not produce a single column of water. And while its outbursts average 20 minutes, one day in May 1920 it remained in continuous eruption for more than 12 hours.

The geysers, supplied by the same subterranean reservoir of superheated water, exhibit an interesting rhythm in their activity. Just before Pohutu erupts, the water in a nearby hot spring begins to boil over; then, when the geyser begins to spout, the water level drops. Similarly, the Prince of Wales Feathers begin to play a few hours before Pohutu erupts, and then die down just before Pohutu does.

Maori villagers living in the area take advantage of the hot springs for bathing, laundering, and cooking just as they have for generations. Residents of the nearby city of Rotorua, in turn, have harnessed the abundant supply of geothermal energy for home heating as well as a multitude of other uses. □

WHAKAREWAREWA. *A cone of silica has accumulated around the narrow vent of this New Zealand geyser.*

WHITE ISLAND. *Clouds of gas and steam rise perpetually from the shattered crater of this volcanic island off the coast of New Zealand.*

White Island

- New Zealand
- Map: page 23, H–5

This seething summit of a large offshore volcano is the scene of continuing internal turmoil.

White Island, in the Bay of Plenty off the coast of North Island, New Zealand, is the exposed tip of a submarine volcano. Some 800 acres (325 hectares) in area, it rises to a maximum of 1,075 feet (328 meters) above the blue Pacific. Captain Cook named the is-land in 1769, probably in reference to the extensive white deposits of guano that once covered it.

Despite its small size, White Island is notable for the many signs of con-tinuing turmoil within its broad crater. Mud pots bubble ceaselessly, ponds boil, geysers erupt, and jets of steam and gas whistle from cracks in the ground. The largest of these openings, known as Roaring Jimmy, regularly emits jets of high-pressure steam with a deafening sound.

Roaring Jimmy is thought to act as a safety valve that permits the accumu-lated gas to escape without mishap. In 1914, for example, debris from a land-slide temporarily clogged the vent, and disaster ensued. Pressure built up until Roaring Jimmy suddenly cleared its throat with an explosion that trig-gered an enormous landslide. In the process, an entire sulfur-mining camp was swept out to sea.

Despite the hazards, there have been occasional proposals to resume the mining of the island's excellent sulfur deposits. But today the unin-habited speck of land is a scenic re-serve visited only by sightseers, who arrive by boat or plane to view the steaming, restless volcanic island. □

Wind Cave

- United States (South Dakota)
- Map: page 10, D–4

Noted for the winds at its entrance, this underground labyrinth is adorned with delicate honeycombs of rock.

Wind Cave, located in the rugged Black Hills of South Dakota, was named for the very strong air currents that pass in and out of its entrance. Changes in barometric pressure apparently trigger these eerie winds. When the atmospheric pressure rises outside the cave, wind rushes in; then when the outside air pressure drops, the air rushes out again.

But Wind Cave is even more remarkable for its unrivaled displays of the delicate rock formation known as boxwork. When the limestone containing the cave was uplifted some 60 million years ago, it was broken up by networks of intersecting cracks. Over long periods of time, seeping water deposited veins of the mineral calcite in the cracks. Later, when the cave was formed, the enveloping limestone was eroded away, while the more resistant calcite in the cracks was left projecting from the ceilings and walls in fragile, beautifully intricate patterns.

The cave, which has been protected since 1903 as the centerpiece of Wind Cave National Park, has a number of unusual attractions above the ground as well. Its superb prairie grassland harbors bison, black-tailed prairie dogs, pronghorns, and a wealth of other wildlife. □

WHITE SANDS NATIONAL MONUMENT. *Yucca and a few other hardy, drought-resistant plants survive on the desert's parched, ceaselessly shifting dunes of snow-white gypsum sand.*

White Sands National Monument

- United States (New Mexico)
- Map: page 10, D–5

The largest gypsum dune field in the world is a billowing, ever-shifting sea of sand that is as white as snow.

White Sands National Monument includes the most scenic part of the world's largest gypsum dune field. Located in a mountain-rimmed basin in southern New Mexico, it is a tremendous expanse of high, billowing dunes. The sand, as white as snow, is composed of fine crystals of gypsum, the same mineral from which plaster of paris is made.

The source of the sand is the San Andres Mountains to the west of the basin and the Sacramento Mountains to the east. Both mountain ranges contain massive deposits of gypsum that was formed as an ancient sea evaporated some 100 million years ago. In a process that has gone on for countless centuries, seasonal rains and melting snow carry dissolved gypsum from the mountains down to Lake Lucero in the lowest part of the basin.

In this harsh desert environment, the water soon evaporates and leaves a glittering crust of gypsum crystals on the lake bed. Weathering reduces the crystals to fine sand grains, which the relentless southwest wind carries off and piles up into dunes. Constantly on the move, the dunes advance up to 33 feet (10 meters) per year.

Life is sparse on the endlessly shifting dunes. Here and there, however, drought-resistant plants such as saltbush and yucca manage to survive. Here too are found highly specialized pocket mice, lizards, and other creatures whose white coloration makes them nearly invisible on the gleaming gypsum sand. □

WIND CAVE. *Like wax poured into a mold, calcite was deposited in cracks in a limestone formation, leaving this delicate boxwork relief when the limestone was later eroded away.*

Yangtze River

- China
- Map: page 21, F–1

China's longest river, slashing across its populous heartland, is also the country's most important waterway.

From its source in the Tibetan highlands to its outlet near Shanghai on the East China Sea, the Yangtze flows a total of 3,430 miles (5,520 kilometers). It is thus the longest river in Asia and among the longest in the world. Only the Nile, the Amazon, and the Mississippi-Missouri travel a greater distance from source to sea.

The Yangtze's drainage basin of some 750,000 square miles (1.9 million square kilometers) encompasses an area almost the size of Mexico. Although the river flows through wild and inhospitable country along much of its upper course, the lower part of its basin is one of the most densely populated areas in the world. It is also China's most highly developed agricultural and industrial region.

Flowing through the heart of such a populous region, the Yangtze is one of the busiest waterways on earth. The country's main east-west transportation artery, it has been called China's Main Street. Ocean liners can travel all the way to the thriving metropolis of Wuhan about 700 miles (1,100 kilometers) from the sea; junks and smaller vessels can sail as far as Ipin, some 1,500 miles (2,400 kilometers) inland from the coast.

The Yangtze rises at an elevation of

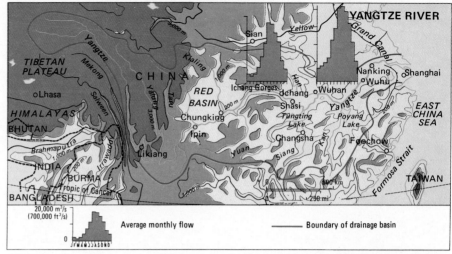

The Yangtze's enormous drainage basin is nearly the size of Mexico. The river's flow reaches its high-water stage in the summer monsoon season and sometimes causes extensive floods.

18,000 feet (5,500 meters) in the Tibetan highlands and flows at first on a southerly course. As it spills off the highlands, it parallels the Mekong and Salween rivers for about 250 miles (400 kilometers). In places the three great rivers lie within 40 miles (65 kilometers) of one another.

And like its companion rivers, the Yangtze makes a rapid descent from the mountains through deep, rugged gorges. Veering northeast, it receives the waters of the Yalung, the first of its major tributaries. By the time it reaches Ipin, the head of navigation, it has dropped to within 1,000 feet (300 meters) of sea level.

Along its middle course, between Ipin and Ichang, the Yangtze winds eastward through the so-called Red Basin of Szechwan, named for the color of its many sandstone hills and rich agricultural soil. As it approaches the city of Ichang, the river passes into its most scenic sector, the famous Ichang Gorges. Over the course of about 120 miles (200 kilometers), the Yangtze is hemmed in by a succession

of three towering limestone gorges bounded by cliffs up to 2,000 feet (600 meters) high. With its flow suddenly constricted in these narrow clefts, the river increases dramatically in depth. In some parts of the gorges the water is 600 feet (180 meters) deep, thus making the Yangtze the deepest river in the entire world.

By the time it emerges from the gorges, the Yangtze is only about 130 feet (40 meters) above sea level. It meanders eastward across a broad, lake-studded plain that is considered the rice bowl of China. A majestic avenue of commerce, it broadens in places to widths of 1 mile (1.6 kilometers) and more.

Of the many canals that crisscross the lower basin, the most famous is the Grand Canal, the longest in China. Completed by Kublai Khan in the 13th century, it is about 1,000 miles (1,600 kilometers) in length and links the Yangtze basin with both the Yellow River and the city of Peking far to the north.

At Wuhu, 200 miles (320 kilometers) from the sea, the Yangtze becomes a tidal estuary. Crossing its broad, ever-growing delta, it divides into two main channels as it enters the East China Sea. Although not nearly as muddy as the Yellow River (the muddiest river in the world), the Yangtze carries so much silt that it extends its delta seaward at a rate of 1 mile (1.6 kilometers) every 64 years.

Supplied by rainfall that averages 43 inches (1,100 millimeters) per year, the Yangtze is susceptible to occasional flooding, especially during the summer rainy season. Extensive flood control measures help keep the high

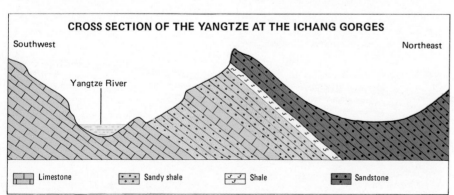

At the famous Ichang Gorges near the end of its middle course, the Yangtze carved a series of deep canyons as it eroded its channel across steeply sloping rock layers.

YANGTZE RIVER. *Within the narrow confines of the magnificent Ichang Gorges, the Yangtze reigns as the deepest river in the world.*

waters in check. But when abnormal rainfall produces rising waters in several tributaries at the same time, the results can be devastating. In 2297 B.C., floodwaters are said to have transformed the entire North China plain into a gigantic inland sea.

In more recent centuries the Yangtze has produced a major flood about once every 50 years. In 1931, more than 35,000 square miles (90,000 square kilometers) of land—an area larger than the state of Maine—were inundated by a catastrophic flood that directly affected the lives of some 40 million people. Even more widespread flooding occurred in 1954, when the water level in places rose almost 5 feet (1½ meters) higher than it had in 1931.

Dams, levees, and other control devices have done much to reduce the hazards of future flooding. Even so, the river's watershed is so huge that total control is probably impossible. The Yangtze is one of China's great economic assets, but like all rivers, it remains unpredictable.　□

Yellowstone National Park

- United States
- Map: page 10, D–4

Pioneering mountain men traversed Yellowstone long before it became a national park—but found few who believed their tales of its wonders.

Yellowstone, established in 1872, is the oldest national park in the world. It encompasses nearly 3,500 square miles (9,000 square kilometers) of high plateau country in the northern Rockies. Most of the park is located in the northwest corner of Wyoming, but parts of it extend into Montana and Idaho as well.

Wonders are everywhere in this unusual wilderness reserve. In addition to the park's famous array of geysers and hot springs, there are rugged mountains, dense forests, deep, cold lakes, and rushing trout streams. Here

too are found the spectacular Grand Canyon of the Yellowstone River, a cliff of solid black obsidian (volcanic glass) where Indians once quarried material for arrowheads, and even entire fossil forests. A loop road provides easy access to most of the park's major features, and miles of trails thread through the backcountry wilderness.

But for most people Yellowstone is first and foremost a superb showcase of geothermal activity. With some 300 geysers and nearly 10,000 hot springs and steam vents, the park boasts the world's largest, most varied collection of geothermal phenomena.

The boiling springs and spouting geysers are a legacy of the region's volcanic past. The high, mountain-rimmed plateau was built up by a long succession of lava flows, the last of which occurred less than 100,000 years ago. Even now a reservoir of molten magma remains quite near the surface beneath the park. Water from rain and melting snow seeps into fissures, where it is heated by contact with

YELLOWSTONE NATIONAL PARK. *The terraces of Mammoth Hot Springs are constantly remodeled by new deposits of dissolved limestone.*

hot rocks. Some then escapes to the surface through hissing steam vents, sputtering mud pots, and scalding hot springs. And some escapes in the intermittent fountains of geysers.

The best-known geyser in Yellowstone—perhaps in the world—is Old Faithful. Named for the regularity of its eruptions, it spouts on the average every 72 minutes, day after day, year in and year out. Its jet of steam and hot water, which lasts for two to five minutes, has been known to reach 184 feet (56 meters) but usually is about 130 feet (40 meters) high.

Riverside Geyser on the bank of the Firehole River is even more predictable, with 5¾-hour intervals between eruptions. Although not as high as Old Faithful, it continues to play for 15 minutes, shooting a graceful plume of spray at an angle over the river.

Other geysers in the park's various geyser basins show a wide range of eruptive activity. Some send up columns of water only three feet (one meter) or less in height and play almost continuously. Others produce much more substantial jets, but they erupt only at intervals of days, weeks, or even months.

Steamboat Geyser, famous for producing the highest jets in the park, has been known to erupt to heights of 400 feet (120 meters). But in 1969 it mysteriously died. Renewed activity in recent years, however, suggests that it may be entering a new phase of spectacular eruptions.

Many other geysers vie for the visitor's attention at Yellowstone. Castle Geyser erupts from an enormous fortresslike cone built from silica that was dissolved in the hot water. Grotto Geyser's cone, penetrated by cavelike openings, resembles a huge abstract sculpture. Grand Geyser and Great Fountain Geyser regularly produce jets up to 200 feet (60 meters) high.

The numerous hot springs, ringed by deposits of geyserite, are more notable for their colors than for any displays of activity. Among the most beautiful is Morning Glory Pool. The sky, reflected in its deep trumpet-shaped basin, produces a startlingly intense blue color.

The lovely hues in other hot springs are the products of various species of algae and bacteria, each adapted to life in water of different temperatures. Grand Prismatic Spring is blue in the center, but algae growing around the edges produce an amazing array of warm tones of yellow, orange, golden

YELLOWSTONE NATIONAL PARK. *In the midst of the forest, a great steaming pool is fringed by deposits of geyserite, formed from dissolved silica in the scalding water.*

brown, and green. And, for reasons that are immediately apparent, Hillside Springs were once known as Tomato Soup Springs.

But the most spectacular by far are Mammoth Hot Springs near the park's northern border. A fantastic structure of stepped pools and terraces, the springs adorn the slope like a gigantic wedding cake. Here the hot water spilling from the pools is saturated with dissolved limestone; it is estimated that 2 tons (1.8 metric tons) are brought to the surface each day. Precipitated from the water, the limestone deposits cause the terraces to change slowly but constantly both in size and shape. As in the other springs, heat-tolerant algae streak the terraces with ribbons of delicate colors.

Although less well known than its hot springs and geysers, Yellowstone's fossil forests are equally impressive. Spread over an area of some 40 square miles (100 square kilometers), they are the most extensive petrified forests existing in the world. The trees, moreover, were buried alive in outpourings of volcanic debris; in contrast to most other petrified forests, where the logs are strewn in a helter-skelter fashion across the ground, the fossilized tree trunks at Yellowstone remained in upright positions.

Nor is there just one petrified forest

at Yellowstone. As one forest was buried, a new forest took root above it in the volcanic debris, only to be buried itself by renewed eruptions. More than 12 separate layers of petrified forests have been unearthed in the park. With details of foliage, twigs, and cones faithfully preserved as fossils, more than 100 different species of trees have been identified, ranging from relatives of modern redwoods to various types of maples, chestnuts, oaks, and figs.

No visit to Yellowstone is complete without a pause to admire the park's own Grand Canyon. Flowing north from Yellowstone Lake, the largest high-mountain lake in North America, the Yellowstone River plunges into an awesome abyss by way of two mighty waterfalls. The first, the Upper Falls, has a drop of 109 feet (33 meters); the Lower Falls are an imposing 308 feet (94 meters) high.

Downstream the bright green water of the Yellowstone River rushes through a canyon 24 miles (39 kilometers) long. Averaging 1,000 feet (300 meters) in width, it is up to 1,200 feet (365 meters) deep. From overlooks on the canyon rim such as Artist Point and Inspiration Point, visitors can readily grasp the size and beauty of this spectacular canyon in this varied and magnificent national park. □

YOSEMITE NATIONAL PARK. *Broken into two plumelike cataracts, Yosemite Falls drop 2,425 feet (739 meters) to the valley floor.*

Yosemite National Park

- United States (California)
- Map: page 10, D–5

Spectacular rock formations, giant sequoias, waterfalls, and wildlife attract countless sightseers to this wonderland in the Sierra Nevada.

One of America's greatest naturalists, John Muir, captured the essence of Yosemite when he wrote, "Its natural beauty cleanses and warms like fire, and you will be willing to stay forever." Since the establishment of Yosemite National Park in 1890, uncounted millions of visitors have come to understand what he meant.

The tremendous impact of Yosemite results partly from its grand scale, partly from the sheer abundance of magnificent scenery. Then too, the senses are heightened by the incredibly clean, sharp air, and—especially at the change of the seasons—by a wonderful clarity of colors in foliage, sky, and massive gray rocks.

The most famous portion of the park is Yosemite Valley, a narrow, sheer-walled cleft in the western flank of the Sierra Nevada. Near the entrance to the valley the looming crag of El Capitan rises 3,604 feet (1,099 meters) above the valley floor. On the opposite side of the valley, Bridalveil Fall—as diaphanous and lovely as its name suggests—spills 620 feet (189 meters) over a granite cliff. Nearby Ribbon Fall, the highest unbroken cataract in the park, drops 1,612 feet (491 meters) in a single leap. The valley, some 7 miles (11 kilometers) long, is lined with other equally awesome wonders: the triple promontory of the Three Brothers, the Cathedral Spires, and Half Dome, which broods over the valley like a sinister hooded figure.

The scenery of Yosemite was shaped primarily by the successive advances of numerous glaciers over the course of the past 2 million years. The greatest of the glacial tongues pushed far down into the ancestral valley of the Merced River (which still flows through Yosemite Valley), filling it to the brim with ice. Only the tops of El Capitan, Half Dome, Eagle Peak, and Sentinel Dome projected above the ice. As the glaciers ground their way down the V-shaped Merced Valley, they plucked chunks of rock from the highly fractured granite walls. When the ice retreated, the valley was left with a broad, U-shaped cross section and sharply defined vertical walls.

The most recent glacier, which may have reached its greatest extent only 10,000 years ago, was smaller than its predecessors. The ice extended about one-third of the way up the valley walls, and the snout advanced only about as far as El Capitan. When it began to melt, glacial debris dammed the valley with a moraine, forming Ancient Lake Yosemite in a scooped-out basin. Silt, sand, and rock eventually filled the lake, creating the present strikingly level valley floor.

But there is much more to Yosemite than this spectacularly scenic valley. The park boundaries embrace 1,200 square miles (3,100 square kilometers) of lush primeval forests, glacial lakes, rushing rivers, ice fields, flower-filled alpine meadows, and groves of giant sequoias. The park also includes areas of true wilderness, where hikers and backpackers can find solitude and unsurpassed vistas.

The highest point in Yosemite is Mount Lyell, at 13,114 feet (3,997 meters) above sea level, and many other peaks exceed 10,000 feet (3,050 meters). Because of this tremendous range, the park encompasses five major life zones, with striking differences in the plant and animal communities at various elevations. The park's famous giant sequoias, for example, do not grow in Yosemite Valley. They grow only in the higher country. Of the three sequoia groves in the park, the largest is Mariposa Grove. There is found the Grizzly Giant, a sequoia with a trunk almost 31 feet (9.5 meters) in diameter and an estimated age of 2,700 years.

The name Yosemite is thought by some to come from the Miwok Indian term for the grizzly bear, *uzu-mati.* Although grizzlies have long since vanished from the area, hikers may still encounter black bears, for there is ample wilderness to support them. Some 220 species of birds have been sighted in the park, the most conspicuous being the bold, bright blue Steller's jay, or "camp robber." Mule deer frequent Yosemite Valley, and golden eagles and red-tailed hawks soar overhead. A glimpse of any of them enhances the awesome experience that is Yosemite, a place both beautiful and wild where, if the visitor ventures beyond the well-trodden paths, he may indeed find himself alone with nature. □

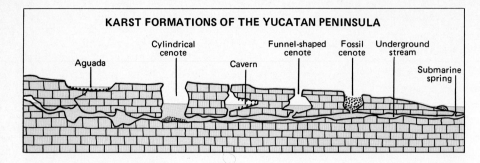

KARST FORMATIONS OF THE YUCATAN PENINSULA

Aguada · Cylindrical cenote · Cavern · Funnel-shaped cenote · Fossil cenote · Underground stream · Submarine spring

Yucatan Karst

- Mexico
- Map: page 13, D–3

In the ancient homeland of the Mayas, great cities were centered around mysterious natural wells.

The Yucatan Peninsula of southeastern Mexico is a land rich in history and tradition. Long before Columbus made his first voyage to the New World, it was the center of the remarkable Mayan civilization. Even today a visitor looking across the flat, dry landscape may see an isolated, steep-sided hill—only to discover on closer examination that it is actually the ruin of a Mayan pyramid.

These imposing monuments were usually built on sites chosen for reasons closely related to Yucatan's distinctive terrain. The peninsula, some 70,000 square miles (181,000 square kilometers) in area, is essentially a massive platform of limestone. Few natural hills interrupt its flat surface. And virtually no streams or rivers course across the land.

Instead the rain seeps quickly into the porous limestone. Charged with carbonic acid (from carbon dioxide in the air), the water dissolves the limestone. As a result, the Yucatan is honeycombed with networks of caves, channels, and other so-called karst features. Near the coast some underground streams even extend beneath the sea, where the water emerges in submarine springs.

Surface karst features include shallow oval basins known locally as *aguadas*. Made watertight by linings of clay (a product of decomposition of the limestone), they serve as natural reservoirs. Even more important are the large, usually cylindrical sinkholes known as cenotes. Up to 65 feet (20 meters) in diameter and 165 feet (50 meters) deep, they often extend below the water table and so are dependable natural wells.

Partially developed cenotes resemble inverted funnels, widening at the bottom, where more limestone has been dissolved. Collapse of the upper limestone layers results in the formation of fully developed cenotes. Older fossil cenotes may in time become filled with debris.

In this dry land with little surface water, cenotes have long been a major source of water. Mayan centers were always built in the vicinity of these natural wells. The Mayas, in fact, considered them sacred and used cenotes for ceremonial purposes. Best known is the great cenote at Chichén Itzá. Used for human sacrifices, it has yielded a wealth of gold and jade ornaments as well as other archeological treasures. □

Yukon River

- Canada—United States
- Map: page 10, A–2

A sprawling, complex river system meanders across one of the last great wilderness areas in North America.

The Yukon, one of the longest and most unspoiled rivers in North America, rises in the wilds of northwestern Canada. It flows in a long arc to the northwest, and then southwest across central Alaska, and ultimately empties into the Bering Sea.

The Yukon proper, originating in Lake Tagish on the border between Yukon Territory and British Columbia, is 1,587 miles (2,554 kilometers) long. But measured from the source of its most distant headwater, the Nisutlin River in the Mackenzie Mountains, the Yukon's length is 1,979 miles (3,185 kilometers). It is thus the third longest waterway in North America, exceeded only by the Mississippi-Missouri and Mackenzie rivers.

The Yukon's drainage basin covers some 320,000 square miles (830,000 square kilometers), an area almost equal to Texas and Oklahoma combined. Most of it is virtually uninhabited wilderness. The only large settlement on the river's upper course is the Yukon's territorial capital, Whitehorse, about 40 miles (65 kilometers) northwest of Lake Tagish.

Whitehorse is also the head of navigation during the brief summer shipping season. From an icebound low in March, the Yukon's volume increases dramatically in June and July as the Pelly and other tributaries carry in the runoff from melting snow and glaciers on distant mountains.

Long before the annual freeze returns in autumn, the water level subsides, and long stretches of the Yukon become a typical braided stream. Meandering across a broad valley, the river breaks up into a multitude of shallow channels that weave in and out between hundreds of islands and sandbars that clog the riverbed.

Shortly before crossing into Alaska, the Yukon passes through Dawson, where it receives one of its smaller but most famous tributaries, the Klondike. It was the discovery of gold on one of the Klondike's feeder streams, Bonanza Creek, in 1896, that triggered the famous Klondike gold rush.

Entering the United States, the Yukon continues on its leisurely course to the northwest. At Fort Yukon it reaches its northernmost point, skirting just to the north of the Arctic Circle. The Yukon then turns to the southwest across the heart of the Alaskan wilderness. Despite the influx of several major tributaries, its shallow channel again is littered with islands for long stretches.

As it nears the sea, the river makes one last abrupt turn toward the north before emptying into Norton Sound, an inlet of the Bering Sea. In its final stages the Yukon forms a delta some 60 miles (100 kilometers) wide, where it fans out into a complex system of branching channels.

Most of them are small and shallow, but one is deep enough for navigation—an important fact, since much of the region's history is intimately linked to the river. In the 1830's its lower course was first explored by Russian traders, and in 1847 agents of the Hudson's Bay Company established Fort Yukon, Alaska's oldest English-speaking settlement. Finally, half a century later, the Yukon took on a brief but special importance as one of the few routes to the Klondike during the legendary 1897–98 gold rush. □

Yunnan Rock Forest

- China
- Map: page 20, E–2

A tropical climate in a time long past resulted in the formation of this bizarre "forest" of gigantic limestone towers and clustered monoliths.

The province of Yunnan in southern China is part of the most extensive limestone region in the world. And like other limestone areas, it exhibits a wide variety of karst landforms. (Karst is a landscape category characterized by limestone that has been etched and eroded through solution by acidic groundwater.)

Among the area's oddest karst features is the Yunnan Rock Forest, on a high plateau some 60 miles (100 kilometers) southeast of the provincial capital, Kunming. At first glance it resembles a strange petrified forest, with thickets of grayish "tree trunks" jutting up from the soil.

In fact these strange-looking turrets and towers are composed of limestone, not fossilized wood. Fancifully compared to enormous mushrooms, clumps of bamboo, and even pagodas, they range from a few feet to nearly 100 feet (30 meters) in height. Some stand alone, while others are grouped in dense clusters laced by labyrinths of deep, narrow ravines.

The columns are the creations of groundwater that seeped through networks of vertical fissures in the rock. Carbon dioxide and the products of decaying humus transformed the water into a dilute acid that dissolved the limestone and gradually enlarged the fissures. In time only the rocky columns were left standing.

Karst landforms of such imposing dimensions are typical of tropical regions. Yet a temperate climate prevails today on the plateau, which is about 6,600 feet (2,000 meters) above the sea. In fact, until it was uplifted about 1 million years ago, the limestone formation was near sea level and the climate was tropical.

It was then that these unusual landforms were created, for the erosion process that sculpted them has now ended. Thus the Yunnan Rock Forest is of particular interest, for here, in effect, the clock has been stopped at an early stage in the evolution of a tropical karst landscape. □

YUNNAN ROCK FOREST. *Thickets of severely eroded limestone towers, reminiscent of giant petrified tree trunks, litter the landscape on a high plateau in southern China.*

Common Karst Formations in Tropical Regions

The term karst refers to landscapes of limestone and similar rock that have been eroded by acidic groundwater. Charged with carbon dioxide from the atmosphere, the water becomes a dilute solution of carbonic acid that is capable of dissolving limestone, creating such typical karst formations as sinkholes, caves, underground streams, and resurgent springs.

Climatic differences, however, result in considerable variety among karst features in different parts of the world. Karst formations in tropical regions, for example, are characteristically much bigger than their counterparts in temperate zones.

This is in large part the result of higher temperatures, which facilitate the bacterial decay of humus in the soil. Great amounts of carbon dioxide are generated in the process, and the groundwater is further enriched with additional acids, making it even more effective in dissolving the limestone. The result is an array of large, strikingly varied tropical karst landforms such as those illustrated here.

1. Natural bridge or arch
2. Lapies (giant ridges and furrows)
3. Towers with giant vertical lapies
4. Conical towers
5. Elongated domes
6. Sinkholes
7. Giant sinkholes
8. Eroded conical towers
9. Domes or haystack hills
10. Tower with base undercut by water
11. Cave in tower
12. Towers flooded by the sea

Z

Zaghouan, Djebel

- Tunisia
- Map: page 24, D–2

Imposing despite its modest height, this North African mountain has played an important role in history.

A craggy limestone massif, Djebel Zaghouan, overlooks the market town of Zaghouan some 30 miles (48 kilometers) south of Tunis, the capital of Tunisia. The mountain (*djebel* is the Arabic word for "mountain" or "hill") is not especially large. A ridge extending from the northeast to the southwest, it is scarcely six miles (nine kilometers) long and two miles (three kilometers) wide. And Ras el-Gassa, its highest summit, rises to only 4,249 feet (1,295 meters).

Yet the mountain is undeniably imposing, for parts of it loom above plains that are only about 400 feet (125 meters) above sea level. The contrast is most conspicuous along the southeastern front of the massif, where steep slopes rise abruptly to a long crest line. Beyond, the land slopes down gradually to the northwest.

The limestone of Djebel Zaghouan was formed about 150 million years ago. In a long, complex history of folding and faulting, the entire formation was thrust southeastward over adjacent rock layers. Hence the asymmetry of the massif, with its steep southeastern face and gentler slopes to the northwest.

Ever since antiquity, Djebel Zaghouan has played a special role in history, for its high slopes are a precious source of water in an otherwise dry land. The ruins of a stone reservoir, built by the Romans, are still found on the mountainside. There are also lines of stone arches, the remains of an aqueduct built by the emperor Hadrian to transport water to the ancient city of Carthage.

Today a modern dam and reservoir on Djebel Zaghouan serve as a water source for the city of Tunis. So valued is this water supply that, according to local folklore, anyone who drinks water from Djebel Zaghouan is certain to return to Tunisia. □

Zagros

- Iran
- Map: page 18, F–5

Lofty, rugged, and austere, the great Iranian range is a superb example of mountains that were formed by folding of the earth's outer crust.

The Zagros is the rugged, lofty mountain barrier that forms Iran's western frontier. The range rises in northwestern Iran near its border with Turkey and the U.S.S.R. It extends southeastward for about 1,100 miles (1,770 kilometers) to the Strait of Hormuz, the strategic narrows linking the Persian Gulf and the Gulf of Oman.

Many of the peaks and ridges in the Zagros exceed 10,000 feet (3,050 meters). The highest, the snowcapped volcanic summit of Mount Sabalan near Tabriz, reaches 15,592 feet (4,752 meters). To the east the Zagros encloses Iran's high central plateau. On the west the mountains drop down to the Mesopotamian plains of Iraq and the Persian Gulf.

The range was born of a collision of two of the crustal plates that drift restlessly about on the surface of the earth's molten interior. Moving slowly but relentlessly northeastward, the so-called Arabian plate collided with the Eurasian mainland. As the leading edge of the Arabian plate was forced down beneath the Eurasian plate, the great mountain range was heaved up along the collision zone.

The results of this impact were far from uniform, however, and the northwestern end of the Zagros contrasts dramatically with its southeastern counterpart. The northwest is a heavily faulted plateau where blocks of rock were thrust up along fractures in the earth's crust to form mountain ridges, while other blocks sank to form basins. Iran's largest lake, salty Lake Urmia to the west of Tabriz, lies in one of these landlocked basins. Lava erupted along many of the fault lines, dotting the countryside with massive volcanic cones such as Sahand and Mount Sabalan. The region, moreover, is still unstable. A few of the volcanoes continue to smolder, and the area is periodically wracked by violent earthquakes.

The southeastern part of the Zagros, in contrast, is one of the most beautifully folded mountain ranges in the world. Here the colliding crustal plates caused the area's thick limestone de-

posits to buckle up in high folds, known as anticlines, separated by downwarps, or synclines. Extending from northwest to southeast is a broad zone of long parallel lines of enormous hogback ridges and deep intervening valleys. In places where compression was very intense, some of the folds were thrust over the tops of their neighbors, like collapsed dominoes.

Despite the rugged terrain and the meager rainfall, people live in the Zagros as they have for centuries. In the more densely populated northern part of the range, grains, fruits, and vegetables are grown in the fertile valleys. Farther south, nomadic tribes continue to make their traditional seasonal migrations. In summer they travel to the highlands to graze their flocks of sheep and goats on alpine meadows; in winter they return to the sheltered lowland valleys. □

ZAGROS. *Virtually devoid of vegetation, the severely eroded slopes of the Iranian mountains are revealed with startling clarity.*

How Folded Mountains Are Formed and Then Altered Over the Course of Time

Rigid though rock is, great horizontal pressure can cause it to bend into wavelike folds. The folds usually occur in long parallel rows of mountain ridges separated by valleys, such as are found in the Zagros. The upward folds are termed anticlines; the intervening downwarped troughs are called synclines.

Erosion in time can mask the basic structure of the folds. The top of a fold may be worn away to form an anticlinal valley (*left*).

Severe erosion can completely wear away the anticline, resulting in inverted relief (*center*). In this case the synclines—once the bottoms of valleys—are left standing high above their surroundings. In the case of so-called Appalachian relief (*right*), the folds are first eroded down to a flat surface. Renewed erosion then wears away the areas of soft rock to produce valleys separated by ridges of more resistant rock.

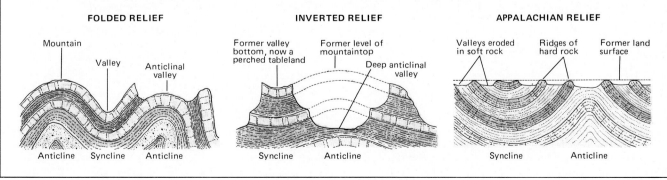

Zardalu Tableland

- Afghanistan
- Map: page 18, H–5

This looming tableland, flat-topped and symmetrical, is the offspring of an explosively erupting volcano.

The Zardalu Tableland is part of a magnificent volcanic landscape in the east of Afghanistan. About two miles (three kilometers) long, the brooding massif looms far above its surroundings on the high plains near Ghazni, southwest of the capital city of Kabul. Its summit, as flat as a tabletop, is crowned by a layer of glassy black volcanic rock. The slopes below are composed of an accumulation of volcanic debris nearly 1,300 feet (400 meters) thick.

Few plants mask the harsh, geometric contours of the tableland; occasional clumps of drought-resistant shrubs and grasses are all that can survive in this cool, dry region. Silhouetted against the cloudless blue sky, the glassy black summit contrasts vividly with the drab gray and ocher tones on the slopes.

The Zardalu Tableland is a by-product of the eruptions of a volcano, Mamikala, located about 10 miles (16 kilometers) to the northeast. Part of a much more extensive volcanic area, Mamikala erupted periodically between 2 and 3 million years ago.

Mamikala was a particularly violent volcano. Instead of emitting oozing streams of fluid lava, it periodically blew its top in enormous explosions. Clouds of incandescent debris were hurled high into the sky. The hot ash then showered down on the surrounding countryside, burying it beneath thick deposits of debris. Most of the Zardalu Tableland is composed of this accumulated debris: ash, tuff (consolidated volcanic ash), and ignimbrite (firmly welded masses of a type of volcanic glass).

The glassy slab that caps the tableland was formed during Mamikala's final paroxysmal eruptive phase. Incandescent lumps of lava were hurled into the air with unbelievable force. Flattened by the impact when they landed atop the present tableland, they rapidly cooled and hardened into sheets of extraordinarily hard, glassy volcanic rock.

Mamikala then expired, and the forces of erosion began stripping away the blanket of volcanic debris that had engulfed the countryside. In periods

ZARDALU TABLELAND. *A thin layer of hard black volcanic rock, like the icing on a cake, caps the tableland and protects it from erosion.*

when the climate was wetter than today, rushing streams gnawed away at the relatively soft deposits of ash and tuff.

The glassy slab that caps Zardalu like the icing on a cake, however, protected it from erosion. As the surrounding terrain was gradually worn away, the tableland remained standing, an isolated remnant of the former land surface.

Cracks caused by shrinkage formed around the margins of the glassy summit as the rock cooled long ago. Today frost forms in the cracks, causing chunks of the rock to chip off and roll down the slopes from time to time. The only other irregularities on the generally smooth slopes of the tableland are hard, glassy masses of ignimbrite that were exposed by the long, slow process of erosion. □

Zion National Park

- United States (Utah)
- Map: page 10, D–5

Colorful canyons and lofty cliffs are prime attractions in this magnificent gem of a national park.

Zion National Park in southwestern Utah boasts some of the finest canyon scenery in the United States. Established in 1919 and then enlarged in 1956, the park encompasses some 230 square miles (600 square kilometers) of canyons, cliffs, and beautifully colored monumental rock formations.

The undisputed centerpiece of the park is Zion Canyon, so named in the 1860's by early Mormon settlers. Carved by the North Fork of the Virgin River, it is about 15 miles (25 kilometers) long and is bounded by sheer cliffs that average some 2,500 feet (760 meters) in height. The massive formation known as the West Temple, one of the highest points in the park, rises 3,800 feet (1,160 meters) above the canyon floor.

A scenic road through the canyon and a network of hiking trails enable visitors to sample the wonders of Zion. One side canyon, the Court of the Patriarchs, is dominated by a line of mountainous rocks known as the Three Patriarchs. Other formations along the canyon walls include the Beehives, the Mountain of the Sun, Lady Mountain, and Angels Landing.

The canyon road ends in a magnificent rockbound amphitheater, the Temple of Sinawava. There, overlooking the depths of the canyon, is one of Zion's most celebrated landmarks, the Great White Throne. Flat-topped and sheer-walled, the majestic monolith looms nearly 2,400 feet (730 meters) above the canyon floor.

Upstream from the Temple of Sinawava the river is hemmed in by the Narrows. In this winding, slotlike chasm, the canyon walls rise straight up for 2,000 feet (600 meters). The first European to explore the cleft called it "the most wonderful defile it has been my fortune to behold."

Not far away is the famous Weeping Rock, where springs high on the canyon wall emit water that trickles like tears down the face of the cliff. At the Hanging Gardens, a similar seepage area, the water nourishes a veritable garden of ferns and other moisture-loving plants that cling to the lofty rocks. Elsewhere in the park a number of streams sometimes spill over the canyon walls in glistening, windblown cascades.

The rocks of Zion in a sense are a continuation of the story revealed in the rocks of the Grand Canyon, some 75 miles (120 kilometers) to the south. The youngest and uppermost layer of rock exposed on the rim of the Grand Canyon, known as Kaibab limestone, extends north, forming some of the lowest and oldest outcrops in the Zion area. Piled layer upon layer atop the Kaibab limestone are thick deposits of younger rock that was formed over the course of 200 million years.

Sediments that accumulated at the bottoms of vast inland seas, lakes, and marshy lowlands were consolidated into multicolored layers of limestone, shale, and sandstone. But the most prominent rock forming the canyon walls is a thick deposit of Navajo sandstone, which was formed at a time when the area was a desert. Sand blown in from present-day Nevada piled up in enormous dunes that were eventually consolidated into the sandstone. Its color ranges from rich vermilion to pink to white near the tops of the cliffs.

Even younger layers of rock were deposited on top of the Navajo sandstone, but in the Zion area they have been partially removed by erosion. In a long, slow process of uplift, which took place over the course of millions of years, the region was elevated to its present position far above sea level. Gradual tilting of the land surface caused streams to flow faster and increased their cutting power. In time the awesome gorges of Zion and other great canyons in the area were formed by the rivers' ceaseless scouring, undercutting, and carrying off of debris.

The process continues even today. In spite of its gentle appearance for much of the year, during the spring thaw and after summer thunderstorms the North Fork of the Virgin River becomes a churning torrent. Laden with boulders and other eroded debris, it has been likened to an endless belt of sandpaper that relentlessly scours away the canyon floor.

Rockfalls are also quite common in the park. In 1958 some 60,000 tons (54,000 metric tons) of rock gave way and came crashing down the cliffs. But even the tiniest chip or pebble that tumbles to the floor of the canyon is a reminder that change is inevitable: slowly but surely the contours of the canyon continue to evolve. □

Ziz Gorges

- Morocco
- Map: page 24, C–2

En route from the mountains to the desert, a small African river flows through a series of impressive gorges.

The Ziz Gorges are a series of canyons on the upper course of the Oued Ziz, a river that rises in the High Atlas range in central Morocco and flows southward toward the Sahara. Traversed by one of the few roads that cross the high mountain barrier, the gorges have had a long history as a strategic pass. The Roman general Paulinus traveled through them when he crossed the High Atlas in the first century A.D. And for hundreds of years they were part of a traditional caravan route to and from the oases and market towns of the northern Sahara.

Tourists traveling the same route today are usually impressed by the rugged beauty of the gorges. In places they are narrow clefts between towering limestone walls. Elsewhere the winding valley broadens enough for palm groves to flourish on the riverbanks. All along the way the blue-green water of the Ziz contrasts with the reddish-brown of the contorted limestone cliffs and reflects the clear blue sky above.

Long before there were any mountains in the area, the Ziz followed much the same course it does today. During the long, slow process of folding and upheaval that created the High Atlas range, the rushing river kept pace with the uplift, etching its bed ever deeper into the limestone as the land rose upward.

The carving of the canyon, moreover, continues even to this day. Melting snow and occasional downpours transform the placid Ziz into a raging torrent. Sweeping away fallen debris that litters its bed, the river relentlessly gnaws its way deeper into the rock. □

Zugspitze

- Austria—West Germany
- Map: page 17, E–4

The loftiest summit in the Bavarian Alps is an irresistible mecca for mountaineers, skiers, and sightseers.

The Bavarian Alps are an imposing mountain rampart stretching approximately 70 miles (110 kilometers) along the border between Austria and West Germany to the south of Munich. Their northern face rises abruptly to heights of 7,000 feet (2,100 meters) and more above the German resort center of Garmisch-Partenkirchen in the broad, glacier-carved Loisach Valley at the foot of the rugged range. To the south, in Austria, the slopes descend even more steeply toward Innsbruck in the valley of the Inn.

Directly astride the international boundary is the Zugspitze, the highest peak in the Bavarian Alps. Its very

ZIZ GORGES. *Traversed today by a modern highway, the rugged mountain gorges are part of a centuries-old caravan route to the Sahara.*

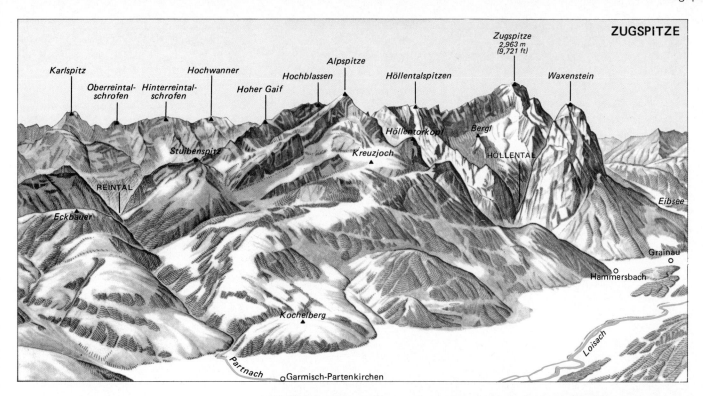

ZUGSPITZE

Karlspitz — Oberreintal-schrofen — Hinterreintal-schrofen — Hochwanner — Hoher Gaif — Hochblassen — Alpspitze — Höllentalspitzen — Zugspitze 2,963 m (9,721 ft) — Waxenstein

Stulbenspitz — Höllentorkopf — Bergl

Kreuzjoch — HÖLLENTAL

REINTAL — Eckbauer — Eibsee — Grainau — Hammersbach

Kochelberg

Partnach — Garmisch-Partenkirchen — Loisach

dramatic, sharply chiseled, pyramidal summit culminates at 9,721 feet (2,963 meters) above sea level and 7,400 feet (2,255 meters) above the Loisach Valley to the north.

Located at the junction of three high mountain ridges, the peak shows signs of severe glaciation. Cirques (deep, glacier-carved amphitheaters) indent its flanks and accentuate the steepness of the summit. Even to this day, remnants of the glaciers persist at the foot of the knife-edged ridges.

The mountain, like the entire range, moreover, is composed primarily of limestone. Attacked over the eons by running water, which erodes limestone by actually dissolving it, the rock is cut up into sharp peaks and crags and riddled with jagged ridges and deep ravines.

But it is the very ruggedness of the terrain that attracts enthusiasts to the beckoning summit of the Zugspitze. Garmisch-Partenkirchen, the site of the 1936 Winter Olympic Games, remains a popular base point for skiers who enjoy the challenge of the slopes. In summer, mountaineers gather there to make the long, fairly difficult climb to the summit.

For the less ambitious, the lofty crest of the Zugspitze is much more easily accessible. A famous cog railway ascends the slopes from Garmisch-Partenkirchen. And there are two aerial tramways visitors can take to the top of the mountain: one from

ZUGSPITZE. *Far above the timberline, the magnificently sculpted limestone summit overlooks sweeping panoramas of the snow-covered peaks of the Eastern and Central Alps.*

the German village of Eibsee to the west, the other from the resort center of Ehrwald in Austria.

However they attain the summit, which is complete with a meteorological station and a restaurant, visitors are rewarded by one of the finest vistas in the Bavarian Alps. Stretching off to the north are the Bavarian lowlands, accented by the glinting surfaces of

the Ammersee, the Starnberger See, and a multitude of smaller lakes. To the east, south, and west, range after jagged range of the Central and Eastern Alps recedes to the distant horizon. On fine days it is even possible to make out the lofty summit of the highest peak in Austria, the Grossglockner in the Hohe Tauern range far to the southeast. □

Glossary

DUNE. Raabjerg Mile Dunes, Denmark

EARTH CHIMNEY. Melnik Badlands, Bulgaria

CRATER. Meteor Crater, United States (Arizona)

SEA STACK. Port Campbell Cliffs, Australia

GLACIER. Mont Blanc, France

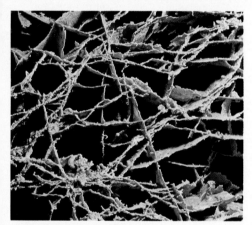

CAVE. Formations in Wind Cave,
United States (South Dakota)

GORGE. Aar Gorge, Switzerland

HOT SPRING. Pamukkale, Turkey

A

AA

Hawaiian term, pronounced ah-ah, referring to *Lava* that has solidified so that its surface is a mass of rough, jagged blocks.

ABRASION

The wearing away of part of the earth's surface by the action of wind, water, or ice, using moving sand or other debris as an abrasive material.

AFFLUENT

A *Tributary*; a stream flowing into a larger stream.

ALKALI FLAT

An alkaline, level area in an arid region into which desert streams may lead. In the dry season it is a barren expanse of hard mud covered with alkaline salts; after heavy rain it becomes a shallow, muddy lake that soon dries out again. See *Playa*.

ALLUVIAL CONE

An *Alluvial Fan* in which the deposit is deep and its surface steeply inclined, owing to the rapid sinking and evaporation of the stream water and the consequent dropping of the entire load.

ALLUVIAL FAN

The deposit of sediment laid down by a swiftly flowing stream as it enters a plain or an open valley; so called because of its shape. An alluvial fan is most common in dry regions, where the alternate drying up and flooding of the mountain stream favors its formation. Alluvial fans are sometimes many miles across, and several fans made by neighboring streams frequently unite to form a continuous plain.

ALLUVIAL PLAIN

A level tract bordering a river on which *Alluvium* is deposited; it may include a *Floodplain*, a *Delta*, or an *Alluvial Fan*.

ALLUVIUM

The surplus material, consisting mainly of sand and silt, which a river has carried in suspension and which it has been forced to deposit. Some of the world's most fertile land consists of alluvium deposited in the valleys and deltas of the great rivers.

ALPINE

Belonging to the Alps, or to the higher regions of any mountain system; the term may be used in reference to climate, flora, and other characteristics of a region.

ALTIPLANO

In the Andes of South America, a series of elevated plateaus between the Western and Eastern *Cordilleras* at an altitude of about 11,500 feet (3,500 meters), mainly in western Bolivia but extending into Peru and Argentina.

ALTITUDE

Vertical distance above mean sea level, usually measured in feet or meters.

ANTECEDENT RIVER

A river that has cut through land that has risen in its path, thus maintaining its course; so called because it is older than the present topography. One of the best-known examples is provided by the Colorado River, which created the Grand Canyon in Arizona.

ANTICLINE

The arch or crest of a *Fold* in rock layers. See *Syncline*.

AQUIFER

A layer of rock that holds water and allows water to percolate through it.

ARETE

A sharp mountain ridge, often formed by the erosion of two adjoining *Cirques*. On many mountains, cirque erosion has taken place from several sides, leaving a series of arêtes radiating from the summit. See *Horn*.

ARROYO

A normally dry streambed in a desert area that is transformed into a temporary watercourse after heavy rain. When the rain has ceased, the water soon subsides and the bed dries up again. The term is used mainly in North and South America. See *Wadi*.

ARTESIAN WELL

A type of well that normally gives a continuous flow, the water being forced upward by hydrostatic pressure; this pressure is due to the outlet of the well being some depth below the level of the source of the water. If the source of the water is sufficiently high, the water in the well will gush out above the ground without the necessity of pumping.

ASH CONE

The conical hill or mountain built up with the ejected material from a *Volcano*. The slopes of a cinder cone are usually steeper than those of an ash cone.

ATOLL

A *Coral Reef* in the shape of a ring or horseshoe, enclosing a lagoon.

AVALANCHE

A mass of snow and ice at high altitude that has accumulated to such an extent that its own weight causes it to slide rapidly down the mountainside, often carrying varying amounts of rock. The term is sometimes used for a fall of purely rock materials, but this phenomenon is better described as a *Landslide*.

B

BADLANDS

An arid region that is seamed and lined with deep gullies by occasional heavy rains, normal precipitation being insufficient to support a protective covering of grass or other vegetation. Such a region is named after the Badlands of western South Dakota.

BANK

(1) A sandy or muddy portion of the seabed raised

above its surroundings but covered with enough water to permit navigation. See *Sandbank*.

(2) The sloping ground along the edge of a river, stream, or lake.

BAR

A ridge of sand formed in the sea across the mouth of a river or the entrance to a bay or harbor, lying approximately parallel to the coast. A bar that remains exposed even at high tide is termed a *Barrier Beach or Barrier Island*. See *Spit; Tombolo*.

BARCHAN

A crescent-shaped sand *Dune*, with the tips of the crescent pointing downwind, formed in a region where the wind direction is virtually constant. The windward slope of the barchan is gentle, while the leeward slope is relatively steep.

BARRANCA

A Spanish term for a ravine or gorge that forms where heavy rains cause torrents to sweep downward and cut through soft rock layers.

BARRIER BEACH or BARRIER ISLAND

A *Bar* that is exposed even at high tide and separated from the coast by a *Lagoon*; common along the Atlantic coast of the United States and along the coast of the Gulf of Mexico.

BARRIER REEF

See *Coral Reef*.

BASALT

A dark-colored, fine-grained *Igneous Rock* formed by the solidification of *Lava*. It is found in many volcanoes and sometimes forms huge plateaus.

BASIN

(1) A region in which the rock layers slope downward from all directions toward a central point.

(2) The total area drained by a river and its tributaries, termed a river basin.

BATHOLITH

A dome-shaped mass of *Igneous Rock*, often consisting of *Granite*, formed by the intrusion of *Magma* into overlying rocks. Often extending over hundreds of square miles, batholiths are revealed when the overlying rocks have been worn away. They form the substructure of many mountain ranges and continue downward to great depths.

BAY BAR

A *Bar* that extends across a bay and is attached to the land at both ends, thus distinguishing it from a *Spit*.

BAYOU

A marshy creek or offshoot of a river or lake; occurring in flat country, it remains swampy because of floods, river seepage, and lack of drainage. The term is used chiefly in the southern United States.

BEACH

The gently sloping strip of land bordering the sea, usually composed of sand, pebbles, boulders, or mud.

BEDDING PLANE

The surface that separates one layer of *Sedimentary Rock* from another.

BEDROCK

The solid rock beneath the soil, subsoil, and other loose rock material that covers most of the earth's land surface. It may lie hundreds of feet beneath the surface, but it is usually found at a much shallower depth and sometimes has no soil cover at all.

BLIND VALLEY

In a *Karst Region*, a valley, either dry or containing a stream, which ends in a cave or sinkhole where the streambed disappears underground.

BLOCK MOUNTAIN

A mountain formed by the uplift of land between *Faults*, or by the subsidence of land outside the faults. See *Horst*.

BLOWHOLE

A hole near the seashore, formed in the roof of a cave, through which air and sometimes water are forced by the rising tide.

BLUFF

A headland or cliff with an almost perpendicular front; usually applied to steep slopes bordering a river. Such bluffs are formed by the action of the river cutting into the valley sides, as on the concave side of a *Meander*.

BOG

An area of soft, wet, spongy ground consisting chiefly of decayed moss and other vegetation. It often forms in shallow, stagnant lakes and ponds.

BRAIDED STREAM

A network of small, shallow, interlaced streams derived from a single stream whose sediment deposits have caused it to divide into several channels that repeatedly separate and then rejoin one another in a braidlike pattern.

BREAKER

A wave breaking into foam as it approaches the shore, where the water is so shallow that there is not enough to complete the wave form.

BREAKWATER

A barrier built into the sea in order to break the force of the waves and serve as a protection against them.

BRECCIA

Rock consisting of angular fragments cemented together in a matrix. Breccia may consist of any type of material and is formed in many different ways. See *Conglomerate*.

BUTTE

A flat-topped hill, formed where a layer of hard rock protects softer layers below it from being worn down. A butte is similar to but smaller than a *Mesa*, and is often produced when a mesa is reduced in size through dissection and erosion. It is characteristic of semiarid regions of the western United States.

C

CALCAREOUS

Containing a substantial proportion of calcium carbonate; the term is generally applied to rocks and soils.

CALDERA

A large basin-shaped *Crater* bounded by steep cliffs, usually formed by the subsidence of the top of a volcanic mountain and sometimes occupied by a lake. If the volcano is not yet extinct, the caldera may contain one or more active cones.

CALVING

The detachment of an *Iceberg* from the front of a *Glacier* that has reached the sea, or the detachment of a portion of a floating iceberg.

CANYON

A *Gorge*, relatively narrow but of considerable size, bounded by steep slopes. It is formed by a river cutting through the rocks of an arid region; the scantness of the rainfall prevents erosion of the canyon walls and so maintains their steepness. A smaller ravine through which a tributary flows into the main river is known as a side canyon.

CAPE

A *Headland*; a more or less pointed piece of land jutting out into the sea.

CATARACT

A large *Waterfall* or series of falls, or sometimes, as on the Nile River, *Rapids*.

CAVE

A subterranean hollow space in the earth's crust. Caves are usually formed in limestone regions where running water containing carbon dioxide dissolves out underground channels and enlarges them in places to the dimensions of caves. See *Karst Region; Speleology*.

CAVERN

A term generally synonymous with *Cave*, though sometimes implying one of large dimensions.

CHAIN

A mountain system consisting of a group of more or less parallel ranges. The term is also applied loosely to islands or other features when several of them are arranged in a line.

CHALK

A soft white or grayish type of *Limestone* composed largely of the calcareous remains of small marine organisms and shell fragments. In its purest form it may contain as much as 99 percent of calcium carbonate.

CHANNEL

(1) A relatively narrow stretch of sea between two landmasses, connecting two more extensive areas of the sea.

(2) A riverbed.

(3) The deep, navigable part of a bay, a harbor, or some other waterway.

CHOTT

A shallow, temporary *Salt Lake* or *Salt Marsh* found in North Africa. The dry basins left behind when the lakes have disappeared are characterized by deposits of salt and often by the absence of vegetation.

CINDER CONE

See *Ash Cone*.

CINDERS, VOLCANIC

See *Lapilli*.

CIRQUE

A deep, rounded, steep-sided hollow on a mountain, formed through erosion by snow and ice and characteristic of regions that have been glaciated. In areas where glaciers still exist, *Firn* often accumulates in the basins of cirques and feeds small glaciers.

CIRQUE GLACIER

A small glacier within a *Cirque*.

CLAY

An extremely fine-grained substance, very retentive of moisture, often becoming pliable when mixed with water. The various types of clay differ according to mineral character and origin.

CLIFF

A high, steep rock face, approaching the vertical, either inland or along a coastline.

CLOUDBURST

An abnormally heavy downpour of rain, usually associated with a thunderstorm. Although short-lived in temperate regions, a cloudburst can cause considerable damage, transforming gullies into raging torrents.

COASTAL PLAIN

A plain that borders the seacoast and extends to the nearest elevated land. It may be formed by the deposition of sediment by rivers, by erosion by the sea, by uplift of the earth's crust, or by the emergence of part of the former *Continental Shelf* as a result of a relative fall in sea level.

COL

A low point in a range of mountains or hills, usually providing a pass through the range. It may be formed by two streams on opposite sides of the ridge cutting back toward each other, or by the erosion of an *Arête* between two *Cirques* on opposite sides of the ridge.

COMPOSITE VOLCANO

The most common kind of *Volcano*: a conical mountain built up by many eruptions of lava alternating with layers of ash, cinders, and other material. Also called a stratovolcano.

CONFLUENCE

The point at which one stream flows into another, or where two streams converge and unite.

CONGLOMERATE

A rock composed of rounded pebbles or boulders cemented together in a matrix of finer material; sometimes called puddingstone. See *Breccia*.

CONTINENTAL DIVIDE
See *Watershed*.

CONTINENTAL DRIFT
The horizontal movement of the earth's continental plates, which are portions of an ancient supercontinent called *Pangaea*, once comprising the world's entire land area. Evidence supporting the theory includes the fact that the shores of opposite continents, such as the western coast of Africa and the eastern coast of South America, often fit together like pieces in a jigsaw puzzle and exhibit geological similarities.

CONTINENTAL GLACIER
A term sometimes used for an *Ice Sheet*.

CONTINENTAL SHELF
The part of the seabed bordering the continents and covered by relatively shallow water. It takes the form of a shelf or ledge that slopes gently downward from the coast and ends in a relatively steep edge that drops abruptly to the depths of the sea.

CONTINENTAL SLOPE
The relatively steep slope that descends from the edge of the *Continental Shelf* to the deep ocean bed.

CORAL ISLAND
An exposed portion of an isolated *Coral Reef*. It may consist simply of a mound of sand on a flat coral reef. When there has been an uplift of the land, however, the reef itself may be above sea level, and the island may reach a considerable altitude.

CORAL POLYP
A small marine animal, constructed like a sea anemone, that has a hard skeleton formed by the solidification of the base and sidewalls of the body, and can live only in shallow tropical seas. The skeleton is made up of calcium carbonate extracted from the seawater. When the coral polyp dies, the softer parts of the body decay and are washed away, but the skeleton is left behind. Large numbers of coral polyps living in colonies cause masses of coral to grow to enormous size, forming *Coral Islands* and *Coral Reefs*.

CORAL REEF
A mass of limestone rising from the ocean floor, built up principally by immense numbers of small marine organisms called coral polyps; fragments of shells, coral, and sand gradually accumulate on and behind the reef to form new land. There are three principal types of coral reefs. Fringing reefs grow near the shore of a continent or island. Ribbonlike barrier reefs lie farther offshore, separated from the land by a broad lagoon. Atolls are ring-shaped reefs enclosing a lagoon.

CORDILLERA
A series of more or less parallel mountain ranges, together with the intervening plateaus and basins. The term refers especially to the Andes of South America, but is also applied to the mountain systems in western North America from the Rockies to the Pacific coast.

CORE
The central part of the earth, below the *Mantle*, about 4,300 miles (6,900 kilometers) in diameter, with a high density and probably consisting of nickel-iron.

CORROSION
The wearing away of rocks by chemical action rather than by mechanical processes of erosion.

CRAG
A rough, steep rock or point of rock. In high mountain regions, crags are often formed by the action of frost in *Weathering*.

CRATER
The usually funnel-shaped hollow at the top of a volcanic cone leading down into the channel or pipe through which erupted material rises to the surface. The term is also applied to the hollow caused by the fall of a *Meteorite* on to the earth's surface.

CRATER LAKE
A body of water collected in the *Crater* of an extinct volcano. See *Caldera*.

CREVASSE
A deep, vertical crack in a glacier, generally caused by a steepening of the slope, a sharp turn, or some other change in the terrain that results in an alteration of the glacier's movement.

CRUSTAL MOVEMENTS
The movements of the outer parts of the solid *Lithosphere*, as manifested by *Earthquakes* and other geological phenomena.

CYCLE OF EROSION
The series of changes through which *Erosion* causes a newly uplifted land surface to pass from youth through maturity to old age. In youth, for example, streams occupy steep-sided, V-shaped valleys; in maturity, the valleys are broad and gentler in slope, and rivers have begun to *Meander*; in old age, valleys are very broad, rivers are sluggish, and the region becomes a *Peneplain*.

D

DEBRIS or DETRITUS
A collection of material formed by the disintegration or wearing away of rocks or vegetation.

DEFILE
A term rather loosely used, but usually applied to a gorge, ravine, or narrow pass.

DELTA
The fan-shaped alluvial tract, often extremely fertile, formed at the mouth of a river when more sediment is deposited there than can be removed by the currents. As the deposits build up, the river divides and subdivides into numerous channels that branch out in a triangular shape. The term was first applied by early Greeks to the alluvial tract created by the Nile, since

its shape resembled the letter Delta of their alphabet. A small delta may also develop where a river enters a lake, or at the confluence of two rivers.

DENUDATION

The wearing away and lowering of the land by various natural forces: heat, wind, rain, frost, chemical solution, running water, moving ice, and the sea. Along with *Deposition*, denudation is one of the two major processes responsible for the changes in form of the earth's surface. See *Transportation; Weathering*.

DEPOSITION

The laying down of solid material that has been carried from another part of the earth's crust by rivers, the sea, the wind, and other natural agents. Deposition is one of the two major processes of earth sculpture, the other being *Denudation*.

DESERT

An almost barren tract of land in which precipitation is so scanty or irregular that it cannot adequately support vegetation. A desert in which absolutely nothing grows, however, is uncommon. A rock desert is one in which the rock has been exposed by strong wind erosion. In a stony desert, the rock surface has been broken up by temperature changes and the ground is covered by a layer of fragments. A sandy desert usually has an undulating surface of *Dunes* with intervening hollows. See *Erg; Hamada; Reg*.

DESERT PAVEMENT

A relatively smooth, mosaiclike area in a desert region consisting of pebbles closely packed together after the removal of finer material by wind erosion.

DIKE

(1) A vertical or near-vertical sheet of *Igneous Rock*, formed when molten rock material, or *Magma*, from the earth's interior forces its way upward through a cleft, then cools and solidifies there. The dike may change direction, branch away into smaller dikes, or give rise to *Sills*. (2) A bank of earth, stones, or other material built to prevent low-lying land from being flooded by the sea or a river.

DISSECTED PLATEAU

A once-continuous *Plateau* into which a number of valleys have been carved by erosion.

DISTRIBUTARY

A branch or outlet that leaves a main river and does not rejoin it, carrying its water to the sea or a lake, usually across the surface of a *Delta*.

DIVIDE

See *Watershed*.

DJEBEL

In Arabic, a mountain or range of mountains.

DOLINA or DOLINE

A closed hollow in a *Karst Region*, formed by the solution of the limestone near the surface and subsequent subsidence; it is often rounded or elliptical in shape and sometimes has a *Sinkhole* into which a stream of surface water flows.

DOLOMITE

A white or gray crystalline mineral composed of the double carbonates of calcium and magnesium; also a rock sometimes known as magnesian limestone.

DRIFT ICE

Detached portions of ice floes or icebergs carried by currents into the open sea. See *Pack Ice*.

DROWNED VALLEY

A valley that has been submerged by the advance of the sea or a lake, owing to a sinking of the land or a rise in the water level; also called a submerged valley.

DRUMLIN

An elongated hill or ridge of glacial debris, usually oval and shaped like half an egg; it occurs in a previously glaciated region, the long axis lying parallel to the direction of the glacier's flow, with the thick, steep end facing the direction from which the ice came.

DUNE

A mound or ridge of sand formed either in a desert or along the seacoast through *Transportation* by the wind. A dune is often begun where an obstacle of some kind exists, the sand piling up and finally covering it, then falling over on the leeward side. While the size and shape of dunes are always changing, desert dunes fall into four main groups: the crescent-shaped *Barchan*; hairpin-shaped parabolic dunes; transverse ridges; and *Seif Dunes*—long, narrow ridges that extend in the direction of the prevailing wind.

DUST

Solid matter consisting of minute particles and occurring everywhere in the atmosphere. Often carried great distances by the wind, it is constantly being deposited on the earth's surface.

E

EARTH CHIMNEY

A tall, slender column of earth, often 20 to 30 feet (6 to 9 meters) high, capped by a large boulder that originally lay on the ground and protected the soil beneath it as the surrounding soil was gradually worn away by erosion. Earth pillars, sometimes known as hoodoos, are frequently found in glaciated mountain valleys.

EARTHQUAKE

A movement or tremor of the earth's crust originating below the surface. It is sometimes caused by a volcanic explosion; earthquakes, in fact, are common in most volcanic areas and often precede or accompany eruptions. It is more likely to be of *Tectonic* origin, however, usually owing to the existence of a *Fault*. A major earthquake is normally followed by a series of other shocks. One that originates below or near the sea may generate large, potentially destructive waves called

Tsunamis. The world's three great earthquake regions are a belt across southern Europe and southern Asia, a belt along the west coast of North and South America, and a belt around the western Pacific Ocean that includes Japan, the Philippines, and most of the East Indies. Worldwide, thousands of earthquakes are recorded annually, but of these only about 100 cause serious damage.

ELEVATION
The raising of a portion of the earth's crust in relation to its surroundings. See *Subsidence.*

ENTRENCHED MEANDER
See *Incised Meander.*

EOLIAN
Relating to or caused by the wind. Eolian deposits are materials transported and laid down on the earth's surface by the wind, including *Loess* and the sand of deserts and dunes.

ERG
In the Sahara, that part of the desert whose surface is covered with sand *Dunes.* See *Hamada; Reg.*

EROSION
The wearing away of the land surface by various natural agencies, particularly sea, river, and rain water, ice, and wind.

ERRATIC
A boulder that has been transported from its source by a glacier, sometimes over a considerable distance, and has been left stranded when the ice melted; thus it is often of a different type from neighboring rocks. In some areas of the northern United States and Europe, erratics have been so numerous as to impede the cultivation of crops.

ESCARPMENT
An inland cliff or a steep slope; also called a scarp.

ESKER
A long, narrow ridge of sand and gravel that was once the bed of a stream flowing beneath or within the ice of a glacier and was left behind when the ice melted.

ESTUARY
The mouth of a river where tidal effects are evident, and where fresh and salt water mix.

EXFOLIATION
A *Weathering* process that consists of the peeling off of thin layers of rock from the surface. It is caused chiefly by chemical weathering, aided by the alternate expansion and contraction of the rock produced by changes in temperature, especially in deserts where such changes are extreme. The formerly rectangular corners of the rock are rounded off, and the surfaces assume a spherical form. Also called onion-skin weathering.

EXTRUSIVE ROCKS
Rocks formed by the solidification of *Magma* above the surface of the earth, such as volcanic *Lava.* See *Intrusive Rocks.*

F

FAULT
A fracture in the earth's crust along which movement has taken place, and where the rock layers on the two sides therefore do not match. The movement may take place in any direction, and the change in position between the two sides may vary from less than an inch to thousands of feet. See *Earthquake; Thrust Fault.*

FAULT SCARP
An *Escarpment* situated where a *Fault* has formed, and owing to the relative downward movement of the rock layers on the lower side of the fault.

FELDSPAR
A widely distributed group of hard white and pink minerals, probably constituting almost half of the earth's crust, consisting of silicates of aluminum combined with potassium, sodium, calcium, and barium. It is typically found in *Granite.*

FINGER LAKE
A long, narrow lake lying in a hollow scooped out by an ice sheet or a glacier and often dammed at the lower end by a *Moraine.*

FIRN
The granular substance, intermediate between snow and ice, formed as accumulated snow at the head of a glaciated valley is being transformed into *Glacier* ice. As the glacier moves down the valley, the firn gradually becomes welded into a completely crystalline mass of ice. Also called névé.

FISSURE ERUPTION
A *Volcanic Eruption* in which *Lava* is ejected through a long fissure or cleft, generally without explosive activity and often producing a *Lava Plateau.*

FJORD
A long, narrow inlet in the seacoast with generally steep sides, formed when a glacier flowing seaward scooped out a deep, troughlike valley that was later invaded by seawater. In most cases a fjord is extremely deep but becomes shallower toward the mouth, possibly because the glacier lost some of its erosive power as it moved down the valley.

FLOE
See *Ice Floe.*

FLOODPLAIN
A plain, bordering a river, that has been formed from deposits of sediment carried down by the river. When the river rises and overflows its banks, the water spreads over the floodplain and deposits a new layer of sediment, so that the floodplain gradually rises. During its formation, a floodplain is often characterized by the presence of *Marshes, Swamps,* meandering streams, and *Oxbow Lakes.*

FOLD
A bend in rock layers, varying greatly in size and struc-

ture, caused by movements of the earth's crust. See *Anticline; Overfold; Syncline*.

FOLDED MOUNTAINS

Mountains that have been thrown up into massive *Folds* or ridges by earth movements. Often the mountains form an *Anticline*, or upfold, and the adjacent valleys are *Synclines*, or downfolds. Most of the important mountain ranges are of this type, including the Himalayan, Alpine, Andean, and Appalachian chains.

FOSSIL

The remains or the form of a plant or an animal that has been buried and preserved for a long period in rocks of the earth's crust. Organisms preserved in this way were usually buried in *Sedimentary Rocks* soon after death, or were encased in a material such as volcanic ash or mud that protected them from decay.

FRINGING REEF

See *Coral Reef*.

FUMAROLE

A hole in the earth's crust from which steam and gases, such as carbon dioxide and sulfur dioxide, are emitted under pressure. It is frequently found in a volcanic region; the steam is produced by *Magma* beneath the surface when the volcano itself has ceased to erupt.

G

GABBRO

A group of dark greenish-black, coarse-grained *Igneous Rocks* consisting essentially of a *Feldspar* and one or more ferromagnesian minerals.

GEOLOGY

The science of the composition, structure, and history of the earth. It includes the study of the materials of which the earth is made, the forces that act upon these materials and the resulting structures, the distribution of the rocks of the earth's crust, and the history not only of the planet itself but also of the plant and animal life of different ages.

GEOTHERMAL

Relating to the heat of the earth's interior as evidenced by the high temperature of its *Magma*. Geothermal energy is utilized in some areas of the world in the form of electricity that is produced by steam raised by drilling from a *Hot Spring*.

GEYSER

A *Hot Spring* that at regular or irregular intervals throws a jet of hot water and steam into the air. The jet 'may rise to a height of well over 100 feet (30 meters).

GEYSERITE

A siliceous deposit produced from the water of a *Geyser* or *Hot Spring*.

GLACIAL LAKE

A small lake enclosed between the margin of a *Glacier* and the valley wall; a lake fed by glacial meltwater.

GLACIATION

The covering of an area, or the action on that area, by an *Ice Sheet* or by *Glaciers*.

GLACIER

A mass of ice that moves slowly down a valley from above the *Snow Line* toward the sea under the force of gravity. It results from the pressure of great depths of snow, which transforms the snow in the lower layers into granular ice and later into clear ice. The glacier may extend far below the snow line, decreasing in size as temperatures increase and ending where the amount of ice melting equals the supply from above. The glacier is usually tongue-shaped and follows the general contours of the valley in which it lies; its surface is often uneven and sometimes cut by deep cracks, or *Crevasses*. A glacier's rate of movement is greatest in the middle, the progress at the bottom and sides being slowed by friction. Along its course the glacier collects rock material that is deposited when the ice melts in accumulations called *Moraines*. See *Piedmont Glacier*.

GLACIER BURST

See *Jokulhlaup*.

GLACIER SNOUT

The tapering, convex end of a *Valley Glacier*, often with an arch from which flows a stream formed by melting ice, and sometimes partially covered by a terminal *Moraine*.

GNEISS

A coarse-grained type of *Metamorphic Rock* with a banded structure, the bands representing alternating layers of different mineral composition.

GONDWANALAND

The southerly of two ancient continents into which the earth's landmass was once divided. According to the theory of *Continental Drift*, Gondwanaland and the other supercontinent, Laurasia, broke up and formed the present continents. Gondwanaland comprised Africa, Madagascar, India, Australia, Antarctica, and parts of South America.

GORGE

An unusually deep and narrow valley with steep walls; generally similar to but smaller than a *Canyon*, although there is no sharp distinction between the two.

GRABEN

See *Rift Valley*.

GRANITE

A coarse-grained white, pink, or speckled *Plutonic Rock* containing *Quartz*, *Feldspar*, and other minerals. It is one of the earth's hardest and most abundant rocks, often occurring in large masses or *Batholiths*. Its structure is so coarse that the different mineral grains can be plainly seen and distinguished from one another.

GRASSLANDS

Those regions of the world where the natural vegetation consists of grass. The rainfall is too light to permit forest growth but is less scanty and irregular than that of the deserts, and the grasslands are thus normally situated between the forest belts and the arid regions.

GRAVEL
A deposit of small rounded stones, usually mixed with finer material such as sand or clay, formed by the action of moving water in a river, a lake, or the sea.

GROTTO
A large cave produced in a limestone region by the solvent action of underground streams and percolating water; the term is sometimes also applied to other types of caves.

GROUNDWATER
Water that exists in the pores and crevices of the earth's crust, having entered them chiefly as rainwater percolating down from the surface. Most groundwater occurs in soil and sedimentary rock within a few hundred feet of the surface. It has important chemical effects on the rocks it penetrates, dissolving rock material, depositing dissolved minerals, or modifying minerals by chemical combination. See *Runoff; Water Table*.

GULCH
A narrow, deep ravine with steep sides, formed by a torrent; the term is used chiefly in the western part of the United States.

GULF
A large, deep bay; an extensive inlet penetrating far into the land. It may have been formed either by fracture of part of the earth's crust or by the sea overflowing depressed land.

GULLY
A long, narrow channel worn out by the action of water, particularly on a hillside; it is smaller than a *Ravine* and much smaller than a *Valley*. The term is often used, too, for a channel produced in *Soil Erosion*; such a gully normally carries water only during or immediately after rain or the melting of snow.

H

HAMADA
A desert area, particularly in the Sahara, in which the surface consists chiefly of bare rock, having been swept clear of debris by the wind. See *Erg; Reg*.

HANGING GLACIER
A *Glacier* that is perched on a high shelf above a valley, appearing to hang over the valley; it is potentially dangerous, since a mass of ice may break off without warning and fall into the valley below.

HANGING VALLEY
A tributary valley that enters a main valley from a considerable height above the latter, so that a stream flowing down it enters the main valley by a waterfall or rapids. Hanging valleys usually occur where a large glacier has scooped out a main valley to a far greater depth than did the smaller tributary glaciers in valleys leading into the main valley.

HARMATTAN
A strong wind blowing southwestward from the Sahara into West Africa; it is hot, dusty, and very dry, but has a cooling effect by promoting evaporation in the normally humid West African climate.

HEADLAND
A steep crag or cliff jutting out into the sea.

HEAD OF NAVIGATION
The farthest point up a river to be reached by vessels for the purposes of trade.

HEADWARD EROSION
The action of a river in cutting back and thus lengthening its valley upstream, in some cases leading eventually to *River Capture*.

HEATH
An extensive tract of open, uncultivated ground that is more or less flat and covered with small shrubs such as heather.

HILL
A small portion of the earth's surface elevated above its surroundings. It is of lower altitude than a *Mountain*, though the distinction between the two is not always clear-cut; indeed, some "hills" in the lower parts of the Himalayas are considerably higher than others commonly known as mountains.

HOODOO
See *Earth Chimney*.

HORN
A pyramidal peak, formed when adjacent *Cirques* separated by sharp *Arêtes* have been cut into a mountain. The best-known example is the peak of the Matterhorn in Switzerland.

HORST
An elevated block of rock between parallel *Faults*, produced either by uplift of the block between the faults or by *Subsidence* of the rock outside the faults.

HOT SPRING
A stream of hot water issuing from the ground, often after being heated by *Magma*, and therefore commonly occurring in a volcanic region when eruptions have ceased. Hot springs are not confined to volcanic regions, however, as water sinking far enough into the earth may become heated and rise to form springs. Mineral substances that have been held in solution are often deposited around the hot springs, which are also known as thermal springs. See *Fumarole; Geyser; Travertine*.

HUMUS
The decomposed and partly decomposed organic matter, of animal and vegetable origin, in the soil. Humus plays an important part in maintaining the fertility of the soil.

I

ICE AGE

A geological period in which *Ice Sheets* and *Glaciers* covered large areas of the continents, reaching the sea in places and lowering the temperature of the oceans. The most recent ice age, during which ice covered much of Europe and North America, ended about 10,000 years ago; the present ice sheets of Greenland and Antarctica are relics of this ice age.

ICEBERG

A mass of land ice that has been broken off, or calved, from the end of a *Glacier* or from an *Ice Shelf*, and is afloat in the sea. When a glacier enters the sea, the ice is buoyed up by the water, and a portion of the glacier is easily broken off and floats away. A glacier berg is irregular in shape; a berg from an ice shelf is rectangular in shape, flat-topped, often very large—sometimes over 40 miles (65 kilometers) long—and is characteristic of the Antarctic. The main sources of icebergs are the great ice sheets that cover Greenland and Antarctica, and the number of icebergs varies considerably from year to year. Only about one-ninth of an iceberg's mass is visible above the water, so that its depth below the surface is far greater than its height above the sea.

ICE CAP

A term often used synonymously with *Ice Sheet*, but sometimes applied specifically to smaller masses of ice and snow, such as those on Spitsbergen and other Arctic islands.

ICE FIELD

A large area of land ice, such as the Columbia Icefield in western Canada. The term is also applied to a uniform, unbroken *Ice Floe* several miles across.

ICE FLOE

A mass of floating ice, detached from the main polar ice and of large or small extent.

ICE SHEET

A vast, nearly flat mass of ice and snow covering a large land area in the polar regions. The ice sheets of Greenland and Antarctica, the only major ones now in existence, have thicknesses of as much as several thousand feet.

ICE SHELF

An extensive sheet of floating ice on the margin of and attached to a coastline, such as the Ross Ice Shelf in Antarctica.

IGNEOUS ROCKS

Rocks that have solidified from molten *Magma* and form one of the three main types of rock that compose the earth's crust. They may have solidified after reaching the surface, or in pipes or channels connecting the molten reservoir with the exterior, or well below the surface under pressure. They do not usually occur in distinct beds or strata, and do not contain fossils. There are many kinds of igneous rocks, owing to the varying conditions under which the original magma solidified. See also *Lava; Metamorphic Rocks; Plutonic Rocks; Sedimentary Rocks*.

IMPERMEABLE ROCKS

Rocks that are nonporous, or practically so, and therefore do not allow water to soak into them; also called impervious rocks.

INCISED MEANDER

An old *Meander* that has become deepened by *Rejuvenation*. In a so-called entrenched meander, vertical erosion has predominated, so that the valley sides are steep, and in cross section the valley is symmetrical. In an ingrown meander, lateral erosion as well as vertical erosion has taken place, so that one valley side is steep and the other much gentler, and in cross section the valley is asymmetrical.

INSELBERG

German for "island mountain." An isolated hill that formed in an arid or a semiarid region, usually with a rounded summit and steep sides of bare rock. It may rise to well over 1,000 feet (300 meters) above the surrounding plain. See *Monadnock*.

INTERGLACIAL PERIOD

A period of relatively warm climate between two periods of glaciation and cold climate during an *Ice Age*.

INTERMITTENT SPRING

A spring from which the flow of the water is not continuous, usually as a result of changes in the level of the *Water Table* caused by a fluctuating seasonal rainfall.

INTERNAL DRAINAGE

Drainage in which the waters have no outlet and so do not reach the sea; it often results in *Salt Lakes*, from which the water continually evaporates or sinks into the ground.

INTRUSIVE ROCKS

Igneous Rocks that solidified from *Magma* beneath the earth's surface.

INVERTED RELIEF

A type of relief in which land that was once at a relatively high level has been eroded so severely that it is now at a lower level than land previously below it.

ISLAND

An area of land surrounded by water in an ocean, sea, lake, or river. It may be formed by an uplift of the seabed, by a drop in the water level exposing parts of the sea floor, or by a rise in the water level isolating parts of the coastline. Alternately, a volcanic cone may be built up until its peak reaches above the sea, or coral polyps may build a *Coral Island*. Islands may also result from the erosion of a coastline, deposits of sediment by a river, or various other natural processes.

ISLAND ARC

A long, curving chain of islands, often associated with a long, narrow trench in the ocean floor on the seaward side. Movements of the earth's crust along the trench are manifested by great earthquakes and frequent volcanic activity.

ISTHMUS

A narrow strip of land joining two large land areas; one of the best-known examples is the Isthmus of Panama.

J

JOINT

A crack in a mass of rock that has formed along a plane of weakness; unlike a *Fault*, little or no movement has taken place between the blocks. Where the rock is exposed to the weather, joints greatly influence the shape of cliffs and crags.

JOKULHLAUP

An Icelandic term for a flood of water with blocks of ice, rocks, and mud. It is caused by the melting of ice in a glacier or an ice cap by hot *Magma* during a volcanic eruption.

K

KAME

A mound of gravel and sand formed by the deposition of sediment from a glacial stream. Kames are often found on the *Outwash Plain* of a glacier. See *Esker*.

KARST REGION

A *Limestone* region in which most of the drainage is by underground channels, the surface being dry and barren; named after the Karst limestone region of Yugoslavia. The calcium carbonate in the limestone is carried away in solution by rain and *Groundwater* containing carbon dioxide, and only the insoluble material is left to form a covering to the rocks. The surface may consist of bare rock or be covered with a thin soil except in the valleys, where a greater depth of soil may accumulate. Few streams are visible on the surface, for the rainwater tends to disappear into underground channels, often through *Sinkholes*. It is the solution of the limestone by this water, both on the surface and underground, that gives rise to the uneven topography typical of a karst region; it also leads to the formation of underground *Caves*. Even when the water does appear at the surface as a *Spring*, the stream often flows for a short distance and then disappears underground once more. See *Blind Valley; Dolina*.

KETTLE

A hollow or depression in a glacial *Outwash Plain*, created where an ice block covered by gravel has melted, allowing the debris to settle. The kettle is often filled by a pond or small swamp.

KEY

A *Sandbank*, *Reef*, or low island; the term, also spelled cay, is most commonly used in the West Indies.

KOPJE

In South Africa, an isolated hill, often formed by *Denudation* of the land around it. A kopje is a small *Inselberg*.

L

LAGOON

A shallow stretch of water that is partly or completely separated from the sea by a narrow strip of land. In the case of a *Coral Reef*, it is the channel of seawater between the reef and the mainland, or the sheet of water enclosed by an *Atoll*; a fringing reef, close to the shore, has a relatively narrow and shallow lagoon, while a barrier reef, far from the shore, has a much wider and deeper lagoon. A lagoon may also be formed by a spit of land closing, or almost closing, the entrance to a bay or an inlet.

LAHAR

A flow of volcanic mud formed by the mixing of water with *Volcanic Ash*, sometimes assuming the destructive power of an avalanche. The water may be supplied by rainfall or by the overflow from a *Crater Lake*.

LAKE

An extensive sheet of water enclosed by land, occupying a hollow in the earth's surface. The name is sometimes loosely applied, too, to the widened part of a river, or to a sheet of water lying along a coast, even when it is connected with the sea. Usually the amount of water entering a lake exceeds that lost by evaporation, and there is an outflowing stream; the water of the lake is thus fresh. In a region of low rainfall and great evaporation, however, the lake may have no outlet, and it may form an inland drainage area. All the salts brought down in solution by the rivers accumulate in such a lake, which thus becomes a *Salt Lake*, such as the Dead Sea or the Great Salt Lake in Utah. When rainfall is seasonal, the level and area of a lake may fluctuate considerably; a lake may also dry up entirely during a drought or in the dry season, leaving only a salt-covered mud flat. A lake remains permanent provided that the amount of water it receives, as rain and as water draining into its hollow, equals the amount lost. See *Crater Lake; Oxbow Lake*.

LAND ICE

Ice formed inland from fresh water, in contrast to ice formed from seawater.

LANDSLIDE

The downward movement of a large mass of earth or rocks from a mountain or cliff. It is often caused by rainwater soaking into the soil and earthy material on a steep slope; their weight is much increased, and they become more mobile. It may also be caused by an earthquake, or on the seacoast by the undermining action of the sea. See *Avalanche*.

LAPIES

A French term for the surfaces of limestone rocks in a *Karst Region* that are grooved and fluted owing to solution by rainwater containing carbon dioxide, the grooves and flutings being the channels where the water runs down the rock faces.

LAPILLI

Small rock fragments ejected from a *Volcano*; they are smaller than *Volcanic Bombs* but larger than *Volcanic Ash*. Also known as cinders, they vary in size from peas to walnuts.

LATERITE

A reddish soil or rock material produced by *Weathering* and occurring near the surface, chiefly in humid tropical regions or in semiarid regions that were once humid. It contains hydrated oxides of iron and aluminum. Laterite is relatively soft when first quarried but hardens on exposure to the atmosphere, and is often used as building material. It occupies considerable areas of India, Malaysia, Indonesia, northern Australia, and equatorial Africa and South America.

LAURASIA

The northerly of the two ancient continents into which the earth's landmass was once divided, the other being *Gondwanaland*.

LAVA

Molten rock, or *Magma*, that has flowed from the interior of the earth onto its surface through the crater of a *Volcano* or through fissures in the earth's surface. On the surface the molten material solidifies more quickly than in the interior of the earth. Some lavas have a high melting point, are very viscous, flow slowly, and do not travel far; such lavas do not lose their gases readily and so cause the volcanoes to erupt explosively, the whole mass sometimes bursting into fragments or even dust. Other lavas have a lower melting point, are very fluid, move rapidly, and may flow for several miles before solidifying; these lavas give comparatively quiet eruptions with a widespread flow of lava. The surface of solidified lava is usually very rough, and the escaping gases often cause the upper layers of the stream to contain numerous cavities. See *Aa; Pahoehoe; Pillow Lava; Scoria.*

LAVA FOUNTAIN

A spout of molten lava rising from a volcanic crater during an eruption.

LAVA PLATEAU

An extensive elevated area consisting of lava deposits, usually formed by a series of *Fissure Eruptions*. An example is the Snake River plateau in southern Idaho.

LEACHING

The process by which soluble substances such as organic and mineral salts are washed out of the upper layer of a soil and into a lower layer by percolating rainwater.

LEVEE

The natural bank of a river formed during flooding by the deposition of sediment. When the flood subsides, the sediment remains, and the levee is thus the highest portion of the *Floodplain* of a river. The height and length of a levee may be sufficient to divert the course of a tributary. A levee continues to be raised by flooding, and as the river also goes on depositing material in its own channel and raises the bed, both levee and riverbed may finally lie above the adjoining country. This is the case, for example, in the middle and lower reaches of the Mississippi River. Occasionally a flood may be heavy enough to break down levees and inundate large areas of land; artificial levees are constructed so as to supplement the work of the natural levees in keeping the water of such rivers as the Mississippi within its proper channel.

LIMESTONE

A *Rock* consisting essentially (at least 50 percent) of calcium carbonate. There are many types of limestone, all of which have certain common characteristics owing to their similar chemical composition, and are distinguished from one another according to texture, mineral content, origin, and geological age. Most of them are partly or wholly of organic origin and contain the hard parts of various organisms such as the shells of mollusks and the skeletons of corals. The calcium carbonate of limestone is readily soluble in water that contains carbon dioxide, and many limestone areas develop underground drainage and other characteristic features. See *Cave; Karst Region.*

LITHOSPHERE

The solid crust that envelops the *Mantle* of the earth. It consists of the thin, loose layer known as the soil and the mass of hard rock on which the soil lies.

LOAM

A rich soil consisting principally of a mixture of sand and clay, together with *Silt* and *Humus*.

LOCH

In Scotland, a freshwater *Lake*, a *Fjord*, or an arm of the sea.

LOESS

A deposit of fine silt or dust that is generally believed to have been transported to its present location by the wind. It is homogeneous and generally yellow in color, but weathers to a brown or reddish hue. One characteristic is its ability to maintain vertical walls in the banks of streams. In some places numbers of small vertical tubes run through it, probably owing to the remains of roots. It covers wide areas around the margins of the arid interior of Asia, especially in northern China, where it has enormous extent and thickness. There are also extensive loess deposits in Central Europe, in the central United States, and in several parts of the Soviet Union.

M

MAELSTROM

A large *Whirlpool*; the term applies specifically to a strong tidal current that occurs between two of the Lofoten Islands off the west coast of Norway.

MAGMA

The molten material that exists below the solid rock of the earth's crust and sometimes appears on the surface as *Lava* on its eruption from a *Volcano*. It does not always reach the surface in a molten state through a volcano, however, but may cool and solidify as it forces its way upward. See *Batholith; Dike; Sill*.

MANGROVE SWAMP

A swampy area occupied chiefly by mangroves, occurring mainly in the low coastal lands of tropical regions, most extensively near river mouths; from the trunks and branches of the trees descend long arching roots, which anchor the trees and form an almost impenetrable tangle at ground level.

MANTLE

The layer of rock below the earth's crust or *Lithosphere*, consisting of rocks of higher density than those of the latter; it extends downward to about 1,800 miles (2,900 kilometers) below the earth's surface. Below the mantle is the *Core*.

MAQUIS

A French term for the low *Scrub* of part of the Mediterranean region, consisting of small drought-resistant trees or shrubs.

MARBLE

A coarse-grained, crystalline *Metamorphic Rock* derived from *Limestone*; the term is applied commercially to any *Calcareous* rock that can be polished.

MARL

A mixture of clay and calcium carbonate, though the term is loosely applied to a wide variety of rocks and soils. Some of the marls are marine deposits, while others are of freshwater origin.

MARSH

A tract of soft, wet land, usually low-lying and at times partly or completely under water; the extreme dampness is due to the impermeable nature of the soil and the poor drainage. See *Salt Marsh; Swamp*.

MASSIF

A major mountainous mass that has relatively uniform characteristics and breaks up into a number of peaks toward the summit.

MEANDER

A curve in the course of a river that repeatedly swings from side to side in wide loops across flat terrain. The meander is continually accentuated as the current wears away the bank on the concave side of a curve while depositing solid material on the convex side. Eventually, the river may bend around in a nearly complete circle, at which time the current often cuts a new channel across the narrow strip of land to bypass the exaggerated curve. See *Oxbow Lake*.

MESA

A flat, tablelike upland that falls away steeply on all sides; the word in Spanish means "table." The harder top layers of rock have resisted erosion, while the surrounding terrain has been worn away. In time, parts of a mesa may be reduced by dissection and erosion to a series of *Buttes*.

METAMORPHIC ROCKS

Rocks that were originally either *Igneous* or *Sedimentary* but have been changed in character and appearance; they form one of the three main types of rocks that constitute the earth's crust. The change may have been due to heat, which sometimes causes the minerals to recrystallize, or to pressure, which alters the rock structure, or possibly to the action of hot water, which dissolves some rock material and deposits other material, thus changing the rock's composition. Most common igneous and sedimentary rocks have a metamorphic equivalent; for instance, *Granite* may be transformed into a *Gneiss*, *Limestone* into *Marble*, and *Shale* into *Slate*.

METEOR

A fragment of solid matter that enters the upper atmosphere from outer space and becomes visible through incandescence caused by the resistance of the air to its passage. Most meteors are very small and disintegrate in the atmosphere, reaching the ground only as dust; occasionally, however, a larger body known as a *Meteorite* falls to the earth's surface.

METEORITE

A *Meteor* of such large size that it does not disintegrate to dust in the atmosphere, but instead reaches the earth's surface. One of the largest meteorites that ever hit the earth created the enormous basin known as Meteor Crater near Winslow, Arizona.

MIDNIGHT SUN

A phenomenon of high latitudes in each hemisphere during part of its summer when, because of the tilt of the earth's axis, the sun remains visible above the horizon 24 hours a day.

MINERAL

A natural inorganic substance with a definite chemical composition and definite physical and chemical properties. Although there are about 3,000 known minerals, relatively few of them are abundant, and less than a dozen are common in most *Rocks*.

MINERAL SPRING

A *Spring* containing a noticeable quantity of mineral matter in solution and usually containing dissolved gases such as carbon dioxide.

MOFETTE

An opening in the ground that emits carbon dioxide,

together with some oxygen and nitrogen. It occurs in a region of former volcanic activity, as in Yellowstone National Park in Wyoming.

MONADNOCK

An isolated hill standing above the surrounding terrain because of the greater resistance of its rock to *Erosion*. The name is derived from Mount Monadnock in New Hampshire.

MONSOON

A type of wind system, occurring chiefly in tropical regions, in which there is a complete or nearly complete reversal of prevailing wind direction from season to season, bringing several months of heavy summer rainfall and hurricane-force winds to large areas.

MOOR

A wild stretch of land, usually elevated and covered with heather, coarse grass, or similar vegetation.

MORAINE

Debris or fragments of rock material transported and finally deposited by the movement of a *Glacier*. Among the common types are lateral moraines, which form along each side of a glacier. When two glaciers merge, two lateral moraines unite to form a medial moraine, visible as a dark longitudinal stripe on the surface of the ice. At the end of the glacier where the ice is melting, all the debris in the ice is dropped, forming a terminal moraine extending across the valley.

MOUNTAIN

A mass of land considerably higher than its surroundings and of greater altitude than a hill. The summit area of a mountain is small in proportion to its base, distinguishing it from a *Plateau*, which might be of similar elevation. The three principal types of mountains are *Folded Mountains*, *Block Mountains*, and *Volcanoes*. See *Chain; Range*.

MUD VOLCANO

A mound of mud, sometimes conical in shape with a crater at the top, formed by hot water issuing from the ground mixed with fine rock material. It is thus not a true *Volcano* but a type of *Hot Spring*.

MUSKEG

A *Bog* or *Swamp*, largely filled with sphagnum moss, in the *Tundra* or the coniferous forest region of northern North America.

N

NATURAL BRIDGE

A bridge or an arch of rock that has been naturally undercut by erosion. It is commonly the remnant of the roof of a cave or tunnel in a *Limestone* region.

NESS

A British term for a promontory or headland.

NEVE

See *Firn*.

NUEE ARDENTE or PELEAN CLOUD

A blast of hot, highly gas-charged, swiftly moving volcanic ash and lava fragments that sometimes sweep rapidly down the slopes of a *Volcano*. The term means "glowing cloud" in French and refers to the intense heat of the moving material.

NUNATAK

An isolated mountain peak or hill projecting like an island from the snow and ice of an *Ice Sheet*.

O

OASIS

An area in the midst of a *Desert* made fertile by the presence of water. It may consist of only a clump of palm trees fed by a small spring, or it may be a much bigger region fed by a major river and supporting a large agricultural population.

OCEAN

The body of salt water that surrounds the great landmasses of the earth; it is divided by them into several large portions, each known as an ocean, and all together they cover about 71 percent of the earth's surface. The individual oceans are the Pacific (the largest), the narrower Atlantic, the Indian, the Arctic (surrounding the North Pole), and the Antarctic.

OCEAN CURRENT

A mass movement of the water of the ocean. The chief causes of ocean currents are the prevailing winds and the differences in density owing to variations in temperature or salinity. Some deflection of currents is caused by the rotation of the earth.

ONION-SKIN WEATHERING

See *Exfoliation*.

ORE

A mineral aggregate containing one or more valuable metal-bearing minerals.

OUTCROP

The portion of a rock layer that projects above the earth's surface and is therefore visible.

OUTLET GLACIER

A *Glacier* that flows out from the margin of an *Ice Sheet* or *Ice Cap*.

OUTLIER

An isolated mass of rock that has been separated by erosion from the main mass of similar rock to which it was once connected.

OUTWASH PLAIN

The *Alluvial Plain* formed by streams originating from the melting ice of a glacier that carry away some of the material of the moraine and deposit it over a considerable area. It usually consists of sand and gravel.

OVERFOLD

A *Fold* inclined so far that some of the rock layers are completely overturned.

OXBOW LAKE

A lake formed when a *Meander* in a river has bent around in a nearly complete circle and the water has cut a new channel across the narrow neck of land, leaving a backwater. The now-bypassed meander is gradually sealed off from the river's flow by deposits of silt, and so becomes a crescent-shaped lake. Such oxbow lakes are very common along the banks of the lower Mississippi River and are often known as *Bayous*.

P

PACK ICE

Large blocks of ice, of greater extent and depth than *Ice Floes*, formed on the surface of the sea when large numbers of ice floes have been driven together to form an almost continuous mass of ice.

PAHOEHOE

A Hawaiian term referring to a mass of *Lava* that has solidified so that its surface is smooth and exhibits ropy or corded shapes, owing to the formation of a thin skin on the surface while the molten lava is cooling; the liquid lava underneath continues to flow for a time and shapes the skin into ropelike lengths, which remain when the lava has completely hardened. Sometimes called ropy lava.

PAMPAS

The South American *Grasslands* or grassy plains, located mainly in Argentina and extending from the Andes to the Atlantic Ocean. The western part of the pampas is largely desert, but the eastern part, with a higher rainfall, has a natural covering of tall, coarse grass. Large areas are now cultivated or are used for raising cattle and sheep. In physical characteristics, the pampas of South America are very similar to the *Prairies* of North America, the *Steppes* of Eurasia, and the *Veld* of South Africa.

PANCAKE ICE

The small, thin cakes of ice, roughly circular in shape, that form on the surface of the sea when the water begins to freeze.

PANGAEA

The vast continent, according to the theory of *Continental Drift*, that once constituted the earth's entire landmass; the term means "all lands."

PASS

A low gap through a mountain barrier; it is usually caused by *Erosion*, either by glaciers or by two streams that rise close to each other on opposite sides of the mountain barrier. Being approached from both sides of the mountains by a steep valley, and being flanked by mountain peaks, a pass is usually saddle-shaped.

PEAK

The more or less pointed top of a mountain, standing above the level of the range or the surrounding country.

It may be formed through the *Erosion* of adjacent rocks that are less resistant than those of which the peak is composed. Sometimes, however, it may be the result of a *Fold* or a *Fault*, or it may be a volcanic cone.

PEAT

A brownish or blackish fibrous substance produced by the decay of vegetation and found in *Bogs*; it is usually considered to represent the first stage in the transformation of vegetable matter into coal, and contains a high proportion of water.

PEDIMENT

In arid and semiarid regions, the gently sloping erosional plain strewn with boulders that borders the mountains.

PENEPLAIN

A region that is almost a plain, or an eroded remnant of such a feature. Its formation is normally due to erosion by rivers and rain, which continues until almost all the elevated portions are worn down; the more resistant rocks frequently stand above the general level of the land, though in time they too will be brought down to that level. When a peneplain is raised, it often becomes a *Plateau*, which is then dissected anew by the rivers as they pass through a fresh cycle from youth to old age. See *Cycle of Erosion*.

PENINSULA

A stretch of land almost surrounded by water.

PERCOLATION

The descent of water into the ground through soil pores and rock crevices. It sometimes leads to *Leaching*.

PERMAFROST

Ground that is permanently frozen, occurring extensively in polar regions, sometimes to great depths. A shallow layer of soil may thaw during the summer while the ground below remains frozen; the contraction and expansion caused by the seasonal thawing and freezing seriously complicates the construction of roads and buildings.

PERMEABLE ROCKS

Porous or fissured rocks that allow water to soak into them. *Sandstone* is an example.

PIEDMONT

Belonging to or related to the foot of a mountain or a range of mountains.

PIEDMONT GLACIER

An extensive sheet of ice that reaches down to low-lying ground at the foot of a mountain range, usually formed by the union of several *Glaciers*. Its width is usually greater than the combined width of the glaciers that form it, and the rate of movement is therefore slow, sometimes practically ceasing. One of the best-known examples is the Malaspina Glacier in Alaska.

PILLOW LAVA

A *Lava* that solidified under water, either because it was erupted under water or because it flowed into the water before solidification, assuming shapes that resemble heaps of pillows.

PLAIN

An extensive area of level or gently undulating land. Plains may be formed in a variety of ways and are often named accordingly, such as *Alluvial Plains*, *Coastal Plains*, and *Floodplains*. On many of the plains of the temperate zone, the natural vegetation is grass, and the plains have thus come to be known as *Grasslands* or, according to their location, *Pampas*, *Prairies*, *Savannas*, and *Steppes*.

PLATEAU

An extensive level, or mainly level, area of elevated land. Sometimes the plateau is traversed by rivers and mountain ranges, and it may be exceptionally high, as in the case of the Tibetan Plateau. If formed of horizontal strata, when young it will be intersected by deep *Canyons*; later the valley floors widen, and it is broken up into *Mesas*; later still, most of the surface becomes a plain dotted with *Buttes*. It is usually called a *Tableland* when it is bordered by steep *Escarpments*. Many of the world's plateaus have an arid climate.

PLATE TECTONICS

See *Continental Drift*.

PLAYA

The Spanish term for a tract of land, such as an *Alkali Flat*, that is temporarily filled with water and becomes a shallow, muddy lake after exceptionally heavy rainfall or the flooding of a river, but soon dries up again in hot weather.

PLUCKING

The action of a *Glacier* in pulling up and carrying away a section of the *Bedrock* on its valley floor as the glacier moves down the valley. Sometimes called quarrying.

PLUTONIC ROCKS

The *Igneous Rocks* that have solidified deep down in the earth, where cooling has been slow and the various minerals have had time to crystallize; these rocks are thus always completely crystalline and coarse-grained. *Granite* is an example.

POLDER

In the Netherlands, an area of land that has been reclaimed from the sea or from a lake. The land is surrounded by *Dikes* to protect it against encroachment, then drained by pumping the water into canals that run along embankments.

POTHOLE

A hole worn in solid rock, often at the foot of a waterfall, by the swirling of stones and gravel that have been kept in continual motion by the eddies of the swiftly flowing stream.

PRAIRIES

The almost flat, generally treeless, grassy *Plains* of North America, covering portions of Canada and the central United States from the foothills of the Rocky Mountains eastward approximately to the longitude of Lake Michigan. The light rains and high temperatures in summer permit a rich growth of natural grasses; these conditions have also made the prairies one of the world's most important grain-producing areas. They form the North American counterpart to the *Pampas* of South America, the *Steppes* of Eurasia, and the *Veld* of South Africa.

PRECIPITATION

The deposits of water, in either liquid or solid form, that reach the earth from the atmosphere. It includes not only rain, sleet, snow, and hail, which fall from the clouds, but also dew and frost.

PREVAILING WIND

The wind, indicated by direction, that occurs more frequently than any other in a given locale.

PROMONTORY

A headland or small peninsula; a cliff or crag projecting into the sea.

PUDDINGSTONE

See *Conglomerate*.

PUMICE

A type of volcanic rock that is light and porous enough to float on water. Its frothy texture is caused by the sudden release of steam and gases during its solidification.

PYRAMIDAL PEAK

See *Horn*.

PYROCLASTIC ROCKS

Fragmented rock materials produced in volcanic eruptions and usually classified according to size; for example, *Lapilli*, *Volcanic Ash*, and *Volcanic Bombs*.

Q

QUARTZ

One of the most common minerals, present in many rocks and soils in a wide variety of forms. A compound of silicon and oxygen, it forms the major proportion of most sands. It is also the colorless glassy material seen in *Granite*.

QUARTZITE

An extremely hard rock consisting mainly of *Quartz* and formed from a *Sandstone*.

R

RANGE

A line of mountain ridges, with or without peaks, in which the crests are relatively narrow.

RAPIDS

Part of a river where the current is flowing with more than normal swiftness and the bed is covered with large rocks and boulders. They may be caused by a sudden steepening of the slope, or by unequal resistance in the successive rocks traversed by the river. They are often due to *Outcrops* of unusually hard rocks that have resisted erosion better than softer rocks downstream.

RAVINE

A long, narrow depression on a mountain or hillside, smaller than a *Valley* but larger than a *Gully.*

REEF

A ridge of rocks, lying near the surface of the sea, which may be visible at low tide but is usually covered by the water. The most common type is a *Coral Reef.*

REG

In the Sahara, the extensive areas of flat desert plain from which the fine sand has been blown away, leaving a surface of small stones and gravel. See *Hamada.*

REJUVENATION

The process by which erosive activity is renewed, especially river erosion. The rejuvenation of a river may result from an uplift of the land over which a river flows, or from a fall in sea level, so that the river begins to cut into its bed once more and a new *Cycle of Erosion* is begun.

RIA

A long, narrow bay or inlet in the seacoast, caused by submergence and the consequent drowning of the valleys in a region of ridges and valleys that are not parallel to the coast and have not been glaciated.

RIFT VALLEY

A valley formed by the sinking of land between two roughly parallel *Faults*; such a valley is long in proportion to its width. The best-known example is the Rift Valley of Southwest Asia and East Africa. An example of a smaller rift valley is the section of the Rhine Valley between the Vosges Mountains in France and the Black Forest in West Germany.

RIVER

A stream of fresh water that for at least part of the year is larger than a brook and flows by a natural channel into the sea, a lake, or another river. In arid regions, however, a river may become no more than a series of pools during the dry season, or may even dry up completely. A river may originate, at the point known as its source, in a number of rivulets, a spring, a lake, or some other body of water; the path it follows is known as its course; it gradually swells as it is joined by *Tributaries*, all the rivers together forming a river system.

RIVER CAPTURE

The action of a river in acquiring the headstreams of a second river by enlarging its drainage area at the expense of the other. The more powerful river erodes its valley more deeply and cuts back into the valley of its weaker neighbor until eventually the headstreams of the weaker river are diverted into the drainage basin of the stronger river.

ROCHES MOUTONNEES

Hillocks of rock in a glaciated valley that have been smoothed and streamlined by the glacier on the up-

stream side and left rough and rugged, with steeper slopes, on the downstream side.

ROCK

One of the solid materials, composed of one or more *Minerals*, that make up most of the earth's crust. Rocks are divided into three major classes: *Sedimentary, Igneous*, and *Metamorphic*. More popularly, a rock is any mass of the harder portions of the earth's crust.

ROCK FLOUR

The finely ground solid matter produced by *Abrasion* of the bed of a glacier by the stones and rocks embedded in its base as they move forward with the glacier down the valley.

ROPY LAVA

See *Pahoehoe.*

RUNOFF

The portion of rainfall that ultimately reaches a stream, chiefly by flowing off the surface instead of sinking into the ground.

S

SALINITY

The degree of saltiness of the water in oceans, seas, lakes, and rivers, usually expressed as the number of parts per thousand. The average salinity of seawater, for instance, is 35 parts per thousand, while that of the Dead Sea is 280 parts per thousand. See *Salt Lake.*

SALT DOME

A mass of salt, often roughly circular in shape, that has been forced upward by subterranean pressures through rock layers that originally lay above it. Also called a salt plug.

SALT LAKE

A lake, situated in an arid region, which has no outlet and so accumulates salts carried in by the rivers that enter it. Loss of water by evaporation at least equals the supply of water by precipitation and inflow, and the lake gradually becomes more salty.

SALT MARSH

A coastal *Marsh* that at times is flooded by the sea, or an inland marsh in an arid region in which the water contains a high proportion of salt.

SALT PAN

A hollow, formerly containing water, in which a deposit of salt has been left behind following evaporation of the water.

SALT PLUG

See *Salt Dome.*

SAND

A mass of small rock particles, most commonly *Quartz*, that are finer than *Gravel* but coarser than *Silt* or *Dust*. It is often heaped up by the wind into mounds called *Dunes*. When consolidated or cemented together, sand forms a *Sandstone.*

SANDBANK

A submerged ridge of sand in the sea or a river, often exposed at low water.

SANDBAR

See *Bar*.

SANDSTONE

A porous *Sedimentary Rock* consisting of grains of sand bound together by such substances as calcium carbonate or silica. Some sandstones are well cemented, containing considerable *Quartz*, and form extremely durable rocks; others are poorly cemented and readily disintegrate on exposure.

SAVANNA

A tropical region bordering the equatorial forests in which the natural vegetation is mainly grass, with only scattered trees. There are distinct wet and dry seasons, and the lack of rainfall during the annual dry season prevents the growth of forests. The most extensive savannas are found in Africa.

SCARP

See *Escarpment*.

SCHIST

A crystalline *Metamorphic Rock* that can easily be divided into many thin flakes. Schists are named for their most conspicuous mineral, such as mica schist.

SCORIA

A volcanic *Lava*, produced during a violent eruption, that is extremely porous as a result of the escape of gases while it was still viscous.

SCRUB

A type of vegetation consisting of low-growing shrubs and stunted trees, with occasional taller trees. It is found in regions that have insufficient rainfall or too poor a soil for forest growth, such as the semiarid areas on the margins of hot deserts.

SEA

One of the smaller divisions of the *Oceans*, especially if partially enclosed by land, such as the North Sea; also a large expanse of inland salt water, even if completely landlocked, such as the Caspian Sea.

SEA LEVEL

The level that the surface of the sea would assume if uninfluenced by tides, waves, or swells; the average level between high and low tide at any place.

SEA STACK

A rocky islet or pillar that has been isolated from a coastline by the erosive action of the waves.

SEDIMENTARY ROCKS

Rocks that have been deposited in layers, often as underwater sediments but sometimes as windblown deposits; one of the three main types of rocks that make up the earth's crust. Among the most common sedimentary rocks are *Sandstone*, *Limestone*, *Shale*, and *Conglomerate*, while coal is a sedimentary rock of organic origin. See *Igneous Rocks; Metamorphic Rocks*.

SEEPAGE

The slow oozing of *Groundwater* onto the earth's surface, as distinct from the more pronounced flow of water from a *Spring*.

SEIF DUNE

A type of sand *Dune*, common in the Sahara, with a long, sharp ridge lying parallel to the direction of the prevailing wind.

SERACS

Pinnacles or pillars of ice of various shapes into which a glacier is sometimes broken up when it reaches a steep slope and numerous crisscrossing *Crevasses* are formed on its surface.

SHALE

A fine-grained *Sedimentary Rock* produced from *Clay*. It is formed by compression owing to the weight of overlying rocks, and is easily split into thin plates.

SHIELD VOLCANO

A *Volcano* formed from basic *Lava* in quiet eruptions with few explosions, taking the shape of a gently sloping dome like an inverted saucer.

SHOAL

A ridge of sand or rocks just below the surface of the sea or a river, and therefore dangerous to navigation.

SHOOTING STAR

See *Meteor*.

SILL

A sheet of *Igneous Rock*, often almost horizontal, formed when *Magma* forces its way between two layers of *Sedimentary Rock* and solidifies there.

SILT

A deposit laid down in a river or lake that is finer than *Sand* but coarser than *Clay*.

SINKHOLE

A saucer-shaped depression in the land surface, also called a swallow hole, through which water may flow into an underground course. It is caused by the solvent action of water on the limestone of a *Karst Region*, and may be enlarged by the collapse of rock above an underground cave.

SIROCCO

The southerly wind experienced from time to time in North Africa and southern Europe that, blowing from the Sahara, is characteristically hot, dry, and sometimes laden with dust.

SLATE

A dense, fine-grained *Metamorphic Rock* produced by heat and pressure from a fine clay; it readily splits into thin, smooth plates suitable for roofing purposes and other uses.

SNOUT

See *Glacier Snout*.

SNOWFIELD

A region of permanent snow found in mountainous areas or in high latitudes.

SNOW LINE

The line on a mountain or hill slope that represents the lower limit of perpetual snow; below the line, any snow that falls is melted during summer.

SOFFIONE

In volcanic regions, a vent in the ground through which steam and certain gases are emitted.

SOIL

The loose material, consisting mainly of very small particles of mineral and organic matter, that covers most of the earth's land area.

SOIL CREEP

The almost imperceptible but continual movement of surface soil and rock fragments down slopes.

SOIL EROSION

The wearing away and loss of topsoil, mainly by the action of wind and rain.

SOLFATARA

A vent in a volcanic region that no longer emits *Lava* or ash but continues to give off steam and sulfurous gases.

SOLIFLUCTION

Soil flow; a more rapid movement of soil and rock fragments down slopes than is the case with *Soil Creep*. It occurs mainly in the *Tundra*, where the top layer of soil remains saturated and alternate freezing and thawing take place.

SOUND

A narrow passage of water, usually wider than a *Strait*; sometimes a narrow inlet in the seacoast.

SPELEOLOGY

The study of caves.

SPIT

A narrow, low-lying tongue of sand and pebbles projecting into the sea or across an inlet.

SPRING

A continuous or intermittent flow of water from the ground, formed when rainwater sinks through the ground and emerges at a site some distance from its point of origin. Its location depends on the position of the *Water Table*, the shape of the land surface, and the types of rock. See *Geyser; Hot Spring; Seepage; Vauclusian Spring*.

STALACTITE

A column of mineral matter, usually calcium carbonate, that hangs like an icicle from the roof of a cave or other elevated point. It is formed by the deposition of dissolved minerals in slowly dripping groundwater. See *Stalagmite*.

STALAGMITE

An upward-pointing column of calcium carbonate formed on the floor of a cave by mineral-laden water that drips from the roof. It is usually shorter and thicker than a *Stalactite*, and is often produced by the water dripping from a stalactite. Sometimes the two meet and form a pillar from the floor to the roof of a cave.

STEPPES

The level, generally treeless grasslands of Eurasia, corresponding to the North American *Prairies* and South American *Pampas*.

STRAIT

A narrow stretch of sea connecting two much more extensive areas of the ocean.

STRATOVOLCANO

See *Composite Volcano*.

STRATUM

A more or less distinct layer of rock, occurring as one of a series of strata in the earth's crust. The term is usually applied only to *Sedimentary Rocks*.

SUBMARINE CANYON

A canyon in the seabed that crosses the *Continental Shelf*, probably formed by a present-day river at a time when the sea level was lower than it is today.

SUBMARINE RIDGE

A ridge rising from the ocean floor. The best-known example is the Mid-Atlantic Ridge, which runs north to south beneath the Atlantic Ocean.

SUBSIDENCE

The sinking of a portion of the earth's crust relative to the surrounding parts.

SWALLOW HOLE

See *Sinkhole*.

SWAMP

A tract of low-lying land that is permanently saturated with moisture and is usually overgrown with vegetation. The term is sometimes applied specifically to wetlands that are partly forest covered, such as the Dismal Swamp of Virginia and North Carolina. See *Marsh; Salt Marsh*.

SYNCLINE

The trough, or inverted arch, of a fold in rock layers; a downwarped area of the earth's crust. See *Anticline*.

T

TABLELAND

A *Plateau* bounded by steep, clifflike faces that lead abruptly down to the sea or the adjoining lowlands.

TALUS

A mass of boulders and broken rocks of all sizes that accumulate at the foot of a cliff or mountain slope, having been broken from the main rocks by *Weathering*. The talus slope is often so steep that a slight disturbance will send the whole mass sliding downward.

TALUS CREEP

The gentle movement of rock fragments down a *Talus* slope. See *Soil Creep*.

TECTONIC

Relating to the processes that tend to build up the various features of the earth's crust. Included, for example, are those forces that break, bend, and warp the crust and create depressions and elevations. Tectonic forces are distinct from those that tend to wear down the surface to a common level.

THERMAL SPRING
See *Hot Spring*.

THRUST FAULT
A *Fault* in which the upper rock strata have been pushed forward, protruding over the lower strata. Also called a reversed fault, it may be formed by the breaking of an overturned fold, or *Overfold*, at the sharply bent crest of the *Anticline*.

TIDAL RANGE
The difference in water level between mean high tide and mean low tide at a given place. It varies considerably in magnitude in different areas.

TIDES
The alternate rise and fall of the surface of the sea, approximately twice a day, caused by the gravitational pull of the moon and to a lesser degree of the sun.

TIDEWATER GLACIER
A *Glacier* that reaches the sea, where portions of it may break off as *Icebergs*.

TIMBERLINE
The boundary line on a mountainside above which trees do not grow. Its height depends on both latitude and local conditions of climate and soil. It is lower in the temperate zone than in the tropical zone, for example, and lower on the shady side than on the sunny side of a mountain. Also called the tree line.

TOMBOLO
A *Bar* of sand or gravel that joins an island to the mainland or to another island.

TOR
An isolated mass of granite or other rock that has been left intact on or near the top of a hill or other upland by the erosion of deeply weathered bedrock.

TRADE·WINDS
The winds that blow regularly from the subtropical belts of high pressure toward the equator, from the northeast in the Northern Hemisphere and from the southeast in the Southern Hemisphere.

TRANSPORTATION
The process by which loose material from the earth's crust is conveyed from one region to another. Some of the agents that wear away the land also carry the material with them. Rivers are the chief agents of transportation, carrying mud, sand, and stones for immense distances. Glaciers also bring material down from the mountains and deposit *Moraines*. The sea and the wind are other agents of transportation. See *Denudation*.

TRANSVERSE VALLEY
A valley that cuts across a mountain range instead of running parallel to it.

TRAVERTINE
A deposit of calcium carbonate produced by a spring, usually a *Hot Spring* or *Mineral Spring*, whose water is rich in lime.

TRENCH
A long, narrow trough, often extremely deep, in the ocean floor. Trenches are not usually found in the middle of the oceans but toward the margins, generally where volcanoes are active and earthquakes common.

TRIBUTARY
A river or stream that discharges its water into another stream at any point along its course.

TSUNAMI
A Japanese term for a large sea wave caused by an *Earthquake* taking place on the ocean bed. It is sometimes wrongly called a tidal wave.

TUFF
A rock formed from *Volcanic Ash* and *Dust* that were emitted during a volcanic eruption.

TUNDRA
The treeless plains of northern North America and Eurasia lying to the north of the coniferous forests. For most of the year the mean monthly temperature is below freezing, though during the brief summer the topsoil thaws (see *Permafrost*), permitting the growth of mosses, lichens, and some flowering plants.

U

UPLAND
The higher land of a region, in contrast to the valleys and plains.

U-SHAPED VALLEY
A *Valley* that is U-shaped in cross section, with a relatively level floor and steep sides, carved by the gouging action of a *Glacier* as it moved down a former river valley. See *V-Shaped Valley*.

V

VALLEY
A long, narrow depression in the earth's surface with a fairly regular downward slope. A river or stream usually flows through it, having carved it out from the surface rocks, and it is then known as a river valley. A young valley is narrow and steep-sided; when mature, it is wider and its sides are often gentler; an old valley is very wide, has a broad *Floodplain* and only a slight gradient. See *Hanging Valley; Rift Valley; Transverse Valley; U-Shaped Valley; V-Shaped Valley*.

VALLEY GLACIER
A *Glacier* that originates at high altitude and flows down a valley; most glaciers are of this kind. It is also known as an Alpine glacier.

VAUCLUSIAN SPRING
In a *Karst Region*, a spring composed of water from an underground stream that emerges at a point where the

limestone overlies a layer of impermeable rock. Named after the Fontaine de Vaucluse in the southern part of France.

VEIN

A crack or fissure in a rock containing mineral matter. The term is also applied to any layer of rock with economic value.

VELD

Elevated, open country in South Africa, much of which consists of *Savannas* or treeless *Grasslands* that correspond to the *Steppes*, *Prairies*, and *Pampas* of other regions.

VENTIFACT

A stone or pebble that has been shaped by windblown sand, usually in a desert, so that its surface consists of flat facets with sharp edges.

VOLCANIC ASH

Fine particles of *Lava* ejected by an erupting *Volcano*; the term is sometimes used interchangeably with *Volcanic Dust*.

VOLCANIC BOMB

A lump of *Lava* ejected from a *Volcano* in a liquid state and solidifying during its fall. It is usually rounded in shape; it may vary from a few inches to several feet in diameter.

VOLCANIC CINDERS

See *Lapilli*.

VOLCANIC DUST

Fine particles of *Lava* that have been ejected from a volcano in eruption, having been blown into small particles by the force of the explosion. Sometimes that dust is shot high into the air and is then carried immense distances by the wind.

VOLCANIC ERUPTION

The forcing of solid, liquid, or gaseous materials from the earth's interior to its surface by a *Volcano*. See *Fissure Eruption*.

VOLCANIC NECK

A mass of solidified *Lava* filling the central vent of a volcano; it is sometimes left isolated after the remainder of the cone has been removed by *Denudation*. Also called a volcanic plug.

VOLCANISM

The range of processes by which *Magma* and associated solid and gaseous materials rise into the earth's crust or are ejected onto its surface; it is thus not limited to the activities of volcanoes.

VOLCANO

A vent in the earth's crust caused by *Magma* forcing its way to the surface. Molten rock, or *Lava*, is finally ejected during an eruption, and often builds up gradually to form a conical hill or mountain. In addition to lava, gases, rock fragments, ash, and dust may be emitted during eruptions. Volcanoes are located on lines of weakness in the earth's crust, usually near the sea, and are regarded as being active, dormant, or extinct. See *Composite Volcano; Shield Volcano*.

V-SHAPED VALLEY

A *Valley* that is V-shaped in cross section, usually the product of downcutting by a river. A young valley is narrow and steep-sided, widening with age until it finally becomes broad, open, and almost flat. See *Cycle of Erosion; U-Shaped Valley*.

W

WADI

A desert watercourse that is usually dry, containing water only after occasional heavy rainfall; the term is used mainly in reference to North African and Southwest Asian watercourses. See *Arroyo*.

WATERFALL

A sudden fall of water, usually occurring where hard rock overlies softer rock in a riverbed; as the softer rock is worn away by the water, the hard layer overhangs and so produces the waterfall. A waterfall is also formed when a stream descends from a *Hanging Valley* or the edge of a *Plateau*. See *Cascade; Rapids*.

WATER GAP

A narrow gorge eroded through a ridge by a river or a stream.

WATERSHED

The elevated boundary line separating the headstreams that lead to different river systems. The term is also used to mean river basin or the entire area drained by a river system. A continental divide is a line that separates the rivers flowing toward opposite sides of a continent.

WATER TABLE

The surface of the *Groundwater*, below which the pores of a rock are saturated with water. This surface is uneven and also varies seasonally, depending on the amount of precipitation in the area.

WEATHERING

The decay and disintegration of the rocks of the earth's crust by exposure to the atmosphere; it is one of the main processes of *Denudation* and may be classified as either mechanical or chemical weathering. The dissolving of *Limestone* by water containing carbon dioxide is an example of chemical weathering, while the cracking of rock surfaces by temperature-related expansion and contraction illustrates mechanical weathering.

WHIRLPOOL

A circular eddy in the sea or a river produced by the shape of a channel, the meeting of two currents, or other causes.

WIND GAP

A narrow notch in a ridge, originally a *Water Gap*, through which a watercourse no longer flows.

Index

Credits and Acknowledgments

Front cover: Delicate Arch, Arches National Park, United States (Utah). Photo by David Muench.
Back cover: Staubbach Falls, Switzerland. Photo by H. Schmocker.

27 *top* Gabriel Camps; *bottom* Robert Wurgler. **28** Grant Heilman. **29** Michel Serraillier/Rapho. **30** *bottom left* Shostal Associates; *bottom right* Philippe Rochot/Atlas Photo. **31** *top* Vulcain/Explorer. **32** Paul Forge/Explorer. **33** *bottom* Vulcain/Explorer. **34** *bottom* Jacques Besançon. **35** Jean-Marie Chourgnoz/Balafon. **36** Matti A. Pitkanen. **37** Sébastien Marmounier. **38** Wide World Photos. **39** *top* & **40** *top* Michel Brosselin. **40-41** *bottom* Pascal Hinous. **42** *top* Gérard Couvreur. **42-43** *bottom* Michel Marenthier/Hoa-Qui. **44** Charles Lenars. **45** *right* Jacques Dejouy/Explorer. **46** Michel Petit. **47** Shostal Associates. **48** *top* René Battistini. **49** *middle* Jean-Marie Adamini/Cedri. **50** *top* Thérèse Anderson/Explorer; *bottom* Edwin Mickleburg/Ardea. **52** *right* Ezio Quiresi. **53** *top* Jean Dresch; *bottom* Editura Stiintifica, Bucharest. **54** *top* Jean-François Ramousse. **55** Georges Papigny. **56-57** Photo Researchers. **58** Shostal Associates. **59** *top* Candelier-Brumaire/Cedri; *bottom* Yves Leloup. **60** Orion Press. **61** Gérard Chedot/A.A.A. Photo. **62** *left* Tom Weir. **63** D.C.H. Plowes. **64** Ray Halin. **65** Photo Researchers. **66** *top* Marie-Louise Maylin. **67** D.C.H. Plowes. **68** Ulrich Wienke/Zefa. **69** Roland Michaud. **70-71** *top* Jean-Claude Tobailen. **71** *bottom* Ludovic Segarra. **72** Hungarian National Tourist Board. **73** *right* Monique Mainguet. **74** Erich Lessing/Magnum Photos. **75** Anne Gael. **76** Drive Publications Limited. **77** *left* Shostal Assoc.; *right* Mireille Vautier-Decool. **78** Shostal Assoc. **79** Monique Mainguet. **81** Giorgio Gualco/Bruce Coleman Inc. **82** Bill Staley/Photo Researchers. **83** *bottom* Russ Kinne/Photo Researchers. **84** *bottom* Jean Bottin. **85** *bottom* Jacques Dubois. **86-87** *top* Mireille Vautier-Decool. **87** *bottom* Editura Stiintifica, Bucharest. **88** Victor Magallon. **89** *top* Claude Laugenie; *bottom* Explorer. **90** Jacques Jolfre. **91** Bruce Coleman Inc. **93** Shostal Associates. **94** Bill Brooks/Bruce Coleman Inc. **95** Daniel Balland. **96** Marie-Louise Maylin. **97** *bottom* Marc Tennevin. **98** *left* Jean-Charles Pinheira; *right* Marc Tennevin. **99** K.W. Fink/Bruce Coleman Inc. **100** *top* Daniel Dreux; *bottom* Sébastien Marmounier. **101** Dominique Darr. **102** Jean Radvanyi. **103** Paolo Koch/Rapho. **105** Holmes-Lebel. **106** Michel Serraillier/Rapho. **107** Mireille Vautier de Nanxe. **108-109** Ray Atkeson. **110** Holmes-Lebel. **111** Walter Schmidt. **112** Robert Everts/Rapho. **113** Pierre Pothier. **114** *top* Victor Englebert/Rapho. **115** *top* Erich Lessing/Magnum Photos. **116** *top* Robert Harding Picture Library. **117** Jean Dresch. **118** Pascal Hinous/Top. **119** Shostal Associates. **120** Ken Dequaine. **121** Gerald Cubitt. **122** *top* André Charpen-

tier. **123** Shostal Associates. **124** & **125** *top* Michel Petit. **126** *top* Véronique Naud/A.A.A. Photo. **127** Johanson/Naturfotograferna. **128-129** Sébastien Marmounier. **130** *top* People's Republic of China; *bottom* André Charpentier. **131** *bottom* Photo Researchers. **132** Gerald Cubitt/Bruce Coleman Inc. **133** Bernardeau/Kutschera. **134** Ziegler/Joachim-Kinkelin. **135** Jean Radvanyi. **137** Monique Mainguet. **138** George Holton/Photo Researchers. **139** *top* Toni Schneiders/Bruce Coleman Inc. **140** *bottom* André Édouard/Studio des Grands-Augustins. **140-141** *top* Uwe Ommer/Top. **143** *bottom* David Muench/Alpha Photo Associates. **144** *top* Ray Halin. **145** *left* Jean Bottin; *right* Louise Slater. **146** François Gohier. **147** Gerhard Klammet. **148** Titus/Cedri. **149** Brian Brake/Rapho. **150** *top* Ezio Quiresi; *bottom* Paul von Baich. **151** Mag. Volker Weissensteiner. **152** *bottom* Jacques Guillard. **153** *top* Shostal Associates. **154** Franke Keating. **156** François Gohier/Pitch. **157** Shostal Associates. **158** *top* J.C. Whalley. **159** *right* Ashvin Mehta. **160** Serge Chirol. **162** *top left* Sébastien Marmounier; *bottom left* Gerald Cubitt. **162-163** Mireille Vautier-Decool. **164-165** David Muench. **166** *bottom* Shostal Associates. **167** Georg Gerster/Rapho. **168-169** Michel Folco/Cedri. **170-171** Paul-Émile Victor/Pitch. **172** Klaus Hackenberg/Zefa. **173** Gene Ahrens/Bruce Coleman Inc. **174-175** Pierre Salama. **175** Serge D'Ydewalle. **176** Gerhard Klammet. **177** H.W. Kitchen/Photo Researchers. **178-179** John DeVisser. **179** *bottom* Robin Smith. **180-181** Jean-Marie Adamini/Cedri. **182-183** *top* Roland Michaud. **183** *right* Gerhard Klammet. **184** *top* François Gohier/Pitch. **185** Ed Cooper. **186** Peter Arnold. **187** Françoise Huguier. **188** Jean-Claude Lozouet. **189** *left* J. Bucher/Photo Researchers. **190** Yves Leloup. **191** *top* Pierre Rias/Vulcain. **192** Francis Jalain/Cedri. **193** *top* Herb & Jan Conn; *bottom* Dennis Stock/Magnum Photos. **195** *top* Edmond van Hoorick. **196** *bottom* Adrien Warren/Ardea. **197** *top* Victor Englebert/Photo Researchers. **198** *top* Roland Michaud. **200-201** Ashvin Mehta. **201** *top* René Battistini. **202** *top* Caroline Weaver/Ardea. **203** *bottom* Shostal Associates. **204** Irish Tourist Board. **206-207** *bottom* Hélène Pagezy/Explorer. **207** *top* Vulcain. **208-209** *top* Heinz Herfort/Zefa. **210** *top* Louis-Yves Loirat/Tetrel. **211** Vulcain/Explorer. **212** *top* Emil Schulthess. **213** Mireille Vautier-Decool. **214** Ezio Quiresi. **215** *left* Ezio Quiresi; *right* Micheline Billaut. **216** *top* Douglas Botting/Bruce Coleman Inc. **217** J.W.E. Simons. **218** *bottom right* Siegfried Eigstler. **219** François Gohier. **220** *bottom* Paolo Koch/Rapho. **220-221** *top* Giuseppe Molteni/S.R.D. **222** *top* Joseph Rychetnik/Photo Researchers. **223** Dirk Schwager. **224** Russ Kinne/Photo Researchers. **225** Temuçin Aygen. **226-227** Kay Lawson/Rapho. **227** *bottom* Jean Dragesco/Atlas Photo. **228**

Daniel Bléneau. **229** Alain Cormontagne/Explorer. **230** Tiofoto. **231** Paisajes Espagnoles. **232** *bottom* Pierre Minvielle. **233** Sekai Bunka Photo. **234** Monique Mainguet. **235** Marie-Louise Maylin. **236-237** Mireille Vautier-Decool. **238** Sébastien Marmounier. **239** Brian Hawkes/N.H.P.H. **240** Photo Researchers. **241** *top* Ed Cooper Photography. **242** *bottom* Jacques Dumas. **243** *right* Micheline Billaut. **244** Vulcain/Explorer. **245** Grant Heilman. **246** Jean-Pierre Charre. **247** Charles Lenars. **248** Michel Serraillier/Rapho. **250** Shostal Associates. **251** Louis Boireau/Rapho. **252** Georg Gerster/Photo Researchers. **253** *bottom* Sébastien Marmounier. **254** Jean-Paul Hervy/Explorer. **255** Charles Lenars. **256** Photo Researchers. **258** Widere Photo. **260** Photo Researchers. **261** *bottom* Ashvin Mehta. **262** Henri de Châtillon/Rapho. **263** André Picou/Fotogram. **264** *top* Louis-Yves Loirat/Tetrel. **265** *top* Jean Bottin; *bottom* Giuseppe Molteni. **266-267** Claude Abron. **268** *bottom* Anne Gael. **269** Jean Bottin. **270** *bottom* Jean-Louis Nou. **271** Néli Bariand. **272** Olivier Magnier/Hoa-Qui. **273** *bottom* Roger Bellone. **274** *bottom* Pierre Rondière/Rapho. **275** Hoa-Qui. **276** Chris Bonington/Bruce Coleman Inc. **277** *bottom* Charles Lenars. **278** Oronoz. **279** *top* Louis-Yves Loirat/Rapho. **280-281** Kiai Sunlines. **281** *bottom* Guillemot/Fotogram. **282** Oronoz. **283** *top* Giuseppe Molteni. **284** Michel Serraillier/Rapho. **285** *bottom* Roland Michaud. **286** Yavuz/Fotogram. **287** Vulcain/Explorer. **288-289** *top* François Gohier. **290** Sébastien Marmounier. **291** *top* Francis Roux/Explorer; *bottom* Michel Binois/Pitch. **292** Jean-Claude Berrier. **293** *top* David Muench; *bottom* Philippe Roy/Explorer. **294** *top* Jacques Fronval. **295** Bernard Landrin. **296** Monique Mainguet. **297** Georg Gerster/Rapho. **298** *bottom* Jean-Noël Reichel/Top. **299** Sébastien Marmounier. **300** *bottom* Suzanne Held. **300-301** *top* Jean-Paul Duchêne/Cedri. **302** *top* David Béal. **303** Michel Brosselin. **304** *top* Lino Pellegrini. **305** Toni Schneiders/Kinkelin. **306** *top* Shostal Associates. **307** Michel Brosselin. **308** Inga Aistrup. **309** Derek C. Ford. **310** *top* Ray Manley/Shostal Associates. **311** Georg Gerster/Rapho. **312** Marie-José Turquin. **313** Paolo Koch/Rapho. **314** *bottom* Edmond van Hoorick. **315** Hans Silvester/Rapho. **316** Gabriel Camps. **317** *bottom* Editora Abril. **318** Caroline Weaver/Ardea. **319** *top* Jocip Ciganovic; *bottom* Ray Manley/Shostal Associates. **320-321** *bottom* Robert Prevost. **323** Suzanne Held. **324** David Muench/Shostal Associates. **325** Michel Petit. **326** Robin Smith. **327** Des Bartlett/Bruce Coleman Inc. **328** Matti A. Pitkanen. **329** Richard Vroom. **330** Gérard Duboutin/Explorer. **331** Freeman Patterson. **333** Matti A. Pitkanen. **335** Georg Gerster/Rapho. **336-337** Jean-Louis Patel/Pitch. **338** *top* Michel Aubert; *bottom* Hektor/Zefa. **339** Mihai Serban/Zefa. **340** Jorge de Brito. **341** *top* Paolo Koch/Rapho. **342** *bottom* Charles Lenars. **343** D.A. Harissiadis. **344-345** Monique Mainguet. **345** *top* Lino Pellegrini. **346-347** Tom Weir. **348** *top* Jean Nicod. **349** Shostal Associates. **350** Maximilien Bruggmann. **351** Daniel Silberstein/Rapho. **352-353** *bottom* J. Dezort/C.T.K. **354** *bottom* Government of British Columbia. **354-355** *top* Christian Kempf. **356** H. Schmocker. **357** Bo Boesen/Tiofoto. **358-359** Russ Kinne/Photo Researchers. **359** *top* Naturfotograferna. **360** André Édouard/Explorer. **361** Henri Veiller/Explorer. **362-363** Kiai Sunlines. **363** *right* Michel Serraillier/Rapho. **364** Dominique Darr. **365** Alain Beauvilain. **366-367** *top* Kay Lawson/Rapho. **368** Daniel Balland. **369** Bernard Desjeux. **370 & 372** Monique Mainguet. **373 & 374** Ginette Cros. **375** Shostal Associates. **376** Roland Maillard/Vloo. **377** Jean Sudriez/A.A.A. Photo. **379** Tass. **380** Jean-Paul Duchêne/Cedri. **381** Christian Errath/Explorer. **382** Charles Lenars. **383** *bottom* Jacques Dubois. **384** Georges Pierre. **385** Jacques Dumas. **386-387** Salmer. **388** Alain St. Hilaire/Atlas Photo. **389** *bottom* Claude Laugenie. **390** *top* Michel Serraillier/Rapho. **391** Roland Michaud. **392** Claude Rives/Cedri. **393** Jean-François Terrasse. **394-395** André Édouard/Studio des Grands-Augustins. **396** Sébastien Marmounier/Diatec. **397** Lino Pellegrini. **398** Francis Jalain/Cedri. **400-401** *bottom* D. Edwards/Freelance Photographers Guild. **401** *top* Michel Yolka/Atlas Photo. **402-403** Photo Researchers. **404** *top* Jean-Pierre Charre. **405** © Stephen J. Krasemann/Canada Wide. **407** Paolo Koch/Rapho. **408** *bottom* Lino Pellegrini. **409 & 410** Charles Lenars. **411** Charles Lenars/Atlas Photo. **412** Michel Serraillier/Rapho. **413** *top* Mireille Vautier-Decool; *bottom* Shostal Associates. **415** Emil Schulthess. **416** Jean-Claude Berrier. **417** Mireille Vautier-Decool. **418-419** David Muench. **421** *top* Marc Riboud/Magnum Photos. **422-423** *top* Georg Gerster/Rapho. **424-425** Daniel Balland. **426** Jean-Jacques Arcis/Rapho. **427** *lower* Gerhard Klammet-Aberl. **428** *top left* Micheline Billaut; *top right* Inga Aistrup; *bottom* Charles Lenars. **429** *top left* David Béal; *top right* Jean-Paul Hervy/Explorer; *middle left* Shostal Associates; *bottom left* Robert Wurgler; *bottom right* Yavuz/Fotogram.

Maps and diagrams: Sélection du Reader's Digest, S.A., Paris.

The Glossary is adapted from *A Dictionary of Geography* © W.G. Moore, 1949, 1952, 1963, 1968, 1974, published by permission of Penguin Books Limited.

The editors wish to express special thanks to the personnel of numerous national, state, and provincial parks and other governmental agencies in the United States and Canada who reviewed portions of the text.